USS MASSACHUSETTS

BB-59

TURNER PUBLISHING COMPANY

Turner Publishing Company

Turner Publishing Company Staff:
Editor: Katherine Sredl
Designer: Heather R. Warren

Editors for the
U.S.S. Massachusetts Association
Edward Palmer
Richard Bowerman

Library of Congress Catalog No.
95-061710
ISBN:
978-1-68162-431-0

2nd Division Dance. Boston MA. Hotel Beaconsfield-1942.

TABLE OF CONTENTS

History

ACKNOWLEDGEMENT

For reasons that will become apparent shortly, there is only one person who can appropriately acknowledge the help which he has had from a great variety of people in all of the work that has gone into the production of all the information you will find in this book. We refer, of course, to Edward W. Palmer whose other efforts and sacrifices on behalf of the USS *Massachusetts* have been appropriately chronicled in Chapter Six - "Save the Ship."

However, quite beyond his efforts in bringing Big Mamie to Fall River, Ed has been, for years, accumulating all of the biographical data presented herein. It goes so far beyond "accumulating." He has personally typed hundreds of the biographies. He has kept in constant touch with shipmates. He has worked out the arrangements with the publisher and editors and with the representatives of the USS *Massachusetts* Association. His efforts on behalf of all of us are beyond enumerating and far beyond the call of duty. His energies are matched only by the tolerance of his dear wife, Grace, who had to sacrifice so much in putting up with all of these diversions from a normal home life.

From all of us who have benefitted so much from all of your efforts, "Thank You, Ed."

R.H. Bowerman

☆☆☆☆☆

Starting with the gathering of "bios" in 1966, and the encouragement and the assistance from hundreds of crew-members, this book became a possibility. As the book grew, the addition of the Editorial Staff, consisting of former Bay Stater editors, staff members and advisors of the ship's former newspaper, deserve the final credit for the book.

Sincerely, Ed Palmer

Ed Palmer

DEDICATION
The Right Reverend Joseph N. Moody
1904-1994

Father Joe was the first Chaplain assigned to the USS *Massachusetts* as it fitted out in 1942 at the South Boston Naval Annex.

Those were the days when hundreds of raw recruits came aboard - officers and enlisted men in a confused state of wonderment. Recently wrenched from their families, instantly thrust from peace to war and relatively untrained, they (more accurately, we) needed a stabilizing influence to help us understand and adjust to this bewildering transition.

That influence was Father Joe Moody who quickly became the Spirit of BB-59. Without fear of contradiction he, more than any other person, helped forge that disparate mass of humanity into a caring, mutually supportive, fully effective group of shipmates.

Joseph N. Moody was born in New York City April 18, 1904, grew up in Mt. Vernon, NY, attended St. Joseph's Seminary in Yonkers and was ordained a Catholic priest May 25, 1949.

Throughout his clerical career, Monsignor Moody was recognized by the church as an extraordinary combination of parish priest and professional instructor. He demonstrated both facets of his character as a naval chaplain.

He was always available to help a shipmate over a tough time - a death in the family, receipt of a "Dear John" letter or just the despondency of homesickness. His battle station was everywhere, as he made the rounds of the ship providing good cheer, and a sense of shared apprehension wherever he went.

Throughout, he was a teacher. He taught us how to grow up, how to adapt to life away from home, how to love and help one another, how to face death. Having heard Adolph Hitler, at Nuremberg in 1938, exhort the youth of Germany to the horrors of his ways, Father Joe knew how vital it was to teach his charges the virtues of moral decency, compassion for fellow man and the worth of democracy.

Following his ordination, he received a doctorate after attending Fordham and Columbia Universities. He spent four years as assistant pastor at Blessed Sacrament Church in New Rochelle and was then assigned to teach at Cathedral College in Manhattan.

He was appointed to the Chaplain Corps of the USN as a lieutenant in 1941. After serving into 1943 aboard the USS *Massachusetts*, he later joined the aircraft carrier USS

This is the photograph of our Chaplain as most of the BB59 Crew-members remember him. 1942-1944.

Yorktown. He was discharged as a Commander in 1946 and returned to Cathedral College where he spent the next 10 years.

He was named a monsignor in 1959-joined the faculty of the Catholic University of America and taught modern French history until retirement in 1974. From 1976-82, he was an adjunct professor at Boston College, teaching also at St. John's Seminary in Brighton, MA. From 1965 until the time of his death, Monsignor Moody was an associate editor of the *Catholic Historical Review* and was also past president (1979) of the American Catholic Historical Assoc.

In the early 1980s, Father Joe moved to Statesboro, GA where the warmer climate better enabled him to cope with his increasing physical disabilities. There, he assisted St. Matthew's Parish and established an adult Sunday school program. He also taught part-time at Georgia Southern University.

Through the years, his physical handicaps grew more extensive and more painful, but his faith, acceptance and cheerful mood never did change. His brilliant mind kept him ever active and contributing to causes for the betterment of human life.

After Thanksgiving 1943, he faced even more serious problems: pneumonia, congestive heart failure, and eventually the amputation of his left leg. He was very aware of the situation and not only gave his consent for the amputation, but said: "When you have something unpleasant to do, get on with it as soon as possible."

He grew to love Georgia and all his Statesboro friends. With them, and under their care, Father Joe passed away in March 1994 at the age of 89 in Bullock Memorial Hospital, Statesboro, GA. He elected to choose the Veterans Section of Statesboro's Bullock Memorial Gardens for his final resting place.

To a beloved friend and shipmate, we express our profound thanks and say: Requiescat in Pace.

FOREWORD

She fired the first 16-inch shell in WWII at Casablanca, Nov. 8, 1942, the start of the European offensive, and fired the last 16-inch shell at Kamaishi, Japan, Aug. 9, 1945, half a world away.

In between, she logged over 225,000 nautical miles, engaged twenty-five times with the enemy and sank or damaged five ships, including the French battleship *Jean Bart*. She participated in nine bombardments of enemy territory, three of which were directed at the Japanese home islands. As a member of Task Force 58 under Adm. Spruance or Task Force 38 under Adm. Halsey, it destroyed or assisted in the destruction of at least 18 Japanese aircraft. Her scout plane pilots rescued seven aviators downed by enemy fire, often under the barrels of Japanese guns.

But a ship is more than a litany of her accomplishments, more than a collection of people or an embodiment of complex machinery, guns and fire power. She has a character, all her own, derived from and always reflecting the leadership of a Capt. Whiting; the inspiration of its rescue-bound aviators; and the dogged determination of Ed Palmer and his compatriots who saved the *Massachusetts* and brought her home. It's the soul of a Father Joe Moody.

In the aggregate, it's all of those things forged into a wonderfully efficient and warmly cohesive team. It's all wrapped up in the affection reflected in the name by which we all called her and loved her - "Big Mamie." Here with is her story.

Big Mamie's Homecoming Crew. Front row (L to R) Comdr. George M. Hall, Needham, MA; Francis Gatley, Foxboro, MA; Joseph Taylor, Fall River, MA; Harry Femino, Roslindale, MA; Edison Beaton Quincy, MA; Edward Allen, Malden, MA; Edward Palmer, Reading, MA; Joseph Olivera, Jr., Fall River, MA. Middle row (L to R) John Garvey, Dorchester, MA; Samuel Elson, Fall River, MA; Roland LaFrance, Fall River, MA; Robert Green, No. Kingston, RI; Earle Allen, Braintree, MA; Paul J. Dias, Braintree, MA; Back row (L to R) John Cassidy, Stoughton, MA; Joseph Reilly, Somerville, MA; Martin Adler, Boston, MA; Lawrence Bennett, Randolph, MA; Fred Knowles, Braintree, MA; Sheldon Titcomb, Agawam, MA; Stirling Oldberg, Framingham, MA; William DeNadal, Westport, MA; Alexander Poulos, Milton, MA; James Burt, Shart Hills, NJ; Victor Brum, Augusta, ME; Harold Nye, Marion, MA.

PROLOGUE
"A Fighting Ship"

At this time, which is the only opportunity I shall have to address the entire crew, I wish to lay down the policy of this vessel. I do not think of this ship as just a battleship—she is more. She is the Massachusetts. Let me tell you what I mean by that.

The Massachusetts has had built into her the intestinal fortitude of the Pilgrim Fathers, the watchfulness of Paul Revere, the discipline of Bunker Hill, the education of John Harvard.

The ancestors of the men who built her, built the first American ship ever to sail around the world. Right here in Quincy, a century and a quarter ago, they built the biggest ship of that day, and her name also, was the Massachusetts.

They built the Flying Cloud and other Clipper ships. They built the immortal frigate Constitution–"Old Ironsides." And they built the Hartford, flagship of Adm. Farragut, who lashed himself to the rigging and called out the command that will never be forgotten: "Damn The Torpedoes: Full Speed Ahead."

These are the traditions handed down to us who walk the deck of the Massachusetts. Traditions of daring, fortitude, character, and a love of liberty so fierce that a man would rather give up his life than give up his freedom. Never forget that only a few

miles from here free government in America had its start. They were poor people, ordinary people. They were not seeking power or gold. They were seeking a place where they could live in liberty. For this ideal they cheerfully crossed the ocean in tiny wooden ships, and landed in a winter wilderness to face hostile savages and wild beast. Half of that brave company died in the first winter but those who died, and those who survived, never had a thought of turning back. They believed that any price was not too great to pay for the privilege of being free.

They chose a motto for the seal of the Commonwealth of Massachusetts. It is a fighting motto—With The Sword It Seeks Peace Under Liberty.

That is our motto, yours and mine. That is our assignment—To win peace under liberty, and to keep on fighting until we do win it. Our only purpose in life at this moment is battle; we must not waste a single hour in getting ready for it.

I quoted a minute ago some American words that I like—"Damn The Torpedoes; Full Steam Ahead." I shall close with some famous words that I do not like—"Don't Give Up The Ship." Those words were uttered by one of the bravest men who ever wore the uniform of the American Navy, your uniform and mine, Capt. James

Lawrence. I honor him, but I resent the words because they were uttered at the end of a fight in which he and his men did not have a chance. They were the words of a dying captain, on a sinking ship, spoken to a brave but untrained crew. Because they were untrained, they were doomed.

So would we be doomed if we had to fight today even in this great ship, one of the biggest and most powerful in the world. We would be doomed because we are untrained. Our first business, our only business now, is to make this ship an efficient fighting unit, and to do it in the shortest possible time. We are going on a 24 hour basis.

I shall be intolerant of shirking. I intend to drive you because I am responsible for your lives. The quicker and better you are trained, the greater your chance for victory is, and the sooner we shall go home to an honorable peace. I shall give you full opportunity, but in the meanwhile "work" is our motto. I would not be doing my duty to you if I did not drive you and drive you hard.

The minute our training is complete, we shall show the world how the Massachusetts can take it and how she can dish it out. We shall prove that we appreciate the great traditions handed down to us. We shall be worthy of the name.

The address of Captain F.E.M. Whiting, USN, first commanding officer, to the crew of the U.S.S. Massachusetts at its commissioning on 12 May 1942.

"The Spirit of BB59"

Chapter One
Massachusetts Warships

1775 - 1939

US NAVAL SHIPS NAMED MASSACHUSETTS

To Capt. Richard H. Bowerman, 4th & L Divs., who compiled old naval records, together with information about ships named Massachusetts, and was the author of this chapter. To a retired Reading, MA teacher, Fred Wales, now associated with the Peabody Essex Museum, for his information about the Hannah. Bowerman was also responsible for the writing of the Foreward, the suggestion for the Dedication to Father Moody, the suggestion for the Prologue, and the Acknowledgement.

In an effort to block the one uncovered approach by the British to Boston, George Washington, as Commander-in-Chief of the American Army, sought to create the beginnings of a Navy. Having had no reply to his proposal toward that end from the Provincial Congress of Massachusetts, he acted on his own, under authority of the Continental Congress.

Gen. Washington commissioned Nicholas Broughton to arm and outfit his vessel, the *Hannah*, which, therefore, became the first armed vessel in the service of the US. It is reputed to have been a Marblehead type of schooner of the size in general use on the northeast coast in 1775.

It was armed with four six-pounder guns and manned by a crew of 30. It subsequently captured the English ship *Unity*, loaded with a cargo of naval stores. It was the first prize taken by the Continental Navy.

Early in October 1775, Gen. Washington instructed Col. Glover of the Marblehead marines to procure, with utmost haste, additional vessels at Newbury or Salem and to prepare them for armed sea duty. By Oct. 29 of that year, Glover had the *Lynch, Franklin, Lee, Warren, Washington* and *Harrison* ready for sea duty—a small navy which was known to some as "Washington's Cruisers." In some Massachusetts history books, these six ships, which replaced the *Hannah*, are referred to as the "Massachusetts Navy."

Of interest to our story is the fact that the ensign proposed by Gen. Washington's secretary, Col. Reed, was "a flag with a white ground, a pine tree in the middle, with the motto: 'An Appeal to Heaven'." This is the same flag which was flown aboard the USS *Massachusetts* (BB-59) on her final voyage from Norfolk, VA to Fall River, MA. It's the ensign which still flies aboard Big Mamie in Fall River today.

While many a gallant vessel has been named *Massachusetts*[2], there have been only four ships commissioned into the service of the U.S. Navy with that name.

The first naval vessel *Massachusetts* was a full-rigged ship constructed in the Boston Shipyard of Samuel Hall for trans-Atlantic service. It had a length of 178 feet; a 32 foot beam; a depth of hold of 20 feet; a draft of 15 feet and a speed of 5 to 8 knots. Its complement was 75 officers

Postcard featuring the third USS Massachusetts.

7th Division, 1942, aboard the USS Massachusetts.

Plank Owners at USS Massachusetts BB-59 decommissioning May 1946. Photo courtesy of Marty Fritz, 6th Div.

and men. It was purchased by the War Department in 1847 for use as an Army transport during the Mexican War. It was sent to the Pacific Coast it was transferred to the Navy in 1849. There, it cruised in support of pioneers against Indian disturbances in the sparsely-settled Washington Territory. Her landing party attacked a band of Indians on Puget Sound, Nov. 21, 1856. It continued its protection of settlers until April 4, 1847.

The second US naval vessel to bear the name *Massachusetts* was an iron steamer purchased in Boston from the Boston & Southern Steam Ship Co. for $172,000. It was 210 feet long; had a beam of 33 feet; tonnage of 1,515; a depth of hold of 25 feet and an average speed of 8 knots. When commissioned in Boston May 24, 1861, its crew numbered 92 men. Its original armament was one 32-pounder pivot gun and four eight-inch guns. During the Civil War, it served with the forces which blockaded the Southern ports, made prizes of numerous Confederate ships and served effectively as a supply and transport ship for the blockading squadrons. It was sold at auction in New York City in October 1867, having been decommissioned Sept. 22, 1865.

The name *Massachusetts* was assigned in 1869 to an iron-clad double-turreted Monitor which was under construction in the Portsmouth, NH Navy Yard but was never completed. Its wooden hull was to have been fitted with side armor, turret and machinery built under contract with the Delamater Iron Works in New York City. It would have displaced 5,600 tons. Its design called for a length of 354 feet, a beam of 56 feet eight inches, and a draft of 17 feet. It was condemned under Act of Congress Aug. 5, 1882, and was broken up in the Portsmouth Navy Yard in 1884.

The third *Massachusetts* was a seagoing coastline battleship (BB-2) whose keel was laid June 25, 1891, was launched two years later and commissioned at Philadelphia Navy Yard June 10, 1896. It had a length of 350 feet; a beam of 69 feet; a normal displacement of 10,288 tons; a mean draft of 24 feet, and a designed

The first USS Massachusetts, built as a merchant ship for the Atlantic trade, was chartered by the U.S. Goverment during the war with Mexico, and later served in the U.S. Navy.

speed of 15 knots. It had a complement of 32 officers and 441 enlisted men. It was armed with four 13-inch .35 caliber guns; eight eight-inch .35 caliber guns; four six-inch .40 caliber guns; 20 six-pounder guns; and six one-pounder guns. The maximum thickness of its armor was 18 inches.

During the Spanish-American War, it bombarded the batteries of Christobal, Colon. It missed the naval battle of Santiago, as it was re-coaling. In other engagements, however, it assisted in sinking other units of the Spanish fleet. It was placed in reduced commission May 2, 1910, and served as a summer practice cruise ship for the midshipmen of the US Naval Academy. Fleet Adm. Chester W. Nimitz who, during WWII was Commander-in-Chief, Pacific Ocean Areas, took his midshipman cruise aboard BB-2.

In 1917, off Yorktown, VA, it was employed in training hundreds of men in heavy gun target practice and was thus used for the remainder of WWI. The name *Massachusetts* was cancelled as of March 29, 1919; and it was designated Coast Battle-

ship Number 2. In 1920, it was loaned to the War Department as a target ship off Pensacola, FL. Now partially sunk, this ship has become a popular Florida tourist attraction and Florida's fourth underwater archaeological preserve. The citizens and tourists of Pensacola still enjoy fishing around the hull of BB-2 which has become a natural habitat for fish.

On April 4, 1921, at the Fore River Plant of the Bethlehem Shipbuilding Corp. at Quincy, MA, a keel was laid for a ship designated to become BB-54 and to have been named USS *Massachusetts*. It was to have had a displacement of 43,200 tons and a speed of 23 knots. This ship was never completed but was scrapped before reaching the launching stage. Her planned armament was 12 16-inch guns; 16 six-inch guns; four three-inch AA guns; other lighter guns and two 21-inch submerged torpedo tubes.

The fourth US naval ship proudly to bear the name *Massachusetts* was Big Mamie (BB-59), whose construction, description, exploits and history are fully described in later pages of this volume.

Chapter Notes
[1] *Following the Revolutionary War, there was no sea force available for the protection of the coast. The Revenue Cutter Service was organized by an Act of the First Congress and approved by President Washington in 1970. It became the only armed force afloat for the new United States until the U.S. Navy was organized a few years later. One such Revenue Cutter was named "Massachusetts."*

Chapter Two
Building BB59

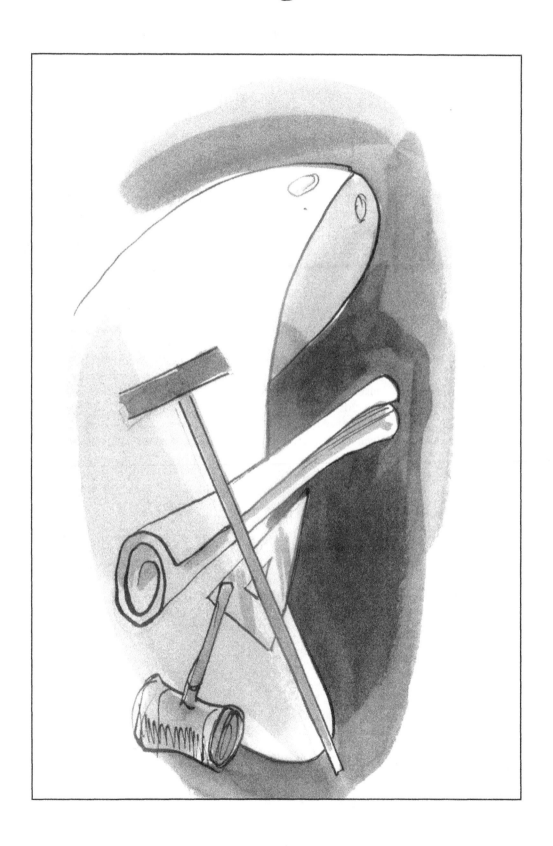

1939 - 1942

A SHIP IS BORN

To Edward W. Palmer, PhoM 2/c, and former Chaplain's Yeoman, who wrote this chapter.
To the Boston Public Library and the Quincy Historical Society, whose files and many news
clippings were made available to provide information for this chapter. To Mrs. Margery Conroy
for loaning her donation card and providing information about the BB-59 school drive in 1941.
To Debbie Collins, and the files of BB-59 at Fall River for photographs for this chapter.

While employment at the Bethlehem Shipbuilding Company's Fore River Plant in Quincy, MA was at a peace-time record with about 6,400 men working in July 1938, the city, like so many other industrial centers of the US, was still trying to shake off the effects of the depression that had beset the country throughout most of 1939. Continued growth in the economy and the long-term improvement in the city itself was, by no means, assured.

Things took an enormous upbeat with the announcement in mid-July 1938 that the Fore River Plant was the probable low-bidder for one of the three battleships to be built for the U.S. Navy. Since only three yards had bid on the vessels, it was generally assumed that each yard would be allowed to build one ship.

The ships, the final three of the quartet of *South Dakota* battleships were to be named the *Alabama*, the *Indiana* and the *Massachusetts*. To the *Quincy Patriot Ledger*, it only made sense to have the *Massachusetts* built at Quincy and to assign the *Alabama* and the *Indiana* to the Newport News and New York shipyards, the only other bidders for the contracts.

In mid-July 1938, the *Patriot Ledger*, under the title "*Massachusetts* in Massachusetts" advanced the foregoing argument. It noted that Fore River was to have built an earlier battleship named *Massachusetts* (BB-54) which, only partially constructed, was junked by the arms limitation treaty in the early 20s.

The paper pointed out that the cruisers *Quincy* and *Northhampton*, both named after Massachusetts towns, had been built at Fore River as had the aircraft carrier *Lexing-*

ton. The arguments proved successful; and the contract for the construction of Big Mamie was awarded to Fore River.

"Battleship *Massachusetts* to be Built Here"

The Bethlehem Shipbuilding Co. had had a great deal of experience in building naval vessels. The ships included six battleships (one for the Republic of Argentina), 92 destroyers, 77 submarines, 10 cruisers and two aircraft carriers. Nevertheless, not an executive at the Fore River yard and very few, if any, of the workmen in early 1939 were present when the USS *Nevada* (BB-36) a 29,000-ton dreadnaught was delivered to the Navy in 1916.

The contract with the Navy called for expenditures of $52,145,000. The anticipated time of construction was 55 months. The city eagerly anticipated steady work for thousands of employees for a minimum period of five years.

While the plans for the design and construction of the ship were prepared and mandated by the Navy, the 15 men in the plant's estimating department, who had spent months together and in consultation with manufacturers and vendors in preparing the bid, formed the nucleus of the plant's planning group which took over a three-story building at Fore River and, with a crew of 250 draftsmen, labored over the blueprints and tracing cloths on the big drawing tables to create the 3500-4000 different plans necessary for the construction of the ship.

The energizing impact upon the economy was to be felt throughout the region commencing in early 1939. While wood aboard the ship was probably to be limited to bread boards, meat chopping blocks in the galley and a few tongue depressors in the sick bay, massive amounts of lumber were needed for scaffolding and staging during construction. Twenty thousand tons of steel would go into the steel plates and shapes

Laying of the keel BB-59.

built into the hull and superstructure. Huge tonnage of aluminum for lining and insulating the walls of the living quarters and other parts of the ship would be needed. About 96 miles of brass tubes in the condensing and heat transfer units - piping for liquids, water, steam and oil-would be required.

Four propellers, each weighing 25 tons; 200,000 turbine blades for the main power plant; 130,000 square feet of linoleum; tiling or other floor coverings in massive amounts; 300 tons of various kinds of paint (60,000 gallons); 450 motor driven units; 350 port lights (windows); 5300-lighting fixtures and 950,000 feet (about 180 miles) of electrical cable were just some of the items required for construction.

"Sea-Going City to be Built in Fore River"

In an article entitled *Sea-Going City to be Built in Fore River*, under the by-line of Carlyle Holt, the author tried to give his readers a civilian's impression of what life, in the form of a 35,000-ton battleship, was all about.

"The electric power plant is big enough to light a large city. Its refrigerating units are large enough to keep a three-month's supply of fresh food for 1500 men. Its telephone switchboard would do to service a fair-sized town. Its hospital is a complete unit with x-ray machines and surgical appliances and supplies; likewise its dentistry establishment, its laundry, cobbler shop, tailor shop, galleys, pharmacy and barber shops.

The ventilating and cooling apparatus is of the most modern type and reaches every part of the ship. Her furniture includes a locker for every man, about 1500; bed springs and mattresses—sailors no longer swing in hammocks, they lie in pipe-bunks, three deep. All the furniture of the *Massachusetts* will be aluminum, as well as the mess kits and most of the galley utensils.

Last and least important, the ship, like most modern American warships, will have a ladies room. After all, officers and men do give parties sometimes and have visitors, so this is not superfluous.

A battleship must be the toughest kind of ship, for it is designed to take more punishment than anything that floats. Not only must its hull and deck be strong to resist torpedoes, shells and air bombs with which enemies attack it, but the ship must also be strong to resist the punishment it gets from its own weapons. A 16-inch gun will throw a one-ton shell about 25 miles. Now

THIS ACKNOWLEDGES

A CONTRIBUTION

BY *Margery Allen*

TOWARD THE PURCHASE OF FLAT SILVER FOR THE U.S.S. MASSACHUSETTS

Leverett Saltonstall
GOVERNOR OF THE COMMONWEALTH

NOVEMBER, 1941

Margery Allen's gift acknowledgement card, Nov 1941.

John F. Matigzeck, Plank owner and former NYC Entertainer.

the thrust of the gun's discharge is just as great against the butt of the gun as it is on the base of the shell. If a 16-inch gun could be mounted on the deck of a large ocean liner and fired, it would tear itself right out of the boat and take a good part of the boat with it. Yet, on a battleship, that tremendous blow must be stopped in a minute fraction of a second in the space of about 10 feet.

So a battleship's hull including the decks is double and sometimes triple and any projectile has to penetrate from a foot and a half to two feet of steel to reach any important part of the ship. Furthermore, the ship is divided into compartments which localize the extent of the damage."

While Mr. Holt gave an interesting description of certain aspects of life aboard

They did not take up much of her total displacement, but her nine heavy 16-inch guns were why Massachusetts was built. Each could elevate independently, as this 11 July 1944 photograph shows. At this time the conning tower was still topped by a spotting glass; other visible elements of the main battery fire control system are the MK 38 director in the foretop with its 26.5-foot steroscopic rangefinder topped by a MK 8 fire control radar, and the armored rangefinder of No. 2 turrets. Note also the sighting ports in the turret sides, a backup against failure of the fire control system.

the *Massachusetts*, her crew members who read that description will chuckle at a few of the discrepancies from fact. Hammocks were swung by those who awaited the assignment of a berth. The Marine detachment aboard Big Mamie would gladly have accepted "pipe-bunks, three-deep." Many of them slept in bunks of five-deep. Perhaps those circumstances resulted from the fact that the ship's normal crew, throughout its career, was numbered just under 2400, not the 1500 projected by Mr. Holt.

"Laying out the Keel"

Mamie's keel was laid July 20, 1939. It was conducted without ceremony and with little fanfare. According to the local newspaper, "Laying the keel for another ship was not a **news worthy event** in this city."

Little did the people of Quincy know that, in two years and five months, the nation would be at war; that the ship whose keel was then laid would become the USS *Massachusetts*, the "Workhorse of the Fleet" and that it would later become the WWII memorial for the Commonwealth of Massachusetts.

While Mamie was being built in Quincy, following a naval tradition, funds were being raised to purchase silverware for the ship. A committee of citizens, under the direction of the State Department of Education, conducted this fund drive throughout schools of the Commonwealth of Massachusetts.

Each contributor was given an acknowledgement of his/her gift. That these were meaningful to those children is evi-

Massachusetts on post refit speed trials, out of Puget Soung Navy Yard, 11 July 1944.

denced by the fact that Marjorie Allen, now Marjorie Conroy of Freedom, NH, never threw her card away but gave it to the editor of the BB-59 newsletter.

As it became more obvious that the ship would be involved in war, the citizens committee decided that the donation of traditional silverware was not particularly appropriate. Instead, the school children's contribution enabled the gift of a Hammond organ that could be tied into the ship's public address system so that the entire ship could enjoy the music. Their reasoning was further motivated by the fact that donated funds were to benefit the entire ship, both officers and crew members, but that the silverware would only be seen, and used, by the officers.

The organ was delivered to the ship in May 1942 and was installed in the band room adjacent to the crew's mess hall. The ship then recruited John Cartright, a graduate of the New England Conservatory of Music, and assigned him to the ship as an organist May 29, 1942.

Somehow, in the dismantling of the *Massachusetts* preparatory to its demolition, the organ ended up in the possession of a church in North Cambridge, MA as an assist to the efforts of the church to rebuild following a fire.

Big Mamie was launched Sept. 23, 1941.

Mrs. Charles Francis Adams, wife of the most distinguished living member of America's most distinguished family, a family whose roots came from the city of Quincy, was her sponsor.

In a speech at the launching, Col. Frank Knox, Secretary of the Navy, pleaded for the repeal of the Neutrality Act. The fall of France had occurred; and America was beginning to recognize that its way of life was increasingly in danger.

Gov. Leverett Saltonstall praised the Fore River shipyard for launching the ship seven months ahead of schedule.

Fueling at sea allowed Massachusetts and other U.S. battleships to remain at sea for long periods of time; here she refuels from the oiler Kaskaskia 17 October 1944.

USS Massachusetts BB-59 at sea.

Adm. Ernest King, Commander-in-Chief of the U.S. Navy, was in attendance as were 75,000 other people, probably the greatest crowd ever assembled at one spot in the 315-year history of Quincy.

While the contract price of the ship was $49,000,000, it was later disclosed that it cost, ready for battle, about $80,000,000; that her standard displacement was 35,000 tons, but that it weighed around 41,000 tons when commissioned; that it was 680 feet long, 108 feet wide and of 36-feet draft; that her main armament included nine 16-inch guns.

A vessel of the so-called South Dakota class, the *Massachusetts* was sister ship to the *Indiana, Alabama* and *South Dakota*, in 1941 the most powerful class of ships in the American Navy. At that time, seven 42,000-tonners were in the drafting room stage, of which four, including the *New Jersey*, were later to be built.

Following the launching in September 1941, Big Mamie remained in the Quincy shipyard for her "fitting out" until the spring of 1942, when it became the Bethlehem Shipbuilding Company's duty to sail her to Boston, and deliver her to the Navy.

Many of the officers and enlisted men came aboard the ship in Quincy. Although this list is not complete, some of the biographies in CHAPTER EIGHT reveal that, in January 1942, Ken Armel came aboard to set up the print shop, and Earl Bledsoe, Victor Brum, Jim Butte, Wallace Davis, Bob Grimes, Russell Lambert, Russ Luckey, M. Madau, Charles Outcall, Bill Thomas, and Don Tucker also reported aboard that month. In February, Jack Lacy, Eugene Lake, Emmett Norwood, Fred Parola and Vic Pellarin came aboard and, in March, Henry Banzhaf, Bob Hill, Max Ludwick, and John Price. In April, a month before it sailed to Boston and was commissioned, Frank Beardsley, Jack Becker, Henry Bedard, Jack Bishop, George Duhamel, Bob Greening, Charles Hopkins, Casimir Kudasik, Ace Mavrogeorge, Ken McLeod, Dale Moudy, Ed Palmer, Ed Pogor and Bob Princeton had been added to the crew.

Most of the officers who were department heads started their duties in Quincy. Most of the enlisted men who were assigned helped to build Big Mamie knew that they would soon be drafted, and therefore enlisted in the Navy, so they could serve aboard the ship. Some of the former Quincy shipyard workers who enlisted became members of the R Div., Ed and Bob Condon, Jack DeChambeau and Bon Huggon. (Jack was a good sax player and later became a member of the band.)

The USS *Massachusetts* formally became part of the USN at its commissioning which took place May 12, 1942. At that time, her first skipper, Capt. F.E.M. Whiting, USN addressed the crew in a speech printed as the Prologue in this volume.

The following sketches of BB-59, both a broadside and an overhead view, were made following her overhaul period at the Puget Sound Navy Yard June-July 1944.

Mamie was built, launched, and commissioned. It was time to create her crew.

Big Mamie, at home in Fall River, MA, January 18, 1972.

Chapter Three
The Building of a Crew

May '42 - October '42

THE BUILDING OF A CREW

To Capt. Richard H. Bowerman for writing this chapter.
To Mary Beth Bowerman for typing all the text written by her
father-in-law. To Edward W. Palmer and the old files of the Bay Stater
and photographs he had taken. To Bill Canfield, CBM, and Big Mamie's
cartoonist who supplied the sketches for each of the title pages of this book.

The keel of Battleship 59 was laid down in Quincy, MA at the Fore River Plant of the Bethlehem Steel Corporation July 20, 1939. Two months later, Germany invaded Poland. Days later, Great Britain and France declared war on Germany. In that same month, Russia crossed the Polish frontier, and Poland was partitioned. In the Far East, Japan had marched into Manchuria in 1931 and landed in Shanghai in 1937. The Second World War began with these Far Eastern and European aggressions. The *Massachusetts* was being rushed to completion when the Japanese attack on Pearl Harbor plunged America into war Dec. 7, 1941. The 35,000-ton ship was commissioned and officially joined the USN May 12, 1942.

Like any new US naval vessel commissioned in the 1940s, the *Massachusetts'* crew was a blend of a cadre of veterans with the majority of her numbers about to go to sea for the first time.

When most of her crew reported aboard in Fore River or in South Boston, she was a tangle of one umbilical lifeline after another—electric cables, hoses, water lines and every other service that a floating city for 2400 people would require until she had been built to self-sufficiency. A myriad of workmen stormed over her, riveting, welding, wiring and doing the hundreds of other operations which go into building a capital naval ship. Huge cranes operated alongside

Training - retrieving our Kingfisher.

THE BAY STATER

Vol. 1, No. 13. U. S. S. MASSACHUSETTS October 3, 1942

WRESTLING TEAM ENTERTAINS

USS Massachusetts newsletter.

of her, lowering massive equipment and machinery aboard.

When the ship was commissioned May 12, 1942, it was painted battleship gray outboard and, for the most part, within. Inside of two months from commissioning, the Navy announced the availability of non-flammable paint and required its use on all ships. As a result, the air was filled, for weeks on end, with the sound of paint chippers and with the smell, in the interior spaces, of paint remover. A more laborious or boring job could hardly be imagined.

The original plan of the day for July 13, 1942, called for the usual in-port activity— "Send mail orderly for mail in station wagon"; "All junior officers of Watch I report to the Ward Room for censorship" and "Liberty for Watch II." A modification of that plan was issued in the very early hours of July 13. It specified, among other things, "Make all preparations for getting underway. Secure all gear for sea"; "Man all special sea details"; "Underway at 1100 to conduct structural firings of secondary batteries."

Big Mamie was finally going to sea on her test trials. The revised plan of the day was part of the process of secrecy which enveloped the movements of naval vessels during the war. Nevertheless, when the wife of an officer took a taxi cab downtown to shop at the department stores July 13 and asked the cab driver what all the excitement and the balloons were about, the cabby answered: "Oh, the *Massachusetts* is going to sea today."

The processes of training had gone on even as the ship was fitting out. For example, the original plan of the day for July 13 called for rigging paravanes and conducting dock trials. Machine gunners had gone off to Rhode Island to learn how to tear down and re-assemble 20mm and 40mm guns and how to load and fire them.

Fr. Moody, in baseball cap, enjoys a softball game with us.

But July 13 marked a distinct change in the training routine. Thereafter, the ship trained with a submarine in Penobscot Bay off the coast of Maine. Her machine gunners trained constantly in firing at sleeves towed behind aircraft. Her main and secondary batteries fired at towed sleds.

Extensive simulated damage-control drills were conducted, teaching how to respond to one emergency after another. The crew learned how to catapult aircraft and recover them by calming the waves with as sharp a turn across the wind as the ship could make.

All of this was designed to enhance the technical, mechanical and professional skills of the crew. Capt. Whiting lived up to his promise or threat, as the case may be, in his commissioning address where he preached reality in saying that "if we had to fight today ... we would be doomed because we are untrained. Our first business, our only business now, is to make this ship an efficient fighting unit, and to do it in the shortest possible time. We are going on a 24-hour basis."

However, a technically proficient crew is not necessarily an efficient and effective crew unless there is, concurrent with the development of technique, the development of a sense of family—an atmosphere

of respect, a sense of mutual caring. That side of things developed in a multitude of ways.

During the many months Mamie was in and out of Casco Bay off Portland, ME, she made use everyday she was in port of the recreational facilities which the Navy had developed on Little Chebeague Island. Our chaplain, Father Moody, would go ashore with a working party early in the day, pick up clams, lobsters and cases of beer and go to Chebeague to build a pit for the clam and lobster bake. The liberty watch would come in the afternoon for football, baseball, basketball, horseshoes or just to swap yarns over a bottle of beer. The truly hardy (perhaps, read that foolhardy) would push a few seals out of the way and go for a swim in the icy waters of the bay.

Later, in the Pacific, spirited competition between the teams of Big Mamie and those of other ships developed.

The creation of friendship started first within divisional lines and then, rapidly, across those lines, as shared experiences created new companionship. Religious services—both Roman Catholic and non-denominational—all were held faithfully every Sunday.

The chaplain's office produced the weekly "*Bay Stater*" (E.W. Palmer, editor and Bill Canfield, art editor). It kept us abreast of what was going on aboard; but, even more importantly, its columns wrote about the background of shipmates all of which told us about some very interesting people and helped us develop a sense of pride in being involved with them in a common effort. The chaplain's office developed a library of both books and phonograph records. Space was allocated in all of the crew's quarters and living spaces for library sub-stations. That office was also busy in pointing the way to get tickets at Fenway Park or at the Boston Symphony concerts and other types of entertainment wherever the ship went.

Ships developed various sporting teams. In early October, the *Massachusetts* wrestling team showed us an assortment of holds that had the crew cheering from start to finish. The chaplain's office also arranged such things as checker tournaments, the organization of a ship's orchestra and a variety of presentations at ship Smokers. A boxing team and a ship softball team were formed.

Ship's dances were a regular feature in helping to develop esprit de corps. The fourth of them was held Sept. 19, 1942, at a local lodge hall, with the ship's orchestra and performers from a local night-club providing the entertainment.

Johnny Matigzeck, a former professional entertainer from Brooklyn, put together a team of entertainers from among the crew which not only did a great job at frequent gatherings aboard ship but, in the Pacific, were eagerly sought by other ships.

All of this was part of the process of building confidence and self-esteem in a bunch of young, basically untrained sailors—the development of a state of readiness and the creation of a family responsible for itself. Traditions and rituals remain essential to the military mystique, and the crew of Big Mamie was developing its own traditions.

But nothing does a better job of bonding a crew than to share the risks of battle—the grist of war stories to be developed and enlarged upon as part of the pride in accomplishment. All of this was shortly to be afforded the crew at the Battle of Casablanca.

"Dedicated to all A.S."

Ed Palmer's Future wife, Grace (center of photo looking up), watches Ed as he takes photo of dance.

Fr. Moody after a softball game.

2nd Division dance, Boston, MA, Hotel Beconsfield, 1942. Photo courtesy of Stanley Campbell.

L Div softball Champions Fall 1942. First Row, L-R: Andrew W. Termyna, Lt. Richard H. Bowerman, Kelly Cougnlih, Gerard J. Boeh, Callahan, J.V. Anderson, Hobbs. Second Row: Edward J. O'Brien, Frank J. O'Brien, Frank J. Marrion, Tom F. Daly, Rubin C. Rand. Third Row: Fr. Joseph N. Moody, Terence Patrick Brady.

Chapter Four
The Battle of Casablanca

November 1942

THE BATTLE OF CASABLANCA

To Capt. Richard H. Bowerman, author of this chapter, and
To Cosmopolitan Magazine for permission to reprint its article written by
John R. Henry, war correspondent, and a guest aboard USS Massachusetts, November 1942.

It was a gorgeous fall day Oct. 24, 1942. The days preceding had been fully occupied with the provisioning of the ship, bringing a fuel barge and later a gasoline lighter alongside to top off our reserves and, in general, doing all those extra busy things which led everyone to realize that the training days were over, at least for a while, and that something big was afoot. That proved to be Operation Torch.

That something unusual was about to happen was confirmed when the crew learned that John Henry, war correspondent for *Cosmopolitan* (then, a far different type of magazine than today's version) was to travel with us. Scuttlebutt aboard, always highly imaginative, reached its ultimate proportions.

Operation Torch, the landing of Allied troops in North Africa in November 1942, was the first major American amphibious assault of the war against European Axis powers. The *Massachusetts* was on her shake-down cruise, but her crew of 2400 men had been welded into a top-notch fighting team during months of intensive training. Not only was Operation Torch the largest amphibious operation ever undertaken, it was the largest overseas expedition that had ever been attempted in the history of man. Later operations would find the US mounting even larger overseas expeditions, but the invasion of North Africa was the beginning—the baptism of fire.

Mamie was designated flag ship for Commander Covering Gp., RAdm. Robert C. Giffen, USN, which was to assist in landing 35,000 Army troops near Casablanca. It sailed from Casco Bay off Portland, ME Oct. 24, 1942, and rendez-voused with TF-34 on the 28th. This was the greatest war fleet ever assembled to that time. The ships stretched over 800 square miles of submarine-infested ocean.

The weather turned bad half-way across the Atlantic. At the height of the bad weather, heavy seas damaged one of the Kingfishers (Mamie's observation planes) and did some other minor damage on deck. At one point, the crew's mess hall had a couple of inches of water sloshing around in it. However, after the storm passed, we sailed for almost an entire day into the arch of a beautiful rainbow.

As we moved eastward, the *Massachusetts* fueled destroyers every few days. On Oct. 28, the crew was directed to prepare for the disposal of all cigarette lighter fluid, hair tonic, face lotions and other flammable liquids. All letters and unnecessary papers were similarly to be disposed of. Church service Nov. 1 produced about twice the usual number of worshippers. The chaplain's office, which had been converted into a confessional, kept Father Moody busy for hours on end.

About 0330 Nov. 2, the sound of depth charges rocked the air. It developed that an enemy submarine had innocuously surfaced inside our destroyer screen. Mamie bent on all boilers and moved out of the area at flank speed.

In lieu of music that had been piped aboard from local radio stations (which were not able to be picked up out in the Atlantic), Ed Palmer became a disc jockey and played recordings from the chaplain's office.

The group took position off the North African coast on the night of Nov. 7-8. Her mission was three-fold:

1. To cover the entire Task Force against possible attack by the formidable French ships stationed at Dakar, further down the African coast;

2. To contain the enemy ships in the harbor of Casablanca and destroy them if they decided to fight; and

USS Massachusetts, just before her departure for the North African Campaign.

3. To knock out the shore batteries around Casablanca, if they resisted.

The French Republic had fallen before Nazi Germany's armed might in 1940. The French fleet and its units in French Morocco, North Africa were under the control of the Vichy regime, which was cooperating with the Nazis.

The political situation ashore was complex. Negotiations had been underway for some time to try to keep the French military from resisting the Allied invasion. It was not known whether the French would attempt to block the invasion or permit the Allies to land without resistance. France had been a traditional friend of the US; but, if the French navy, now under German control, chose to fight, there would be no alternative but to shoot it out.

The overall plans called for the destroyer *Wainwright* (DD-419), with RAdm. H. Kent Hewitt, USN, commander of the Western naval Task Force (TF 34) aboard, to steam into Casablanca Harbor (if the French did not resist) to arrange the terms of surrender. It wasn't until the invasion force was well at sea that someone realized that there was no one aboard the *Wainwright* who spoke French. The back-up plan, in the event that the *Wainwright* was not able to go in, called for Mamie's Executive Officer, Cmdr. E.M. Thompson, USN, to go ashore in a *Massachusetts'* whaleboat with an interpreter for the same purpose. Lt. Renouf Russell, USNR, and Lt. G. Barron Mallory, USNR, volunteered as the interpreters.

One day, just after lunch, Adm. Giffen (whose Nom De Guerre was "Alkili Ike") met with Russell and Mallory in his cabin to draft the surrender terms and message. He was stunned when he returned to his cabin about three hours later to find that the two officers were still there. When he asked what the problem was, they replied: "We can't decide whether to use the subjunctive at this point in the message." The admiral tossed them out of his cabin shortly thereafter with appropriate references to the relative immateriality of the subjunctive.

When the *Wainwright* stood in, it was fired upon by all local French batteries. Capt. Whiting is reputed to have turned to Adm. Giffen and said "The *Wainwright* is retreating at flank speed—I repeat flank speed."

As dawn approached on the morning of Nov. 8, 1942, the *Massachusetts* catapulted her two spotting planes, increased speed to 25 knots and joined the cruisers *Wichita* and *Tuscaloosa* in battle formation. With four

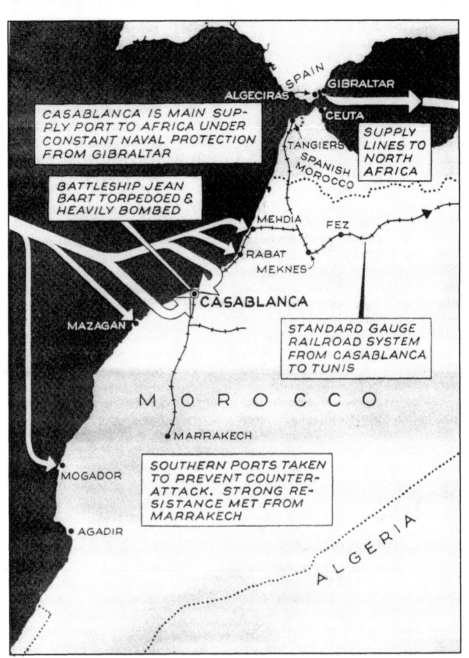

The Casablanca campaign is shown above. The Moroccans, last to be conquered by France and still unreconstructed, may fight on from inaccessible mountion hideouts. Railway from Casablance can transport supplies east on inland railway safe from Mediterranean submarines and planes.

destroyers some 3,000 yards ahead, the Force steamed for Casablanca with battle flags flying. The American Forces were under orders not to fire unless there was resistance. "Batter Up" was the code phrase to signal that local resistance had begun and "Play Ball" the signal for our forces to open fire.

Task Force 34[1]

RAdm. H. Kent Hewitt,
Commander, in Augusta

WESTERN NAVAL TASK FORCE,
Adm. Hewitt

Embarking Western Task Force US
Army, MGen. George S. Patton Jr., USA

TG 34.1 COVERING GROUP., RAdm.
Robert C. Giffen

BB-59 *MASSACHUSETTS*
Capt. F.E.M. Whiting

CA-45 *Wichita*
Capt. F.S. Low

CA-37 *Tuscaloosa*
Capt N.C. Gillette

Screen, Capt. P.D. Moon
(ComDesRon 8)

DD-419 *Wainwright*

Lt. Cmdr. R.H. Gibbs
DD-402 *Mayrant*
Lt. Cmdr. E.K. Walker
DD-404 *Rhind*
Cmdr. H.T. Read
DD-447 *Jenkins*
Lt. Cmdr. H.F. Miller

Tanker
AO-30 *Chemung*
Capt. J.J. Twomey

At 0400 that morning, a message from President Roosevelt was beamed by radio into all of North Africa, urging the French to cooperate. The answer arrived just after dawn when French gun emplacements ashore opened fire on the American scout boats, landing craft, the landing troops and their patrolling destroyers. Almost immediately, Adm. Giffen sent the message "Play Ball." Thus did the battle for Casablanca start.

Wherever the *Massachusetts*, *Wichita* and *Tuscaloosa* went in firing upon French ships and shore batteries, a group of fishing trawlers would move right along with them. The enemy firing was so accurate that Adm. Giffen strongly suspected that the trawlers were serving as spotters for the French guns. Lt. Franklin D. Roosevelt Jr., USNR, from the USS *Mayrant* (DD-402) was sent aboard to investigate but reported that he could find no indication of radio equipment. Further examination after the battle revealed that each of the trawlers had a false bottom beneath which highly sophisticated radio equipment had been hidden to enable them to spot the French gunfire. While the *Massachusetts* took three direct hits and a shell passed through its ensign, it managed, by some lively zig-zagging, to avoid dozens of enemy shells which fell into the water on all sides of it. The tattered ensign now adorns the Crew Members' Memorial Room.

The drama of the battle is captured in the following excerpts from the Talkers' Log maintained on the bridge of the *Massachusetts* as the action unfolded:

TELEPHONE TALKER'S NOTES

Nov. 8, 1942

0545	General Quarters
0547	It has been reported resistance has been met by landing force.
0604	Ammunition and powder up to all guns.

0614	Two vertical lights, bottom one blinking can be seen on the beach.
0618	Port plane off.
0620	Starboard plane off.
0625	Seven planes off port quarter.
0634	Paint locker flooded with CO2 also the gas tanks.
0638	Four destroyers, two cruisers, and the *Massachusetts* are together.
0644	Admiral requests 20 knots on first fire run. Admiral and Captain reported on open bridge.
0652	AA opened up on the beach at our aircraft.
0655	Fishing schooner dead ahead.
0656	Message from plane, "I have encountered hostile aircraft."
0657	Enemy planes approaching us.
0659	One of our own planes coming in on starboard bow—from Doerflinger: "Hostile aircraft following, pick up hostile planes."
0701	We opened fire. Light bombers coming at us.
0702	*Jean Bart* has opened fire on us.
0706	Changed to flank speed.
0707	Turret 1 fired - - - Turret 3 fired - - shell hit the target.
0709	Changing to 060 to avoid aircraft. Salvo landed on end of jetty.
0710	Changed to 080 - - - small bombs dropping around us. Hits in the water bearing 95.
0713	Two bombs on port - - - looks like shell fire.
0716	Four planes bearing 060. No flame but a lot of smoke on our objective.
0717	Plane approaching starboard— Torpedo plane approaching from east.
0719	We are opening up on El Hank (shore battery).
0723	Have not been hit as yet.
0726	Dive bombers going at one of our cruisers.
0727	Enemy planes approaching.
0728 0.070	Plane dove into water bearing 070.
0730	A fire on the Jetty reported.
0732	Transport and destroyer bearing 345.
0735	All three turrets reported in smooth operation.
0736	Range on *Jean Bart* 29000.

0740	Last salvo looks like hit on *Jean Bart*—ceased firing on main battery, temporarily.— Changed to 180—speed 27 knots.
0744	Landing barges are in sight off port bow about 10,000 yards off. El Hank is not firing.
0747	Four landing barges on port quarter—Cruiser *Augusta* is dead astern. Standby to fire on *Jean Bart*.
0803	Shell fire landing between tin cans and us.
0805	Our sub spotted with gun aft— reported as the unidentified war ship.
0807	20mm #15 damaged—repair gang dispatched there.
0812	*Jean Bart* firing secondary battery.
0817	Enemy subs leaving harbor.
0828	Shells off port bow.
0830	French blowing up ammunition dumps.
0845	Sub crossing from port to starboard—unidentified. Turrets all in fine condition. Standby to recover plane.
0855	Transports being attacked by enemy cruiser—we are going to their aid. Enemy shell went through our colors (our commissioning flag).
0914	Orders to destroy enemy cruisers between Casablanca and Fedala.
0916	Three French cruisers are firing bearing 200.
0917	Turrets get word to load.
0918	Standby for firing.—Aloft observers report haze and mist—visibility about 4 miles—we are firing into the sun.
0921	Cruiser is returning fire.
0923	We believe we have hit on one cruiser—it is smoking.
0924	Two cruisers smoking.
0925	They all seem to be hit—there is plenty of smoke—their shells are falling 1000 yds. short.
0929	Their shells are about 500 yds. off.
0930	Planes overhead friendly— shells coming closer—hit 70 yds. off beam.—French cruiser and can bearing 166 True— Our course is
140.	—Captain asked navigator

how long he can keep on this course—Wants to know navigation situation—We just crossed the 50 fathom curve.

0931 Shell went right over us.

0934 —Turret 1 fired and we really were shaken up.—Aloft observers can see cruisers smoke and splashes—Cruisers are slowing down.

0938 Report one cruiser sunk.—Our planes directly overhead.

0939 Standby to fire on cruiser bearing

190 Shells are falling closer to us.

0941 Two cruisers opening fire on us.

0943 New Range 15200—Shells on port and starboard about 50 yds. off—New course 295—Two of their cruisers are hit.

0944 Destroyer is at 250—believe we hit her—much smoke pouring out of her.

0945 Shrapnel falling short of frame 41, can't see any damage.

0946 Range 15500—A good hit on one of the large destroyers.

0948 Two close misses on starboard beam.

0951 Fire is getting heavy—Target lost in the smoke.

0953 Picked up another French cruiser

254 —Changing course to 260.

0955 Destroyer bearing 260 heading this way—Enemy mine fields exist about 8 miles east of beach Xray and about one mile off beach.

1000 Hit on the port bow abreast of Turret II. Compt. A208L. No casualties or fire.

1002 Enemy cruiser sinking.

1003 Three torpedo wakes on port side.

1006 Three torpedoes missed.

1007 Torpedo on port side—missed by 10 feet—fire on our main deck—We have water.

1010 Sub on port bow 207—Warship bearing 205, unidentified, is firing

1015 Small fire under control.

1016 Enemy cruiser smoking—It is safe to say cruiser or destroyer 243, is burning from bow to stern, looks like cruiser we have been firing on.

1021 Shells are being fired at us—

Torpedo wake on port bow bearing

335 —Missed.

1024 Keep a sharp lookout everywhere—Fire is completely out—Everything under control.

1030 French destroyer leader is firing on us, bearing 52. *Wichita* is now firing.

1034 Two ships bearing 50 and 45 are firing on us. Ship bearing 95 is firing on us.

1041 Lt. Doerflinger reports 15 minutes of gas left. We are 6-1/2 miles off coast, bearing 230.

1050 Shell splashes are moving in closer on port bow.

1051 Small fire at frame 112, a piece of canvas on main deck port. Quick acting door to Executive Officer's cabin is blown out.

1052 Firing from shore bearing 50. Shells are coming close. Five planes coming in forward, unidentified. Friendly planes. French cruisers are in range of 5" guns. Nine inch shell from beach hits about 25 yards off starboard beam.

1058 Believe hit on starboard side aft of conning tower.

1100 French destroyer coming at us dead ahead very fast.

1101 Hit at 20mm group 13. Direct

hit on destroyer. We are now firing at a cruiser.

1104 No. 4 machinery space filled with smoke; everything is under control.

1105 Firing at destroyer. Shell did not penetrate through the second deck. Hit on 20mm is under control. Fire at frame 85 is under control, where shell had hit. No casualties at 20mm.

1115 Repair 5 reports no smoke in passageways near machinery #3.

1150 Sunk two cruisers, some cans, one cruiser is on fire. The landing is not going too well. *Jean Bart's* main battery is out of commission.

1155 Watch 1 is to go for chow.

1200 Give the galley steam, orders from Conn.

1230 Plane dropping depth charge bearing 355.

1300 Two fishing boats bearing 325.

1310 General quarters sounded on alarm.

1312 Cruiser bearing 100. Expect to catapult plane starboard.

1315 We may engage three cruisers who have escaped to the north.

1327 Starboard catapult is out of commission, must change to port.

A lull in the battle of Casablanca allowed Massachusetts' crewmen to move about on deck, and afforded a photographer the opportunity for a detailed view of her superstructure. Note the open side ports of both main and secondary battery directors, and the "mushroom" ventilator set into the main deck just abaft No. 3 turret.

1328 Plan to engage El Hank at 1345. Tracking enemy destroyer into Casablanca.

1339 Fired to starboard on destroyer leader.

1340 Several very near misses around us.

1345 Our shot went right on. Misses to us are closer.

1350 Cease firing.

1353 Conn to control, "Search for other targets."

1400 French cruiser is apparently now on fire.

1405 French cruiser that was headed for harbor was beached.

1410 Heavy black smoke on horizon bearing 317. Gunnery officer reports 41 or 42 rounds per gun left.

1420 Watch 2 went for chow

1445 *Tuscaloosa* and *Wichita* are firing to port. Target is not visible. *Wichita* got another cruiser on the last salvo. El Hank is in flames. Cruiser is listing terribly. One of our oil tanks has been hit.

1500 We are going to investigate a ship on the starboard beam.

1505 Getting the range on El Hank.

1515 General quarters.

1518 Lt. Doerflinger reports no activities inside of harbor.

1528 Two subs have surfaced and are headed into the harbor.

1605 Enemy cruiser has caught fire at the mouth of Casablanca Harbor. The last salvo hit military stores at El Hank.

1610 Secure from general quarters.

TELEPHONE TALKER'S NOTES

Nov. 10, 1942

0900 General quarters.

0909 Fishing boat, relative bearing 290.

0938 Fishing boat is coming on parallel course with *Massachusetts*.

0940 El Hank, relative bearing is 104. Rounds of fire left—Turret 1, 127—Turret 2, 130—Turret 3, 128.

1014 Plane, relative bearing 260 is a PBY. Message from Texas plane, "We are encountering no enemy aircraft and unable to find targets of opportunity."

1021 Ship on starboard bow—a big burst of water near it and smoke coming from the left of it. PBY is passing over it. There are six destroyers in that area.

1023 Investigate white smoke on horizon.

1038 Destroyer is going into Casablanca without being fired upon.

1040 Start chow. Give the galley water and steam.

1105 AA seems to be fired from the beach, relative bearing 40. Ranger had dodged four torpedoes.

1116 Report wake across our bow about 1,000 yds.

1123 *Wainwright* reports submarine contact. *Wainwright* is off starboard bow.

1129 Wake dead across port bow about 800 yds.

1130 Smoke visible from city.

1133 Nothing is standing out of the harbor.

1138 *Texas* just opened fire.

1139 *New York* is firing.

1140 Some firing coming at our destroyer but it is falling short. Someone is dropping smoke screen in between.

1142 Anti-aircraft firing coming from one of our battleships.

1143 Heavy fire on the beach.

1144 It is reported that *Jean Bart* may be shooting. A cruiser inside harbor is firing, not the *Jean Bart*. Relative bearing on cruiser is 303.

1145 Looks like *Jean Bart* is firing aft 6" battery. Yellow splash in water,

150 feet high near *New York*. Relative bearing on *Jean Bart* is 302.

1146 Smoke over one of our ships. It looks like the *Jean Bart* has been hit. El Hank is firing. Smoke over one of our battleships.

1148 Small fishing boat, relative bearing is 300.

1149 Firing from El Hank.

1155 Yellow splash around *Augusta*, relative bearing 200.

1157 Fishing boat turning back to Casablanca, think it may be spotting.

1158 *Jean Bart* has been silent since last salvo.

1203 Ranger has dodged two more tin fish.

1220 Plane reports *Jean Bart* firing.

1223 Prepare to make full speed at 1300.

1230 Plane bearing 25. French destroyer standing out of harbor one mile.

1250 Fishing boat bearing relative 340.

1259 Expedite dinner.

1310 Fishing boat, relative bearing 263 heading this direction.

1342 All hands who have not eaten dinner, lay below to mess hall immediately.

1344 Ship on port side looks like trawler.

1352 Keep sharp look-out for all fishing boats.

1404 Coming to 145.
Ships bearing 275 relative—are fishing boats.

1406 Damage control manned and ready.

Fishing boat at 335 relative.
Fishing boat bearing 55 relative.

1446 Object looks like ship and we are heading for it. Object between can and us. Destroyer dispatched after fishing boat.

1455 Two ships bearing 290 relative. Report French submarine MED-USA surrendered.

1506 Secure from Condition Zed and Set Material Condition Yoke. Secure from general quarters. Set Condition II, Watch II.

USS Massachusetts BB-59 at work.

CASABLANCA DEAD AHEAD

"Where are you going?" we asked this famous I.N.S. war correspondent one day last October. "I don't know," he said. "Our destination is secret but we expect action." "Write what you see," we told him. Here it is . . .

Thanks to the courtesy of Cosmopolitan *magazine, we reproduce here with the article written by its war correspondent, John R. Henry, who sailed as a guest aboard the* Massachusetts *during the course of the battle.*

The cool, moonless night was quiet. The sea was miraculously calm. It was a strangely placid setting for the death and destruction of war.

Over there within shooting distance was the coral-fringed coast of Morocco. There, under the star-specked autumn sky, lay the land that would become an American fighting front—the palm trees, rivers, jungles, plains and white vistas of sand; the pink minarets, towns and villages of French West Africa.

Misty, Herculean forms of American battle craft and transport ships slipped silently in toward the shore line. The zero hour was near. The climax to the greatest amphibious operation in US military history was at hand.

You could feel the tension. Conversation was speculative and subdued. Everybody seemed to be wondering and waiting, fidgety to find out what the dawn would bring.

"Say, mate," wisecracked a sailor from Missouri to his buddy, "there's no telling whether we'll have to fight here tomorrow or not. Remember that girl you were squiring around last time in port? Well, just in case we fight, how 'bout giving me that chickadee's address; you know—just in case we fight, and just in case one of us don't come back."

"Okay, it's a deal," his pal replied, forking over some sweet little thing's street and telephone number. Thus, in one particular instance, the tension was lifted momentarily.

Thousands of other little conversation pieces kept men in high spirits, offsetting the otherwise somber trend of thought. In this manner did American fighting men go forth to battle.

Girded for combat and supported from the sea by nearly all the striking force in the Atlantic Fleet, Army troops were ready now to launch their monumental campaign along the Mediterranean. Nothing had ever been attempted before on such a vast scale. Never in military annals had so many troop vessels and naval ships transported so many men so far on such a mission. Every lad in khaki and blue realized the sweeping significance of the task ahead.

Stern questions gripped the minds of all present.

Would the French oppose American occupation of Africa? Or would they accept our overtures of friendship?

You could sense the imminent possibility that France would fight. It was evident, moreover, that a prolonged campaign against forces of the Vichy government would thwart a swift, surprise blow against Axis armies in Libya and along the southen coast of the Mediterranean.

Would the daring landing operation be successful?

What would the French choose to do?

Soldiers and sailors wondered as they waited at their battle stations on the night of Nov. 7th.

Nerve-twisting time was to pass before they had their answers. It would seem ages before the ships could creep closer to shore and disembark their soldier cargoes. Twelve gruelling hours were to tick away, converting darkness into daybreak, before the French showed their hand.

Meanwhile, soldiers and bluejackets had their orders.

The suspense of the afternoon was broken when RAdm. Robert C. Giffen delivered a message to his men. The commander of the Navy's force, protecting the convoy from surface opposition, asserted:

"If circumstances force us to fire on the French, let it be done with the firm conviction that we are striking not at the French people, once our victorious Allies, but at the men who prefer Hitler's slavery to freedom. If we fight, hit hard and break clean. Good luck. Go with God."

In similar words other Navy officers and Army leaders had given "pep talks" to their men. The rugged, redheaded captain of one of the fighting ships told his officers and crew:

"If we wield the sword, do so with all the strength in this mighty ship to destroy completely and quickly."

I saw officers and bluejackets react to the captain's statement. They exchanged understanding glances. Some seemed pensive. Others nodded approvingly. Their expressions were those of football players just before the kickoff, anxious to get on with the game.

After the captain's voice had faded from the ship's loudspeaker, men on deck, gunners at stations in the turrets, officers who had gathered in the wardroom and the black gang crawling around the throbbing engines essayed their own predictions regarding the events of the morrow.

"I'll lay you two to one the French won't fight," one sailor said to his pal.

"Yeah—that's easy money," came the reply, and another nautical wager was made.

Across their coffee cups in the wardroom, small groups of officers huddled. One, seated around the end of the long dining board, discussed French history. They agreed that the present situation was incredible. None would believe that America's historic friendship with France could crumble now. Some predicted the French would fight only halfheartedly and briefly, offering a token defense to satisfy their German oppressors.

"These fellows haven't got anything against us," remarked a fresh-faced young ensign barely out of Annapolis. "I don't think they want to fight us any more than we want to fight them, and I'll bet they'll be glad to see our soldiers going after the Nazis."

The suspense, the tension, all the eagerness and dry nervousness that embraced minds and bodies were the cumulative effect of more than two weeks at sea. The 3,000-mile ocean trail which led to this date with destiny had seemed endlessly long. These climactic moments on the eve of action were bringing an end to months of careful preparation and planning.

More than a day was required for the conception and birth of the African campaign.

As far back as last spring, the military minds in Washington and London were laying the groundwork and studying the theory of the Allied move along the southern Mediterranean coast. Everything was thought and said in secrecy.

Thousands of details had to be ironed out. There was the problem of procuring sufficient ships to transport the Army in one huge armada. Material and supplies for the troops had to be obtained, and preparations made to keep them flowing even while we maintained other life lines to our forces in the Pacific and to our Allies.

Without fanfare and public acclaim, the Army general staff and the Navy general board solved each problem connected with the maneuver. They planned to make the expedition as foolproof as humanly possible. Their paper work, however, was not enough. The operations were carried out in actual practice.

Troops were brought to the Eastern Seaboard from their training camps. Loaded aboard transport ships, they didn't know whether their next stop was to be the Solomon Islands or the rugged shore line of Norway. They were surprised to find themselves anchored "somewhere off the East Coast," and put ashore again in landing barges.

These practice landings were carried out in the strictest secrecy and under conditions that closely simulated the surf-lashed shores of Morocco. Combat troops learned how to go from ship to shore.

Meanwhile, Navy ships maneuvered in small forces along the coast. Some went through strange battle drill; others uncorked full salvos at moving targets in the air and on the surface. A chief petty officer aboard one of the ships later told me, "Those were the strangest fleet maneuvers I'd ever seen, and of course none of us knew what they were all about. We knew something big was brewing, though."

Day by day, troop ships with their telltale landing barges hanging from davits over the side moved into a number of eastern seaports. Unusual concentration of naval power assembled up and down the coast from Maine to Hatteras. You'd never have known, though, that all these ships were to sail almost simultaneously and form the largest military convoy in history.

With orders to report for assignment, I boarded a Navy airplane in New York one evening, and the next day found myself in a lazy little resort village "somewhere on the East Coast." It was a brisk fall afternoon when our station wagon rolled into the driveway of a sprawling, roomy hotel. The armed forces had taken over this one-time mecca for seashore vacationists. An admiral's flag waved at the entrance. Here was headquarters for the American expedition to Africa.

Trailed by three press association correspondents, including myself, a Marine colonel walked past stiffly attentive sentries into the lobby. We climbed a flight of stairs. Another sentry directed us to the office of RAdm. Henry Kent Hewitt. Army and Navy staff officers hurried busily along the hallways. In the rooms, you could see others studying charts and operational plans. Pistol-belted sentries stood in the doorways. How Hitler would have loved this scene!

Adm. Hewitt, commander of the amphibious force, bade us enter his sanctum. The admiral, a man of stately bearing and courtly manner, conversed with us in generalities. The nature of the African mission, so far as the press was concerned, still remained a heavily shrouded secret.

Capt. Lee P. Johnson, the admiral's rollicking, good-natured chief of staff, assigned each correspondent to a fighting ship, and in a matter of hours I was en route to my port of embarkation.

With a new set of orders signed by Adm. Hewitt in my wallet, I set out with an indelible impression of the momentous behind-scenes activity that precedes any large-scale military operation. The work that had been done in that faraway resort hotel was unsung heroism of dramatic proportions. A vital miscalculation by this group of officers would have been as costly as the concentrated fire of the entire French Fleet.

The "armchair" officers had carefully studied weather conditions, conditions of terrain, intelligence reports and other data, weaving them all into a gigantic, workable form. The Navy plans alone, stacked one atop the other, made a pile of paper more than four feet high.

One morning at eight o'clock, our fighting ships rolled in the rumbling anchor chains and we sailed out to sea, one following the other in a long line. The flagship of Adm. Giffen led the way. Elsewhere, at other eastern ports, more Navy craft got under way, escorting large concentrations of transports and supply ships.

Each of these forces sailed alone for about two days, all steaming toward a little dot on their charts. The dot was marked "Rendezvous." There were about 100 ships in the convoy when finally it was fully assembled.

Stretching for miles into the dim, hazy horizon, the great American armada made a picture that nearly defied the imagination. Far ahead of the troop transports was the Navy's screen of protective ships—first the swift, trim little destroyers, ever alert against Axis submarines; then more powerful battle craft, prepared to slug it out with any seagoing force the enemy might send to intercept us. Farther behind steamed the transports, their pulsating

Battered French warship Jean Bart, which fiercely resisted U.S. landings at Casablanca.

decks jammed with combat troops half-hidden behind their landing barges. There, too were supply vessels, tankers and more Navy ships, including aircraft carriers and tenders. Other Navy vessels protected the rear and sides of the convoy from surface, undersea or air attack.

The convoy barely was out of sight on land before Axis U-boats struck their first futile blow.

Messages came crackling in code across the intership communications system. "Am investigating submarine contact, bearing 80 degrees," reported a destroyer skipper, and through our glasses we could see the tiny "tin can" veer from its position in the protective force.

A rumble and thud rolled across the water. The tin can now was dropping depth charges. You could see it plainly. The sleek little destroyer was moving in at full speed, its bow standing out of the water and its stern leaving a foaming wake. Here was a hound chasing a hare. The charges rolled off the fantail or were catapulted into the air from Y guns on the sides. You could see them plummet into the water, churning up white geysers where they hit. Then there was the thud and rumble as they exploded deep beneath the choppy waves.

The tin can turned, crossed back over the spot where the U-boat was believed to be. More depth charges went overboard, and more explosions churned the ocean. Another destroyer wheeled into the attack.

Hardly a day passed that the fiery little destroyers did not report submarine contacts and dump their dynamite toward the enemy undersea. Even the eerie blackness of night was punctuated frequently by the flashes of depth charges.

So thoroughly did the destroyers beat off the U-boats that not a single submarine penetrated the protective screen far enough to fire its torpedoes. The vigil against subs also was kept by naval aircraft. In good weather, the carrier-based scouting planes swarmed into the air and maintained an anti-sub patrol for miles around the convoy.

It was estimated that at least 50 enemy submarines lurked in the path of the convoy. It is doubtful whether some of them ever returned to their bases.

Soldiers and sailors liked nothing better than to watch the destroyers in action. They seemed to be so fascinated by the twisting maneuvers of the fast little sea hounds that they had no time to think about the chances of being torpedoed. One doughboy, who had never been to sea before, told me:

"I thought I'd be scared when a sub got near us. But those durned little destroyers made me forget there was any danger for me."

Morale of the men was high all the way. Like all soldiers at sea, they played games of chance, read everything available from novels to comic strips, wrote letters home to be mailed "sometime, somewhere," and wished they'd get to wherever they were going.

The course of the convoy was changed from time to time, making it appear first as if we were going toward England, then toward the Cape of Good Hope. The maneuvers extended the period at sea, but they probably tricked Axis leaders.

What started out as fair weather turned foul after several days of cruising. Heavy swells crashed across the tough noses of the Navy ships. The little destroyers bounced about like dead leaves in the eddies of a creek. The bulky transport vessels pitched and rolled. Rain squalls dropped over the force like a heavy gray curtain, limiting vision. Some of the storms were so serious that officers began to grow apprehensive.

At best, the beaches along the Moroccan coast are fringed with a roaring, heavy surf. The storms, beating down on us from north and south, surely would whip the big swells into crashing canyons of water, making the navigation of landing barges practically impossible.

Two days off Morocco, however, the ocean lost its turbulence. The surface rippled like a calm mountain lake. God seemed to be with us.

But now came the afternoon of Nov. 7th—the end of the trail to Africa—and what lay ahead was a mystery.

That Saturday night the chaplains aboard the troopships and larger naval craft held prayer services and the Catholic clergymen said Mass. American fighting men crossed their Rubicon praying for a peaceful reception but prepared for battle if the French refused to yield. The French soldiers and sailors were the last people on earth that these lads would have preferred to fight. The French, they remembered, had been side by side with their fathers in WWI. Moreover, the French had befriended America in its first crisis.

Adm. Hewitt ordered the large convoy to deploy along the Moroccan coast Saturday afternoon. Before the large orange sun dipped behind the cloudy blue horizon, troopships and naval escorts were moving shoreward over a 200-mile area from Rabat in the north as far down as Safi in the south.

Adm. Hewitt's flagship led a group of transports in toward Cape Fehdala, some 14 miles north of Casablanca. The vital port city of Casablanca, meanwhile, was the objective of Adm. Giffen's contingent of fighting ships, because the units of the French Fleet lay at anchor in the harbor. A force approaching Rabat and the surrounding areas, including Port Lyautey, was under command of RAdm. Monroe Kelly, and the southern group at Rabat was commanded by RAdm. Lyal A. Davidson. The carrier group steamed offshore in charge of RAdm. Ernest D. McWhorter.

Adm. Giffen's force, to which I was attached, operated alone, unencumbered by troop transports. As we moved in toward shore, in the darkness of Saturday night, the suspense spawned that gnawing nervous tension.

Did the French know we were out there? How successful had the negotiations of Gen. Mark Clark been? The answers were not available yet.

Down in the wardroom, a group huddled over the radio. They heard President Roosevelt's message broadcast to the French people. They heard the instructions of Gen. Dwight Eisenhower put on the air. If the French were friendly, they would show a vertical beam from a searchlight as a sign of welcome.

I went back to the flag bridge. An orderly came to Adm. Giffen, saluted, and said, "Casablanca is dead ahead, sir."

It was a message from the navigator that we were on course. You could even see the flashing shaft of light swinging from the lighthouse at Casablanca.

Moments later, the lighthouse was blacked out. Not a pin point of illumination was visible now on shore. There was no sign of the signal of friendship.

At least, we knew that the French were aware of our presence now. What would they do about it? We were under strict orders not to fire unless they did.

Elsewhere along the long coastline, American combat troops were swinging into action. Landing barges were made ready; soldiers unsheathed their guns.

A flicker of light showed from the shore. It came from soldiers who had reached the beach several hours earlier, making the trip across in American submarines. They had located the exact landing spots, and these dots of light were signals.

Soldiers scrambled down the net-draped sides of the transports and into the landing barges that had been lowered alongside. The barges were jam-packed with men, and looked like water-going porcupines with the soldiers' rifles sticking up like quills.

Flashes were visible at Cape Fehdala. Gunfire! French shore batteries opening up. Our naval ships returned their fire. The landings continued.

A report trickled in from Adm. Davidson. The landings at Safi had been carried out bloodlessly, before the French had time to resist.

Sunday's pale dawn streaked the African sky, and now the low, undulating coastline was plainly visible. Adm. Giffen's force continued steaming near Casablanca, ready to block the French naval force in the event it came out to attack our troopships. The suspense at Casablanca was intense, for we had been moving around there for nearly six hours waiting for something to happen.

At 4:00 a.m., the ship turned to for breakfast. Nearly everybody had spent a restless night.

"Boy, these fighting French-fried potatoes are going to go good," wisecracked an officer. We also ate steak, whole-wheat bread and coffee. Then came the klaxon sound of the general alarm.

"All hands ... Man your battle stations ... Make all preparations for battle," were the words a bluejacket from somewhere down South drawled into the microphone. He repeated the call in a monotone that seemed almost morbid. "All hands ... Man your battle stations ... Make all preparations for battle."

I grabbed the day's emergency rations—a can of sardines, a candy bar and a package of chewing gum—stuffed them into my gas mask and joined the officers and bluejackets scurrying to their battle posts. You adjusted your steel helmet as you climbed the ladder and lugged along a lifejacket—just in case.

Adm. Giffen already was on the flag bridge. "Looks as if they may fire a few at us," he said. "I'm sending our observation planes over Casablanca to see what they're doing."

The planes were catapulted with a sharp, explosive bang, soaring in single file into the gray, splotchy sky.

They were still in sight and buzzing shoreward when suddenly, up ahead, a swarm of French fighter planes appeared and roared down at our slow reconnaissance craft. A screaming dogfight ensued. One of our fliers was forced to land in the water. He was wounded.

Up in our radio shack, they were taking in a message from one of the pilots. He started with his code name and ours.

"This is Blondie. Calling Cobra ... Look, I'm bringing these bums across the ships. Pick 'em off as we come over, but don't forget I'm leading them."

"Rajah," replied our radioman.

So the birdman wheeled out of the fight and headed toward the surface ships with the French in hot pursuit.

Instructions had been relayed to ComDesRon (Commander of the Destroyer Sqdn.).

Once within range, the French airmen were greeted by an angry crescendo of ack-ack fire from the destroyers. The larger ships joined in the rattle and boom, and the sky swiftly filled with the black plumy bursts of anti-aircraft shells. The Frenchmen fled.

Our observation planes turned back toward Casablanca.

Time seemed to stand still now. All hands stood at their guns awaiting the next development in the incipient battle.

The stillness, so strange in contrast with the sputtering of AA guns only a few minutes before, was punctuated sharply by the whining scream of a shell. Over near the shoreline we could see the bright flash of gunfire. Heavy missiles splashed uncomfortably close to our ship. The reconnaissance planes radioed that the battleship *Jean Bart* had taken us under fire. It was 7:03 a.m. Sunday, Nov. 8th, when the first shot was unleashed in the battle of Casablanca.

What followed was a blaze of compact action. You stuffed cotton in your ears, anticipating the thunder of the American guns. French shore batteries uncorked a hail of smaller shells at the task force, which by now was twisting and turning and changing course in a desperate effort to throw the French gunnery off range. Another siren-like salvo from the 35,000-ton battleship, the most modern fighting machinery in the French navy, whistled through the air. The shells landed on both sides of the flagship. It was a "straddle."

Adm. Giffen, meanwhile, was roaring out orders, and directing the task group the way a musical maestro leads a band. "Play ball!" the admiral shouted.

A yeoman standing near him, equipped like a telephone girl with earphones and mouthpiece, relayed the message to the fire-control tower and the gunnery officer. "Play ball!" he repeated. It was the secret signal to return the French fire.

Our turrets turned toward the *Jean Bart* like gigantic iron hands with their round, steel fingers jutting out as though ready to clutch a foe in the death grip.

Those few inches of steel deck beneath us vibrated with the force of the ensuing explosion. Our forward turret belched shells from all guns. Red, sulphurous flame spouted from the heavy barrels. Thick wisps of smoke and the stench of powder enveloped the flying bridge.

I lost my notebook in the roaring blast of the next shot. Funny how minor matters upset a person at the most impossible moments! The admiral's quick-footed chief signalman, "Sandy," saw my plight and thrust a wad of scratch paper in my hand. The words I scrawled from then on looked like a Wall Street chart in the middle of a financial crisis, but they were strangely coherent.

Shells were flying thick and fast.

One gashed through our large battle flag, flying from the tower. American steel was hurled back, punch for punch, at the Frenchmen. It was eight o'clock, and nobody had noticed how time had flown. Fire control, by this time, had a report from our observation planes that the *Jean Bart* had been hit in the stern and had ceased firing from her main batteries. Smaller shore guns continued hammering at us, and were subjected to bombardment.

"If they keep this up," Adm. Giffen said, "there'll be nothing left of Casablanca." Our task group pulled away from the action, obviously to give the French a chance to surrender.

One of the "talkers," as they call the lads with earphones, blurted out a report from the radio shack. Units of the French fleet—submarines, a cruiser, two light cruisers or destroyer leaders, and three destroyers—were steaming out of Casablanca. Leaving the *Jean Bart* behind, smoking at the docks in the harbor, the French ships apparently were headed northward to attack our troopships at Fehdala. Nearly all the soldiers were ashore, however, and sporadic fighting had begun on land.

American fighting ships moved in to intercept the French craft. The blast and roar of rapid-firing batteries tugged at your clothing. Shells from the French ships whistled and whined overhead, some splashing close by.

Repeatedly, their salvos bracketed our beam. Blossoms of yellow, purple and green splashed out of the water where they landed. The French shells were dyed, a different color being used by each of their ships in order to spot the accuracy of their shots.

Adm. Giffen was striding about the flying bridge in a near sprint, almost bowling over his aides and myself. He bellowed encouragement to all within hearing. You could hear his husky voice above the din and roar of battle. "Keep firing!" he said. Then he yelled, "Let them have it! Pour it on 'em!"

The devilish scream of another shell pierced the air, so loudly that you were sure it would hit.

A tin-hatted bluejacket, sternly standing by one of the pom-pom guns, spoke his first words during the fight.

"Close one, eh?" he inquired.

"Yep," I said, and that was a conversation. Those clipped phrases lifted the strain. Another howling shell came near, and we felt a slight tremor through the ship. It was a hit.

But the explosion sent shrapnel clattering across the steel decks like dice rolled on a tin roof, and did little damage. The French had the range.

Then a new note sounded in the shattering symphony of battle. A shell thudded into the armor plating forward, penetrating into the Marine compartment below. You wondered if anybody had been hurt, but the activity on topside held your attention and you forgot about being hit until a report came in from the damage-control party. The shell had burst in the Marine compartment, caused a fire which was quickly extinguished, and since nobody was in there, none were hurt. In the course of the battle, our ship got two more direct hits, but damage and casualties were slight.

Our guns had been pitching steadily all the while, and at 9:48 a.m., the fire-control tower made its first report of success. Two light cruisers had been hit. All I could see over there was smoke and, at intervals, a flash of fire. Only the men with powerful glasses could observe all the destruction caused by our fire. One of the French ships was down by the stern. Another had sunk.

Loss of life on the sunken vessel must have been tremendous. Observers said it went down in less than a minute. There was no time to rescue survivors.

Word of our success passed from man to man, but no one cheered. This was grim business. Frenchmen—men whom Americans didn't want to kill—were dying.

But there wasn't much time to think it over. Suddenly there came the scream of a lookout: "Torpedoes approaching off the port bow!"

They were 5,000 yards away. You could see their foaming, slithering wakes.

The mighty ship came about in a swift turn to port. The vessels following us executed the same maneuver, all heading into the direction from which the surface missiles had been fired. It was a dramatic, all-out effort to parallel the approaching torpedoes. It seemed they would hit before we could extricate ourselves from that fast, dizzy turn. You forgot all about the shells plopping into the ocean so close by.

"Stand by for torpedoes!" cried the yeoman at the ship's loudspeaker. An order like that means the torpedoes are about to score a bull's-eye.

Men all around me fell to the deck, and so did I: we were clawing at bulkheads and stanchions for a death grip, bracing ourselves for the blast.

We waited—silently, no man said a word.

Nothing happened! Two minutes passed and the suspense died out. We all got to our feet to find that the torpedoes had gone by—one some 10 feet to starboard and the other three to port. A horrible nightmare was finished.

At this juncture, the French naval force was on the verge of demolition. At least two of their ships were sunk, and the others had been badly battered.

Nevertheless, they refused to surrender. The French admiral at Casablanca spurned all armistice suggestions; moreover, he dispatched another light cruiser of the Primauguet class and two more destroyers out to sea in a do-or-die effort to reinforce the French naval units.

The "fresh meat" in the fight also was taken under fire by our ships, and the running sea fight continued unabated.

The rumbling thunder of our own gunfire was broken by the crash of a French shell on the forward deck.

"Damn near got me," chirped a young signalman crouching next to me.

"You hurt?" I asked.

No, he wasn't wounded, but he was fingering a gaping slash in his trousers where a piece of shrapnel had torn through them without touching his skin.

You didn't have time then to consider the proximity of death, because the whine and whistle and thunder and turmoil of battle continued. Our ships were pouring it on.

Another French vessel was reported sunk, and over there along the horizon you could see the remnants of their crippled fleet staggering, reeling and creeping away. One French man-of-war was flaming from stem to stern. The battle was finished. They had ceased firing and were moving back toward Casablanca.

In all, 10 French warships were sunk or damaged in the course of the fighting.

The American vessels then took up the chase, following the Frenchmen toward the port. Some of them failed to get in, and their officers and crews turned the battered ships into the beach and left them stranded there. Our guns unleashed a deadly barrage against the shore installations, which continued to pepper us whenever we were within range.

The last devastating salvo was fired into the shore guns at 4:00 p.m., and the rest of that quiet Sabbath evening our ships maintained a patrol along the opening to Casablanca harbor.

Monday found the American warships hammering again at the shore batteries.

An old battleship, pride of the fleet in WWI, waddled in toward the beach to fire a series of salvos, then struggled away proudly, as though it had proved herself to be as tough and rugged as it was in 1917.

Navy bombers roared across the Casablanca harbor late in the afternoon, unleashing a devastating coup de grace, and with the dawn of Tuesday, Casablanca capitulated.

American losses, during the landing of troops and in the naval duel, were a minimum. We lost five ships altogether, all of which were troop transports. Torpedoes from enemy submarines sank them—but not before they had unloaded nearly all of their men and materiel.

The remarkable success principally was due to the long-range preparation and planning. Except for the seven-hour sea fight at Casablanca, the French received us as friends, as is evident in the fact that French troops now have joined the Allies in their smashing drive against the Axis armies on the southern Mediterranean coast.

"BIG MAMIE'S" FLAG, SHELL-TORN
AT CASABLANCA, GIVEN TO STATE

The *Boston Daily Globe*, Friday, Feb. 11, 1944

The $75,000,000 USS *Massachusetts*, manned by many local boys and launched at Bethlehem Steel's Fore River Yards in September 1941, exchanged shots with the French battleship *Jean Bart* as the flagship of RAdm. Robert C. Giffen and under colors presented by the Crosscup-Pishon Post, A.L. during the invasion at Casablanca, it was revealed by the Navy yesterday afternoon.

Its battle-scarred American flag, may now be viewed at the State House Hall of Flags. It was presented to Gov. Saltonstall yesterday at the annual mid-winter luncheon of the Crosscup-Pishon Post attended by 700 members and guests at the Hotel Statler.

The story of the 35,000-ton battleship, affectionately known as "Big Mamie," was told by Cedric Foster over a nationwide radio hookup from a report written by war correspondent John Henry, only reporter on the flagship at the time. Quoting Henry, Foster said:

"It's all over now. You feel as if you'd awakened from a weird, kaleidoscopic dream. You have seen America's greatest sea victory in the Atlantic since the days of Sampson and Schley. Your ship, bearing the flag of RAdm. Robert C. Giffen, directed the fight and was in the thick of it all the way."

"Play Ball" was Signal

"The events started when a clarion call to general quarters came over the loud speaker system soon after the 4 a.m. breakfast. The French had not shown the designated symbol of friendship. Fighting had broken out in nearby areas where our troops landed. Day began to break and you got your first good glimpse of the Moroccan coast. You also could observe the expressions of men near you. Adm. Giffen, the picture of a fighting man, his lieutenant, chief signalman and Marine orderly climbed to the flying bridge.

"You looked up in time to see French fighter planes roaring down on our observation craft. A brief dogfight ensued. One of our flyers was forced to land in the water, but two Frenchmen, in a smoking tailspin, crashed into the sea. Our ack-ack opened up. The French flew away.

"Adm. Giffen meanwhile refused to open fire upon the harbor. He was ordered only to protect American troop ships from attack. Moments later you heard the eerie scream of a shell. It plunged into water uncomfortably close. Another fell on the opposite side. The *Jean Bart* had opened fire. It was 7:03 a.m. Another flash brightened the shoreline as French batteries swung into action. You stuffed cotton in your ears, anticipating the shuddering blasts of our big rifles. Adm. Giffen was roaring out orders.

"Play ball!" he exclaimed. This was the secret signal for American ships to open fire.

Crossfire Decimated Enemy

"A terrific explosion nearly rocked you to the deck as your forward turret belched shells from all guns. Someone said the *Bart* was afire. Shore batteries continued pounding at us, but fire control, meanwhile, received a report that the *Bart* had been hit and had ceased firing. It was 8:04 a.m.

"Our ships then laid a concentrated bombardment on the shore emplacements. Minutes later a kid blurted out a report from our observation planes. Units of the French fleet—submarines, a cruiser of the Primagauget class, at least two light cruisers and three destroyers—were steaming out from Casablanca to attack our troop ships.

"'All right, if they want to come out for a fight we'll let them come,' the admiral said. What followed was a flame of compact action. The blast and roar of our rapid-firing batteries tugged at our clothing. Shells from the French ships whistled and whined overhead and we were witnessing a naval duel no one had expected.

"Soon, however, firing was seen dead ahead. Our cruisers, standing by the transports, came up to head off the French craft. Our guns boomed again and the hapless foe was ensnared in a withering crossfire.

"It was 2:05 p.m., however, before the depleted foe withdrew and staggered under the protection of shore batteries which had opened up anew. We steamed away toward Casablanca on the heels of the reeling French fleet to unleash a final nearly devastating salvo at the beach guns."

Capt. Barleon Returns Ensign

'Keep firing!' the admiral said. 'Let them have it, pour it on them!' The French ships' salvos repeatedly bracketed our beam. At 9:48 the fire control tower reported two French destroyers had been hit. One French ship was down by the stern. Another had sunk. There was no time to rescue survivors.

"You got a dim vision of one of their destroyers just as our shells crashed into it amidship, and 45 seconds later the vessel had sunk. The shriek of another shell and everyone sprawled on the deck. Shrapnel tore a gaping slit in the trousers of a sailor next to you. Our main batteries were hammering hard at the Frenchmen. The ships behind were closing in for the kill. 'Tell them to move in,' Adm. Giffen hollered to his signalman. He was perspiring. You were looking at a fighting admiral. Another shell zoomed into our forecastle. Fire was reported in the Marine compartment below decks, but the damage control party quickly doused it.

"With at least two of their number sunk and others badly damaged, the French vessels, in a few more salvos, had their fill. There was a lull in the battle as our ships moved toward the shore batteries on Point El Hank. Our turrets uncorked more than 30,000 pounds of steel into the shore guns, and, one by one, they fell silent."

The flag, with a gaping shell hole and stained from the *Massachusetts'* smoke gases was returned to the Legion post at the request of RAdm. F.E.M. Whiting, formerly captain of the battleship. It was returned to Post Commander Edward P. Keefe by Capt. John S. Barleon, chief of staff of the 1st naval District. Gov. Saltonstall, in turn, accepted the flag from Cmdr. Keefe in behalf of the state and declared "it will hold a sacred and honored place in the heart of the Commonwealth."

Another speaker, Lt. James Britt, USNR, former local radio sports announcer just returned from action in the Pacific, took issue with Army and Navy men who declare that there is too much complacency on the home front. He expressed the opinion that Americans and industry have done a fine job and should not be blasted."

Casablanca managed to put up stiff resistance to the US invasion. Gen. George S. Patton landed three tank columns ashore east and west of the sprawling city and lit out first for an outlying reservoir. With that in his hands, he hoped to cripple Casablanca, if necessary. Soon parachutists seized the city's main airdrome, and the tank force advanced.

The *Massachusetts* withdrew from the naval Battle of Casablanca at 1105 on Nov. 8; because it had expended nearly 60% of her 16-inch armor-piercing ammunition. The remainder would be needed if the *Richelieu* (another massive French battleship) made an appearance from Dakar. The men of the *Massachusetts* were at general quarters from 0545 to 1610 on Nov. 8, showing unusual endurance in handling 16-inch shells for hours on end. Out of her 113 officers and 2203 men, only three were in sick bay during the action. It expended 786 rounds of 16-inch .45 caliber ammunition during the battle, firing 134 salvos, for an average of almost six shots per salvo.

A cease-fire was reached with the French in North Africa on Nov. 11, changing the whole complexion of the European war. With the unqualified success of Operation Torch, the stage was set for Allied Forces to drive the Axis from North Africa. Bases had been secured which would be used to protect the Straits of Gibraltar and adjacent areas of the Atlantic. Northwest Africa was no longer a potential site for an Axis submarine base, and the area was no longer a source of supplies for the enemy. Gen. Patton's troops were ashore, and the French military forces, which had been fighting the Americans so recently, became allies in the common cause against the Axis powers.

On the 12th, Mamie steamed off for the States. Her battle-tested crew returned to Norfolk, VA on Nov. 22, 1942, for a well-earned liberty. Mamie had gone to Casablanca untried and untested; it left as a veteran, credited with having put the battleship *Jean Bart* out of action, having sunk two destroyers and having silenced shore batteries.

Massachusetts on-loaded supplies and 278,082 gallons of fuel from a pier at Norfolk; shifted to the Boston Navy Yard and then returned to Casco Bay off Portland, ME. Until her departure for the Pacific, the crew was constantly being trained and drilled into an even more efficient fighting machine.

About the battle for Casablanca, *Time* Magazine published a letter written by the Casablanca representative of the American Friends Service Committee (the Quakers). He wrote:

"It has been truly marvelous that the town has suffered practically no damage with all of the hell in the port. A Frenchman who had been caught in a hotel near the port told me he had never seen such superb gunnery in his life—that every shot that came in landed in the port and none lit in the town. Some shell fragments did scatter, naturally, and in at least one other locality, some houses were hit and a number of Arabs were killed. However, I would not have believed it possible for operations on such a scale to cause so little harm to civilians. Certainly the Americans did everything to avoid injuring the town."

Gen. Dwight D. Eisenhower, Commander-in-Chief of the Allied Expeditionary Forces, wrote to Commander TF 34 as follows:

"With successful completion of your task under Allied Hqs. and your return to normal American command I want to express my grateful appreciation of the splendid services you and the forces operating under your command had rendered. I am making immediate official report to Washington to this effect but in the meantime I hope it is proper for a soldier to say to a sailor 'well-done'."

Appendix

TASK FORCE 34

RAdm. H. Kent Hewitt, Commander, in Augusta

WESTERN NAVAL TASK FORCE, Adm. Hewitt

Embarking Western Task Force US Army, MGen. George S. Patton, Jr., USA

TG 34.1 COVERING GROUP., RAdm. Robert C. Giffen

BB-59 *Massachusetts*
Capt. F.E.M. Whiting

CA-45 *Wichita*
Capt. F.S. Low
CA-37 *Tuscaloosa*
Capt. N.C. Gillette

Screen,
Capt. P.D. Moon (ComDesRon 8)

DD-419 *Wainwright*
Lt. Cmdr. R.H. Gibbs
DD-402 *Mayrant*
Lt. Cmdr. E.K. Walker
DD-404 *Rhind*
Cmdr. H.T. Read
D-447 *Jenkins*
Lt. Cmdr. H.F. Miller

Tanker

AO-30 *Chemung*
Capt. J.J. Twomey

TG 34.8 NORTHERN ATTACK GROUP., RAdm. Monroe Kelly

Embarking 60th Inf. Regt. (Reinforced) of 9th Div.; 1st Bn., 66th Armd. Regt., 2nd Armd. Div.; 1st Bn., 540th Engrs.; and special units. Brig. Gen. Lucian K. Truscott Jr., USA, commander. 9,099 officers and men, 65 light tanks.

Fire Support Group

BB-35 *Texas*
Capt. Roy Pfaff
CL-42 *Savannah*
Capt. L.S. Fiske

Northern Attack Gp. Transports,

Capt. Augustine H. Gray
(ComTransDiv 5)
AP-30 *Henry T. Allen*
Capt. P.A. Stevens
AP-51 *John Penn* (ex-Excambion)
Cmdr. Charles Allen
AP-57 *George Clymer*
(ex-African Planet)
Capt. A.T. Moen
AP-72 *Susan B. Anthony*
(ex-Santa Clara)
Capt. Henry Hartley
AK-21 *Electra* (ex-Meteor)
Cmdr. J.J. Hughes
AK-25 *Algorab* (ex-Mormacwren)
Cmdr. J.R. Lannom
AP-70 *Florence Nightingale*
(ex-Mormacsun) Capt. E.D. Graves Jr.
AP-76 *Anne Arundel* (ex-Mormacyork)

Capt. L.Y. Mason Jr.
Screen, Cmdr. D.L. Madeira
(ComDesRon 11)
DD-418   *Roe* (also fire support)
Lt. Cmdr. R.L. Nolan Jr.
DD-429   *Livermore*
Cmdr. Vernon Huber
DD-432   *Kearny* (also fire support)
Cmdr. A.H. Oswald
DD-440 *Ericsson* (also fire support)
Lt. Cmdr. C.M. Jensen
DD-604   *Parker*
Lt. Cmdr. J.W. Bays
Beacon Submarine
SS-235 *Shad*
Lt. Cmdr. E.J. MacGregor

Air Group

ACV-26 *Sangamon*
(ex-Esso Trenton)
Capt. C.W. Wieber
VGS-26: 9 TBF-1 (Avenger),
9 SBD-3 (Dauntless),
Lt. Cmdr. J.S. Tracy
VGF-26: 12 F4F-4 (Wildcat),
Lt. Cmdr. W.E. Ellis
ACV-28 *Chenango*
(ex-Esso New Orleans)
Capt. Ben H. Wyatt
Carrying 76 Army P-40Fs
(Curtis) for future basing at Casablanca
Air Group. Screen,
Capt. Charles Wellborn Jr.
(ComDesDiv 19)
DD-455   *Hambleton*
Cmdr. Forrest Close
DD-458   *Macomb*
Cmdr. W.H. Duvall

Special Units

DD-199   *Alexander Dallas*
Lt. Cmdr. R. Brodie Jr.
DD-430   *Eberle*
Lt. Cmdr. K.F. Poehlmann
AO-36 *Kennebec* (ex-Corsicana)
Cmdr. S.S. Reynolds
AM-55 *Raven*
Lt. Cmdr. C.G. Rucker
AM-56 *Osprey*
Lt. Cmdr. C.L. Blackwell
S.S. (Honduran) *Contessa*
Lt. A.V. Leslie, USNR
William H. John (Br.) (Mr. John the
Master) (Naval Liaison)
AVP-10   *Barnegat*
Cmdr. J.A. Briggs
TG 34.9 CENTER ATTACK GP.,
Capt. Robert R.M. Emmet in
Leonard Wood

Embarking 3rd Inf. Div. (7th, 15th,
30th Regts. reinforced), 1st Bn., 67th
Armd. Regt., 2nd Armd. Div., and spe
cial units. MGen. J.W. Anderson, USA,
commander. 18,783 officers and men,
79 light tanks.

Fire Support Group.

CA-31 *Augusta*
Capt. Gordon Hutchins
CL-40 *Brooklyn*
Capt. F.C. Denebrink

Control and Fire Support Destroyers,

Cmdr. E.R. Durgin (ComDesDiv 26)
DD-441   *Wilkes*
Lt. Cmdr. J.B. McLean
DD-443   *Swanson*
Cmdr. L.M. Markham Jr.
DD-438   *Ludlow*
Lt. Cmdr. L.W. Creighton
DD-603   *Murphy*
Lt. Cmdr. L.W. Bailey

Center Attack Group. Transports,
Capt. Emmet

AP-25 *Leonard Wood* (ex-Western
World) Cmdr. Merlin O'Neill, USCG
AP-60 *Thomas Jefferson* (ex-President
Garfield) Cmdr. C.R. Crutcher

TransDiv 3, Capt. R.G. Coman

AP-58 *Charles Carroll* (ex-Del Uru
guay) Cmdr. H. Biesemeier
AP-26 *Joseph T. Dickman*
Cmdr. C.W. Harwood, USCG
AP-15 *William P. Biddle* (ex-city of
San Francisco) Cmdr. P.R. Glutting
AP-50 *Joseph Hewes** (ex-Excalibur)
Capt. R. McL. Smith
AP-42 *Tasker H. Bliss**
(ex-President Cleveland)
Capt. G.C. Schetky
AP-52 *Edward Rutledge** (ex-Exeter)
Capt. M.W. Hutchinson Jr.
AP-43 *Hugh L. Scott** (ex-President
Pierce) Capt. H.J. Wright
*Sunk by enemy action.

TransDiv 9, Capt. W.M. Quigley

AP-66 *Ancon*
Capt. P.L. Mather

Christian Endeavor Unit, an international, interdenominational young people's organization. The USS Massachusetts unit was the only unit on any Navy ship, according to Association records.

5'' Gun Mount #8 Division 6. Photo courtesy AG Simpson.

AP-69 *Elizabeth C. Stanton*
(ex-Mormacstar)
Capt. Ross A. Dierdorff
AP-77 *Thurston*
(ex-Del Santos)
Capt. Jack E. Hurff
AK-19 *Procyon* (ex-Sweepstakes)
Cmdr. L.P. Padgett Jr.
AK-56 *Oberon* (ex-Del Alba)
Cmdr. Ion Pursell
AK-18 *Arcturus*
(ex-Mormachawk)
Cmdr. J.R. McKinney

Screen

Capt. John B. Heffeman
(ComDesRon 13)
DD-453 *Bristol*
Cmdr. J.A. Glick
DD-437 *Woolsey*
Cmdr. B.L. Austin
DD-439 *Edison*
Lt. Cmdr. W.R. Headden
DD-641 *Tillman*
Cmdr. F.D. McCorkle
DD-600 *Boyle*
Lt. Cmdr. E.S. Karpe
DD-405 *Rowan*
Lt. Cmdr. R.S. Ford

Minecraft

Cmdr. A.G. Cook Jr.
(CoMinRon 7)
DMS-5 *Palmer*
Lt. Cmdr. J.W. Cooper

DMS-6 *Hogan*
Lt. Cmdr. U.S.G. Sharp Jr.
DMS-8 *Stansbury*
Lt. Cmdr. J.B. Maher
CM-10 *Miantonomah* (ex-Quaker)
Lt. Cmdr. R.D. Edwards
AM-57 *Auk* Lt.
Cmdr. W.D. Ryan, USNR
CM-5 *Terror*
Cmdr. H.W. Fitch
TG 34.2 *Air Gp.*,
RAdm. Ernest D. McWhorter
CV-4 *Ranger*
Capt. C.T. Durgin

Air Gp.9, Cmdr. D.B. Overfield, 1 TBF

VF-9: 27 F4F-4,
Lt. Cmdr. John Raby
VF-41: 27 F4F-4,
Lt. Cmdr. C.T. Booth II
VS-41: 18 SBD-3,
Lt. Cmdr. L.P. Carver
ACV-27 *Suwannee* (ex-Markay)
Capt. J.J. Clark
VGF-27: 11 F4F-4,
Lt. Cmdr. T.K. Knight
VGS-27: 9 TBF,
Lt. Cmdr. M.A. Nation
VGF-28: 12 F4F-4,
Lt. Cmdr. J.I. Bandy
VGS-30: 6 F4F-4,
Lt. Cmdr. M.P. Bagdanovitch

Air Gp. Screen

CL-55 *Cleveland*

Capt. E.W. Burrough
DesRon 10,
Capt. J.L. Holloway Jr.
DD-454 *Ellyson*
Cmdr. J.B. Rooney
DD-461 *Forrest*
Capt. T.L. Wattles
DD-462 *Fitch*
Lt. Cmdr. Henry Crommelin
DD-463 *Corry*
Lt. Cmdr. E.C. Burchett
DD-464 *Hobson*
Lt. Cmdr. R.N. McFarlane
Beacon Submarines
SS-253 *Gunnel*
Lt. Cmdr. J.S. McCain
SS-233 *Herring*
Lt. Cmdr. R.W. Johnson

Tanker

AO-38 *Winooski* (ex-Calusa)
Cmdr. J.E. Murphy

TG 34.10 SOUTHERN ATTACK
GROUP.,

RAdm. Lyal A. Davidson in
Philadelphia
Embarking 47th Regt. Combat Team,
9th Inf. Div.; 3rd and elements of 2nd
Bn., 67th Armd. Regt., 2nd Armd. Div.,
and special units; MGen. E.N. Harmon,
USA, Commander. 6,423 officers and
men, 54 light and 54 medium tanks.

BB-34 *New York*
Capt. Scott Umsted
CL-41 *Philadelphia*
Capt. Paul Hendren
Control and Fire Support Destroyers
Capt. C.C. Hartman (ComDesRon 15)
DD-489 *Mervine*
Lt. Cmdr. S.D. Willingham
DD-633 *Knight*
Lt. Cmdr. R.B. Levin
DD-640 *Beatty*
Lt. Cmdr. F.C. Stelter Jr.

Southern Attack Group. Transports

Capt. Wallace B. Phillips
AP-8 *Harris* (ex-President Grant)
Capt. O.M. Forster
AP-65 *Calvert* (ex-Delorleans)
Capt. J.W. Whitfield
AK-55 *Titania* (ex-Harry Culbreath)
Cmdr. V.C. Barringer Jr.
AP-67 *Dorothea L. Dix* (ex-Exemplar)
Cmdr. L.B. Schulten
AP-71 *Lyon* (ex-Mormactide)

At sea in the pacific.

Empty shells surround 5" guns following battle.

Capt. M.J. Gillan Jr.
APM-9 *Lakehurst* (ex-Seatrain
New Jersey) Cmdr. H.J. McNulty

Screen, Cmdr. H.C. Robison
(ComDesDiv 30)
DD-632 *Cowie*
Lt. Cmdr. C.J. Whiting
DD-490 *Quick*
Lt. Cmdr. R.B. Nickerson
DD-634 *Doran*
Lt. Cmdr. H.W. Gordon Jr.

Assault Destroyers

DD-155 *Cole*
Lt. Cmdr. G.G. Palmer
DD-153 *Bernadou*
Lt. Cmdr. R.E. Braddy Jr.

Minecraft

CM-9 *Monadnock* (ex-Cavalier)
Cmdr. F.O. Goldsmith
DMS-7 *Howard*
Lt. Cmdr. C.J. Zondorak
DMS-18 *Hamilton*
Lt. Cmdr. R.R. Sampson

Tankers

AO-35 *Housatonic* (ex-Esso Albany)
Cmdr. A.R. Boileau
AO-37 *Merrimack* (ex-Caddo)
Capt. W.E. Hilbert

Beacon Submarine

SS-220 *Barb*
Lt. Cmdr. J.R. Waterman

Air Group.

ACV-29 *Santee* (ex-SeaKay)
Capt. W.D. Sample
VGF-29: 14 F4F-4,
Lt. Cmdr. J.T. Blackburn
VGS-29: 8 TBF, 9 SBD (Douglas),
Lt. Cmdr. J.A. Ruddy Jr.

Air Group. Screen

DD-456 *Rodman*
Cmdr. W.G. Michelet
DD-457 *Emmons*
Lt. Cmdr. H.M. Heming

Ocean Tug

AT-66 *Cherokee*
Lt. J.H. Lawson

Bill Canfield's New Year's cartoon, January 1943.

Chapter Five
On to the Pacific

1943 - 1945

ON TO THE PACIFIC

*To the author, Capt. Richard H. Bowerman, an officer aboard the Massachusetts, who also served
as the Flag Secretary and Operations Officer when Big Mamie became the flagship of RAdm.
Glenn B. Davis in command of Battleship Div. 8. To Reader's Digest and the New York Times
for their permission to reprint the article, When the Third Fleet Met the Great Typhoon. To
Ken Armel Prtr1/c, X Div. for suggesting most of the subtitles for this chapter.*

It was bitterly cold in Portland, ME Feb. 5, 1943. The plan of the day for the sixth indicated that the ship would be doing pretty much what it had been doing since its return from Casablanca—further training and alterations to improve her military efficiency. Beyond that, every time the German battleship, *Tirpitz*, blew her stacks in Altenfjord near Tromso, Norway, the *Massachusetts* would charge out into the Atlantic in case the Nazi behemoth got loose, as had her sister ship, the *Bismark*.

The *Massachusetts* was moored a couple of miles off shore in Casco Bay, about a 40-minute ride for the liberty parties to go ashore on the local island steamer. When the whaleboat or motor launch had to make the run, the coxswain and the crew often came back caked with ice. In Portland, *The Major and The Minor*, starring Ginger Rogers and Ray Milland, played at the local movie house; and Squeeze Box Bev entertained with her accordion in the bar room of the Lafayette Hotel on Congress Street.

Departure for the Pacific

In the early hours of Feb. 6, a new Plan of the Day was issued calling for the ship to depart that day for the Pacific. Against the cold of the winter, many a beard had been grown with the consent of Capt. Glover, but with the understanding that, if a beard were grown, it had to be maintained in the South Pacific.

At 1158, Mamie, escorted by USS *Phillip* (DD-498), USS *Eaton* (DD-510) and USS *Renshaw* (DD-499) departed Casco Bay en route to Colon, Panama Canal Zone.

The southerly journey was relatively uneventful until the ship arrived off Cape Hatteras. There, it ran into the heaviest storm that it had encountered in the Atlantic. So great was the force of the water that it tore two of the three heavy leather bloomers on Turret One which surrounded the huge guns as they entered the turret. As a result, water entered the turret at such a rate that three large submersible pumps going full time just about kept up with the intake.

In an effort to reduce the flooding, the turret was trained to port, but that merely exposed a ventilator through which even more water poured in. With Turret One athwartship, it experienced initial difficulty in entering the Panama Canal. By a complex arrangement of heavy electric cables, the power from Turret Two was used to drive Turret One back into position.

Thanks to a superhuman effort by the electricians assigned to Turret One, the motors were all cleaned up and dried without material or personnel casualty. What should have been a job for a navy yard was taken care of, without incident, by what had become a well-coordinated, well-trained team of professionals.

Panama Canal

The ship transited the Panama Canal Feb. 12 and 13, having moored at the DeGaussing Range in Gatun Lake on the night of the 12th. While on the East coast, the darkening of ship at sunset had been religiously observed as had the rendering of honors to other ships.

It was a peaceful Sunday as the ship lay moored at Balboa, Canal Zone. The afternoon watch was sleepy and uneventful when, suddenly, the British carrier HMS *Victorious* came down the channel. Mamie's officer of the deck, anxious to accord the proper and then required honors, called out the Marines and the band. When the first hawser from the *Victorious* hit the dock, the band struck up "God Save the King." To the consternation of the skipper of the *Victorious*, all British seamen dropped everything they were doing and stood at attention, so

At Joe Kelly's, L to R: C warrent gunner deGruchy (USS Black), Henry Kloss, Lt. James Burt, Lt. John Mahoney, Lt. Arthur Machen (USS Massachusetts). Photo Courtesy of James Burt.

that his ship started to drift out with the tide. At the conclusion of the British anthem, the band struck up our national anthem, and every US sailor on dock stood at attention, dropping everything he had been doing.

When Capt. Glover returned to the ship later that afternoon, he explained that he had had quite a discussion with the skipper of the *Victorious* about the need for conferring honors in time of war. Glover promptly issued orders that, henceforth and for the duration, the rendering of honors would be dispensed with on the *Massachusetts*.

The ship departed from Balboa Feb. 13, 1943, repelling simulated torpedo attacks by motor torpedo boats and torpedo planes, as well as simulated horizontal, dive bombing and strafing attacks by US Army planes. It crossed the Pacific still under the escort of the *Phillip, Eaton* and *Renshaw* and reached Noumea, New Caledonia March 4, 1943. Her entry into that beautiful anchorage gave the crew an inkling of the growing power of the Pacific fleet, for there, in formidable array, were the carriers USS *Saratoga* and HMS *Victorious*, the US battleships *Washington* and *Indiana* and a host of other warships.

At dusk, in accordance with standard procedures, all external lights were extinguished on Mamie, while, on the other hand, her crew saw moving pictures being shown topside on virtually every other ship in the anchorage.

Guadalcanal - The Slot

The effort of the US to retake Guadalcanal from the Japanese, which commenced with landings in August 1942, was the first US offensive land effort in the Pacific. The USN suffered heavy losses in a series of actions with the Japanese in the inter-island channel which became known as The Slot. Among other reasons for Allied set-backs was the fact that the Japanese enjoyed the advantage of the Type 93 Long Lance torpedo, the best in the world, and superior flares for night fighting. The USN never suffered a defeat as resounding as that administered by the Japanese in the Battle of Savo Island Aug. 9, 1942. The Japanese early successes supported their claim that, at that time, they knew no peer in night fighting.

Ironbottom Sound

Coming back from the depths of that defeat, American forces fared better and, from the perspective of the Navy, reached the pinnacle of success on the night of Nov.

6th Division mark 37 Director Crew, L-R, Back Row: Lt. James Burt, Royal Estel Puffy (Rangefinder), Ens Zizer (Asst Officer) Front Row: Boshears (Trainer), Bowens (Pointer and Firecontrolman), Roby Jarrett (Radar Operator). Photo courtesy James Burt.

5th Division Gunner's Mates, left to right: Washington, Cardinares, Bullock, Shoemaker, Ch. GM. Fee, Lt. James Burt, Smitty. Photo courtesy James Burt.

14. Then, two American battleships, the *Washington* and the *South Dakota* and four destroyers, under the overall command of RAdm. Willis A. Lee, USN, took on an invading Japanese force of one battleship, the *Kirishima*, two heavy cruisers, *Atago* and *Takao*, two light cruisers, *Nagara* and *Sendai*, and 14 destroyers, guarding four troop transports. In the ensuing slugfest in Ironbottom Sound[1], commencing just after midnight on the 15th, the *South Dakota*, in the words of Adm. Lee, was rendered "deaf, dumb, blind and impotent" by the loss of all of its radios, all but one radar and its radar plot. At one time, there were 23 fires in the superstructure of the *South Dakota* resulting from 27 hits. It was forced to leave the

battle area shortly thereafter. The destroyer *Preston* was lost to enemy cruiser and destroyer gunfire, and the *Walke* was abandoned after enemy gunfire caused her number two magazine to explode. The other US destroyers, *Benham* and *Quinn*, fought valiantly after sustaining serious damage. The *Benham* went down later in the day.

The USS *Washington*, under the command of Capt. Glenn B. Davis, USN, was the sole US vessel left to fight the battle. It successfully dodged torpedoes and engaged the cruisers and the *Kirishima* which, at 0325, rolled over and sank. The Japanese also lost the destroyer *Ayanami* in what was a clear-cut American victory.

In his engaging book *Guadalcanal*, Ri-

RAdm Glenn B. Davis, USN.

chard B. Frank describes Lee's actions as the result of "audacious planning and execution" and gives his highest accolade to "the skillful touch of Capt. Davis at the conn of *Washington*," whose performance is described by Frank as the "vital role" in the battle. For that superb performance, Davis was awarded the Navy Cross. These men assumed roles of great significance to the *Massachusetts*.

On April 29, 1943, Mamie became the flagship of RAdm. Glenn B. Davis as he took command of Battleship Div. 8, comprised of the *Massachusetts* and the *Indiana*. Subsequently, as a vice admiral, Lee was to assume command of the Battle Line, ultimately comprised of 10 new fast battleships.

Coral Sea Operations

Between March and October 1943, while based first at Noumea and later at Havannah Harbor, Efate, in the New Hebrides Islands, Mamie sailed, in company with the *Saratoga* and *Victorious*, other new battleships and destroyers. Their mission was to guard convoy lanes and to provide combat air patrols for ships and forces operating in the Solomon Islands. These operations, under the overall command of Adm. William F. ("Bull") Halsey, USN, were carried out, for the most part, in the Coral Sea in support of operations against the Russell Islands between April 5 and 15, operations at Munda between June 27 and July 25 and thereafter at Vella Lavella and Kolombangara, all in the Solomon Islands.

The objective of Halsey's advance up the Slot was to deny airbases to the Japanese and to acquire them for US forces. The ultimate strategic purpose was to deny the enemy continued effective use of Rabaul, a strong naval and air fortress, at the northeastern tip of New Britain. This was essentially achieved with the successful invasion of Bougainville Nov. 1, 1943. Our strategic

planners then learned that it wasn't necessary to occupy strongholds like Rabaul. Their isolation, after being bypassed, effectively eliminated their strategic effectiveness.

While the battleships and carriers provided air support from the Coral Sea, it was the cruisers and destroyers which did the ship-to-ship slugging against the enemy's Tokyo Express in the darkened waters of the Slot, north of Savo Island. A series of bitterly contested night naval battles ensued in which both sides fought valiantly and both sides lost heavily, but the net effect of which was that, by the end of 1943, the whole area was rendered unusable by the Japanese.

These operations in the Solomons under Halsey and the operations against the Makin Islands late in 1943 were really the proving grounds of modern carrier warfare and for the allocation of specialized duties to various classes of ships making up the fleet.

Task Force 58 and Task Force 38

New *Essex*-Class carriers and light carriers of the *Independence* Class came west in ever-increasing numbers. These, of course, became the heart and core of the fast carrier groups which operated as a part of TF 58 when RAdm. Raymond A. Spruance, USN, was in overall command of the operation as Commander of the Fifth Fleet and as TF 38 when Adm. Halsey had the same ships as the Third Fleet. New battleships and cruisers, for the most part, became the anti-aircraft fire support for the attack carriers in those task groups.

The older, slower battleships which had been badly mauled at Pearl Harbor were resurrected and refitted and rejoined the fleet in a different role. They became the experts in shore bombardment in direct support of troop landings. The newer, faster battleships, such as the *Massachusetts*, took part in some bombardments; but they were often, as in the case at Saipan and Okinawa, bombardments a week or so before D-day at places where landings were not intended to take place, but in the hope that the Japanese would be deceived into strengthening those areas, rather than the actual landing beaches.

A carrier task group would normally have three or four carriers at the center. The fleet axis would be oriented in the direction from which the wind was expected to blow. With reference to that axis, one carrier would be at 12 o'clock, one at 3 o'clock, one at 6 o'clock and one at 9 o'clock. Therefore, when the task group turned into the wind to launch or recover planes, each carrier would have the maximum air space for its planes that the fleet dimensions permitted.

Immediately surrounding the carriers would be battleships and cruisers whose anti-aircraft fire was supposed to be virtually the last carrier defense against enemy plane attack. Around the outside of the whole, in a circular screen, perhaps 16 destroyers would be stationed. Their principal purpose was to detect and protect the force from submarine attack and to add their anti-aircraft guns to the protection of the carriers. The diameter of such a task group would be about 6 nautical miles.

The Nippon air force, until June 1944, was a very competent and worthy foe. Their pilots were experienced, knew how to use weather and cloud cover, and their Zeros

(their premier fighter planes) had flying qualities and speed which, in many respects, were superior to the F4F Wildcats then operating with the US carriers.

Often, the Carrier Task Gp. would be detected by Japanese scout planes the afternoon before the group commenced its high speed run to the launch area. As the sun set, a Japanese Snooper could be seen ducking up and down beyond the horizon to be ready, after dark, to guide the attacking bombers to their targets.

Night Attacks - Lamplighters

After dark, the Lamplighters would show up and drop flares in the sea around the outside perimeter of the task group. Other Lamplighters would release aerial flares which illuminated the attacking ships as though it were daylight. Japanese flares

were extremely bright, descended slowly and illuminated an area for a longer period than ours, all to their great advantage.

The enemy attacking bombers would circle the task force, much as Indians around settlers' wagons, and successively peel off to make a torpedo or bomber attack. While these attacks, although pressed with amazing fortitude and skill, were indeed frightening to the crews of the target ships, they were not particularly effective. Over the course of a year and a half, relatively few ships were hit either by torpedo or bomb as a result of these night attacks.

Central Pacific Offensive - Gilbert Islands.

If the operations in the South Pacific into the fall of 1943 can be said to be the end of the beginning of the war in the Pacific, the

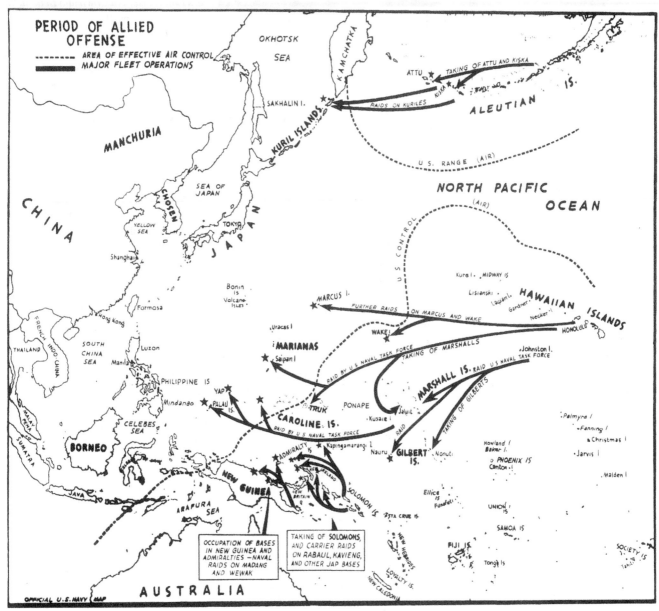

Map of advance across Pacific.

Scratch one Zero!

mission on which the *Massachusetts* set out on Nov. 11, 1943, can certainly be described as the beginning of the end—the first strong offensive move in the Central Pacific under the overall guidance of Adm. Chester W. Nimitz, USN, Commander-in-Chief, Central Pacific Ocean areas.

The *Massachusetts* sortied Oct. 31, 1943, from Havannah Harbor en route to Nandi Bay, Viti Levu, Fiji Islands which it entered Nov. 7, having rendezvoused with an *Essex*-Class Fast Carrier Task Gp. The task group, under the command of RAdm. A.W. Radford, USN, and comprised of the *Enterprise*, the light aircraft carriers *Belleau Wood* and *Monterey*, battleships *Massachusetts, North Carolina, Indiana* and six destroyers, stood out of Nandi Bay Nov. 11, 1943, to participate in the landings at Makin, Tarawa and Apanama in the Gilbert Islands, the first large-scale US amphibious assault against a heavily-fortified Japanese bastion.

During these operations, the fast carrier forces were subjected to repeated night attacks. On Nov. 26, 1943, our forces sustained the heaviest night air attack up to that time against the Pacific fleet. By this time, however, naval aviation had developed night fighter "Bat Teams" which, through the use of sophisticated radar equipment, were able effectively to intercept and shoot down Japanese planes in darkness.

Marshall Islands

The task force then headed north to the Marshall Islands where, on Dec. 4, the carriers launched air strikes on Kwajalein Atoll. One Japanese transport and five cargo ships were sunk, two light cruisers and other enemy ships were damaged and at least 55 enemy aircraft were destroyed.

On the nights of Dec. 4-5, one of the carrier task groups was hit by enemy aircraft which scored a torpedo hit on the carrier *Lexington*. It was believed that these enemy bomber and torpedo planes had taken off from the island of Nauru. Thus, a task force, under the leadership of RAdm. Lee, consisting of the carriers *Bunker Hill* and *Monterey*, with five fast new battleships, including the *Massachusetts*, and 12 destroyers was dispatched to conduct a bombardment of Nauru Dec. 8.

At 0702, the *Massachusetts* opened fire with a full nine-gun salvo from her main battery and then closed the range to bring her secondary five-inch battery into action on the enemy air strip. Mamie threw 136 16-inch and 400 five-inch projectiles into the island from ranges as close as only 1500 yards; while carrier planes dropped 51 tons of bombs and strafed enemy positions. Following the bombardment, the group set course for the New Hebrides where, on Dec. 12, it re-entered Havannah Harbor.

The US landing force suffered heavy

casualties at Tarawa in November. While the preparatory bombardment, most notably by the old battleships, was heavy, gunners and aviators tend to believe that the impressiveness of their fire is matched by the results at their targets. At Tarawa, that wasn't so; and the Marines fought a bloody battle before overcoming their foe. The battle literally hung in the balance for the first day and a half. The situation was exacerbated by the fact that the landing force experienced an unexpected low tide and had to wade 600 yards between a coral reef and the beach against heavy opposition.

However, the lessons learned at the Gilberts helped make the next operation against the Marshall Islands much more effective. On Jan. 23, 1944, TF 58, under the overall command of RAdm. Marc A. Mitscher, USN, stood out of Funa Futi Atoll. The *Massachusetts'* task group was comprised of the carriers *Enterprise, Yorktown* and *Belleau Wood*, other battleships *Washington* and *Indiana*, together with a destroyer screen. The force conducted air strikes in the Marshalls Jan. 29. The following morning, Mamie, the *Indiana* and *Washington* bombarded Kwajalein, the largest atoll in the world. When her guns opened up, it was straddled by five-inch salvos from shore batteries, the first enemy salvo passing directly overhead. Her return fire not only silenced this battery, but one of her salvos struck an ammunition dump, causing a tremendous explosion which sent smoke and debris hurtling thousands of feet into the air. The captain of another ship promptly messaged: "You hit the jackpot that time!" By afternoon, the *Massachusetts* had fired 362 16-inch and 1902 five-inch projectiles on coastal defense guns, enemy troop concentrations and landing strips at the air fields which were made temporarily useless, unlike Tarawa, the landings proceeded "according to the book."

On the morning of Feb. 1 at 0338, the *Indiana*, pulling out of formation in order to fuel destroyers, collided with the *Washington*, putting both ships out of action for many months. To illustrate the speed with which things were happening in the Pacific, the Marines had occupied Majuro Atoll on that very morning at about the precise time the collision had occurred. When the *Indiana* and *Washington* (able to make only 6 knots because of gaping wounds) limped into the Majuro lagoon in the dark at about 2000, they were given charts which had been prepared that day by the US Hydrographic Forces, no other charts of the area having ever been available to them prior thereto. On Feb. 4,

1944, the *Massachusetts* and the balance of the fleet anchored at Majuro—the first pre-war Japanese territory to be occupied by American forces—which became a major fleet anchorage for many months thereafter.

The capture of the Gilbert and Marshall Islands provided the US with anchorages, air strips and staging areas for further westward advances and denied these resources to the enemy.

Caroline Islands - Truk

On Feb. 12, 1944, the *Massachusetts* was part of a fast carrier task group under the leadership of RAdm. F.C. Sherman, USN, which set forth for the Caroline Islands. The three-group task force was apparently undetected as it arrived off Truk on the night of Feb. 16. Truk, 700 miles from Eniwetok and Rabaul, was to the Japanese what Pearl Harbor had been to the US—an allegedly impregnable naval base. Before dawn Feb. 17, the first night radar bombing attack in the history of US carrier operations left the deck of *Enterprise*, the start of a continuing series of strikes. These cost the enemy 200,000 tons of shipping, including two light cruisers, four destroyers, three auxiliary cruisers, two submarine tenders, two submarine chasers, an armed trawler, a plane ferry and 24 auxiliaries, including six tankers. Between 250 and 275 enemy planes were destroyed which, thereafter, rendered the "impregnable" Truk totally useless to the Japanese and decimated its capacity to threaten the American forces engaged in the capture and occupation of the Marshall Islands. During these operations, our forces were subjected to some of the heaviest enemy air attacks yet encountered; and all hands spent two days and two nights at battle stations.

A new use for battleship and cruiser Kingfisher Scout Planes had been devised. They were catapulted with instructions that, entirely at the option of the pilot, they were authorized to land, pick up downed fighter pilots and return to the ship. During the attack on Truk, Lt. Charles C. Ainsworth, USNR, head of the flight detachment on the *Massachusetts*, flew into Truk Lagoon and made a daring rescue of a fighter pilot who had been forced down. The Japanese were so surprised at his daring that they failed even to shoot at him. Ainsworth was awarded the Distinguished Flying Cross for that extraordinary feat.

By this time, a pattern was evolving for fast carrier operations. Even as one target

was being occupied by a landing force, the fast carriers would be sent to attack the next major Japanese base "up the line" towards Japan. Thus it was that the *Massachusetts* accompanied TF 58 in a series of air strikes on Feb. 21 and 22 against Saipan, Tinian, Ota and Guam in the Mariana Islands, causing the destruction of 135 Japanese planes during the operation. During these strikes, Marines landed on Eniwetok Atoll, 300 miles farther west of the Marshalls and, with the assistance of heavy bombardment by the older battleships, soon won control of the atoll.

Hollandia - New Guinea

While things were heating up in the Central Pacific under the overall leadership of Adm. Nimitz, the forces of the South West Pacific area under Gen. Douglas A. MacArthur, USA, started their offensive in New Guinea. The *Massachusetts* operated with the carrier task force out of Seeadler Harbor, Manus, in the Admiral Islands. It assisted MacArthur's troops in leapfrogging over and beyond the Japanese in the capture and occupation of Lae, Salamaua and the Hollandia area of New Guinea, and gave close support to the amphibious landings at Tanahmerah Bay and at Cape Gloucester at the western end of New Guinea, from which MacArthur was enabled to plan his move westward to the Philippines. On April 29-30, Mamie, steaming with the carrier groups, participated in further air strikes on Truk. Once again, Lt. Ainsworth rescued a downed fighter pilot within range of shore batteries.

During the operations westward along the coast of New Guinea, TF 58 conducted

repeated air attacks deep into Japanese territory, hitting Palau (another enemy stronghold), Yap, Ulithi and the Woleai Islands in the Western Carolines. During the course of these attacks, 160 Jap planes and 29 ships, with a gross tonnage of 130,000 tons, were destroyed and sunk.

Puget Sound and Leave

On May 1, *Massachusetts* joined in the aerial-surface bombardment of Ponape Island after which it, the carrier *Yorktown* and two screening destroyers set sail for repairs, rest and recreation at the Puget Sound Naval Shipyard, Bremerton, WA. Mamie was at Bremerton from May 19 until July 15. In the meantime, Capt. T.D. Ruddock, USN, who had relieved Capt. Glover, was promoted to rear admiral and was replaced by Capt. William W. Warlick, USN.

During her stay at Puget Sound, the Fifth Fleet occupied all of the Mariana Islands after bitter battles in which large segments of the Japanese army committed Hara Kiri.

The Marianas Turkey Shoot

During the occupation of the Marianas, major elements of the Japanese fleet, consisting of five carriers and four light carriers and escorting cruisers and destroyers, left their base at Tawi Tawi, southwest of the Philippines. On June 19, Adm. Ozawa, the enemy task force commander, launched four successive strikes against the American carriers from just east of the Philippines. Ozawa's force had not yet been detected by US forces. Because of the prevailing wind out of the

Task force 58 at Majuro.

49

USS Massachusetts, Indiana, and South Dakota (Battleship Division Egypt) Bombarded Japanese Homeland 1 July 1945.

Massachusetts Returns to Battleline

By Aug. 8, 1944, when the *Massachusetts* dropped the hook at Eniwetok and thereby rejoined the Pacific Fleet, the war had taken a great turn for the better for the US forces. The occupation of the Marianas enabled the construction of massive airfields from which B-29s could raid the Japanese homeland, the Turkey Shoot had largely destroyed the effectiveness of the Japanese naval airforce[2]; and the US carrier attacks had further severely damaged the enemy fleet.

Overall Pacific Strategy - A Division of Opinion

So swift had been the advances of the US forces that the strategists had not been able to keep up with events. An essential conflict had developed between the views of Gen. MacArthur, on the one hand, and those of Adms. King (Chief of Naval Operations) and Nimitz, on the other. The general believed in what he called the "New Guinea-Mindanao Access" approach to Japan, liberating the Philippine Islands from south to north before attacking Japan itself. Adms. King and Nimitz believed in a two-pronged approach to Japan. The right prong would be an aerial assent by B-29 bombers "up the ladder of the Bonins"; and the left prong would capture Formosa and a base on the coast of China. In the King-Nimitz plan, MacArthur's role would be to liberate Mindanao in the Philippines and set up air bases from which the Far Eastern Air Forces could pound Japanese air power on Luzon, after which he would help the Pacific Fleet capture Formosa.

In July, President Roosevelt conducted an inspection tour of the Pacific and summoned Gen. MacArthur and Adm. Nimitz to meet with him aboard the heavy cruiser *Baltimore* on which the president had crossed the Pacific. Subsequent high level discussions were conducted at a private residence at Waikiki. At the center of the debate lay the question of whether the Philippines, or at least Luzon, should not be bypassed. Nimitz felt that the occupation of Formosa was the best way to sever Japanese lines of communication southward, thus cutting off the home islands from essential supplies to their economy and their war-making capacity. On the other hand, MacArthur felt that both national honor and sound strategy required the liberation of the Philippines. Ever present in the general's mind was his promise, as he had departed the Philippines in early 1942, that "I shall return."

east, he was able to launch while closing our forces; whereas Mitscher, whenever he launched or recovered aircraft, had to turn east, therefore away from the Japanese fleet. The relatively fragile Japanese planes had a superior range—about 300 miles, as opposed to their sturdier US counterparts' comfortable 200. Ozawa's first strike was at a range of 300 miles. The ensuing air battle, which became known as the "Marianas Turkey Shoot," led to the destruction of 219 attacking Japanese planes out of a total force of 326. US forces lost only 29 aircraft; while the battleship *South Dakota* sustained a hit which, while it killed 27 sailors, caused no structural damage.

Mission Beyond Darkness

Before Ozawa retreated west of the Philippines, he lost the big carrier *Taiho*, torpedoed by the US submarine *Albacore* and another large carrier *Shokaku*, torpedoed by the US submarine *Cavalla*. On the evening of June 19, Mitscher launched 216 planes against the enemy force at maximum striking distance in what has become known as the "Mission Beyond Darkness." In this Battle of the Philippines Sea, the attacking planes sank the large carrier *Hiyo* and a couple of oilers and damaged the carriers *Zuikaku* and *Chiyoda*.

Well after darkness, as our planes struggled back to the fleet, often low on gas and seriously damaged, Mitscher ordered all of his ships to turn on their search lights to help his pilots find their way home. About 80 planes ditched or crashed on deck, but almost all of the pilots and crews were saved. Thus ended one of the most significant naval battles in WWII, a decisive victory for the US fleet.

Agreement on Overall Strategy

The basic agreements and understandings reached at this high-level meeting led the Joint Chiefs of Staff (whose responsibility it was to determine strategy and planning) to the adoption, in September, of an overall strategy embracing the following time-table and concepts:

Sept. 15, Southwest Pacific Forces (MacArthur) to occupy Morotai. Central Pacific Forces (Nimitz) to occupy Peleliu Oct. 5, with Yap and Ulithi to follow.

Oct. 15, Southwest Pacific Forces to occupy Salebaboe Island.

Nov. 15, Southwest Pacific Forces to land at Sarangani Bay, Mindanao, in the Philippines.

Dec. 20, Southwest Pacific Forces to occupy Leyte.

Thereafter, Southwest Pacific and Central Pacific forces to combine to occupy Luzon in the Philippine Islands by Feb. 20, 1945, or Formosa and Amoy on the China coast by March 1, 1945.

The *Massachusetts* operated with one of the four carrier task groups as those groups made air attacks in late August and early September against Yap, the Palaus and Mindanao in the Philippines. Their object was to destroy Japanese air forces which might otherwise challenge the up-coming landings on Morotai and Peleliu. Palau was bombed Sept. 6-8 and the Mindanao airdromes near Sarangani Bay Sept. 9 and 10. These attacks were virtually unopposed by the Japanese who lost about 200 planes shot down or destroyed on the ground, with many ships sunk and numerous installations destroyed. In strikes on Sept. 20 and 21, US carrier aircraft sank 40 enemy ships and destroyed 375 Jap planes in the air and on the ground.

Halsey Advances Schedule

All of this led Adm. Halsey who, by that time, had assumed command of the Third Fleet, to recommend that the foregoing time-table in effect be scrapped and that the calendar be substantially advanced. He recommended that the Palau, Yap, Morotai, and Mindanao landings be cancelled as unnecessary and that the troops which would otherwise have been used in these operations, as well as TF 38, be made available to Gen. MacArthur for an immediate seizure of Leyte in the central Philippines.

After promptly studying the recommendation, MacArthur agreed with Halsey's suggestion. The most significant element of his agreement lay in his recognition that the fast carrier forces had effected a tactical revolution. Their ability to maintain station off enemy-held territory for long periods of time and to maintain control of the air caused MacArthur to realize that it was no longer necessary to develop airfields in the southern Philippines before invading Leyte or Luzon to the north. In effect, the Navy could furnish all the air support that the Army would require until it acquired new fields of its own after the invasion.

Fortunately, at this time, the Joint Chiefs of Staff were meeting with President Roosevelt, Prime Minister Churchill and Premier MacKenzie King of Canada at Quebec. Within 90 minutes after receipt in Quebec of the MacArthur-Nimitz recommendation, the Joint Chiefs of Staff issued their instructions to execute the Leyte operation, with a target date of Oct. 20. Thus, the three intermediate landings at Yap, the Talauds and Mindanao were cancelled. Subsequent strategic planning focused upon the occupation of Luzon in the northern Philippines at the end of December, the occupation of Iwo Jima (lying between the Marianas and the home islands of Japan) in late January or early February and the occupation of Okinawa in April as a suitable base from which to launch the final invasion of the Japanese home islands.

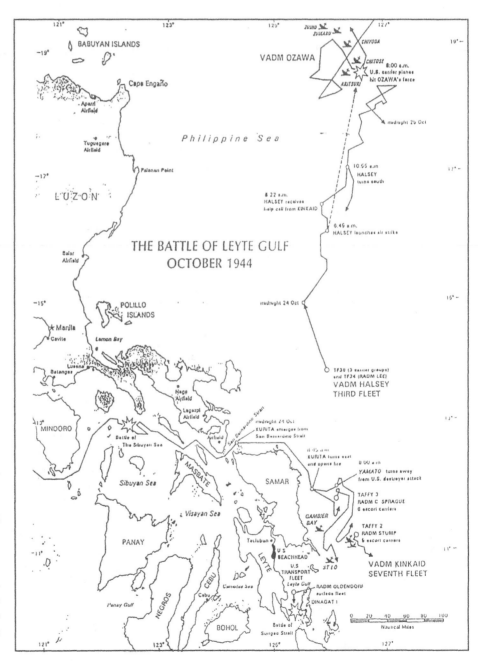

Map of Battle of Leyte Gulf, October 1944.

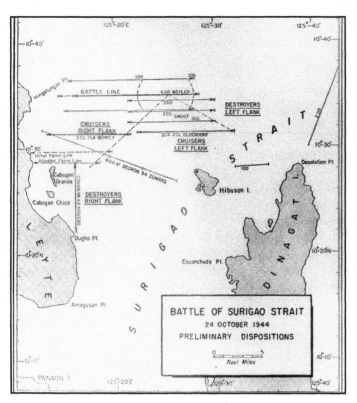
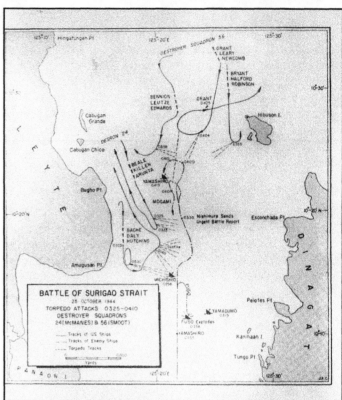

Map of Surigao Strait.

Softening the Philippines - Luzon

On Aug. 30, 1944, Big Mamie sortied from Eniwetok in the company of two *Essex*-Class carriers, two light carriers, three other fast new battleships, four light cruisers and 14 destroyers as part of TG 38.3 under the overall command of RAdm. Frederick C. Sherman, USN. Attacks against the Palaus and throughout the central Philippines were intensified, designed to gain domination of all airfields in the Philippines preparatory to the invasion for the liberation of those islands. All airfields were hit hard, along with shipping and shore installations, in a move to support the seizure of Morotai and Peleliu and to soften up the enemy for the landings at Leyte in October. During one of these strikes, one of Mamie's Kingfisher's, piloted by Lt. G.A. Robinson, USNR, successfully performed yet another sea rescue of a downed pilot.

Luzon, with its important harbor of Manila and a whole network of airfields, was the object of a devastating strike starting at dawn Sept. 21. After replenishing at Saipan Harbor between Sept. 24 and 28, the task force moved on to Ulithi Atoll, recently captured in the Caroline Islands Oct. 1. The force then departed Ulithi Oct. 6 in direct support of the landings of MacArthur's Southwest Pacific Forces in Leyte Gulf.

Formosa and Okinawa

Consistent with the pattern of carrier operations which had been developed, the mission of TF 38 was to render useless the staging airfields between the Japanese home islands and the target area, in this case the Philippines. Consequently, Oct. 10 found the *Massachusetts*, as part of Adm. Sherman's TG 38.3, off Okinawa, about 300 miles from Japan proper. This highly significant enemy base, 10 times as large as Saipan, with several good harbors, was the Japanese staging point for aircraft flown from the home islands southward to Formosa and thence to the Philippines and the East Indies. Strikes on Okinawa were completed Oct. 11, during which operation Mamie's pilots effected still another rescue of a downed pilot.

Halsey's assessment that the enemy air force had been rendered ineffective, as evidenced by its failure to resist attacks in the Philippines in September, proved quite inaccurate. The enemy was husbanding its planes in anticipation of the ultimate battle on the Japanese homeland. As carrier attacks hit closer and closer to those islands, as with Formosa and Okinawa, the enemy's resistance stiffened enormously.

The *Massachusetts* assisted in driving off enemy aerial attacks the night of Oct. 12. Further attacks by our air forces were conducted against Formosa on the 13th.

Canberra and *Houston* Torpedoed

On the 13th, the cruiser *Canberra* was torpedoed. It became dead in the water, with both engine rooms flooded. It was taken in tow by the cruiser *Wichita* accompanied by the cruiser *Houston* and a few destroyers. Halsey withdrew the remainder of the fleet, leaving the damaged ships under tow as bait in the hope that the Japanese high command would believe Tokyo Rose and the enemy attacking forces which had claimed a massive victory and the destruction of almost the entire US Pacific Fleet. Unfortunately, the ruse didn't work, but the damaged American ships were subjected to further aerial attacks during which the *Houston* suffered a very damaging torpedo hit.

Enemy air attacks continued throughout the day; and, at dusk, another group of enemy planes attacked and succeeded in breaking through our Combat Air Patrol to force an attack upon the task group. One enemy torpedo plane launched an unsuccessful attack on the carrier *Langley* and then approached the *Massachusetts* whose gunners shot it down. It splashed a short distance off Mamie's starboard bow. Moments later, Mamie's gunners downed another enemy aircraft on her starboard quarter; while the cruiser *Reno* suffered an enemy suicide crash on her fantail causing a few casualties and minor damage. By Oct.

15, the carrier task force was on its way to a fueling rendezvous while conducting long-range searches for the enemy fleet. Although successfully located, it was too far distant to attack. During these pre-landing attacks by TF 38, our forces sank 40 Japanese ships and destroyed 325 enemy planes at a cost to our forces of 89 planes.

"I Have Returned"

As American troops stormed the shores of Leyte Gulf Oct. 20, 1944, Sherman's TG 38.3 operated as the northernmost of the four task groups; while TG 38.1 under VAdm. John S. McCain, USN, TG 38.2 under RAdm. G.F. Bogan, USN, and TG 38.4 under RAdm. Ralph E. Davison, USN, operated to the south in closer proximity to Leyte Gulf. All of the task groups continued the process of neutralizing enemy aircraft and airfields in direct support of the landing operations. Gen. MacArthur was finally able to proclaim "I have returned."

These operations made it abundantly clear to the Japanese high command that, unless the US advance could be stopped, Japan's ultimate defeat was inevitable. With the Philippines in American hands, all fuel supplies from the East Indies, as well as the supply of other essential war and home consumption materials and equipment would be cut off. In desperation, the Japanese threw their entire fleet into one last desperate gamble aimed at wiping out the transport fleet disembarking troops around Leyte. That decision led to the greatest naval engagement ever fought, involving nearly 190,000 men on board 216 US, two Australian and 64 Japanese warships and encompassing an area in excess of 100,000 square miles.

The Japanese Plan of Attack

The Japanese planned a two-pronged attack on the Gulf, one through Surigao Strait to the south, with the major force as the second prong sweeping through San Bernardino Strait to the north. Our previous capture of Japanese war plans revealed that one essential element of an operation, as decisive and complex as the Japanese envisioned, required the use of a third force to serve as a decoy to try to draw US' attention away from the primary objective of enemy activity. For further details of this great battle, it is recommended that one consult any of the many detailed studies of the Battle for Leyte Gulf which have been written. Probably, the most definitive of these is

Samuel Eliot Morison's Volume XII of his *Official History of US Naval Operations in WWII*. Space considerations allow the inclusion here of only highlights of that enormous and complex battle.

US Submarines Attack Enemy Main Force

Confirmation of the enemy's commitment to a major engagement occurred at 0116 Oct. 23 when the US submarines *Darter*

and *Dace* made contact with the Japanese Center Force in Palawan Passage southwest of the Philippines. That force consisted of 10 heavy cruisers, five battleships (including the two largest in the world—the *Musashi* and *Yamato*, each armed with a main battery of nine 18-inch guns), two light cruisers and 12-14 destroyers screening the flanks. The enemy force was under the command of VAdm. T. Kurita who, from the perspective of the enemy, made many unfortunate mistakes in the course of the next few days. The

BB-59 Contributes to another naval victory.

Repelling Japanese air attack.

USS Bunker Hill hit by Kamakazi 11 May 1945.

first of these was that, although he was making only 16 knots, he had not stationed picket destroyers ahead of his disposition. Between 0500 and 0700, our submarines made repeated torpedo attacks upon this force, sinking the heavy cruiser *Atago* (Kurita's flag ship), the heavy cruiser *Maya* and so damaging the heavy cruiser *Takao* that it had to retire to its base at Brunei. All of this was dutifully reported to Halsey who then firmed up his own welcoming reception for the attacking Japanese forces.[3]

The total Japanese force consisted of four separate groups. Gp. 1, under the command of VAdm. Ozawa, sailed out of the home islands, and was comprised of four carriers (but with only 116 aircraft on their decks), two old battleships partially converted to carriers, three light cruisers and nine destroyers.

The second enemy group was under the command of VAdm. Nishimura and consisted of a pair of old battleships, a heavy

cruiser and four destroyers. That force came out of Brunei Bay, in the Southeast Asian area.

The third group, under the command of VAdm. Shima, consisted of two heavy cruisers, a light cruiser and four destroyers. It came from the home islands.

The fourth group was Kurita's major force described above. The overall Japanese plan called for the second and third groups to force their way through Surigao Straits, the southern entrance to Leyte Gulf, in the early hours, and for the fourth main group to force its way through San Bernardino Strait north of Leyte Gulf. The carrier group (Gp. 1) was to dangle itself out as bait to lure TF 38 away from Leyte Gulf and to allow Gps. 2, 3 and 4 to savage the landing force.

Halsey immediately recalled TG 38.1 under McCain from its intended refueling at Ulithi, concentrated TG 38.2 under Bogan and 38.4 under Davison east of San Bernar-

dino Strait and had TG 38.3 under Sherman up north opposite Luzon. The *Massachusetts* was operating as part of Sherman's TG 38.3.

The *Princeton* is Hit

Before Halsey got off a strike, Japanese naval planes on Luzon fields conducted one of the most vigorous and successful air attacks of the Leyte operation. The Japanese raids, each of 50-60 planes, focused their attack upon TG 38.3. For the most part, these were masterfully intercepted and destroyed by the US fighter pilots. However, the group's Combat Air Patrol missed the one enemy plane that mattered. Just as the light carrier *Princeton* was recovering its air group, a lone Judy glide bomber flashed out of the clouds at 0938 and planted a 550-pound bomb on the *Princeton* flight deck. The blast entered the hangar deck which was soon blazing with burning gasoline which enveloped torpedo bombers, with their loaded torpedoes aboard. These exploded one-by-one and tossed the 25 foot square forward elevator up as high as the mast head. Notwithstanding heroic efforts by the destroyers *Gatling*, *Erwin* and *Cassin Young* and the heavy cruiser *Birmingham*, the *Princeton* could not be saved. At 1600, after more than 600 survivors of her crew had been rescued, the gallant ship was hit by two torpedoes from the cruiser *Reno* which exploded 100,000 gallons of gasoline and literally blew the *Princeton* out of the water.

Aerial Attacks on Japanese Fleet

While the *Princeton* was struggling for its life, our carriers were punishing Kurita's main force. Since Kurita had very little, if any, air protection, the losses of his force were impressive and significant. The Japanese air defense was ineffective. There were an enormous number of anti-aircraft guns in the Japanese fleet—120 in each battleship. The enemy battleships even fired their main batteries of 18-inch guns at attacking planes. Nevertheless, only 18 American planes, of the hundreds that attacked Oct. 24, were shot down.

The aerial attack concentrated on the giant battleship *Musashi* which took a total of 19 torpedo and 17 bombing hits during the day. It rolled over and sank at 1935, with a loss of 39 of her 112 officers and 984 of her 2287 man crew.

Her sister ship, *Yamato*, and the older battleship *Nagato* received two bomb hits; and the old battleship *Haruna* was damaged by five near-misses. Heavy cruiser *Myoko* was damaged by torpedoes and forced to return to Brunei Bay.

By late afternoon, the Japanese force had been reported by our aviators as seriously crippled and was seen to be heading west. However, the enemy ships were merely milling around in order to re-group, hopefully after the Japanese land-based air forces had been able to strike the attacking US fleet. However, there were really no land-based air forces left to the Japanese to accomplish anything. Notwithstanding the reported damage to the main force, a night-flying pilot from the *Independence* spotted the major enemy force at 1935 heading 120 degrees, a direct shot at San Bernardino Strait. Kurita's force had been battered, mauled and wounded, but not destroyed.

In the meantime, Ozawa's carrier force, which, for the better part of the day, had deliberately broken radio silence in its attempt to lure Halsey north, was finally sighted at 1640, not too many miles north of the *Massachusetts*' TG 38.3.

Halsey's Fateful Decision

At this point, Adm. Halsey made the fateful decision with respect to the Battle for Leyte Gulf. At 2022, Oct. 24, Halsey ordered Bogan's TG 38.2 and Davison's TG 38.4 to steam north at 25 knots, join Sherman's group and attack Ozawa. By midnight Oct. 24-25, all those carrier groups, with all of their fast new battleships and cruisers, were dashing north, just as the Japanese wanted them to do, leaving the San Bernardino Strait unguarded.

The next night, after the battle was over, Halsey gave his justification in a dispatch to Adm. Nimitz and Gen. MacArthur:

"Searches by my carrier planes revealed the presence of the Northern Carrier Force on the afternoon of Oct. 24, which completed the picture of all enemy naval forces. As it seemed childish to me to guard statically San Bernardino Strait, I concentrated TF 38 during the night and steamed north to attack the Northern Force at dawn. I believed that the Center Force had been so heavily damaged in the Sibuyan Sea that it could no longer be considered a serious menace to Seventh Fleet."

This decision of Halsey's was reached, notwithstanding strongly-worded recommendations on the part of Adms. Bogan and Lee to concentrate on San Bernardino Strait and notwithstanding the expressed reservations of Adm. Mitscher, the overall air commander. No advice was solicited, and that which was volunteered was ignored.

Action in Surigao Strait

While our carriers concentrated their fury on Kurita's force during the 24th and chased the Japanese carriers during the night of Oct. 24-25, the two southern enemy forces, under Nishimura and Shima, continued to make their way through Surigao Strait, with Shima trailing Nishimura. In the narrow, darkened waters of the Strait, just before 0300, 39 US motor torpedo boats, in three successive raids, attacked without making any hits. These attacks were followed by US destroyer torpedo attacks which blew the old battleship *Fuso* into two parts and sank one of Nishimura's destroyers, also damaging his flagship, the old battleship *Yamashiro*, and two other destroyers. The remnants of the attacking Japanese forces pressed on.

Ahead of them were six old American battleships, eight cruisers and nine destroy-

4th Division aboard BB-59. Photo courtesy of Ed Metzel.

ers, many of them, including five of the battleships, the relics of the Pearl Harbor attack, all under the command of VAdm. Jesse B. Oldendorf, USN. All these forces were armed principally with bombardment shells, although the few rounds of armor-piercing shells which they did have were put to great use. The US force was strung out along the neck of the bottle, thereby automatically crossing the T of the Japanese force. In that classic naval maneuver, all guns of the US forces were able to be trained upon the head of the enemy force which, being in column, was limited to utilizing only its forward turrets. Nishimura's force was almost entirely destroyed; while Shima's was severely damaged and retired without inflicting any damage on US forces. The battle of Surigao Strait was decisively won by the US; but the elation of victory was short-lived.

San Bernardino Strait and Leyte Gulf

While Halsey was chasing the bait north, Kurita, whose force still consisted of four battleships, six heavy cruisers, two light cruisers and several squadrons of destroyers, had passed through San Bernardino Strait and, at 0658 on Oct. 25, commenced firing upon what Kurita thought was the main US battle force.

His opposing force proved to be three task groups made up entirely of small escort carriers built upon thin-skinned cargo ship hulls, and their escorting destroyers and destroyer escorts. The battle which ensued for the next two and a quarter hours was the most extraordinary naval battle ever conducted. In short, the three escort carrier groups and their screen took on the major Japanese force under Kurita. Kurita was completely taken aback by the fierce attack

of the escort carrier pilots who used bombs, torpedoes, rockets and machine guns and, when their weapons were gone, made dry runs. (This from aviators trained to support troop landings, not take on enemy fleets). He was confused by the charge of the escorting destroyers and destroyer escorts which launched torpedoes in profusion, fired their guns at anything visible, laid down smoke screens and, when all ordnance had been consumed, made feigned attacks on the vastly superior enemy force.

All of this so befuddled Kurita that, at 0911, he issued orders to break off the action. In an unbelievable demonstration of indecisiveness, Kurita milled around for three hours, while the landing force in Leyte Gulf lay open to attack. It was defended only by the old battleships and cruisers which had won at Surigao Strait and which were virtually out of armor-piercing ammunition.

L-R, Back Row: Cyril A. Fochs, Gene R. Hill; front row: Thomas Meyers, person unidentified. (Photo courtesy of Cyril A. Fochs.)

Given the fact that he had had to swim for his life when his flagship was torpedoed by the *Dace-Darter* group, without radar and with his optical equipment made useless by repeated smoke screening from the escort carriers' escorts; having learned of the destruction of the Nishimura and Shima forces; having heard nothing from Ozawa; and, finally, believing that he was about to take on the entire US fleet for which he had mistaken the escort carriers, one can perhaps sympathize with Kurita's plight. At 1236, he made the incredible decision to head back, at maximum speed, to what he hoped would be the friendlier waters of San Bernardino Strait.

Adm. Kinkaid, overall commander of the naval forces under MacArthur, and the general, himself, were under the mistaken impression that Halsey had formed TF 34, (consisting of six new battleships, seven cruisers and 17 destroyers, under Adm. Lee) and that TF 34 was eagerly awaiting Kurita off San Bernardino Strait as the main Japanese force streamed out. This was a natural assumption based upon Halsey's orders from Nimitz to engage the enemy fleet if and when an opportunity occurred and from a somewhat poorly drafted message from Halsey that he would form TF 34. Unfortunately, Halsey's message did not state when or under what circumstances this would occur. Consequently, the US defenders of Leyte Gulf were absolutely stunned when they first saw the Pagoda masts of the Japanese battleships and the flashes of the enemy guns as they opened fire on the escort carriers.

"Where is TF 34?"

While the major action between the escort carriers and the main Japanese fleet was unfolding, and while McCain's TG 38.1 was racing north from Ulithi to attack Kurita's force, the balance of TF 38, including all of TF 34, got as close as 42 miles to Ozawa's cripples. However, by mid-morning, Halsey had heard Adm. Kinkaid's plain-language pleas for assistance[4] and, at 1000, had received Nimitz's dispatch inquiring "Where is TF 34?" Halsey's biographers say that it was the Nimitz dispatch[5] which finally caused him to order Bogan's TG 38.2 and the major part of Lee's Battle Line

to reverse course and steam south to help Kinkaid. This order was executed at 1115. Even by making the best speed they possibly could, this force could not expect to reach San Bernardino Strait before 0100 on the following day—far too late.

While the battleships and TG 38.2 were racing south, Mitscher sent the balance of his carriers and escorts to deal with Ozawa. Mitscher had his search planes out before dawn and launched his first strikes between 0540 and 0600 on the assumption that the search planes would have done their job and be in position to vector the strikes to the enemy carriers.

For several days, Ozawa had tried to be seen and to attract attention to himself and away from Kurita. He succeeded with a vengeance on the morning of Oct. 25. Ozawa's flagship was the carrier *Zuikaku*, a thorn in the USN's side throughout the war. It took a torpedo early on, thus causing the admiral to shift his flag to the *Oyodo*. (The battle for Leyte Gulf was not good for Japanese flagships nor a dry experience for Japanese admirals.) Before the air strikes were completed, the enemy lost the *Zuikaku*, the small carriers *Zuiho* and *Chitose* and the destroyer *Akitsuki*; while the carrier *Chiyoda* was left dead in the water and abandoned.

Mitscher had dispatched the cruisers *Santa Fe*, *Mobile*, *Wichita* and *New Orleans*, with nine destroyers, under RAdm. Lawrence T. Dubose, USN, to continue north to engage the carriers. This force sank the damaged carrier *Chiyoda* with gunfire and later the destroyer *Hatsuzuki*.

Leyte Gulf Summary

During the prolonged battle for Leyte Gulf, the Americans had lost seven ships—a light carrier, two escort carriers, a submarine, two destroyers and a destroyer escort, aggregating 33,118 tons. The Japanese lost 26 ships—two large and two light carriers, three battleships, seven heavy and four light cruisers and nine destroyers, aggregating 302,782 tons. Thereafter, no Japanese carrier ever went to sea on a combat mission, and only once more would a battleship do so.

The end result was an enormous victory for the US naval forces. However, for the battleship sailors, the result left much to

be desired. Battleships were built to be a part of the battle line and to bring the enemy's ships under their guns. As Morison observes: "The mighty gunfire of the Third Fleet's Battle Line, greater than that of the whole Japanese Navy, was never brought into action except to finish off one or two crippled light ships." Cruising across the throat of the San Bernardino Straits, TF 34 would have already "crossed the T" as the Japanese forces came single-file out of the Strait. For the battleships, San Bernardino was the last chance. It was the lost chance.

Kamikaze Attacks

One of the seven US vessels lost during the battle was the escort carrier *St. Lo*. It was part of the escort carrier group which had fought off Kurita's main body. On Oct. 25, that group was the recipient of the first deliberate Kamikaze ("Divine Wind") suicide plane attack of the war. While many a Japanese pilot had theretofore attempted to crash himself on a US ship, Oct. 25 was the inaugural of a deliberate policy, born of desperation, by the enemy. From then on, little-trained pilots were sent on these missions with just enough gasoline to make a one-way trip. They were not only expected to crash into US ships but looked forward to the glorious distinction of having the privilege of doing so. Dealing with this threat became a major pre-occupation of the US naval forces. As a steward's mate on the cruiser *Wichita* is reported to have said: "We don't mind them planes which drops things, but we don't like them what lights on you!"

With the Japanese fleet rendered virtually inoperable, the *Massachusetts* continued with the carrier task force in extensive raids on enemy airfields throughout the Philippines.

On Dec. 17, 1944, the force reached a fueling rendezvous, but rising winds and seas forced abandonment of that operation. Along with the rest of the fleet, Mamie soon found herself plowing into the teeth of a howling typhoon, bucking monstrous seas brought on by a titanic gale estimated at 120 knots. Mamie sustained only minor damage which was repaired by her own force. However, one of her scout planes was damaged beyond repair.

When the Third Fleet Met the Great Typhoon

Condensed from

The New York Times Magazine

Hanson W. Baldwin

Military editor, *The New York Times*

A dark December blow, aided by "large errors," humbled a proud armada in its hour of triumph.

Through the courtesy of The Reader's Digest, we reprint here Hanson W. Baldwin's vivid description of that weather-induced nightmare entitled When the Third Fleet Met the Great Typhoon.

It was the greatest fleet that had ever sailed the seas, and it was fresh from its greatest triumph. But the hand of God was laid upon it and a great wind blew, and it was scattered and broken upon the ocean. The inexorable law of storms was neglected, and the Third Fleet, Adm. William F. Halsey commanding, paid the penalty: more men lost, more ships sunk and damaged than in many of the engagements of the Pacific war.

In mid-December 1944 the battle for Leyte Gulf was history; the Japanese Empire only a few weeks before had been dealt a fatal blow. The invasion of Mindoro started Dec. 15 and the Third Fleet was weary from three days of wide-ranging strikes against the island of Luzon. As the fleet retired to refuel, the beginning of the end was in sight. Adm. Halsey, flying his flag on the battleship *New Jersey*, dispatched the refueling rendezvous—about 500 miles east of Luzon—to the oilers and to TF 38, the carriers. But on the night of Dec. 16-17 the sea made up and there was the queasiness of impending storm.

Sunday, Dec. 17: This day dawns dark and brooding, the sea choppy, the wind brisk but fickle, the ships fretful. Across hundreds of miles of ocean the Third Fleet steams, the masts, the flight decks bowing and dipping, swinging in wide arcs across the horizon. Here in all its majesty is the fleet that has humbled Japan—a score of carriers, eight "battlewagons," numerous cruisers, dozens of destroyers. Third Fleet makes contact with the 24 big fleet oilers and their escort, and despite the querulous swells refueling starts. The compulsion of combat, the support needed by those GIs back on Mindoro, permits no concession to nature.

The destroyers—the little ships that dance in any sea, the ships with maws empty from their days of high-speed steaming—come alongside the tankers. But the ocean will have none of it. Some ships get aboard hundreds of gallons before the lines break and the ships swing wildly apart, but most part line after line as boatswains curse and the water boils aboard the well decks and the steel plates run with oil.

In early afternoon fueling is suspended, and a course is set to northwest, later to southwest to escape the center of the approaching storm which is not clearly located. The barometers drop, the winds moan, but the Third Fleet steams on in cruising formation.

Monday, Dec. 18: The night is haggard; aboard the destroyers the sideboards are on the wardroom tables, the sleepers are braced in their bunks, but the sharp motion of the aroused ocean makes sleep fitful. Barometers fall steadily. Rain squalls and flung spray and spume reduce visibility; station-keeping is difficult—at times almost impossible. The winds beat and buffet, "but no estimates of the storm center were in agreement" and not until dawn does Third Fleet realize it is in the path of the granddaddy of all typhoons. Fleet course is changed to 180 degrees—due south—but it is too late; the fury is upon them.

The forenoon watch opens, in the words of an old seagoing term, "with the devil to pay and no pitch hot." The violence of the wind is terrible; it shrieks and whinnies, roars and shudders, beats and clutches. The ships are laboring deeply—laid over by the wind, rolling rapidly through tremendous arcs with sharp violent jerks, pounding and pitching, buried deep beneath tons of water, rising heavily, streaming foam and salt from gunnels and hawse pipes. Violent rain gusts, spindrift blown with the sting of hail, a rack of scud blot out visibility. Third Fleet is scattered; few ships see others; only on the radar-scopes do the pips of light loom up to show in wild confusion man's panoply of power.

The deeply laden oilers, the heavy battleships, the larger carriers roll and plunge deeply and violently, but not dangerously, through the towering seas; but for the escort carriers, the light carriers and the destroyers, the struggle is to live. Some of the fleet is in the "dangerous semicircle" of the typhoon, where stronger winds drive them toward the storm's center, and at least one task unit is directly in the center, where the funnel of wind and the boiling ocean leap to climax. Ship after ship falls away into the terrible troughs and will not answer her helm.

Aboard the light carrier *Cowpens*, an F6F$_5$ airplane, triple-lashed on the flight deck, breaks loose on a 45-degree roll and smashes into the catwalk, starting a fire. Men fight it as a wall of solid green water rips open, like a can opener, the steel-roller curtains on the port side of the hangar deck. Men fight it as the wind and sea pull out of its steel roots the forward 20mm gun sponson. Men fight it as bombs break their battens in the magazine and skitter about the deck; as jeeps and tractors, a kerry crane and seven planes are flung and blown off the flight deck into the writhing sea. But in the end it is the sea which extinguishes the fire, as it was the sea which started it; the F6F₅ breaks clear of the catwalk and falls into the tumult of water.

As the day wears on, the log books run out of nautical superlatives. The barometer drops as no seaman there had ever seen it fall before. Several ships record a flat 28 inches; *Dewey* reads hers at 27.30—possibly the world's lowest recorded reading. Oiler *Nantahala*, with other ships of a fueling unit to the northeast of the main body near the storm center, records a wind velocity of 124 knots. [A knot is approximately 1.15 mph.]

The wind shifts rapidly as the typhoon curves, blowing from north and south and east and west—backing and filling as do all circular storms—and increasing in intensity to Force 17, far beyond that ancient nautical measuring stick of mariners, the Beaufort scale—which defines Force 12, its maximum, as a "hurricane above 65 knots."

The wind has a thousand notes—the bass of growling menace, the soprano of stays so tautly strained they hum like bowstrings. The tops of the waves—70 feet from trough to crest—are flattened off by the wind and hurled straight before its violence; rain and spindrift mix in a horizontal sheet of water; one cannot tell where ocean stops and sky begins. Over all is the cacophony of the racked and groaning ships, the creaking of the bulkheads, the working of the stanchions, the slide and tear and roar of wreckage slipping from bulkhead to bulkhead.

Attempts to keep station or to change course to ease pounding spell havoc for some. Several of the lighter destroyers are derelicts; all possible combinations of rudders and screws fail to take them out of the troughs; they are sloughed and rolled and roughed far on their sides by wind and water, and drift out of control downwind.

The light and escort carriers fare little better. Their hangar decks are infernos of flame and crashing metal, of fire and wind and sea.

Aboard the light carrier *San Jacinto* men of the damage-control and fire-fighting parties lash themselves to lines suspended from the overhead of the hangar deck and, swinging and slithering like pendulums across the slippery deck, risk their lives to secure the mass of sliding, groaning wreckage. *Monterey's* Nos. 1 and 2 firerooms are abandoned because of heavy smoke from a hangar-deck fire; the boilers are manned by skeleton crews using rescue breathing masks; a gasoline vapor explosion kills one seaman; another, trapped by the flames, is burned to death; a third asphyxiated; many injured.

Destroyer *Dewey* labors almost to the death. With the storm howling like a banshee, the quartermaster on watch scribbles on the deck log, as casualty reports funnel to the bridge:

1020—Lost bridge steering control; steering aft.

1130—Main engines stopped—main switchboard shorted from salt water. Five hundred to 1000 gallons of water entering No. 2 main forced draft intake on every big roll ... Dead in the water. All hands told to remain on port side. Rolling and pounding worse. Inclinometer to 73 degrees to starboard and stopped for a few seconds.

But *Dewey*, as the morning dies, still lives. Not so destroyers *Monaghan* and *Spence*.

Monaghan, with 12 battle stars on her bridge, lunges to her doom—the fleet unknowing. Her 1500 tons of steel are racked and strained; her starboard whaleboat drinks the sea as the davits dip into green water. But there's little intimation of disaster.

About eight bells the wind pushes *Monaghan* far on her starboard side. It struggles to rise again—and makes it, but sluggishly. In the after deck house 40 or 50 men cling to stanchions and pray: "Bring it back, oh, God! Bring it back!" Slowly the ship recovers. But the lights go out; again the deep roll to starboard, again and again it struggles back, shudderingly, from disaster.

Finally the wind brutalizes her; heavily *Monaghan* rolls to starboard—30, 40, 60, 70 degrees—tiredly it settles down flat on her side to die amid a welter of white waters and the screaming Valkyries of the storm. Eighteen officers and 238 men go with her.

Spence goes about the same time. Deballasted, light in fuel, it rides like a cork and is flung like a cork in the terrible canyonlike troughs. The ship goes over 72 degrees to port—and stays there. The lights are out; the pumps are stopped—the ship's heart dead before the body dies. Sometime before noon *Spence*—2100 tons of steel with the power of 60,000 horses—is done.

The fleet is widely dispersed; some ships have felt the full fury of the storm; others are still to feel it. Between 1100 and 1400 of that day the peak is reached.

For destroyer *Hull*, with much of the fleet's mail aboard, the afternoon watch is her last. As the wind increases to an estimated 110 knots "its force lays the ship over on her starboard side and holds her down in the water until the seas come flowing into the pilot house." Young Lt. Cmdr. James Alexander Mark steps off his capsized ship, his first command, into a sea "whipped to a froth," a sea so ravening for life that lifejackets are torn from the back of the few survivors.

Destroyer *Dewey* makes it though hurt almost mortally. Green water slops over the starboard wing of the bridge as the ship lies over an estimated 80 degrees to starboard—and lives to tell about it—the first vessel in the history of the sea to survive such a roll.

At 1300 the barometer hits "bottom." But the typhoon has done its worst; at 1340 the barometer registers a slight rise, and at 1439 the wind slackens to about 80 knots. The storm curves on into the wide open spaces of the Pacific the rest of that day—Monday. Even on Tuesday the seas are huge—but the great typhoon is over.

Survivors of *Monaghan* and *Hull* and *Spence* are pitifully few. Ships scouring the ocean, find a handful of spent and injured sailors, who will forever comprehend more fully than any living men the meaning of the fury of the sea.

The great typhoon cost 790 dead or missing. More than 80 men were injured; 146 planes were blown overboard or damaged beyond repair. The small ships were battered and spent; the list of *Monterey's* damages alone covered nine closely typed pages. Thirteen vessels required major repair, while nine others sustained minor damage. The planned strikes against Luzon were canceled and the Third Fleet straggled—cockbilled and askew—into the atoll of Ulithi.

A Navy Court of inquiry, summoned to solemn post-mortem, found that "large errors [had been] made in predicting the location and path" ... of the typhoon. Adm. Chester W. Nimitz pointed out that the damage done "represented a more crippling blow to the Third Fleet than it might be expected to suffer in anything less than a major action." And from Commander Service Force, a sobering comment from man, arrogant in his victory against man: "...there is no ship afloat that cannot be capsized in a seaway."

China Coast Raids

For the balance of the year and most of January 1945, TF 38 continued its onslaught against Japanese air power in the Philippines and Formosa, including raids on shipping and airfields in the Saigon-Kamranh Bay area of Indo-China and the Hong Kong, Swatow and Amoy areas of the China Coast. This phase of operations, in support of landings by troops of the South-West Pacific Command at Lingayen Gulf, was concluded Jan. 23 with new air strikes against Formosa and Okinawa.

On Dec. 24, 1944, Adm. Davis was relieved by RAdm. John F. Shafroth Jr., USN, as commander Battleship Div. Eight.

Iwo Jima

When B-29s first started raiding the Japanese homelands from airfields in the Marianas, they were frequently harassed by Japanese fighter planes from the island of Iwo Jima, lying about halfway between the Marianas and Japan. Iwo Jima had long been identified as a primary target for the US forces, both to deny its use to Japan and to permit our B-29s to be escorted by our fighters to be based there. Thus it was that the *Massachusetts* was part of one of four carrier task groups which, with aerial bombing, softened up the island for invasion by the Marines in early February 1945. Its capture was one of the hardest fights in the history of the Marine Corps about which Adm. Nimitz said: "Uncommon valor was a common virtue."

At Iwo Jima, the Japanese airforce severely damaged its navy's favorite target, the US aircraft carrier *Saratoga*, and also sank the escort carrier *Bismark Sea*; but that was about the extent of US losses in terms of ships. Iwo Jima was declared secured March 16; although fighting lasted until May. Its landing fields became a haven for crippled B-29s.

First Raid on Tokyo

In mid-February, the *Massachusetts* took part in an operation that had been the goal of naval planning and strategy for years—the first raids by carrier-based planes on Tokyo. Mamie was part of a task group under the command of RAdm. "Jocko" Clark, USN, who always asked to be placed in the van of the attacking forces, thus bringing his group and the *Massachusetts* only 70 miles from the coast of Honshu and 117 miles from Tokyo itself.

Each of these major operations put a great strain on the crews of the various ships. Beyond the stress of the battles themselves, the crews were called to General Quarters at all hours of the day and night. Keeping a home for 2400 men in tip-top fighting condition left little time for rest. For example, the fleet was at sea for 108 straight days before, during and after the occupation of the Marianas.

While the Navy provided recreational facilities at the various bases as we moved westward through the Pacific, there was little time to enjoy them. Big Mamie was in port for a total of only 70 days from the beginning of the Philippine operation, Aug. 30, 1944, until the end of the war—almost a year later.

Back to Okinawa

Following the successful conquest of Iwo Jima, it was back to Okinawa and the Japanese home islands. On March 1, Lt. Robinson was catapulted from the *Massachusetts* to rescue a fighter pilot from the carrier *Bennington* off southeastern Okinawa. The rescue was undertaken under extremely adverse weather conditions. For this, Robinson was awarded the Distinguished Service Medal, while Lt. A.B. Cenedella, USNR, and aviation radioman first class Stanley J. Krejeski (both of whom were in an assisting communications plane) were awarded Air Medals.

On March 18, the *Massachusetts* Task Gp. was off Kyushu, the southern-most Japanese home island, where it helped drive off determined enemy aerial attacks, assisted the carrier *Wasp* in downing one suicide plane and shot down another that tried to dive-bomb the carrier *Hornet*. It shot down another enemy aircraft the night of March 18 and scored hits on another, while the badly damaged carrier *Franklin* put up an epic and successful fight for her life off the southern tip of Kyushu[6]. Air strikes were made on Okinawa March 23; and, on the following day, Mamie participated with other fast battleships in the bombardment of the southeastern coast of Okinawa preparatory to the American invasion of that "last stepping stone" to Japan itself. Off Kyushu, another successful rescue operation was completed by Mamie's aviators, the first by any ship in enemy homeland waters.

It was at Okinawa that the British Pacific Fleet, consisting of heavy surface forces, including battleships and at least

four aircraft carriers, first became our partners in the assault upon Okinawa and the Jap home islands. The British force was designated as TF 57 when functioning under Spruance and as TF 37 when functioning under the overall command of Halsey.

American troops stormed the shores of Okinawa on Easter Sunday, April 1, 1945. The overall operation was under the command of RAdm. Raymond S. Spruance, commander of the Fifth Fleet; and, therefore, the carriers operated as TF 58. Because of the furious resistance by the enemy following the relatively easy landing itself, the fleet was required to operate for a prolonged period in close support of Okinawa.

Okinawa Secured

Thus, it was constantly in reach of whatever planes the enemy had to throw at it from the home islands. Kamikaze attacks occurred almost daily and were carried out with fierce determination. The fleet suffered its heaviest losses in ships and personnel during the securing of Okinawa. One-seventh of all casualties suffered by the Navy in WWII were taken at Okinawa.

On April 6 and 7, 355 kamikazes and 341 other aircraft attacked the fleet. They sank three destroyers, an LST and two ammunition-laden freighters and damaged 17 other ships, some so badly that they were scrapped as soon as the war was over. By the end of June, 21 US ships had been sunk and 66 others severely damaged. No big combat ships were among those sunk, but there were plenty of them among those damaged. Big Mamie, fortunately, came through unscathed.

It was at Okinawa, and especially on the radar picket stations[7], that American sailors showed that they could endure. They took it for three months amid the constant threat of death and where the action was always intense. As an example, in a period of one hour and 20 minutes, the picket destroyer *Laffey* came under 22 separate attacks. Her crew shot down eight of her attackers; but six more crashed into her, and four bombs hit her. More than a third of her crew were casualties; but they brought the ship home, and it served for many years thereafter.

On April 6, an enemy suicide plane made a dive for the carrier *Bennington* and was downed by the fire of *Massachusetts*. Another, in a shallow dive above the carrier *Hornet*, was taken under fire by the *Massachusetts*, lost enthusiasm, pulled up sharply to gain altitude, burst into flames, and fell in a slow spin into the sea. About the same time, another suicide plane dove towards the cruiser *Vincennes* on Mamie's starboard hand. That Kamikaze was downed by *Massachusetts* gunners before reaching the cruiser. That same afternoon, an enemy plane dove out of a cloud towards the carrier *San Jacinto* and was set afire by gunners of the *Massachusetts* who knocked off a wheel of the aircraft before it crashed into the sea just forward of the *San Jacinto's* bow.

The Enemy Fleet's Last Effort

When the Okinawa operation started, there were four carrier task groups in TF 58. Normally, refueling arrangements would leave at least two of those groups in direct support of Okinawa while the other two went down to refuel. As a result of the damage to some of the carriers, it developed that, on April 6, 1945, only TG 58.1 under Jocko Clark, consisting of the carriers *Hornet, Wasp, Bennington, Belleau Wood, San Jacinto,* Battleship Div. 8 (*Massachusetts* and *Indiana*), Light Cruiser Div. 14[8] (*Vincennes, Miami, Vicksburg* and *San Juan*) and Heavy Cruiser Div. 10 (*Baltimore* and *Pittsburgh*), with a screen of 22 destroyers, was the only task group immediately off of Okinawa.

In the morning of April 6, word was received from Adm. Nimitz that a message had been decoded by his cryptographers that the remnants of the Japanese fleet were to come out of the Inland Sea, hug close to the China coast so as to avoid TF 58 and fall upon the US troop transports at Okinawa. These enemy ships are reputed to have been carrying virtually all of the oil remaining in Japan. By January 1945, American submarines had sunk most of Japan's deep-water merchant ships. Mainly as a result of the work of our submarines, no oil reached Japan after March 1945.

TG 58.1 was ordered north at flank speed to intercept the enemy force off the coast of Kyushu. In the afternoon, the battleships and cruisers, with appropriate screen, pulled ahead and left the carriers behind, although their planes continued to fly combat air patrol over the battle force. There was uncertainty as to the makeup of the Japanese force, but it was known that it included the biggest battleship afloat, the *Yamato,* whose 18-inch guns could outrange those of the *Massachusetts* and *Indiana.* Furthermore, the enemy force was expected to stay close to the southern tip of Kyushu where the US task group was to meet it after dark. There was the likely prospect that the effectiveness of our ships' radar would be substantially diminished by the mountainous background of the Japanese homeland.

As dusk approached, with all battle preparations made, the carriers' search planes were mystified by the fact that they were unable to locate any enemy force. That situation was shortly clarified by a second dispatch from Nimitz to the effect that his cryptographers had misinterpreted the first message and that the Japanese were not due until the following day.

Yamato Sunk

TG 58.1 withdrew to the south, as the other task groups came north for an engagement April 7. However, once again, aircraft carriers (in this case our own units and not the bait of the Japanese fleet) prevented a surface engagement between battle lines. The Japanese force, consisting of the *Yamato,* light cruiser *Yahagi* and eight destroyers, was spotted by Mitscher's planes early on the 7th. Carrier aircraft subjected the enemy fleet, and particularly the *Yamato,* to relentless and constant attacks. It took at least 12 torpedoes and countless bombs (in one air strike alone, 10 bombs hit the *Yamato*) to cause that mighty vessel to roll over and sink to the bottom. The cruiser *Yahagi* and four destroyers were also lost. With a complement of 2,767 officers and men, only 269 from the *Yamato* survived. The *Yahaki* lost 446 men, and the destroyers lost 391. Our losses were 10 planes and 12 men.

The Japanese coordinated the ill-fated *Yamato* mission with one of the heaviest Kamikaze attacks of the war. On April 7, an enormous formation of 380 Japanese planes clouded the sky above the task force. The majority of these were dispatched by our carrier planes. Many others were shot down by ship's gunfire; but many completed their mission as flaming pyres aboard US ships.

Until the end of April, the *Massachusetts* remained in support of the Okinawa operation, helping to repel the frequent air attacks. Back in Ulithi, Capt. Warwick, who had been promoted to commodore, was relieved in early May by Capt. John R. Redman, USN.

In mid-May, TF 58 returned to its job of punishing the airfields of Kyushu and destroying the remnants of the Japanese fleet in the Inland Sea of Japan. At midnight, May 29, Adm. Spruance hauled down his flag as commander of the Fifth Fleet and again relinquished the command to Adm. Halsey.

June 1945 Typhoon

Once again, the fleet under Halsey was to meet its other adversary in the Pacific— a typhoon, which is the Pacific's version of a hurricane, cyclone and tornado all mixed into one raging, boiling manifestation of the elements. At 0100, June 4, the barometer dropped to 29.42. The force of the wind rose to an estimated 100 knots by 0630 June 5 at which time some ships were having serious difficulties, including the heavy cruiser *Pittsburgh* which lost her bow and the cruiser *Duluth* whose bow buckled under the force of the storm.

At about 0700 June 5, the *Massachusetts* passed through the "eye" of the typhoon, and the barometer dropped to 28.30; the wind decreased to 26 knots, and visibility increased from a few hundred feet to about 10,000 yards. The ceiling rose from zero visibility to an estimated 5,000 feet, and the circular structure of the swirling typhoon was clearly discernable.

The seas in the typhoon's 12-mile diameter eye were mountainous, being much greater even than those encountered when the wind was estimated at 100 knots. Mamie's anemometer carried away when the wind reached 158 knots. At the edge of the typhoon's eye, the waves were 50-60 feet from crest to trough in long curving swells radiating from the typhoon's center; but, within the eye itself, they were pyramidal and confused.

The ship experienced rolls of up to 34 degrees to each side, an arc of almost 70 degrees. The wind was so strong that it seriously blurred the definition between the sea and the air. A scud of water and air prevented radar from working properly. Again, solid green water swamped the foredeck. The plunging was so severe that green water was thrown over Spot One, more than 150 feet above water-line. When Mamie emerged on the other side of the eye, it found the seas subsiding, and the barometer rose steadily. It suffered only minor damage; but one of her Kingfisher planes was destroyed by the battering waves.

One cannot fully comprehend the power of a storm such as this until he has stood on the deck and felt a 35,000-ton behemoth shudder throughout its length as it fights to shake off the impact of solid green water back to Turret 2.

Following the typhoon, the carrier task groups reformed to the southeast of Okinawa where air strikes were conducted June 9 against Okino Daito Jima and Minami Daito Jima, the latter being hit on the morning of June 10 by a fierce bombardment from the main batteries of the *Massachusetts, Alabama, Indiana* and five destroyers.

This was followed by a refurbishing visit at San Pedro Bay, Leyte June 13 after almost three months of nearly continuous operations at sea in support of the Okinawa Campaign. There, June 19, 1945, Adm. Shafroth, commander of Battleship Div. Eight, transferred his flag from the *Massachusetts* to the *South Dakota*.

Final Offensive Action

On July 1, 1945, there started what was to become the final offensive action of the war—the Third Fleet's month and a half of savaging operations in Japanese waters directly against the Japanese homeland. On July 10, carrier-based planes of the task force blasted airfields and installations in the Tokyo area with the launching of 1200 sorties. July 14 saw another attack on the island of Honshu, this time farther north. Then, shortly after noon, Japan's civilian and military population along the coast near Kamaishi saw a line of big, fast battleships, including Mamie, escorted by cruisers and destroyers, bombard the Empire's largest iron and steel-producing center.

While the activity of the Third Fleet was directed at military targets, one of the principal purposes of these operations after July 1 was to demonstrate conclusively to the leaders as well as to the civilian population of Japan that that nation had nothing left with which to defend itself against continuing ravaging by the Allied forces. The bombardment force included the *Massachusetts, South Dakota* and *Indiana* and the heavy cruisers *Quincy* and *Chicago*, all under the command of Adm. Shafroth.

Carrier strikes in the Kure-Kobi areas of the Inland Sea continued. On July 29, *Massachusetts* joined another naval gunfire force in the bombardment of the industrial city of Hamamatsu, Honshu, blasting the Japanese Musical Instrument Co. with 270 rounds of 16-inch shells in an effort to halt production of airplane propellers there. On Aug. 9, Battleship Div. Eight under Shafroth, with two more

heavy cruisers (*Boston* and *St. Paul*), bombarded Kamaishi a second time. In this effort, they were joined by a Royal Navy bombardment unit which included the light cruisers HMS *New Foundland* and HMNZS *Gambia*, with a screen of three destroyers.

Atomic Bombs on Hiroshima and Nagasaki

On Aug. 6, the first atomic bomb was dropped on Hiroshima by the AAF and a second on Nagasaki three days later. These and the pounding which the home islands had received throughout 1945 had their desired affect. Air strikes Aug. 15 were called back to the aircraft carriers when word was received from Adm. Nimitz that hostilities with Japan had ceased.

Destination—US

After embarking passengers from various ships in waters south of Tokyo, including a landing force of its own Marines, the *Massachusetts* set course for the US. Accompanied by the carriers *Essex* and *San Jacinto* and the cruiser *Astoria*, it anchored off the Puget Sound Navy Yard at Bremerton, WA, Sept. 13, 1945, after a 5,000 mile non-stop voyage from the waters off Japan. That concluded 75 days of continuous steaming at sea.

Mamie remained in the Puget Sound Naval Shipyard until Jan. 28, 1946, when it set course for operations at Long Beach and San Francisco, CA. It cleared San Francisco Bay April 4 and was assisted through the Panama Canal by three tugs on her way to Lynnhaven Roads, VA where it anchored on the morning of April 22, 1946. At 0942 on that day, the crew of the *Massachusetts* manned the rail to render honors to President Harry S. Truman embarked in the new heavy aircraft carrier *Franklin D. Roosevelt* standing out of the harbor.

Mamie entered the Norfolk Naval Shipyard for inactivation overhaul May 20, 1946, and was decommissioned March 27, 1947. It was assigned to the Norfolk Gp., US Atlantic Reserve Fleet where it remained inactive until it was boarded by a small but dedicated group of her former crewmen who would not be daunted, who would not give up the ship and, through whose persistence, it was brought to Fall River, MA as shall be more fully described in Chapter Six.

Total Success

One cannot conclude the story of Mamie's active military service without putting it into a broader context.

The principle draftsman of War Plan Orange, the USN's strategic plan for defeating Japan following the opening of hostilities by an enemy attack, told this author, on the day following the Pearl Harbor attack:

"The only mistake I made in that plan was the assumption that we would have, surviving the enemy's opening attack, a fleet with which to fight him."

The Japanese attack on Pearl Harbor Dec. 7, 1941, except for the aircraft carriers which fortuitously escaped, could hardly have been more effective in destroying the US fleet. When one adds to that catastrophe the strategic decision that the highest military priority for the US was determined to be success in Europe, the fact that we prevailed so completely in the Pacific ranks as the greatest naval success in the history of warfare.

No less a naval authority than England's noted historian, John Keegan, in his *Warpaths, Travels of a Military Historian in North America*, grants the highest accolade to the USN:

"In its victories it is outdone by no other navy and equalled by few: the surprise of Midway was as complete as that of Nelson's at the Nile, the risk taken at Coral Sea as bold as that of Hawke's at Quiberon Bay, the triumph of Leyte Gulf even greater than that of Trafalgar."

One can ascribe many reasons for that success, which reasons would certainly include the nation's industrial military capacity and the cadre of trained professionals turned out by our military and naval academies. However, to this author, particular credit must be given to two particular components of the winning team.

The first is the quality of the professionalism of the naval officers of flag rank—King, Nimitz, Spruance, Mitscher and Halsey. Undaunted by the reverses suffered up to the time of Midway, these outstanding leaders, with rare exception, led us from the brink of defeat to total victory.

The second element is the non-professional—the kid who, in a state of bewilderment, was plucked from whatever he or she was doing as a civilian and, in short order, became a highly efficient sailor, soldier, marine or aviator. To them, enlisted person or officer, is owing our highest and most profound gratitude.

Captain Wm. W. Warlick presenting Citations on board USS Massachusetts BB-59. L-R: Capt. John R. Redmon, Capt. Wm. W. Warlick, S.J. Krajeski, ARM2/c, Lt. Alfred Cenedello, Jr., and Lt. George A. Robinson.

Massachusetts just prior to decommissioning at the St. Helena Annex of the Norfolk Navy Yard. She is being "mothballed" and preparations are being made to place her in reserve.

As Frank Delano Roosevelt, the Commander-in-Chief, put it:

"In all the far-flung operations of our Armed Forces, the toughest job has been performed by the average, easy-going, hard-fighting young American who carries the weight of battle on his young shoulders. It is to him that we and all future generations of Americans must pay grateful tribute."

During her active military service, the USS *Massachusetts* earned 11 Battle Stars and other awards for the operations listed below:

One star/NORTH AFRICAN OCCUPATION: Algeria-Morocco Landings: Nov. 8-11, 1942; actions off Casablanca: Nov. 8, 1942.

One star/GILBERT ISLANDS OPERATION: Nov. 19-Dec. 8, 1943.

One star/MARSHALL ISLANDS OPERATION: Occupation of Kwajalein and Majuro Atolls: Jan. 29-Feb. 8, 1944.

One star/ASIATIC-PACIFIC RAIDS - 1944: Truk Attack: Feb. 16-17, 1944; Marianas Attack: Feb. 21-22, 1944; Palau, Yap, Ulithi, Woleai Raid: March 30-April 1, 1944; Truk, Satawan, Ponape Raid: April 29-May 1, 1944.

One star/HOLLANDIA OPERATION (Aitape, Humboldt Bay-Tanamerah Bay): April 21-24, 1944.

One star/WESTERN CAROLINE ISLANDS OPERATION: Capture and occupation of southern Palau Islands: Sept. 6-Oct. 14, 1944.

One star/LEYTE OPERATION: Third Fleet supporting operations, Okinawa Attack: Oct. 10, 1944; Northern Luzon and Formosa Attacks: Oct. 11-14, 1944; Luzon Attacks: Oct. 15, 1944, Oct. 17-19, 1944, Nov. 5-6, 1944, Nov. 13-14, 1944, Nov. 19-22, 1944, Dec. 14-16, 1944; Battle off Cape Engano: Oct. 25-26, 1944; Visayas Attack: Oct. 21, 1944.

One star/LUZON OPERATION: Formosa Attacks: Jan. 3-4, 1945; Jan. 9, 1945; Jan. 15-16, 1945; Jan. 21, 1945; Luzon Attacks: Jan. 6-7, 1945; China Coast Attacks: Jan. 12, 1945, Jan. 16, 1945; Nansei Shoto Attack: Jan. 22, 1945.

One star/IWO JIMA OPERATION: Assault and Occupation of Iwo Jima: Feb. 15-March 4, 1945; Fifth Fleet Raids against Honshu and the Nansei Shoto: Feb. 15-16, 1945, Feb. 25, 1945, March 1, 1945.

One star/OKINAWA GUNTO OPERATION: Fifth and Third Fleet Raids in support of Okinawa Gunto Operation: March 17-June 11, 1945.

One star/THIRD FLEET RAIDS AGAINST JAPAN: July 10-Aug. 15, 1945.

PHILIPPINE REPUBLIC PRESIDENTIAL UNIT CITATION BADGE: Oct. 10-15, 17-19, 21, 1944; Nov. 5-6, 13-14, 19-22, 1944; Dec. 14-16, 1944; Jan. 3-5, 6-7, 9, 12, 15-16, 21-22, 1945.

COMMANDING OFFICERS

Capt. Francis E.M. Whiting, USN - May 12, 1942-Dec. 12, 1942; Capt. Robert O. Glover, USN - Dec. 12, 1942-Sept. 27, 1943; Capt. Theodore D. Ruddock, USN - Sept. 27, 1943-April 8, 1944; Capt. William W. Warwick, USN - April 8, 1944-May 2, 1945; Capt. John R. Redman, USN - May 2, 1945-Jan. 22, 1946; Capt. Heber H. McLean, USN - Jan. 22, 1946-Aug. 5, 1946; Cmdr. Harry M.S. Gimber Jr., USN - Aug. 5, 1946-Sept. 9, 1946; Cmdr. Charles B. Carroll, USN - Sept. 9, 1946-Jan. 4, 1947; Lt. Marion L. Buchan, USN - Jan. 4, 1947-March 27, 1947.

COMMANDERS BATTLESHIP DIVISION EIGHT

RAdm. Glenn B. Davis, USN - April 29, 1943-Dec. 24, 1944 and RAdm. John F. Shafroth Jr., USN - Dec. 24, 1944-Jan. 28, 1946.

Chapter Notes

[1] *So named because of the great number of ships which went to their grave there in 1942-43.*

[2] *The carrier air strength of the Japanese Mobile Fleet had been reduced to 35 planes, a blow from which it never really recovered.*

[3] *It would be nice to be able to report that both submarines went on to further successful missions against the Japanese, as did the Dace. Unfortunately, having had to operate submerged for close to 24 hours and operating only by dead reckoning in these tortuous channels, Darter ran fast aground on Bombay Shoal, a coral reef on the China side of Palawan Passage. Her crew was transferred to Dace; and Darter ultimately was destroyed by a combination of Dace torpedoes and shelling and by aerial bombing by the Japanese.*

[4] *Among others, "Where is Lee x Dend Lee.*

[5] *To mislead cryptographers, coded U.S. messages were preceded and followed by words not related to the text, itself. Unfortunately, Nimitz's encoders used the trailer 'the World Wonders." When the message was handed to Halsey, it read "Where is rpt where is TF 34 the whole world wonders." Halsey took this as a rebuke from Nimitz.*

[6] *The Franklin's wounds were more severe than those suffered by any other ship which survivrd World War II. More than 800 of her crew were killed.*

[7] *Often a single ship well north of the landing beaches whose function was to give early warning of the approach of Japanese planes.*

[8] *Of interest is the fact that Cruiser Division 14 was under the command of Rear Admiral F.E.M. Whiting, the first skipper of the Massachusetts.*

Chapter Six
Bring Back Big Mamie

1962 - 1965

BRING BACK BIG MAMIE

*To Lt. Harold L. Wattel for writing this chapter.
To the ship riders who rode Big Mamie, under tow, from Norfolk, VA to
Fall River for photos and information about the "Homecoming."
To the hundreds of crew members, citizens and schoolchildren who made this project
a success. We are unable to include the names of everyone who helped; so we say
THANKS to all who helped in any way.*

*"The history of the world is but the biography of great men." Thomas Carlyle, 1830 (1795-1881)
"There is properly no history; only Biography." Ralph Waldo Emerson, 1841 (1803-82).*

Thousands of men manned Big Mamie through her WWII battles - from the shelling of the French battleship *Jean Bart* in the Atlantic (Nov. 8, 1942) to the bombardment of Kamaishi, Japan in the Pacific (Aug. 5, 1945.) The task of bringing her home, however, fell to a few men - devoted, resourceful and persevering. In telling this tale of Mamie's homecoming, we pay homage to those who succeeded in establishing BB-59 as a fitting memorial to the nation's successful defense of Freedom, to all of the Commonwealth of Massachusetts' WWII

veterans and especially to the men who served aboard BB-59. We are proud to have been able to make their biographies an integral part of this volume.

Mamie's homecoming was, in some ways, as harrowing as some of the engagements it experienced as a fighting ship. At the end of WWII in 1945, it was refitted in Bremerton, WA for further service. Between January 1946 and April 1946, it operated off the California coast; and, in the latter month, it was assigned to the Atlantic Fleet. On May 20, 1946, it was ordered to Norfolk, VA for decommissioning and moth-balling. On March 27, 1947, it was attached to the Norfolk Gp., US Atlantic Reserve Fleet. For 15 months, it languished in Norfolk, while some of her crew dreamed of bringing her home.

This part of the BB-59 saga ended at

6:31 p.m. June 13, 1965, when it tied up at the State Pier, beneath the Braga Bridge in Fall River, MA. As a memorial, it lives on; but that is another tale to be told by those who come after us.

Faith in Their State

The Navy had prepared to strike BB-59 from its Register of Ships as of June 1, 1962. The crew members were not surprised by that fact, but most of the crew had faith in their state and were sure that it would be saved. The former crew members living in Massachusetts knew that the Texas and the North Carolina politicians had saved their battleships from scrapping, and they assumed that the BB-59, NAMED for their state and BUILT in their state, would be saved by the leaders of their state.

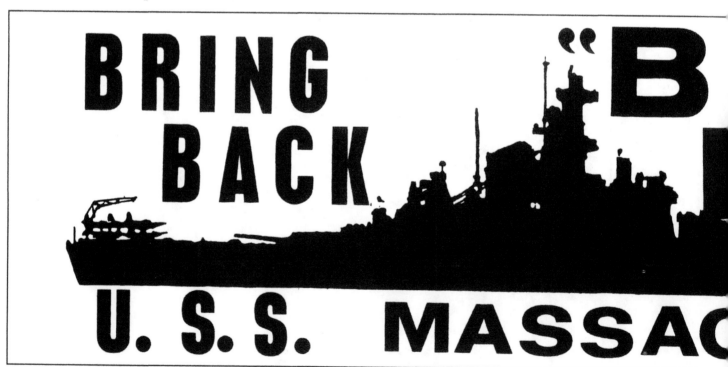

Big Mamie bumper stickers spread the word throughout the state.

The men interested in bringing her home knew that the battleships USS *North Carolina* and the USS *Texas* had been "saved as memorials" when the Navy acceded to the petitions of the State Commissions for the custody of these ships. In these cases, state monies were pledged to support these memorials - which was not the case in Massachusetts. While Gov. Endicott Peabody of Massachusetts gave moral support to the efforts of the USS *Massachusetts* Memorial Committee, Inc., which was petitioning the Navy for the custody of BB-59, he, unfortunately, was unwilling to commit public monies to the enterprise, thereby creating difficulties for the committee and lengthening the entire recovery process.

News from Norfolk, VA

A small three or four-line news item on the bottom of a page of a New York newspaper in early 1963 caught the eye of Ed Palmer one morning. (Ed was vice president of the USS *Massachusetts* Associates.) The clipping, with a Norfolk, VA date line, mentioned that oil was being pumped out of the battleship USS *Massachusetts* in preparation for its scrapping. This information was quickly relayed to two other former crew members, Frank Letourneau of the Fourth Div. and president of the Associates, and to Jack Hayes of the Sixth Div. This group of three, who

worked in downtown Boston, met together for lunch and agreed that the state should take some action to save the ship and that they should find out from the Navy what the state needed to do to accomplish this. It was suggested that Ed, who worked for the telephone company, should call the Navy and find out what should be done. The Navy Dept. said that all the governor had to do was to form a State Commission and apply for the donation of the ship, the same as North Carolina and Texas governors did to acquire the ships named for their states.

Palmer was the prime mover of the undertaking to establish Big Mamie as a war memorial. When aboard, he had been yeoman for Father Joseph N. Moody, BB-59's first chaplain. After the war, in civilian life, he worked for the New England Telephone Co. which generously allowed him, as a member of the Public Relations Department, to use its facilities and their personnel for this undertaking. For example, its house organ *Telephone Topics*, in its August-September 1963 issue, featured an article, *Bring Back Big Mamie*, of which 10,000 copies were made available for the committee's fund-raising distribution.

Off to the Governor's Office

After learning what the Navy required to save their ship, Frank, Jack and Ed walked up to the State House to see the governor.

After receiving an appointment, they were ushered into Gov. Endicott Peabody's office. For response to their plea for the formation of a State Commission to save Big Mamie, they received a very quick, NO. The governor said, "We already have Old Ironsides, and we don't need any more ships for tourist attractions." The group of three stood their ground and asked the governor if he would be willing to send a telegram to the Navy Dept. to delay the scrapping of BB-59 for six months so that the crew members could conduct a drive to save their ship. He agreed to send the telegram, if they would write it for him but added that he didn't believe that the crew members could save their ship. The three stepped outside of the governor's office long enough to write out the telegram message and then walked back into his office and presented it to him. The governor then added this comment, "It's too damn big!." The visitors realized that they had not done their "homework" because the governor, a former submarine officer, hated battleships. (Ironically one of the submarines that Gov. Peabody served aboard, the USS *Lionfish*, was also saved from scrapping, and is a tourist attraction in Battleship Cove in Fall River, MA guarded by Big Mamie.)

BB-59 Reunion in 1963

At BB-59's reunion in 1963, many ideas were suggested on just how the campaign to save the ship should be conducted. The group agreed to design and sell bumper stickers, contact local leaders and state representatives, and contact local newspapers. Most of the crew members who attended the reunion agreed to volunteer their efforts. Funds were not made available from the Associate's treasury, but it was agreed that fund raising information would be mailed by the Associates to its members. Ed's friend in the printing business, John Hutchenson a WWII vet, agreed to print a supply of two-color bumper stickers and would not bill for them until donation money became available to pay the bill. Crew members then started a drive to sell the stickers at $1.00 each and were able to pay the bill in three weeks. A number of favorable news items began to appear. One of the most helpful was the feature article mentioned above, written by Alice Lavin, the editor of *Telephone Topics* an in-house publication of the New England Telephone Co. that was mailed to 24,000 of its employees. (See Appendix #1 of this chapter)

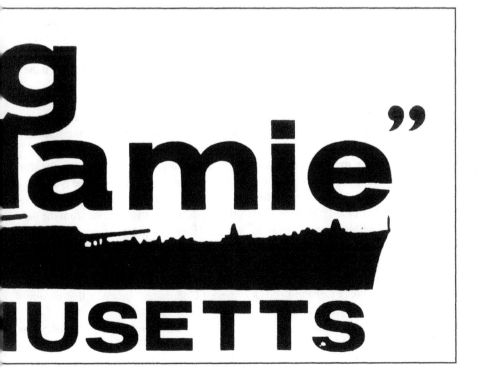

Members of the Board of Directors of the U.S.S. Massachusetts Memorial Committee, Inc. show the "pine tree flag," the first fighting flag of the Massachusetts Navy, to governor John A. Volpe. From left to right: Edward Palmer, Vice President; Governor Volpe; Jack Cassidy, Secretary; Martin Adler, Director.

Contact the Politicians

Although this small group of former crew members was successful in reaching a growing number of citizens, they felt that it was important to reach those in public office who, in turn, could convince others to save Big Mamie. Alfred Cenedella, a former aviator aboard BB-59, who represented his city of Milford, MA in the Massachusetts Senate, and Paul Vaitses, of the A & R Divs. and the mayor of Melrose, MA were two important contacts who could help. Personal letters and *Bring Back Big Mamie* flyers were mailed to all of the state's US senators and representatives in Washington D.C. to request their support.

A unanimous return of replies to support the project was received with the exception of one senator. Sen. Leverett Saltonstall, who was chairman of the Naval Affairs Committee, and had been governor of the state when BB-59 was launched in Quincy, was away on business. His son, William Saltonstall, who worked in the senator's office, answered the letter for him and did what the senator would have done that is, contact the Navy for advice. The Navy's reply to the Saltonstall letter reported that no citizen's group, or former crew members of a naval ship, had ever been successful in saving a "Capital Ship," and that it did not believe it could be done without the support of a state committee.

This letter was the committee's greatest disappointment, because they needed the senator's support; but this didn't stop them, and they applied for the donation of the ship in the name of the committee. The USS *Massachusetts* Associates Inc., being a nonprofit organization, thought it could be the agency to request the donation of Big Mamie.

Associates Request the Donation of BB-59

"The USS *Massachusetts* Associates requests the transfer of the former battleship USS *Massachusetts*, to this association - to be maintained as a memorial in Boston, MA according to the conditions and the regulations as prescribed by the Department of the Navy."

The Navy was reluctant to turn the ship over to civilians when there was no documentation that there were funds available for memorial purposes. Consequently, following the rule book (Title 10 Section 7308 of the US Code), it withheld its approval. In a letter dated Dec. 31, 1963, RAdm. B.E. Moore reminded the USS *Massachusetts* Associates of the costs involved by citing the case of the USS *North Carolina* - costs for which the state of North Carolina was prepared to pay. As noted above, similar monies were not available in Massachusetts. The admiral wrote;

"Unfortunately, your letter does not meet all of the provisions required by Title 10 Section 7308. You are aware of the costs involved in accepting the *Massachusetts* as a memorial. The ex-USS *Massachusetts* was stricken from the naval vessel register in June 1962. Since then it has been subjected to the ravages of time and the elements. You can anticipate some costly restoration to make the ship fit as a memorial and safe for visitors. The Navy Department intends to proceed with disposal action if a formal application/formally complete/is not received prior to Feb. 1, 1964."

Without summarizing the entire set of rules under Section 7308, it is sufficient to cite the germane details - mainly relating to costs:

1. The vessel has to be maintained in a condition satisfactory to the Department of the Navy.

2. The US would bear no expense of the transfer.

3. There has to be a clear statement regarding the facilities and personnel available for the maintenance of the vessel.

4. The receiver must agree to take delivery at its berthing site and pay all charges incident to the delivery.

Clearly, the Association was being forced to raise considerable monies to meet the Navy's demands. For example, in the case of the USS *North Carolina*, the Navy estimated that the preparation costs would be greater than $200,000 and that annual maintenance costs would run in the neighborhood of $100,000. The Associates recognized the size of this monetary obstacle but was prepared to move forward. It wrote to the Navy Jan. 31, 1964, informing it that, among other matters:

1. It had three temporary berthing sites and a committee working on the selection of a permanent site.

2. It was prepared to maintain the ship in conditions satisfactory to the Navy.

3. It was prepared to pay the acquisition costs within two months from the date of the letter.

4. A Citizens Committee for the purpose of raising funds was in the process of formation. (The USS *Massachusetts* Memorial Committee, Inc. was that committee.)

5. It had plans to acquire BB-59 as soon as possible (Feb. 3, 1964) and to have the "ship ready for public display by early fall 1965."

The Navy acknowledged the intent of the Associates as written in the letter just summarized and promised to give the Associates until May 1, 1964, to demonstrate its financial abilities and to remedy any defects in its application. Nevertheless, the Navy pointed out that two embarrassing years had passed since the original postponement of scrapping, that the present berthing space occupied by the ship was needed for other purposes, that security personnel assigned to BB-59 were needed elsewhere and that other government programs awaited the scrap steel from the ship. In other words, the heat was on the Associates.

Advisory Board

To assist this new committee, an advisory board was created, and the following persons agreed to help and to let the committee use their names as advisors: Leslie M. Buckingham Jr.; Frank S. Christian; Hon. John F. Collins; Ralph H. Colson; Richard Cardinal Cushing; Hon. Roland Desmarais; Henry Dormitzer; Rabbi H. Bruce Ehrmann; Cmdr. George M. Hall USN; Hon. Edward M. Kennedy; Owen B. Kiernan; Hon. Torbert H. Macdonald; Hon. John W. McCormack; Douglas J. Mitchell; Brig. Gen. John E. Murray, USAF Ret.; Hon. Endicott Peabody; Asa E. Phillips Jr.; Elliot L. Richardson; Rand Smith; Clifford A. Somerville; John J. Spencer; Rt. Rev. Anson Phelps Stokes; Hon. Paul S. Vaitses Jr.; Hon. John A. Volpe; and William N. Ward. Ed Palmer was pleased to have these leaders accept his request to serve as "advisors" but was disappointed when RAdm. Samuel Eliot Morison, the official historian of the Navy in WWII, would not allow his name to be used as an "advisor."

The committee had already been functioning for about a year with an impressive roster of members. In addition to public officials, it had, as members, professionals from the field of public relations, insurance, finance, education, planning and publishing. The Greater Boston and Attleboro Chambers of Commerce were staunch supporters. The Boston Chamber had a Military Affairs Committee which initially attempted to preserve "certain ship's items which would be enshrined as part of the proposed maritime museum on Boston's downtown waterfront." Their "Relics Committee" had to be guided so that it did not undermine the Memorial Committee's effort. In June 1963, the Relics Committee

shifted its support to the establishment of the BB-59 War Memorial.

However, Gov. Peabody, as late as February 1964, continued to appoint people to the Governor's Advisory Committee, USS *Massachusetts* Relics. Gov. Peabody assigned one member of his staff, John T. Sweeney, to attend these relics meetings and to do everything possible to obtain the ship's bell. A new state office building, under construction at that time, had a space designed in its lobby for the ship's bell.

A New Committee Formed

A new committee, The USS *Massachusetts* Memorial Committee, was incorporated in Melrose, MA on Feb. 10, 1964, with the help of many former crew members. Mayor Paul Vaitses recruited Cmdr. H. Leland Haskell, USN (Ret.) as president of the new organization and Ed Palmer as vice president.

In recruiting additional volunteers to serve on the committee, it sought help from those with special talents. Ray Gosselin, a former naval officer from Wellesley, MA, became secretary of the committee and later became its vice president. Francis G. Shepard, vice president of the State St. Bank and Trust Co., became the treasurer.

When Ed Palmer went to Mayor Collins of Boston to try to locate a berth for the ship in Boston Harbor, the mayor assigned the

task to the Waterfront Planning Gp. of the Boston Redevelopment Authority (BRA). Dan Ahern, who led this group as an initiative of the Chamber of Commerce, assigned this task to the principal planner of the BRA, Martin Adler of Newtonville, MA. Another BRA staffer, Jack Cassidy, approached Adler and volunteered to become a member of the "team." He later became the committee's "site chairman," and both Adler and Cassidy became "ship riders" on the "homecoming" trip.

Ed also contacted a long time friend, Ken MacRae, his insurance man from Somerville, MA, to head up the effort to meet any needs for insurance that the Navy might request.

When the school drive for funds got underway, the committee received a letter from a senior at Wellesley High School, Alan Tait, who volunteered to become the "school drive representative" of the committee. (Alan later attended the Naval Academy, served on the battleship USS *New Jersey*, and is now Lt. Cmdr. Tait, USN Ret., living in San Diego, CA.)

(Appendix #2 contains a list of the other committee members)

Tactics and Strategy

Senate Bill #1000 was introduced in the Massachusetts Senate in September 1963 to make the battleship the official WWII memorial for the state. In Washing-

Governor Volpe signs a bill to make BB59 the state's WWII Memorial. L to R: William Torpey, Fallriver; Frank Tanner, State Representative, Reading; Ed Palmer; Ted Thompe; Gov. Volpe; Jack Cassidy, Comdr. H LeLand Haskell (Hidden) Martin Adler.

ton, Sen. Edward M. Kennedy was a tireless petitioner for this action. (Appendix 2)

While the new organization brought new hands and minds to the problem of reclaiming BB-59, a detailed plan for saving the ship had yet to be developed. The ultimate overall plan included a public relations campaign, a fund-raising campaign, a media campaign to reach out to prominent persons, the physical delivery of the ship from Norfolk to Massachusetts, the securing of appropriate berthing and the renovation, use and administration of the ship as a museum. Innumerable meetings were held, demanding time freely donated by the committee members, in many cases supported by their employers. A letter dated July 1, 1963, from Ed Palmer to crew members in Massachusetts noted that the Memorial Committee had met over 25 times with "leading Bostonians" to obtain "ideas and assistance."

Berthing

Boston was the original berthing choice and was so described in all communications with the Navy. One plan submitted to the Boston Development Authority in a letter dated Feb. 21, 1964, suggested placing the battleship between Piers One and Two in Boston Harbor. Martin Adler, of the Memorial Committee, foresaw harbor development in these words;

"We would have then at the mouth of Fort Point Channel, across from a new Boston Yacht Club and the Downtown Waterfront, a public recreational facility that would be self-supporting, a dockage facility, ground rent for marine sales, restaurants, and admissions to the USS *Massachusetts*."

Given the berthing requirements, alternative sites were not eminently suitable. Boston at Atlantic Avenue, Charlestown, Pier Four in South Boston, US Naval Annex in South Boston, Castle Island Terminal and East Boston were ruled out for various reasons. As of March 3, 1964, the committee was to explore further Piers One and Four, the Army base and Castle Island, Wiggin Terminal. Anchorages in Massachusetts waters which would require the hydrofoil transportation of visitors might have to be acceptable if all other alternatives were unavailable. When deeper studies were made of the Boston pier sites, it was found that the longshoremen's union was concerned about the use of ANY Boston pier to berth Big Mamie for fear it might cut into its members' activity and livelihood. Ed Palmer was invited by "Red" Moran, the union's leader, to speak to the union at the Hotel Essex early one Sunday morning but Ed was unable to change their minds. Every useable harbor in the state of Massachusetts was contacted but no town or city was the least bit interested in providing a pier for BB-59.

The "memorial effort," which started in 1962, was not successful until the spring of 1964. On June 24, 1964, C.F. Elliott, assistant to the Navy's chief of the Bureau for Legislation and Special Matters, informed Ed Palmer that the Navy had notified Congress May 15, 1964, that the Navy intended to donate BB-59 to the USS *Massachusetts* Memorial Committee; further, he said that it was expected that the Congress would approve giving the Navy the appropriate authority to donate the ship July 15, 1964. This letter forced the committee to renew its efforts to find a berth for Big Mamie)

In July 1964, with the new scrapping date now only 48 hours away, Ed Palmer asked Jack Cassidy, site chairman, if all possible sites had been reviewed. In response to Jack's affirmative reply, Palmer remarked that he had not seen any report on Fall River. Cassidy's reply was that Fall River had been ruled out because it only had one pier, and it would require an additional day of towing up Narragansett Bay. This did not deter Palmer from phoning Fall River's Mayor Desmarais whose interest rose when he heard that his city was being offered a "million dollar tourist attraction." At the mayor's suggestion, the next call went to Bill Torpey, manager of the city's pier, and a former public relations professional, who immediately recognized the tourist possibilities for the city. He agreed to meet the next day with Ed Palmer and the Navy Department in Washington, D.C. to document that Big Mamie could be accommodated in Fall River, MA. The meeting was successful; the site problem solved.

When Fall River was selected as the berthing site, the committee was reorganized by adding Fall River residents to its membership. By 1965, Joseph H. Feitelberg had become president, Martin Adler vice president, John Cassidy secretary, John S. Brayton treasurer and Ed Palmer chairman of the board of directors. (Feitelberg and Brayton were Fall River residents.)

Financing

From the beginning of the campaign to bring the $75 million dreadnought home, the bottom line had been money and more money. The long-term activities of the committee had to be funded; but the initial "Big Bucks" had to be raised to pay for towing and other costs incident to bringing the ship from Norfolk to Fall River. Long range, the Navy had to be satisfied that additional monies were available for the maintenance of the ship and the establishment and administration of it as a museum.

Sam Huff, former football star, a guest attraction at a boat show in Milford, CT. Standing beside one of the Courtesy Wagons on loan from the Buick Dealers of Massachusetts. Huff on left, Ed Palmer on Right.

Alex Poulos

Those paint cans got heavier during the past 20 years!

The proud veteran of World War II retired from the active fleet on March 27, 1947.

Committee visits Big Mamie in Norfolk, VA.

Ken MacRae leaves for Boston.

Joe Reilly.

Twelve former WWII crew members - part of the "Homecoming Crew."

Muster at 0700 and 1900, Homecoming Trip.

As time passed, the sums needed became both better defined and larger in scope. In March 1964, it was discovered that the ship had no light bulbs in any of its light fixtures. The Sylvania Co. heard of this need and donated cartons of bulbs to replace the missing ones.

The Navy insisted that insurance cover the scrap value of the hull, which was valued at $500,000 before it could be towed to Fall River. Insurance man Ken MacRae had to turn to Lloyd's of London which was willing to insure only one-half of that sum. Solicitations were required to get five American insurance companies to insure the remaining $250,000. Final insurance expenses covered the hull, disability, crew, liability after mooring, utility trailer and the State St. office and its contents.

Original money targets were a total of $300,000, with $60,000 to be available by May 1, 1964, to convince the Navy that there would be adequate funds to support the museum plan. When efforts to reach this goal failed, the firm of Paget & Beakey, Inc. was hired as a consultant to assist the committee to raise funds in the period Sept. 1, 1964-April 30, 1965, this time with a goal of $250,000. The consultant would not solicit funds.

Theodore Thomte, who served as executive director of the Memorial Committee, was employed by Burdette & Co. of Boston, MA; and this firm generously underwrote some of the printing costs. The Hutchenson Co. of Boston printed much of the stationery and small brochures at cost for the Associates and the committee. The committee hired the New England Newsclip Agency Inc. Feb. 24, 1964, to clip news items about BB-59.

Raising funds took almost three full years; because, as noted earlier, the state of Massachusetts did not underwrite any of the costs of bringing the ship home or establishing the museum. In fact, Palmer's notes show that last minute dollar deficit had to be remedied on an ad hoc emergency basis. For example, the committee was shy $25,000 for the towing costs. Ten committee members each pledged $2500 to meet this crisis. Fortunately, this "emergency fund" was never needed.

To raise funds, there was a plan to "sell honorary Massachusetts Navy ranks and commissions," a technique used by the North Carolina Battleship Commission but enlarged by this committee to appeal to adults and children.

The "Massachusetts Navy"

A donation of $100 provided an admiral's commission in the North Carolina plan. In the "Massachusetts Navy," one could become a rear admiral or a fleet admiral, depending upon the size of the donation.

A list of the ranks, donations and number of passes awarded follows:

Rank	Donation	Passes	Number of Guests Allowed	
Fleet Admiral	$1,000	Lifetime		25
Admiral	$500	"		10
Vice Admiral	$250	"		5
Rear Admiral	$100	"		1

All admiral commissions were signed by the governor and the secretary of the Commonwealth and included the official seal of the Commonwealth.

Captain	$75	10 years	
Commander	$50	5 years	

Lieutenant Commander	$40	4 years
Lieutenant	$30	3 years
Lieutenant (j.g.)	$20	2 years
Ensign	$10	1 year

Recruiters were also rewarded with ranks and passes according to the sums they were able to raise. See Appendix #3

Ed Palmer received a negative comment from Bob Graham, a historian in Ed's hometown of Reading, MA, claiming that the "Massachusetts Navy" had never been taken off the state's records since George Washington's time, therefore the committee was selling commissions in an EXISTING "Navy." Ed responded by saying, "Bob, why don't you tip off the media - we could use any news, negative or not, at this time!" This news never reached the newspapers.

This program was fairly successful, but trying to reach adults with this approach was not an easy project. It did provide a method of saying "Thank You" by presenting a "commission" in return for services or volunteer work. The actual amount raised was near $42,000.

However, offering schoolchildren "petty officer" rates for their donations was much more successful and raised over $53,000.

School Drive

Before starting on the school drive, the committee again contacted the North Carolina campaign people to learn how they had conducted their very successful drive. They reported that their state department of education had sent a letter to all North Carolina schools suggesting that the school children assist the state in its drive to save the battleship named for their state.

This was not the response when the Massachusetts Department of Education was approached. It did give the committee "permission" to contact each and every local school committee to request individual fund drives. Most schools in Massachusetts did not condone such fund drives, so each school committee in the Commonwealth of Massachusetts had to vote on these requests. This became another assignment for the crew members of Big Mamie located in many of the state's towns and cities and, in most cases, knew the school committee members in their community.

Raising money from the school children was not an easy task. The committee's problems were exacerbated by the fact that we had recently lost President John F. Kennedy, and there was now a plan to build a Memorial

Library in Boston to honor him. Its sponsors also approached all of the schools in Massachusetts with a fund drive to build that memorial. Now these local school committees had TWO problems: should they give to one without giving to the other, or should they take the easy way out, stick to the rules, and not give to either? The BB-59 crew members were successful in many of their communities; and the school children of Massachusetts provided more than one-half of the funds needed for towing. (See Appendix #4 for the list of participating schools)

Advertising

One of the committee's greatest needs was money for advertising, and it was not in the budget. Through the courtesy of its president, Carl H. Haffenreffer, the Narragansett Brewing Co., in Rhode Island, solved the problem. It offered radio spot announcements, subway posters, 24 sheet billboards, and display cannisters to be placed in all liquor stores and barrooms for contributions to "Save Big Mamie."

The cost of this publicity was estimated to be over $55,000 and became one of the committee's most important contributions to "Save Big Mamie."

During one of the Red Sox baseball games, Ed Palmer was invited to watch the game from the broadcasting booth with Curt Gowdy and to add a few words about Big Mamie, as Curt gave his spot announcements. To thank Curt Gowdy, he was later given an honorary "admiral's commission" in the "Massachusetts Navy" and Carl Haffenreffer was made an honorary "fleet admiral."

Local, State and Navy Department Assistance

The local residents of Fall River and their organizations supported the museum drive in many ways. For example, the Master Barber's Association of Fall River offered to refurbish the ship's barber shop, and the local Camera Club volunteered to renovate the photo darkroom. An entrance sign was the gift of a local display organization. Legal costs were donated by various legal firms, including $2700 in services by former BB-59 officer, Robert A. Grimes of Hardy, Hall, Grimes and Murphy of Waltham, MA and the firm of Lobell and Lobell. The Firestone Rubber and Latex Co. contributed three parking areas accommodating 450 cars contiguous to the berthing pier for an annual rent of $3000. (The lots were

valued at $63,750). Most of the site preparation costs were contributed by the state of Massachusetts. Dredging costs of $23,800 were contributed by the city of Fall River and the Fall River Line Pier. The Fall River Line also provided $1000 in clerical services for which it made no charge. Earlier, the state had also picked up the tab ($6,500) for preliminary engineering and testing.

It should also be noted that firms in Boston were helpful. The Boston Tugboat Co. reduced the cost of towing by $13,000. The Workingmen's Cooperative Bank of Boston donated office space valued at $2,750. Newsome and Co. provided $2000 of public relations services at no charge to the committee. Burdette and Co. underwrote $5,000 of the executive director's services. Office equipment worth $1,000 was provided by Boston equipment firms. Billboards and subway poster space throughout the Boston area was provided free of charge (valued at $4,500) by Transit Advertising. Smaller donations, such as; printing services by Hutchenson & Co.; photo services by Fay Foto Service and Airport Photo Services; picture and poster mounting for displays by DeMille Garey Co. of Reading helped to keep expenses at a minimum.

On March 8, 1965, Gov. Volpe established a Governor's Advisory Committee to assist in the establishment of the WWII memorial. However, months passed before the financial and insurance problems which would free the ship were solved.

The Navy's largesse must not be neglected. It cooperated fully in establishing the Massachusetts Memorial. It loaned the museum the following marine equipment ("relics" was the Navy term) on an indefinite basis: two anchors, the ship's bell, a US ensign, two signal flags, a life ring buoy, a machinery label plate for a boiler, a builder's plaque, six steering wheels, two megaphones and 10 sections of deck planking. The Navy was unsuccessful in its attempt to locate the ship's organ. Finally, it was a Navy destroyer which took the families of the ship's riders into Narragansett Bay to meet the *Massachusetts* on its way home. Also the Navy's Quonset, RI captain's gig brought one of the ship rider's family and its relatives out to meet Big Mamie in the Bay.

Commanding Officer

One of the final actions of the committee was set forth in a letter dated April 13, 1965, offering the job of commanding officer/ship's superintendent of BB-59 in its memorial status to Cmdr. George M. Hall, USN (Ret.). Among his duties were the following:

1. To have full responsibility on a 24 hour basis for the safety and security of the ship, the site, ship property, visitors and other personnel.
2. To be the operational manager of the ship.
3. To maintain the ship-shape appearance of the ship.
4. To enhance the attractiveness and interest of BB-59 as a memorial and tourist attraction.
5. To develop programs to attract visitors.
6. To establish and maintain files.
7. To undertake other duties as prescribed by the board of directors.

Cmdr. Hall responded affirmatively in a letter four days later.

The following excerpts from the minutes of meetings of the committee in June 1965 will give the reader an idea of the pressing matters which continued to require the attention of the committee.

June 16: Problems relating to the painting of the bridge over the *Massachusetts*; hiring of workmen; appointment of new members to the Ship Preparation Committee; a towing report; and insurance program for the ship.

June 30: Appointment of liaison between the committee and the First Naval District; matters regarding the preparation of the ship; establishment of a ship address for personnel; policies covering acquisitions and short and long-term funding; admission fee schedule; concession stand policies and staffing; bud-

gets; and travel policies. In other words, the committee was hard at work up to the dedication ceremonies.

Cmdr. Hall detailed for the Memorial Committee the tasks that had to be planned out and accomplished to ready the ship for visitors. For example: One anchor had been obtained in Norfolk where it was hoisted aboard - a job that might not have been accomplished by limited equipment in Fall River. Work on board had to be determined and then scheduled. Supplies, tools and other equipment had to be procured, including paint and tools for the ship riders to use on the towing trip from Norfolk to Fall River. (These "riders" would become a "work party" during the "Homecoming" trip.) Personnel for the restoration had to be hired on both temporary and permanent basis. Signs had to be designed, produced and erected. To meet the requirements for signs on state highways, Kay Krekorian of the state highway department suggested the committee accept the name "Battleship Cove" for the area. Parking lot attendants, concession managers and ticket takers had to be employed. Electricity and phone service had to be installed.

Conclusion

Big Mamie could not have been saved without the enormous contributions detailed above. From those of us who were not direct participants, we say: **TARE VICTOR GEORGE** - the Navy's signal for "Well Done." We are profoundly grateful for your efforts and sacrifices.

Homecoming

Following an overnight bus ride on one of Cmdr. J. Alex Michaud's Salem, MA busses, the homecoming crew arrived in Norfolk to make preparations for towing to Fall River. The huge cranes in Portsmouth, VA removed more than 100' of BB-59's masts so the ship could pass under the Mt. Hope and Braga Bridges, and also hoist one of Big Mamie's anchors onto the deck for future display purposes. The crew, dressed in their white shirts, had a photo taken on the pier as they signed a receipt for Big Mamie, representing the Memorial Committee.

With the help of four additional tugs, the new ocean-going tug, *Margaret Moran*, was able to move away from its pier and then took charge of her towing job to Massachusetts.

The following five days at sea, including two days in fog, the crew was busy chipping and scraping paint and then added new paint to help make her presentable for Fall River. Some of the crew, with the aid of flashlights, were able to locate the gun barrels and enough parts to reassemble a 40mm quad.

In both Norfolk, and in Narragansett Bay, USN helicopters brought Navy photographers out to record Big Mamie's homecoming.

Tears of joy rolled down the cheeks of the crew as the thousands of persons lined the shores and the bridges to cheer Big Mamie as it was towed up Narragansett Bay to Fall River.

"Slats" DeNadal.

Nye and Roland LaFrance.

Appendix 1
Bring Back "Big Mamie"

Reprinted from Telephone TOPICS, August-September1963.

Once before something like this happened. Once before men of heart with a love of the sea and of ships, and of one ship, and with a flag-waving unashamed pride in their country's history—once before such a group rallied round a cause. If you were a youngster in the 30s you might remember going home from school one day, emptying your piggy bank and counting the pennies that fell on the bed. The inflamed patriotism of the group had reached you, too. And, although you weren't sure why, you knew you must give all your pennies to save Old Ironsides.

And the pennies of millions of children did it. They, and some 24 lines of unabashed sentiment from the masterful Mr. Holmes. And since then children and their parents have felt the wind in their faces as they strode the decks where their forefathers repulsed the Barbary Pirates and, young and old, they could hear the battle cry echo down the decades—*Millions for defense, but not one cent for tribute!*

Perhaps it's an omen that the old 44-gun frigate has blasted the front pages again. The Lady still has the power to cause a battle—albeit verbal—when someone suggests removing her even temporarily from Massachusetts.

Once again the same kind of fever spreads through the state ... and from such an unlikely source. For the "fight to save the ship" is coming from a corps of men—fortyish, settled, steeped in the problems of getting ahead on the job, meeting mortgage payments, seeing the kids through school. But when word came that the USS *Massachusetts* was to be scrapped, 20 years vanished. There were once again no mortgages, no kids, and the only job was one of war.

They called their ship the "Big Mamie." It fought in a kamikaze war. It fought the sea. Amid torpedo bursts, her big guns silenced the *Jean Bart* at Casablanca. Then, her job completed in the Atlantic, it headed west, inching through the Panama Canal, heading for the Pacific.

Suddenly, vividly, these men remember swimming at Noumea and how Nauru looked before and after the blast of a 16-inch barrage. They remember the direct hit at Ebeye and the planes that screamed down in flames. They feel the water squish through their toes while they scrub down the deck. They hear the off-key music of merry minstrel shows. Their nostrils fill with the smells of shot-up buddies in sick bay. They laugh again at Shell-backs and King Neptune and assuming the proper angle. They remember shore leave on Saipan, Japanese pagodas and destroyed sugar mills. There's Mog Mog—the island of Paradise with sand and beer and water. That prayerful Christmas on Ulithi. Formosa and Iwo and Tokyo. The towers of smoke rising from the Imperial Iron Works during the bombardment of Kamaishi.

When peace came to the Pacific, "Big Mamie" could be proud. From commissioning May 12, 1942, until war's end in mid-August 1945, it had logged over 225,000 nautical miles from Casablanca to Tokyo and the China coast. It had taken part in some 35 engagements. It had sunk or damaged five ships. It had been part of nine bombardments of enemy territory, three on the Japanese home islands. It had destroyed or assisted in the destruction of at least 18 Japanese aircraft.

Her scout Kingfisher planes had rescued seven aviators downed by enemy fire, often as not within sight and range of Jap guns. Her firepower and speed had lent invaluable support to the fast carrier task forces that crippled Japanese air power and seized control of blackened Pacific skies. It had been a work-horse of the fleet, always in there fighting when there was fighting to be done.

And just the sound of her name could fill her crew with a pride too big to contain. Any sea-going man will tell you, it's a mighty hold a ship can get on the heart and the brain of a man. It's a hold that can wash away 20 years and give a man again the feel of a deck beneath his feet and the strength of a mission in his heart.

This is what an ordinary ship can do. And "Big Mamie" wasn't ordinary. Such an esprit de corps flourished among her crew that a nucleus formed the USS *Massachusetts* Associates, Inc., who have met in reunion every year since 1946. There are now 335 dues-paying associates, 126 living in Massachusetts, 34 in other parts of New England, the rest from 25 other states.

This is the crew that is spreading the fever once again through Massachusetts. Such a ship, they say, with her record, and built by the Bethlehem Steel Co. and the workmen at the Fore River Yard at Quincy, such a ship has a body and a spirit that belong in the Bay state. They see her here, side by side with Old Ironsides, the first and the last battleships built in Massachusetts, part of Boston's new waterfront, a permanent historic shrine and tourist attraction.

On June 27 they launched a $300,000 fund-raising drive to Bring Back "Big Mamie" to Boston. It's a fight against time because the Navy Department has granted only a "six months stay of execution." If, at the end of that time, the people of Massachusetts have not raised the funds to bring her back from dry-dock in Virginia, "Big Mamie" will be sold for scrap.

Vice president of the USS *Massachusetts* Associates, Inc., is Edward W. Palmer of our company's Public Relations Department. Eddie has already carried his story to the people of New England over radio stations WBZ, WNAC, WEEI's Opinion Please, and WHDH-TV. The committee has won the support of Gov. Peabody, Mayor Collins, Sen. Kennedy, and the Boston Chamber of Commerce from which you can now order, for one dollar, a red, white and blue bumper sticker that proclaims the refrain in so many hearts—Bring Back "Big Mamie."

Soon you'll hear of a committee of prominent citizens who will supervise the funds and tackle the problems of relocation. Come fall school children will learn about the USS *Massachusetts* just as their parents learned about the USS *Constitution*. Maybe your son will empty his piggy bank and count the pennies that fall on the bed. And watching him you may even feel a touch of the fever yourself.

It's a big job that's facing the crew of the *Massachusetts*, but not so big as one they licked 20 years ago. And the way the fever is raging you and your son may soon roam the decks that both your pennies saved—that frigate that tamed the pirates and proved that Britannia didn't always rule the waves, berthed alongside the "Big Mamie" who tossed the first 16-inch shell of the European offensive and fired the last big naval bullet in the Pacific campaign.

Quite a pair.

Appendix 2

Many of the BB-59 crew members and officers became regional, city and town committee chairmen, who assisted in the drive for funds, and became contacts with newspapers, school committees and leading citizens.

The following persons became "Active Members" of the committee:

Leslie M. Buckingham Jr.,
    engineer
Ralph H. Colson, Citizens Committee
    Massachusetts Dept. of Education
Henry Dormitzer,
    Citizens Committee
    Electro Powerpacs, Inc.
Robert A. Grimes, treasurer
    BB-59 Associates
Frank Letourneau, president
    BB-59 Associates
Hon. Torbert H. Macdonald,
    member US Congress
Douglas J. Mitchell, Burdette & Co.,
Brig. Gen. John E. Murray,
    USAF (Ret.)
Asa E. Phillips Jr.,
    Navy League, president
Rand Smith,
    Advertising Club of Boston,
Clifford A. Somerville
    Citizens Committee, Boston &
    Maine RR
William N. Ward,
    Citizens Committee and
    vice president
    Attleboro Chamber of Commerce

Many citizens, businesses and associations provided campaign assistance:

Anthony Athanas,
    owner of Pier Four Restaurant
Lester Bowles,
    American Legion
Buick Dealers of Massachusetts
Kiwanis & Lions Clubs,
New England Telephone Co.
Publicity Club of Boston
Rotary Club of Wakefield, MA
Arthur F.F. Snyder,
Greater Boston Chamber of Commerce
William J. Torpey,
    Fall River Line Pier Inc.

The Navy Dept. and other "Memorialized Naval Ships" provided assistance in many ways to help make this drive a success:

Flags flying - we head for "Big Mamie's" new home.

RAdm. E.M. Eller,
    director of Naval History
Cmdr. George M. Hall,
    First Naval District
Capt. Blish C. Hills, USN
F. Kent Loomis, USN
RAdm. B.E. Moore, USN
Hugh Morton, USS *North Carolina*
    Battleship Commission
George F. Murphy, USS *Alabama*
    Battleship Commission
Capt. L.S. Orser, USN
    VAdm. John Sylvester, USN.

A guide and advisor at the State House for making contacts and for the submitting of bills was:

Rep. Frank Tanner, of Reading, MA

Many encouraging letters from the following Massachusetts US Senators and Representatives helped the efforts of the committee:

Sen. Edward M. Kennedy
Rep. William H. Bates
Rep. Edward P. Boland

Rep. James A. Burke
Rep. Silvio O. Conte
Rep. Harold D. Donahue
Rep. Hasting Keith
Rep. Torbert H. Macdonald
Rep. Joseph W. Martin
Rep. John W. McCormack - speaker
Rep. F. Bradford Morse
Rep. Thomas P. O'Neill
Rep. Philip J. Philbin

Appendix 3
The Massachusetts Navy

Fleet Admirals

Carl W. Haffenreffer
Hon. John A. Volpe

Admirals

Cmdr. H. Leland Haskell
Ozzie Ingram
Capt. Arthur Knight
Edward W. Palmer CM
Richard O. Palmer
William S. Stuhr
William J. Torpey

Vice Admirals

Martin Adler
American Legion #288
John S. Brayton Jr.
John Nicholas Brown
Jack Cassidy
Frank S. Christian
Hon. Roland G. Desmaris
Joseph H. Feitelberg
Edward M. Guild
Cmdr. George M. Hall
Sidney L. Hathaway
Jack T. Hayes
Holiday Lanes, Somerset
Hon. Edward M. Kennedy
Frank LeTourneau
Hon. Torbert MacDonald
Kenneth A. MacRae
Mason Box Co.
Strafford Morss
Grace S. Palmer
Judith M. Palmer
Thomas A. Rodgers
Clifford A. Somerville
Paul S. Vaitses

Rear Admirals

Donald P. Babson
Paul T. Babson
David W. Boland
Mrs. D.W. Boland
Joseph E. Boutilier
John S. Brayton Jr.
Philip S. Brayton
Mrs. Walter Broughton
Dr. Roger E. Cadieux
Eugene H. Clapp III
Tim Clark
John B. Cole CM
Roger L. Currant
Ross H. Currier
Cmdr. Charles Donaldson
Lewis W. Dunton
Fall River National Bank
Frank S. Feitelberg
Henry J. Feitelberg
Peter G. Femino
Joseph E. Fernandes
Forrester Clark Foundation
Howard F. Furness
Paul A. Giroux
W.J. Godlewski
Collins Graham
Edward M. Guild
George Hall
George D. Hammond
R.L. Hammons
Patrick H. Harrington
Ernest K. Henderson

Donald Hirst
Fred A. Herrick
R.A. Gosselin
Alden C. Kefauver
Vincent J. Kelley
Lester H. King
John Kosier
Jack C. Lacy CM
Normand J. LeComte
Kenneth List
Samuel J. Lovit
Somerled A. MacDonald
Henry J. Matarazzo
Cmdr. I.L. McNally
Melrose Lions Club
Melrose Trust Co.
J. Alex Michaud
Hollis P. Nichols
Harold F. Nye CM
Albert J. Oliva
Thomas W. O'Reilly
Carol Palmer
Constance Palmer
Donald M. Palmer
William K. Palmer
Patterson, Wylde & Windeler
George E. Pelletier
Lt. Col. Charles H. Phillips
Richard D. Phippen
James C. Raleigh
Louis J. Roehr
John F. Ryan CM
William E. Shawcross
Alan Shepard
Cmdr. Kathleen F. Smith
Raymond E. Smith
Miss G. Frances Souther
Bernard C. Stuhr
James J. Sullivan
Capt. A.E. Tuttle

William Vaughn
George P. Wahn
Henry W. Wakeman
Christopher M. Weld
Lt. Col. A. Turner Wells
Asa P. White
William T. Whitney
Charles E. Wood CM
Charles R.O. Wood

Captains

Leslie M. Buckingham Jr.
Betsy Coldewey
William Coldewey
Hon. John F. Collins
Ralph H. Colson
Richard Cardinal Cushing
Natale G. DeMarco
Henry Dormitzer
Rabbi H. Bruce Ehrmann
Frank H. Gatley CM
Capt. James Gavin
Robert A. Grimes CM
Gilbert D. Guimond
M.O. Levesque
Douglas J. Mitchill
Brig. Gen. John E. Murray
Jeff B. Palmer
Joanne Palmer
John H. Palmer
Rosemary Palmer
Hon. Endicott Peabody
Asa E. Phillips Jr.
Elliot L. Richardson
Andrew G. Schofield
Rand Smith
John L. Spencer
Alan Tait
Theodore Thomte

Big Mamie at sea... we may never see this sight again...All dressed up for her arrival back to the old Bay State...Our twenty six men did a wonderful job of making her look presentable.

Harold Nye.

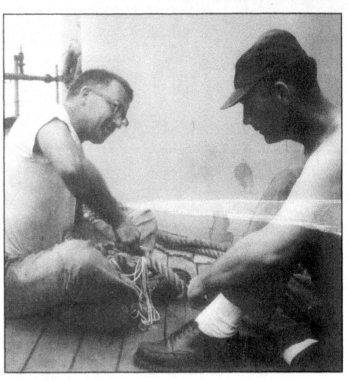

Earle Allen listens to "Seadog" Cassidy tell about the Artic while watching Jack do some fancy rope splicing.

Bob Green takes aim on Big Mamie's superstructure.

Jim Garvey.

Fred Knowles all about lights being Edison man.

Somewhere off there is "home."

Victor Brum.

Ed Allen.

Commanders

40 Names

Lieutenant Commanders

20 Names

Lieutenants

50 Names

Lieutenants (j.g.)

43 Names

Ensigns

366 Names

Appendix 4
Massachusetts School Drive
(Contributing Schools)

Andover	$492.
Athol	$285.
Attleboro	$994.
Baldwinville (Union)	$62.
Barnstable	$579.
Bedford	$185.
Bellingham	$38.
Belmont	$546.
Berkley	$48.
Berlin	$57.
Beverly	$315.
Beverly (Private)	$207.
Boston	$4798.
Boylston	$145.
Boylston Reg-H.S.	$123.
Braintree (Private)	$128.
Brockton	$2600.
Burlington	$290.
Cambridge	$411.
Canton	$400.
Charlmont	$63.
Chester	$12.
Chicopee	$745.

Clinton	$276.
Conway	$5.
Dartmouth	$206.
Dedham	$919.
Deerfield	$16.
Dighton	$101.
Dover	$207.
Dracut	$131.
Duxbury	$105.
Eastham	$39.
Easton	$50.
Fall River	$2966.
Fairhaven	$518.
Fitchburg	$196.
Fitchburg (Private)	$57.
Freetown	$188.
Greenfield	$487.
Groton (Private)	$43.
Hadley	$10.
Hanover	$59.
Haverhill	$387.
Holbrook	$69.
Holden	$10.
Holyoke	$352.
Hopedale	$210.
Hull	$617.
Lakeville	$189.
Lowell	$315.
Lowell (Private)	$75.
Lynn	$1891.
Malden	$1143.
Manchester (Private)	$38.
Maynard	$62.
Medfield	$66.
Medford	$1829.
Melrose	$1605.
Mendon	$25.
Middleboro	$450.
Millbury	$337.
Milton (Private)	$122.
Needham	$111.
New Bedford	$2664.
Northfield	$187.
Northampton (Private)	$115.
Norwood	$861.
Orange	$195.

Otis	$7.
Peabody	$883.
Pittsfield	$346.
Plainville	$35.
Quincy	$1401.
Raynham	$74.
Reading	$1475.
Rehoboth	$145.
Rehoboth (Private)	$36.
Revere	$1124.
Rockland	$49.
Salem	$640.
Saugus	$966.
Sharon	$50.
Shrewsbury	$616.
Shrewsbury (Private)	$48.
Somerset	$804.
Somerville	$1717.
Southbridge	$68.
S. Lancaster	$55.
Spencer	$17.
Springfield	$1217.
Stoneham	$860.
Stoneham (Private)	$28.
Stoughton	$99.
Swansea	$151.
Taunton	$833.
Templeton	$23.
Tewksbury	$202.
Wakefield	$931.
Wellesley	$997.
Westfield	$107.
W. Newton (Private)	$13.
Westport	$289.
W. Springfield	$386.
W. Bridgewater	$74.
Winchendon	$195.
Winchendon (Private)	$25.
Winthrop	$524.
Worcester	$1631.
Worcester (Private)	$18.

Grand Total All Schools
$53, 186.

Frank Gately.

Stirling Olberg.

Old Glory and the Massachusetts Navy Flags fly from BB59's mast.

Hard to believe, after three long years of work, we are really bringing Big mamie home. Ed Palmer stands watch on the bridge.

Our "wide awake" crew arrived via Adm. Michaud's land yatch.

Chapter Seven
The Fall River Navy

1966 - 1996

THE FALL RIVER NAVY

LCDR Paul S. Vaitses Jr., a key person in the campaign to save "Big Mamie" and later the executive director of the ship in Fall River from 1970-90 provided the help in checking the information for this chapter. The USS Massachusetts Memorial Committee Inc. and the present staff of the ship, under the direction of Capt. Guy Archambault, are to be commended for interest and help for this book. Some of the minutes of the Memorial Committee's reports and a report of the "Field Day" work aboard the ship submitted by one of the field day workers is also included in this chapter.

When the battleship arrived in Fall River June 12, 1965, it was the biggest event in the city since the infamous Borden murders in 1892. More than one-half a million people lined the shores of Narragansett Bay and the Taunton River to cheer the ship's arrival.

The arrival brought tremendous publicity in the New England media with front-page news and heavy television and radio coverage.

Once the ship was safely moored at the pier in Fall River, the task of preparing her for public visitation began. Since it had been in mothballs for 15 years before the Navy decided to scrap her, it was a sorry sight on the exterior. After the 1962 scrapping date the Navy allowed active fleet ships to strip her of any useful equipment.

When BB-59 was first berthed in Fall River the State Highway Department did not allow "activity signing" on the highways, however, Kay Krekorian of Reading, MA, traffic engineer for the state, suggested the name "Battleship Cove" and it has been known as BB-59's "home" since 1965.

The Memorial Committee contracted to have the hull and superstructure painted and a number of volunteers from the former crew members association began the monumental task of picking up, cleaning up and painting the interior compartments of the ship. Active in this process were Edward Allen and Francis Gately and his two sons. Work was centered in the wardroom and adjoining compartments on the main deck. Later, the work spread to the captain's quarters, adjoining officers staterooms, the crew's living compartments and the main galley area on the second deck.

The memorial committee hired businessman Theodore Thomte as executive director and Cmdr. George Hall as ship's superintendent. They hired several retired Navy personnel as ship's staff to work on getting the ship open to the public.

After feverish efforts of all hands, the ship was ready to receive visitors by the first week in August 1965. The visitors were restricted to the main deck of the battleship and the charge was $1.00 per person. With the assistance of the State Department of Public Works, a wooden covered walkway was built to protect the visitors who approached the ship walking underneath the still uncompleted Braga Memorial Bridge spanning the Taunton River.

The USS Massachusetts War Memorial, Battleship Cove, Fall River, MA, 1965.

The USS Massachusetts BB-59 is dedicated as Massachusetts' World War II Memorial.

Dedication

On Saturday, Aug. 14th, the USS *Massachusetts* was officially dedicated. The Dedication Program included:

US Naval Band from Boston.

Flyover of aircraft from Quonset Air Station.

Invocation by Rev. Robert R. Hansel, rector St. Luke's Episcopal Church.

Introductory remarks by master of ceremonies, Col. Milton T. Miller.

Introduction of Joseph H. Feitelberg, president USS *Massachusetts* Memorial Committee.

Introduction of distinguished guests in audience.

Introduction of speakers

US Rep. Joseph W. Martin.
US Sen. Leverett Saltonstall.
Gov. John A. Volpe.

Prayer of memorial and dedication by Rev. Robert L. Stanton, rector, St. Mary's Cathedral.

Dedication of ship, Feitelberg and Gov. Volpe, representing the commonwealth.

Taps by US Naval Band, First Naval District.

Raising of the ship's colors, National Anthem.

Raising of Pine Tree Flag, official state naval flag, by Gov. Volpe.

Presentation of ship's plaque by RAdm. William B. Seiglaff, commandant, First Naval District to Edward W. Palmer, chairman of the board, USS *Massachusetts* Memorial Committee.

Tour of the ship by official guests and public.

Civic reception for dignitaries and guests at White's restaurant.

In the two months the ship was open until the end of the fiscal year Sept. 30,

1965, the ship hosted some 65,000 visitors. During the fall and winter months, the ship's small staff and volunteers continued cleaning and painting more of the second deck compartments to be opened for public visitation.

About this time, Harold Putnam of Needham, former state representative, became interim executive director and Richard Sullivan became public relations director. Edward J. Ward of Somerset was brought on board as hospitality director.

An auxiliary low-pressure boiler heating system was installed using the ship's combination steam coils and ventilation ducts to heat compartments within the superstructure and the second deck. This was very important to make these areas of the ship useful in the fall, winter and spring for continued renovation of the ship and for the comfort of the visitors.

RAdm. William Seiglaff presents Ed Palmer the ship's plaque.

1966

During 1966, a full-time executive director, Capt. James F. Gavin, USNR (Ret.) of Newport, RI was hired. In the ensuing three years he expanded the ship's staff and more decks were opened to the public.

The USS *Massachusetts* Associates, Inc. submitted an entry in the Public Relations Society of America's 22nd Silver Anvil Awards Competition in the Special Events and Observances category. (The "Oscar" of Public Relations) The Associates were successful and received their "Silver Anvil" at the New York Hilton Hotel on May 19th.

For the next three years attendance soared to over 200,000 per year due to radio advertising donated by the Haffenraffer family through their Narragansett Brewing Co. and many special events, celebrity visita-

tions and public appearances by Capt. Gavin and others on radio and TV shows. Peak attendance of 265,000 was reached in 1966.

Meanwhile, under the legislation of 1964 to establish the battleship as the official WWII Memorial for the Commonwealth of Massachusetts, a three-man commission was named by Gov. John Volpe to plan and erect a suitable memorial to the more than 13,000 citizens of the state who died in WWII in all services.

1968

Commission members, Paul S. Vaitses Jr., of Melrose, chairman; Joseph H. Feitelberg, of Fall River, businessman and corporation president; and Charles N. Collatos, state veterans' agent, pressed ahead with the development of the memorial. By early summer of 1968 the memorial was completed on the main deck of the battle-

ship, within the superstructure, aft of the wardroom. It is a stunning memorial, with all 13,000 WWII deceased veterans listed by county and by service.

The battleship was the beneficiary of some unique publicity by appearing on the covers of all New England Telephone Co. directories for all of the cities and towns in Massachusetts during the years of 1965-67. This promotion was arranged by Ed Palmer, an employee of the telephone company's public relations department in Boston. There is no question that these phone-book covers were a very effective method of placing a painting of Big Mamie into every home and business in the state of Massachusetts.

1969

Big Mamie was turned, so that she was at a right angle to Braga Bridge and helped to create "Battleship Cove." With the help of the Smithsonian Institution the "land-based version" of the OS2U airplane, muh to the delight of our former aviator, Lt. Alfred Cenedella. The Smithsonian took the OS2U back, after a loan of 11 years.

1970

For a short while, Mr. Kieth Heifer served as the Executive Director for the ship. He was replaced by Paul S. Vaitses Jr., chairman of the board of directors of the corporation and former junior officer aboard the battleship during WWII.

The decade of the 1970s featured the development of new exhibits, new programs and the acquisition of more ships at Battleship Cove. Both management and the board of directors felt the need to broaden the appeal of the historic naval ship's museum.

1972

1972 was a pivotal year in the history of the committee, with three key developments occurring that would have long-term effects on the operation of Battleship Cove. The USS *Lionfish* SS-298, arrived in Fall River, adding to the core exhibit of the battleship and encouraging the further development of the complex. Negotiations began with the 4 year old Marine Museum on joint programs and ticket sales; both were approved and a formal business relationship with the museum continued for 19 years.

Perhaps most important was the initiation of the Overnight Youth Group Camping Program. Beginning with fewer than 100 young people and their chaperones sleeping on the deck in the battleship's wardroom, the program grew rapidly, to the point where the ship now can berth up to 500 people a night during

the program season. Over 250,000 people have participated in the overnight program, and it has been copied by other historic ships as well as by such institutions as Boston's Museum of Science. It is also the ship's most profitable special program.

In 1972, another significant event took place when the number one main engine room was opened to the public. This was a major achievement by the maintenance staff led by Joseph Oliveira, retired Navy chief shipfitter, with the help of Herbert H. Collins, retired Coast Guard chief electrician and Wayne Copass, retired Navy shipfitter.

The possibility of obtaining the WWII PT-796 came after contacting the national PT Boats organization, an independent organization of some 8,500 members under the colorful leadership of WWII PT boater, James "Boats" Newbury of Memphis, TN. President Joseph H. Feitelberg and execu-

USS Massachusetts in Battleship Cove, 18 January 1972.

tive director Vaitses travelled to Memphis to work out an agreement with Mr. Newbury.

1973

The Massachusetts Legislature signed into law an education grant, amounting to $50,000 per year, permitting Massachusetts school groups aboard at no charge. They also signed the Korea-Vietnam Memorial Bill; this memorial was to be placed aboard the battleship, but in September it was decided to accept the Gearing-class destroyer USS *Joseph P. Kennedy Jr.* DD-850, a destroyer that had been in service during the Vietnam War, and it was deemed to place the memorial aboard this ship.

During this year negotiations were completed with the PT Boats, Inc. of Memphis, TN to develop a PT boat exhibit at Battleship Cove.

1974

This year saw the beginning of a powerful phase of physical plans for the Cove. The USS *Kennedy* arrived in January, providing three major warship types

(equalled at the time only by Patriot's Point in Charleston, SC) plus plans to add a PT boat and other exhibits in the future. This year also brought two state Bicentennial grants—$7,000 for the emplacement of the bow of the cruiser USS *Fall River* on the grounds of the complex and $10,000 for an exhibit aboard the destroyer entitled *The Kennedys and the Sea.*

1975

This year marked the 10th anniversary of the arrival and opening of battleship USS *Massachusetts*. An agreement had been reached for the development of a PT boat museum and library aboard the battleship and the placement of the 78-foot Higgins-built PT-796. Tin Can Sailors, a national organization of destroyer veterans, was founded here in 1975 and would remain aboard until removing to Somerset, MA in 1991. A grant from the Massachusetts Bicentennial Commission funded half of the cost of the creation of a student orientation center on the battleship's second deck.

1976

The Bicentennial Year of 1976 saw development extending beyond the battleship to the waterfront, with the conceptual planning for Fall River Heritage State Park; members of the Memorial Committee were named to the Park's steering committee. Our exhibit ships drew the benefits of $68,000 in maritime preservation grants. The Memorial Committee hired a director of development to implement organized fund-raising programs.

1977 - 78 - 79

- The involvement of the battleship corporation in the development of the waterfront outside of the cove.
- The first phase of the Fall River Bicentennial Park dedicated.
- Four members of the corporation singled out for credit.
- Destroyer and PT boat exhibit programs, "bull sessions" and reunions helped to increase activity at Battleship Cove.

1980

The 15th Anniversary of Battleship Cove was marked by basic planning for the acquisition of land and themes for the Heritage State Park, and once again this initiative involved members of the Memorial Committee. A more aggressive marketing effort was directed at tour groups and schools. An appeal to the battleship's former crew members resulted in donations totalling $6,500 from 154 contributors.

A member of the "Field Day" crew writes;

Restoration Effort by the "Field Day" Crew

Sometime in 1980, during the very lean years of available budget, our esteemed shipmate, and executive director of the USS *Massachusetts* Memorial Committee, Inc., Mr. Paul Vaitses, at an annual crew members reunion, stated the need for help in restoring of viewable parts of the ship. His appeal fell on the receptive ears of Arion "Ace" Mavrogeorge from Manchester, NH (formerly of the 4th Div. - also known as the "work" division). "Ace" decided to launch a drive to enlist the help of former crew members, and anyone who would partici-

James Burt, President, and Edward Palmer, Past President of the USS Massachusetts Associates, receive the Silver Anvil from Robert B. Wolcott, Jr., National President of the Public Relations Society of America.

New England Telephone Directory for

PLYMOUTH

including CARVER, DUXBURY, KINGSTON,
MANOMET, MARSHFIELD

Area Code 617

USS MASSACHUSETTS WAR MEMORIAL

July 1967

This phone book cover brought Big Mamie into every home and business in Massachusetts.

pate in volunteering their time and effort in restoration areas of the ship, for tourist viewing. His success was immediate. It started with a small group, but grew with every "working party." It didn't take long before dedicated ex-crew members and their friends were spending four or five weekends each year. (Consisting of Fridays, Saturdays and Sundays.) Even though this meant giving up a week from their vacation time, it was a small sacrifice. All thought the same. Here was a ship in need, and they could make a difference. After all, here was the ship that took them to many battles in the Atlantic and Pacific oceans during WWII, and brought them home safely to their loved ones. How could they refuse this call.

These acts of "love" by the crew members and their friends, continued on for about 14 years, until Father Time caught up to many of them and rendered them unable to continue this very hard and vigorous effort. Their main contribution came in the form of scraping the many years of rust from the decks and bulkheads of areas that could not be shown to tourists, and then painting same. The work was very demanding of muscles not used for a long time, and knees not accustomed to kneeling on cold steel decks for days at a time.

The memories of those "work parties" and the social time at the end of the day will be forever remembered. It was a wonderful feeling to gather at these social gatherings aboard our great warship after a day of physical work, and reminisce about our experiences on board 50 years ago. Some of the stories seemed to be magnified as the night grew on. To walk the decks, stand at your battle station, and relive some of your wartime experiences at that exact location, and move about familiar areas of the ship that you served on some 50 years ago, is an experience that very few warriors of WWII can ever relive.

During one of those work weekends, a small group of Ace's workers were chipping paint on the quarter deck, dressed in their dungarees, when a group of tourists passed by, and was heard to say ... my! "these sailors are quite old to be doing that type of work." Always with a quick comeback, Bernie Silveria asked one elderly lady, "Is the war over??" The flabbergasted lady replied, "yes, a long time ago!!" Bernie then called out very loud.."All right shipmates, we can all go

home now, the war is finally over." We all had a great laugh over the expression on that lady's face.

The executive director of Battleship Cove recognizing how symbolic it was to have a group of ex-crew members aboard, asked us if we would allow ourselves to be presented to the overnight Boy Scouts that came to visit the ship, and inform them about our duties while serving aboard, and also answer any questions they might have. What an experience!!!!! The kids (and their leaders) were mesmerized by the presence of this aged group, and being told "real" stories about life aboard this warship during the war. We thrived on these encounters, because when we looked out into the audience's eyes, we could see among these scouts, the very reason why we fought in WWII ... we could see, feel and taste the juices of patriotism from these young people, who will be responsible for carrying on our great sense of duty to our country.

The below listed crew members deserve recognition for their outstanding dedication throughout the years. As they all have professed ... it was a great privilege to have performed such a work of LOVE.

A salute to Ace Mavrogeorge, "Field Day" crew member coordinator, and his working crew members: Doug Autsolief, New York; Ted DeLesdernier, Massachusetts; Chips Duhamel, Massachusetts; Skip Sande, Florida; John Buckley, New York; Mickey Dempsey, New Jersey; (*)Frank Dunbar, New Hampshire; Bernie Silveria, Florida; John Bullock, Massachusetts; Bob Doran, New Jersey; and Harold Nye, Massachusetts. (*)Deceased.

And their friends: Rick DeLesdernier, Cris Giotopoulos, Billy Giotopoulos, Nick Kacavas, Arthur Raymond and Roland Lappierne.

Recognition must be afforded Armand Vigeant, another former crew member who lives in Fall River. Armand has dedicated himself to just about a "full time" volunteer and has contributed an enormous amount of time in the restoration of the ship.

We apologize to any other of our crew members for inadvertently neglecting to give them recognition in this tribute. We know there were many, but time and memories have clouded our ability to remember their names. Let it suffice to say, that the depth of affection displayed by the above mentioned crew members for "Big Mamie" is unique. We all feel

our love affair with this ship is just another way of expressing our thanks for taking us to battle the enemy and taking us home safely to our loved ones.

A member of the "Field Day" crew ...
1981

Ground breaking for the Heritage State Park occurred in August of this year. A second PT boat, 617, was under restoration at Melville, RI and slated for exhibit at the Cove, and a landing craft, mechanized (LCM) was dedicated in the fall. The cruise ship, SS *Veracruz*, resumed visits to the State Pier.

1982

Included in the 1982 Annual Report of the Memorial Committee was a positive statement; "Battleship Cove is no longer to be just a brief stopover, it is about to become a destination." It would take almost 10 more years for this to happen, but happen it would. Restoration of the LCM and the relocation of the submarine and the destroyer took place this year improving the viewing and the development of the Cove.

1983

The physical appearance of the Cove had changed significantly with the relocation of the submarine between the battleship and the destroyer and the addition of a Navy T-28 Trojan aircraft on the pier.

1984

A new ship's store was completed and opened this year and a walkway past the Quonset Hut and a new gangway onto the pier helped to make this operation more professional-looking. National History Day was celebrated in April with more than 400 students and educators participating.

The Fall River Heritage State Park was opened in August with Gov. Michael Dukakis as featured speaker.

1985

The first full year of the operation of the State Park, the arrival of PT-617, the continued visits of SS *Veracruz*, and a grant from the Commonwealth for maritime preservation were some of the highlights this year. The grant of $2,500,000 was sponsored by Rep. Robert Correia and the work of members of the Memorial Committee. Another important milestone at the Cove in November was the National Park Services designation of the battleship, the submarine and PT-796 as NATIONAL HISTORIC LANDMARKS, giving Battleship Cove the highest concentration of landmarks in southeastern Massachusetts.

1986

The committee's use of the state's preservation grant was based on the Navy's superintendent of ships survey that the destroyer badly needed hull restoration and the ship was towed to Boston for drydocking. Part of this grant was also used for painting the superstructure of the battleship and to completely refurbish and modernize the heads used by both visitors and camping groups. The Tin Can Sailors completed the construction of the Arleigh Burke National Destroyermen's Museum on the destroyer prior to that ship's temporary removal to Boston. A new building to house PT-617 was virtually completed this year.

1987

The first year of "Fall River Celebrates America" proved to be a very successful event in which the members of the Memorial Committee were prime movers, and would become a yearly event. This was also the first year in which the committee participated in the American Youth Hostel program.

1988

The National Park Services conducted surveys of the destroyer and PT-617 and other Cove exhibits for possible designations as landmarks.

A critically important development, overshadowing others that year, was the successful passage of a six million dollar appropriation for the drydocking of the battleship USS *Massachusetts* in Boston for needed hull work. During the course of the year specifications and contracts were developed for this project. The monumental task of preparing the ship for this work including plans for the removal of the topmasts and radar and all office equipment took many months of work, however, the project had to be postponed in deference to the state's fiscal crisis.

1989

It took just over a year to place the ship back in order. Virtually all office equipment, files, exhibits, in fact all materials not literally a part of the ship's structure, had been removed and placed in storage.

Two National Historic Landmarks were designated by the National Park Services this year at Battleship Cove. In June the destroyer, DD-850 *Joseph P. Kennedy* was named, and in December PT-617 became a "Landmark."

This makes Battleship Cove one of the highest concentrations of Landmarks in the northeast.

1990

A major change took place this year. The executive vice president, Paul S. Vaitses Jr. retired after 20 years. During the next 10 months the Selection Committee advertised for and interviewed candidates for the position of executive director.

1991

In April of this year the board of directors concluded an exhaustive search for a new executive director and named former Navy captain Guy A. Archambault to this position. Capt. Archambault, a native of West Warwick, RI, retired from active duty in 1987 following almost 30 years of naval service, which included command of Destroyer Sqdn. 30, the destroyer USS *Corry*, and the destroyer tender USS *Prairie*.

In 1991 the Raytheon Co. donated a full size model of a Patriot Missile, the Aetna Insurance Co. awarded a grant of $9,500 to the battleship to assist in the purchase and development of educational materials. The Memorial Committee adopted the name and the masthead of "*The Bay Stater*," with permission from the USS *Massachusetts* Associates. This was the name of the ship's original newspaper starting in 1942.

In December a two page spread in *Yankee Magazine* featured *The Sailors of the USS Massachusetts* with a photograph of Alex Poulos, Ace Mavrogeorge, Ed Palmer and Bernie Silveria standing underneath the 16" guns of turret #3.

1992

The Marketing Department designed a new brochure, initiated specialized tour itineraries, distributed information items on group programs and discounts, worked with hostelries in Massachusetts and Rhode Island, and filled thousands of requests for information with everything from an attractive presentation folder to directions for travelers, lists of area hotels and motels and information on the overnight camping program. The department was recognized as a powerful promoter of the Battleship Cove and of area tourism, and by the end of the year this work yielded excellent results.

One of the highlights of this year was the celebration of the 50th Anniversary of the commissioning of Big Mamie. It also marked the 50th year since the keel of the USS *Lionfish* was laid and its 20th year at Battleship Cove. In October of this year the official Gulf War Memorial of the Commonwealth of Massachusetts was dedicated on board the battleship.

The crew members memorial was renamed in 1992. Formerly known as Casablanca Hall, it was renamed, USS *Massachusetts* Crewmembers' Memorial.

1993

The former flag secretary's room became the USS *Boston* Shipmates Memorial Room aboard BB-59. The ceremony featured remarks by Julien F. Paul, president of the Memorial Committee, and Allan W. Morgan, president of USS *Boston* Shipmates Inc. The *Rhode Islander* Sunday Magazine featured a story about Big Mamie's crew and included a photo of former crew members, Francis Dunbar, Ace Mavrogeorge, George "Chips" Duhamel and Bernie Silveria.

Volunteers Ray Portella, Chris Nardi and staff member Paul Gosselin visited Portsmouth, VA and boarded the guided missile destroyers USS *Preble* and USS *Dahlgren*, both marked for disposal by the Navy. They were able to obtain many items that could be used on Battleship Cove ships. They were also able to obtain WWII items from the Naval Historical Center in Washington, D.C.

A replica of HMS *Bounty*, built in 1960, arrived in Fall River this year, and although it will make trips to other ports, Battleship Cove will become her regular "Home Port."

1994 - 95 - 96 - 97

News events of these three years included:

- Battleship's "Father Joe" passing away in 1994.

- Big Mamie's crew members celebrate their 50th Reunion in 1995.

- The Drydocking Bill clearing the house vote of the Massachusetts House of Representatives, thanks to the work of Fall River Rep. Robert Correia in 1996, but it died before the end of the legislative session.

The 30th anniversary of the founding of the Historical Naval Ships Association (HNSA) is now referred to as "The World's Third Largest Navy." As the size of the USN shrinks, the floating memorials of the (HNSA), assume a more visible role in reminding the public of the importance of sea power. Founded in 1966, the battleship USS *Massachusetts* was one of the five original members. Among the organization's past presidents are Martin Adler and Paul Vaitses of the Memorial Committee. Its directors included committee members Joseph Feitelberg, John Brayton and James Gavin who were instrumental in forming the association. BB-59's executive vice president, Guy Archambault, serves as a current HNSA trustee. HNSA includes four aircraft carriers, four battleships, four cruisers, 20 submarines, Coast Guard vessels, and an armada of other combatants from the US, Canada and France. Another ship was added to "The Fall River Navy" in 1997. An East German patrol gunboat, built in Russia during the 1960's, has become an added attraction in Battleship Cove. This gunboat was equipped to fire rockets and missiles. This has become an added historical attraction for the boy scouts and overnighters to inspect. Most of these young people know very little about 16" guns, but rockets and missiles are part of their world today.

Summary

When the former crew members of Big Mamie attended their reunions each year, they can look back for 30 years, and can be proud of the fact, that they did not "give up their ship" without a great fight. Fall River and Southeastern Massachusetts have a strong tourist attraction, and a collection of National Historic Landmarks, that is the envy of many New England towns and cities, thanks to "Big Mamies Boys."

Bring back Big mamie was a state wide effort. Children, business professionals, and veterans raised money and volunteered their time.

Chapter Eight
Big Mamie's Boys

BIG MAMIE'S BOYS

To the hundreds of crew members and officers who sent stamps and funds so that we could mail survey forms to crew members and their families to obtain these bios.

To the most important "volunteer" who made it possible to produce this chapter - Howard Burkhalter, E Div., of Auburn, NY, who offered to use his computer and type most of these bios during a four year period of time - 1992-96. We regret that his death in 1996 did not allow him to see the work of this book completed. Howard was an active and later "life member" of the Telephone Pioneers of America, who encourage employees of the telephone companies in the USA and Canada to be "volunteers" in their communities. Howard was a GREAT BB-59 "volunteer."

USS Massachsetts beginning the long tow from Norfolk to her new home at Fall River. Note the extent to which she has been stripped: The cocoons over the 40mm mounts have been removed and the 40mm barrels have also been removed and stored. Also note that she is already flying the Massachusetts Navy flag.

AARON, OTTIS, (n), 360-24-82, enlisted Oct. 25, 1940, Houston, TX. He is a plankowner and served aboard BB-59 as F2/c at commissioning May 12, 1942, and was on board on its third anniversary, May 12, 1945.

ABBOTT, CHARLES BENTON, 242-72-35, enlisted Feb. 24, 1941, Newport, RI. He is a plankowner and served aboard BB-59 as CSK, May 12, 1942.

ABLES, WILLIAM J., resides at PO Box 270, South Pittsburg, TN 37380 (1995).

ACKERMAN, HERBERT EDWARD, was in hull maintenance. Served aboard BB-59 as ChCarp R Div., December 1942 and was on board on its second anniversary May 12, 1944.

ACKERMAN, THOMAS E., enlisted USMC, May 8, 1942, at Norfolk Navy Yard. He is a plankowner and served aboard BB-59 as PFC. 7th Div. May 12, 1942. He resides at 197 Mountain Ave., Revere, MA 02151 (1995).

ACKERSON, OWEN EDWARD, 342-54-47, enlisted Oct. 20, 1941, Kansas City, MO. He is a plankowner and served aboard BB-59 as S2/c at commissioning May 12, 1942 and was on board on its second anniversary, May 12, 1944.

ADAMS, HARRY PETER, 412-19-44, enlisted on Oct. 17, 1940, San Diego, CA. He is a plankowner and served aboard BB-59. He served in music at time of commissioning on May 12, 1942. He resides at 1717 Morena Blvd., San Diego, CA 92110 (1993). Memory List 1996.

ADAMS, LEROY, (n) 258-29-59, enlisted July 31, 1940, Baltimore, MD. He is a plankowner and served aboard BB-59 as S1/c at commissioning May 12, 1942.

ADAMS, WALLACE NORMAN, 646-34-36, enlisted Jan. 7, 1942, New York, NY. He is a plankowner and served aboard BB-59 as AS at commissioning, May 12, 1942.

ADDICKS, CLIFTON EUGENE, 359-97-01, enlisted Nov. 12, 1937, Houston, TX. He is a plankowner and served aboard BB-59 as SM2/c at commissioning May 12, 1942.

ADLER, HAROLD HERMAN, 648-02-65, enlisted on Oct. 7, 1941, Omaha, NE. He is a plankowner and served aboard BB-59 as S2/c at commissioning May 12, 1942.

ADLER, MARTIN, (n) (BRA-Boston), was on USS *Massachusetts* Memorial Committee and 1965 Homecoming Crew.

ADOLPH, ARTHUR WILLIAM, 600-20-79, enlisted March 11, 1942, Albany, NY. He is a plankowner and served aboard BB-59 as AS CR Div. at commissioning, May 12, 1942, and also as S2/c FR Div. on March 10, 1943, and was on board on its second and third anniversaries. He was RdM2/c (I Div. Capt.) on May 12, 1945.

AGURKIS, JOSEPH ANTHONY, 666-19-33, enlisted March 2, 1942, Springfield, MA. He is a plankowner and served aboard BB-59 as AS 6th Div.

at commissioning, May 12, 1942 and was on board for its second and third anniversaries. From 1963 to 1965 was on BBBM committee as RAdm MA Navy. Was on USS Massachusetts Memorial Committee; BB-59 Associates Pres, 1981-83, Bd. of Dir. 1984-93. He resides at 13 Hilltop Dr., Millbury, MA (1993).

AHE, GEORGE FREDERICK, 618-15-84, enlisted Jan. 20, 1942, Denver, CO. He is a plankowner and served aboard BB-59 as an AS at commissioning May 12, 1942.

AHEARN, WILLIAM THOMAS, 212-58-42, enlisted Sept. 3, 1940, Springfield, MA. He is a plankowner and served aboard BB-59 as a S1/c at commissioning, May 12, 1942. Ahearn passed away; Memory List 1990.

AINSWORTH, CHARLES CARROL, served aboard BB-59 as LT. V Div. January 1943 and as senior aviator, October 1943.

ALBERG, CLYDE WILLIAM, 328-71-19, enlisted July 16, 1940, Minneapolis, MN. He is a plankowner and served aboard tBB-59 as GM3/c at commissioning, May 12, 1942.

ALBIN, THOMAS BRUNS, is a plankowner and served aboard the BB-59 as LT. at the time of commissioning, May 12, 1942; as Asst. DC officer, March 1943; as Asst. 1st LT., Oct. 1, 1943; and Comdr. Sr. Plankowner, May 12, 1945.

ALBONDI, PHILIP ANTHONY, 606-49-96, enlisted on March 13, 1942, Boston, MA. He is a plankowner and served aboard BB-59 as AS at commissioning, May 12, 1942, and was on board for its 2nd and 3rd anniversaries.

ALCOTT, CHARLES, (n), Memory List, 1977.

ALCOTT, FRANK, (n), Memory List, 1991.

ALDERSON, JAMES VINCENT, 342-63-90, enlisted January 21, 1942, Kansas City, MO. He was a plankowner and served aboard BB-59 as AS at commissioning May 12, 1942, and was on board on its 2nd anniversary, May 12, 1944. Listed on 1990 Memory List, Independence, MO, and mail returned, 1992.

ALDRICH, DALE LEWIS, 311-23-93, enlisted on Nov. 11, 1941, Pearl Harbor, HI. He is a plankowner and served aboard BB-59 as F1/c at commissioning, May 12, 1942.

ALEYAHIS, GEORGE WILLIAM, 646-82-25, enlisted Feb. 19, 1942, New York, NY. He is a plankowner and served aboard BB-59 as AS CR Div. at commissioning May 12, 1942 and on March 10, 1943, as RDM3/c FR Div.

ALEXANDER, MERRIL, (n) 279-71-17, enlisted Aug. 19, 1940, Cincinnati, OH. He is a plankowner and served aboard BB-59 as F1/c at commissioning May 12, 1942.

ALFORD, CHARLES RICHARD, 622-44-49, enlisted Jan. 28, 1942, Detroit, MI. He served aboard BB-59 as AS at commissioning May 12, 1942 and is a plankowner. He was on board for its 2nd anniversary May 12, 1944.

ALIPRANTI, WILLIAM JOHN, 207-38-19, enlisted March 6, 1942, New Haven, CT. He is a plankowner and served aboard BB-59 as AS at commissioning, May 12, 1942, and on 3rd anniversary as 6th and R Div. Received Meritorious Mast April 1944. From 1963 to 1965, on BBBM Committee (RAdm MA Navy). He resides at 92 Lockwood Ave., Stamford, CT (1993).

ALLEN, BILLY JAMES, 356-48-32, enlisted on Jan. 16, 1941, Dallas, TX. Allen is a plankowner and served aboard BB-59 as S1/c at commissioning May 12, 1942.

ALLEN, BOBBY JOE, 337-71-64, enlisted Sept, 30, 1941, St. Louis, MO. He is a plankowner and served aboard BB-59 as S2/c at commissioning, May 12, 1942.

ALLEN, EARLE, (n) Member of Homecoming Crew, 1965. He resides in Braintree, MA.

ALLEN, EDWARD HENRY, 381-41-10, was born October 1922 in Hackensack, NJ. He enlisted on March 20, 1941, San Diego, CA, served aboard the USS *Minneapolis*. Allen is a plankowner and served aboard BB-59 as S1/c at commissioning May 12, 1942. In March 1943 the US Marines as Medical CPhmM; Associates Pres. 1969 and served from 1963-65 on BBBM Committee as (RAdm. MASS Navy). Member of Homecoming Crew, 1965. His post war work was at Boston Navy Yard. Allen married Carol Charchoodian and had two children and two grandchildren. He passed away Nov. 14, 1992.

ALLEN JOHN WESLEY, 265-92-15, enlisted on Feb. 5, 1942, Pearl Harbor, HI. He is a plankowner and served aboard BB-59 as MM2/c at commissioning May 12, 1942.

ALLEN, WALTER EDWARD, 606-49-21, enlisted March 12, 1942, Boston MA. He is a plankowner and served aboard BB-59 as AS at commissioning May 12, 1942, and was on board for its 2nd and third anniversaries. He resides at 510 Belmont St., Watertown, PA (1967).

ALLEN, WOODROW, (n) 291-56-65, enlisted Oct. 18, 1938, Indianapolis, IN. He is a plankowner and served on board BB-59 as S1/c at commissioning May 12, 1942.

ALLRED, ALVIN EARL, 368-41-50, enlisted July 12, 1938, Salt Lake City, UT. He is a plankowner and served on board BB-59 as GM3/c at commissioning May 12, 1942.

ALMOND, DAVID DELMAR, 262-64-26, enlisted Aug. 8, 1940, Raleigh, NC. He served aboard BB-59 as F2/c at commissioning and was on board for its 2nd and 3rd anniversaries.

ALTIERIE, FREDERICK ALEXANDER, 244-09-21, enlisted March 18, 1942, Philadelphia, PA. He is a plankowner and served aboard BB-59 as AS 4th Div. at commissioning May 12, 1942, and was on board for its 2nd and 3rd anniversaries. He resides at 55 Harborview Lane 102, Belleair Bluffs, FL (1993).

ALYK, GEORGE JOSEPH, 642-12-43, enlisted Feb. 9, 1942, in New Haven, CT. He is a plankowner and served aboard BB-59 as AS at commissioning May 12, 1942.

AMARO, G.L., on BB-59 Mailing List, 1966. RFD Ferndale, CA.

ANDERSON, THORLEIF, (n), 224-71-76, enlisted March 2, 1942, New York, NY. He is a plankowner and served aboard BB-59 as AS 6th Div. at commissioning May 12, 1942, was on board for its 2nd and 3rd anniversaries. (Mrs.) resides at 149 96th St., #B5, Brooklyn, NY (1993).

ANDERSON, WALTER, was on 1990 BB-59 Mailing List, 4th Div. (Mrs.) resides at 7N 35th St., St. Clear Lake, IA (1992).

ANDERSON, ALBERT ROBERT, 311-50-93, enlisted Sept. 24, 1940, Detroit, MI. He is a plankowner and served aboard BB-59 as S1/c at commissioning May 12, 1942.

ANDERSON, DUANE VERDY, 368-39-69, enlisted Dec. 17, 1941, San Francisco, CA. He is a plankowner and served aboard BB-59 as COX in January 1942. Was also X and CR Div. BM2/c, BM1/c to CMB (Laundry Chief). Anderson retired into Fleet Reserve after 21 years in Navy (1957). His post war work was in Boston School Dept. at the Girl's Latin School. He married Ethel (died 1968). He is an active fund raiser for the BBBM Campaign and resides in Dorchester, MA (1993).

ANDERSON, FRANK CHARLES, served aboard BB-59 as LT (jg) in Supply Dept. January 1945.

ANDERSON, GARTH B., E Div., address is PO Box 964, Crestline, CA (1993).

ANDERSON, HOWARD CHARLES, 647-00-79, enlisted Feb. 20, 1942, New York, NY. He is a plankowner and served aboard BB-59 as AS F Div. at commissioning. He also served the Ship's Armory and Magazines. Left BB-59 in November 1945 as GM1/c. His post war work was as lithographer for Litho Art, New York, NY. Anderson has four children and resides at 32 Belmohr St., Belleville, NJ (1993).

ANDERSON, JOHN HELDING, 666-19-64, enlisted March 4, 1942, Springfield, MA. He is a plankowner and served aboard BB-59 as AS at commissioning May 12, 1942, and was on board for its 2nd anniversary May 12, 1944. He resides at 99 Elm St., Southbridge, MA (1964).

ANDERSON, WILLIAM PINCKNEY, LT(jg), served aboard BB-59 as Asst. Chaplain in September 1943 and on May 12, 1944 Anniversary Committee. (Mrs.) resides at 308 Willow Winds Dr., Columbus, SC (1993).

ANDERSON, WOODROW, ST.G, Enlisted USMC May 8, 1942, Norfolk Navy Yard. He is a plankowner and served aboard BB-59 as PFC 7th Div. at commissioning May 12, 1942.

ANDREWS, ALFRED DEAN, 372-15-20, enlisted June 11, 1940, Denver, CO. He is a plankowner and served aboard BB-59 at commissioning May 12, 1942.

ANDREWS, THOMAS J., resides at 802 Shagbark Rd., New Lenox, IL (1993).

ANDRIOPOLOS, PAUL JOHN, 202-18-01, enlisted Jan. 7, 1942 as AS. He is a plankowner and served aboard BB-59 at commissioning May 12, 1942. (Mrs.) resides at 5600 Mossberg Dr., New Port Richey, FL, 34655-1137.

ANDRYSIK, STANLEY, 7th Div., resides at 502 Carls Path, Deer Path, Long Island, NY, 11729 (1993).

ANGELINI, ALBERT ANTHONY, 650-33-22, enlisted Feb. 25, 1942, in Philadelphia, PA. He is a plankowner and served aboard the BB-59 as AS at commissioning May 12, 1942.

ARBANAS, MONTE, (n), 234-26-66, enlisted Aug. 26, 1940, Buffalo, NY. He is a plankowner and served aboard BB-59 as F2/c at commissioning May 12, 1942, and was on board for its 2nd anniversary May 12, 1944.

ARCHER, WILLIAM BURBERRY, 647-02-26, enlisted Feb. 21, 1942, New York, NY. He is a plankowner and served aboard BB-59 as S2/c at commissioning May 12, 1942.

ARCHIBALD, CHARLES RICHARD, 647-00-80, enlisted Feb. 20, 1942, New York, NY. He is a plankowner and served aboard BB-59 as AS at commissioning May 12, 1942, and was on board for its 2nd and 3rd anniversaries.

ARENA, OROZZIO J., is a member of 1963 Membership Roster. (Mrs.) resides at 7 Manor St., Natick, MA (1993).

ARENDS, STANLEY R. SR., resides at PO Box 233, Ellsworth, MN (1993).

ARENELLA, ARTHUR T., is a member of the 1966-1970 Membership Roster. He married Dorothy and has two children. He resides at 410 Main St. #14, Farmingdale, NY (1993).

ARMEL, KENNETH, (n), 626-05-78, was born on May 9, 1919, in Indianapolis, IN. He enlisted on Dec. 11, 1941, Indianapolis, IN; Great Lakes (three weeks) Prtr 2/c; Rec/Sta Pier 92 NYC (three weeks). He is a plankowner and served on board tBB-59 on Jan. 28, 1942 (Quincy) and on Feb. 10, 1943 as Prtr 1/c X Div. Left BB-59 at sea on May 24, 1945.

Armel attended Photo-Lithography School in Washington DC; received a BS from Carnegie Tech with a BS and MS from Butler University. Taught graphic arts at Mishawaka High School, retiring in 1984. He married Mary and has a son Donald who is assistant professor at Eastern Illinois University. Resides at 739 N Wenger Ave., Mishawaka, IN (1993). He is a member of the Editorial Board for this book.

ARMSTRONG, KENNETH DOW, 411-30-61, born July 22, 1919, Red Oak, IA. Enlisted Oct. 20, 1940, Naperville, IL; attended Radio and Radar schools in Great Lakes, IL; MM and Diesel Engine School, Dearborn, MI; R/S Boston. He is a plankowner and served aboard BB-59 as S2/c at commissioning May 12, 1942, and as F3/ c Eng. in January 1943. Left BB-59 Jan. 18, 1943, then to YMS-105 until discharge at Great Lakes, IL.

Worked 35 years in production department, Chicago American & Chicago Tribune; also worked part-time PBX operator and relief driver for retirement home. In his spare time, he is church/trustee, golfs three times weekly and builds doll houses for service clubs to raffle off as fund-raisers. Resides at 5442 Creeping Hammock Way, Sarasota, FL (1993).

ARMSTRONG, PAUL HENRY, ENS, 4th Div. Served aboard BB-59 in May 1943.

ARNOLD, CLYDE BENJAMIN, 291-57-26, enlisted Jan. 10, 1939, Indianapolis, IN. Stationed at Pearl Harbor Dec. 7, 1941, aboard the USS *St. Louis*. He is a plankowner and served aboard BB-59 as S1/c 5th Div. at commissioning May 12, 1942. Transferred to the USS Mid*way* and later had shore duty in Bloomington, IN, until the end of WWII.

Post war activities include the owner of Arnold Motel, Waterville, ME; fund raiser for BBBM Campaign; and RAdm Massachusetts Navy. He married Theresa and has one son and one grandson. They live at 4803 Calamondin Circle, Coconut Creek, FL 33063 (1993).

ARNOLD, JOHN L. SR., L Div., Newsletter/survey booster. He has a son and a daughter and two grandchildren and resides at 855 Phyllis Way, Cocoa, FL (1993).

ARNOLD, WILLIAM JAMES, 341-63-42, enlisted Jan. 30, 1942, Mare Island, CA. He is a plankowner and served aboard BB-59 as WT1/c at commissioning May 12, 1942, and was aboard on its 2nd anniversary on May 12, 1944, B Div.

ARNONE, ANGELO ANTHONY, 646-82-27, enlisted Feb. 19, 1942, in New York, NY. He is a plankowner and served aboard BB-59 as AS at commissioning on May 12, 1942, and on her 2nd anniversary, May 12, 1944. Memory List 1977.

ARONOLD, JOHN L., 263-51-98, enlisted on Dec. 16, 1941, Raleigh, NC. He is a plankowner and served aboard BB-59 as S2/c at commissioning May 12, 1942.

ARRUDA, JOSEPH THOMAS, 202-26-65, born on Jan. 3, 1920, in Fall River, MA. Graduated from high school and enlisted on March 2, 1942, in Boston, MA. He attended training in Newport, RI (six weeks). He is a plankowner and served aboard BB-59 as AS E Div., at commissioning May 12, 1942. Left BB-59 on May 1945 to Shore Patrol, Long Beach, CA; Maryland Pawt. Naval Station until 1949.

His pre-war work included candlestick maker in silver in jewelry shops. After the war, he was a commercial electrician for 12 years and worked for Texas Instruments Company for 22 years. Other activities include BBBM Campaign as fund raiser; "Lt Cmdr" in Massachusetts Navy and is an active Field Day member. He has two sons and resides at 45 Beagle Club Rd., Attleboro, MA (1993).

ASHBY, WILLIE ELLIS, 287-57-05, enlisted July 15, 1941, Louisville, KY. He is a plankowner and served aboard BB-59 as S2/c at commissioning May 12, 1942, and was on board on its 2nd anniversary May 12, 1944.

ASHTON, CYRIL JOHNSON, 201-78-49, enlisted Oct. 8, 1940, Boston, MA. He served aboard BB-59 as S1/c and is a plankowner.

ATHANASAS, THOMAS, (n) 223-77-97, enlisted Aug. 2, 1940, New York, NY. Served aboard BB-59 as S1/c at commissioning May 12, 1942, and is a plankowner.

ATKINSON, GILBERT AARON, 622-27-55, enlisted Dec. 30, 1941, Detroit, MI. He served aboard BB-59 as EM3/c at commissioning May 12, 1942, and was on board for its 2nd anniversary May 12, 1944. He is a plankowner.

AUFIERO, DONALD ANDREW, 224-73-07, enlisted March 9, 1942, New York, NY. He is a plankowner and served aboard BB-59 as AS.

AULDRIDGE, GEORGE A., (old membership list) Prince, WV.

AUSTIN, HARRY GARDNER, 311-50-43, enlisted Sept. 17, 1940, in Detroit, MI. He is a plankowner and served aboard BB-59 as S1/c at commissioning May 12, 1942, and on its 2nd anniversary May 12, 1944. He resides at 11563 Lindale St., Norwalk, CT (1963).

AUSTIN, WARREN ERWOOD, 223-76-43, enlisted July 16, 1940, New York, NY. He is a plankowner and served aboard BB-59 as S1/c. He resides at 54 Little River Rd., Hampton, NH (1993). Memory List 1996.

AUTSOLIEF, EDWARD DOUGLAS, 600-16-60, born Oct. 1, 1921, in Troy, NY. Attended Lansingburg High School and Siena College. He enlisted Feb. 14, 1942, at Albany, NY, and attended boot camp Newport, RI. He is a plankowner and served aboard BB-59 as AS 1st Div. from Quincy to Boston and later N Div. He left BB-59 in May 1945 via breeches buoy to tanker off Okinawa.

His post war work is for the US Postal Service. In his spare-time he golfs; is a member of the VFW (past commander and past county commander) and is Field Day worker and newsletter booster. Autsolief has four children and eight grandchildren. He resides at 333 White Spring Rd., Troy, NY (1993).

AVERY, ROBERT CLARENCE, 642-02-10, enlisted on Nov. 25, 1941, New Haven, CT. He is a plankowner and served aboard BB-59 as S2/c.

AVIS, WILLIAM ALBERT, 244-08-20, enlisted March 31, 1942, Philadelphia, PA. He served aboard BB-59 as AS 4th Div. at commissioning May 12, 1942, and was on board for its 2nd and 3rd anniversaries. He was a plankowner. Part of the BBBM Campaign as fund-raiser and ENS in the Massachusetts Navy. In 1966, he resided in Pitman, NY. Memory List 1977.

AYERS, HOWARD FRANKLIN, 244-07-09, enlisted March 2, 1942, Philadelphia, PA. He is a plankowner and served aboard BB-59 as AS at commissioning May 12, 1942, and was on board for its 2nd and 3rd anniversaries. Memory List, 1984. (Mrs.) resides at 215 Edgewater Ave., Westville, NJ (1993).

AYLING, GEORGE LeROY, 650-32-35, enlisted March 31, 1942, Philadelphia, PA. He is a plankowner and served aboard BB-59 as AS CR Div. at commissioning May 12, 1942 and in March 1943 to FR Div. S1/c and was on board for 3rd anniversary. He resides at 125 Chestnut St., Tuckerton, NJ (1993).

BABCOCK, CHARLES WELLS, 224-72-44, enlisted March 4, 1942, New York, NY. He is a plankowner and served aboard BB-59 as AS.

BACON, JACK G., SR., on March 10, 1943 was RT2/c CR to FR Div. Transferred Feb. 3, 1945 to Radio Material School T.I., San Francisco, CA. He resides at 1218 South 4th St., Terre Haute, IN, 47802 (1993).

BAER, GARTH ARTHUR, 382-33-02, enlisted Dec. 11, 1940, Los Angeles, CA. He is a plankowner and served aboard BB-59 as EM3/c.

BAILEY, GUY F., served aboard BB-59 from January 1943 as B Div. to September 1946 as boilerman, Oil King and was Div. Petty Officer BT2/c. After the war worked for the Potomac Edison Company in the reproduction department. and married Florence. Memory List, 1977.

BAILEY, VIRGIL CALVEN, 608-10-96, enlisted Feb. 17, 1942, Buffalo, NY. He is a plankowner and served aboard BB-59 as AS at commissioning May 12, 1942, and was also on board May 12, 1944 and May 12, 1945.

BAILEY, WADE JUNIOR, 356-34-93, enlisted Aug. 10, 1940, Dallas, TX. He is a plankowner and served aboard BB-59 as S1/c at commissioning May 12, 1942. He is deceased; Memory List, 1977.

BAIN, GEORGE M., resides at PO Box 390, Mechanicsville, VA (1993).

BAIRD, JAMES WENDELL, 328-95-57, enlisted Aug. 29, 1941, Minneapolis, MN. He is a plankowner and served aboard BB-59 as S2/c at commissioning May 12, 1942.

BAIRD, WILLIAM RUSSELL, 295-99-54, enlisted June 16, 1941, Nashville, TN. He served aboard BB-59 as S2/c at commissioning May 12, 1942 and is a plankowner.

BAK, ANTHONY MARTIN, 600-20-97, enlisted March 13, 1942, Albany, NY. He is a plankowner and served aboard BB-59 as AS at commissioning May 12, 1942, and was also aboard May 12, 1944 and May 12, 1945.

BAKER, RAYMOND FRANKLIN, 600-21-03, enlisted March 13, 1942, Albany NY. He is a plankowner and served aboard BB-59 as AS at commissioning May 12, 1942, and on board on May 12, 1944.

BALAO, TERIBLE, (n), 497-88-53, enlisted Jan. 9, 1940, San Diego, CA. He is a plankowner and served aboard BB-59 as OC2/c at commissioning May 12, 1942.

BALD, LEROY, USMC, born Nov. 8, 1918, in Baltimore, MD. He graduated from Forest Park High School, 1937 and received a BA from Colgate University, 1942; a JD from the University of Maryland Law School, 1947. He enlisted in the USMC in 1940 at Colgate University. Served aboard BB-59 in February 1944 as XO Marine Detachment 1st LT 7th Div.; CO Marine Detach. Capt. May 12, 1945. He left BB-59 in California. His USMC assignments include: 4th Marine Div., Pacific and Korea September 1950 to April 1952.

His post war work activities include attending the University of Maryland Law School LLB-JD 1949 and maintaining a law practice to the present time. During his spare time, he is on the YMCA Board of Directors; past president of Rotary Club; Military Order World Wars; president Anne Arundel Company and Maryland Bar Assoc. His honors include the Bronze Star. He married Harriet (deceased 1990) and has three children; and seven grandchildren. He resides at 192 Duke of Gloucester St., Annapolis, MD (1993).

BALDAUF, RICHARD BIRGE, born Nov. 9, 1915, and attended Dartmouth College, 1939 and Trinity College, Hartford, CT, 1952. Baldauf enlisted Jan. 2, 1942, and attended Midshipman School in Chicago Sept. 1, 1942. He served aboard BB-59 as ENS 4th Div. in June 1943; as 1st LT's Div. 2nd year LT(jg). He left BB-59 in California in June 1945 for Damage Control School in Philadelphia. His assignments include: serving aboard the USS Honolulu as Lieutenant.

After the war he worked in the War Assets Administration, 1946-47 and Hartford Insurance Company, 1947-48. In his spare time he enjoys making duck decoys. He is married to Sue Warley and has three children and six grandchildren. He resides at 33 Pearl St., Englewood, FL 34223-5771 (1993).

BALDUZZI, DANIEL F., Enlisted USMC, 1942. He served aboard the BB-59 as Pvt. 7th Div. at commissioning May 12, 1942. He is a plankowner.

BALDWIN, HENRY WILSON, 263-52-14, enlisted Dec. 16, 1941, in Raleigh, NC. He is a plankowner and served aboard BB-59 as S2/c at commissioning May 12, 1942.

BALESTRERI, SALVATORE A., 224-78-11, enlisted April 1, 1942, in New York, NY. He is a plankowner and served aboard BB-59 as AS at commissioning May 12, 1942, and was on board May 12, 1944.

BALINT, ANDREW JOSEPH, 385-75-28, enlisted on October 13, 1937, in Seattle, WA. He is a plankowner and served aboard BB-59 as S1/c at commissioning May 12, 1942.

BALTRAMITIS, CLEMENT J., USMC, enlisted May 8, 1942, at Norfolk Navy Yard. He is a plankowner and served aboard BB-59 as Pvt. 7th Div. at commissioning May 12, 1942. He resides at 330 W. Valerio St., Santa Barbara, CA, 93101.

BAMBINO, ANTHONY ALBERT, 646-82-28, enlisted Feb. 19, 1942, in New York, NY. He served aboard BB-59 as AS at commissioning May 12, 1942, and is a plankowner.

BANAS, ALBERT EDWARD, 666-16-06, enlisted Feb. 10, 1942, in Springfield, MA. He served aboard BB-59 as AS at commissioning May 12, 1942, and is a plankowner. Banas resides at 50 Springside, Pittsfield, MA (1993).

BANAS, BRUNO JOHN, 650-26-09, enlisted Feb. 11, 1942, in Philadelphia, PA. He is a plankowner and served aboard BB-59 as AS at commissioning May 12, 1942.

BANE, LAWRENCE MARION, 355-71-73, enlisted May 3, 1942, in Boston, MA. He served aboard BB-59 as RM1/c at commissioning May 12, 1942, and is a plankowner.

BANGHAM, CLIFFORD FORREST, 224-71-79, enlisted March 2, 1942, in New York, NY. He is a plankowner and served aboard BB-59 as AS at commissioning May 12, 1942.

BANKS, CHESTER CLARK, 606-75-79, born July 23, 1921, in Quincy, MA. He enlisted May 12, 1942, in Boston, MA, and served aboard BB-59 as EMC3 E Div. Left the BB-59 in 1944 at Bremerton, WA. He attended the University of Colorado and worked for the Amoco Corporation for 35 years. He married Doris. Banks died March 31, 1996. (Mrs.) resides at 25846 S. Flame Tree Dr., Sun Lakes, AZ. Memory List 1996.

BANKS, MARVIN ROGER, 328-96-70, enlisted Oct. 7, 1941, in Minneapolis, MN. He served aboard BB-59 as S2/c at commissioning May 12, 1942, and is a plankowner.

BANNON, FRANCIS XAVIER, 652-25-17, born April 23, 1917, in Pittsburgh, PA. Graduated from high school and attended Carnegie Tech. University. He enlisted on March 5, 1942, Pittsburgh, PA, and trained in Newport, RI. Bannon is a plankowner and served aboard BB-59 as AS L Div. at commissioning May 12, 1942, and as ComBat Div. 8 Staff Adm. Davis Y2/c. Left BB-59 on March 5, 1945, off Iwo Jima, also Philadelphia Navy Yard and Patux Naval Air Station. After the war became vice-president for Swift Industries. Married to Olive and has two sons and six grandchildren. They reside at 311 Karen Dr., Elizabeth, PA (1993).

BANOLEWICZ, THADEUS, 642-02-83, enlisted Dec. 13, 1941, in New Haven, CT. He is a plankowner and served aboard BB-59 as MM2/c at commissioning May 12, 1942.

BANZHAF, HENRY FREDERICK, born Sept. 17, 1911, in Milwaukee, WI. Attended University of Wisconsin. Graduated from the Naval Academy Class of 1933 and served aboard the USS *Pensacola*. Resigned in August 1934 and was employed at Cutler-Hammer Company Milwaukee. Was supervising application engineer for Navy and Marine equipment and served as Cutler-Hammer representative to War Production Board.

Banzhaf returned to the Navy in 1942 and was assigned as a commissioning officer in the engineering department to the USS *Massachusetts*. He served aboard BB-59 in Quincy, MA at commissioning May 12, 1942, and is a plankowner. Made E Div. Officer on May 12, 1942, and B Div. Officer in March 1943. He left the BB-59 on Jan. 14, 1944, at Efate Island, New Hebrides, and served aboard the USS *Wisconsin* at commissioning March 10, 1944 to Sept. 10, 1944 as Asst. Eng. Officer; resident inspector Naval Materials, E. Pittsburgh, PA, from Sept. 20, 1944, to July 1945.

After the war he was employed with Allis Chalmers Mfg. Company as executive assistant to senior vice-president of Industries Group; Touche Ross & Company management consulting division. In 1964 he formed his own firm, Henry Banzhaf & Assoc., investment advisors. In his spare time he is a member of Financial Analysis Federation; the Milwaukee Investment Analysis Society and the Milwaukee County Council Boys Scouts of America. Also holds a patent on electric cargo wenches. He semi-retired on July 1, 1992. Married to Barbara Badet (died 1960) in 1939 and had four children and nine grandchildren. Died May 27, 1993, at Columbia Hospital, Milwaukee, WI.

BAPTISTA, MANUEL ANDREW, 606-47-02, enlisted March 6, 1942, in Boston, MA. He is a plankowner and served aboard BB-59 as AS 6th Div. at commissioning May 12, 1942, and made S1/c in February 1943. After the war he was employed at Campelli Brothers Construction. Married Ruth and had two children. Memory List 1992.

BARAK, H., served aboard BB-59 as ENS in March 1943.

BARBER, CHARLIE RAYMOND, 287-50-61, enlisted on Jan. 14, 1941, in Louisville, KY. He served aboard the BB-59 as S1/c at commissioning May 12, 1942, and is a plankowner.

BARBETTO, GEORGE CARL, 243-59-20, enlisted on April 7, 1942, in San Francisco, CA. He is a plankowner and served aboard BB-59 as COX 2nd Div. at commissioning May 12, 1942. Left BB-59 in November 1943 as BM1/c and later became CBM.

After the war was employed at the Court House of Atlantic, in charge of boiler room in courthouse buildings. He is commander VFW Post 5341, Egg Harbor Boys Club and the Republican Club in his spare time. He has a son, George Barbetto.

BARDSLEY, CARROLL S., served aboard BB-59 as SK3/c S Div. at commissioning in 1942 and left BB-59 in 1945. Post war employment was as assistant manager of H.C. Pond Lumber Company. In his spare time he has been past counselor UCT, past president MA Lumberman's Assoc. and past president of Square Dance Club. He married Gertrude and has three children. They reside at 22 Johnson Lane, Yarmouth, MA (1992).

BARENE, HAROLD, (n) 647-00-82, enlisted on Feb. 20, 1942, in New York, NY, and served aboard BB-59 as AS at commissioning May 12, 1942. He is a plankowner.

BARGOIL, JAMES, 4th Div. (1966) Winston Salem, NC.

BARKER, L.E., served aboard BB-59 and on Mailing List (1966) Perry, OK.

BARKHIMER, CHARLES LEWIS, 652-14-54, enlisted Jan. 22, 1942, in Pittsburgh, PA. He is a plankowner and served aboard BB-59 as S2/c at commissioning May 12, 1942. On Memory List 1990. In 1992 (Mrs.) resided in Columbia, MD, and on Feb. 6, 1993, mail returned.

BARNES, RAYMOND JOSEPH, 243-74-09, enlisted Aug. 14, 1940, Philadelphia, PA. He is a plankowner and served aboard BB-59 as S1/c at commissioning May 12, 1942.

BARNETT, CHARLES LEE, 262-63-82, enlisted Aug. 7, 1940, in Raleigh, NC. He served aboard BB-59 as S1/c at commissioning May 12, 1942, and is a plankowner.

BARNEY, JOHN J., served aboard BB-59 and now resides at 11 Wheeler Ave., Carteret, NJ (1992).

BARNHILL, WILLIAM JAMES, served aboard BB-59 as LT(jg) at commissioning May 12, 1942, and is a plankowner.

BARRAGER, KENNETH LESLIE, 650-29-42, enlisted Feb. 18, 1942, in Philadelphia, PA. He is a plankowner and served aboard BB-59 as AS.

BARRETT, GEORGE HENRY, JR., 204-43-20, enlisted Nov. 16, 1937, in San Pedro, CA. He is a plankowner and served aboard BB-59 as EM1/c at commissioning May 12, 1942.

BARRETT, HERBERT NELSON, 224-78-50, born Aug. 19, 1920, in Yorktown Heights, NY. He enlisted April 2, 1942, in New York, NY and served aboard BB-59 as AS 1st Div. at commissioning May 12, 1942. Left BB-59 on March 8, 1945, as F1/c F Div. at Ulithe. He is a plankowner. His assignments include: 1945-47 Treasure Island; 1947 to Jan. 19, 1948, Pearl Harbor. After the war he was an electrician for the NY Central Railroad. Was an active member of the American Legion Post 1009, and loved to golf and travel. Married to Alice. He died Feb. 13, 1993. (Mrs.) resides at 636 N. Terrace Ave., Mt. Vernon, NY (1993).

BARRETT, HORACE MITCHELL, 650-05-79, born July 14, 1924, in Cleveland, OH. Graduated from Lago Community High School and attended colleges in Aruba, Netherlands Antilles and Lynchburg College, Lynchburg, VA. Enlisted Oct. 22, 1941, in Philadelphia, PA, and received training Ford Motor, Dearborn, MI, Mach-Mate Trade School. He is a plankowner and served aboard BB-59 as S2/c P Div. at commissioning May 12, 1942. Left BB-59 in September 1944 at Bremerton, WA, and assigned to USS *Gosselin APD 126* on Dec. 30, 1944 for commissioning in New Orleans. Was aboard till the end of the war. Discharged at Camp Shelton, VA, Oct. 24, 1945.

Post war: from 1946-1960 worked for various architectural firms in Virginia, Massachusetts, Florida and Texas. Took NCARB examination in 1959 and from 1960-1987 had a general architectural practice. Retired on Jan. 1, 1987. Was honored with Emeritus Membership in the American Institute of Architects. Married Nancy Holloran and has three sons, three daughters and 16 grandchildren. They reside at PO Box 92, Prudence Island, RI (1993).

BARRETT, JOHN LINDSAY, 600-02-70, enlisted on Dec. 16, 1941, Albany, NY. He is a plankowner and served aboard BB-59 as SF3/c at commissioning May 12, 1942.

BARRINGTON, WALTER RALEIGH, 262-28-51, enlisted April 28, 1938, in Raleigh, NC. He is a plankowner and served aboard BB-59 as Y2/c at commissioning May 12, 1942.

BARRUZZI, JAMES, (n) On Aug. 30, 1993 name submitted by Bob Princeton, (Connecticut) relayed to Bob by Wally Davis, California. No further data. Memory List 1996.

BARTKUS, AUGUSTUS EDWARD, 207-28-51, enlisted Sept. 3, 1940, New Haven, CT. He is a plankowner and served aboard BB-59 as SK3/c at commissioning May 12, 1942. Left BB-59 in 1944 as SK1/c. Post war, he worked in shipping and receiving for Consolidated Tube Fabricating Corp. He has four children and resided in Waterbury, CT (1993) (mail returned).

BARTLETT, RALPH RICHARD, 368-47-40, enlisted Feb. 7, 1940, in Salt Lake City, UT. He is a plankowner and served aboard BB-59 as FC2/c at commissioning May 12, 1942, and was on board May 12, 1944.

BARUZZI, JOSEPH MARCE, 283-62-10, enlisted Oct. 23, 1941, in Cleveland, OH. He is a plankowner and served aboard BB-59 as S2/c.

BASILLE, FRANCIS JOSEPH, 652-19-25, enlisted Feb. 8, 1942, in Pittsburgh, PA. He is a plankowner and served aboard BB-59 as AS 2nd Div. He resides at 5415 Glenwood Ave., Pittsburgh, PA (1993).

BASS, REGINALD H., served aboard BB-59 (no dates) in FC and X Divs. He resides at PO Box 57, Kingston, WA (1993).

BASTIAN, RALPH WESLEY, served aboard BB-59 as LT 3rd Div. in July 1944 (source: July 1945 roster).

BASTIAN, ROBERT OWEN, served aboard BB-59 in April 1943 as 2nd LT USMC 7th Div. (source: October 1943 roster).

BATES, GEORGE N., born Nov. 23, 1921, in Grand Rapids, MI. Graduated from Creston High School and attended Morehead State College. Enlisted July 1942 in Great Lakes, IL, and received training at Great Lakes Naval Training & Electrician School, Morehead, KY. Bates served aboard BB-59 as EM3/c E Div. January 1943 and left BB-59 in October 1945 in Bremerton, WA.

His post war work was 30 years employment with Michigan Bell Telephone and 12 years with Southern Bell Telephone (Miami and Miami Beach). Retired on Dec. 31, 1982. Spare time activities include photography and cine/photography. He is married to Blanche and has three children and two step-children. They reside at 6716 NW 59th St., Tamarac, FL (1993).

BATES, PARKER WILLARD, 606-56-11, enlisted March 28, 1942, in Boston, MA. He is a plankowner and served aboard the BB-59 as S2/c at commissioning May 12, 1942, and was on board on May 12, 1944. Memory List 1977.

BATES, THOMAS ALBERT, 250-67-13, enlisted Nov. 5, 1941, in Pittsburgh, PA. He is a plankowner and served aboard BB-59 as S2/c at commissioning May 12, 1942, and was on board on May 12, 1944.

BATSON, CLIFTON DELAINE, 337-44-47, enlisted Nov. 5, 1940, in St. Louis, MO. He served aboard BB-59 as F2/c at commissioning May 12, 1942, and was on board on May 12, 1944. He is a plankowner.

BAUER, OMER WILLIAM, 316-57-74, enlisted March 8, 1939, in Omaha, NE. He served aboard BB-59 as RM1/c at commissioning May 12, 1942. He was a plankowner. Memory List 1992.

BAUGH, WILLIAM THOMAS, JR., 382-43-52, enlisted April 4, 1941, in Los Angeles, CA. He is a plankowner and served aboard BB-59 as S1/c at commissioning May 12, 1942. Memory List 1992.

BAUMGARTNER, FLOYD, (n) 647-00-84, born April 20, 1922, in Perth Amboy, NJ. Graduated Voc. High School and attended Drake's Business College. He enlisted Feb. 20, 1942, in New York, NY, and is a plankowner. Served aboard the BB-59 as A Div. Machine Shop, at commissioning May 12, 1942. Left BB-59 in the fall of 1943 as MM2/c. Assignments included serving aboard the USS *Prince George* until two days before VJ Day; USNA Oakland, CA; USNA Carona, CA; and USNH Sampson, NY.

After the war he had several jobs such as beer sales, liquor salesman and retired in 1964. He enjoyed bobsledding and represented the USA at Innsbrook, Austria in the World Games in 1963 and in the Olympics in 1964 while living in Saranac Lake, NY. He was post commander, county sergeant at arms and district chaplain of the American Legion. Married Jean Weber. He died July 22, 1991. (Mrs.) resides 1824 Monroe St. #12, Hollywood, FL (1993).

BAUMIESTER, WILLIAM, (n) 650-14-16, enlisted Jan. 28, 1942, in Philadelphia, PA. He is a plankowner and served aboard BB-59 as AS at commissioning May 12, 1942.

BAUMLEY, FRANK, (n), 224-73-48, enlisted March 10, 1942, in New York, NY. He is a plankowner and served aboard BB-59 as AS on May 12, 1942 and was on board for her 2nd anniversary. He resides in Hopelawn, NJ (1966).

BAXTER, ARTHUR ALTON, 279-87-44, enlisted Oct. 8, 1941, Cincinnati, OH. He is a plankowner and served aboard BB-59 as S2/c CR Div. at commissioning May 12, 1942. He resided at 1022 S. Third St., Louisville, KY (1993). Memory List 1996.

BAY, WILLIS EDWARD, 279-47-82, enlisted Jan. 3, 1942, in Cincinnati, OH. He is a plankowner and served aboard BB-59 as S1/c at commissioning May 12, 1942.

BAYLESS, JERRY WATSON, 258-37-01, enlisted Aug. 27, 1941, in Baltimore, MD. He is a plankowner and served aboard BB-59 as S2/c at commissioning May 12, 1942. He resides at 1367 Stewart St., Mineral Ridge, OH (1993).

BAZA PRESBETERIO ALVAREZ, 421-04-31, enlisted May 3, 1939. He is a plankowner and served aboard BB-59 as MATT1/c at commissioning May 12, 1942.

BEACH, CHARLES, J., 600-15-42, born March 27, 1913, in Syracuse, NY. He enlisted on Feb. 10, 1942, in Albany, NY, and received training on the USS *Orca-NTS* in Newport, RI, and RS Boston. He is a plankowner and served aboard BB-59 as AS 3rd Div. and left BB-59 on June 16, 1945, as GM2/c.

His assignments included RS PSNY Bremerton, WA; USS Orca RS NYD Washington, DC; AATRA and TST Cen, Dam Neck, VA; and USNH Portsmouth, VA. After the war he worked for the US Postal Service. Married Elizabeth and had two sons, three daughters and one step-son. Beach died Jan. 7, 1992. (Mrs.) resides at 8025 Casilina Dr., Clay, NY (1993).

BEAM, BROWSLAS L., served aboard BB-59. He resides in Black Mountain, NC (1966).

BEAN, H., (n) served aboard BB-59. He resides at 1700 Washburn Ave., Topeka, KS (1966).

BEARDEMOHI, JOHN, Memory List 1996

BEARDLSEY, FRANKLIN H., JR., born Oct. 11, 1914, in Philadelphia, PA. He earned a BS in 1938 from West Chester University; attended the University of Pennsylvania, 1938-41 and 1946-1948; New York University, MBA, 1953, MBA degree. Enlisted on Aug. 20, 1941 in the USN V-7 Program in Philadelphia, PA, and in the US Naval Reserve Midshipman School and on the USS *Prairie State* (Columbia University) earning ENS in January 1942.

Assignments included USN Communication School, Noroton Heights, CT, from January 26 to March 28, 1942. He is a plankowner and served aboard the BB-59 as Communications Watch Officer, Quincy, MA, at commissioning May 12, 1942. Left BB-59 on June 14, 1942. From 1942-43 aboard the USS *Big Horn* (a USN "Q" ship) Communication and Div. Officer; 1943-45 USS *PC* 1140 Commanding Officer (LT April 1, 1944); 1945 USS *PCE* ® 858 Commanding Officer (Pacific); 1946 USNH Philadelphia, PA, as Welfare and Recreation Officer. In April 1946, separated from active duty.

Beardsley joined the Naval Reserve in 1951 in Volunteer Indus. Rela. Unit 4-1; 1951-52 Surface Div., April 26 Philadelphia, PA, Commanding Officer; July 1, 1954 (CDR); 1954-55 NRO School, New York, NY, Admin. Office; 1956-59 (NROS 3-8), Elizabeth, NJ, Director; Jan. 1, 1962, CAPT; 1964-65 Naval Reserve Group (5-1) Baltimore, MD, Chairman of Counciling Board and Staff Program Assistant ACDUTRA.

Civilian work: April 1946 to 1952, Ins. Company of North America (CIGNA); 1952-57, American Metal Company LTD (AMAX), personnel director; 1957-59 Great American Ins. Company, personnel director; 1959-65 Commercial Credit Corp., Baltimore, MD, personnel director; 1965-80 Ward Howell Intl. Inc. (executive search bus.), senior partner and director. In his spare time he is part of the No. Jersey Council; president of Navy League, 1992; past president of Exchange Club, Morristown, NJ; past president of New York Personnel Mgt. Assoc.; and Silver Bay Assoc. Human Relations Conference, past chairman. Married Amy Street on Feb. 21, 1942, in Wilmington, DE, and has three children. They reside at 19 Lake Dr. Lake Intervale, Boonton, NJ, 07005 (1993).

BEATON, EDISON H., 606-90-33, born Oct. 2, 1908, in Fall River, MA. Attended Mechanic Arts, Boston & Wentworth Institute. Worked as a turbine operator at Boston Edison before the war. Enlisted on May 15, 1942, in Boston, MA, and served aboard BB-59 as CMM M Div. #1 Engine Room at commissioning May 12, 1942. Left BB-59 in September 1945 as CMM(AA) (T) (CR1/14.5). Beaton was active in the BBBM Campaign as fund-raiser and committee member; a Commander in the Massachusetts Navy and part of 1965 Homecoming Crew. Married Isabelle. Died Aug. 4, 1988. (Mrs.) resides at 1 Sherwood Lane, Apt. #123, Kingston, MA, 02364 (1993).

BEATON, WILLIAM CAMPBELL, 250-27-64, enlisted March 7, 1942, in Pittsburgh, PA. He is a plankowner and served aboard BB-59.

BEATTIE, ALBERT KEIR, 606-41-51, enlisted Feb. 26, 1942, in Boston, MA. He was a plankowner and served aboard BB-59 as SF3/c R Div. at commissioning May 12, 1942. Left BB-59 in September 1943. After the war he worked at the National Press Company as a printer. Was part of BBBM Campaign as LT Cmdr Massachusetts Navy. Beattie died in 1987 and has two daughters. His daughter Ms. Janice Beattie resides at 1051 Orleans Rd., Harwich, MA (1993).

BEAUCHAMP, CURTIS PATRICK, 300-77-90, born March 17, 1924, in Nahma, MI. He enlisted on Jan. 29, 1942, in Chicago, IL, received training at Great Lakes, Chicago, IL. He is a plankowner and served aboard BB-59 as AS 4th Div. at commissioning May 12, 1942. He left BB-59 on March 16, 1946, at Bremerton, WA.

After the war he worked for the Bay de Noc Lumber Company and in 1951 was head painter for American Playground Device Company, Nahma, MI. He married Rose on April 7, 1951, and has 10 children, losing one son at 4 months to pneumonia. He has 14 grandchildren and resides at Box 52, Nahma, MI (1993).

BEAULIEU, HENRY PAUL, 606-46-58, enlisted March 6, 1942, in Boston, MA. He is a plankowner and served aboard BB-59 as AS at commissioning May 12, 1942.

BEBEAU, ARNOLD HAROLD, 300-20-86, enlisted October 16, 1940. He is a plankowner and served aboard BB-59 as S1/c at commissioning May 12, 1942.

BECAN, ARTHUR FRANK, 647-00-85, enlisted Feb. 20, 1942, in New York, NY. He was a plankowner and served aboard BB-59 as AS at commissioning May 12, 1942, and on its 2nd and 3rd anniversaries. Deceased; Memory List 1992.

BECKER, ELLSWORTH, (n), 321-43-23, enlisted June 18, 1940, in Des Moines, IA. He is a plankowner and served aboard BB-59 as EM3/c at commissioning May 12, 1942.

BECKER, JACK HARDING, 224-72-66, born March 24, 1922, in South Bend, IN. Graduated from high school and enlisted on March 6, 1942, in New York, NY. Received training at Quonset Point, RI. He is a plankowner and served aboard BB-59 as AS 1st Div. at commissioning May 12, 1942 and later as QM3/c N Div. He left BB-59 in 1945 at Norfolk, VA. Other assignments included serving aboard the USS Princeton (CV 37) until Jan. 7, 1948. Married Ruth on Sept. 25, 1954, in New Brunswick, NJ. They reside at 250 Crestwood Dr., Milltown, NJ, 08850 (1993).

BECKER, MARLIN ELSWORD, 243-22-18, enlisted March 8, 1939, in Santiago, Cuba. He is a plankowner and served aboard BB-59 as CM1/c at commissioning May 12, 1942.

BECKER, WILLIAM GEORGE, JR., 224-77-43, enlisted March 30, 1942, New York, NY. He is a plankowner and served aboard BB-59 as AS at commissioning May 12, 1942.

BEDARD, HENRY PAUL, 606-36-08, enlisted Feb. 16, 1942, in Boston, MA. He is a plankowner and served aboard BB-59 as AS F Div. at commissioning May 12, 1942, Quincy. Left BB-59 in March 1945 to Fleet Fire Control School at US Naval Repair Base, San Diego, CA, from May 1945 to Aug. 14, 1945. He was discharged Oct. 10, 1945, Boston, MA.

Married Doris Marchand, his school sweetheart from Lowell, MA, on June 27, 1944, at Naval Chapel, Bremerton, WA. It was a double wedding with James C. Murphy of Reading, MA (also of the F Div.). Weddings were performed by BB-59 Chaplain McBlain. After the war worked for the New England Power Company and is involved in the K of C. He has five sons, one daughter and seven grandchildren. They reside at 119 Forest St., Danvers, MA (1993).

BEDNAR, WILLIAM, (n), 658-07-53, enlisted on Nov. 6, 1941, Richmond, VA. He is a plankowner and served aboard BB-59 as S2/c at commissioning May 12, 1942, and was on board May 12, 1944.

BEEBE, DONALD JOSEPH, 316-49-22, enlisted Feb. 16, 1937, in Omaha, NE. He is a plankowner and served aboard BB-59 as GM2/c at commissioning May 12, 1942, and was on board on its 2nd and 3rd anniversaries. In 1945 was CGM FC Div.

BEER, DONALD RAY, 612-03-87, born May 21, 1920, graduated from high school and Ohio State University in 1950. He enlisted on Oct. 26, 1941, in Cincinnati, OH, and trained in Great Lakes, IL. He is a plankowner and served aboard BB-59 as S2/c A Div. at commissioning May 12, 1942. In November 1942 was F2/c and vice-president of CE Group - WT1/c "Oil King." He left BB-59 in September 1945.

After the war became a manufacturing rep. for Hofferberth Machinery Company and a lay minister for the United Church of Christ for 30 years. Married Katherine and has three children and six grandchildren. Memory List 1992. (Mrs.) resides at 878 Rosetree Lane, Cincinnati, OH (1993).

BEGAY, JOHN, JR., 238-65-53, enlisted April 23, 1940, in Albany, NY. He is a plankowner and served aboard BB-59 as S1/c at commissioning May 12, 1942.

BEHREND, LOUIS MICHAEL, JR., 642-13-93, enlisted on Feb. 23, 1942, New Haven, CT. He served aboard BB-59 as AS 6th Div. at commissioning May 12, 1942, and was on board on its 2nd and 3rd anniversaries. He is a plankowner.

BEILKE, ORVILLE RALPH, 610-24-67, enlisted Jan. 2, 1942, in Chicago, IL. He is a plankowner and served aboard BB-59 as S1/c at commissioning May 12, 1942, and was on board May 12, 1945.

BELIVEAU, ROGER L., born Sept. 22, 1920, in Salem, MA. He graduated from Salem High School in 1939 and enlisted in the USMC on April 4, 1940, Boston. He received training at Paris Island, SC; St. Juliens Creek, Naval Ammo, Portsmouth, VA; NOB Norfolk, VA, Navy Yard; Gunnery School Nags Head, VA. Served aboard BB-59 as Pvt. 1/c 7th Capt. Whiting's orderly. Was injured on board after shakedown, Casco Bay, ME.

Transferred to Chelsea Naval Hospital, Chelsea, MA. He is a plankowner. His assignments included: light and heavy machine gun instructor, Stony Bay, NC; Coco Solo Navy Base, Christobal Panama, CZ. After the war he worked for GTE Sylvania Electric Products for 25 years. He married Mabel and has one daughter, two step-daughters, two step-sons and two grandchildren. He resides at 25 Liberty St., Beverly, MA (1993).

BELL, ALEX J., born Dec. 4, 1925, Detroit, MI. Trained at Farragut, ID, for seven or eight weeks. Served aboard BB-59 in May 1944 at Puget Sound and left BB-59 on May 4, 1946, Norfolk, VA. After the war he worked for General Motors as a wood model-maker and retired in 1982 with 32 years of service. In his spare time he plays golf two times a week and does volunteer work. He married Anne and has one son and two granddaughters. He resides at 19194 Kingsville St., Detroit, MI (1993).

BELL, JAMES D., enlisted USMC, May 8, 1942, Norfolk Navy Yard. Served aboard BB-59 as FM 7th Div. at commissioning May 12, 1942, and is a plankowner.

BELL, JESSE FRANKLIN, 111-25-90, enlisted March 12, 1942, Jacksonville, FL. He is a plankowner and served aboard BB-59 as MM2/c at commissioning May 12, 1942.

BENDER, BERNARD B., BBBM Campaign; fund-raiser. Memory List 1992. (Mrs.) resides at 348 Farnum Rd., Rd. 1, Media, PA 19063 (1993).

BENDINGER, WARREN FRED, 321-70-61, enlisted Oct. 8, 1941, Des Moines, IA. He is a plankowner and served aboard BB-59 as S2/c at commissioning May 12, 1942.

BENNETT, GILES JAMES, 600-22-23, enlisted March 19, 1942, Albany, NY. He was a plankowner and served aboard BB-59 as AS on commissioning May 12, 1942, and was on board on May 12, 1944. Memory List 1992.

BENNETT, JOHN ARCHER, 265-85-08, enlisted Dec. 8, 1938, in Richmond, VA. He was plankowner and served aboard BB-59 as S1/c at commissioning May 12, 1942.

BENNETT, LAWRENCE, rode ship from Norfolk, VA, to Fall River, MA.

BENNETT, ROBERT HARGRAVES, 647-26-27, enlisted Feb. 21, 1942, in New York, NY. He was a plankowner and served aboard BB-59 as AS. Memory List 1992.

BENNETT, WALTER EDWARD, 650-26-01, enlisted Feb. 11, 1942, Philadelphia, PA. He is a plankowner and served aboard BB-59 as AS and was on board May 12, 1944. He resides at 4231 Maywood St., Philadelphia, PA (1993).

BENSIE, V.R., served aboard BB-59. He resides at 510 Columbia Ave., Burlington, IA.

BENTEL, CARR EUGENE, served aboard BB-59 from Nov. 24, 1944 to Oct. 1, 1945, as Senior Medical Off. Cmdr. to Capt.

BENZIE, PAUL, (n), 647-02-28, enlisted Feb. 21, 1942, in New York, NY, and served aboard BB-59 as AS at commissioning May 12, 1942, and is a plankowner.

BERGER, ARLIN HENRY, 337-21-38, enlisted on Oct. 18, 1939, in St. Louis, MO. He is a plankowner and served aboard BB-59 as S1/c at commissioning May 12, 1942.

BERGER, CLAY, (no data) resides at 132 Savannah St., Mattapan, MA (1966).

BERGER, DAVID, USN, CHMACH, P Div. and M Div. Served aboard BB-59 from Jan. 1, 1943, to Aug. 21, 1945. Memory List 1992.

BERGERON, JUNIUS PAUL, 1st LT, USMC, served aboard BB-59 from May 18, 1943, to June 14, 1945. He is part of Memory List 1992.

BERGESEN, JOHN CATTO, 224-77-44, enlisted on March 30, 1942, New York, NY. He is a plankowner and served aboard BB-59 as AS at commissioning May 12, 1942, and on BB59's 2nd and 3rd anniversaries.

BERGEVIN, NED HOMER, 375-89-79, enlisted Jan. 6, 1942, in New York, NY. He is a plankowner and served aboard BB-59 as MM2/c at commissioning May 12, 1942.

BERGHAHN, EUGENE AUGUST, 337-23-90, enlisted on Dec. 11, 1939, St. Louis, MO. He is a plankowner and served aboard BB-59 as S1/c at commissioning May 12, 1942.

BERHOW, JAMES OLIVER, 620-33-59, enlisted on Feb. 3, 1942, in Des Moines, IA. He is a plankowner as AS at commissioning, May 12, 1942.

BERKOWICZ, WALTER CARL, 666-16-59, enlisted on Feb. 14, 1942, in Springfield, MA. He received training in Newport, RI, and served aboard BB-59 as AS A Div. at commissioning date May 12, 1942. He left the BB-59 after the treaty and was a plankowner. Married to Agnes and had three children and two grandchildren. Berkowicz is part of Memory List 1992. (Mrs.) resides at 157 Blackstone St., Blackstone, MA (1993).

BERNEY, CARROLL LAVERNE, 648-02-77, born June 13, 1920, in Wolback, NE. Graduated from high school and enlisted on Oct. 9, 1941, in Omaha, NE. He attended USN Machinist School in Dearborn, MI. Berney is a plankowner and served aboard BB-59 as S2/c M&P Div. Left BB-59 at Pearl Harbor during the summer of 1944. He was assigned to APA PICKAWAY.

After the war he returned to the farm and then entered civil service from 1957-80 in soil conservation service and Army Corps of Engineering. In his spare time he played baseball for 20 years as a pitcher for the Legion Baseball. He married Lois Nelson on June 3, 1947, and has two boys. They reside at Rt. 1, Box 78, Clifton Hill, MO (1993).

BERO, THOMAS, (n) 600-13-22, enlisted Feb. 2, 1942, in Albany, NY. He is a plankowner and served aboard BB-59 as AS commissioning date May 12, 1942.

BERRY, DANIEL EDWARD, 202-28-48, enlisted on April 2, 1942, in Boston, MA. He is a plankowner and served aboard BB-59 as AS 3rd Div. at commissioning May 12, 1942. Left BB-59 in November 1945 as a GM2/c Turret 3. After the war became a partner in Hampton Heating Supply, Inc. Was part of the BBBM Campaign as fund raiser in "Massachusetts Navy" RAdmr. Berry has three children and resides at 33 Ryders LA., Marion, MA (1993).

BERRY, PAUL, (no data), Memory List 1992.

BERSIE, VERNON RAY, 321-31-62, enlisted on May 3, 1939, in Des Moines, IA. He is a plankowner and served aboard BB-59 as GM3/c at commissioning May 12, 1942.

BEST, WAYNE ROBERT, 632-25-82, enlisted on Jan. 8, 1942, in Los Angeles, CA. He is a plankowner and served aboard BB-59 as FC3/c at commissioning May 12, 1942.

BETTENCOURT, STEPHEN, (n) 202-26-75, enlisted on March 5, 1942, in Boston, MA. He is a plankowner and served aboard BB-59 as an AS S Div. as a cook, butcher and baker. Left BB-59 at Norfolk, VA (Mothballs). After the war he owned and operated the Wampanoag Diner in E. Providence, RI. Member of the American Legion Post 10. He has three daughters, one son and eight grandchildren. He resides at 192 Vincent Ave., E. Providence, RI (1993).

BETTGER, MILES CHRIST, enlisted on Jan. 3, 1942, at Pearl Harbor. He was a plankowner and served aboard BB-59 as Y3/c E Div. May 12, 1942, and was aboard on May 12, 1944. Was ship's clerk for CY A Div. on June 18, 1944. He resided at LT. P.O. Box 187, Altaville, CA (1993). Memory List 1996.

BEVINS, CLEVELAND, CR Div., resides at P.O. Box 404, Williamson, WV (1993).

BEYL, HARRY L., CBM B Div., served aboard BB59 (no data). On May 3, 1945 he transferred to the USS *Intrepid.*

BEILINSKI, JOHN JOSEPH, 244-07-12, enlisted on March 2, 1942, in Philadelphia, PA. He is a plankowner and served aboard BB-59 as AS at commissioning May 12, 1942.

BIERI, RUBEN VANCE, 341-82-43, enlisted on Nov. 22, 1939, in Lisbon, Portugal. He wa a plankowner and served aboard BB-59 as a CFC (AA) at commissioning May 12, 1942. Memory List 1996..

BISAILLON, GORDON WILSON, 201-61-89, enlisted on Jan. 31, 1938, in Boston, MA. He was a plankowner and served aboard BB-59 as S1/c at commissioning, May 12, 1942. Memory List 1996..

BISAILLON, ROBERT W., born Oct. 15, 1918, in Bourbonnais, IL. He enlisted on March 20, 1942, in Great Lakes, IL. Attended Gunnery School – Armed Guard. Served aboard BB-59 in June 1942 as S1/c 4th Div. and L Div. He left BB-59 at USN R/S Seattle, WA, US Naval Hospital, Bremerton, WA.

After the war he became a carpenter. In his spare time he enjoys gardening and swimming with a local senior's group. He is married to Dorothy and they have three sons, three daughters, 12 grandchildren and six great-grandchildren. They reside at 560 Stockton Heights Drive, Bourbonnais, IL 60914.

BISH, ROBERT, 4th Div. resides at 3500 82nd Ave., Brooklyn Park, MN.

BISHOP, HAROLD PAYNE, 606-36-35, enlisted on Feb. 14, 1942, in Boston, MA. He is a plankowner and served aboard BB-59 as AS at commissioning May 12, 1942, and was on board on 2nd and 3rd anniversaries.

BISHOP, JASPER J. "JACK," 207-38-17, born on March 5, 1925, in Wilmington, NC. He graduated from high school and attended one year of college. He enlisted on March 5, 1942, in New Haven, CT, and received training at Newport, RI. Bishop served aboard BB-59 on April 20, 1942, in Quincy, MA, as AS. Became F1/c Fwd. Emergency Diesel Elec. Engine Room in June 1942. Was in charge of aft emergency diesel electrical engine room air compressors and main drain pipes. Also furnished 3,000 lb. per sq. inch compressed air to blow gases out of 16 inch guns after each firing.

In October 1942 was MM2/c Engineering Force. Ship's electrical hydraulic power steering gear room, plus all hydraulic systems used for operating all 16 inch guns. He left BB-59 in June 1945 during a transfer at sea close to Japan to a freighter to return to USA. His assignments include: GM Diesel Electrical School, Cleveland, OH. From August 1945 to March 1946 served aboard the USS *Itara* as chief engineer (tug boat, Charleston, SC). After the war he worked for Hearshey Steel, Manheim, PA, (March 6, 1946).

He re-enlisted in the USN on April 16, 1946, as MM2/c at Philadelphia Navy Station, USS *Holder* (DD), in charge of engine room. Occupation duty in Italy and Yugoslavia; April 1947 was aboard USS *Witek* (DD) engine room in Cuba, Caribbean, West Indies and Atlantic. He was honorably discharged on Feb. 10, 1948, in Brooklyn, NY.

As a civilian he was outside journeyman machinist from February 1948 to January 1950 for the Harbor

Boat & Yacht Company and the National Steel Ship Building Yard, San Diego, CA. He enlisted in the US Army on Feb. 1, 1950 as corporal, US Marine Base, Camp Pendleton, CA; February 1950 Co. L 4th Inf. Div. Fort Ord, CA; July 1950 HQ 930th Eng. Batt. SFC, E6 (Korean War); Dec. 24, 1951, Off. School/ Eng. Fort Bellvoir, VA; February 1952 (Training Troops) 1st Field Art. 5th Armored Div. Ft. Chaffee, AK; November 1956 740th AAAMSL Bn. Platoon Sgt. – Launcher Platoon – Ft. Scott, CA; December 1957 Aircraft Maint. School. Ft. Rucker, AL; February 1958 Operations Sgt., Ft. Barry, CA (HQ 30th); January 1959 SFC E7 HQ Co., Yukon Comd. APO 731 at Ladd Air Force Base, Fairbanks, AK, Maint. Supv. (Fixed wing aircraft and helicopters); April 1961 Ft. Wainwright, Fairbanks, AK, 1st Sgt. E8 568th TransCoArmyAircraft Heavy Maint./Serv.; April 1963 Ft. Rucker, AL, HQ Co. USAAUNTBD (8605); April 12, 1963, Sgt. Maj. E8 HQ US Army Aviation Test Board (8605); May 1, 1964, Ft. Rucker, AL.

Retired from the US Army as Sgt. Maj. with 20 years service. After retirement he was a member of the US Navy Civil Service 1965 to Sept. 13, 1976. US Naval Air Station, San Diego, CA, plus other Navy sites in California. Was a foreman repair inspector of heavy mobile equipment.

Married to Elsie E. Pratt of Kenosha, WI, and has one daughter, one son and four grandchildren. They reside at 610 Douglas St. Chula Vista, CA 91910-6507 (1993).

BLACK, CHARLES OSCAR, JR., 243-31-00, enlisted on Nov. 19, 1941, in San Francisco, CA. He is a plankowner and served aboard BB-59 as MM1/C A Div. at commissioning May 12, 1942, and was on board May 12, 1944. He left BB-59 on July 13, 1944 as CMM to R/S PSNY in Bremerton, WA.

BLACK, JAMES FYFE, JR., 647-09-89, enlisted on Feb. 20, 1942, in New York, NY. He is a plankowner and served aboard BB-59 as AS at commissioning May 12, 1942, and was on board on its 2nd and 3rd anniversaries.

BLACK, JOSEPH, (n), 647-02-32, born July 7, 1924, in Brooklyn, NY. He graduated from high school and enlisted on Feb. 21, 1942, in New York, NY. Received training in Newport, RI. He is a plankowner and served aboard BB-59 as AS 5th Div. at commissioning May 12, 1942.

Left BB-59 in 1942 after Casablanca to R/S NY to Amph. Tr. Base Portsmouth, VA; LST 386; Amph. Tr. Bs. Little Creek, VA; ATB Ft. Pierce, FL; ATB Camp Bradford, VA; USS *Dorothea L. Dix* USNH Horva R/S Charleston, SC, MTCT Little Creek, VA; R/S Chickasaw, AL; USS *Nucleus;* R/S PSNY Bremerton, WA; R/S NY; R/S San Francisco, CA; R/S Navy 3964; PSC Lido Beach, NY.

After the war he worked for the New York Police Dept. from 1955 to 1979. Married to Julia and has three children and seven grandchildren. They reside at 81-60 261 St., Floral Park, NY (1993).

BLACK, WILEY SMITH, 262-69-26, enlisted on Sept. 28, 1940, Raleigh, NC. He is a plankowner and served aboard BB-59 as SM3/c at commissioning May 12, 1942.

BLACKBURN, CLIFFORD WALTER, 652-25-72, enlisted Aug. 8, 1942, in Pittsburgh, PA. He served aboard BB-59 as AS at commissioning May 12, 1942, and was on board on May 12, 1944. He is a plankowner.

BLACKBURN, HORACE STANLEY, 244-07-98, enlisted on March 4, 1942, in Philadelphia, PA. He is a plankowner and served aboard BB-59 as AS at commissioning May 12, 1942, and was on board on May 12, 1944.

BLACKMAN, LYLE H., Enlisted USMC, May 8, 1942, Norfolk Navy Yard. He was a plankowner and served aboard BB-59 as Pfc. 7th Div. at commissioning May 12, 1952. Memory List 1993.

BLACKWELL, FRED, (n) 647-00-90, enlisted Feb. 20, 1942, in New York, NY. He is a plankowner and served aboard BB-59 as AS at commissioning May 12, 1942.

BLACKWOOD, WALKINSHAW STEVENSON, served aboard BB-59 as ChBosn on May 21, 1944.

BLAIR, HUSTON PAUL, 668-00-32, enlisted on May 27, 1941, in St. Louis, MO. He is a plankowner and served aboard BB-59 as PhM3/c at commissioning May 12, 1942, and was on board on May 12, 1944.

BLAIR, OSCAR TABOR, JR., 205-56-61, born July 20, 1922, in Kepple Hill, PA. He enlisted July 30, 1940, in Pittsburgh, PA, and received training at NTS, Newport, RI. Was stationed aboard the USS *Flusser DD368* and then BB-59 as S1/c 5th Div. at commissioning May 12, 1942. He is a plankowner. Left BB-59 in 1943 off New Caledonia to the USS Tulagi *CVE 72;* Island of Mog Mog, Torpedo Shop, Guam.

After the war he was employed by Allegheny Ludlum Steel Mill for 37 years and was a constable for 12 years. In his spare time he was a volunteer fireman for 45 years; ambulance driver and attendant; Ground Observer Corps USAF, head of airplane spotters, Civil Defense. Was honored as Fireman of the Year. He married Lois on Oct. 16, 1943, and had two sons and 10 grandchildren. They reside at 206 Whitter St., Vandergrift, PA 15690.

BLAIR, RONALD E., CAPT. (no other data). Memory List 1992.

BLAIS, DAVID J., S Div., after the war worked for Walter Lux Landscaping. Married Eva and had 10 children, 20 grandchildren and one great-grandchild. Memory List, 1992. (Mrs.) Blais resides at 15 Apollo Ave., Box 221, Billerica, MA.

BLAIS, FREDERICK LEWIS, 638-11-62, enlisted on Jan. 3, 1942, Minneapolis, MN. He served aboard BB-59 as F2/c at commissioning May 12, 1942, and is a plankowner.

BLANCHETTE, GERALD P., (no data) Memory List 1992.

BLAND, WILLIAM LEE, 266-53-48, enlisted Oct. 11, 1941, in Richmond, VA. He is a plankowner and served aboard BB-59 as S2/c at commissioning May 12, 1942, and was on board on May 12, 1944.

BLANK, ROY BENJAMIN, 652-19-03, enlisted on Feb. 7, 1942, in Pittsburgh, PA. He is a plankowner and served aboard BB-59 as AS at commissioning May 12, 1942.

BLANKENSHIP, CECIL, (n) 295-73-52, enlisted on Aug. 30, 1940, in Nashville, TN. He served aboard BB-59 as S1/c at commissioning May 12, 1942. He is a plankowner.

BLANTON, ARTHUR, (no data) resides at 2003 Park Ave., St. Louis, MO (1966).

BLEDSOE, EARL FRANK, 320-66-96, born July 24, 1909, in Davenport, IA. He enlisted on Jan. 4, 1927, in Des Moines, IA. He received training in Great Lakes, IL in 1927. Assignments include: USS *Macdonough 331*; USS *Southard 209*; Shore Duty at Indianapolis, IN, 1940-41; USS *Casco* from January 1941 to June 1941.

Served aboard BB-59 from June 30, 1941, at Quincy, MA; made BM2/c on May 12, 1942 (he is a plankowner), 4th Div.; made BM1/c MAA and BM1/c L Div. He left BB-59 on July 24, 1942 as warrant officer. He transferred to USS *Butternut* (a net tender). He retired on July 24, 1959 as CWO (commissioned 357010). After the war he worked for Los Angeles County from 1959 to 1980. Married LaRene on Nov. 28, 1957, and resides at 15135 Ashley Glen Dr., Victorville, CA 92392 (1993).

BLOCK, JEROME, enlisted USMC May 8, 1942, at Norfolk Navy Yard. He was a plankowner and served aboard BB-59 as Corp. 7th Div. at commissioning May 12, 1942.

BLOODGOOD, CHARLES FRANCIS, 646-82-33, enlisted on Feb. 19, 1942, in New York, NY. He is a plankowner and served aboard BB-59 as AS at commissioning May 12, 1942, and was on board on its 2nd and 3rd anniversaries.

BLOODGOOD, STANLEY LEON, 223-78-70, enlisted on Aug. 8, 1940, at New York, NY. He is a plankowner and served aboard BB-59 as F2/c at commissioning May 12, 1942.

BLOOM, PHILLIP, (n) 606-H6-99, enlisted on March 4, 1942, in Boston, MA. He served aboard BB-59 as AS at commissioning date May 12, 1942. He is a plankowner.

BLOUIN, WALTER PETER, 600-20-92, enlisted on March 12, 1942, in Albany, NY. He served aboard BB-59 as AS at commissioning May 12, 1942, and was on board on its 2nd and 3rd anniversaries. He is a plankowner.

BLYSKAL, JOSEPH JAMES, 650-31-75, enlisted on Feb. 21, 1942, in Philadelphia, PA. He was a plankowner and served aboard BB-59 as AS at commissioning May 12, 1942, and was on board on its 2nd and 3rd anniversaries. Memory List 1996..

BLYTHE, JAMES ANTHONY, 224-77-77, born Aug. 2, 1924, in Woodside, NY. Graduated from Newtown High School, Elmhurst, NY, and enlisted on March 31, 1942, in New York, NY. Received training at Newport, RI. He is a plankowner and served aboard BB-59 as AS 3rd Div., S2/c, S1/c, COX Gun Capt. Left Gun Turret 3. He left BB-59 on Oct. 1, 1945, Lido Beach, LI, NY.

After the war he worked for the American Stage Equipment Company, Manhattan; and owner of Blythe Iron Works, Miller Place, NY. In his spare time he was past president of the Chamber of Commerce; VFW Rocky Point, NY; past president of NY Ornamental Metals Assoc., Long Island Chapter. Married Katherine on June 29, 1946, and has three children and six grandchildren.

BOATES, JACK, (no data) resides at 97 Florence St., Brockton, MA (1992).

BOATMAN, ALEC CARSON, 346-88-86, enlisted Dec. 17, 1940, Little Rock, AR. He served aboard BB-59 as S1/c at commissioning May 12, 1942, and is a plankowner.

BOATRIGHT, HAROLD MOMON, served aboard BB-59, Oct. 27, 1943, CPC S Div. and on May 12, 1944, as a member of the Anniversary Committee. He left BB-59 on Jan. 12, 1946.

BOBEL, JOSEPH, 647-00-91, born in Carteret, NJ, graduated from high school and attended one year of college. He enlisted on Feb. 20, 1942, in New York, NY. Received training at Newport, RI, and served aboard BB-59 as AS S Div. at commissioning May 12, 1942. He left BB-59 in October 1945 in Seattle, WA, as SK1/c. He is a plankowner. After the war he was employed as a purchasing assistant to sales manager. Married Helen in 1950 and has one son and two granddaughters. They reside at 19 Tennyson St., Carteret, NJ.

BOCACCIO, GEORGE C., Enlisted USMC May 8, 1942, at Norfolk Navy Yard. He is a plankowner and served aboard BB-59 as Pvt. 7th Div. at commissioning May 12, 1942.

BOEH, GERARD JOSEPH, 652-25-66, born Sept. 1, 1922, in Pittsburgh, PA. He graduated from high school and enlisted on March 8, 1942, in Pittsburgh, PA. Received training at Newport, RI, and is a plankowner. He served aboard BB-59 as AS L Div. at commissioning May 12, 1942. Left BB-59 in November 1945 at Bremerton, WA. Married Mildred on June 22, 1946, in Pittsburgh. They have four children (one deceased) and four grandchildren. They reside at 139 Meade Ave., Pittsburgh, PA (1993).

BOESIGNER, DAVID ORVILLE, 648-16-46, born in Cortland, NE, and graduated from high school. He enlisted on Feb. 2, 1942, in Omaha, NE, and received training at Great Lakes, IL. He is a plankowner and served aboard BB-59 as AS 4th Div. at commissioning May 12, 1942.

Left BB-59 in November 1943 at Bremerton, WA, and went to machine gun school, Tacoma, WA. Then to Astoria, OR, and was assigned to the aircraft carriers USS Tulagi and USS *Munda.*

Married Jean Drent on Nov. 19, 1943, at Navy Chapel, Bremerton, WA. They reside at Box 35, Clatonia, NE 68328 (1993) and have four children and eight grandchildren. He returned to farming and raising livestock after the war.

BOGEN, HERBERT LOUIS, 642-14-03, enlisted Feb. 24, 1942, in New Haven, CT. He served aboard BB-59 as AS at commissioning May 12, 1942, and was on board on its 2nd and 3rd anniversaries. He is a plankowner.

BOHACK, JOSEPH, (n) 650-31-67, enlisted Feb. 21, 1942, in Philadelphia, PA. He was a plankowner and served aboard BB-59 as AS at commissioning May 12, 1942, and was on board on its 2nd and 3rd anniversaries. Memory List 1992.

BOHAR, WILLIAM T., born Sept. 6, 1922, in Cementon, PA. He enlisted Sept. 17, 1942, in Philadelphia, PA. Training was at Newport, RI and Diesel School, Richmond, VA. He served aboard BB-59 in December 1942; April 1, 1944, as MoMM2/c A Div.; Sept. 16, 1946 as MoMM1/c.

He left the BB-59 in December 1945 in San Francisco, CA, and was part of Operation "Crossroads" (nuclear bomb tests); was stationed on the USS

Rockwall APA 230, USS Oklahoma City CL91 and the USS Shangri-La CV 38, Sub Grp. One.

After the war he was employed at Bethlehem Steel Company in Bethlehem, PA, Structural Steel Rolling Mill. He married Anne on May 1, 1947, in Northampton, PA. They reside at 203 W. 33rd St., Northampton, PA (1993).

BOHE, ELMER ELBANUS, 328-74-48, enlisted Sept. 10, 1940, at St. Paul, MN. He is a plankowner and served aboard BB-59 as S1/c at commissioning May 12, 1942. He resides in Fort Rice, ND (1966).

BOLAND, "C" "B" JR., 274-71-66, enlisted Sept. 25, 1941, in New Orleans, LA. He is a plankowner and served aboard BB-59 as Bkr3/c at commissioning May 12, 1942. He resides at 5455 16th Ave. Apt. T-3, Hyattsville, MD (1966).

BOLOCK, JOSEPH, (no data) resides at 308 Bradford St., Wilmington, DE (1966).

BOLT, WILBUR REED, 234-13-77, enlisted Dec. 11, 1941, at Pearl Harbor. He is a plankowner and served aboard BB-59 at commissioning May 12, 1942, and was on board on May 12, 1944.

BOLTON, FRANK HARTWELL, born Feb. 25, 1918, in Nashville, TN. Graduated from E. Nashville High School; Peabody College with a BS, 1941; CAA Flight Training, Vanderbilt University; Nashville Flying School, 1942; Grad Studies Middle Tennessee State College, 1951-53. Joined the Navy on Feb. 2, 1942, Naval Air Corps, Atlanta, GA, and attended NAS Jacksonville, FL, Nov. 17, 1942. Served aboard BB-59 as ENS V Div. April 2, 1943. In the Pacific was "down at sea" (rescued). In March 1944 was LT(jg).

Left BB-59 on Oct. 11, 1944, and joined the USS Guadeloupe (AO32); Oct. 18, 1944, served aboard the USS Mauna Loa (AE8); NAS Alameda, CA; Dec. 12, 1944, NAS Pensacola, FL, multi-engine training; May 1, 1945, LT; May 21, 1945, NAS Jacksonville, FL; Aug. 11, 1945, Patrol Bombing Squad 91, Seattle, WA; inactive duty, Dec. 12, 1945. Worked as deputy, Tennessee State Employment Dept. from January 1946 to May 1946; recruitment officer, VA Hospital, Murfreesboro, TN, from May 1946 to January 1949, later served as assistant personnel; personnel officer, for the same VA Hospital; April 1954, held a number of positions in the USDA – ASCS offices in Cincinnati, Minneapolis and Washington DC.

In his spare time he serves on the Board of Deacons, Presbyterian Church; International Exchange Club; Masonic Lodge; American Legion and board of directors of Cincinnati Chapter Personnel Admin. He married Ruth A. Crump, ENS NNC, NAS Pensacola, FL, Dec. 12, 1945. They have one son and three daughters and seven grandchildren. Bolton passed away; Memory List 1992. (Mrs.) Bolton resides at 6814 Bluefield CT., Springfield, VA, 22152.

BOMBA, MICHAEL ALEX, 238-84-52, enlisted March 4, 1942, Albany, NY. He is a plankowner and served aboard BB-59 as AS at commissioning May 12, 1942.

BONDE, GORDON RALPH, 368-69-95, enlisted Oct. 7, 1941, in Salt Lake City, UT. He is a plankowner and served aboard BB-59 as S2/c at commissioning May 12, 1942.

BONEKEMPER, R.C., served aboard BB-59 as LT(jg) 4th Div. July 1942.

BONER, GEORGE, Memory List, 1992, resided at 5768 Penn Ave. Detroit, MI (1966).

BONHAGE, WILLIAM, (n) 258-25-57, enlisted Nov. 2, 1939, in Baltimore, MD. He is a plankowner and served aboard BB-59 as F1/c at commissioning May 12, 1942.

BONN, HUGH EDWARD, 647-00-92, enlisted Feb. 20, 1942, in New York, NY. He is a plankowner and served aboard BB-59 as AS at commissioning May 12, 1942.

BOOHER, HAROLD EDWIN, 342-64-44, born April 27, 1924, in Hooser, KS. Graduated from high school and enlisted on Dec. 12, 1940, Wichita, KS. He received training at Great Lakes, IL. He served aboard BB-59 in L Div. at commissioning May 12, 1942; Qm2/c N Div. Left BB-59 in September 1945, Bremerton, WA. He was a plankowner

After the war Booher worked on the Santa Fe train crew; Struthers Thermo-Flood Steel Fabrication for 33 years and Commandar Laraby Flour Mills. Married Betty on Oct. 30, 1928; died Dec. 22, 1989. They have three children, eight grandchildren and four great-grandchildren. Resides at RR4, Box 308, Arkansas City, KS.

BORUSIEWCZ, WALTER EUGENE, 647-00-93, enlisted on Feb. 20, 1942, in New York, NY. He is a plankowner and served aboard BB-59 as AS at commissioning May 12, 1942.

BOSHEARS, FRED ADAMS, 295-40-81, enlisted Jan. 18, 1938, in Nashville, TN. He is a plankowner and served aboard BB-59 as S1/c at commissioning May 12, 1942, and was on board on its 2nd and 3rd anniversaries.

BOTKA, ALEXANDER GUS, 224-77-45, enlisted on March 30, 1942, in New York, NY. He is a plankowner and served aboard BB-59 as AS A Div. at commissioning May 12, 1942. Memory List 1992. (Mrs.) Botka resides 5655 North 9th Ave. P-207, Pensacola, FL 32504.

BOTHNER, RAYMOND MOYER, 244-07-99, enlisted March 4, 1942, in Philadelphia, PA. He is a plankowner and served aboard BB-59 as AS at commissioning May 12, 1942.

BOUDREAUX, DAVID ELIRICE, 341-72-88, enlisted Feb. 6, 1942, in San Diego, CA. He served aboard BB-59 as a GM1/c at commissioning May 12, 1942, and is a plankowner.

BOURASSA, ADRIEN AMIE, 606-49-06, enlisted March 11, 1942, in Boston, MA. He served aboard BB-59 as AS at commissioning May 12, 1942, and is a plankowner. He resides at 242 Newport Ave., Rumford, RI (1966).

BOUTON, WILLIAM HOLMES, 662-22-61, enlisted Dec. 29, 1941, in San Francisco, CA. He is a plankowner and served aboard BB-59 as Mus2/c at commissioning May 12, 1942.

BOWEN, PERRY EUGENE, 283-56-02, enlisted June 9, 1941, in Cleveland, OH. He is a plankowner and served aboard BB-59 as HA1/c at commissioning May 12, 1942, and was on board on May 12, 1944.

BOWEN, REGINALD INGRAM, 262-98-67, enlisted Nov. 4, 1941, in Raleigh, NC. He is a plankowner and served aboard BB-59 as EM3/C at commissioning May 12, 1942, and was on board on May 12, 1944.

BOWERMAN, RICHARD H., born April 29, 1917, Newark, NJ. BA degree, Yale University 1939; LLB Yale University, 1942; Hon Doc of Laws Uni-

versity of New Haven, 1982. Commissioned ENS June 1939, Yale NROTC. Assigned CNO in Washington DC, Aug. 4, 1941-June 1, 1942. Aboard BB-59 June 8, 1942 as LT(jg) 4th Div.; L Div., Off as LT July 1942, transferred to Staff of Combat Div. 8 as Ass't Op. Off. May 8, 1943. Flag LT; Flag Sec'y., Op. Off. as Lt. Comdr. Left BB-59 April 21, 1945 at sea off Okinawa to become Chief of Staff Cru. Div. 20. November 1945 awarded Bronze Star for outstanding work in five bombardments of Japanese Territory. Retired as Capt. USNR.

After the war he was a member of the firm of Tyler, Cooper, Grant, Bowerman & Keefe, New Haven, CT. Was active in Bar Assoc. work; founder of Young Lawyers of Connecticut 1949; National Chairman ABA Young Lawyers Div., 1953; Ass't Sec'y and Member House of Delegates ABA, 1954; President Conecticut Bar Association, 1964. Chairman of the Board and CEO Southern Connecticut Gas Co. and Connecticut Energy Corp., 1969-88; Chairman N.E. Gas Assoc., 1974. Chairman Yale-New Haven Hospital; Science Park, New Haven and Quinnipack Council of Boy Scouts.

Bowerman married Frances Whitney March 7, 1942, and has one son and two daughters. They reside at 830 Bayberry Lane, Orange, CT. He is the associate editor of this book.

BOWIE, GORDON H., Memory List 1996.

BOWMAN, HARRIS J., born July 8, 1915, in Downey, Bannod County, ID. Graduated from high school and enlisted March 23, 1944, in Boise, ID. Received training at the Naval Center, Farragut, ID. Bowman served aboard BB-59 in April 1944 and left BB-59 on Dec. 2, 1945 at Bremerton, WA.

After the war he was employed with Union Pacific Railroad for 39 years. In his spare time he is active in church work, LDS Temple in Idaho Falls, ID. He has three children and eight grandchildren. He resides at 204 Randolph Ave., Pocatello, ID, during the summer months. From November to May 1, he resides in Quartzsite, AZ. Because of a cardiac problem in 1984, which left Harris with only half a heart; he cannot breathe in the cold air of Idaho.

BOWMAN, HENRY CLAY, 346-37-70, enlisted July 7, 1938, in San Diego, CA. He is a plankowner and served aboard BB-59 as CY X Div. at commissioning May 12, 1942, and was on board on May 12, 1944. He left BB-59 on July 14, 1944, to Comdt 13th Naval District.

BOWMAN, K.L., Served onboard BB-59 as AOM3/c V Div. March 8, 1943, transferred to Comdt. Fleet Air in Noumea ("Ken"). Moved from Bayyard, NE (1967) (no other data).

BOWMAN, WARREN EUGENE, 610-07-69, enlisted Oct. 16, 1941, in Chicago, IL. He was a plankowner and served aboard BB-59 as S2/c at commissioning May 12, 1942, and was on board on its 2nd and 3rd anniversaries. On May 12, 1945 was MM2/c (M Div. Capt.). Memory List 1992.

BOYD, GILBERT JOHN, 650-25-94, enlisted Feb. 11, 1942, in Philadelphia, PA. He served aboard BB-59 as AS at commissioning May 12, 1942, and is a plankowner.

BOYD, JOHN WILLIAM, JR., 268-33-81, enlisted March 30, 1942, in Boston, MA. He is a plankowner and served aboard BB-59 as BM2/c at commissioning May 12, 1942.

BOYD, WILLIAM HOWARD, 201-58-22, enlisted March 16, 1942, in Boston, MA. He is a plankowner and served aboard BB-59 as SK2/c at commissioning May 12, 1942.

BOYER, HARRY, was aboard BB-59 in 1945, West Coast to Norfolk, VA.

BOYLE, JAMES VINCENT, 606-44-12, enlisted March 6, 1942, in Boston, MA. He served aboard BB-59 as AS at commissioning May 12, 1942, and left BB-59 in October 1945 as S1/c. He is a plankowner. After the war he worked for Raytheon Mfg. Precision Grinder and resides in Lunenberg, MA (1966). He has three children.

BOYLE, ROBERT L., resides at Dorchester, MA (1966) and has four children.

BOYLE, ROYCE RAYMOND, 337-06-08, enlisted Dec. 17, 1941, at Pearl Harbor. He is a plankowner, served aboard BB-59 as S1/c on commission May 12, 1942, and was on board on its 2nd and 3rd anniversaries.

BRACKEN, DONALD JAMES, 321-50-03, enlisted Oct. 22, 1940, in Des Moines, IA. He is a plankowner and served aboard BB-59 as SK3/c at commissioning May 12, 1942.

BRADFORD, J.D., resides at Box 91, Kellyville, OK (1966).

BRADLEY, PHILIP H., after the war he worked for IBM Corp. and resides at 110 Hampshire Rd., Wellesley Hill, MA (1966). He has three children.

BRADY, LEWIS HAWLMAN, 267-63-22, enlisted on Jan. 8, 1942, in Birmingham, AL. He is a plankowner and served aboard BB-59 as MM2/c at commissioning May 12, 1942.

BRADY, ROBERT JOSEPH, 224-78-52, enlisted April 2, 1942, in New York, NY. He is a plankowner and served aboard BB-59 as AS X Div. at commissioning May 12, 1942, and was on board on May 12, 1944, as S1/c 1st Div. Resided at Lombardo Ave., Freeport, NY (1992). Mail returned (1993). Memory List 1996.

BRADY, TERRANCE PATRICK, 224-78-12, enlisted on April 1, 1942, in New York, NY. He is a plankowner and served aboard the BB-59 as AS at commissioning May 12, 1942, and was on board on its 2nd and 3rd anniversaries. Received note from Terry's mom, Mrs. Anna C. Orr, informing us that Terry died Jan. 19, 1963 (Rockaway Beach, NY.)

BRAMLEY, RAY ALVIN, 393-09-95, enlisted Jan. 3, 1942, in San Francisco, CA. He is a plankowner and served aboard BB-59 as MM1/c at commissioning May 12, 1942.

BRANCO, HENRY THOMAS, 376-29-86, enlisted April 2, 1941, in San Francisco, CA. He is a plankowner and served aboard BB-59 as S1/c at commissioning May 12, 1942.

BRAND, WALTER EUGENE, 258-19-68, enlisted March 25, 1942, Boston, MA. He is a plankowner and served aboard BB-59 as MM2/c at commissioning May 12, 1942, and on March 8, 1943, transferred to ComSerForSoPac.

BRANDON, W.G., served aboard BB-59 in January 1943 as ENS F Div.

BRAUSS, NORMAN ROBERT, S2/c, received Meritorious Mast, May 12, 1942.

BREEZE, RANDALL MYRON, 282-95-43, enlisted Oct. 31, 1935, Philadelphia, PA. He is a plankowner and served aboard BB-59 as BM1/c at commissioning May 12, 1942.

BRETTENBACH, CARL GRAFF, 113-08-74, served aboard BB-59 as CGM X Div. at commissioning May 12, 1942, and was aboard on its 2nd and 3rd anniversaries. He is a plankowner. Resided at Cristobal, Canal Zone (1966). Memory List 1992.

BRENNAN, E.L., (no data).

BRENNAN, PHILIP LEO, 650-31-47, enlisted Feb. 21, 1942, in Philadelphia, PA. He is a plankowner and served aboard BB-59 as AS at commissioning May 12, 1942, and was on board on its 2nd and 3rd anniversaries.

BRENNAN, THOMAS CHRISTOPHER, 606-49-30, enlisted March 12, 1942, in Boston, MA. He is a plankowner and served aboard the BB-59 as AS at commissioning date, May 12, 1942, and was on board on its 2nd and 3rd anniversaries.

BRENZ, GEORGE EDWARD, 600-05-89, enlisted Jan. 4, 1942, Albany NY. He is a plankowner and served aboard BB-59 as AS at commissioning May 12, 1942.

BRIDGES, RALPH, (n) 337-65-00, enlisted July 14, 1941, St. Louis, MO. He is a plankowner and served aboard BB-59 as Matt3/c at commissioning May 12, 1942.

BRIGGS, HENRY ISAAC, 337-35-46, enlisted Aug. 20, 1940, and served aboard BB-59 as SK3/c at commissioning May 12, 1942. He is a plankowner.

BRISCUSO, AMLETO JOHN, 603-03-05, enlisted Sept. 25, 1941, Washington, DC. He is a plankowner and served aboard BB-59 as Yeo3/c at commissioning May 12, 1942.

BRISSON, REGINALD JOSEPH, 66-19-87, enlisted March 6, 1942, in Springfield, MA. He is a plankowner and served aboard BB-59 as AS at commissioning May 12, 1942.

BRITT, ROBERT THOMAS, 647-02-35, enlisted Feb. 21, 1942, in New York, NY. He is a plankowner and served aboard BB-59 as S1/c 3rd Div. at commissioning May 12, 1942, and was on board on its 2nd and 3rd anniversaries. Left the BB-59 in December 1945.

After the war he worked as a US Government Administrative Officer. He has one daughter and one son. Memory List 1992. (Mrs.) resides at 283 Proctor Ave. Revere, MA.

BRITTEN, CLARENCE ERNEST, 223-64-03, enlisted Jan. 23, 1940, New York, NY. He is a plankowner and served aboard BB-59 as F1/c at commissioning May 12, 1942, and was on board on its 2nd and 3rd anniversaries.

BRITTON, ROBERT ELWIN, served aboard BB-59 in June 1944 as PhM2/c H Div. Left the BB-59 in October 1944 as an X-ray Tech. After the war he worked for Western Engineers Inc. Refrigeration Engineer. In his spare time he belongs to the ABA and

Aircraft Owners & Pilots Assoc. He has two sons and resides at 5330 SW 87th St., Portland, OR (1966).

BRODERICK, WALTER SAMUEL, 201-53-70, enlisted Dec. 9, 1941, Pearl Harbor. He is a plankowner and served aboard BB-59 as S1/c at commissioning May 12, 1942.

BROEKSTRA, ROBERT STANLEY, served aboard BB-59 as LT(jg) CR Div. on July 14, 1944, and left on Jan. 25, 1946.

BROMM, ROBERT, (n) enlisted Dec. 16, 1940, in St. Louis, MO. He is a plankowner and served aboard BB-59 as F2/c at commissioning May 12, 1942.

BROOKS, GEORGE OTHA, 359-67-67, enlisted April 3, 1942, San Francisco, CA. He is a plankowner and served aboard BB-59 as CBM at commissioning May 12, 1942.

BROOKS, RUSSELL BURNERD, 393-36-67, enlisted June 18, 1940, in Portland, OR. He served aboard BB-59 as S1/c at commissioning May 12, 1942. He is a plankowner.

BROOM, VAIL THERON, 337-37-86, enlisted Sept. 10, 1940, St. Louis, MO. He is a plankowner and served aboard BB-59 as S1/c at commissioning May 12, 1942.

BROUGHTON, CHESTER, (n) 287-43-47, enlisted Aug. 20, 1940, Louisville, KY. He is a plankowner and served aboard BB-59 as S1/c at commissioning May 12, 1942.

BROWDER, RICHARD ARNOLD, 224-77-46, enlisted March 30, 1942, New York, NY. He is a plankowner and served aboard BB-59 in 3rd Div. at commissioning May 12, 1942. He resides at 68 Bayside Place, Amityville, NY.

BROWN, JOHN A., resided at 1444 N. 4th St. Apt. 9, Columbus, OH, in 1956. In 1957 was in charge of USS *Washington* 3rd reunion in July 1957 in New York City. Last place of residence was P.O. Box 362, Nelsonville, OH. Memory List 1996..

BROWN, LOREN BURTON, 632-27-41, enlisted on Jan. 10, 1942, in Los Angeles, CA. He is a plankowner and served aboard BB-59 as C.SP at commissioning May 12, 1942.

BROWN, L.F., (no data) resides 1240 3rd St. NW, Cedar Rapids, IA (1966).

BROWN, ROBERT N., born Feb. 23, 1921, in Old Westbury, NY. Graduated from high school and attended Harvey School, Choate and Columbia. Enlisted in the USMC with training at Parris Island. He served aboard BB-59 as Pvt. 1/c 7th Div. After the war was president of Bob Brown Color Labs NYC, 1957-70 (color printing). Between 1970-80 became a sales rep. for Tru-Color-Greenfield, MA. His spare time was spent as treasurer and coach of Franklin County Hockey Assoc.; general manager of Mohawk Men's Hockey Team, Greenfield.

Married Florence in 1955 in Yonkers, NY and had six children and 11 grandchildren. He died on Sept. 7, 1990, after suffering from kidney failure, but with the help of dialysis, he kept up with his hobby of woodworking. Lived in Florida for three years. (Mrs.) resides

31 D Country Club Dr., New Smyrna Beach, FL 82168 (1993).

BRUGERE, LESTER, born Dec. 22, 1925, in St. Louis, MO. A high school graduate with training at an electronics school, he enlisted in March 1944. Received training at Farragut, ID. Brugere served aboard the BB-59 as F2/c M Div. in May 1944. He left BB-59 in January 1946 and went to USS *Logan* for two months on LCS ship. Took into mothballing in Astoria, OR.

After the war he owned a TV repair business for 12 years. Worked for Montgomery Ward TV repair for two years and Monsanto electronic division for 27 and a half years. He retired in 1991. Was also a volunteer for 4-H. Married Marie June 24, 1950, in St. Louis, MO, and they have three daughters, one son, five grandsons and one granddaughter. They reside at 15 Doris, Rt. 1, O'Fallon, MO.

BRUM, VICTOR CARL, 201-84-89, born April 3, 1923, in Lawrence, MA. Graduated from high school and received a master's and doctorate at George Washington University Medical School. He enlisted on Dec. 19, 1940, in Boston, MA. He served aboard BB-59 in January 1942 in Quincy, MA, as H Div. HA1/c. Left BB-59 on April 12, 1943, as PhM3/c to the USS *Casablanca* (CVE 550) PhM2/c; Officers Training, Dartmouth College. He is a plankowner and part of Homecoming Crew June 8-13, 1965.

After the war went to VA Hospital, Medical Research, 1953-76. Taught medical courses and consultation in Medical Research Techniques in Brazil. Brum is also a partner in the Americas Clinical Assistance and medical training in Nayal, Brazil. He married Jean in Methuen, MA, on July 25, 1953 (she died in 1983). They have two daughters, one son and three grandchildren. Resides at 16 Tracy St., Augusta, ME (1993).

BRUNJES, GEORGE J., Enlisted in USMC, May 8, 1942, Norfolk Navy Yard. He served aboard BB-59 as Pvt. 7th Div. at commissioning May 12, 1942. He is a plankowner.

BRUSHELL, VERTILL I., Enlisted in USMC, May 8, 1942, Norfolk Navy Yard. He is a plankowner and served aboard BB-59 as Pvt. 7th Div. at commissioning May 12, 1942.

BRYAN, JOSEPH, III, born April 30, 1904, in Richmond, VA. Graduated from high school and received AB from Princeton University, 1927. He joined the Navy in 1942 with training at Washington, DC, at NAS Quonset Point, RI. Prior to BB-59 he was with COMAIRSOWESPAC and COMSOPAC as lieutenant, March 1942. Served aboard BB-59 with COMBATDIV-8 as Asst. Flag Sec, Asst. Gunner, Staff, LCDR, August 1943-Oct. 1, 1943. After the war he worked as a free-lance writer. He married Elizabeth Mayo Atkinson (McIntosh), Joppa, MD (1991). He had three children, six grandchildren and two great-grandchildren. He resided at 5301 Brook Rd., Richmond, VA. Memory List 1996.

BRYAN, JOSEPH E., born April 2, 1926, Roxbury, MA. Attended Boston Public schools, Newman Prep. and Massasoit Community College. Enlisted June 9, 1943, in Boston, MA, and received training at NTS Newport, RI. Prior to BB-59, he served aboard USS *Alabama.* He served aboard BB-59 as S2/c 6th Div. in October 1943 and left BB-59 in January 1946 as GM3/c, Bremerton, WA.

After the war he worked as a salesman for Jordan Marsh and as a real estate broker. Was active in the Retail Clerks Union, Local 1291 as president and was vice-president of the same union after it merged with Food & Commercial Workers Union. In his spare time he was active as Grand Knight in K of C, 1966-67. Married Dorothy on June 30, 1946, in St. Patrick's Church, Roxbury, MA. They have one son and five daughters and 10 grandchildren. They reside at 52 Russell Rd., Whitman, MA.

BUCELLO, SEBASTIAN, (n)642-13-82, enlisted Feb. 21, 1942, New Haven, CT. He is a plankowner and served aboard BB-59 as AS at commissioning May 12, 1942, and was on board on its 2nd and 3rd anniversaries.

BUCHAN, MARION L., LT, Commanding Officer from Jan. 4, 1947 to March 27, 1947.

BUCHANNAN, DONALD, (no data) resides at 2917 West Jenkins Ave., Sandusky, OH 44870 (1993).

BUCHANNAN, JAMES JOSEPH, 342-28-78, enlisted Sept. 17, 1940, in Kansas City, MO. He is a plankowner and served aboard BB-59 as S1/c at commissioning May 12, 1942. He resides at 8020 Meadow St., Kansas City, MO (1966).

BUCKLEY, JOHN, (n) 600-15-59, born April 2, 1920, in Binghamton, NY. He enlisted Feb. 10, 1942, in Albany, NY, and received training in Newport, RI. He served aboard BB-59 as AS B Div. at commissioning May 12, 1942, and in 1943 as WT1/c B Div. He is a plankowner.

He left BB-59 in May 1945 at sea, transferred to Ships Boiler Engineer Course in Philadelphia, PA. In 1965 attempted to become a "Ship Rider" on "Homecoming Trip" but employer would not give the time. Later became a member of "Field Day" gang, along with "Skip" Sande, they re-commissioned # 1 Engine fire room. They replaced all missing equipment gauges and name plates and repainted. Was aboard eight or nine field days to finish.

After the war he worked for New York State and Electric and Gas Company as a switchboard operator at Goudey Station. Worked in the Power Plant for 38 years. In his spare time he loves to bowl and has built two homes. He married Dorothy at St. Paul's Church in Binghamton, NY, on June 5, 1944. He has two sons, one daughter and four grandchildren. They reside at 38 Hayes Rd., Binghamton, NY.

BUCKLEY, RALPH TIMOTHY, 606-48-71, enlisted March 10, 1942, in Boston, MA. He was a plankowner and served aboard BB-59 as AS at commissioning May 12 1942, and was on board on its 2nd and 3rd anniversaries.

BUFFUM, JOHN PHILBRICK, 600-08-88, enlisted on Jan. 11, 1942, in Albany, NY. He is a plankowner and served aboard BB-59 as EM2/c at commissioning May 12, 1942, and was on board on its 2nd and 3rd anniversaries as CEM E Div.

BUFORD, E. CLIFFORD, B Div., Memory List 1977. (Mrs.) resides in Woodville, GA 30670.

BUIE, G.F., JR., AerogM1/c, March 11, 1943, transferred from V to N Div.

BUKOVSKY, JOSEPH FRANK, 610-62-69, enlisted on Feb. 11, 1942, in Chicago, IL. He served aboard BB-59 as AS at commissioning May 12, 1942. He is a plankowner.

BULL, THOMAS, Memory List 1986.

BULLARD, JOHN RUDOLPH, 244-10-84, enlisted March 31, 1942, in Philadelphia, PA. He is a plankowner and served aboard BB-59 as AS at commissioning May 12, 1942.

BULLIS, HARVEY CHARLES, 642-14-00, enlisted Feb. 24, 1942, in New Haven, CT. He is a plankowner and served aboard BB-59 as AS at commissioning May 12, 1942, and was on board on its 2nd and 3rd anniversaries.

BULLOCK, JOHN EARL, 291-55-07, born April 20, 1919, in New Harmony, IN. Took Gen. Apt. Test and attended Navy E. College for two years. Enlisted on May 24, 1938, in Indianapolis, IN. Received training in Great Lakes, IL.

Served aboard USS *Maryland BB-46* and was assigned to BB-59 on the way back from Pearl Harbor (December 1941) to advanced Gunnersmate School Washington Gun Factory to Fargo Barracks, April 12, 1942. He was a plankowner and served aboard the BB-59 as GM2/c 5th Div. 5" GM1/c and CGM. Left the BB-59 on Sept. 16, 1945, at Tokyo Harbor and was discharged Oct. 1, 1945.

After the war was BB-59 fund raiser and field day worker; Jack Madden Ford Sales as a mechanic 1966;1970 to Fitzmaurice - Lincoln, Mercury and Mazda. He is still working (1993). He married Claire on March 2, 1946, in Boston. They have three sons and three grandsons. He resided at 404 West St., Randolph, MA. Memory List 1997.

BULMER, PAUL ABBOT, 647-00-97, enlisted Feb. 20, 1942, in New York, NY. He is a plankowner and served aboard BB-59 as AS at commissioning May 12, 1942, and was on board on its 2nd and 3rd anniversaries in 4th and S Div. Left BB-59 in January 1945 as SK3/c. After the war worked for Met Life Ins. Company in the publication division and is a member of the volunteer fire department in Glen Ridge, NJ. He has three children. Part of Memory List, 1993.

BURCHART, HENRY A., 644-21-86, born Jan. 21, 1920, in New Orleans, LA. He graduated from high school and enlisted on his birthday, in New Orleans. Training at Great Lakes for two weeks and Ford Carpenters School for 14 weeks, CM3/c. He served aboard the BB-59 in June 1942 as R Div. CM3/c; 1943 CM2/c and in 1944 as CM1/c R Div. Left BB-59 in 1945 in Bremerton, WA, transferred for discharge at NAS.

After the war founded Design Kitchens, Inc., as partner. Designed and built plastic kitchen cabinets; sold the business and retired in 1982. In his spare time he was a Scoutmaster for 12 years; a member of the AARP Chapter # 3757, held all offices and is still active; tax aid for the elderly for eight years; received AARP National Community Service Award and Lions Club Civic Award for Scouting; and a member of American Legion Post #366. He has two sons and four grandchildren. He resides at 12 Hermitage Dr., Destrehan, LA.

BURDA, MORRIS ROLLAND, 393-49-01, enlisted Jan. 20, 1941, in Portland, OR. He served aboard BB-59 as S1/c at commissioning and is a plankowner.

BURDULIS, ALPHONSE BENJAMIN, 650-26-00, enlisted Feb. 23, 1942, in Philadelphia, PA. He is a plankowner and served aboard BB-59 as AS at commissioning May 12, 1942. Memory List 1978.

BURGESS, RAY EDWARD, 295-08-17, enlisted Jan. 26, 1937, in Long Beach, CA. He is a plankowner and served aboard BB-59 as CM1/c at commissioning May 12, 1942.

BURGESS, WINSTON O., resides at 1 Jerusalem Rd., Cohasset, MA.

BURK, PARKER, 606-48-86, enlisted March 8, 1942, in Boston, MA. He is a plankowner and served aboard BB-59 as S2/c at commissioning May 12, 1942, and was on board on its 2nd and 3rd anniversaries. Resided at 24 Prescott St., Cambridge, MA (1966). Memory List 1989.

BURKAS, JAMES, (n) 224-78-53, born in New York City, NY and graduated from high school. He enlisted April 2, 1942, in New York, NY, with training at Newport, RI. He is a plankowner and served on board BB-59 as AS A Div., F2/c, F1/c, WT3/c and WT2/c. Left BB-59 in March 1945 at sea and was transferred to Brooklyn Navy Yard.

After the war he worked as meat cutter from 1946 to 1950 and was a meat salesman from 1950-83. He is a member of the American Legion, VFW, Moose Lodge and Elks Lodge as Exhalted Ruler (1993). Married Antoinette in 1944 and Marie in 1960 (died of cancer 1986). He has three children and four grandchildren and resides at 421 NE 1st St., #216, Hallandale, FL 33009.

BURKE, F.J., resides at 2608 Ohio St., St. Louis, MO (1966).

BURKE, HOWARD V., Marine, resided at 364 Belmont Ave., Kenmore, NY (1963) and at 917 M and T Bldg., Buffalo, NY (1966).

BURKE, JOSEPH MARK, 224-77-78, enlisted March 31, 1942, in New York, NY. He is a plankowner and served aboard BB-59 as S1/c 5th Div. at commissioning May 12, 1942. Left BB-59 in February 1944. After the war worked for Public Service Gas Company as supervisory inspector in 1966. Was also part of American Legion #1651, K of C as 3rd and 4th degree; assistant director of St. Andrew Drum and Bugle Corps. He had one son and one daughter and five grandchildren. He died on May 6, 1992, and son Mark lives at 41 Newman Ave., Bayonne, NJ.

BURKE, MARTIN, (n) 224-78-14, enlisted April 1, 1942, in New York, NY. He is a plankowner and served aboard BB-59 as AS at commissioning May 12, 1942, and was on board on its 2nd and 3rd anniversaries. Resides at 201 E 114th St., New York, NY (1966).

BURKE, PAUL IRVING, 263-07-40, enlisted Dec. 17, 1939, in San Francisco, CA. He is a plankowner and served aboard BB-59 as CGM at commissioning May 12, 1942, and was on board on May 12, 1944.

BURKETT, JOSEPH ALLEN, 382-79-48, enlisted Dec. 26, 1941, in Los Angeles, CA. He is a plankowner and served aboard BB-59 as FC3/c at commissioning May 12, 1942.

BURKEY, HERBERT ALDEN, 291-47-28, enlisted Oct. 16, 1940, in Cincinnati, OH. He is a plankowner and served aboard BB-59 as Bkr2/c at commissioning May 12, 1942.

BURKHALTER, HOWARD JOHN, 646-04-65, born April 9, 1920, in West Orange, NJ. Graduated from West Orange High School and enlisted on Aug. 5, 1941, in New York, NY. Received training at Newport, RI, Electric School in St. Louis, MO and Gyro Comp. School, Brooklyn, NY. He served aboard the BB-59 as EM3/c E Div. at commissioning on May 12, 1942, and from May 1942 to November 1942 worked in Electrical Repairs. Assignments: November 1942 to May 1944 was aboard the USS *Bear*, ice breaker - EM3/c to EM1/c; May 1944 Minecraft training, Little Creek, VA; June 1944 to October 1945, USS *Pledge* (AM 277) as EM1/

c to CEM. Left the BB-59 on Nov. 30, 1942, in Boston, MA and was discharged at Lido Beach, NY (CEM). He is a plankowner.

After the war he was a switchman for New York Telephone Company, Auburn, NY from November 1945 to May 1965; May 1965 to May 1985 was central office supervisor for NY Tel.; retired in May 1985 with 40 years of service. In his spare time he enjoys teaching stamp collecting to school Stamp Clubs; building and repairing model railroad equipment. He is president of Stamp Club Federation; treasurer of Model Railroad Clubs; a member of Telephone Pioneers of America and active in Boy Scouts.

Married Mildred on Feb. 14, 1942, in New York (deceased) and then married Susan on Dec. 1, 1973. He has three sons, three daughters and five grandchildren. He died on March 22, 1996. Memory List 1996. (Mrs.) resides at 28 Fleming St., Auburn, NY 13021-5422. Burkhalter was a member of the Editorial Staff for this book and typed most of the bios.

BURKS, MELVIN NOEL, JR., 266-00-21, enlisted Nov. 6, 1939, in Richmond, VA. He is a plankowner and served aboard BB-59 as S1/c at commissioning May 12, 1942 and was aboard on its 3rd anniversary.

BURNETT, CLARENCE FREDERICK, 238-84-46, enlisted on Feb. 28, 1942, in Albany, NY. He is a plankowner and served aboard BB-59 as AS 6th Div. at commissioning May 12, 1942, and was on board on its 2nd and 3rd anniversaries. He resides at 95 E. Main St., Afton, NY 13730.

BURNETT, ROBERT W., Enlisted USMC, May 8, 1942, Norfolk Navy Yard. He waa a plankowner and served aboard BB-59 as Pfc. 7th Div., at commissioning May 12, 1942. Memory List 1996.

BURNETT, WILLIAM EWING, 646-52-99, born Nov. 3, 1919, in Philadelphia, PA. Graduated from Middletown, NY, High School, in 1937 and Columbia University in 1941. He enlisted on Jan. 23, 1942, in New York, NY, and received training at USNTS Newport, RI. He is a plankowner and served aboard BB-59 as AS S Div. paymaster's office SK3/c at commissioning May 12, 1942. Left the BB-59 on March 11, 1943, at Noumea, New Caledonia to USA on board Army transport.

Was commissioned ENS(SC) USNR at Treasure Island and assigned LST outfitting pool at Mare Island. Sent to Naval Supply School at Harvard University and ordered to Lion 4 at Little Creek, VA to California via troop train. Was assigned Disbursing Officer for Lion 4, advanced echelon bound for Guam (first paymaster to carry $1 million, West of Pearl Harbor). After paymaster duties, he was assigned to Naval Supply Depot, Guam (LT jg). Awarded a Pacific Fleet Commendation. Released from active duty in December 1945.

After the war rejoined US Steel Corp. from December 1945 to October 1946 as accountant; October 1946 to January 1961 Standard Oil of California as secretary, treasurer and assistant to president (East Coast) sub.; January 1961 to October 1962, PR Consultant; October 1962 to October 1967 Dime Savings Bank, New York; October 1967 to October 1971 Grumman Aerospace Corp.; October 1971 to December 1977 Bethpage Federal Credit Union as director of marketing; WEB Enterprises from January 1978 to November 1981; retired in December 1981.

He married Dorothy McGrath "Tots" on Dec. 1, 1942, in New York, NY, and had one daughter, Ann. In 1983 he was severely injured in auto accident and totally disabled. They reside at 1809 Seaman Dr., Merrick, LI, NY.

BURNHAM, IRWIN LOUIS, 393-36-06, enlisted on May 20, 1940, in Portland, OR. He is a plankowner and served aboard BB-59 as F1/c at commissioning May 12, 1942.

BURNS, JOHN W., Enlisted USMC, May 8, 1942, Norfolk Navy Yard. He is a plankowner and served aboard BB-59 as Pfc. 7th Div. at commissioning May 12, 1942.

BURT, DONALD HAYHURST, 606-49-44, enlisted on May 12, 1942, in Boston, MA. He is a plankowner and served aboard BB-59 as AS at commissioning and was on board on its 2nd and 3rd anniversaries.

BURT, JAMES ELLIOTT, born June 2, 1918, in East Orange, NJ. He graduated from high school and attended NYC School of Commerce receiving a BS in marketing. Joined USN as 9th Class (Prairie State), Columbia University Midshipman School for three months. Had one month indoctrination at Notre Dame.

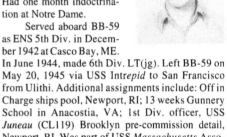

Served aboard BB-59 as ENS 5th Div. in December 1942 at Casco Bay, ME.

In June 1944, made 6th Div. LT(jg). Left BB-59 on May 20, 1945 via USS *Intrepid* to San Francisco from Ulithi. Additional assignments include: Off in Charge ships pool, Newport, RI; 13 weeks Gunnery School in Anacostia, VA; 1st Div. officer, USS *Juneau* (CL119) Brooklyn pre-commission detail, Newport, RI. Was part of USS *Massachusetts* Associates as vice president in 1967, president in 1968 and a member of Homecoming Crew in 1965. Part of USS *Massachusetts* Memorial Committee for four years.

After the war worked for a number of coffee-tea firms in purchasing, sales and trading production. Retired in 1987. He is also a member of NY Coffee & Sugar Exchange (13 years). Was official coffee grader for 27 years; a member of US Power Squadron; US Golf Assoc.; board member of Green Coffee Assoc. of NYC and honorary life member.

Married Peggy Eyre and had two children (son died at an early age) and two grandchildren. They reside at 39051 12th Ave., Zephyrhills, FL.

BURTON, JOHN WESLEY, 265-28-18, enlisted Jan. 28, 1942, in San Francisco, CA. He is a plankowner and served aboard BB-59 as S1/c at commissioning May 12, 1942.

BURZDAK, FRANK STANLEY, 224-78-54, enlisted April 2, 1942, in New York, NY. He is a plankowner and served aboard BB-59 as AS N Div. at commissioning May 12, 1942. He resided in Furrowtown Rd., Westfield, MA.

BUSH, HAMILTON CARL, 668-44-59, born Feb. 2, 1919, in New Hebron, MS. Graduated from high school and attended Mississippi State. He enlisted on Feb. 17, 1942, in St. Louis, MO, and received training in Great Lakes, IL. He is a plankowner and served aboard BB-59 as Y3/c XO Div. at commissioning May 12, 1942. Left BB-59 in November 1942 to midshipman school at Notre Dame University. Assignments include: USS Dora*n* (DD634) in the Atlantic two years; LST 600 in the Pacific.

After the war was a rural letter carrier from 1948 to 1981. He is also a tree farmer. In his spare time was involved in the American Legion, Baptist Church, Boy Scouts, Lions Club also a blood donor with 197 donations. He married Hazel on March 11, 1949, in Nashville, TN, and has one son and two grandchildren. He resides at PO Box 30, New Hebron, MS.

BUSH, ROBERT CHARLES, 311-42-34, enlisted March 13, 1940, in Detroit, MI. He is a plankowner and served aboard BB-59 as F1/c at commissioning May 12, 1942.

BUTCHER, RALPH S., Enlisted USMC, May 8, 1942, Norfolk Navy Yard. He is a plankowner and served aboard BB-59 as PFC 7th Div. at commissioning May 12, 1942.

BUTLER, CHARLES J., Memory List 1993.

BUTLER, DOUGLAS PARKER, born June 29, 1920, in Worcester, MA. Graduated from North High School in Worcester and attended Amherst College with an AB in 1942. Joined the Navy on July 8, 1942, in Boston, MA. Training received at Navy Supply Corps School, Harvard, May 1943 (120 days). Assignments include: Navy Port Director's office, NYC, NY; Naval Air Station, Quonset Point, RI; Harvard Business School.  He served aboard the BB-59 in August 1943 as LT(jg), S Div., and was promoted to lieutenant in 1944. Left the BB-59 on Jan. 26, 1945, at Ulithi. Other assignments: Outgoing Stores Officer NAS Pensacola, FL. Was released from active duty in March 1946.

After the war worked for National Broadcasting Company, NYC, NY, in advertising from 1946-49; Butler-Dearden Paper Service, Worcester, MA, from 1949-86; Navy Ready Reserve; retired from Navy in June 1985 with the rank of LCDR. In his spare time he is a member of the Northboro Planning Board; Consumers Bank as director; Northboro Board of Appeals; and Preservation of Worcester as director. He married Virginia Knox and has one son, one daughter and two grandchildren. They reside at 75 Cherlyn Dr., Northbrough, MA.

BUTLER, FRANK ERIC PAGET, 385-40-95, enlisted on June 11, 1938, in San Diego, CA. He is a plankowner and served aboard BB-59 as CEM E Div. at commissioning May 12, 1942.

BUTLER, JAMES FRANCIS, JR., 610-22-34, enlisted Dec. 30, 1941, in Chicago, IL. He is a plankowner and served aboard BB-59 as EM3/c E Div. at commissioning May 12, 1942.

BUTSKO, PETER, (n) 650-33-19, enlisted on Feb. 25, 1942, in Philadelphia, PA. He is a plankowner and served aboard BB-59 as COX 5th Div. at commissioning May 12, 1942, and was on board on its 2nd anniversary May 12, 1944, as shell loader, Mount Capt. Left the BB-59 in November 1945. After the war he became a state trooper for the Commonwealth of Pennsylvania. He has one daughter, Linda (1966 survey). He resides at Teaberry Hill, Minersville, PA.

BUTTE, JAMES JOHNSON, 383-02-47, born in 1919 in Harrisburg, AR. Graduated from high school and joined the Navy in Aug. 13, 1937, in Los Angeles, CA. Served aboard the USS *Detroit* CL 8 from 1937 to 1942. He is a plankowner and served aboard BB-59 in Quincy, MA, as BM2/c MAA at commissioning May 12, 1942.

Transferred to 4th Div. Then left BB-59 in Norfolk, after North Africa to USS *Baltimore* CA68 to the end of the war. Retired BMC 1957. Sent brass belaying pin from USS *Detroit* to BB-59. After the war guarded atomic bombs at the Nevada test site from 1962 to 1983. Worked for LVMPD at the pistol and rifle range. Married Dorothy and resides at 5303 E. Twain Ave., Sp. 127, Las Vegas, NV.

BUTTERFIELD, JACKSON B., Enlisted USMC, May 8, 1942, Norfolk Navy Yard. He is a plankowner and served aboard BB-59 as Capt. 7th Div. at commissioning May 12, 1942.

BUTZINGER, CHARLES L., 337-08-23, enlisted Aug. 9, 1938, in St. Louis, MO. He is a plankowner and served aboard BB-59 as MM2/c at commissioning May 12, 1942.

BYERS, ROBERT WESLEY, 291-64-09, enlisted Feb. 23, 1938, in Indianapolis, IN. He is a plankowner and served aboard BB-59 as S1/c at commissioning May 12, 1942.

BYNUM, DARREL T., E Div., resides at 12306 Dorwayne, Houston, TX. He has three daughters and seven grandchildren.

BYRNE, JAMES FRANCIS, Bat. Div. 8, Oct. 1, 1943, Flag Sec and Aide, Ops Off. Retired as RADM. Memory List 1983.

BYRNE, MICHAEL CHARLES, JR., 650-26-20, enlisted Feb. 23, 1942, Philadelphia, PA. He is a plankowner and served aboard BB-59 as AS at commissioning May 12, 1942, and was on board on its 2nd and 3rd anniversaries.

BYRNE, CHARLES FRANCIS, 224-72-15, enlisted March 3, 1942, in New York, NY. He served aboard BB-59 in 5th Div. at commissioning May 12, 1942, and was a plankowner. Memory List 1989. (Mrs.) resides at 341 Stewart Ave., Bethpage, NY.

CABLE, EUGENE CHARLES, 223-18-23, enlisted on Feb. 5, 1942, at Pearl Harbor. He is a plankowner and served aboard BB-59 as MM1/c at commissioning May 12, 1942.

CAHILL, EDWARD W., served aboard BB-59 as AOM2/c. Latest address is 151 So. 10th St., Newark, NJ 07101.

CAIN, WILLIAM IRVING, resides at 6340 38th # 29, Wheatridge, CO 80033.

CALANDRA, ANDREW J., served aboard BB-59 as SF2/c. Calandra was discharged on Oct. 11, 1945, in Lido Beach, LI, NY. Married Onalee and resided at 700 Mease Plaza #942 Dunedin, FL 34698. He died on Nov. 16, 1983: Memory List 1993.

CALANENNO, ANTHONY, (n) resides at 31 Buckland Drive, Waterbury, CT 06704.

CALE, DOUGLAS, served aboard BB-59 in 1st Div. He has one daughter and one grandchild. Latest address (daughter) is 5007 Red Oak Court, Jacksonville, NC 28546.

CALHOUN, CHARLTON "H," JR., LT(jg), served aboard BB-59 in 2nd Div. on May 20, 1944. He left BB-59 on Oct. 15, 1945 as FC Div. JO

CALHOUN, DUNCAN NELSON, born Nov. 30, 1920, in Wilmington, NC, graduated from high school and enlisted in May 1941, at Wilmington, NC. Was NOB (Base Police) Norfolk, VA, Patrol Wing 9, Quonset Point, RI, US Naval School of Photography. He served aboard BB-59 in V Div. and left BB-59 at Naval Air Station, Seattle, WA. After the war he was a news photographer for 25 years. He married Eloise in Wilmington, NC, and has one son and one daughter. Latest address is 113 Sherwood Road, Box 261 Jacksonville, NC 28540.

CALKINS, WILLIAM ERNEST, 311-32-86, enlisted June 21, 1939, Detroit, MI. He served aboard BB-59 as S1/c at commissioning May 12, 1942. He is a plankowner.

CALLAHAN, JAMES JOSEPH, JR., 642-12-39, enlisted Feb. 9, 1942, in New Haven, CT. He is a plankowner and served aboard BB-59 as AS at commissioning May 12, 1942, and was on board on its 2nd anniversary.

CALLAHAN, JOSEPH GABRIEL, 646-65-56, enlisted Feb. 5, 1942, in New York, NY. He is a plankowner and served aboard BB-59 as AS at commissioning May 12, 1942.

CALVERT, HENRY, latest address is 24740 Meadow Creek, Harrison Township, MI.

CAMERA, JOSEPH LOUIS, 647-02-36, born April 21, 1923, in White Plains, NY. A high school graduate and some college experience in electronics, he enlisted on Feb. 21, 1942, in New York, NY. He received naval training at Naval Training Station, Newport, RI; USN Medical School, Bethesda, MD. He served aboard BB-59 as AS in Sick Bay at commissioning May 12, 1942, and is a plankowner. Assignments include Hospital Corpsman Striker. He left BB-59 in October 1942 at Casco Bay, ME. Other Naval assignments include: 2nd Beach Bn. ETO (North Africa, Sicily, Salerno), D-Day Normandy Invasion, Battle of Germany. He was discharged as Phm2/c.

Post war employment as bacteriogist, bio assayist for Burrough Welcome; data control systems, field service engineer space program, telemetry (space to ground mechanical information); Pulse Code Modulation (PCM); Local Electronic Systems, Electronic Counter Measures (ECM), SR Design Assist Systems, Engineer Tech. In his spare time he holds a patient's Bible study authorized by Father Donahue, Harlem Valley Psychiatric Center, Winedale, NY. Camera has two sons, four daughters, 12 grandchildren and seven great-grandchildren.. Latest address is 41 Barker Ave. Apt. 3E, White Plains, NY 10601-1638.

CAMMETT, RALPH WINSOR, 606-46-20, enlisted March 6, 1942. He was a plankowner and served aboard BB-59 as AS F Div. at commissioning May 12, 1942, and was on board on its 2nd anniversary. Other assignments include Range Keeper OPR FC3/c F Div. Left BB-59 in April 1945. After the war he worked as fire lieutenant in Lynn, MA. He has one son, one daughter and two grandchildren. Latest address was 106 Allerton St. Lynn, MA 01904. He died Dec. 22, 1981; Memory List 1983.

CAMP, HORACE ROLAND, 272-36-89, enlisted July 31, 1940, in Birmingham, AL. He is a plankowner and served aboard BB-59 as S1/c at commissioning May 12, 1942.

CAMPBELL, CLAYTON EDWARD, 606-18-10, enlisted Jan. 10, 1942, in Boston, MA. He served aboard BB-59 as EM2/c E Div. at commissioning May 12, 1942, and was on board on its 2nd anniversary. He is a plankowner. His assignment aboard was Electric Lighting Shop. Left BB-59 on Oct. 25, 1945, as an EM1/c After the war he worked as an electrician for Hanscom Air Force Field, Bedford, MA. In his spare time he is part of NEFCA Campers Chapter # 96. He resides at 32 Vineland St., Brighton, MA.

CAMPBELL, LESTER JAY, JR., 647-00-98, enlisted Feb. 20, 1942, in New York, NY. He is a plankowner and served aboard BB-59 as AS at commissioning May 12, 1942.

CAMPBELL, RONALD JOHN, 224-72-16, enlisted March 3, 1942, in New York, NY. He is a plankowner and served aboard BB-59 as AS at commissioning May 12, 1942.

CAMPBELL, STANLEY, 646-68-45, born Aug. 24, 1924, and graduated from high school. He enlisted Feb. 7, 1942, in New York, NY. Received training at Newport Naval Training Station, Newport, RI; April 1942 at Fargo Barracks, Boston, MA. He served aboard BB-59 as AS at commissioning May 12, 1942, and was on board on its 2nd and 3rd anniversaries. He is a plankowner and assignments were as S1/c 2nd Div., 5th Div. He left BB-59 in November 1945 in Seattle, WA.

After the war he worked as US Postal Clerk, Newark, NJ; Surface Transportation Spec., ALO, Hackensack, NJ; Distribution and Routing Spec., Transportation Management Office, Northeast Region, New York, NY. Retired in January 1980. In his spare time belongs to the American Legion Post #300, Newark, NJ; VFW Post # 9503, Bayville, NJ; National Assoc. of Retired Federal Employees Chapter # 1619. Received Outstanding Award for Services. He is married to Myrtle and has two daughters, and four grandchildren. Latest address is 713 Morningside St., Toms River, NJ 08757.

CAMPBELL, WILLIAM N., Memory List 1977.

CANAVAN, ARNOLD FRANCIS, 606-49-80, born Oct. 23, 1922, in Francestown, NH. Graduated from high school and received an associate degree in mechanical engineering from Lowell Technical College. Enlisted on March 11, 1942, in Boston, MA, and received training at Newport Naval Training Station. Served aboard BB-59 as AS 3rd Div. at commissioning May 12, 1942, and was a plankowner. Assignment in Turret #3.

Post war work included: Design Draftsman for Nashua Industrial Machine Inc., International Paper Box Machine Company for 20 years. In his spare time he is involved in Boy Scouts and Our Lady of Mercy Church. Married Alice on Aug. 31, 1946, in Wilton, NH. They have four sons, four daughters and 15 grandchildren. Canavan died on Jan. 2, 1991; Memory List 1993. (Mrs.) resides at 9-68 Blackstone Drive, Nashua, NH 03063.

CANFIELD, WILLIAM NEWTON, 647-02-37, born Oct. 8, 1920, in East Orange, NJ. Graduated from high school and attended American School of Design, New York. Enlisted Dec. 10, 1941, Newark, NJ, and attended Newport Naval Training Station, Fargo Barracks, Boston, MA. He is a plankowner and served aboard BB-59 as AS 5th Div. at commissioning May 12, 1942, and was on board on its 2nd anniversary. Was assigned 5th Div. Yeoman BM2/c. Left BB-59 in November 1945.

Other Naval assignments include: BM PLA6 Admiral Staff, USS Alab*ama*, USS *Indiana*, Japan duty for one month then returned to USA November 1945. After the war worked as a newspaperman in editorial, sports cartoonist for *Newark News-Star Ledger*, Newark, NJ. In his spare time he is part of First Aid Squadron, Tinton Falls, NJ - 15 years. Honors include: Who's Who "BB-59 Award," 1991. He has one son and one daughter. Latest address is 143 Wayside Road, Tinton Falls, NJ 07724.

CANNON, RAYMOND JEROME, 647-02-38, enlisted on Feb. 21, 1942, in New York, NY. He is a plankowner and served aboard BB-59 as AS at commissioning May 12, 1942 and was on board on its 2nd and 3rd anniversaries.

CANNON, WILLEY SPENCER, 342-11-99, enlisted on June 9, 1939, in Kansas City, MO. He is a plankowner and served aboard BB-59 as BM2/c, L Div. at commissioning May 12, 1942.

CANOVA, LIBERO, served aboard BB-59 as CCM Hull Maintenance CH Carp. on Jan. 27, 1945. Left BB-59 on Sept. 19, 1945.

CAPEK, FRANK, served aboard BB-59 in Band as 1st alto sax. Latest address is 47 Pine Grove Court, Peekskill, NY 10566.

CARAWAY, LEVY VIVIAN, 359-99-44, enlisted June 10, 1938, in Houston, TX. He is a plankowner and served aboard BB-59 as SK2/c S Div. at commissioning May 12, 1942, and was on board on its 2nd and 3rd anniversaries. Assignments: May 12, 1945 as CSK S Div. Capt.

CARBONE, JOSEPH BENJAMIN, 382-26-55, enlisted on Sept. 25, 1940, in Los Angeles, CA. He is a plankowner and served aboard BB-59 as F2/c at commissioning May 12, 1942.

CARBONE, ROBERT LEO, 606-37-05, enlisted on Feb. 20, 1942, in Boston, MA. He is a plankowner and served aboard BB-59 as AS at commissioning May 12, 1942, and was on board on its 2nd anniversary. Latest address is 21100 Highway 79 # 16 San Jacinto, CA 92383.

CARDENAS, ARTHUR JOE, 383-35-81, enlisted Jan. 11, 1941, in Los Angeles, CA. He is a plankowner and served aboard BB-59 as S1/c at commissioning and was on board on its 2nd and 3rd anniversaries.

CARDUCCI, JOHN GABRIEL, 244-08-00, enlisted March 4, 1942, Philadelphia, PA. He served aboard BB-59 as AS at commissioning May 12, 1942, and was on board on its 2nd anniversary. He is a plankowner.

CAREY, EDWARD MICHAEL, 646-67-02, enlisted Feb. 6, 1942, in New York, NY. He is a plankowner and served aboard BB-59 as AS at commissioning May 12, 1942, and was on board on its 2nd anniversary.

CAREY, HOMER, born March 24, 1926, in Winfield, KS. He enlisted in St. Louis, MO. Served aboard BB-59 on April 4, 1944, as S1/c 5th Div. with assignments as S1/c R Div. Left BB-59 on May 1, 1946, in Norfolk, VA. After the war he has been self-employed as president of his insulation company. He married Ruth Sept. 28, 1946, in Minneapolis, MN. They have two sons and five grandchildren. They reside at 6307 Indiana Ave. N., Minneapolis, MN 55429.

CAREY, JOSEPH J., COMDR, served aboard BB-59 on March 5, 1944. Assignments were in Dept. Head Engineer. Left BB-59 on May 30, 1945 as Capt.

CARLETON, ROLAND A., served aboard BB-59 in 5th Div. Latest address is 38241 South Farm Lane, Northville, MI 48167.

CARLL, EDWARD, (n) 202-25-83, born in Brighton, MA, and graduated from Brighton High School. He enlisted Feb. 23, 1942, in Boston, MA, and attended Newport Naval Training Station, Naval Gunnery School, RI, and Fargo Barracks, Boston, MA. Served aboard BB-59 as AS 1st Div. at commissioning May 12, 1942, and was on board on its 2nd and 3rd anniversaries. He is a plankowner and assignments were Turret #1 GM3/c 1st Div.; 1945 Master at Arms GM3/c. Left BB-59 in 1946 at Norfolk, VA.

Other Naval assignments include Rec. Station ERB, New Orleans, LA, USS LSN 485. After the war he was employed as foreman for Matheson-Higgins; Graphic Arts, police officer, Needham, MA. In his spare time he is a private pilot and a boats and plane modeler. He married Ann Nigro on Sept. 26, 1945, in Newton, MA. They have two sons and four grandchildren. He resided at 81 Roberts Road, Ashland, MA 01721. Memory List 1997.

CARLON, QUINN ALVAN, 654-31-84, enlisted Feb. 3, 1942, in Portland, OR. He is a plankowner and served aboard BB-59 as S1/c at commissioning date, May 12, 1942.

CARLSON, DANIEL, COMDR, was a graduate of US Naval Academy, Class of 1929. He was a plankowner and served aboard BB-59 at commissioning May 12, 1942, and was on board on its 2nd anniversary. Was assigned Navigator on Oct. 1, 1943; Public Relations, Education's Officer. Left BB-59 on Aug. 1, 1944. Memory List 1994.

CARLSON, GEORGE E., born April 9, 1924, in Hastings, MN. Graduated from high school and attended junior college for two years. He enlisted July 3, 1942, in Minneapolis, MN. Attended Great Lakes Naval Training Center, IL, Naval School, St. Louis, MO YMS 79. Carlson served aboard BB-59 as S2/c 5th Div. He left BB-59 in February 1943. Other Naval assignments include NAS Recife, Brazil, USS *Memphis CL13*.

He was discharged November 1945. After the war he worked for US Postal Service Management from 1949-1979. Worked part-time electronic service and repair. Married Edell on Sept. 6, 1947, in St. James, MN, and has one son, three daughters and six grandchildren. They reside at 16653 Mt. Acomo Circle, Fountain Valley, CA 92708.

CARLSON, HAROLD JOHN, served aboard BB-59 as P Div. MM, B Div. W. and JO ChMach Oct. 1, 1943. Left the BB-59 on Aug. 14, 1945.

CARMAN, LEON WILLIAM (NICKNAME "WINK"), born Sept. 18, 1922, Freeport, LI, NY. Graduated from Freeport High School and enlisted on March 3, 1942, in New York, NY. Attended Newport Naval Training Station, RI. He is a plankowner and served aboard BB-59 as EM2/c E Div. at commissioning May 12, 1942. Assignments aboard include: lighting shop, boats and batteries, 36 inch searchlights.

Left the BB-59 at sea off Okinawa. Other Naval assignments were shore duty and discharge, Point Lookout, NY. After the war he was employed as captain of tug boats on the river, coast and Great Lakes. Is a sport fishing boat owner, Freeport, LI, NY, and Montauk Point, LI, NY.

Married Patricia Grayson, in Merrick, NY, and divorced in 1965. Remarried to Joan Keene in 1977 in Freeport, LI, NY. He has two sons, one daughter and six grandchildren. His latest address is 4601 SE Boatyard Drive, Stuart, FL 34997.

CARPENTER, WILLIAM DEMPSEY, enlisted June 4, 1940, in St. Louis, MO. He is a plankowner and served aboard BB-59 as F2/c at commissioning May 12, 1942.

CARPENTIERI, JOSEPH G., is a plankowner and served aboard BB-59 as X Div. at commissioning May 12, 1942, and was on board on its 2nd and 3rd anniversaries. Memory List 1993.

CARPER, BILLY HALE, born March 30, 1925, in Pulaksi, VA. Graduated from high school and had two years of college. Enlisted on April 13, 1942, in Norfolk, VA, and attended Norfolk Naval Training Station, and Butler University Signal School. He served aboard BB-59 as SM3/c CS Div. He left BB-59 on Dec. 5, 1945 in Seattle, WA.

After the war he was employed with Appalachian Power Company from 1946-47; 1947-49 National Business College; 1949-57 Chesapeake & Potomac Telephone Company; 1957-65 Southern Bell Telephone Company; 1965-83 Chesapeake & Potomac Telephone Company. Retired on Dec. 31, 1983 at 58 years old and 36 years service and in real estate sales. He is president of Life Member Club Telephone Pioneers of America; president of Rinke Council Salvation Army; Easter Seals and Cancer Society.

He married June Young on Aug. 15, 1946, in Pulaksi, VA. They have three sons and four grandchildren. They reside at 5827 Arcturus Drive SW, Roanoke, VA 24018-6603.

CARR, D.J., served aboard BB-59 at commissioning May 12, 1942, and was a plankowner.

CARREKER, JOEL, served aboard BB-59 as CM R Div. CARP on Oct. 1, 1943.

CARROLL, BERTRAM K., Memory List 1993. Latest address is (Mrs.) 94 Grove St., Melrose, MA 02176.

CARROLL, COMMANDER CHARLES B., Commanding officer from Sept. 9, 1946 to Jan. 4, 1947.

CARTER, MELVIN L., born June 14, 1924, in Beloit, WI. A high school graduate, he enlisted on July 22, 1942, in Chicago, IL. Training at Great Lakes Training Station and Electrical School, Morehead, KY. He served aboard the BB-59 as F1/c E Div. in December 1942. Assignments include EM3/c E Div. He left BB-59 in September 1943.

Other Naval assignments: SCTC Terminal Island, CA; Mine Sweeping School, Santa Barbara, CA; USS *Captivate AM156*, USS *Antona IX133*. After the war he worked as an electrician for Beloit Corporation, Beloit, WI. He married Esther Harju on Feb. 8, 1946, Jesup, GA. They have one son, one daughter, four grandchildren and one great-grandchild. They reside at 1868 Greenview Drive, Beloit, WI 53511.

CARTER, MILLARD, resided at Rt. 1 Box 227H, Ashland, MO 65010. Memory List 1997.

CARTER, WALTER R., is a plankowner and served aboard BB-59 at commissioning May 12, 1942, and was on board on its 2nd and 3rd anniversaries. Received a Meritorious Mast in April 1944. Resides in Gloucester, MA (1965).

CARTWRIGHT, JOHN FREDERICK, 606-78-09, educated at New England Conservatory, Boston; and received MA at Julliard Musical School, New York, NY. He enlisted on May 25, 1942, in Boston, MA. He is a plankowner and served aboard the BB-59 as Mus2/c X Div. at commissioning May 12, 1942, and was on board on its 2nd and 3rd anniversaries. Assignments include Mus1/c, organist and chaplain's assistant. He left BB-59 in August 1945 and was in Naval Reserve. After the war he was organist and choirmaster for Church of Epiphany, New York and organist Temple Israel, New York. He resides at 446 East 85th St., New York, NY 10028.

CARUSO, ARNOLD J., born Nov. 8, 1911, in Kearny, NY, graduated from high school and attended New York University for three years. He enlisted Feb. 21, 1942, New York, NY, and training at Newport Naval Training Station, Rec. Station, Boston, MA. He is a plankowner and served aboard BB-59 as FCM3/c F Div., and was on board on its 2nd and 3rd anniversaries. As FCM1/c he left BB-59 on July 1, 1945.

After the war worked as a pension trust specialist for Mutual Benefit Life Insurance Company. He is a commander VFW, Livingston, NJ. He married Dorothy P., on April 19, 1962, Newark, NJ, and has one stepson and two grandchildren. Died on June 8, 1976; Memory List 1977. (Mrs.) resides at 13 Davidson Road, Bloomfield, NJ 07003.

CARUSO, WESLEY, born June 2, 1921, Newark, NJ. Graduated from high school and enlisted on March 31, 1942, in New York, NY. Attended Newport Naval Training Station, RI; Fargo Barrack, Boston, MA. He is a plankowner and served aboard BB-59 as AS 4th Div. at commissioning May 12, 1942, and was on board on its 2nd and 3rd anniversaries. Assignments: 1942-46 as S1/c 4th Div. and 1946 as S1/c 3rd Div. He left BB-59 in July 1946. After the war he was a butcher for A&P and married Dorothy on Feb. 9, 1952, in Elizabeth, NJ. They have two sons and two grandchildren. Latest address: 961 Potter Ave., Union, NJ 07083.

CARWAN, L.W., is a plankowner and served aboard BB-59 at commissioning May 12, 1942, and was on board on its 2nd anniversary.

CASE, ROBERT E., resides at 102 Dahlin Ave., #103 Isanti, MN 55040.

CASE, ROBERT STARBUCK, 666-16-14, enlisted Feb. 11, 1942, Springfield, MA. He is a plankowner and served aboard BB-59 as AS B Div. at commissioning May 12, 1942, and was on board on its 2nd and 3rd anniversaries. Was assigned to #4 fireroom WT3/c B Div. Left BB-59 in July 1946. After the war he was a pattern maker for Taylor & Fenn Manufacturing. He is also a member of Boy Scouts of America, Institutional Representative. He married Helen and has one son and two daughters. They reside at 485 Hillcrest Lane, Ellenton, FL 34222.

CASHMAN, BRUCE ASHLEY, 647-01-00, enlisted Feb. 20, 1942, in New York, NY. He is a plankowner and served aboard BB-59 as AS at commissioning May 12, 1942.

CASSEL, DOUGLAS WATTS, LT(jg) served aboard BB-59 as V Div. JO Aviator. He was assigned as aviation instructor and JFD officer Oct. 1, 1943. Left BB-59 on June 12, 1944, as lieutenant.

CASSELS, ROBERT QUARTERMAN, LT(jg) born on Aug. 12, 1918, in Atlanta, GA. Graduated from high school and received a BS in commerce from Georgia University, he enlisted in February 1941. Received training in V-7 Program, Inshore Patrol, Cockspur Island, Savannah, GA. He served aboard BB-59 as ENS S Div. and was assigned JW and Military to SO, March 1943; LT(jg) R Div. JW and JD, DC Material Officer, LT X Div.; October 1943 FC Div. JO.

He left BB-59 on Sept. 15, 1945 in Seattle, WA. After the war became president of Draper-Owens Realty Company (commercial sales and leasing) for 48 years. Married Donata Horne on Aug. 8, 1942, in Atlanta, GA, and had three sons, two daughters and two grandchildren. They reside at 11 Ivy Chase, Atlanta, GA 30342.

CASSIDY, JACK, is part of USS *Massachusetts* Memorial Committee Inc., Site Committee chairman and 1965 Homecoming Crew Member.

CASSILE, ROLL RUCKES, 234-61-08, enlisted April 19, 1938, in Philadelphia, PA. He is a plankowner and served aboard BB-59 as EM1/c E Div. at commissioning May 12, 1942.

CASTAGLIOLO, JOSEPH, is a BBBM Fund Raiser and resides at 43 Franklin St., East Paterson, NJ 07514.

CASTLE, WILLIAM, (n) born in 1925 in Bronx, NY. Graduated from high school and enlisted on Oct. 14, 1942, in New York, NY. Received training at Newport Naval Training Station, RI, Fargo Barracks, Boston, MA. He served aboard BB-59 as S2/c 4th Div., Portland, ME. Assigned S1/c L Div. and Y3/c Capt. Office. He left BB-59 on July 3, 1946. Other Naval assignments: 1952 Naval Reserve CBS, Heavy equipment operator chief MCB19, trained with Marines at Parris Island and Camp LeJeune, MCB19 disbanded and joined National Guard 101st Cavalry A Troop, Dining Facility Mgr.

Retired in 1977 from reserves as Sgt. 1st Class E7. Honors: USS *Massachusetts*, Captain's Meritorious Mast, Expert Lookout, Marine Corps and Navy CBS Expert Pistol, Marine Corps Expert Rifle, Army Black Barett for proficiency in rank and title. After the war was a New York City bus driver, 1950; police officer, New York City, 1957; Fire Dept., New York City, 1959; retired from NYFD in August 1983.

Married Frances Marie on June 5, 1948, New York, NY, and had three sons and five grandchildren. They reside at 143 Milton Ave., Staten Island, NY 10306.

CATAPANO, PASQUALE ALOYIUS, 647-01-02, enlisted Feb. 20, 1942, in New York, NY. He is a plankowner and served aboard BB-59 as AS at commissioning May 12, 1942, and was on board on its 2nd and 3rd anniversaries. Memory List 1996.

CAUFIELD, LAWRENCE MARTIN, 647-01-03, enlisted Feb. 20, 1942, in New York, NY. He is a plankowner and served aboard BB-59 as AS at commissioning May 12, 1942.

CAUFMAN, JAMES WILLIAM, 265-58-18, enlisted on April 2, 1932, and received training at Boot Camp Hampton Roads, VA. Had assignments: USS *Oglala, William B. Preston, Farragut* and *Moffett*. He re-enlisted Feb. 27, 1942, Boston, MA. He served aboard BB-59 as CMM at commissioning May 12, 1942, and was a plankowner. Also served aboard the USS *Walker, Tranquillity, Heywood, Shangri-La, Boxer,*

Valley Forge and *Carmick.*. Transferred to Fleet Reserve on Dec. 7, 1949. Caufman died Dec. 19, 1978 (Information supplied by son, James L. Caufman via *USS KIDD Newsletter.*)

CAULKINS, CHARLES DOUGLAS, 223-79-09, enlisted Aug. 9, 1940, in New York, NY. He served aboard BB-59 as S1/c 4th Div. at commissioning May 12, 1942, and was on board on its 2nd anniversary. He is a plankowner. Assigned as COX 5th Div., Feb. 25, 1943, MAA X Div. Latest address is 431 Delaware Ave., Longhorne, PA 19047.

CAUSSEE, LLOYD, Memory List 1978.

CAVANAH, BENJAMIN RUSSELL, 295-33-60, enlisted Nov. 2, 1940, in San Diego, CA. He is a plankowner and served aboard BB-59 as COX at commissioning May 12, 1942.

CAWELTI, LESLIE ROBERT, 620-10-87, enlisted Nov. 26, 1941, in Des Moines, IA. He is a plankowner and served aboard BB-59 as SF3/c 3rd Div. at commissioning May 12, 1942, with assignments in R Div. Cawelti died; Memory List 1993. (Mrs.) resides at 927 West 16th St., Cedar Falls, IA 50613.

CEHOWSKI, JOHN EDWARD, 600-21-65, enlisted on March 16, 1942, Albany, NY. He is a plankowner and served aboard BB-59 as AS at commissioning May 12, 1942.

CELIBERTI, PETER JAMES, 647-01-04, enlisted on Feb. 20, 1942, in New York, NY. He is a plankowner and served aboard BB-59 as AS at commissioning May 12, 1942, and was on board on its 2nd and 3rd anniversaries. Assigned as SKD2/c Disbursing Office, S Div. Left BB-59 in December 1945.

After the war worked as Senior Workmen's Compensation Examiner, New York State Compensation Board, New York, NY. He has five sons and two daughters. Memory List 1987. Latest address is (son, Peter) 67 Carman Ave., East Rockaway, NY 11518-1138.

CENEDELLA, ALFRED BERNARD, JR., LT, served aboard BB-59 as LT V Div. in June 1944. Was assigned as aviator, staff aviator, Bat. Div. 8. Left the BB-59 in July 1945. After the war worked as attorney at law and a former state senator. Was president of USS *Massachusetts* Assoc. in 1970. In his spare time is a member of Rotary Club and various fraternal organizations. Married Jeanne and had two sons, two daughters and four grandchildren. Memory List 1981. Latest address is (Mrs.) 107 Congress St., Milford, MA 01757.

CERENZIA, ANTHONY, Memory List 1986.

CERLING, ROBERT GLENN, ENS, served aboard BB-59 as R Div. JO Asst. ChemWarOff on June 14, 1945.

CERNY, ANDREW, (n) 283-37-82, enlisted Aug. 21, 1940, in Cleveland, OH. He is a plankowner and served aboard BB-59 as F1/c at commissioning May 12, 1942.

CHABOT, JOSEPH E., born Feb. 3, 1925, in Amesbury, MA. Enlisted on May 1, 1942, in Amesbury, MA, and received training at Newport Naval Training Station, RI, USS *Alabama*, and USS *Indiana*. Served aboard BB-59 and left on Feb. 3, 1946, Seattle, WA, discharged.

After the war worked as a sheet metal shear operator. Was a volunteer Newton NH, Fire and Police Dept. He retired in 1970. Married Louisa S. on Oct. 26, 1947, Haverhill, MA, and had four children and six grandchildren. Latest address is PO Box 214, Newton Jct., NH 03859.

CHABOT, LEO ALBERT, 606-51-74, born March 29, 1921, Rollinsford, NH. Graduated from Somersworth, NH, High School and attended McIntoch Business College, Dover, NH. He enlisted on March 18, 1942, in Boston, MA. Attended Newport Naval Training Station, RI, for training. He is a plankowner and served aboard BB-59 as AS 2nd Div. at commissioning May 12, 1942. Assigned as GM3/c 2nd and 3rd Div. He left BB-59 in February 1944, Guam. Other Naval assignments: GM3/c USS *Makin Island* CVE.

After the war was assistant sales manager for A.L. Textile Inc.; a field underwriter for New York Life Insurance for 28 years. He is now retired. Spare time activities are 1950-75 Kiwanis Club, president in 1965 chairman 1961-66; Somersworth Housing Authority, NH; 1987 to current treasurer of Great Falls Development Corp.

Married to Barbara M. on Feb. 10, 1944, in Somersworth, NH, and has one daughter and one grandchild. They reside at 96 West High St., Somersworth, NH 03878.

CHAISSON, JOSEPH ARTHUR, born July 31, 1919, Portland, ME. Attended Boston schools and St. Anthony's Allston, MA. Enlisted on March 5, 1942, in Boston, MA, and attended Newport Naval Training Station, RI. He is a plankowner and served aboard BB-59 as AS 4th Div. at commissioning May 12, 1942. Later assigned EM2/c E Div. He left BB-59 in September 1943 in the South Pacific.

Other Naval assignments: USS *North Carolina*, USS *Pennsylvania*, USS *Spangenberg DD223*, French Interpreter Pre-Comm. Detail. After the war was electrical power house operator, 1945-77, Generating Chief Watertown Arsenal. Retired in 1977. In his spare time he enjoys bowling, golf and other sports. Married Mary C. Rago in September 1942, in Boston, MA. They have two daughters and five grandchildren. They reside at 39 Litchfield St., Brighton, MA 02135.

CHALE, WARREN EDWARD, ENS, born July 25, 1923, Minneapolis, MN. Graduated from high school and attended one year of college. He enlisted Aug. 29, 1942, in Minneapolis, MN, with active service Jan. 14, 1943. Received Aviation Cadet Training V5, Corpus Christi, TX; ENS March 1, 1944, Naval Air Station SOSUI Ford Island, CA. Served aboard BB-59 as ENS V Div. on July 25, 1944, and assigned Aviator V Div. Left BB-59 on Sept. 15, 1945, Bremerton, WA.

Other Naval assignments: Jan. 29, 1945 to Jan. 6, 1946, Naval Air Station, Astoria, OR. After the war became a lieutenant in Portland Fire Dept., Portland, OR. Married Betty Dickerson Dec. 29, 1946, Portland, OR, and has one son, one daughter and three grandchildren. They reside at 1817 SW Dickinson Lane, Portland, OR 97219-9604.

CHAMBERLAIN, GEORGE MELVIN, JR., 320-91-35, enlisted April 14, 1938, Los Angeles, CA. He is a plankowner and served on board BB-59 as F1/c at commissioning May 12, 1942.

CHAMBERS, JAY WALTON, JR., 650-32-77, enlisted Feb. 14, 1942, Philadelphia, PA. He is a plankowner and served aboard BB-59 as AS at commissioning May 12, 1942, and was on board on its 2nd anniversary.

CHAMBLISS, JOE "E," 266-02-13, enlisted Nov. 15, 1939, in Norfolk, VA. He is a plankowner and served aboard BB-59 as FC3/c at commissioning May 12, 1942.

CHAMPAGNE, MAURICE EDWARD, 666-19-34, enlisted March 2, 1942, Springfield, MA. He is a plankowner and served aboard BB-59 as AS at commissioning May 12, 1942, and was on board on its 2nd and 3rd anniversaries. Assigned as SK1/c GSK S Div. Left BB-59 Nov. 19, 1945. After the war was president and owner of Elwood Adams Hardware. He resides at 42 Briarwood Circle, Worcester, MA 01606.

CHANDLER, CHARLES RICHARDSON, graduated Naval Academy, 1939; served aboard BB-59 on staff, Bat. 8th Div. in May 1943. Assignments include Oct. 1, 1943 Flag LT and aide, Assistant Comm. Officer. Made lieutenant June 1942.

CHANDLER, HIRAM FRANCIS, 360-20-17, enlisted Aug. 6, 1940, in Houston, TX. He is a plankowner and served aboard BB-59 as F2/c at commissioning May 12, 1942, and was on board on its 2nd and 3rd anniversaries. Assigned B Div. March 1, 1944, WT2/c to WT1/c later to CWT.

CHANI, GEORGE WILLIAM, Memory List 1989.

CHAPMAN, ARTHUR JOEL, 606-20-06, enlisted Jan. 10, 1942, Boston, MA. Served aboard BB-59 as EM3/c E Div. at commissioning May 12, 1942, and was on board on its 2nd and 3rd anniversaries. He was a plankowner. Latest address 26 London St., Lowell, MA 01853. Memory List 1987.

CHAPMAN, CHARLES, (n) born May 21, 1921, in Arma, KS. Graduated from high school and enlisted Oct. 13, 1942. Received training at Great Lakes Naval Training Station, IL. Served aboard BB-59 as S1/c 4th Div. at commissioning November 1942. Assigned Pointer on 40 mm Quad. Left BB-59 on Oct. 9, 1945, on discharge.

After the war he worked various jobs as delivery man for Dad's Root Beer; carpenter/supervisor, Pittsburg State University, KS for 34 years. In his spare time he enjoys fishing and bowling winning 1st place Team State Bowling Tournament. Married Pauline Dolores Spangler on June 1, 1944, in Pittsburg, KS. They have five sons, one daughter and 11 grandchildren. They reside at 106 West Kansas, Pittsburg, KS 66762.

CHAPMAN, WILLIAM EUGENE, 368-49-61, enlisted July 11, 1940, Salt Lake City, UT. He is a plankowner and served aboard BB-59 as F2/c at commissioning May 12, 1942.

CHAPPINA, ERNEST, (n) 224-72-72, enlisted on March 6, 42, in New York, NY. He is a plankowner and served aboard BB59 as AS 4th Div. at commissioning May 12, 1942, and was on board on its 2nd and 3rd anniversary. Last address was 158 Oakwood Ave., Edison, NJ 08837. Memory List 1996.

CHAREST, MAURICE GEORGE, 202-28-86, enlisted April 2, 1942, Boston, MA. He is a plankowner and served aboard BB-59 as AS at commissioning May 12, 1942.

CHARLTON, HUBERT HUDDLEN, 274-45-51, enlisted June 4, 1940, New Orleans, LA. He is a plankowner and served aboard BB-59 as S1/c at commissioning May 12, 1942.

CHARRON, LLOYD HAMPTON, born July 9, 1919, in Grand Forks, ND. He enlisted Dec. 8, 1941, in Grand Forks, ND, and received training at Great Lakes Naval Training Station, IL; Naval Service School, Dearborn, MI; Cooks and Bakers School, Dearborn, MI. He served aboard BB-59 as S1/c S Div. and assigned to SC3/c, SC2/c and SC1/c. Left BB-59 on April 9, 1945 in the Pacific.

Other Naval assignments include Submarine Base, New London, CT; Naval Hospital, Newport, RI. After the war he worked for B & B Freight House, Great Northern RR, Clerk Burlington Northern RR; was ticket clerk Amtrak, carpenter, Sugar Beet Factory, East Grand Forks, MN. In his spare time he enjoyed planting trees and mechanic work.

Married Clara Helen Moe on July 7, 1945, New London, CT, and had two sons, one daughter and three grandchildren. They resided at Route #4 Box 161, Minot, ND 58701. Memory List 1997.

CHASE, KENNETH JOSEPH, 224-72-17, enlisted March 3, 1942, New York, NY. He is a plankowner and served aboard BB-59 as AS on commission date May 12, 1942, and was on board on its 2nd anniversary.

CHAUSSEE, LLOYD, Memory List 1977.

CHEMA, MICHAEL ROBB, JR., 647-02-42, enlisted Feb. 21, 1942, New York, NY. He served aboard BB-59 as AS at commissioning May 12, 1942, and was on board on its 2nd anniversary. He is a plankowner. Latest address was 7 Rudolph Terrace, Yonkers, NY 10701. Memory 1985.

CHEMA, THOMAS, 647-02-43, born in Yonkers, NY. Graduated from high school and attended Columbia University. Enlisted Feb. 21, 1942, New York, NY. He is a plankowner and served aboard BB-59 as AS R Div. at commissioning May 12, 1942. Assigned to YM1/c and left BB-59 in 1943 USN V12 Program.

Other Naval assignments: transferred US Navy to US Army, retired US Army as colonel. In his spare time he is board member, Collier County Retired Officers Club. He has one son and one daughter. Latest address: 1845 Tiller Terrace, Naples, FL 33940.

CHEVASSUS, EDOUARD, born Aug. 14, 1924, graduated from high school and attended California University, Class of 1948, Davis, CA. He enlisted in July 1943 in Sacramento, CA, and attended USNR V-12 Program, Radio Operator School, Madison, WI. He served aboard BB-59 as RM1/c CR Div. May 1945. Left BB-59 on April 4, 1946, in Bremerton, WA.

Other Naval assignments include: Communication Technical School, Bainbridge, Island, WA; CT2/c Adak, AK. He was discharged April 1952 in San Francisco, CA. After the war he worked for the California State Dept. of Food & Agriculture, Sacramento, CA for 26 years and retired. Married Nancy Lee in February 1949, San Francisco, CA. They have two sons, two daughters and six grandchildren. They reside at 144 Brady Court, Sacramento, CA 95820.

CHILDRESS, PAUL VINCENT, 600-18-51, enlisted Feb. 28, 1942, Albany, NY. He is plankowner and served aboard BB-59 as AS at commissioning May 12, 1942, and was on board on its 2nd and 3rd anniversaries.

CHILDS, JAMES COULIE, JR., 650-21-08, enlisted on Jan. 28, 1942, Philadelphia, PA. He is a plankowner and served aboard BB-59 as AS 5th Div. at commissioning May 12, 1942, and was on board on its 2nd and 3rd anniversaries. Assigned COX Boat Crew, Crane Operator and Shellman. Left BB-59 on Nov. 28, 1946.

After the war worked as security guard for General Company. His spare time is spent in VFW, assistant fire chief Darby, PA, Fire Dept., Delaware County, PA Fire Assoc., 4th District, Fire Chief's Assoc. and Penna. State Fire Chief's Assoc. His family consists of three sons, four daughters and 14 grandchildren. His latest address is 228 Reese St., Sharon Hill, PA 19079.

CHILDS, ROBERT EDGAR, 268-39-94, born May 16, 1921, in Jenkinsburg, GA. He enlisted Nov. 28, 1939, Macon, GA. Attended Naval Training Station, Norfolk, VA, and stationed aboard USS *Pennsylvania.* He is a plankowner and served aboard BB-59 as S1/c 6th Div. at commissioning May 12, 1942, and was on board on its 2nd and 3rd anniversaries. Married Ann on April 5, 1947, in Jenkinsburg, GA, and has one daughter and one grandchild. Childs died on Dec. 17, 1988; Memory List 1989. (Mrs.) resides at 539 Cowan Trail, Stockbridge, GA 30281.

CHIMBOR, JOHN EDMUND, 642-14-34, enlisted Feb. 26, 1942, New Haven, CT. He is a plankowner and served aboard BB-59 as AS at commissioning May 12, 1942. Memory List 1989. Latest address: 102 Knowles Ave., Plantsville, CT 06479.

CHOTE, RALPH JAMES, 632-35-98, enlisted Jan. 22, 1942, Los Angeles, CA. He is a plankowner and served aboard BB-59 as S1/c at commissioning May 12, 1942.

CHRISTENSEN, HOWARD, (n) 121-29-38, enlisted April 6, 1940, San Diego, CA. He is a plankowner and served aboard BB-59 as CSF at commissioning May 12, 1942.

CHRISTENSEN, MURRAY DAVID, 606-36-86, enlisted Feb. 17, 1942, Boston, MA. Served aboard BB-59 as AS at commissioning May 12, 1942, and is a plankowner. Assigned on March 10, 1943, S1/c CR Div. to FR Div.

CHRISTIANSEN, CLAYTON LEROY, 654-19-54, enlisted Jan. 5, 1942, Portland, OR. Served aboard BB-59 as S1/c at commissioning May 12, 1942, and is a plankowner.

CHRISTOPHER, EUGENE LESLEY, 342-17-18, enlisted Dec. 27, 1939, Kansas City, MO. He is a plankowner and served aboard BB-59 as COX at commissioning May 12, 1942.

CHRISTY, JAMES VINCENT, 646-82-40, enlisted Feb. 19, 1942, New York, NY. A plankowner he served aboard BB-59 as AS at commissioning May 12, 1942, and was on board on its 2nd and 3rd anniversaries. Assigned on May 12, 1944, to S1/c.

CHUDY, JOHN STANLEY, 642-14-07, born Aug. 11, 1920, Hartford, CT. Enlisted Feb. 24, 1942, New Haven, CT, and received training at Newport, RI. He is a plankowner and served aboard BB-59 as AS 1st Div. at commissioning May 12, 1942, and was on board on its 2nd and 3rd anniversaries as GM3/c. Left BB-59 in Bremerton, WA, September 1945 and discharged at Lido Beach, NY, November 1945.

After the war he worked for the US Postal Service (finance) and now retired. Works at VA Hospital in his spare time. Married to Frances Jan. 26, 1946, Hartford, CT, and has two sons and two grandchildren. They reside at 111 Wilmont St., Wethersfield, CT 06109.

CHURCH, FRANK WHEATLEY II, ENS, served aboard BB-59 as N Div. JO at commissioning Sept. 29, 1944, and "Bay Stater" Staff May 1945. Left BB-59 on Dec. 8, 1945.

CHURCH, VIRGIL, (n) 342-07-91, enlisted July 12, 1938, Kansas City, MO. He is a plankowner and served aboard BB-59 at commissioning May 12, 1942, and was on board on its 2nd anniversary.

CHYLKO, PETER JAMES, 646-64-53, enlisted Feb. 4, 1942, New York, NY. He is a plankowner and served aboard BB-59 as AS at commissioning May 12, 1942.

CIAMILLO, ELMER, JR., (n) 647-02-44, born July 7, 1921, Orange, NJ. Attended West Orange High School and enlisted on Feb. 21, 1942, New York, NY. A plankowner, he served aboard BB-59 as AS 1st Div. at commissioning May 12, 1942; assigned 5th Div. and left BB-59 in 1944. Other assignments include USS *Midway* and USS *St. Louis.*

After the war, he was employed with Public Works Dept., Township of West Orange, NJ. Retired on Jan. 31, 1991 after 53 years of service. In his spare time he is head usher and ran bingo at the Parish of St. Raphael, Livingston, NJ.

Married Ruth O'Neil on May 2, 1953, Holy Name Church, East Orange, NJ. They have four sons, four daughters and five grandchildren. They reside at 35 Lorelei Road, West Orange, NJ 07052.

CICCONE, ALBERT ANTHONY, 207-33-55, enlisted March 11, 1941, New Haven, CT. He is a plankowner and served aboard BB-59 as HA1/c at commissioning May 12, 1942.

CIOLA, KONSTANTINE JOSEPH, 642-14-27, enlisted Feb. 26, 1942, New Haven, CT. He is a plankowner and served aboard BB59 as AS E Div. at commissioning May 12, 1942. Latest address: 605 Ridge Road, Orange, CT 06477.

CLANCY, JAMES MICHAEL, 642-03-11, enlisted Dec. 15, 1941, New Haven, CT. A plankowner, he served aboard BB-59 as SF3/c at commissioning May 12, 1942.

CLARDY, JESSE OLIVER, 606-32-72, enlisted Feb. 7, 1942, Boston, MA. He is a plankowner and served aboard BB-59 as AS at commissioning May 12, 1942.

CLARK, HENRY HAROLD, 356-25-60, enlisted April 4, 1940, Dallas, TX. He is a plankowner and served aboard BB-59 as S1/c at commissioning May 12, 1942.

CLARK, JAMES L., served aboard BB-59 in 4th Div. Latest address: PO Box 56666 Jacksonville, FL 32241.

CLARK, JOHN F., Enlisted USMC, May 8, 1942, Navy Yard, Norfolk, VA. He is a plankowner and served aboard BB-59 as PVT 7th Div. at commissioning May 12, 1942.

CLARK, LOUIS HENRY, 646-33-89, enlisted Jan. 7, 1942, New York, NY. He served aboard BB-59 as SK3/c at commissioning May 12, 1942, and is a plankowner.

CLARK, ROBERT FRANCIS, 618-15-10, enlisted Jan. 17, 1942, Denver, CO. He was a plankowner and served aboard BB-59 as AS at commissioning May 12, 1942, and was on board on its 2nd anniversary. Was assigned SF2/c Plumbing and General Shipfitting. Left BB-59 in January 1945. After the war he worked as a plumber. He had five sons. Memory List 1977.

CLARK, ROBERT NORMAN, 244-07-14, enlisted March 2, 1942, Philadelphia, PA. He is a plankowner and served aboard BB-59 as AS at commissioning May 12, 1942, and was on board on its 2nd and 3rd anniversaries.

CLARKE, CHARLES HARRISON, 238-85-12, born June 5, 1923, Fort Covington, NY. A high school graduate he enlisted on April 1, 1942, Albany, NY. Attended Newport Naval Training Station, RI. A plankowner, he served aboard BB-59 as AS 1st Div. at commissioning May 12, 1942, and assigned S2/c, S1/c, GM3/c and GM2/c 1st Div. Left the BB-59 in October 1946. Other Naval assignments include: USS *Kershaw*, Norfolk Naval Station. He was discharged Dec. 17, 1946.

After the war he returned to his old job from 1946 to March 1947; an ice cream maker from March 1947 to 1949; auto mechanic from 1949-50, parts manager from 1950 to June 1988 Ford/Mercury Dealer, Potsdam, NY, now part-time. In his spare time he enjoys painting, gardening, carpenter work for church and neighbors.

Married Nora K. on July 30, 1955, at St. Mary's Catholic Church, Potsdam, NY, and has one son and one daughter. They reside at 5 Cottage St., Potsdam, NY 13676.

CLAYTON, FRANK BURTIS, JR., 224-78-15, born Sept. 22, 1924, Spring Lake, NJ. He enlisted April 1, 1942, New York, NY. He is a plankowner and served on board BB-59 as AS at commissioning May 12, 1942. He is divorced and has two sons and one daughter. He died March 21, 1993; Memory List 1993. (Son) Frank Clayton resides at 2540 Huntington Woods Dr., Winston Salem, NC 27103.

CLINTON, GEORGE STANTON, 224-37-00, born Feb. 16, 1923, Kingston, NY. Graduated from high school, received a BA from Boston University and MA from Adelphi University. Enlisted July 1, 1941, Washington, DC. Training at Norfolk Naval Training Station, USN Music School, Washington, DC, Sept. 1, 1941 to May 4, 1942. He is a plankowner and served aboard BB-59 as MUS1/c X Div. at commissioning May 12, 1942. Assigned to Sick Bay, Band and 5" Guns. Left BB-59 on Aug. 3, 1945, Leyte Gulf. Other Naval assignments: Sept. 1, 1945 to Sept. 3, 1946 US Naval Separation Center, Minneapolis, MN; Sept. 3, 1946 to July 1, 1947, US Navy Band, Washington, DC.

After the war he was chairman of music department Bennington College, 1951-55; faculty Adelphi University, 1956-70, Garden City, NY; 1971-74 consultant and department head, New York City Public Schools; 1975-86 president of Food Services Inc., Long Island, NY. In spare time he participates in Meals on Wheels; president Nassau County Music Educators; American Legion; Veterans of Foreign Wars; president Boston University Alumni Assoc. School for the Arts; and chairman of Alumni Committee.

He married Marie E., Oct. 25, 1945, Norfolk, MA, and has three daughters and four grandchildren. They reside at 29 Needham St., Norfolk, MA 02056.

CLOSE, J.S., Memory List 1977.

COATE, H.H., served aboard BB-59 on May 12, 1944.

COATES, ROBERT, JR., (n) 646-82-41, enlisted Feb. 19, 1942, New York, NY. He is a plankowner and served aboard BB-59 as AS at commissioning May 12, 1942, and was on board on its 2nd and 3rd anniversaries.

COATES, WILLIAM EARL, 272-38-00, enlisted Aug. 8, 1940, Birmingham, AL. A plankowner, he served aboard BB-59 as S1/c at commissioning May 12, 1942.

COCHRAN, CHARLES FRANKLIN, 250-72-62, enlisted March 5, 1942, Pittsburgh, PA. He is a plankowner and served aboard BB-59 as AS at commissioning May 12, 1942, and was on board on its 2nd anniversary.

CODORI, EDWARD GERARD, 652-25-36, enlisted March 6, 1942, Pittsburgh, PA. He is a plankowner and served aboard BB-59 as AS at commissioning May 12, 1942, and was on board on its 2nd and 3rd anniversaries. He resides at 355 Logan Rd., Bethel Park, PA.

COFFELT, JACK HALE, 632-19-86, enlisted Dec. 30, 1941, Los Angeles, CA. He is a plankowner and served aboard BB-59 as FC3/c at commissioning May 12, 1942.

COFFEY, ARTHUR BERNARD, 666-19-82, enlisted March 5, 1942, Springfield, MA. Served aboard BB-59 as AS F Div. at commissioning May 12, 1942, and is a plankowner. Was assigned as FC3/c Fire Control Repair 5" Battery. Left BB-59 in December 1943.

After the war he worked as an impulse technician for General Electric Company. In his spare time he was a member of Deputy Sheriff's Assoc., member of Uniform Forces of Berkshire County Deputies; past commander VFW Post 445; commander VFW District 9 Berkshire County; and adjutant Allied Vets' Council, Pittsfield, MA. Memory List 1989. (Mrs.) resides at Pierce Road, Windsor, MA 01270.

COGSWELL, BYRON J., served aboard BB-59 in 3rd Div. He resides at 114 East Coffren Ave., Greenville, MI 48838.

COHAN, JOHN LAWRENCE, 606-46-10, enlisted March 6, 1942, Boston, MA. He is a plankowner and served aboard BB-59 as AS at commissioning May 12, 1942.

COLE, HOWARD BERTON, 642-12-21, enlisted Feb. 7, 1942, New Haven, CT. A plankowner, he served aboard BB-59 as AS at commissioning May 12, 1942. He resides at PO Box 1035 Charlestown, NH 03603.

COLE, JOHN BOWMAN, 606-12-81, enlisted Dec. 29, 1941, Boston, MA. He is a plankowner and served aboard BB-59 as Y3/c CR Div. at commissioning May 12, 1942. Was assigned CYM, Captain's Writer, Captain's Office. He left BB-59 in September 1945. After the war he was professor of accounting at Bentley College, CPA. He has five children and resides at 2211 So., Flagler Drive, West Palm Beach, FL 33401.

COLEMAN, CARL PARKER, 600-21-06, enlisted March 14, 1942, Albany, NY. He is a plankowner and served aboard BB-59 as AS at commissioning May 12, 1942, and was on board on its 2nd and 3rd anniversaries.

COLEMAN, EDWARD, (n) 287-37-54, enlisted Feb. 8, 1940, Louisville, KY. He served aboard BB-59 as MATT2/c at commissioning May 12, 1942, and is a plankowner.

COLLIER, EDWARD IRVINE, 287-48-50, enlisted Dec. 10, 1940, Louisville, KY. He is a plankowner

and served aboard BB-59 as SK3/c at commissioning May 12, 1942.

COLLINS, FRANK APPLETON, 223-81-70, enlisted Aug. 29, 1940, New York, NY. He is a plankowner and served aboard BB-59 as SC3/c at commissioning May 12, 1942.

COLLINS, MICHAEL THOMAS, 606-35-82, born March 17, 1924, Fall River, MA. Graduated from high school and received an associate's degree in civil-structural in 1953; BBA in engineering and management from Northeastern University, 1955; from 1964-65 extensive courses hydraulics, MIT University.

He enlisted March 17, 1942, Boston, MA, and received training Newport Naval Training Station, RI. He served aboard BB-59 as S2/c FC Div. at commissioning May 12, 1942, and is a plankowner. Assigned FC2/c Secondary Battery Plot, Computer Operator, Calibrated all 20 and 40 mm sights, Main Battery Turret II Director, Turret II computer operator. Left BB-59 in June 1945 in Philippines. Other Naval assignments: Master at Arms, Fargo Barracks, Boston, MA.

After the war he became a town engineer, Wakefield, MA Highway designer E & R Consultant Engineers, Assistant track supervisor, New York, New Haven RR In his spare time he is a member of the Knights of Columbus and Municipal Engineers Assoc. Honors include: Co-op Students Admission Citation, Northeastern University, Citations from Massachusetts House of Rep., Senate and Secretary of State upon retirement.

He married Katherine in 1946, West Newton, MA, and has four sons, four daughters and 15 grandchildren. They reside at 183 Winding Pond Road, Londonderry, NH 03053-3377.

COLLOPY, WILLIAM J., served aboard BB-59 in CR Div. He resides at 2760 Linshaw Court # 8 Cincinnati, OH 45208.

COMO, VIRGIL, Memory List 1996.

COMPANERO, EMITERO, (n) 435-01-83, enlisted Nov. 29, 1937, San Diego, CA. He is a plankowner and served aboard BB-59 as MUS1/c at commissioning May 12, 1942, and was on board on its 2nd anniversary. Memory List 1977.

COMPERATORE, FRANK JOHN, 608-12-69, enlisted March 4, 1942, Buffalo, NY. He served aboard BB-59 as AS 2nd Div. at commissioning May 12, 1942, and was on board on its 2nd anniversary. He is a plankowner and resides at 95 Stonehenge Road, Rochester, NY 14609.

CONDON, EDWARD PAUL, 606-07-19, enlisted March 17, 1942, Boston, MA. He was a plankowner and served aboard BB-59 as SF3/c R Div. at commissioning May 12, 1942, and was on board on its 2nd anniversary. Was assigned SF2/c R Div. After the war he was employed in milk sales, H.P. Hood.

In his spare time he was active in Holy Name Society, Knights of Columbus, Boy Scouts, Little League, chairman of Youth Activity, Committee Chairman Advisor Basketball. He had three sons and three grandchildren. He resided at 77 Bromfield St., Wollaston, MA 02170. Memory List 1997.

CONDON, ROBERT WATSON, 606-62-11, was born in Wallington, CT, and attended Western Washington State College. He enlisted on April 13, 1942, Boston, MA. He is a plankowner and served aboard BB-59 as CM3/c R Div. at commissioning May 12, 1942. Was assigned to CMM Carpenter Shop and Damage Control.

Left BB-59 in November 1945. Other Naval assignments: retired Warrant Officer, 1960.

After the war he was employed as a teacher of special education high school, Everett School District 2, Washington, from 1966-77 and in his spare time is part of US Naval Institute. Married Betty Jean on Nov. 9, 1945, Seattle, WA, and had two sons and two grandchildren. He died Oct. 21, 1980; Memory List 1981. (Mrs.) resides 21227 96th Ave. W, Edmonds, WA 98020.

CONDON, WILLIAM J., Memory List 1983.

CONE, ROGER R., served aboard BB-59 in I Div. Memory List 1996. Latest address: (Mrs.) 3501 S. Quillian Court, Kennewick, WA 99336.

CONN, ARNOLD, latest address is Box 342 Hendersonville, NC 28739 (1966).

CONNELL, DONALD E., latest address is 116 4th St., Troy, NY 12181 (1966).

CONNELLY, THOMAS FRANCIS, JR., 652-29-27, enlisted March 29, 1942, Pittsburgh, PA. He is a plankowner and served aboard BB-59 as AS at commissioning May 12, 1942.

CONNORS, GILBERT DANIEL, 202-28-65, enlisted March 30, 1942, Boston, MA. He is a plankowner and served aboard BB-59 as AS at commissioning May 12, 1942, and assigned S1/c 1st Div., primer man Turret #1. Left BB-59 September 1943. After the war worked as an assembler for Elliot Business Machines. Married Alice and has four sons and one daughter. Latest address is 260 Brookline St., Cambridge, MA 02139.

CONRAD, CARLTON SAM, 393-44-57, enlisted Dec. 2, 1940, Portland, OR. He is a plankowner and served aboard BB-59 as F2/c at commissioning May 12, 1942.

CONSENTINO, CLYDE, served aboard BB-59 as EM2/c. He last resided in Peoria, IL. Memory List 1974.

CONTARDO, DOMINIC A., born in Boston, MA, and graduated from Medford High School. Attended Franklin Union Tech. and Lincoln Tech. He enlisted in 1942 at Boston, MA, and trained at Norfolk Naval Training Station. He served aboard BB-59 as F1/c M Div. Was assigned as F2/c, F1/c and MM3/c, and left BB-59 in December 1945 in Okinawa. Other Naval assignments: USS *Columbia* and discharged at Fargo Barracks, Boston, MA.

After the war he worked as a laborer and foreman for Everett Construction Company and Bouel Brothers General Contractors, MA. He married Charlotte in 1949 in Medford, MA. They have two sons, one daughter and five grandchildren, and reside at 35 Dudley St., Medford, MA 02155. Contardo died Feb. 8, 1996. Memory List 1996.

CONWAY, THOMAS EVERETT, 202-28-75, enlisted March 30, 1942, Boston, MA. He is a plankowner and served aboard BB-59 as AS 5th Div. at commissioning May 12, 1942. Was assigned as MaM1/c mail clerk CR Div., and left BB-59 in December 1944.

After the war was self-employed as a Roto Rooter Service man. In his spare time he is a member of the Elks Lodge #25, New Haven, CT. He has one son and one daughter, and resides at 114 Hundred Acre Pond Road, Box 342, West Kingston, RI 02892.

COOK, ABNER HUGH, 647-02-49, enlisted Feb. 21, 1942, New York, NY. He is a plankowner and served aboard BB-59 as AS at commissioning May 12, 1942, and was on board on its 2nd anniversary.

COOK, BRUCE ALLEN, 328-75-09, enlisted Sept. 18, 1940, Minneapolis, MN. He is a plankowner and served aboard BB-59 as S1/c at commissioning May 12, 1942.

COOK, RALPH JOSEPH, 646-67-09, enlisted Feb. 6, 1942, New York, NY. He is a plankowner and served aboard BB-59 as AS at commissioning May 12, 1942, and was on board on its 2nd and 3rd anniversaries. Resides at 26 Center Ave., Cedar Grove, NJ 07009.

COOKE, SAMUEL GEORGE, 650-31-65, enlisted Feb. 21, 1942, Philadelphia, PA. He is a plankowner and served aboard BB-59 as AS 5th Div. at commissioning May 12, 1942, and was on board on its 2nd and 3rd anniversaries.

COOKERLY, JAMES M., served aboard BB-59 in E Div. Memory List 1994. His latest address was 624 4th St., New Cumberland, PA 17070.

COOLEY, LEON WILLARD, 328-92-50, enlisted June 10, 1941, Minneapolis, MN. He is a plankowner and served aboard BB-59 as S2/c at commissioning May 12, 1942, and was on board on its 2nd and 3rd anniversaries.

COONEY, MALCOLM T., served aboard BB-59 in A Div. Latest address is RR2 Box 13 Powell Road, Dover Plains, NY 12522.

COOPER, LEO EDWARD, 316-88-10, enlisted Jan. 12, 1942, Omaha, NE. He is a plankowner and served aboard BB-59 as S2/c at commissioning May 12. 1942.

COOPER, LESLIE R., JR., latest address is 1526 Buffalo St., Dayton, OH 45432.

COOPER, PRIDE A., JR., born May 16, 1919, Haddock, GA. Graduated from high school and attended Georgia Tech one year. Enlisted August 1942, Macon, GA. He served aboard BB-59 as S3/c M Div. on October 1942. Was assigned to Fire Rooms; March 1943 E Div.; June, EM3/c; June 1944 EM2/c; and October 1944 EM1/c. Left BB-59 in November 1945 in Bremerton, WA.

After the war he worked as an electrician, chief electrician, department head of maintenance and construction for Eastman Kodak, Peabody, MA. He retired after 36 years of service. In his spare time he is involved with Boy Scouts and church activities.

He married Lillian Mae on Oct. 22, 1945, at St. Paul's, and has two daughters and one grandchild. They reside at 249 Lynn St., Peabody, MA 01960.

COOPER, SAMUEL RUEBEN, 606-73-75, enlisted May 11, 1942, Boston, MA. He is a plankowner and served aboard BB-59 as SF3/c at commissioning May 12, 1942, and was on board on its 2nd anniversary.

COOPER, SIMON, (n) 244-07-46, enlisted March 2, 1942, Philadelphia, PA. He is a plankowner and served aboard BB-59 as AS at commissioning May 12, 1942.

COOTS, LOUIS, Memory List 1993.

CORBETT, F.S., ENS, served aboard BB-59 in 1st Div. on June 14, 1945.

CORBIN, RALPH VICTOR LEON, 342-30-58, enlisted Sept. 11, 1940, Kansas City, MO. He is a plankowner and served aboard BB-59 as S1/c at commissioning May 12, 1942.

CORCETTI, LOUIS NICKOLAS, 652-17-42, born March 27, 1917, Vandergrift, PA. Graduated from high school and enlisted on Feb. 1, 1940, Pittsburgh, PA. Received training at Great Lakes Naval Training Station. He is a plankowner and served aboard BB-59 as AS at commissioning May 12, 1942, with assignments to magazine, BK2/c. Left BB-59 on Jan. 4, 1944, at sea. Other Naval assignments include: BK1/c Treasure Island, CA; USS *Roi*, Sea Bees CASU F#33; CASU F#69 Acorn, CA.

After the war he owned and operated his own bakery in Apollo, PA, for 25 years. In his spare time he coached Colt Baseball, manager for Senior Slow Pitch Softball Team, planted 500 pine trees, did volunteer work, St. George Church; American Red Cross Disaster Service, Montdora, FL; treasurer Knights of Columbus; Faithful Navigator 4th Degree Knights of Columbus, Fort Lauderdale, FL.

Married Eleanor on Nov. 24, 1944, Apollo, PA. They reside at 11735 Starwood Lane, Clermont, FL 34711-9557.

CORLISS, MALCOLME PATTERSON, 204-45-37, enlisted Feb. 14, 1942, Boston, MA. He is a plankowner and served aboard BB-59 as MM1/c M Div. at commissioning May 12, 1942, and was on board on its 2nd anniversary. Was assigned to CMM #2 Engine Room. Left BB-59 on April 17, 1945, and transferred to USS *Kaskaskia*.

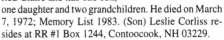

After the war he worked at the New Hampshire State Prison, Concord, NH. Married Claire and has one son, one daughter and two grandchildren. He died on March 7, 1972; Memory List 1983. (Son) Leslie Corliss resides at RR #1 Box 1244, Contoocook, NH 03229.

CORMIER, EDWIN A., USMC, enlisted May 8, 1942, Navy Yard, Norfolk, VA. He is a plankowner and served aboard BB-59 as PVT 7th Div. at commissioning May 12, 1942.

CORMIER, LAWRENCE DOUCETTE, 606-63-88, born Aug. 30, 1912. He enlisted April 23, 1942, Boston, MA. He was a plankowner and served aboard BB-59 as EM3/c E Div. at commissioning May 12, 1942, and assigned EM2/c E Div. He left BB-59 in March 1945.

After the war he worked as a tester and inspector for Western Electric Company. He married Irene and had six children. He died March 5, 1994. (Mrs.) resides at 20 Kendall Road, Lexington, MA 02173.

CORN, ARNOLD, served aboard BB-59 in 4th Div. Resides at 512 1st Ave. W. Hendersonville, NC 28739-4908.

CORNEIL, JOHN FORREST, 642-14-42, enlisted Feb. 27, 1942, New Haven, CT. He is a plankowner and served aboard BB-59 as AS N Div. at commissioning May 12, 1942, and assigned as F3/c P Div. Left BB-59 on March 8, 1943. Other Naval assignments were at Command Services for South Pacific. He resides at 14 Rolling Hill Ave., Plaistow, NH 03865-2537.

CORORI, EDWARD GERARD, 652-25-36, enlisted March 6, 1942, Pittsburgh, PA. He is a plankowner and served aboard BB-59 as AS at commissioning May 12, 1942, and was on board on its 2nd and 3rd anniversaries. He resides at 355 Logan Road, Bethel Park, PA 15102.

CORYELL, JOHN ROSCOE, 646-68-51, enlisted Feb. 7, 1942, New York, NY. He is a plankowner and served aboard BB-59 as AS X Div. at commissioning May 12, 1942, and was on board on its 2nd and 3rd anniversaries. He resides at 634 Oakwood Drive, Forked River, NJ 08731.

COSENS, DONALD, 557-82-98, born Aug. 8, 1927, Miami, FL. Graduated from high school in Miami, FL, and enlisted in July 1944. Attended San Diego Naval Training Station. He served aboard BB-59 as S2/c F Div. on March 1945 and assigned as F1/c in 1946. Left BB-59 at decommissioning, Portsmouth, VA.

After the war he worked as a traveling electrician, worked in Saudi Arabia in 1977 and 1984. He retired in 1988. In his spare time he enjoys travel, fishing, woodworking and yard work. He married La Verne and has two daughters and one grandchild. They reside at 2851 Indian Trail, Morristown, TN 37814-5824.

COSHOW, JOHN MILTON, 375-91-35, enlisted Sept. 7, 1938, San Francisco, CA. He is a plankowner and served aboard BB-59 as COX at commissioning May 12, 1942, and was on board on its 2nd anniversary.

COSTA, PETER DENNIS, 606-38-03, enlisted Feb. 18, 1942, Boston, MA. He is a plankowner and served aboard BB-59 as AS at commissioning May 12, 1942, and was on board on its 2nd and 3rd anniversaries. He resides at 63 Fenwood Road, Roxbury, MA 02120 (1966).

COSTAGLIOLA, JOSEPH ANDREW, 647-01-07, enlisted Feb. 20, 1942, New York, NY. He was a plankowner and served aboard BB-59 as AS at commissioning May 12, 1942, and was on board on its 2nd and 3rd anniversaries. Memory List 1977.

COSTELLO, JOSEPH JOHN, 646-64-58, enlisted Feb. 4, 1942, New York, NY. He is a plankowner and served aboard BB-59 as AS at commissioning May 12, 1942. He resides at 342 Hawthorne Ave., Brooklyn, NY 11235.

COSTELLO, LEO JOHN, 244-07-16, enlisted March 2, 1942, Philadelphia, PA. He is a plankowner and served aboard BB-59 as AS CR Div. at commissioning May 12, 1942, and assigned as S2/c FR Div. and EM2/c E Div. Left BB-59 on Jan. 6, 1946. After the war he worked as an electrician, Alan Woo. He had three sons and resided at 108 W. 10th Ave., Conshohocken, PA 19428. Memory List 1997.

COTE, HENRI HERVE, 202-28-89, AS, born March 17, 1925, Manchester, NH. Graduated from high school and attended one year of Hesser Business College. He enlisted March 30, 1942, Boston, MA, and attended Newport Naval Training Station.

Served aboard BB-59 as AS at commissioning May 12, 1942, and is a plankowner. Assigned to GM3/c #2 Turret and left BB-59 in the Philippines. After the war he worked for Coates Automobile Repair, Manchester, NH.

He has three sons, two daughters and 15 grandchildren. He resides at The Heather 7470 Allen Drive, Brooksville, FL 33512.

COTTON, JAMES A., ENS, served aboard the BB-59 as an aviator V Div. Memory List 1977.

COUGHLIN, THOMAS FRANCIS, 646-82-44, enlisted March 19, 1942, New York, NY. He is a plankowner and served aboard BB-59 as AS at commissioning May 12, 1942, and was on board on its 2nd and 3rd anniversaries.

COUILLARD, JOHN, served aboard BB-59 in 4th Div. Resides at 311 12th St., Brooklyn, NY 11215.

COURTNEY, ROBERT ARTHUR PAUL, 201-54-96, enlisted March 4, 1940, Boston, MA. He is a plankowner and served aboard BB-59 as PHM1/c at commissioning May 12, 1942.

COVERSTONE, LLOYD R., served aboard BB-59 FC Div. He resides at 7433 Sandalwood Drive, Indianapolis, IN 46217.

COWSINS, WILLIE CLIFTON, 266-18-36, enlisted Aug. 30, 1940, Richmond, VA. He is a plankowner and served aboard BB-59 as S1/c at commissioning May 12, 1942.

COX, DUANE, Memory List 1977.

COX, ERNEST BERNARD, 375-83-42, enlisted Feb. 6, 1942, Bremerton, WA. He is a plankowner and served aboard BB-59 as SC3/c at commissioning May 12, 1942. Also assigned to USS *Tennessee.*

COX, IRVIN DUANE, 228-32-94, enlisted Oct. 15, 1938, Long Beach, CA. He is a plankowner and served aboard PHM1/c at commissioning.

COYLE, FRANK MARION, JR., 337-29-59, enlisted April 16, 1940, St. Louis, MO. He is a plankowner and served aboard BB-59 as SC3/c at commissioning May 12, 1942, and was on board on its 2nd and 3rd anniversaries.

CRANSTOUN, HOWARD F., born June 6, 1924, Penns Neck, NJ. A high school graduate, he enlisted July 12, 1942. Attended Newport Naval Training Station, Gunners Mate School, Newport, RI. He served aboard BB-59 as S2/c 4th Div. on March 1943. Left BB-59 on Dec. 2, 1945, in Bremerton, WA.

After the war he worked as a maintenance mechanic-facilities supt., Electronic Manufacturing, Silicon Valley, CA, for 30 years. In his spare time he enjoys woodworking and golf.

He married Heleni Gallimae on Aug. 21, 1976, Lake Tahoe, NV. He has two sons, one daughter, two stepsons and two stepdaughters. He resides at 6109 Edenhall Drive, San Jose, CA 95129.

CRAVEN, JOHN THOMAS, 223-02-81, enlisted June 19, 1939, Brooklyn, NY. He is a plankowner and served aboard BB-59 as BM1/c at commissioning May 12, 1942.

CRAYTON, BILLIE LINWOOD, 262-31-62, enlisted Oct. 19, 1938, Raleigh, NC. He is a plankowner and served aboard BB-59 as FC3/c at commissioning May 12, 1942.

CRENSHAW, WILLIAM POWELL, ENS, served aboard BB-59 in I Div. on Sept. 29, 1944, and left BB-59 on Dec. 26, 1945.

CRESSON, HAROLD, Memory List 1977.

CRIMMINGS, FRANK HOLBROOK, 202-27-02, enlisted March 4, 1942, Boston, MA. He is a plankowner and served aboard BB-59 as AS at commissioning May 12, 1942, and was on board on its 2nd anniversary. Memory List 1991.

CRIST, LEMERTON EDSON, JR., Graduate Naval Academy, Class of 1923; COMDR, served aboard BB-59 as gunnery officer March 1943. Was assigned as Capt. on Oct. 1, 1943 Exec. Officer,

Welfare and Training. Additional Navy assignments were RADM, Ret.. Memory List 1977.

CROFT, WILLIAM CROSSWELL, LT CDR, graduated US Naval Academy Class of 1940. In 1940 Turret Officer USS *California* until sunk at Pearl Harbor, Dec. 7, 1941; February 1942 Turret, Division and Deck Officer USS *Indiana.* Served aboard BB-59, 1st Div. in July 1944. Assigned as commanding officer during mothballing of ship, Norfolk, VA. Left BB-59 in July 1946. Resigned form Navy in December 1946.

After the war, worked for Anaconda Wire & Cable Company, California; 1950 was plant manager for Pyle National Company, Chicago, IL; 1955 elected president until 1977; purchased a small company in 1971; 1973 started another company, now has six companies. In 1987 chairman of his company Clements National Company and CEO of First Illinois Corp. Married Helen Barbara April 1942 and resides at 2150 W. 16th St., Broadview, IL 60153.

CROKEN, WILBERT WENDELIN, 600-21-04, enlisted March 13, 1942, Albany, NY. He served aboard BB-59 as AS at commissioning May 12, 1942, and was on board on its 2nd and 3rd anniversaries.

CRONAN, STEPHAN A., Enlisted USMC, May 8, 1942, Navy Yard, Norfolk, VA. Served aboard BB-59 as P1 Sgt. 7th Div. at commissioning May 12, 1942, and was a plankowner. Resided at 856 Mass Ave., Cambridge, MA 02139. Memory List 1996.

CRONIN, CHARLES JOSEPH, SR., born March 30, 1919, Albany, NY. Attended St. James School and Christian Brothers Academy 1937. Enlisted March 13, 1942, and attended Newport Naval Training Station, RI. Served aboard BB-59, X Div. in January 1943. Was assigned as Y3/c chaplain's yeoman and left BB-59 in February 1944 at sea. Other Naval assignments: DE School, Norfolk, VA; Camp Wallace, Galveston, TX; Bainbridge Training School, Hampton Roads, VA; and in October 1945 Y1/c Teaching Yeoman School, Great Lakes, IL.

After the war he worked as salesman for National Biscuit Company, 1945-64; supt. of salesman Charles Freehofer Bakery, 1966-78; sales rep. Lobel Food Brokers and now retired. In his spare time was director of CYO Sport at St. James School; president and founder Whitehall Little League; president Whitehall Babe Ruth League; phone-o-thon for Alumni CBA; and earned Sportsmanship Catholic Award, CYO.

Married Elizabeth on Sept. 3, 1942, at St. Patrick's Church, Albany, NY, and had one son, one daughter and five grandchildren. They reside at 63 O'Connell St., Albany, NY 12209. Memory List 1997.

CROSBY, RAY CHARLES, 300-19-38, enlisted Oct. 8, 1940, Chicago, IL. He is a plankowner and served aboard BB-59 as S1/c at commissioning May 12, 1942.

CROSS, RALPH EVERETT, 202-39-60, enlisted Jan. 13, 1942, Recife, Brazil. He is a plankowner and served aboard BB-59 as WT1/c at commissioning May 12, 1942.

CROTTY, CARLTON EDMUND, LT(jg) served aboard BB-59 as ENS CR Div. at commissioning May 12, 1942, and was a plankowner. Assigned to Coding Room Oct. 1, 1943, Asst. Radio Officer, CMDR. Memory List 1989.

CROUCH, CHARLES CALLAGHAN, JR., served aboard BB-59 as ENS X Div. (laundry off.), July 8, 1942, and 3rd Div. LT(jg) on Oct. 1, 1943. He left BB-59 on June 5, 1944 as LCDR. Resides at PO Box 3182, Roanoke, VA 24015.

CROUSE, HARRY FRANKLIN, JR., 650-33-18, enlisted Feb. 25, 1942, served aboard BB-59 as AS 5th Div. at commissioning May 12, 1942, and was on board on its 2nd and 3rd anniversaries. Resides at Box 5143 RD5, Stroudsburg, PA 18360.

CROW, CHARLES E., H Div. CPhM.

CROWDER, JONATHAN J., JR., Graduated USNA; ENS N Div., served aboard BB-59 on Oct. 26, 1943. Left BB-59 on Aug. 1, 1944.

CROWELL, PHILIP HOLMES, JR., LT (jg), served aboard BB-59 as ENS CR Div. at commissioning May 12, 1942, and is a plankowner. Assigned as ship's secretary, radar plot March 1943 and Oct. 1, 1943, as JD, CWO. He resides at 21 Sycamore Lane, Hingham, MA 02043.

CRUMBAUGH, ROBERT L., born Dec. 4, 1925, Holden, MO. Graduated from high school and obtained master's degree in education, Bachelor's College. He enlisted February, 1944, Seattle, WA, training at Naval Training Station, Idaho. Served aboard BB-59 as S1/c 3rd Div., Bremerton, WA, July 1944. Left BB-59 May 1947.

After the war, he worked as a teacher at Everett School District, 1951; assistant principal Everett High School, 1960-67; director of counseling, director of financial aid and placement, Everett Community College, WA, 1968; and retired 1989. In his spare time, he is involved in VFW, Exchange Club, YMCA, National Education Assoc., church, board of directors Everett Housing Authority.

Married Beverly in November 1951, Everett, WA, and has two daughters. Resides at 1025 Lombard Ave., Everett, WA 98201.

CRUNK, JAMES GROVER, 287-42-08, enlisted July 15, 1940, Louisville, KY. He is a plankowner and served aboard BB-59 as F1/c at commissioning May 12, 1942.

CUBBERLY, JOHN ANTHONY, 647-03-76, enlisted Feb. 23, 1942, New York, NY. He is a plankowner and served aboard BB-59 as AS at commissioning May 12, 1942.

CUCCIA, CARLO, 8th Flag. Resides at 23 Dillingham Way #1, Hanover, MA 02339.

CULLEN, GILBERT WILLIAM, 647-01-09, enlisted Feb. 20, 1942, New York, NY. He is a plankowner and served aboard BB-59 as AS S Div. at commissioning May 12, 1942. Assigned to SK2/c clothing, small stores and supply office GSK. Left BB-59 in February 1945. After the war he was self-employed for an insurance agency. He has four sons and one daughter and resides at 165 Perry St.

CUMMINGS, CLIFFORD EMBURY, 400-56-48, born April 2, 1915, Springfield, MA. Graduated from high school and a horticulture graduate from Massachusetts University, 1937. Enlisted Feb. 5, 1942, New Haven, CT. Served aboard an unknown reserve destroyer. He was a plankowner and served aboard BB-59 as AS CR Div. at commissioning May 12, 1942, and was on board on its 3rd anniversary. Assigned to S1/c FR Div. on March 10, 1943. Other Naval assignments: Naval Facility, Argentia, NFLD, Roosevelt Roads, Puerto Rico, Korean War – USS *Bataan*. Retired from the Navy with 25 years of service.

Worked for the state of Florida from 1969 until retiring in 1980. In his spare time he was active in First Baptist Church, St. Cloud, FL; Audubon Society; Fleet Reserve #442; Humane Society, Boy Scout Leader, Glen Falls, NY. Married Marion on March 15, 1947, West Springfield, MA, and has two sons and one daughter. He died on June 29, 1986; Memory List 1989. (Mrs.) resides at 1001 Louisiana Ave., St. Cloud, FL 32769.

CUMMINGS, JOSEPH JOHN, 606-38-50, enlisted Feb. 19, 1942, Boston, MA. He is a plankowner and served aboard BB-59 as AS at commissioning May 12, 1942.

CUNNINGHAM, WILBUR EUGENE, 652-24-53, born Sept. 27, 1922, Smock, PA. Enlisted March 3, 1942. and served aboard BB-59 as AS at commissioning May 12, 1942. Left BB-59 as BM2/c. He also served on board USS *North Carolina*, USS *Tulagia* and USS *Ketchun*.

Employed with Boston (MA) Police Force October 1953-1987 and was an active member of many organizations. Married Esther M. (Grill) (Fermon) and had two sons and one daughter. Lived in Peabody, MA, 25 years, moved to Tewksbury, MA in 1995. He died June 23, 1997. Memory List 1997.

CURLEY, JOHN WILLIAM, 224-72-18, enlisted March 3, 1942, New York, NY. He is a plankowner and served aboard BB-59 as AS 6th Div. at commissioning May 12, 1942. He resides at PO Box 56, Etna, CA 96027.

CURRAN, JOHN PATRICK, 224-78-56, enlisted April 2, 1942, New York, NY. He is a plankowner and served aboard BB-59 as AS at commissioning May 12, 1942, and was on board on its 2nd and 3rd anniversary. Resides at 167 Radford St., Yonkers, NY 10170.

CURRIE, JAMES ALEXANDER, 652-20-20, enlisted Feb. 11, 1942, Pittsburgh, PA. He served aboard BB-59 as AS at commissioning May 12, 1942, and was on board on its 2nd and 3rd anniversaries. Assigned to SF1/c R Div. Capt. on May 12, 1945 He is a plankowner.

CURRIE, JAMES W., SF2/c, received Meritorious Mast April 1944.

CURRIER, CHARLES D., aboard BB-59 in N Div. Resides at 2418 N. Eastwood St., Santa Ana, CA 92701.

CURTIN, JOHN WILLIAM, 606-48-31, enlisted March 9, 1942, Boston, MA. Served aboard BB-59 as AS at commissioning May 12, 1942, was on board on its 2nd anniversary and is a plankowner.

CURTIS, WILLIAM ANDREW, 265-90-72, enlisted Dec. 14, 1937, Richmond, VA. He is a plankowner and served on BB-59 as F1/c, at commissioning May 12, 1942.

CUTLER, CHARLES FREDERICK, JR., 400-87-17, enlisted Sept. 26, 1940, Boston, MA. He was a plankowner and served aboard BB-59 as F1/c at commissioning May 12, 1942, and was on board on its 2nd and 3rd anniversaries. Memory List 1977.

CUTRONE, FRANK, (n) 646-67-11, enlisted Feb. 6, 1942, New York, NY. He is a plankowner and served aboard BB-59 as AS at commissioning May 12, 1942, and was on board on its 2nd and 3rd anniversaries.

CUTTER, RALPH THERON, JR., 346-69-26, enlisted Feb. 11, 1938, Little Rock, AR. He is a plankowner and served aboard BB-59 as BM2/c at commissioning May 12, 1942.

CYR, ARMAND ADELARD, 606-40-29, enlisted Feb. 23, 1942, Boston, MA. He served aboard BB-59 as AS at commissioning May 12, 1942, and was on board on its 2nd anniversary. He is a plankowner.

CZEHATOWSKI, A.W., LT, served aboard BB-59 in F Div. February 1943. Assigned March 1943 to duty JD, radar and Comp. 4.

DABAL, TOM, served aboard BB-59 in A Div. He resides at 12 Paronya Court, Clifton, NJ 07013.

DACEY, W.J., JR., served aboard BB-59 as S1/c V Div. and left BB-59 on March 8, 1943, to Commandant Fleet Noumea.

DAFFON, DANIEL BENNETT, 341-98-35, enlisted July 23, 1940, San Diego, CA. He is a plankowner and served aboard BB-59 as COX at commissioning May 12, 1942.

DAILEY, HARRY EARLE, 652-26-02, enlisted March 10, 1942, Pittsburgh, PA. He is a plankowner and served aboard BB-59 in A Div. at commissioning May 12, 1942.

DAILEY, T.F., served aboard BB-59 at commissioning May 12, 1942, and was on board on its 2nd anniversary.

DAIUTE, CARROL F., enlisted Oct. 21, 1942, Boston, MA, and attended Diesel School, Richmond, VA, for eight weeks. Served aboard BB-59 as F1/c A Div. and assigned diesel engines. Left BB-59 on Dec. 12, 1945, discharged. After the war worked in the restaurant business for 40 years and three years part-time grocery store. He resides at 140 Hollis Ave., Braintree, MA 02184.

DALEHITE, WILLIAM HUGH, 295-40-38, enlisted Dec. 15, 1937, Nashville, TN. He is a plankowner and served aboard BB-59 as S1/c at commissioning May 31, 1942.

DALTON, GEORGE FRANCIS, born Dec. 14, 1916, Chelsea, NJ. Enlisted and attended US Naval Academy class of 1938 and Naval War College. Was ensign USS *Colorado* (BB-45), 1st lieutenant and gunnery officer USS *Moffett* (DD-362), XO USS *Charles F. Hughes* (DD-428), XO USS *Cooper* (DD-695). Pre-commissioning and move to Pacific, Comm. USS *Gridley* (DD-380), Comm. USS *Paul Hamilton* (DD-590). Served aboard BB-59 until end of WWII, West Coast. Assigned as a navigation officer. Left BB-59 at Norfolk, VA.

Other Naval assignments: US Naval War College, USS *Fort Mandan* LSD-21), Atlantic Amphibious Force, Comm. Destroyer Div. 22, Comm. Destroyer Squadron 28, Plans Officer Comm. Antisubmarine Force, chief of staff Comm. Antisubmarine Force Pacific Area of Operation. Retired in 1967.

After the war he worked for General Electric Company, Valley Forge, PA, 1967, for three and a half years; ran antisubmarine related research program at Franklin Inst. Philadelphia, PA. He retired again. In his spare time he was active in Navy League; Masonic Veterans of Foreign War (MOFW) Commander 1988-89; member of boards Racquet, Rittenhouse & Philadelphia Clubs, Philadelphia, PA; member Merion Cricket Club.

He married Miriam on Dec. 28, 1943, New York, NY, and has one son, two daughters and five grandchildren. They reside at 322 Ithan Ave., Rosemont, PA 19010.

DALY, THOMAS F., 647-01-10, born Sept. 20, 1920, Passaic, NJ. A high school graduate with a BS from Loyola U. and MSR from Ohio State U. He enlisted on Feb. 20 1942, in New York, NY, and attended Newport Naval Training Station.

He served aboard BB-59 as AS CS Div. at commissioning May 12, 1942, and was on board for its 2nd and 3rd anniversaries. He left BB-59 on Oct. 15, 1944 as SM2/c and is a plankowner. Other Naval assignments: Coronado ATB and San Diego, CA.

After the war he worked as a grad assistant for Ohio State University, 1953; assistant zoology instructor Ohio State, 1954 – academic counselor, tutored football and other sport players, Ohio State – 1972 assistant dean Kent State College – retired 1986. In 1986 taught biology at West Liberty State, WV; assistant professor Kent State College; and has National Science Fellowship, Williams College.

Married and divorced in 1962 with one son. He resides at Box 46, West Liberty, WV 26074.

DAMON, RUSSELL PACKARD, 606-40-95, enlisted March 21, 1942, Boston, MA. He is a plankowner and served aboard BB-59 as F2/c at commissioning May 12, 1942, and was on board for its 2nd and 3rd anniversaries.

D'AMORE, AMERICO MARSHALL, 606-35-41, enlisted Feb. 14, 1942, Boston, MA. He is a plankowner and served aboard BB-59 as AS at commissioning May 12, 1942.

DAMPIER, DOUGLAS LEON, 360-19-53, enlisted Aug. 2, 1940, Houston, TX. He is a plankowner and served aboard BB-59 as F2/c at commissioning May 12, 1942.

DANET, PIERCE MARCEL, 224-78-16, enlisted April 1, 1942, New York, NY. He is a plankowner and served aboard BB-59 as AS at commissioning May 12, 1942.

DANIELS, EARL HOWARD, 606-46-76, born Sept. 26, 1918, Wickford, RI. Enlisted on March 7, 1942, Boston, MA. He is a plankowner and served aboard as AS 2nd Div. on May 31, 1942, and was on board for its 2nd and 3rd anniversaries. Left BB-59 Sept. 26, 1945, Seattle, WA.

After the war he was a commercial fisherman and boat yard worker. He retired in 1980 and now enjoys bowling in his spare time.

He married Ethyl Stone on Oct. 22, 1948, Rhode Island and has three daughters and three grandchildren. He resides at 23 Comfort Lane., Tuckertown Village, Wakefield, RI 02879.

DANILUK, PAUL, 224-16-27, enlisted March 11, 1942, Washington, DC. He is a plankowner and served aboard BB-59 as Mus2/c at commissioning May 12, 1942.

DANKO, JOHN, JR., (n) 337-03-70, enlisted Dec. 31, 1941, San Francisco, CA. He is a plankowner

and served aboard BB-59 as EM2/c at commissioning May 12, 1942.

DARLING, CHARLES GEORGE, 130-24-42, enlisted July 8, 1941, Cape May, NJ. He is a plankowner and served aboard BB-59 as CBM at commissioning May 12, 1942.

DAUGHERTY, PATRICK FRANCIS, JR., 652-20-22, enlisted Feb. 11, 1942, Pittsburgh, PA. He served aboard BB-59 as AS at commissioning May 12, 1942, and was on board for its 2nd and 3rd anniversaries. He is a plankowner.

DAVAULT, ELDRIDGE MACON, 356-29-71, enlisted June 12, 1940, Dallas, TX. He is a plankowner and served aboard BB-59 as S1/c at commissioning May 12, 1942, and was on board for its 2nd anniversary.

DAVAULT, MIKE, Memory List 1992.

DAVE, JOHN IRWIN, 274-46-78, enlisted July 2, 1940, New Orleans, LA. He is a plankowner and served aboard BB-59 as Matt1/c at commissioning May 12, 1942.

DAVIDOFF, M.A., LT CDR, served aboard BB-59 in H Div. on Oct. 10, 1943. Left BB-59 on Dec. 24, 1944.

DAVIDSON, JOHN FRANCIS, 600-21-84, enlisted March 17, 1942, Albany, NY. He served aboard BB-59 as AS at commissioning May 12, 1942, and was a plankowner. Memory List 1997.

DAVIS, ERWIN TIMOTHY, 600-20-83, enlisted March 11, 1942, Albany, NY. He is a plankowner and served aboard as AS at commissioning May 12, 1942, and was on board for its 2nd anniversary.

DAVIS, GLEN BENSON, Graduated from the United States Naval Academy, Class of 1913. Served aboard BB-59 as RADM, ComBatDiv 8 in April 1943 and left BB-59 Dec. 24, 1944. Memory List 1977.

DAVIS, JESSE, Memory List 1977.

DAVIS, JOSEPH WILLIAM, 647-02-55, born Nov. 11, 1921, Brooklyn, NY. A high school graduate, he enlisted Feb. 21, 1942, New York, NY, and attended Newport Naval Training Station, Advance Gunnery School, Quonset, RI.

He is a plankowner and served aboard BB-59 as AS 1st Div. at commissioning May 12, 1942, and was on board for its 2nd and 3rd anniversaries. Was assigned to Turret #1 Gunlayer, 20 and 40 mm Guns GM2/c. He left BB-59 in September 1944 Bremerton, WA, to Gunnery School, Treasure Island, CA. Other Naval assignments: NATCA Patuxent River, MD. Has 20 years flight testing, Supvr. Test Pilot School.

After the war he was supervisor for Gyrodyne Company of America, St. James LI, NY; supervisor, Kenyon Institute, Huntington, LI, NY; production supervisor, Fairchild Engineering Div., and machine shop, Kollsan Institute, Syosset, LI, NY. In his spare time he is involved with Suffolk Lodge AF&AM #60, Port Jefferson, LI, NY; DAV 100 percent disabled VA rated; VFW Post 9482, LI, NY; and Masonic War Vets, Suffolk Post #23, LI, NY.

He married Margaret and has one daughter and two grandchildren. He resides at 1941 Maple Drive, Mechanicsville, MD 20659.

DAVIS, ROBERT EDWARD, 295-18-23, enlisted Dec. 4, 1935, San Diego, CA. He is a plankowner and served aboard BB-59 as BM1/c R Div. on May 31, 1942, and was on board for its 2nd anniversary. He left BB-59 May 22, 1944, Bos'n.

DAVIS, SEBASTIAN WILLIAM, 202-26-38, enlisted March 2, 1942, Boston, MA. He is a plankowner and served aboard BB-59 as AS 4th Div. at commissioning May 12, 1942. He has two sons and one grandchild and resides at Higgins Hollow Rd., Box 42, Truro, MA 02666.

DAVIS, WALLACE EUGENE, 375-67-44, born July 31, 1916, Newman, CA. A high school graduate, he enlisted first on Dec. 10, 1934, San Francisco, CA, and discharged in December 1938. He enlisted a 2nd time on Jan. 2, 1942, San Francisco, CA. Was stationed in Quincy, MA, Jan. 12, 1942.

He is a plankowner and served aboard BB-59 as WT2/c A Div. at commissioning May 12, 1942, and was on board for its 2nd and 3rd anniversaries. Was assigned to WT1/c A Div. in August 1943 and CWT A Div. "Oil King" in November 1944. He left BB-59 on Oct. 10, 1945, Seattle, WA, and discharged in October 1945 at Shoemaker, CA. Other Naval assignments: 1st enlistment San Diego Training Station, California April 10, 1935, USS *California*.

After the war he worked as an engineer for Southern Pacific Railroad for 35 years. In his spare time he enjoys hunting and fishing and is founder of the San Joaquin, CA, Gun Club, 1979; and president of Red Wave Sports, Fresno State Univ.

He married Edith on June 9, 1946, Madera, CA, and has two daughters and three grandchildren. He died on July 24, 1994, and latest address is (Mrs.) 4321 N. 4th St., Fresno, CA 93726.

DAVIDSON, JOHN FRANCIS, Memory List 1997.

DAVIDSON, NORMAN, born Feb. 2, 1922, New York, NY. Attended Pace University and enlisted on Oct. 10, 1942, New York, NY. Attended Great Lakes Naval Training Station, Diesel School.

He served aboard BB-59 as F1/c A Div. Jan. 23, 1943, Boston, MA. He was assigned to EM2/c E Div. and left BB-59 in December 1945, Bremerton, WA. After the war he worked for the Otis Elevator Company in the financial department for 42 years.

He married Lenore on July 1, 1977, New York, NY, and has one daughter and two grandchildren. He resides at 17 Walnut Lane., Avon, CT 06001

DAWSON, JAMES THOMAS, 274-46-51, enlisted June 22, 1940, New Orleans, LA. He is a plankowner and served aboard BB-59 as SM3/c at commissioning May 12, 1942.

DAWSON, RICHARD C., Enlisted USMC, May 8, 1942, Norfolk Navy Yard. He served aboard BB-59 in 7th Div. at commissioning May 12, 1942, and is a plankowner.

DAWSON, THOMAS JOSEPH, 224-78-57, born Sept. 24, 1923, Philadelphia, PA. He enlisted April 2, 1942, New York, NY. He is a plankowner and served aboard BB-59 as AS N Div. at commissioning May 12, 1942, and was on board for its 2nd and 3rd anniversaries. Was assigned to QM2/c N Div. and left BB-59 in August 1944, Bremerton, WA. He had 20 years Naval service and transferred to Fleet Reserve as CET.

After the war he worked for Hewlett Packard Company, Palo Alto, CA, and retired in November 1987. In his spare time he volunteers in the Food Bank of Santa Clara, CA, and is involved in pet therapy with retarded children and in convalescent homes.

He married Regina in November 1956 at Treasure Island Naval Station. He resides at 1102 Kelly Drive, San Jose, CA 95129.

DAY, JACK E., served aboard BB-59 in I Div. and now resides at 2400 SW 4th Ave., Portland, OR 97201.

DAY, PAUL ADDISON, 279-82-95, enlisted June 16, 1941, Cincinnati, OH. He is a plankowner and served aboard BB-59 as EM3/c E Div. at commissioning May 12, 1942.

DEAMCIS, VICTOR EDWARD, 606-45-58, enlisted March 5, 1942, Boston, MA. He is a plankowner and served aboard BB-59 as AS at commissioning May 12, 1942, and was on board for its 2nd anniversary.

DEAN, JACK L., born March 17, 1928, Birmingham, AL Attended college for two years and enlisted in November 1945 Birmingham, AL. Attended San Diego Naval Training Station.

He served aboard BB-59 as S1/c 2nd Div. in November 1945. He left BB-59 in November 1947 Norfolk, VA.

After the war he worked for B.F. Goodrich Company in machine and process development department. He is now retired. Married Lyn on March 16, 1945, Akron, OH, and has one son and one daughter. He resides at 507 Hillpine Dr., Simpsonville, SC 29681.

DEARDEN, JAMES LINCOLN, 650-33-23, born Feb. 12, 1924, Easton, PA. Attended Lafayette College and enlisted Feb. 25, 1942, Philadelphia, PA. He was a plankowner and served aboard BB-59 as F Div. at commissioning May 12, 1942, and was on board for its 2nd and 3rd anniversaries. Was assigned to FC3/c Pointer and Radar Operator – Fire Control Tower. He left BB-59 on Nov. 20, 1944. He was also assigned to the USS *Baltimore*.

After the war he worked for Bethlehem Steel, Bethlehem, PA, as an accountant and retired in 1983. He was an active participant in the American Legion Post #588, Easton, PA.

He married Gladys Nov. 26, 1947, Easton, PA, and had one son, one daughter and three grandchildren. He died in September 1986; Memory List 1989. (Mrs.) J.L. Dearden resides at 315 Old Orchard Drive, Easton, PA 18042.

DEATHERAGE, CHARLES WILLIAM, 360-56-91, enlisted Jan. 27, 1942, Houston, TX. He is a plankowner and served aboard BB-59 as AS at commissioning May 12, 1942, and was on board for its 2nd anniversary.

DEBERG, DONALD J., resides at 3931 Scenic Drive, Waterloo, IA 50701.

DEBOSE, JAMES, (n) 272-85-98, enlisted March 3, 1942, Birmingham, AL. He is a plankowner and served aboard BB-59 as Matt3/c at commissioning May 12, 1942, and was on board for its 2nd and 3rd anniversaries.

DEBROSSE, FRANCES PATRICK, 295-45-16, enlisted March 7, 1939, Nashville, TN. He is a plankowner and served aboard BB-59 as PhM2/c at commissioning May 12, 1942.

DEBRUYN, CHARLES E., resides at 6909 46th Place North, Crystal, MN 55428.

DE CHAMBEAU, JOHN EVERETT, 606-38-78, enlisted Feb. 19, 1942, Boston, MA. He is a plankowner and served aboard BB-59 as Ptr3/c at commissioning May 12, 1942, and was on board for its 2nd and 3rd anniversaries. Played tenor sax in band. He resides at 167 Atlantic Ave., Indialantic, FL 32903.

DECKING, EDWARD C., served aboard BB-59 in S Div. and resides at 4910 Charles St., Easton, PA 18042.

DECOLA, ARTHUR JOHN, 606-41-30, enlisted Feb. 26, 1942, Boston, MA. He is a plankowner and served aboard BB-59 as AS at commissioning May 12, 1942.

DEES, CARL LEMAR, served aboard BB-59 in 3rd Div. He resides at 108 Massee Drive, Dothan, AL 36301.

DE FREES, JOHN WILLIAM, 626-19-87, enlisted Jan. 26, 1942, Indianapolis, IN. He is a plankowner and served aboard BB-59 as AS at commissioning May 12, 1942, and was on board for its 2nd anniversary.

DEGERLAMO, ARNOLD, Memory List 1986.

DEGORIO, ANGELO LOUIS, 606-38-84, enlisted Feb. 20, 1942, Boston, MA. He is a plankowner and served aboard BB-59 as AS at commissioning May 12, 1942.

DE GRECHIE, EDWARD PAUL, 238-84-54, enlisted March 5, 1942, Albany, NY. He is a plankowner and served aboard BB-59 as AS at commissioning May 12, 1942. Resides at 165 Turnpike Rd., Westboro, MA 01581.

DELESDERNIER, THEODORE P., born April 29, 1927, Needham, MA. He attended Northeastern University in 1953. He enlisted in March 1945 Boston, MA, and attended Samson Naval Training Station, USS *Alabama*. He served aboard BB-59 as F1/c A Div. in March 1946 and was assigned to evaporators. He left BB-59 in July 1946 Norfolk, VA.

After the war he worked for MIT as a draftsman to engineer in power plant piping design coordinator on inertial guidance contracts and was physical plant engineer for the University of Massachusetts, Amherst, MA. In his spare time he was involved in music/history for the Volunteer VA Hospital, Northampton, MA.

He married Elizabeth on April 23, 1949, Waban, MA, and has two sons and one daughter. He resides at PO Box 206 50 Leverett Road, Shutesbury, MA 01072.

DELPHIA, MARIO DONALD, 652-24-90, enlisted March 4, 1942, Pittsburgh, PA. He is a plankowner and served aboard BB-59 as AS 6th Div. at commissioning May 12, 1942, and was on board for its 2nd and 3rd anniversaries. He resides at 1026 Woodall Drive, Altamonte Springs, FL 32714.

DELUCA J.D., LT USN, served aboard BB-59 in A Div. July 20, 1945.

DE MARCO, NATALE GEORGE, 647-02-56, born May 10, 1915, New Rochelle, NY. Graduated from high school and enlisted Feb. 21, 1942, New York,

NY. He is a plankowner and served aboard BB-59 as AS A Div. at commissioning May 12, 1942, and was on board for its 2nd and 3rd anniversaries. He was assigned MM2/c and left BB-59 in July 1945.

After the war he worked as a service station dealer, 1932-70; and building services, 1970-81, New Rochelle, NY, Medical Center. In his spare time he is active in the American Legion as a hospital volunteer.

He married Marcy and has one son and one daughter. He resides at 54 Archer Drive, Bronxville, NY 10708.

DEMAREST, HARRY ROBERTS, 647-02-57, enlisted Feb. 21, 1942, New York, NY. He was a plankowner and served aboard BB-59 as AS 3rd Div. at commissioning May 12, 1942, and was on board for its 2nd and 3rd anniversaries. He resided at 4254 Tamargo Drive, New Port Richey, FL 34652. Memory List 1997.

DE MENOCAL, RICHARD ALLAN, 647-02-58, enlisted Feb. 21, 1942, New York, NY. He was a plankowner and served aboard BB-59 as AS at commissioning May 12, 1942, and was on board for its 2nd and 3rd anniversaries. He resided at 2 Mt. Auburn St. # 1105, Cambridge, MA 02138. Memory List 1996.

DE MORANVILLE, WILLIAM, 642-12-29, enlisted Feb. 7, 1942, New Haven, CT. He is a plankowner and served aboard BB-59 as AS at commissioning May 12, 1942.

DEMPSEY, MICHAEL THOMAS, 647-02-59, enlisted Feb. 21, 1942, New York, NY. He is a plankowner and served aboard BB-59 as AS 6th Div. at commissioning May 12, 1942, and was on board for its 2nd and 3rd anniversaries. He has two sons, two daughters and seven grandchildren. He resides at 25 Lafayette Ave., Summit, NJ 07901.

DEMPSEY, WILLIAM, resides at 30 Cutting Ave., Cranston, RI 02878.

DEMPSKO, JOHN, born Jan. 20, 1915, Shenandoah, PA. Graduated from high school and enlisted on Sept. 15, 1942, New Haven, CT. Attended Newport Naval Training Station, RI. He served aboard BB-59 as AS S Div. and was assigned S1/c to SK2/c. He left BB-59 in Seattle, WA.

After the war he worked as an inspector for Alum. Company of America for 23 year and was a toll collector for the State of Connecticut for 17 years. In his spare time he has been a volunteer for Griffin Hospital, Derby, CT, for six years. He resides at 187 Meadow St., #5-2, Shelton, CT 06484.

DE NADAL, WILLIAM, 1965 Homecoming Crew,. His latest address was 47 Old Bedford Rd., Westport, MA 49304. Memory List.

DENDIS, JOHN STEVE, 224-27-24, born May 27, 1924, Franklin, NJ, and graduated from Metuchen High, Metuchen, NJ. He enlisted June 10, 1941, New York, NY and attended Newport Naval Training Station, June 11, 1942; Hospital Corps School, Brooklyn, NY, Aug. 2, 1941; and Sub Base, New London, CT, Oct. 3, 1941.

He served aboard BB-59 as HA1/c H Div. He is a plankowner and was on board for BB59's 2nd and 3rd anniversaries. Was assigned from May 12, 1942, to Aug. 1, 1942 HA1/c PhM3/c H Div.; Sept. 16, 1943 S1/c 5th Div. and left BB-59 on Sept. 27, 1944, at sea off Manila. Additional Navy assignments on Dec. 24, 1944, C77429 Crash Boat Army #QS-74, Fort Lauderdale, FL.

After the war he worked for the Central Railroad of New Jersey; electrician, construction electrician, retired in 1988; part-time Special Police Piscataway, NJ; part-time fire commissioner and chairman of board 15 years. In his spare time he worked as a volunteer fireman, New Market, Piscataway, NJ, for 37 years holding positions of lieutenant, captain, assistant chief, deputy chief and chief.

Married Julia and has one son and two grandchildren. He resides at 125 Hamilton Blvd., Piscataway, NJ 08854.

DENMAN, WILLOW, (n) 300-81-48, enlisted March 31, 1942, Chicago, IL. He is a plankowner and served aboard BB-59 as Matt3/c on May 12, 1942.

DENNIS, FRANK E., served aboard BB-59 in A Div. He has two sons, two daughters, eight grandchildren and four great-grandchildren. He resides at 3238 Mahaska, Des Moines, IA 50317.

DENNISON, WILLIAM REED, JR., LT(jg) served aboard BB-59 in CS Div. on March 23, 1943. He was assigned CWO October 1943 Ass't Signal Officer, March 23, 1944-Nov. 30, 1944. Left BB-59 Nov. 30, 1944 LT.

DENSMORE, SAMUEL WINSLOW, LT CMDR, Naval Academy Class of 1926, is a plankowner and served aboard BB-59 in 4th Div. at commissioning May 12, 1942, and was on board for its 2nd and 3rd anniversaries. He was assigned in March 1943 Mach. Gun Off. and in October 1943 Special Equip. Officer. Left BB-59 Aug. 14, 1945. Memory List 1986.

DEORSAY, RALPH HENRY, MD, LT CMDR, served aboard BB-59 on June 30, 1944. He was assigned Senior Asst. Medical Officer July 1945 and left BB-59 on Jan. 3, 1946. Memory List 1986.

DEPOT, ALFRED A., served aboard BB-59 in S Div., and resides at 2 Vista Drive, Cumberland, RI 02864.

DERCZO, FRANK, 647-02-60, enlisted Feb. 21, 1942, New York, NY. He is a plankowner and served aboard BB-59 as AS at commissioning May 12, 1942, and was on board for its 2nd and 3rd anniversaries.

DERNAGO, FRED, born Sept. 1, 1924, Providence, RI. Graduated from high school and enlisted September 1941 Springfield, MA. Attended Newport Naval Training Station, USS *Emmons* (DD-457), USS *Elison* (DD-454). He served aboard BB-59 as S1/c 4th Div. at commissioning November 1942 and left BB-59 in November 1945.

After the war he worked in radio/TV repair and in his spare time he is active in the American Legion. Married Eileen on June 12, 1948, Chicopee, MA, and has one son, one daughter and four grandchildren. He resides at 599 Newbury St., Springfield, MA 01104.

DERRY, A.G., is a plankowner and served aboard BB-59 at commissioning May 12, 1942, and was on board for its 2nd anniversary.

DERSIN, CLEMENT, 250-47-63, enlisted July 18, 1938, Pittsburgh, PA. He is a plankowner and served aboard BB-59 as EM1/c E Div. at commissioning May 12, 1942.

DERY, ARAM GERARD, 606-47-53, born Aug. 12, 1911, Central Falls, RI. He enlisted March 7, 1942, Boston, MA, and served aboard BB-59 as AS at commissioning May 12, 1942, and was on board for its 2nd and 3rd anniversaries. He is a plankowner. He left BB-59 Sept. 26, 1945, Norfolk, VA.

After the war he worked as a twister tender, textile shipping Corning Fiberglass.

He married Roberta on April 23, 1949, Central Falls, RI, and has one son, one daughter and two grandchildren. He resides at 179 Shawmut Ave., Central Falls, RI 02863.

DE STEFANO, JOSEPH, 646-67-15, enlisted March 6, 1942, New York, NY. He is a plankowner and served aboard BB-59 as AS at commissioning May 12, 1942, and was on board for its 2nd and 3rd anniversaries.

DE TURRIS, FRANK JOSEPH, JR., 646-65-70, enlisted Feb. 5, 1942, New York, NY. He is a plankowner and served aboard BB-59 as AS at commissioning May 12, 1942, and was on board for its 2nd anniversary.

DEVINE, JAMES CONLON, 668-29-31, enlisted Jan. 19, 1942, St. Louis, MO. He is a plankowner and served aboard BB-59 as AS CS Div. at commissioning May 12, 1942, and was on board for its 2nd anniversary. Memory List 1994. (Mrs.) resides at 3372 Marbury Drive, St. Louis, MO 63129.

DEVLIN, THOMAS JOSEPH, 375-23-78, enlisted June 28, 1941, San Francisco, CA. He is a plankowner and served aboard BB-59 as Y2/c at commissioning May 12, 1942.

DE WEES, RAYMOND LEROY, 321-71-02, enlisted Oct. 27, 1941, Des Moines, IA. He is a plankowner and served aboard BB-59 as S2/c at commissioning May 12, 1942, and was on board for its 2nd and 3rd anniversaries. He resides at 107 Second Ave., Red Oak, IA 51572 (1966).

DEWEESE, THOMAS EVAN, 300-78-08, enlisted Jan. 29, 1942, Chicago, IL. He is a plankowner and served aboard BB-59 as AS at commissioning May 12, 1942.

DEWESTER, CLARENCE PFLUGARD, 244-10-88, born March 22, 1925. A high school graduate, he enlisted March 31, 1942, Philadelphia, PA, and attended Newport Naval Training Station, Fargo Receiving Station, Boston, MA. He is a plankowner and served aboard BB-59 as AS 2nd Div. at commissioning May 12, 1942. Was assigned S2/c July 1, 1942; S1/c 2nd Div. Dec. 2, 1942. He left BB-59 on Dec. 3, 1942. Other Naval assignments: USS *Asheville* (PF-1) GM2/c; USS *Guadalupe* (AO-32); and six years in the USN.

After the war he worked for American Motors Corp. in Kenosha, WI, for 31 years in machine set-up and maintenance departments. Retired in September 1978. In his spare time he is active in Veterans Foreign Wars Post 1865, Kenosha, WI.

Married Marilyn on March 5, 1947, Kenosha, WI, and has three sons, one daughter and five grandchildren. He resides at 12227 Chancellor Blvd., Port Charlotte, FL 33953.

DE WITT, LEO VENSON, 628-14-51, enlisted Jan. 4, 1942, Kansas City, MO. He is a plankowner and served aboard BB-59 as EM2/c E Div. at commissioning May 12, 1942, and was on board for its 2nd anniversary.

DE WOLF, MAURICE MORTIMER, Comdr., attended Naval Academy, Class of 1924. He is a plankowner and served aboard BB-59 at commissioning May 12, 1942, and was on board for its 2nd and 3rd anniversaries. Was assigned Oct. 1, 1943, 1st LT damage control officer, ship stores officer and photo officer. Left the BB-59 on June 30, 1944.

DEXTER, HAROLD GEORGE, 628-24-64, enlisted Jan. 29, 1942, Kansas City, MO. He is a plankowner and served aboard BB-59 as S1/c at commissioning May 31, 1942.

DIAS, PAUL J., Homecoming Crew, June 1965.

DICKEY, BLAIR, Memory List 1987.

DICKINSON, HONORABLE FRED A., born March 21, 1915, Brewster, NY. He holds degrees from Hobart College, Boston University and Harvard Law School. Enlisted Feb. 1943 in New York, NY, Seabees. As Y3/c October 1943 commissioned USNR; Transport Officer on transport ship *General W.F. Hase.* He served aboard BB-59 as staff officer to Commander Battleship Div. 8, Eniwetok August 1944. Left BB-59 in 1945. Other Naval assignments: staff officer to Admirals G.B. Davis, J.F. Shafroth and I.C. Sowell and swearing in officer.

After the war he was attorney at law New York State; Dist. Atty. Putnam County, NY; County Judge, Putnam County; Family Court and Surrogate Court Judge, Putnam County; Supreme Court Judge, State of New York 1975 to present.

He married Ruth in 1941 (deceased 1978) and remarried to Florence July 8, 1985, Carmel, NY. He has three daughters, six grandchildren and two great-grandchildren. He resides at PO Box 1149, Carmel, NY 10512.

DICKSON, GEORGE RICHARD, 647-17-32, enlisted March 14, 1942, New York, NY. He served aboard BB-59 as AS at commissioning May 12, 1942, and was on board on its 2nd anniversary. He is a plankowner.

DI CRISTO, MICHAEL, (n) 238-41-26, enlisted May 12, 1937, Washington, DC. He is a plankowner and served aboard BB-59 as S1/c at commissioning May 12, 1942.

DIETHORN, EDWARD BERNARD, JR., 652-26-39, enlisted March 12, 1942, Pittsburgh, PA. He is a plankowner and served aboard BB-59 as AS at commissioning May 12, 1942.

DI FILIPPO, VITO VINCENT, 606-43-99, enlisted March 3, 1942, Boston, MA. He is a plankowner and served aboard BB-59 as AS at commissioning May 12, 1942, and was on board on its 2nd and 3rd anniversaries.

DIFRANCESCO, JOHN B., resides at 4128 Park Lane, Dallas, TX 75220.

DIGIROLAMO, ARNOLD JOHN, 606-48-15, enlisted March 9, 1942, Boston, MA. He is a plankowner and served aboard BB-59 as AS at commissioning May 12, 1942, and was on board on its 2nd anniversary.

DILKS, DAVID H., born March 21, 1926, Royersford, PA. A high school graduate, he enlisted March 17, 1944, Philadelphia, PA. Attended Radio School, Bainbridge, MD.

He served aboard BB-59 as RM2/c CR Div. in

November 1944 and was assigned as radio operator. Left BB-59 in May 1946 Norfolk, VA. Other Naval assignments: Naval Reserve 1946-58; Korean War, 1951-52; and USS *Earl K. Olsen* DE-765.

After the war he worked as a machinist for 10 years; in industrial management for 34 years and retired in 1991. He has two sons and two daughters. He resides at B16G Sussex Lane, Millsboro, DE 19966.

DILLEHAY, BRUCE WALTER, 316-59-14, enlisted July 26, 1939, Omaha, NE. He is a plankowner and served aboard BB-59 as F1/c at commissioning May 12, 1942, and was on board on its 2nd anniversary.

DILLON, EDWARD, (n) 646-82-22, enlisted Feb. 18, 1942, New York, NY. He is a plankowner and served aboard BB-59 as AS at commissioning May 12, 1942.

DIMEGLIO, JOHN EDWARD, 647-02-63, enlisted Feb. 21, 1942, New York, NY. He is a plankowner and served aboard BB-59 as AS at commissioning May 12, 1942, and was on board on its 2nd and 3rd anniversaries.

DI NITTO, RAYMOND JAMES, born Nov. 13, 1921, Jamestown, NY. With two years college, he enlisted Aug. 31, 1942, Macon, GA. Attended Norfolk Naval Training Station, VA. He served aboard BB-59 in the 4th Div. Oct. 23, 1942, and assigned 1st Loader 40 mm Oct. 24, 1942. Left BB-59 Bremerton, WA, Dec. 3, 1945.

Enlisted in the Army in 1948 and was involved in the Korean War, 1950-53; criminal investigator 772nd MP Batt., Army duty in Korea, Japan, Germany and France.

Married by proxy while he was in Korea and Marjorie was in Atlanta, GA, Feb. 6, 1952. They had their marriage blessed at St. Matthew Catholic Church, Statesboro, GA, June 30, 1952. Father Moody was rector at this church. He had two sons, three daughters and one grandchild. He resided at 510 Eisenhower Drive, PO Box 421, Hinesville, GA 31313. Memory List 1996.

DINKINS, ROY ELWOOD, 381-29-06, born Sept. 20, 1920, Chaonia, MO. Graduated from high school in Greenville, MO. He enlisted Oct. 6, 1939, San Diego, CA, and attended San Diego Naval Training Station.

From December 1939 to March 1942 stationed aboard USS *Tennessee*; and in March 1942 Fargo Receiving Station, Boston, MA. He is a plankowner and served aboard BB-59 as F1/c M Div. at commissioning May 12, 1942, and was on board on its 2nd and 3rd anniversaries. Left BB-59 after being discharged in November 1945. In January 1946 he re-enlisted in the Navy for two years.

After the war he was sales rep. for General Mills, St. Louis, MO, for 39 years and retired in 1986.

Married Virginia in January 1946 Benton, IL, and has one son, one daughter and three grandchildren. He resides at RR#1 Benton, IL 62812.

DIRRICK, FREDERICK WILLIAM, ENS, I Div. JO, served aboard BB-59 in 4th Div. March 28, 1945.

DIRTZ, JOSEPH K., Memory List 1985.

DITOMMASO, PHILIP, (n) 650-31-45, enlisted Feb. 21, 1942, Philadelphia, PA. He is a plankowner

and served aboard BB-59 as AS at commissioning May 12, 1942.

DITTMER, FREDERICK HARRY, 224-78-58, enlisted April 2, 1942, New York, NY. He is a plankowner and served aboard BB-59 as AS at commissioning May 12, 1942, and was on board for its 2nd and 3rd anniversary.

DIXON, BRYAN GRIMES, 262-46-61, enlisted Dec. 13, 1939, Raleigh, NC. He is a plank-owner and served aboard BB-59 as EM2/c E Div. at commissioning May 12, 1942. He resides at 12620 Willamette Meridan Rd., NW, Silverdale, WA 98383.

DIXON, MAYNARD HARRY, LT, born July 14, 1918, Mayfield, NY. Attended school at Brooklyn Prep. School, US Naval Academy Class of 1941, RPI Troy, NY, with master's degree. He enlisted in 1937 US Naval Academy.

He is a plankowner and served aboard BB-59 as ensign at commissioning May 12, 1942, and was on board for its 2nd anniversary. He was assigned on Jan. 10, 1943, fueling officer; March 1943 battle station and damage control officer. Left BB-59 on Dec. 30, 1943.

Other Naval assignments: USS *Tuscaloosa* (CA-37), USS *Wichita* (CA-45), USS *Washington;* 1942-43 div. officer USS *Massachusetts* (BB-59); 1944-46 asst. engineer USS *Hancock* (CV-19); promoted to LCDR as engineering officer; 1945; elected for PG School Annapolis for Gas Turbine & Jet Propulsion Engineering, 1946; master of science degree at RPI, Troy, NY; 1947-48 Gas Turbine & Thermoelectric Labs engineering experiment station, Annapolis, MD; 1948 Selected Engineering duties; 1948-51 engineering officer USS *Manchester* (CL83); 1952-53 maintenance off. Service Div. 31, Japan; 1953-57 maintenance off. Pacific Fleet Service Force, Hawaii; 1957-59 Bureau of Ships; 1959-61 Inspector of Naval Material Southeast Dist. Cincinnati, OH; 1961-62 Project Eng. US Army operating Nuclear Reactors; 1962-78 Industrial Eng. Watervliet Arsenal, Watervliet, NY; and retired in 1978 as CDR.

After the war he worked from 1978 to 1982 as equipment manager Watervliet Arsenal, NY and retired in 1982. Loved to travel in his spare time.

He married Rose on April 21, 1942, Boston, MA, and has one son and one grandchild. He died March 27, 1992, and was buried April 3, 1992 at Arlington National Cemetery. Latest address (Mrs.) 1199 Hedgewood Ave., Schenectady, NY 12309.

DOANE, EDWARD GORDON, 413-38-60, enlisted Feb. 7, 1939, Fresno, CA. He is a plankowner and served as S1/c V Div. at commissioning May 12, 1942. He left BB-59 on March 8, 1943, to Comm. Fleet Air-Noumea.

DOERFLINGER, CARL R., LT, enlisted in 1933 in the US Naval Academy and graduated Class of 1937. He served aboard BB-59 in July 1942 and was assigned Senior Aviator in Feb. 1943. Memory List 1994. Latest address was 10 Mansion Court, Menlo Park, CA 94025.

DOHERTY, CHARLES, Revere, MA (1963).

DOHERTY, GEORGE FRANCIS, 201-51-51, enlisted April 11, 1942, Boston, MA. He is a plankowner and served aboard BB-59 as SK3/c at commissioning May 12, 1942, and was on board for its 2nd and 3rd anniversaries. Left BB-59 on Nov. 30, 1944, to Receiving Station, Pearl Harbor for duty in Advanced Base. He married

Pearl and has three sons. Memory List 1977. Latest address was 109 Moreland St., Somerville, MA 02145.

DOHERTY, JOSEPH, Memory List 1984.

DOLE, JOHN ETHELBERT, LT, served aboard BB-59 in I Div. Oct. 30, 1944, and left BB-59 on Jan. 25, 1946. Memory List 1987.

DOMINEY, HARLAND BETFORD, 234-19-23, enlisted Dec. 29, 1938, Buffalo, NY. He is a plankowner and served aboard BB-59 as F1/c at commissioning May 12, 1942.

DOMINITIS, THOMAS ANTHONY, 212-72-33, enlisted June 15, 1941, Springfield, MA. He is a plankowner and served aboard BB-59 as S2/c at commissioning May 12, 1942.

DOMOZIK, JOHN JOSEPH, 650-31-94, enlisted Feb. 21, 1942, Philadelphia, PA. He is a plankowner and served aboard BB-59 as AS at commissioning May 12, 1942.

DONAIS, PAUL EARL, 328-52-26, enlisted April 12, 1938, Minneapolis, MN. He is a plankowner and served aboard BB-59 as S1/c at commissioning May 12, 1942.

DONALDSON, ROBERT JAMES, 201-56-81, enlisted Nov. 18, 1936, Boston, MA. He is a plankowner and served aboard BB-59 as EM1/c E Div. at commissioning May 12, 1942, and was on board for its 2nd and 3rd anniversaries. He left BB-59 on July 12, 1944 (CEM) to Receiving Station, San Francisco, CA.

DONELON, CHARLES, (n) 647-01-14, enlisted Feb. 20, 1942, New York, NY. He served aboard BB-59 as AS at commissioning May 12, 1942, and is a plankowner.

DONNELLY, JAMES JOSEPH, 642-14-24, born Sept. 29, 1919, Waterbury, CT. Graduated from Wilby High School, Waterbury, CT, and enlisted Feb. 25, 1942, New Haven, CT. Attended Newport Naval Training Station. He is a plankowner and served aboard BB-59 as AS FC Div. at commissioning May 12, 1942, and was on board for its 2nd anniversary. Was assigned to Y3/c FC Tower on Dec. 8, 1943, and left BB-59 in March 1944 at Efate, New Hebrides. Other Naval assignments: July 23, 1944, USS *Lowry* (DD-770); Oct. 5, 1944, Y2/c USS *Lowry* (DD-770); and 1956-59 three years US Marines Reserve.

After the war he worked from December 1945 to Jan. 31, 1992 in the engineering department, was draftsman to senior product designer. He has three patents from A.W. Haydon Co. Timex and Carling Switch Company. In his spare time he coached baseball little league-senior league, "Mickey Mantle," midget football and basketball from 1968-1989. Received "Sportsman of the Year" Award, Oct. 28, 1972.

He married Claire on Sept. 4, 1948, Waterbury, CT, and has one son and two daughters. He resides at PO Box 6078, 37 Todd Road, Wolcott, CT 06716.

DONORAS, PAUL E., resides at 1919 8th St., North Claire, Minneapolis, MN 55440 (1966).

DONOVAN, JAMES NOEL, 224-78-60, enlisted April 2, 1942, New York, NY. He is a plankowner and served aboard BB-59 as AS at commissioning May 12, 1942, and was on board for its 2nd and 3rd anniversaries. Received Meritorious Mast (GM3/c) March 1945.

DOOLAN, ARTHUR JOSEPH, 606-49-35, enlisted March 12, 1942, Boston, MA. He is a plankowner and served aboard BB-59 as AS 4th Div. at commissioning May 12, 1942, and was on board for its 2nd and 3rd anniversaries. Was assigned S1/c R Div. and Meritorious Mast April 1944. Left BB-59 in 1946. After the war he worked as a machinist for Worthing Controls, Norwood, MA, and has two children. Memory List 1992. Latest address: 176 Prospect St., Norwood, MA 02062.

DOOLEY, ROBERT HARDCASTLE, 202-28-71, born Feb. 12, 1924, Wollaston, MA, and graduated from high school. He enlisted March 31, 1942, Boston, MA. He served aboard BB-59 as AS 3rd Div. at commissioning May 12, 1942, and is a plankowner. Was assigned to USS *Osage* and discharged on Dec. 5, 1946, Memphis, TN.

After the war worked for the Dept. of DEOS state employee for 29 and a half years. Worked for a car dealer in Milton, CT, and retired in 1985. In his spare time he was involved in the Veteran Foreign Wars #3169, Scituate, MA, and was commander for three years.

He married Kathleen on April 30, 1950, Milton, MA, and has one son, four daughters and nine grandchildren. Memory List 1990. Latest address: 20 6th Ave., Scituate, MA 02066-2814.

DORAN, ROBERT THOMAS, 647-02-66, born June 21, 1919, Morristown, NJ. A high school graduate, he enlisted Feb. 21, 1942, New York, NY, and attended Newport Naval Training Station, Fargo Receiving Station.

He is a plankowner and served aboard BB-59 as AS 5th Div. at commissioning May 12, 1942, and was on board for its 2nd and 3rd anniversaries. Was assigned to Power Shop EM2/c E Div. in June 1943 and left BB-59 on Dec. 15, 1944. Other Naval assignments to USS *LSMR 507* on May 1, 1945.

After the war he worked as a switchman for New Jersey Bell Telephone for 44 years including two and half years for AT&T. In his spare time he is involved with Veterans.

He married Catherine on April 30, 1949, and has one son, two daughters and five grandchildren. He resides at 53 Fairchild Ave., Morris Plains, NJ 07950.

DORAN, WILLIAM P., served aboard BB-59 in C Div. and assigned to R Div. Memory List 1993. Latest address: 165 Pexton St., Sherrill, NY 13461.

DORF, PHILIP, 224-77-47, born Aug. 11, 1922, Brooklyn, NY. Graduated from high school and enlisted March 30, 1942, New York, NY. Attended Newport Naval Training Station. He is a plankowner and served aboard BB-59 as AS S Div. at commissioning May 12, 1942, and was on board for its 2nd and 3rd anniversaries. Was assigned to Baker 2/c, Charge of Bakery. Left BB-59 in June 1946. Was also assigned to two months on transport USS *General Anderson.*

After the war he worked as an operator for New York City Transit Authority. Retired and worked for Bankers Trust in the mail room and security department. Worked part-time during registration at a local college. In his spare time is involved in Jewish War Veterans, is a stamp collector and belongs to a local stamp club.

He married Eha and has one daughter. He resides at 2940 Ocean Parkway, Brooklyn, NY 11235.

DORRES, ROBERT, Memory List 1987.

DOUGHERTY, THOMAS A., CMDR, born Feb. 2, 1916, Hibbing, MN. Graduated from Hibbing High School and attended Hibbing Jr. College and Minne-

sota University. Enlisted on March 1, 1941, Naval Air Station, Minneapolis, MN, and attended Naval Aviation Cadet, Naval Aviator, Pensacola, FL.

He is a plankowner and served aboard BB-59 as ENS V Div. at commissioning May 12, 1942, and assigned aviator-aircraft. He left BB-59 in March 1943 Boston, MA. Other Naval assignments as instrument instructor, chief flight instructor, Corpus Christi Naval Air Station, VP73 Squadron San Juan, P.R.

After the war he worked as an owner and operator of a funeral home. He is a volunteer in his spare time. He married Jeanne on Feb. 11, 1942, and has three sons and 10 daughters. He resides at 600 East 2nd St., Duluth, MN 55805.

DOUNAR, WENCESLAUS A., resides at 3646 E. Underwood Ave., Cudahy, WI 53110.

DOVE, PHILLIP, (n) 201-81-05, enlisted Nov. 4, 1940, Boston, MA. He is a plankowner and served aboard BB-59 as HA1/c H Div. at commissioning May 12, 1942. He resides at 1123 Timber Ridge, Prescott, AZ 86303.

DOWELL, HENRY RICHARD, 287-52-09, enlisted Jan. 24, 1941, Louisville, KY. He is a plankowner and served aboard BB-59 as S1/c at commissioning May 12, 1942.

DOWNING, GEORGE WILLIAM, JR., 204-21-81, enlisted Jan. 26, 1942, Boston, MA. He is a plankowner and served aboard BB-59 as GM3/c at commissioning May 12, 1942, and was on board for its 2nd and 3rd anniversaries.

DOWNING J., Memory List 1977.

DOX, WILLIAM M., JR., resides at 11 Hammond Rd., Falmouth, ME 04105.

DRAPER, ALFRED S., 652-25-30, enlisted March 6, 1942, Pittsburgh, PA. He is a plankowner and served aboard BB-59 as AS 6th Div. at commissioning May 12, 1942, and was on board for its 2nd and 3rd anniversaries. Was assigned to GM3/c Mount Captain MT #2 538. Left BB-59 in December 1945.

After the war he worked for Sears Roebuck Company, Pittsburgh, PA, in watch and jewelry repair. He has two sons and one daughter and resides at 307 Birmingham Ave., Pittsburgh, PA 15210.

DRENG, ROLF OVE, 620-36-46, enlisted Feb. 11, 1942, Des Moines, IA. He is a plankowner and served aboard BB-59 as Bug1/c at commissioning May 12, 1942, and was on board for its 2nd anniversary. Memory List 1977.

DRENNAN, PAUL WILLIAM, 299-74-70, enlisted June 13, 1935, Philadelphia, PA. He is a plankowner and served aboard BB-59 as GM2/c at commissioning May 12, 1942.

DREYFUS, ALBERT AARON, 646-78-63, enlisted Feb. 16, 1942, New York, NY. He is a plankowner and served aboard BB-59 as AS S Div. at commissioning May 12, 1942, and was on board for its 2nd and 3rd anniversaries. Memory List 1991. Latest address was 40-14 79th St., Elmhurst, NY 11373.

DRUMMOND, GEORGE LEMUEL, JR., 646-65-75, enlisted Feb. 5, 1942, New York, NY. He is a plankowner and served aboard BB-59 as AS at commissioning May 12, 1942.

DRURY, WILLIAM FRANCIS, 646-82-49, enlisted Feb. 19, 1942, Naval Receiving Station, NY. He served aboard BB-59 as AS at commissioning May 12, 1942, and was on board for its 2nd and 3rd anniversaries. Was assigned to SK3/c Clothing and Small Stores. Left BB-59 in October 1944.

After the war worked as a clerk to General Foreman for Erie-Lackawanna Railroad. He has three sons and one daughter. Memory List 1985. Latest address was 21 Waldwick Ave., Waldwick, NJ 07463.

DUFFY, DONALD JAMES, 606-47-50, enlisted March 7, 1942, Boston, MA. He is a plankowner and served aboard BB-59 as AS at commissioning May 12, 1942, and was on board for its 2nd and 3rd anniversaries. Memory List 1989.

DUFFY, EDWARD BERNARD, 606-13-72, enlisted Jan. 2, 1942, Boston, MA. He is a plankowner and served aboard BB-59 as SK3/c at commissioning May 12, 1942. He resides at 11114 Lund Place, Kensington, MD 20895

DUHAMEL, GEORGE ALFRED, born Nov. 3, 1919, Taunton, MA, and holds a master's degree from Fitchburg State College. He enlisted April 27, 1942, Boston, MA, and was stationed at Fore River Shipyard.

He is a plankowner and served aboard BB-59 as CM2/c R Div. at commissioning May 12, 1942. Left BB-59 in Noumea, New Caledonia. Other Naval assignments to USS *Midway.*

After the war he was a teacher at Brockton High School. In his spare time he is involved in BB-59 Field Days Gang. He has two sons and one daughter, and resides at 11 Wilson St., Brockton, MA 02401.

DUNBAR, FRANCIS, served aboard BB-59 in 4th Div. Memory List 1995. Latest address was PO Box 575 Shore Drive, Alton, NH 03809.

DUNCAN, EDGAR LLOYD, 328-81-44, enlisted Dec. 17, 1940, Minneapolis, MN. He is a plankowner and served aboard BB-59 as S1/c at commissioning May 12, 1942, and was on board for its 2nd anniversary.

DUNCAN, FRANK ELWOOD, LT(jg) served aboard BB-59 in V Div. J.O. Oct. 30, 1944, and was assigned as an aviator. He left BB-59 in July 1945.

DUNCAN, GEORGE STANLEY, 303-52-94, enlisted March 18, 1941, Portland, OR. He is a plankowner and served aboard BB-59 as S1/c at commissioning May 12, 1942, and was on board for its 2nd anniversary. He resides at Route #1 Kennewick, WA 99336 (1966).

DUNCAN, R.L., B Div., April 7, 1944 F2/c transferred to E Div.

DUNHAM, CLARENCE OCTAVE, served aboard BB-59 as CEM E Div. in November 1942 and left BB-59 on Nov. 1, 1944.

DUNHAM, EDWIN MELVIN, 262-62-76, enlisted July 23, 1940, Raleigh, NC. He is a plankowner and served aboard BB-59 as S1/c at commissioning May 12, 1942.

DUNIGAN, EDWARD BRYAN, JR., ENS, served aboard BB-59 in 4th Div. J.O. May 27, 1945, and left BB-59 Jan. 26, 1945.

DUNKELBERGER, RICHARD FRED, 311-32-93, enlisted June 21, 1939, Detroit, MI. He is a plankowner and served aboard BB-59 as GM2/c at commissioning May 12, 1942.

DUNLAP, CLARENCE WILLIAM, 666-19-65, enlisted March 4, 1942, Springfield, MA. He is a plankowner and served aboard BB-59 as AS at commissioning May 12, 1942.

DUNN, EMERSON LEO, 652-05-34, enlisted Dec. 19, 1941, Pittsburgh, PA. He is a plankowner and served aboard BB-59 as SF3/c at commissioning May 12, 1942.

DUNN, FRANK, (n) 368-67-59, enlisted June 18, 1941, Salt Lake City, UT. He is a plankowner and served aboard BB-59 as S1/c at commissioning May 12, 1942.

DUNN, HANK, Memory List 1977.

DUPERIER, WILLIAM CASPER, 360-47-46, born Nov. 7, 1919, Beaumont, TX. Graduated from high school and enlisted Sept. 18, 1941, Houston, TX. Attended San Diego Naval Training Station, Great Lakes, Machinist School, Ford Motor Company, Dearborn, MI.

He is a plankowner and served aboard BB-59 as S2/c M Div. at commissioning May 12, 1942, and was on board for its 2nd and 3rd anniversaries. Was assigned CMM in charge of #3 Engine Room and left BB-59 in 1947 Norfolk, VA.

After the war he worked as maintenance supt. Mobil Chemical Nitrogen Company, Beaumont, TX. He retired in 1981. He married Evelyn March 14, 1947, Beaumont, TX, and has one son and one daughter. He resides at 5 Cheska Drive, Beaumont, TX 77706.

DUPREE, GLENN STEWART, 268-43-30, enlisted March 14, 1940, Macon, GA. He is a plankowner and served aboard BB-59 as SM3/c CS Div. May 12, 1942, and was on board for its 2nd and 3rd anniversaries. He was assigned to flag bridge with COMBATDIV8 and left BB-59 in December 1944.

After the war he worked for the Colonial Radio TV Company in Arlington, MA. He was also involved in BBBM Campaign (vice admiral Massachusetts Navy); USS *Massachusetts* Assoc. (V Pres. 66-65; Pres. 66-67, V Pres.-Sec. 1967); and BB-59 Award 1978 and member of Memorial Committee.

He married Elvira and has one son, one daughter and four grandchildren. He resides at 9 Nelson Rd., Burlington, MA 01803.

DUPUIS, EMILE, Memory List 1990.

DURANT, CHARLES E., born April 4, 1910, St. Petersburg, FL. Graduated from high school and attended Alabama Poly Tech. He enlisted Feb. 14, 1942, St. Petersburg, FL, and stationed at NOB Norfolk, VA, Radio Communication School.

He served aboard BB-59 as S2/c CR Div. at commissioning June 1942 Annapolis, MD. He was assigned to RM3/c, RM2/c and RM1/c, and left BB-59 on Sept. 25, 1945, Bremerton, WA.

After the war he worked for Stromberg Carlson Company, Rochester, NY for two years; 10 years as

senior engineer aide in advance technology department, General Dynamics Electronics, Rochester, NY; one year Hawaii and two trips to South Africa running and maintaining transmitter equipment. He made several stops in 12 countries. He retired in October 1970 after 25 years of service.

Loved to travel in his spare time. Memory List 1992. Latest address: 2200 Greentree N #2327, Clarksville, IN 47129-8970.

DURGIN, HARRY EVERETT, JR., 381-40-02, enlisted Jan. 30, 1940, San Diego, CA. He is a plankowner and served aboard BB-59 as EM3/c E Div. at commissioning May 12, 1942, and was on board for its 2nd anniversary.

DURKIN, JOHN FRANCIS, 614-22-88, enlisted Feb. 2, 1942, Cleveland, OH. He is a plankowner and served aboard BB-59 as AS at commissioning May 12, 1942.

DUSSAULT, MAURICE JOSEPH, 202-28-62, enlisted March 31, 1942, Boston, MA. He is a plankowner and served aboard BB-59 as AS 2nd Div. at commissioning May 12, 1942, and was on board for its 2nd and 3rd anniversaries. Was assigned to GM2/c, gun captain, Left Gun Turret #2 and left BB-59 in July 1945. After the war he worked as a caretaker for Osiason Bros. He has three sons and resides at 96 Emmett St., Fall River, MA 02721.

DUTY, DONALD R., resides at PO Box 607 Holden, WV 25625.

DWIGHT, JOHN RICHARD, 620-06-47, enlisted Sept. 24, 1941, Des Moines, IA. He is a plankowner and served aboard BB-59 as S2/c at commissioning May 12, 1942.

DWYER, JOHN PATRICK, 647-02-67, enlisted Feb. 21, 1942, New York, NY. He is a plankowner and served aboard BB-59 as AS at commissioning May 12, 1942, and was on board for its 2nd and 3rd anniversaries. Was assigned to MM2/c A Div. maintained steering gear, anchor windlass and cranes. Left BB-59 on Aug. 1, 1945. After the war he was a bartender at Dwyer Tavern and was involved in Holy Name Society. He resides at 216 North 3rd St., Harrison, NJ 07029.

DWYER, ROBERT A., resides at 20 Fall St., Port Jervis, NJ 12771.

DYESS, J.E., served aboard BB-59 as S2/c 4th Div. March 8, 1943. Was killed on board on March 7, 1945. (Mrs.) resides at Route #27, Bismark, AR 71929 (1966).

DYKES, JOSEPH G., QM3/c aboard BB-59 on Sept. 22, 1945, transferred from USS *Sederstrom* DE-31.

DZIEDZINA, THEODORE WILLIAM, 650-26-15, enlisted Feb. 24, 1942, Philadelphia, PA. He is a plankowner and served aboard BB-59 as AS at commissioning May 12, 1942, and was on board for its 2nd anniversary.

DZIENE, THEODORE W., is a plankowner and served aboard BB-59 in A Div. at commissioning May 12, 1942, and was on board for its 2nd anniversary. Was assigned to MM2/c evaporators and left BB-59 in 1944. After the war he worked for A&P Tea Company and married Grace. They have two daughters. Memory List 1983. Latest address 45 Beechwood Ave., New Rochelle, NY 10801.

EARLY, JOSEPH MATTHEW, 650-45-26, enlisted March 31, 1942, Philadelphia, PA. He is a plankowner and served aboard BB-59 as AS at commissioning May 12, 1942, and was on board on its 2nd anniversary. Memory List, 1986.

EARLY, LEO, Memory List 1979.

EASTLAND, VANLEE, JR., 295-73-64, enlisted Aug. 30, 1940, Nashville, TN. He is a plankowner and served aboard BB-59 as EM3/c at commissioning May 12, 1942.

EATON, RALPH JOSEPH, 606-45-52, enlisted March 5, 1942, Boston, MA. He is a plankowner and served aboard BB-59 as AS at commissioning May 12, 1942. He resides at 261 Kilburn St., Fall River, MA (1966).

EBERWEIN, HAROLD EDGAR, CCS S Div., July 13, 1944, appointed APC.

ECHOLS, WILLIAM, resides at PO Box 210331, Montgomery, AL.

EDWARDS, F.H., served aboard BB-59 as LT(jg) in March 1943.

EDWARDS, FRANK LEROY, 666-19-45, enlisted March 3, 1942, Springfield, MA. He is a plankowner and served aboard BB-59 as AS at commissioning May 12, 1942, and was on board on its 2nd and 3rd anniversaries.

EDWARDS, JAMES L., born Feb. 17, 1923, Heavener, OK, and has BS from the University of Oklahoma. Enlisted in November 1941 in Oklahoma City, OK. Received training in San Diego, CA at Aviation Ordnance School. He is a plankowner and served aboard BB-59 as S2/c 6th Div. at commissioning May 12, 1942, in 1944 as BM3/c 6th Div. and in 1945 as BM2/c 6th and S Div.

He left BB-59 in June 1945, Norfolk, VA. Was also assigned to USS *Yolo* and USS *Gilbert Islands*. After the war became a pharmacist in Oklahoma City, a pharmaceutical rep. in Tulsa, OK, and a drug store owner. He has three children and four grandchildren. He resides at 6130 E. 52nd St., Tulsa, OK (June 1993).

EDWARDS, ROBERT JAMES, 356-33-02, enlisted July 16, 1940, Dallas, TX. He is a plankowner and served aboard BB-59 as F2/c at commissioning May 12, 1942.

EGAN, PATRICK, Memory List, 1990. (Mrs.) resides at 3755 Estates Drive, Florissant, MO 63033.

EGAN, RICHARD THOMAS, CR Div. CH.SH.CLK, served aboard BB-59 in ship's sec. coding office on Dec. 4, 1942. He left BB-59 on Oct. 11, 1944.

EGNOTYAK, PAUL JOSEPH, 223-77-24, enlisted July 25, 1940, New York, NY. He is a plankowner and served aboard BB-59 as F1/c at commissioning May 12, 1942.

EHLERT, D.S., served aboard BB-59 as S2/c 4th Div. on March 8, 1943.

EKRE, SHERMAN ERNEST, 385-88-96, enlisted July 22, 1940, Seattle, WA. He is a plankowner and served aboard BB-59 as FC3/c at commissioning May 12, 1942.

ELAM, GERALD WAYNE, 279-87-06, enlisted Feb. 28, 1941, Cincinnati, OH. He is a plankowner and served aboard BB-59 as S2/c at commissioning May 12, 1942.

ELFERS, PAUL LAVERE, LT I Div. served aboard BB-59 on Dec. 14, 1943. Left BB-59 on Sept. 15, 1945. Resided at 1138 Lake St. So., Renton, WA. Memory List 1996.

ELLEGOOD, GEORGE HORSEY, 650-31-63, enlisted Feb. 21, 1942, Philadelphia, PA. He is a plankowner and served aboard BB-59 as AS at commissioning May 12, 1942. Memory List 1997.

ELLENWOOD, KENNETH DONALD, 648-10-27, enlisted January 1942 in Omaha, NE. He is a plankowner and served aboard BB-59 as FC3/c at commissioning May 12, 1942.

ELLIOTT, DONALD P., Memory List, 1991.

ELLIOTT, EUGENE EARL, 291-54-23, enlisted March 5, 1942, as SF2/c. He is a plankowner and served aboard BB-59 at commissioning May 12, 1942.

ELLIOTT, JOHN WALKER, 606-46-07, enlisted March 6, 1942, Boston, MA. He is a plankowner and served aboard BB-59 as AS at commissioning May 12, 1942. He resides at 52A Marion St., East Boston, MA.

ELLIS, ALFRED BENEDICT, Graduated US Naval Academy, Class of 1943, served aboard BB-59 as LT(jg) 1st Div., 3rd Div. Off. and Turret III Off. on July 4, 1942. He left BB-59 on July 21, 1944, as lieutenant.

ELLNER, SEYMOUR, born May 12, 1922, Newark, NJ. Attended Seton Hall College and enlisted on Oct. 13, 1942, New York, NY. Attended Great Lakes and Diesel School, Richmond, VA. He served aboard BB-59 as F1/c A Div. Evaporators in December 1942. He left BB-59 in December 1942 and assigned to various Navy tugboats in San Francisco Harbor MoMM1/c.

After the war he worked for Met Life as an agency manager 28 years. In his spare time he is active in the Knights of Pythias.

He married Lillian on Jan. 26, 1947, in Newark, NJ, and has three daughters and four grandchildren. He resides at 1746 Cheshire Way, Escondido, CA.

ELSON, SAMUEL, served aboard BB-59 and was part of 1965 "Homecoming Crew."

ELSTON, CHARLES, (n) 224-77-49, enlisted March 30, 1942, New York, NY. He is a plankowner and served aboard BB-59 as AS I Div. at commissioning May 12, 1942, and as S2/c CR to FR Div. on March 10, 1943. He resides at 105 N. 10th St., Wausau, WI.

ELZER, ROBERT WALKER, 646-82-52, enlisted Feb. 19, 1942, New York, NY. He is a plankowner and served aboard BB-59 as AS A Div. at commissioning May 12, 1942, and was on board on its 2nd and 3rd anniversaries. Was made MM3/c A Div. Capt. May 12, 1945. He resides at 30 Livermore Ave., Staten Island, NY.

EMANUEL, HENRY, resides at Box 97, Ozona, FL 33560.

EMCO, WILLIAM G., Memory List, 1981. (Mrs.) resides at RFD #1 Spencer, MA 01562.

EMERICK, ROBERT, 651-85-41, born April 3, 1922, Lincoln, PA. Graduated from high school and enlisted Oct. 25, 1942, Lancaster, PA. Attended training at Great Lakes, IL, and Diesel School, Richmond, VA. He served aboard BB-59 as WT3/c A Div. in Boston and left BB-59 in Bremerton, WA.

After the war he was a shoemaker and married Polly M. in 1945. They have one daughter and two granddaughters. They reside at 27 E Pine St., Ephrata, PA.

EMMANUEL, MICHEL, Esq. CDR, Memory List, 1993 R Div. (Mrs.) resides at 2806 Terrace Dr., Tampa, FL.

EMMETT, ALBERT CRAFT, JR., 244-10-59, enlisted March 25, 1942, Philadelphia, PA. He is a plankowner and served aboard BB-59 as AS at commissioning May 12, 1942.

EMMONS, ROBERT C., born Aug. 29, 1921, Hardin, MT, graduated from high school and enlisted Sept. 18, 1942, Seattle, WA. Aviation Cadet training; Flight School, Ontario, OR; University of Washington, Seattle; Murray, KY; Grand Junction, CO; and NAS Seattle, WA. He served aboard BB-59 as QM3/c N Div. on Dec. 5, 1943. Left BB-59 on Dec. 5, 1945, Bremerton, WA.

After the war was a grocer and meat cutter in Weiser, ID, owned the store for 35 years. Was on the city council in Weiser for 12 years and president of the city council for four years. In his spare time he was on the school board for 10 years and chairman for eight years.

He married LaRene on June 9, 1946, in Payette, ID. They have two daughters and two grandchildren and reside at 54 Mobile Lane, Ontario, OR.

EMS, W.M., served aboard BB-59 as S2/c 4th Div. on March 8, 1943.

ENGILKI, ERNOLD, resides at 2407 S. Burrell St., Milwaukee, WI (1966).

ENGLER, O.J., Memory List, 1981.

ENGLISH, DONALD, 551-81-41, born May 30, 1925, Jacksonville, FL. Graduated from Robert E. Lee High School, Jacksonville, FL, and enlisted June 7, 1942, Jacksonville, FL. Training at NTC Norfolk, VA. Platoon 280 R/S Naval Base, Norfolk. Was assigned to USS *Alabama* (BB-60) from Aug. 15, 1942 to Sept. 21, 1943.

He served aboard BB-59 as S2/c L Div., S1/c and QM3/c N Div. on Sept. 21, 1943. Left BB-59 in May 1946 Norfolk, VA, and discharged from USN. Other USN assignments: Re-enlisted in 1947 as S1/c (1953) NTC Bainbridge, MN, QM1/C Amphibious Force (requested "sea duty") USS *Newport News* (CA-148), 1953 TO 1956 QM1/c; USS *Des Moines* (CA-139), 1956; USS *Furse* (DDR-882) 1956-57 QM1/c; USS *Coolbaugh* (DE-217) 1957; NAS Pensacola, FL, Special Services; Gen. *T.C. Breckinridge* (TAP-176) 1960-61 QMC US Naval Support, Taipei, Taiwan-Operations; emergency transfer to USS *Tuluga* (Military Police) for Cuban Missile Crisis.

After the war he was able seaman for US Merchant Marine; SS *American Forrester* US Lines to Bremen-Bremerhaven-Hamburg-Rotterdam; SS *Anardarko* Victory-Lykes Lines (ammunition ship from Sunny Point, NC); to Vietnam; SS *African Star*-Farrell Lines to Sidney and Melbourne, Australia and SS Marine Chemical Transporter. In his spare time he enjoys working in his workshop, electrical and woodwork, garden work and fruit trees. He married Myrtle Nov. 4, 1953, in Darlington, MD, and has one stepson, grandson, great-grandson and great-granddaughter. They reside at 6504 Savannah Hwy., Ravenal, SC.

ENNIS, HAROLD T., born Jan. 28, 1914, West Eminence, MO. He enlisted March 9, 1944, Mason City, IA, and attended training at Farragut, ID. He served aboard BB-59 in 1944 and left BB-59 in December 1945 Bremerton, WA.

After the war he worked as an expressman, Railway Express Agency, assistant funeral director for Major Funeral Home; Iowa State Liquor Comm., clerk; Lehigh Portland Cement Company as crane operator. He is involved in the Elks and VFW in his spare time. He has two sons, four grandchildren and three great-grandchildren (as of April 8, 1993). He died July 1, 1986, and son, Roger, resides at 328 20th Pl., Mason City, IA 50401.

ENTWISTLE, WILLIAM AUGUSTUS, 204-50-41, enlisted March 17, 1942, Boston, MA. He is a plankowner and served aboard BB-59 as S2/c CS Div. at commissioning May 12, 1942, and as SM1/c. Left BB-59 in October 1943 later with ComBatDiv 8 (Admiral Davis). After the war he owned Victory Tap, Warwick, RI. Memory List, 1977. (Mrs.) resides at 2690 West Shore Rd., Warwick, RI.

EPLEY, RICHARD, E Div. resides at Sunshine River Park, 1900 Grace Ave. #200, Harlington, TX 78550.

ERICKSON, WALTER, E Div. Memory List, 1989. (Mrs.) resides at 52 Bickford Rd., Gardner, MA.

ERTEL, THOMAS E., resides at 35 20th Ave., Irvington, NJ (1966).

ERTER, W.G., served aboard BB-59 as S2/c 6th Div.

ESPOSITO, SALVATORE CARL., resides at 3074 Westside Ave., Schenectady, NY (1966).

ESTEPP, WILLIAM MAURICE, served aboard BB-59 as S2/c 4th Div. on March 8, 1943. Resides in Burnet, TX (1966).

ETHRIDGE, ROBERT C., born June 5, 1921, Lawton, OK. Graduated from high school and had one year of college. He enlisted Sept. 20, 1939, Dallas, TX, and trained at Norfolk, VA. Was assigned to USS *Quincy* January 1940 to May 3, 1942, Aviation Unit, Quonset Pt., RI, May 4, 1942.

He served aboard BB-59. Left ship at sea with pilot ENS Tom Dougherty ARM2/c V Div. and Nov. 8, 1942, taken prisoner in Casablanca. Was assigned to Naval Hospital, Norfolk, VA; Sqdn. 152 USS *Intrepid*.

After the war he worked for Pacific Telephone Company, 1946-62, Lakewood, CA; Continental Telephone 1962-80 in California, New Mexico and Arizona. He retired in 1980. In his spare time he enjoys golf, gardening and travel. He was director for Union Hills Country Club 1983-86; director of Arizona Golf Assoc. 1987-94; and SecAffairs Comm. US Golf Assoc.

He married Ina Grissom on June 28, 1944, and has three children and four grandchildren. He resides at 19017 Concho Circle, Sun City, AZ (January 1994).

ETTINGER, CHARLES EDWIN, 647-01-19, enlisted Feb. 20, 1942, New York, NY. He is a plankowner and served aboard BB-59 at commissioning May 12, 1942.

ETTINGER, RALPH G., JR., enlisted USMC, May 8, 1942, Norfolk Navy Yard. He is a plankowner and served aboard BB-59 as PVT 7th Div. at commissioning May 12, 1942.

EVANS, GRANVILLE WALTER, 257-87-97, enlisted Dec. 8, 1941, Baltimore, MD. He is a plankowner and served aboard BB-59 as SK2/c at commissioning May 12, 1942.

EVANS, JAMES WILLIE, 224-77-40, enlisted March 28, 1942, New York, NY. He is a plankowner and served aboard BB-59 as MATT 3/c at commissioning May 12, 1942.

EVANS, ROBERT ERNEST, 243-91-42, enlisted April 30, 1941, Philadelphia, PA. He is a plankowner and served aboard BB-59 as Y3/c at commissioning May 12, 1942.

EVANS, ROBERT SUTHERLAND, 212-53-94, enlisted Dec. 11, 1939, Springfield, MA. He is a plankowner and served aboard BB-59 as S1/c at commissioning May 12, 1942.

EVANS, WILLIAM MCKINLEY, 283-30-34, enlisted Nov. 15, 1939, Cleveland, OH. He is a plankowner and served aboard BB-59 as COX at commissioning May 12, 1942.

EVERETT, FRED WALTON, 265-59-82, enlisted Feb. 17, 1940, San Diego, CA. He is a plankowner and served aboard BB-59 as GM1/c at commissioning May 12, 1942.

EVERHART, M., (n) S2/c, served aboard BB-59 in 5th Div. on March 8, 1943.

EVERTS, H.W., S2/c, served aboard BB-59 in 4th Div. on March 8, 1943.

EWING, ALBERT LEON, 650-28-89, enlisted Feb. 17, 1942, Philadelphia, PA. He is a plankowner and served aboard BB-59 as AS 5th Div. at commissioning May 12, 1942. He has two sons and one granddaughter (March 1992), and resides at 13 Delaware Ave., Somers Point, NJ.

EXWORTHY, JOHN, resides at 28 Ripley St., Malden, MA (1966).

FADELEY, CHARLES F., resides at 111 Beechwood Place, Lexington Park, MD 20653.

FAGGOTTI, ANTHONY JOHN, 647-01-21, enlisted Feb. 20, 1942, New York, NY. He is a plankowner and served aboard BB-59 as AS at commissioning May 12, 1942.

FAIR, RICHARD, EDWARD, 612-07-43, enlisted Dec. 15, 1941, Cincinnati, OH. He is a plankowner and served aboard BB-59 as S2/c 5th Div. at commissioning May 12, 1942, and was on board on its 2nd and 3rd anniversaries.

He was assigned to S Div. and left BB-59 in September 1945. After the war he worked for R.B Fair Company and resides at 3034 Old Dayton-Yellow Springs Rd., Fairborn, OH 45324.

FAIR, WILLIAM GRADIE, 380-54-14, enlisted Nov. 14, 1940, San Francisco, CA. He is a plankowner and served aboard BB-59 as CTC at commissioning May 12, 1942, and was on board on its 2nd anniversary.

FAIRBANKS, K.B., served aboard BB-59 as S2/c 5th Div. on March 8, 1943.

FAIRCHILD, ILER J., JR., LT, US Naval Academy, graduated Class of 1939, is a plankowner and served aboard BB-59 in F Div. at commissioning May 12, 1942, and was on board on its 2nd anniversary.

He was assigned to W4D March 1943, senior watch officer, CIC, LCDR. He left BB-59 in August 1944. He has one son, two daughters and resides at 3084 Bridgeton Court, Woodbridge, VA 22192.

FAIRCLOTH, HORACE S., Memory List 1985.

FALANGA, ANTHONY JOSEPH, 647-01-22, enlisted Feb. 20, 1942, New York, NY. He is a plankowner and served aboard BB-59 as AS at commissioning May 12, 1942, and was on board on its 2nd anniversary. Memory List 1992.

FALGE, FRANCIS MARION, LCDR, born in Reedsville, WI, he graduated from the US Naval Academy, Class of 1924. He entered the Navy August 1919, USS *Oklahoma*; NAPC Newport; and stationed aboard USS *Arizona* from Feb. 5, 1941, to Dec. 7, 1941.

He served aboard BB-59 *Quincy*, February 1942 and at commissioning May 12, 1942, and is a plankowner. On Oct. 1, 1943, assigned communications officer, LT COMDR; COMDR; and assistant 1st LT. He was senior staff officer and flag secretary, Com.Batt.Div. 4 (Maryland, Colorado and West Virginia). He resides at 3093 Fox Run, Appleton, WI 54915.

After the war he worked as a sales district manager for General Electric, lamp division. He was vice-mayor and councilman of Carmel By The Sea, 1968-72.

He married Rose Cleveland, OH, 1919, and has children, grandchildren and great-grandchildren with total offsprings of 36. He retired captain and resides at Box 7556 Carmel, CA.

FALLETTA, THOMAS DOMINICK, 647-02-68, enlisted Feb. 21, 1942, New York, NY. He is a plankowner and served aboard BB-59 as AS at commissioning May 12, 1942.

FANCUILLI, ERNEST THOMAS, 244-10-83, enlisted March 31, 1942, Philadelphia, PA. He is a plankowner and served aboard BB-59 as AS at commissioning May 12, 1942.

FANNING, E.J., served aboard BB-59 as S2/c 4th Div. at commissioning March 8, 1943.

FARIS, L.C., served aboard BB-59 as S2/c 4th Div. on March 8, 1943.

FARLEY, DARIS W., enlisted USMC, May 8, 1942, Norfolk, VA, Sea School. He is a plankowner and served aboard BB-59 as PFC 7th Div. at commissioning May 12, 1942.

FARNSWORTH, JAMES LEE, 680-04-53, enlisted Jan. 5, 1942, San Diego, CA. He is a plankowner and served aboard BB-59 as FC3/c at commissioning May 12, 1942, and was on board on its 2nd anniversary.

FARRAN, ELSTON MATHEW, 375-49-96, enlisted Jan. 1, 1942, Pearl Harbor, HI. He is a plankowner and served aboard BB-59 as SK1/c at commissioning May 12, 1942.

FARRELL, CHARLES JOSEPH, LT, served aboard BB-59 in July 1944. Was assigned chaplain (Catholic) in July 1945.

FARRELL, JAMES WILLIAM, 224-77-81, enlisted March 31, 1942, New York, NY. He is a plankowner and served aboard BB-59 as AS at commissioning May 12, 1942, and was on board on its 2nd and 3rd anniversaries.

FARRINGER, JOSEPH A., JR., resides at Robeson Ext., Williamsburg, PA 16693.

FARRINGTON, DERBY WILLIAM, 214-47-67, enlisted Nov. 10, 1938, San Diego, CA. He is a plankowner and served aboard BB-59 as CYeo at commissioning May 12, 1942.

FARRIOLA, ANTHONY LOUIS, 646-82-54, enlisted Feb. 19, 1942, New York, NY. He is a plankowner and served aboard BB-59 as AS at commissioning May 12, 1942, and was on board on its 2nd and 3rd anniversaries. Left BB-59 in August 1945.

After the war he worked for Columbia President Medical Center. He resides at 172 Daves Ave., Staten Island, NY 10314.

FARRIS, CHARLES D., served aboard BB-59 in CR Div. Memory List 1990. (Mrs.) resides at PO Box 246 Rt. 468, Shady Side, MD 20764.

FARRY, FRANCIS ANTHONY, 650-32-41, enlisted Feb. 24, 1942, Philadelphia, PA. He is a plankowner and served aboard BB-59 as AS at commissioning May 12, 1942.

FASHING, JOHN WILLIAM, 632-03-90, enlisted Oct. 7, 1941, Los Angeles, CA. He is a plankowner and served aboard BB-59 as F2/c P Div. at commissioning May 12, 1942. Left BB-59 on March 8, 1943 to ComSer. South Pacific.

FAUGHT, CHARLES EDWARD, 295-30-77, enlisted March 17, 1942, Kodiak, AL. He is a plankowner and served aboard BB-59 as BM2/c at commissioning May 12, 1942, and was on board on its 2nd anniversary. He left BB-59 on Aug. 14, 1944, CBM transferred to USS *General Hase*.

FAULK, JOSEPH BRUCE, served aboard BB-59 in 4th and S Div.. He married Mattie and has three sons and five grandchildren. He resides at 700 North Lane Wells St., Longview, TX 75604.

FAZIO, CHARLES ANGELO, 224-78-64, born May 9, 1920, Brooklyn, NY. Graduated from high school and enlisted April 2, 1942, New York, NY. He is a plankowner and served aboard BB-59 as AS 3rd Div. at commissioning May 12, 1942, and was on board on its 2nd and 3rd anniversaries. Assigned to COX 3rd Div. CAPT BM2/c May 1945 and left BB-59 Portsmouth, VA. Other Naval assignments: USS *Calvert* APA-32.

After the war he worked as a homicide detective for the New York City Police Department.

He married Carolyn in Brooklyn, NY Nov. 26,

1949. He resided at 9508 Foster Ave., Brooklyn, NY 11236. Memory List 1996.

FEE, FRED DAVE, 346-67-15, enlisted Jan. 21, 1942, Little Rock, AR. He is a plankowner and served aboard BB-59 as GM2/c at commissioning May 12, 1942, and was on board on its 2nd anniversary. Memory List 1984.

FEENEY, JOSEPH, (n) 647-01-23, enlisted Feb. 20, 1942, New York, NY. He is a plankowner and served aboard BB-59 as AS at commissioning May 12, 1942.

FEENEY, K.A., served aboard BB-59 as S2/c CR to FR Div. on March 10, 1943.

FEENEY, KERMIT HENRY, 647-01-24, enlisted Feb. 20, 1942, New York, NY. He is a plankowner and served aboard BB-59 as AS at commissioning May 12, 1942, and was on board on its 2nd anniversary.

FEITELBERG, JOSEPH, (n) (Honorary BB-59 Officer) born in Fall River, MA. From January 1965 to March 1975 was president of USS *Massachusetts* Memorial Committee, Inc., Received "BB-59 Award" 1971. Is president of The Feitelberg Company (insurance) and now lives in Westport, MA.

FELDER, RICHARD W., served aboard BB-59 as EM3/c E Div. and left BB-59 on Dec. 11, 1945. After the war he worked as supt. of grounds and building, Alexandra Central School. In his spare time he was past adjutant and commander of American Legion. Memory List 1977. (Mrs.) resides at RR1 Redwood, NY 13679.

FELLHAUER, HAROLD EUGENE, LT, served aboard BB-59 in I Div. on Nov. 24, 1944, and left BB-59 in July 1945, Div. JO CIC.

FELLOWS, JOHN RICHARDS, 647-01-25, enlisted Feb. 20, 1942, New York, NY. He was a plankowner and served aboard BB-59 as AS 5th Div. at commissioning May 12, 1942, and was on board on its 2nd and 3rd anniversaries. He resided at 3305 Perimeter Drive, Lake Worth, FL 33467. Memory List 1996.

FEMINO, HARRY ANTHONY, 606-47-05, enlisted March 6, 1942, Boston, MA. He is a plankowner and served aboard BB-59 as AS at commissioning May 12, 1942, and was on board on its 2nd and 3rd anniversaries.

Was assigned to GM2/c in charge of catapults, magazines and ordnance, 2/c deep sea diver FC Div. He left BB-59 Oct. 10, 1945.

After the war was self-employed and has one son and two daughters. He resides at 80 Durnell Ave., Roslindale, MA 02131.

FENDER, GEORGE SAMUEL, 269-79-10, enlisted Jan. 28, 1942, Jacksonville, FL. He is a plankowner and served aboard BB-59 as AS at commissioning May 12, 1942.

FERGUSON, CHARLES MITCHEL, 224-77-82, enlisted March 31, 1942, New York, NY. He is a plankowner and served aboard BB-59 as AS at commissioning May 12, 1942.

FERGUSON, DARYL A., Ensign, served aboard BB-59 in 1959 and assigned to decommissioning and maintenance at Portsmouth, VA. Left BB-59 in 1960.

After the war he worked as staff marketing supervisor for C&P Telephone Company. In his spare time he is involved as a member of USS *South Dakota* Memorial Commission. He has one son and resides at 222 Landsdowne Westport, CT 06880.

FERGUSON, THOMAS MCDONALD, 646-82-56, enlisted Feb. 19, 1942, New York, NY. He is a plankowner and served aboard BB-59 as AS at commissioning May 12, 1942.

FERNANDES, ANTONE (n), resides at 337 Nash Rd., New Bedford, MA 02741 (1966).

FERNANDEZ, TONY, served aboard BB-59 as S2/c 4th Div. on March 8, 1943. He resides at 1701 18th St., Galveston, TX 77553 (1966).

FERRARO, BENJAMIN DENNY, 223-09-82, enlisted Dec. 2, 1938, Newport, RI. He is a plankowner and served aboard BB-59 as SC1/c at commissioning May 12, 1942.

FERREIRA, MAURICE L., enlisted USMC, May 8, 1942, Navy Yard, Norfolk, VA. He is a plankowner and served aboard BB-59 as PVT 7th Div. at commissioning May 12, 1942.

FERRIER, N.B., served aboard BB-59 as S2/c 4th Div. on March 8, 1943.

FERRY, VIRGIL W., served aboard BB-59 in R Div. He resided at RR7 Box 123, Lenoir City, TN 37771. Memory List 1996.

FETTER, C.E., served aboard BB-59 as S2/c 4th Div. on March 8, 1943.

FIEGAL, WILLIAM DAVID, 291-64-01, enlisted Aug. 12, 1940, Indianapolis, IN. He is a plankowner and served aboard BB-59 as EM3/c E Div. at commissioning May 12, 1942.

FIELD, HARRY SHERWOOD, 650-30-74, enlisted Feb. 20, 1942, Philadelphia, PA. He is a plankowner and served aboard BB-59 as AS at commissioning May 12, 1942, and was on board on its 2nd and 3rd anniversaries.

FIELD, WELLS L., Captain, resides at Old Bennington, VT.

FIELDING, RULON WAYNE, 372-26-34, enlisted Jan. 28, 1941, Denver, CO. He is a plankowner and served aboard BB-59 as S1/c at commissioning May 12, 1942.

FIELDS, GORDON B., served aboard BB-59 as S2/c 4th Div. on March 8, 1943. He resides at Mount Calm, TX 76673.

FIELDS, WILLIAM NATHAN, 385-82-99, enlisted Oct. 10, 1939, Seattle, WA. He is a plankowner and served aboard BB-59 as FC3/c F Div. at commissioning May 12, 1942. Was assigned as FC2/c F Div. and left BB-59 in August 1943.

After the war he worked as motorcycle officer of Metropolitan Police Dept., Washington, DC. He has one daughter and resides at 13 Armand Ave., Washington, DC 20013.

FIERNAN, FRANK, (N) resides at 95-1177 St., Ozone Park, NY 11416 (1966).

FIFFE, WILLIAM JAMES, 600-20-94, enlisted March 13, 1942, Albany, NY. He is a plankowner and served aboard BB-59 as AS at commissioning May 12, 1942, and was on board on its 2nd and 3rd anniversaries. Memory List 1987. He resided at 341 Madison Ave., Albany, NY 12201.

FILBEY, ROBERT ARNO, 610-43-89, enlisted Jan. 21, 1942, Chicago, IL. He is a plankowner and served aboard BB-59 as AS at commissioning May 12, 1942, and was on board on its 2nd and 3rd anniversaries.

FILINA, A.E., served aboard BB-59 as S2/c 4th Div. on March 8, 1943. He resides at 39230 Bridge Ave., Cleveland, OH 44101 (1966).

FILOSA, CHARLES WILLIAM, 212-60-61, born in Milford, MA. Graduated from high school and attended one year Union Course, Framingham State College. He enlisted Oct. 21, 1940, Springfield, MA, and attended Naval Training Station, Newport, RI. In December 1940 served aboard USS *Pennsylvania*; on Feb. 1, 1942, Fargo Barracks.

He is a plankowner and served aboard BB-59 as S1/c S Div. at commissioning May 12, 1942, and was on board on its 2nd anniversary. Left BB-59 in May 1945 Pearl Harbor for carrier duty and was assigned to Sea Bee Base, Eastport, ME.

After the war he was manager for Western Auto Store, Parcel Post shipper for North America Rockwell, United States Post Office. He is also steward, president of Union.

Married on Oct. 4, 1947, Milford, MA, and has two son, one daughter and seven grandchildren. He resides at 82 Poinsettia Drive, South Yarmouth, MA 02664.

FINNICUM, OLEN A., born in Columbiana County, OH. Graduated from high school and enlisted Dec. 28, 1941, Canton, OH. Attended Cook & Bakers School, Dearborn, MI; Republic Steel, Canton, OH.

He is a plankowner and served aboard BB-59 as S2/c S Div. at commissioning May 12, 1942, and was on board on its 2nd anniversary. Left BB-59 in March 1945 in the Pacific. Other Naval assignments: 1945-47 Boston Dry Dock; 1947-48 Grandell, Greenland; 1948-53 USS *Perry* DD-844; 1953-56 Support Unit Naples, Italy; 1956-57 USS *Mississineva* AO-144; 1957-59 Receiving Station, Philadelphia, PA; 1959-60 Kinetra, Morocco; 1960-64 USS *Marias* AO-57; Feb. 3, 1964, retired as master chief commissary.

After the war he worked for M & M Cafeteria, Perin, FL; Alliance Manufacturing; Republic Steel; Post Office for one year; 7-Eleven for one year; Justice Dept. Bureau of Personnel five years.

He married Aubre on May 21, 1944, Houston, TX, and has two daughters and five grandchildren. He resides at Star Rte. # 4 Box 103, Waverly, VA 23890.

FINUF, HARRISON ALNIN, 342-38-36, born Oct. 20, 1921, Topeka, KS. Graduated from high school and enlisted Jan. 22, 1941, Kansas City, KS. Attended Great Lakes Training Station, USS *Dale* DD-353.

He is a plankowner and served aboard BB-59 as F2/c M Div. at commissioning May 12, 1942. Was assigned to MM1/c steam maintenance and steam turbines. Left BB-59 in November 1942. Was assigned to USS *Chicago* CA-136.

After the war he worked as a clerk in various places. Married his first wife (deceased Dec. 25, 1975) and then married 2nd wife Betty Lou March 6, 1976, Garden City, KS. He has one son, two daughters and four grandchildren. He died Jan. 18, 1994; Memory List 1994. Latest address was 1614 Jan. St., Garden City, KS 67846.

FIORENTINO, VITO, (n) served aboard BB-59 in 2nd and R Div. Died in April 1991; Memory List 1991. Latest address (Sol Glicksman) 16 N. Allegheny St., Cumberland, MD 21502-2739.

FISCH, HARRY JOHN, 299-92-08, enlisted Sept. 20, 1938, Chicago, IL. He is a plankowner and served aboard BB-59 as GM3/c at commissioning May 12, 1942.

FISCHER, RAY, (n) born Dec. 5, 1925, Lorain, OH. Graduated from high school and attended ICS Electrical Engineering Power Distribution. He enlisted Feb. 8, 1944, Cleveland, OH, and attended Electrical School, St. Louis, MO.

He served aboard BB-59 as EM3/c E Div. on July 5, 1944, and left BB-59 on April 15, 1946, Norfolk, VA. Also assigned to Submarine Base, St. Louis Electrical School.

After the war he was operator of an electric power station and supervisor of power distribution for US Steel. He married Emma Dec. 7, 1946, Chicago, IL, and has one son, one daughter and one grandchild. He resides at 830 Osborne Ave., Loraine, OH 44052.

FISH, HERBERT JOSEPH, 201-61-08, enlisted Dec. 28, 1941, San Francisco, CA. He is a plankowner and served aboard BB-59 as MSM1/c A Div. at commissioning May 12, 1942, and was on board on its 2nd and 3rd anniversaries.

Was assigned CMSM in charge of metal shop and left BB-59 on Oct. 3, 1945. After the war he was self-employed in metal fabrication. He has one daughter and resides at 21 Hudson St., Warrensburg, NY 12885.

FISHER, FLETCHER D., served aboard BB-59 as S2/c 4th Div. on March 8, 1943. He resides in Boise, ID.

FITZGERALD, E.D., served aboard BB-59 as BM2/c 1st Div. on May 12, 1945.

FITZPATRICK, JOHN FRANCIS, 224-74-51, enlisted March 30, 1942, New York, NY. He is a plankowner and served aboard BB-59 as AS at commissioning May 12, 1942, and was on board on its 2nd anniversary. He resides at 109 Riveredge Rd., New Shrewsbury, NJ 07724.

FITZPATRICK, PAT D., served aboard BB-59 as PhM3/c H Div.on May 12, 1945. He resides at R#1 Box 219, Cedar, MI 49621.

FLANAGAN, ARTHUR A., served aboard BB-59 as S2/c 4th Div. in January 1943. Was also assigned S1/c, SK3/c SK2/c S Div. Left BB-59 in October 1945.

After the war he was employed as park keeper for the City of Boston. In his spare time he was active in the American Legion Post 154, Dorchester, MA.

He had three sons and resided at 6 Coleman St., Dorchester, MA 02124. Memory List 1989.

FLANAGAN, JOSEPH THOMAS, 244-10-85, enlisted March 31, 1942, Philadelphia, PA. He is a plankowner and served aboard BB-59 as AS at commissioning May 12, 1942.

FLANNERY, ROBERT CHARLES, 646-82-57, enlisted Feb. 19, 1942, New York, NY. He is a plankowner and served aboard BB-59 as AS at commissioning May 12, 1942, and was on board on its 2nd and 3rd anniversaries.

FLEURANT, PAUL DELPHIS, 666-18-95, enlisted Feb. 26, 1942, Springfield, MA. He is a plankowner and served aboard BB-59 as AS at commissioning May 12, 1942, and was on board on its 2nd and 3rd anniversaries. He resides at 131 Regan St., Gardner, MA 01440.

FLYNN, FRANCIS BERNARD, 646-77-15, born May 18, 1918, Brooklyn, NY. Graduated from high school with two years Pace College, he enlisted Feb. 14, 1942, New York, NY. Attended Naval Training Station, Newport, RI

He is a plankowner and served aboard BB-59 as AS F Div. at commissioning May 12, 1942, and was on board on its 2nd anniversary. Was assigned as S2/c, S1/c, Y3/c Gunnery Office, F Div., Y3/c Navigation Office N Div. He left BB-59 in March 1945 at Ulithi Harbor. Other Naval assignments were Receiving Station, San Pedro, CA; Personnel Office Pier 6, Staten Island, NY.

After the war he worked for Inland Marine Insurance in 1946 and as an adjuster for three firms. He retired in 1989. Was involved with the Catholic War Veterans from 1946 to 1959. He married Dorothy March 15, 1942, Brooklyn, NY, and has three sons, one daughter and eight grandchildren. He resides at 389 East 357th St., Brooklyn, NY 11203.

FLYNN, GERARD EDWARD, 224-78-20, enlisted April 1, 1942, New York, NY. He is a plankowner and served aboard BB-59 as AS at commissioning May 12, 1942.

FLYNN, ROBERT MICHAEL, 321-59-95, enlisted Feb. 11, 1941, Des Moines, IA. He is a plankowner and served aboard BB-59 as S1/c 5th Div. at commissioning May 12, 1942, and was on board on its 2nd anniversary. He resides at RR1 Keota, IA 52248.

FLYNN, WILLIAM J., served aboard BB-59 in E Div. He resides at 138 Travel Park Dr., Springhill, FL 34607.

FOCHS, CYRIL A., born in Evanston, IL. He enlisted Dec. 11, 1942, and attended Great Lakes Training Station, Steam Engineering School, Minnesota University MM3/c. He served aboard BB-59 as MM3/c M Div. in March 1943. Left BB-59 on Jan. 1, 1946.

After the war he worked various jobs as maintenance for juke box route; operator of Wisconsin Power & Light Company; assembler Gilman Engineering; instrument repairman; restaurant operator; repairman Lianco Container Company; plant electrician Hussmann Refrigerator Company.

He enjoys gardening in his spare time. He has three daughters seven grandchildren and resides at 117 Sue Lane, St. Charles, MO 63301.

FOGELIN, LELAND GEORGE, 606-46-16, enlisted March 6, 1942, Boston, MA. He is a plankowner and served aboard BB-59 as AS at commissioning May 12, 1942, and was on board on its 2nd anniversary. Latest address was Stockholm, ME 04783. Memory List 1979.

FOGLE, ROBERT FRANCIS, 650-32-54, enlisted Feb. 24, 1942, Philadelphia, PA. He is a plankowner and served aboard BB-59 as AS at commissioning May 12, 1942.

FOLEY, FRANCIS R., USMC, served aboard BB-59 in the 7th Div. He resides at 1164 Wanaka St., Honolulu, HI 96818.

FOLEY, WILLIAM MICHAEL, 202-28-83, born April 27, 1920, Wakefield, MA. Graduated from high school in Malden, MA, and enlisted on March 31, 1942, Boston, MA. Stationed at Naval Base, Providence, RI.

He is a plankowner and served aboard BB-59 as AS 5th Div. at commissioning May 12, 1942, and was on board on its 2nd and 3rd anniversaries. Was assigned as BM2/c and left BB-59 in Philadelphia, PA, after being discharged.

After the war he was a salesman for Egar P. Lewis Company and spent his free time as chief steward of Fraternal Order of Eagles.

He married Lillian in Boston, MA, and has one son, one daughter and one grandchild. Foley died Aug. 15, 1984; Memory List 1987. (Mrs.) resides at PO Box 777, Pocasset, MA 02559.

FOLLA, JOSEPH RICHARD, born Sept. 21, 1922, graduated from Balboa High School, San Francisco, CA. Enlisted on Sept. 7, 1942, San Francisco and attended Naval Training Station, San Diego, CA, and Diesel School, Iowa State College, Ames, IA.

He served aboard BB-59 as F1/c A Div. on Jan. 5, 1943. Was assigned MOMM3 and MOMM2 and left BB-59 on Feb. 5, 1945. Other Naval assignments were Diesel School, Richmond, VA; USS *PCE-894* and MOMM1/c USS *PCE-880.*; and Submarine Base, New London, CT.

After the war he worked for the Pacific Telephone Company, San Francisco, CA, and retired. He married Frances Sept. 9, 1948, Boston, MA, and they reside at 243 Live Oak Dr., Petaluma, CA 94952.

FOLLA, RICHARD T., served aboard BB-59 in S Div. and resides at 143 Westridge Drive, Petaluma, CA 94952.

FONTANAZZA, TONY EDWARD, 243-22-23, enlisted Dec. 28, 1941, San Francisco, CA. He is a plankowner and served aboard BB-59 as MM1/c on at commissioning May 12, 1942.

FORSTIK, EDWARD JOSEPH, 647-01-27, enlisted Feb. 20, 1942, New York, NY. He is a plankowner and served aboard BB-59 as AS at commissioning May 12, 1942.

FORTIER, EDMOND GEORGE, 202-28-55, enlisted March 30, 1942, Boston, MA. He is a plankowner and served aboard BB-59 as AS at commissioning May 12, 1942, and was on board on its 2nd anniversary.

FOSHA, R. LEON DR., born in 1921 in Woodriver, IL. He holds a BS, MS and Ph.D. He enlisted Jan. 29, 1942, Washington, DC and attended Navy School of Music.

He served aboard BB-59 as Mus1/c X Div. on Nov. 25, 1942, and was assigned trumpet player, pianist and arranger. Left BB-59 in June 1945 Uluthi. Was assigned from June 1945 to November 1945 Wold-Chamberlin Separation Center, Minneapolis, MN.

After the war he was music consultant, Secondary School Music, music department of Wisconsin University and music department of Indiana University. In his spare time he was involved in many community youth organizations, community music organizations, fine art activities, teaching adult reading. Honors include president of Wisconsin Music Educators Assoc.; Outstanding Hoosier Musician, 1992; Who's Who in the Midwest; and Who's Who in American Education.

He married Dorothy on Nov. 13, 1946, Bloomington, IN, and has two sons and one daughter. He resides at 3618 Sowder Square, Bloomington, IN 47401.

FOSTER, ROBY ROBERT, 356-31-29, enlisted June 26, 1940, Dallas, TX. He is a plankowner and served aboard BB-59 as F2/c at commissioning May 12, 1942.

FOSTER, ROSS, (n) 283-60-85, enlisted Sept. 18, 1941, Cleveland, OH. He is a plankowner and served aboard BB-59 as S2/c at commissioning May 12, 1942.

FOSTER, ROY ALLISON, served aboard in FC Div. JO in December 1942. Left BB-59 as ChGun on Oct. 22, 1944.

FOUCHE, D.G., served aboard BB-59 as S2/c 4th Div. in March 8, 1943.

FOULIS, GEORGE ANDREW, 606-47-31, enlisted March 7, 1942, Boston, MA. He is a plankowner and served aboard BB-59 as AS at commissioning May 12, 1942.

FRANCE, CARL E., resides at RD #2 Pavonia W. Road, Mansfield, OH 44903.

FRANCIS, POMEROY TUCKER, 647-02-70, enlisted Feb. 21, 1942, New York, NY. He is a plankowner and served aboard BB-59 as AS at commissioning May 12, 1942. He resides at 901 Parke's Run Lane, Villanova, PA 19085.

FRANK, IGNATIUS J., born Nov. 16, 1914, Milwaukee, WI. He enlisted March 4, 1944, Denver, CO, and attended Naval Training Station, Farragut, ID.

He came aboard BB-59 on May 20, 1944 as F1/c assigned to M Div. He was became MM1/c April 24, 1945, and left BB-59 on Dec. 11, 1945, Shoemaker, CA.

After the war he worked as a carpenter and cabinetmaker. From 1947-76 he was a farmer and rancher and retired in 1976. In his spare time he was a commander Boys State Chairman, American Legion Heart Mountain Post 91, Life Member Veteran of Foreign Wars Post 5054; 3rd and 4th Degree Knights of Columbus.

He married Lola Caskey Dec. 27, 1938, Julesburg, CO. He has two sons, two daughters, 10 grandchildren, and 5 great-grandchildren. He resides at 1566 Highway 14 S.R., Powell, WY 82435.

FRANKLIN, JOHN, (n) resides at PO Box 176 Cross Anchor, SC 29331.

FRASER, WILLIAM GEORGE, 606-44-73, enlisted March 4, 1942, Boston, MA. He is a plankowner and served aboard BB-59 as AS at commissioning May 12, 1942.

FRASIER, ROBERT E., resides at HCR-2 Box 70M Goliad, TX 77963.

FRAZIER, J.T., served aboard BB-59 as S2/c 4th Div. on March 8, 1943.

FRAZIER, RICHARD LAVERNE, 337-67-93, enlisted Aug. 14, 1941, St. Louis, MO. He is a plankowner and served aboard BB-59 as S2/c at commissioning May 12, 1942, and was on board on its 2nd and 3rd anniversaries.

FRAZIER, THOMAS DWIGHT, 337-16-81, enlisted Aug. 8, 1939, St. Louis, MO. He is a plankowner and served aboard BB-59 as S1/c at commissioning May 12, 1942.

FRAZIER, VERNON, (n) 266-18-76, enlisted Sept. 16 1940, Richmond, VA. He is a plankowner and served aboard BB-59 as S1/c at commissioning May 12, 1942, and was on board on its 2nd and 3rd anniversaries as 6th Div. GM (1945).

FREDERICK, H.A., served aboard BB-59 as S2/c 4th Div. on March 8, 1943.

FREDERICKS, JOSEPH J., 238-26-98, born March 19, 1905, East Kingston, NY. Graduated from St. Mary's, Saugerties, NY. Enlisted first on April 27, 1925, and second time Jan. 8, 1942, Albany, NY. Was

stationed in 1928 USS *Concord;* 1928 Nicaraguan Campaign; 1929 Sandino Uprising. The second enlistment Electrical School, Hampton Roads, VA.

He is a plankowner and served aboard BB-59 as EM1/c E Div. at commissioning May 12, 1942, and left BB-59 in 1943 San Francisco, CA. Other Naval assignments were USS *Lexington,* USS *Natoma Bay,* USNH League Island, USS *Mercy,* USS *Grasp,* Feb.. 2, 1944 CEM.

After the war he worked in electrical plant engineering for Ford Motor Company, owned a garage and service station and was taxi limousine driver New York City, Larchmont, NY. In his spare time he was active in VFW, Niagara Frontier Chapter and the Retired Officer's Assoc.

He married Irene Kalinowski, St. Mary's, Saugerties, NY. They have one son, one daughter, two grandchildren and one great-grandchild. Memory List 1984. (Mrs.) resides at 105 South Lane, Angola, NY 14006.

FREEMAN, CHARLES FREDERICK, LCDR, is a plankowner and served aboard BB-59 in M Div. at commissioning May 12, 1942. He was assigned engineer watch officer and propulsion officer. He left BB-59 in February 1943.

After the war he worked as bank guard for L.R. Trust. In his spare time he was active in Retired Officer's Assoc. and Fleet Reserve Assoc. He has one son. Memory List 1984. Latest address was 15 Hambly Rd., Tiverton, RI 02878.

FREESE, GEORGE HENRY, 328-43-48, enlisted July 18, 1940, San Diego, CA. He is a plankowner and served aboard BB-59 as COX 6th Div. at commissioning May 12, 1942, and was on board on its 2nd and 3rd anniversaries. He resides at 132 D Ave., Coronado, CA 92118.

FRENCH, WAYNE GOFFREY, 272-39-27, enlisted Sept. 7, 1940, Birmingham, AL. He is a plankowner and served aboard BB-59 as S1/c at commissioning May 12, 1942.

FREVOLA, RALPH, (n) 646-82-61, born April 19, 1916, Brooklyn, NY. Graduated from high school and enlisted Feb. 19, 1942, New York, NY. Attended Naval Training Station, Newport, RI.

He is a plankowner and served aboard BB-59 as AS S Div. at commissioning May 12, 1942, and was on board on its 2nd and 3rd anniversaries. Assigned to SK2/c S Div. and left BB-59 in September 1945 Puget Sound, WA.

He married Margaret April 17, 1948, Brooklyn, NY, and has three sons, three daughters and nine grandchildren. He resides at 240 Marilynn St., East Islip, NY 11730.

FRICH, R.W., served aboard BB-59 as S2/c 4th Div. on March 8, 1943.

FRIEDMAN, DAVID DONALD, 650-30-62, enlisted Feb. 20, 1942, Philadelphia, PA. He is a plankowner and served aboard BB-59 as AS at commissioning May 12, 1942.

FRIEL, EDWARD JOSEPH, 647-02-71, enlisted Feb. 21, 1942, New York, NY. He is a plankowner and served aboard BB-59 as AS at commissioning May 12, 1942, and was on board on its 2nd anniversary.

FRIEL, PAUL, (N) served aboard BB-59 in V Div. Resides at 27 Thornton St., Newton, MA 02158.

FRISOLI, LAWRENCE E., resides at 150 Erie St., # 210, Cambridge, MA 02139.

FRITZ, MARTIN GERARD, 666-19-46, born May 22, 1920, Greenfield, MA. Enlisted March 3,

1942, Springfield, MA, and attended Naval Training Station, Newport, RI.

He is a plankowner and served aboard BB-59 as AS 6th Div. at commissioning May 12, 1942, and was on board on its 2nd and 3rd anniversaries. Assigned to GM3/c 6th Div. and left BB-59 at sea in the Pacific July 1945. Was also assigned to New London, CT.

After the war he worked as a construction worker, truck driver and dairy farmer. In his spare time was active at VFW, American Legion, Plank Owner, US Navy Memorial, Washington, DC.

He married Sophie April 24, 1948, Turners Falls, MA, and has three daughters and one grandchild. He resides at Beers Plain Rd., Northfield, MA 01360.

FRUITS, ROBERT GRIER, 381-09-33, enlisted Dec. 21, 1939, Bremerton, WA. He is a plankowner and served aboard BB-59 as EM1/c E Div. at commissioning May 12, 1942, and was on board on its 2nd anniversary. Left BB-59 on Dec. 28, 1944, CEM.

FRYXELL, ANDREW HOWARD, 614-22-18, enlisted Jan. 30, 1942, Cleveland, OH. He is a plankowner and served aboard BB-59 as AS at commissioning May 12, 1942, and was on board on its 2nd and 3rd anniversaries. He resides at 30720 Lake Rd., Bay Village, OH 44140.

FUELLHART, HOWARD HENRY, 256-19-05, enlisted Sept. 3, 1938, San Pedro, CA. He is a plankowner and served aboard BB-59 as CMM at commissioning May 12, 1942.

FUGILL, ROBERT JAMES, 646-79-82, enlisted Feb. 17, 1942, New York, NY. He is a plankowner and served aboard BB-59 as AS at commissioning May 12, 1942.

FUHST, ROLAND SIEGFRIED, 622-17-00, enlisted Dec. 12, 1941, Detroit, MA. He is a plankowner and served aboard BB-59 as AS at commissioning May 12, 1942.

FULLFORD, OLIVER DUNDEC, 336-76-32, enlisted March 19, 1942, Washington, DC. He is a plankowner and served aboard BB-59 as FC1/c at commissioning May 12, 1942.

FUNALOCK, HENRY ERNEST, 652-25-08, enlisted March 5, 1942, Pittsburgh, PA. He is a plankowner and served aboard BB-59 as AS at commissioning May 12, 1942. He resides at 193 Shackelford Dr., Monroeville, PA 15146.

FUSTON, HOYT L., 295-90-55, enlisted Jan. 20, 1941, Nashville, TN. He is a plankowner and served aboard BB-59 as HA1/c at commissioning May 12, 1942.

FYALLA, MATTHEW CONSTANTINE, 253-22-75, enlisted Dec. 14, 1941, Albany, NY. He is a plankowner and served aboard as MM2/c at commissioning May 12, 1942.

GABRYSZEWSKI, EDWARD JOSEPH, 300-73-47, enlisted Jan. 9, 1942, Chicago, IL. He is a plankowner and served aboard BB-59 as S2/c at commissioning May 12, 1942.

GADBERRY, EDWIN, JR., enlisted USMC, May 8, 1942, Norfolk Navy Yard. He is a plankowner and served aboard BB-59 as PVT 7th Div. at commissioning May 12, 1942.

GADD, LEONARD GLADDING, 257-99-27, enlisted Jan. 8, 1941, Los Angeles, CA. He is a plankowner and served aboard BB-59 as QM2/c at commissioning May 12, 1942.

GAGNON, RENALD HENRY, 208-61-66, enlisted April 3, 1942, Portland, ME. He is a plankowner and served aboard BB-59 as AS at commissioning May 12, 1942.

GAGNON, THOMAS J., transferred from the USS *Sederstrom* DE-31 and served aboard BB-59 as SM3/c on Sept. 22, 1945.

GAINER, LLOYD DANIEL, 642-16-61, enlisted April 1, 1942, New Haven, CT. He is a plankowner and served aboard BB-59 as AS at commissioning May 12, 1942.

GAINEY, CARL E., enlisted USMC, assigned May 8, 1942, Norfolk Navy Yard. He is a plankowner and served aboard BB-59 PVT 7th Div. at commissioning May 12, 1942.

GAISFORD, ROBERT KENNETH, 386-46-17, enlisted Nov. 10, 1939, Salt Lake City, UT. He is a plankowner and served aboard BB-59 as SK3/c at commissioning May 12, 1942.

GALE, C.R., ENS, served aboard BB-59 in 3rd Div. March 5, 1944, and left BB-59 on Nov. 7, 1944.

GALKO, VICTOR JOHN, 250-73-11, enlisted April 2, 1942, Pittsburgh, PA. He is a plankowner and served aboard BB-59 as AS at commissioning May 12, 1942.

GALLAGHER, JAMES ANDREW, 650-32-51, enlisted Feb. 24, 1942, Philadelphia, PA. He was a plankowner and served aboard BB-59 as AS 3rd Div. at commissioning May 12, 1942. He resided at 1459 S. Euclid Ave. #9, Ontario, CA 91761. Memory List 1997.

GALLAGHER, WALTER T., 224-77-52, born Nov. 11, 1924, Brooklyn, NY. A high school graduate. he enlisted March 30, 1942, New York, NY. He is a plankowner and served aboard BB-59 as AS 6th Div. at commissioning May 12, 1942.

After the war he worked for the New York City Police Dept. as a detective 1st Class. He retired in 1977. In his spare time he was active in the Knights of Columbus.

He married Margaret Moriarty Jan. 23, 1948, in Brooklyn, NY, and had one daughter and one granddaughter. He died of lung cancer on July 21, 1988; Memory List 1989. (Mrs.) resides 220 Wakeman Place #2, Brooklyn, NY.

GALLANT, WENDELL PAUL, 606-47-79, enlisted March 7, 1942, Boston, MA. He is a plankowner and served aboard as AS 3rd Div. at commissioning May 12, 1942, and was on board on its 2nd and 3rd anniversaries. He left BB-59 on Oct. 6, 1945. After the war he worked for the Monsanto Company and resides at 283 Proctor Ave., Revere, MA.

GALLAWAY, MARVIN, (n) 668-22-96, enlisted Jan. 6, 1942, St. Louis, MO. He is a plankowner and served aboard BB-59 as S2/c at commissioning May 12, 1942.

GALLIGHER, RALPH EDWARD, 279-07-69, enlisted July 16, 1940, Bremerton, WA. He is a plankowner and served aboard BB-59 as CMM at commissioning May 12, 1942.

GALLOWAY, JAMES, resides at Box 445, Newton, NC (1966).

GALLUP, CLAIR PURD, 650-32-36, enlisted Feb. 24, 1942, Philadelphia, PA. He is a plankowner and served aboard BB-59 as AS at commissioning May 12, 1942. Memory List, 1992.

GALM, JOSEPH HENRY, JR., 650-32-56, enlisted Feb. 24, 1942, Philadelphia, PA. He is a plankowner and served aboard BB-59 as AS at commissioning May 12, 1942. He died March 30, 1993; Memory List 1994. (Mrs.) resides at 417 W. 3rd St. Runnemede, NJ.

GALVIN, JOHN EDWARD, JR., 201-69-78, enlisted Dec. 11, 1939, Boston, MA. He is a plankowner and served aboard BB-59 as Y2/c at commissioning May 12, 1942.

GANDY, CHARLES WILLIAM, 355-82-03, enlisted Dec. 13, 1937, San Francisco, CA. He is a plankowner and served aboard BB-59 as F1/c at commissioning May 12, 1942.

GANN, RICHARD VALDE, 360-20-13, enlisted Aug. 6, 1940, Houston, TX. He is a plankowner and served aboard BB-59 in 1st Div. at commissioning May 12, 1942. He resides at 3713 Hillrock Drive, Round Rock, TX 78681.

GANNON, BERNARD MICHAEL, 224-78-21, enlisted April 1, 1942, New York, NY. He is a plankowner and served aboard BB-59 at commissioning May 12, 1942.

GANNON, WAYNE L., resides at 512 South Meldown, Fort Collins, CO (1966).

GARDNER, P.W., served aboard BB-59 as S2/c 4th Div. on March 8, 1943.

GARRETT, WILLIAM ROBERT, 342-38-39, enlisted Jan. 23, 1941, Kansas City, MO. He is a plankowner and served aboard BB-59 as S1/c at commissioning May 12, 1942.

GARRISS, JOHN ELLSWORTH, 258-17-79, born Dec. 4, 1919, Catonsville, MD. He enlisted the first time May 10, 1937, and the second time Jan. 6, 1942, in Baltimore. Had training at NTS Norfolk, VA. Stationed aboard the USS *Yorktown* CV-5 from Sept. 30, 1937 to Nov. 15, 1940 as plankowner.

He served aboard BB-59 as plankowner and MM2/c M Div. at commissioning May 12, 1942, and was on board on its 2nd and 3rd anniversaries. Left BB-59 in 1944 Bremerton, WA, as CMM. He was also an instructor at APA School, Astoria, OR, and aboard USS *Sanborn* APA-193.

After the war he worked for Baltimore Gas & Electric Company and the US Army Edgewood Arsenal. He married Betty at Catonsville, MD, in 1944. He has two sons and two daughters and resides at 2919 Salford Dr., Abington, MD.

GARVEY, JOHN JOSEPH, JR., 606-46-84, born May 8, 1919, Dorchester, MA. He enlisted March 5, 1942, Boston, MA. He served aboard BB-59 as AS B Div. at commissioning May 12, 1942. He was a plankowner and was on board on its 2nd and 3rd anniversaries. Was F3/c-F2/c-F1/c to Boilermaker 2/c and left BB-59 in June 1945.

After the war he worked for the Boston Police Dept. as signal service and motor equipment operator. He married Ann on Feb. 23, 1946, Dorchester, and had

two children, six grandchildren and one great-grandchild. (One son Robert died on June 30, 1979.) Garvey died Dec. 14, 1990; Memory List 1992. (Mrs.) resides at 12 Woodland Rd., Holbrook, MA.

GARVEY, LENNY, Memory List; 1992.

GASSAWAY, DAVID BRUCE, 372-11-38, enlisted Nov. 15, 1939, Denver, MA. He is a plankowner and served aboard BB-59 as SM3/c at commissioning May 12, 1942.

GATLEY, FRANK H., born May 3, 1918, Boston, MA. Attended Boston Trade High School and enlisted May 3, 1944, Boston, MA. Attended training at Sampson, NY; Firemens School, Philadelphia, PA; and Engineer School, Gulfport, MS.

He served aboard BB-59 in B Div. in December 1944, and left BB-59 as WT3/c in March 1946.

After the war he worked as a plumbing designer for Robert W. Sullivan Company, Boston. He has two sons and three grandchildren. His sons were member of ship's "Turn-Around" crew. He was in "Homecoming Crew" 1965 and part of USS *Massachusetts* Assoc. as board of directors, 1967 to present; president 1971; and "BB-59 Award" 1980. He resides at 115 Dutcher St., Hopedale, MA.

GATZ, TED, (n) resides at 1630 N. Whipple St., Chicago, IL (1966).

GAUGLER, LEONARD GEORGE, 207-20-13, enlisted Jan. 6, 1942, New Haven, CT. He is a plankowner and served aboard BB-59 as MM2/c M Div. at commissioning May 12, 1942, and was on board on its 2nd and 3rd anniversaries. Was propulsion and engine room watch.

Left BB-59 in June 1945 MM1/c. After the war he became an automation specialist for US Time Corp. and resides at 3400 Mary Lane, Mount Dora, FL 32757.

GAUT, JOSEPH FRANK, 244-07-55, enlisted March 31, 1942, Philadelphia, PA. He is a plankowner and served aboard BB-59 at commissioning May 12, 1942.

GAUTHIER, EUGENE EDMOND, 212-42-55, enlisted Feb. 27, 1942, Boston, MA. He is a plankowner and served aboard BB-59 as MM1/c M Div. at commissioning May 12, 1942, and was on board on its 2nd and 3rd anniversaries CMM.

GAY, CHESTER, Bkr3/c, resides in Mobile, AL (1964).

GAYLOR, GEORGE W., enlisted USMC, May 8, 1942, Norfolk Navy Yard. He is a plankowner and served aboard BB-59 as Corp. 7th Div. at commissioning May 12, 1942.

GASOFI, WILLIAM, (n) 647-02-72, enlisted Feb. 21, 1942, New York, NY. He is a plankowner and served aboard BB-59 as AS at commissioning May 12, 1942. He resides at 5 Buttercup Lane, Willingboro, NJ 08046.

GEBSKI, PETER, (n) enlisted USMC, May 8, 1942, Norfolk Navy Yard. He is a plankowner and served aboard BB-59 as PVT 7th Div. at commissioning May 12, 1942, and was on board on its 2nd and 3rd anniversaries as captain's orderly 20 mm guns. Left BB-59 on July 7, 1944. After the war worked as a screen printer for River Edge Company, Fall River. He had one son, Walter. Memory List, 1985.

GEILER, HERBERT S., Memory List 1996.

GEISSLER, HOWARD ALBERT, 650-30-80, born Oct. 29, 1919, Philadelphia, PA. Graduated from high school and enlisted on Feb. 20, 1942, Philadelphia, PA. Training at Newport, RI.

He is a plankowner, served aboard BB-59 as AS X Div. at commissioning May 12, 1942, and left BB-59 in 1943 Noumea, New Caledonia.

Was also assigned to USS *Relief*; USN Hospital # 4 Auckland, NZ; USNH Oakland, CA; USNHA Bethesda, MD; (NRL Washington, DC Sea Guard); Rec.Sta. NYD Washington, DC.) He was discharged on Aug. 27, 1945.

After the war he worked for the C&P Telephone Company, Washington, DC, Sept. 17, 1945, retiring in April 1978. In his spare time he is involved in Telephone Pioneers; Masons; 32nd Degree Scottish Rite; Shriner-Provost Guard.

He married Letha on Feb. 28, 1942, Philadelphia, PA, and has three daughters, four-grandchildren and three great-grandchildren (Aug. 25, 1993). He resides at 1011 Magnolia Lane, Falling Waters, WV 25419.

GEHRIS, NORMAN RICHARD, 650-33-16, enlisted Feb. 25, 1942, Philadelphia, PA. He is a plankowner and served aboard BB-59 as AS at commissioning May 12, 1942.

GENTILE, ALBERT JOSEPH, 650-30-75, born Feb. 12, 1921, CrumLynn, PA. Graduated from high school and had one year Brown Prep. School, Philadelphia, PA. He enlisted Feb. 20, 1942, Philadelphia, PA, and attended training Newport, RI, for three weeks.

He is a plankowner and served aboard BB-59 as AS 5th Div. at commissioning May 12, 1942, and was on board on its 2nd anniversary. Left BB-59 in April 1944 Mog Mog Island. Was also assigned as plankowner on CVE-93, aboard till the end of the war.

After the war he worked for Atlantic City Electric Company as a lineman, trouble shooter and in management retiring in 1986. He enjoys golf in his spare time and is involved in the American Legion Post #0095 and Catholic War Vets Post #1578.

He married Sophie in 1947 New Jersey and has three children (New Jersey, California and Maine). He resides at 651 Parvin Mill Rd., RD 6 Box 552, Bridgeton, NJ.

GENTRY, C.M., March 8, 1943, S2/c 4th Div.

GEORGE, DONALD ANDREW, 381-05-29, enlisted Jan. 2, 1942, Pearl Harbor. He is a plankowner and served aboard BB-59 as SK1/C at commissioning May 12, 1942.

GEORGE, JOE, Memory List 1994.

GEORGE, S.J., served aboard BB-59 as S2/c F Div. on May 8, 1943.

GERGLEY, BENJAMIN, (n) 646-82-64, enlisted Feb. 19, 1942, New York, NY. He is a plankowner and served aboard BB-59 as AS at commissioning May 12, 1942.

GETSCHER, ELMER D., 648-10-16, born May 25, 1923, Omaha, NE. Attended Omaha Tech. and enlisted in November 1941, Omaha, NE. Attended Great Lakes Gunnery School. He is a plankowner and served aboard BB-59 at commissioning May 12, 1942, and left BB-59 in 1945 Bremerton, WA.

After the war he was a truck driver with Ryders and a cement finisher. In his spare time he was with YMCA Indian Guides for 10 years; and active in scouting, merit counselor and scoutmaster with the Cub Scouts and Boy Scouts.

He married Ardith Dec. 3, 1940, Long Island, CA, and has one son, one daughter, and two grandchildren. His son, Michael, is in the Merchant Marines. Elmer,

his wife and son attended the BB-59 50th Reunion. He died on Aug. 23, 1995. (Son) resides at 990 E. Carson St., Apt. A, Long Beach, CA 90807.

GEWERTZ, MANNING, (n) 380-53-54, enlisted Oct. 12, 1939, San Pedro, CA. He was a plankowner and served aboard BB-59 as CRM CR Div. at commissioning May 12, 1942. In July 1942 ENS CR Div. He resided at 4994 Whitfield Ave., Freemont, CA 94536. Memory List 1996.

GIANNETTO, FRANK JOHN, 620-33-26, enlisted Feb. 2, 1942, Des Moines, IA. He is a plankowner and served aboard as AS at commissioning May 12, 1942. Married Evelyn and resides at 602 N. 5th Ave. Marshalltown, IA 50158.

GIBBS, EUGENE, (n) 355-82-03, enlisted May 28, 1938, San Pedro, CA. He is a plankowner and served aboard BB-59 as BM1/c at commissioning May 12, 1942.

GIBBS, WILLIAM R.., (info. from crew) died in 1989. Information received from Bob Princeton (August 1993) and Bob Emerlik (November 1994). Wife, Margaret was a singer with the Fred Waring band. (Mrs.) resides at 410 Sigler St., Hebron, IN 46341.

GIBSON, JACK HOLMES, 650-32-37, born Dec. 7, 1923. Attended Ursinus College 1964 business science. Enlisted Feb. 24, 1942, Philadelphia, PA, and trained at Newport, RI.

He is a plankowner and served aboard BB-59 as AS X Div. at commissioning May 12, 1942. He left BB-59 in 1943 in E Div. Was also assigned to Gyro Compass School, San Diego, CA, and served aboard USS *Boggs* (destroyer).

After the war he owned and operated a service stationed. He married Marge in 1955 North Hills, PA, and has three children living in Pennsylvania. They reside at 1907 Bustard Rd., Harleysville, PA 19438.

GIDDINGS, RALPH EDWARD, 606-54-76, enlisted March 31, 1942, Boston, MA. He is a plankowner and served aboard BB-59 as AS B Div. at commissioning May 12, 1942, and was on board on its 2nd and 3rd anniversaries. He resides at 3rd St., Claire Rd., Neponset, MA 02122.

GIFFEN, ROBERT C., VADM, Commander Support Force aboard BB-59 at Casablanca. Memory List 1982.

GIGLIOTTI, ROSS JOSEPH, 650-32-02, enlisted Feb. 28, 1942, Philadelphia, PA. He is a plankowner and served aboard BB-59 as AS 4th Div. at commissioning May 12, 1942, and as BM 6th Div. Memory List 1977. He resided in Pennsauken, NJ (1966).

GILBERT, ARTHUR RAYMOND, 282-96-71, enlisted April 2, 1942, Cleveland, OH. He is a plankowner and served aboard BB-59 as MM2/c at commissioning May 12, 1942.

GILDER, GEORGE JOHN, 224-78-67, enlisted April 2, 1942, New York, NY. He is a plankowner and served aboard BB-59 at commissioning May 12, 1942.

GILKEY, CHARLES FREEMAN, 381-21-08, enlisted Sept. 16, 1939, Bremerton, WA. He is a plankowner and served aboard BB-59 as FC1/c at commissioning May 12, 1942, and on March 10, 1943 F Div. to FR Div. CFC.

GILL, EDWARD THEOS, 356-15-11, born Nov. 13, 1921, Farmersville, LA. Graduated from high school and had one year of college. He enlisted March 20, 1940, Dallas, TX, and was assigned to USS *New Mexico* and USS *Lemberton* for gunnery duty.

He is a plankowner and served aboard BB-59 as S1/c FC Div. at commissioning May 12, 1942, GM3/c, GM2/c (2nd anniversary) and GM1/c. He left BB-59 in September 1944 in the Philippines as 1/c diver. Later taught Gunnery School in 1945.

After the war he worked as an electrician for Texas Power and Light Company, 1945-50; electrical foreman Katy RR 1950-59; and electrical supervisor for General Tire & Rubber Company, 1959-85. He was active in Little League as coach and a Boy Scout leader. Was awarded the BSA Award of Merit and Silver Beaver Award.

He married Myrline on May 11, 1946 in Stephenville, TX, and has six children, nine grandchildren and one great-grandchild (as of August 1993). He resides at 3836 N. 20th St., Waco, TX.

GILLIAM, GIDEON LAMB, ENS, USNR, served aboard BB-59 AS 2nd Div. at commissioning June 14, 1945. Retired as LCDR and resides at 114 N. Forest Ave., Lookout Mt., TN 37350.

GILLIGAN, WILLIAM F., 706-21-59, born Jan. 14, 1926, New York, NY. Enlisted Aug. 3, 1942, New York, NY and attended training at Newport, RI GRI (B)GM School Newport 16 weeks.

He served aboard BB-59 November 1942 as S1/c 4th Div. 20 and 40 mm Gun Pointer-Trainer 40 mm Mount CAPT GM3/c. Left BB-59 in Bremerton, WA, Nov. 15, 1945, Lido Beach, LI, NY, for discharge and joined active reserve on Aug. 4, 1947, and inactive in 1949.

After the war he worked for Reeves Instruments as a time keeper for 22 years, a doorman for three years; for the Metropolitan Museum of Art for 15 years (still worked as a security officer September 1993). In his spare time he is active in American Nautical Cadets (five years); umpire in Little League (three years); bowling, swimming, etc.

He married Irene July 9, 1950, in New York City and had four children and seven grandchildren (with one on the way September 1993). He resided at 250 W. 78th St., Apt. #3ER, New York, NY. Memory List 1997.

GILLIS, JOHN ANDREW, 400-19-14, enlisted Jan. 23, 1939, Boston, MA. He is a plankowner and served aboard BB-59 as GM2/c 6th Div. at commissioning May 12, 1942. He resided at 4 Gerry St., Marblehead, MA (1992). Memory List 1996.

GILLIS, JOSEPH EDWARD, JR., 201-47-41, enlisted March 6, 1941, Seattle, WA. He served aboard BB-59 as WT1/c at commissioning May 12, 1942. Memory List 1983.

GILMORE, DAVID ROBERT, 650-30-83, born April 18, 1924, Toledo, OH. He enlisted Feb. 20, 1942, Philadelphia, PA. He is a plankowner and served aboard BB-59 as AS 3rd Div. at commissioning May 12, 1942, and was on board on its 2nd and 3rd anniversaries. He left BB-59 in 1945 Bremerton, WA.

After the war he worked for Horn & Hardent Res. and Kieffer Cont. Company. He married in 1945, Maple Shade, NJ, and has two daughters and two grandchildren. He resides at PO Box 70 Buena, NJ 08210.

GILOT, ABEL J., enlisted USMC, assigned May 8, 1942, Norfolk Navy Yard. He is a plankowner and served aboard BB-59 as PVT 7th Div. at commissioning May 12, 1942.

GILSTRAP, ERNEST G., 3rd Div., resides at Lakeview Dr., Brevard, NC.

GIMBER, HARRY M.S COMMANDER., commanding officer from Aug. 5, 1946 to Sept. 9, 1946.

GIRARDI, FRANK JOSEPH, 600-21-87, enlisted March 17, 1942, Albany, NY. He is a plankowner and served aboard BB-59 as AS at commissioning May 12, 1942.

GIUFFRE, JOSEPH JOHN, 375-98-48, enlisted Nov. 10, 1939, San Francisco, CA. He is a plankowner and served aboard BB-59 as SK3/C at commissioning May 12, 1942.

GIUNTA, ALBERT ANTONEY, 642-14-22, enlisted Feb. 25, 1942, New Haven, CT. He is a plankowner and served aboard BB-59 as AS 2nd Div. at commissioning May 12, 1942, and was on board on its 3rd anniversary May 12, 1945. (Mrs.) resides at 7 Tamarac Rd., Westport, CT 06880.

GIUNTA, MATTHEW J., born 1915 in Salem, MA. Educated at St. James, Salem High School and Beverly Coop Trade School; and enlisted Sept. 24, 1942, Boston, MA. Received training at Newport, RI, and assigned to USS *Cony*, Casco Bay, ME; USS *Hulick* and USS *Relief*. He served aboard BB-59 as MM2/C A Div. and machine shop (also 2nd Div.) in Jan. 29, 1943. He left BB-59 in October 1945.

After the war he worked for United Shoe Mach. Corp. as a machinist and in his spare time he is active in the American Legion, golf, Salem Council on Aging. From 1987-93 made toys etc. to sell for fundraising to benefit the patients at Shaughnessy Kaplan Hospital.

Married Pauline in 1946 at St. Mary's, Salem and has three sons and two grandsons. They reside at 117 Highland St., Salem, MA.

GLADSTONE, DANIEL

GLASSMAN, IRVING, March 1943 LT(jg) F Div.; Oct. 1, 1943 LT FC Div.

GLEBE, J.L., F2/c A Div., March 8, 1943, transferred to ComSerForSoPac.

GLOOR, PAUL WILLIAM, 360-09-93, enlisted Dec. 12, 1939, Houston, TX, and assigned USS *Oklahoma*, Pearl Harbor. He is a plankowner and served aboard BB-59 as F1/c at commissioning May 12, 1942. According to Louis Mathieson in April 1994, Paul made MM1/c and introduced Louis to Vera, his wife.

GLOVER, EVERETT RAYMOND, 342-08-72, enlisted Oct. 5, 1938, Kansas City, MO. He is a plankowner and served aboard BB-59 as GM2/c at commissioning May 12, 1942, and was on board on its 3rd anniversary. Memory List 1991.

GLOVER, RAY E., 1st Div., Everett, WA. (Mrs.) resides at 1201 Marine Drive #188, Marysville, WA 98270. Memory List 1966.

GLOVER, ROBERT OGDEN, RADM, graduated US Naval Academy, 1915. Commander from Dec. 12, 1940, to Sept. 27, 1943. 2nd Com. Off. BB-59. Memory List 1979.

GODIN, JOSEPH CLIFFORD, 208-61-67, enlisted April 3, 1942, Portland, ME. He is a plankowner and served aboard BB-59 as AS at commissioning May 12, 1942.

GODWIN, WINFIELD, Memory List 1981.

GOETZ, PETER V., 871-49-41, born Nov. 3, 1924, Selz, ND. Graduated from high school and enlisted March 20, 1944, Minneapolis, MN, with training

at Farragut, ID. Was assigned to Rec. Station, Bremerton, WA.

Served aboard BB-59 as S2/c May 23, 1944; S1/c January 1945; Y3/c Feb. 1, 1945; Y2/c (chaplain) Sept. 21, 1945; and Y1/c (Exec.). Left BB-59 on May 20, 1946, Norfolk, VA.

After the war he was employed as a baker for six years; carpet layer for six years; manager and sales for Sears & Roebuck for 28 years; and retired in 1986. He enjoys woodcraft hobbies and playing in a concert and dance band (five piece) for Elks for 30 years.

He married Pearl Aug. 4, 1947, in Minot, ND, and has four children and eight grandchildren. He resides at 1602 Northwest Ave., Minot, ND.

GOEWEY, RAYMOND, (n) 647-02-75, enlisted Feb. 21, 1942, New York, NY. He is a plankowner and served aboard BB-59 as AS at commissioning May 12, 1942.

GOFORTH, WILLIAM H., resides at 603 Evergreen Dr., Clarksville, IN.

GOLAMBESKI, ANTHONY JOHN, 666-19-72, enlisted March 5, 1942, Springfield, MA. He is a plankowner and served aboard BB-59 at commissioning May 12, 1942.

GOLDMAN, JACOB ISAAC "JACK," 600-11-77, enlisted Jan. 24, 1942, Albany, NY. He is a plankowner and served aboard BB-59 as AS SK Div. Ship's Store on commissioning and was on board on its 2nd and 3rd anniversaries. Left BB-59 in 1945.

After the war he was president of Goldman, Walter & Tillman Advertising. He has two children (1966 survey). Memory List 1982. He resided at 19 Clinton Ave., Albany, NY (1966).

GOLDSMITH, MAX, 600-22-25, born June 10, 1913, Kiev, Russia. Graduated from high school and enlisted March 20, 1942, Albany, NY. He is a plankowner and served aboard BB-59 as AS 2nd Div. on commissioning and later as Gunners' Mate. Left BB-59 in December 1943 as S1/c.

He was also assigned to USS *Makin Island* CVE-93; R/S Bremerton, WA, and discharged Sept. 14, 1945.

After the war he was a restaurant and grill manager for 23 years. In his spare time he ran American Legion bingo. He has two daughters and one grandson, and resides at 98 Kenosha St., Albany, NY.

GOLDSTEIN, MELVIN AUGUSTUS, 300-77-96, enlisted Jan. 29, 1942, Chicago, IL. He is a plankowner and served aboard BB-59 as AS at commissioning May 12, 1942.

GOLEMBESKI, ANTHONY, Memory List 1984.

GOMBASH, AL, (n) Memory List 1982.

GONZALEZ, E.R., resides at 1610 San Fernando St., San Antonio, TX (1966).

GOODRUM, URBAN GUY, 287-48-70, enlisted Dec. 13, 1941, Louisville, KY. He is a plankowner and served aboard BB-59 at commissioning May 12, 1942.

GORDON, C.E., JR., COMDR, served aboard BB-59 in communications on May 21, 1944, and left Nov. 16, 1944.

GORE, ERNEST F., enlisted USMC, May 8, 1942, Norfolk Navy Yard. He is a plankowner and served aboard BB-59 as GY SGT 7th Div. at commissioning May 12, 1942.

GOROW, H.G., served aboard BB-59 as S2/c F Div. on March 8, 1943.

GOSSELIN, RAY, (Honorary BB-59 Officer), secretary and later vice-president of USS *Massachusetts* Memorial Committee 1963-65. Retired lieutenant USNR ("Exercise Tiger" April 1944).

After the war he was president of Massachusetts College of Pharmacy, 1972-87; publisher-editor-in-chief of *Pharmacy Times*; received Ph.D. at University of South Carolina (age 73); board of directors of ASTRA Pharmaceuticals, USA; and contributing editor of *Drug Topics*. Received Silver Star Medal and Purple Heart.

GOULD, MARVIN ELROY, 311-31-36, enlisted March 1, 1939, Detroit, MI. He is a plankowner and served aboard BB-59 as FC2/c at commissioning May 12, 1942.

GOWER, EDWIN, (chief or WO) 1966 letter from A.H. Pearson East Providence, RI, trying to locate. Claimed he served on the "original crew." He is believed to be living in Florida (no other data).

GRACE, JOHN ANTHONY, 606-49-18, enlisted March 12, 1942, Boston, MA. He is a plankowner and served aboard BB-59 as AS at commissioning May 12, 1942, and was on board on its 2nd anniversary.

GRAHAM, ARTHUR IRA, 291-43-29, enlisted Nov. 19, 1938, San Diego, CA. He is a plankowner and served aboard BB-59 as SK2/c at commissioning May 12, 1942.

GRAHAM, GEORGE GORDON, 408-71-48, enlisted Jan. 8, 1942, Indianapolis, IN. He is a plankowner and served aboard BB-59 as MM2/c at commissioning May 12, 1942.

GRALEY, DALLAS H., 560-13-04, born June 30, 1922, Sumerco, WV. He enlisted Aug. 26, 1942, Charleston, WV, and served aboard BB-59 in 6th Div. in October 1942. He left BB-59 in early 1944. Was also assigned to USS *Virgo* (cargo-supply) and the USS *Mercury*.

After the war he worked for Union Carbide as a rigger, boilermaker and ironworker for 15 years. Was a realtor for 30 years and is now retired. He is involved in church work in his spare time.

He married first Violet Perry (died 1990) on March 7, 1947, and 2nd Dorothy Bird on Jan. 4, 1991, Charleston, WV. He has two daughter, two grandchildren, three stepdaughters and two step-grandchildren. He resides at 822 Baier St., St. Albans, WV.

GRANT, ROALD NORMAN, served aboard BB-59 as LT COMDR H Div. at commissioning in May 1942. He was a plankowner. Memory List 1977 CAPT

GRANT, WILLIAM ALGER, 262-10-89, enlisted Dec. 9, 1938, San Pedro, CA. He is a plankowner and served aboard BB-59 as CSK at commissioning May 12, 1942.

GRAPENTIN, RICHARD F., served aboard BB-59 in 4th and R Div. He has two sons and three daughters (1992). Memory List 1993. (Mrs.) resides at 622 Jefferson St., Little Chute, WI 54140.

GRAY, CHESTER, resides at 12000 Lewis Lane, Harrisburg, MO.

GRAY, N.J., resides at 1925 Moody Rd., Virginia Beach, VA 23455.

GREEN, CLARK J., enlisted USMC, May 8, 1942, Norfolk Navy Yard. He is a plankowner and served aboard BB-59 as PVT 7th Div. at commissioning May 12, 1942.

GREEN, ROBERT B., part of "Homecoming Crew," 1965 and awarded "BB-59 Award," 1968.

GREEN, ROBERT L., E Div., served aboard BB-59 in 1943 and left in December 1945. After the war he worked at South Station, Boston and resides at 24 Guild St., Medford, MA (1994).

GREENE, R.S., served as F3/c P Div. on March 8, 1943, transferred to ComSerForSoPac.

GREENFIELD, LLOYD C., Memory List 1996.

GREENING, ROBERT, 223-79-75, born June 15, 1922, Newfoundland, Canada. Graduated from high school and enlisted Aug. 15, 1940, New York, NY, with training at Newport, RI. He was assigned to the USS *Balch* DD-363 Mare Island and Pearl Harbor.

He is a plankowner and served aboard BB-59 Quincy, MA, April 1942 as S1/c F Div. at commissioning May 12, 1942, and was on board on its 2nd anniversary (16" Direc). Left BB-59 in 1945 Bremerton, WA. Was also assigned to USS *Fall River* CA-131 (plankowner); (was flagship for atomic bomb tests, Bikini Atoll). Discharged 1946.

After the war, January 1947 worked for Consolidated Edison of New York for 38 years. Retired on June 30, 1984. In his spare time he is a South Farmingdale volunteer fireman for 31 years. Rescue Company Field Day crews on BB-59 and other battleship cove ships. His main hobby fancy knot tying and teaching woodwork and handling of tools to 11 and 12 year old children in public school.

He married Doris Larson Sept. 25, 1948, in Brooklyn, NY, and has five children and two grandchildren (as of June 25, 1994). He resides at 7 Eagle Lane, Farmingdale, NY.

GREENLEE, JOHN ERNEST, 320-82-45, enlisted May 12, 1942, Des Moines, IA, and served aboard BB-59 as GM3/c at commissioning May 12, 1942. He is a plankowner.

GREENWALD, RAY, resides at 2981 Bret Drive, Grand Junction, CO 81504.

GREER, GLENWOOD, (n) 295-70-95, enlisted July 16, 1940, Nashville, TN. He is a plankowner and served aboard BB-59 as F2/c at commissioning May 12, 1942.

GREITENS, AUGUST ROBERT, 337-02-15, enlisted Nov. 16, 1937, St. Louis, MO. He is a plankowner and served aboard BB-59 as GM2/c at commissioning May 12, 1942.

GRIBBIN, DANIEL FRANCIS, JR., 652-11-22, enlisted Jan. 12, 1942, Pittsburgh, PA. He is a

plankowner and served aboard BB-59 as EM3/c at commissioning May 12, 1942.

GRIFFIN, JACK E., Enlisted USMC, May 8, 1942, Norfolk Navy Yard. He is a plankowner and served aboard BB-59 as SGT 7th Div. at commissioning May 12, 1942.

GRIFFIN, WILLIAM R., A Div., resides at 168 Newton Rd., Haverhill, MA.

GRIFFITH, ROBERT LEE, 612-02-37, enlisted Sept. 23, 1941, Cincinnati, OH. He is a plankowner and served aboard BB-59 at commissioning May 12, 1942.

GRIGGS, WILLIAM H., 216562 LT, served aboard BB-59 in communications division LT(jg) June 1943. Left BB-59 in October 1945. After the war he was professor of pomology at the University of California. He married Ruth on May 24, 1944, and has three children and eight grandchildren (February 1992). He resides at 633 A St., Davis, CA 95616.

GRIGSBY, HARRY R., resides in Youngstown, OH, (1966). On Memory List 1977.

GRIMALDI, JOHN ANDREW, 636-04-80, enlisted Aug. 22, 1941, Macon, GA. He is a plankowner and served aboard BB-59 as EM3/c at commissioning May 12, 1942.

GRIMES, FRANCIS VERNON, 376-03-25, enlisted March 8, 1940, San Francisco, CA. He is a plankowner and served aboard BB-59 as F2/c at commissioning May 12, 1942.

GRIMES, ROBERT A., born Sept. 19, 1915, South Boston, MA. Attended Boston Latin 1933; Harvard with an AB 1937 and Harvard Law LLD 1940. He enlisted in June 1940 and assigned to USS *Quincy*; Prairie State Midshipman; Naval Intelligence, Boston; Recruiting Station, Richmond, VA.

He served aboard BB-59 in January 1942, Quincy, MA, Boston. He is a plankowner and served as ENS 4th Div. at commissioning May 12, 1942, and LT(jg) 1st Div. Left BB-59 in January 1943. Also assigned to USS *Boston* LT(jg), 1st Div.; USS *Detroit*; and discharged LCDR.

After the war was past assistant DA for Middlesex County, 1955-56; Board of Review, City of Boston, chairman 1960-61; founder and president of Middlesex Family Coop Bank, Waltham, MA; trial and bank lawyer. In his spare time was founder and past president of USS *Massachusetts* Assoc. Inc. Was awarded BB-59 in 1969.

He married Martha Nov. 28, 1942, and has seven children and 10 grandchildren (August 1993). He resides at 33 Casey Circle, Waltham, MA.

GROCHMAL, JOHN FRANK, 606-47-73, enlisted March 9, 1942, Boston, MA. He is a plankowner and served aboard BB-59 as AS at commissioning May 12, 1942. He resides at 86 Bryant St., N. Dartmouth, MA.

GROESBECK, WALTER PATTEN, 238-36-38, enlisted Dec. 13, 1941, Albany, NY. He is a plankowner and served aboard BB-59 as EM2/c at commissioning May 12, 1942. Memory List 1993.

GROHOWSKI, MICHAEL JOHN, 650-30-63, enlisted Feb. 19, 1942, Philadelphia, PA. He is a plankowner and served aboard BB-59 as AS at commissioning May 12, 1942.

GROOP, HERBERT RODNEY, 606-49-32, enlisted March 12. 1942, Boston, MA. He was a plankowner and served aboard as S2/c F Div. at commissioning May 12, 1942. He resided at 41 Pine St., Fitchburg, MA. Memory List 1997.

GROSS, DANIEL J., 2nd Div. Last residence was W. Ramsey Ave., Milwaukee, WI 53221. Memory List 1996.

GROTTE, EDWARD JOHN, 610-51-00, enlisted Jan. 28, 1942, Chicago, IL. He is a plankowner and served aboard BB-59 as AS at commissioning May 12, 1942.

GROVE, MICHAEL J., served aboard BB-59 as S1/c N Div. in 1942. He is active in the American Legion, DAV and VFW, and resides at 863 North St., Luzerne, PA.

GROVER, OSCAR L., enlisted USMC May 8, 1942, Norfolk Navy Yard. Served aboard BB-59 as PFC 7th Div. at commissioning May 12, 1942, and is a plankowner.

GRUBB, LEWIS, resides at 315 Valley St., Abingdon, VA (1966).

GRUNSKI, BENJAMIN, (n) resides at 101 Brooklyn St., Rockville, CT (1966).

GUEST, JAMES LIONEL, 368-43-32, enlisted March 14, 1939, Salt Lake City, UT. He is a plankowner and served aboard BB-59 as F1/c at commissioning May 12, 1942.

GUILL, RICHARD ABNER, served aboard BB-59 as LT(jg) on July 25, 1943, and left as LT March 2, 1945.

GULART, JOHN RICHARD, 376-10-23, enlisted Aug. 20, 1940, San Francisco, CA. He is a plankowner and served aboard BB-59 as F2/c at commissioning May 12, 1942.

GULLATT, LINTON, JR., (n) 5th Div., resides at 2366 E. Brown Rd., Mesa, AZ.

GUMBRECHT, GEORGE A., Memory List 1993. (Mrs.) resides at 30205 Austin Drive, Warren, MI 48092.

GUNNELS, CHARLES W., JR., CDR, served aboard USS *California* (BB-44) then aboard BB-59 in 1942. Left BB-59 for USS *Ticonderoga* (CV-14) also USNA. Stationed at NAS JAX, CO VBF43, BuAir and Opns. Officer of USS *Shangri-La* (CV-38). Received the DFC, Air Medal and Navy Commendation Medal. Note: Was flying a SNB-5 that crashed on the Isu Peninsula, Japan, April 27, 1957. He married Phyllis O'Brien and has five sons and two daughters. He is on Memory List 1982.

GUTHRIE, WILLIAM HENDERSON, JR., 269-00-28, enlisted Oct. 27, 1941, Macon, GA. He is a plankowner and served aboard BB-59 as F3/c at commissioning May 12, 1942.

GUTTERON, THOMAS BRINDELEY, 381-13-42, enlisted Jan. 13, 1942, Pearl Harbor. He is a plankowner and served aboard BB-59 as FC2/c at commissioning May 12, 1942.

HAAS, ROLAND WARREN, 262-47-63, enlisted Dec. 20, 1939, Raleigh, NC. He is a plankowner and served aboard BB-59 as S1/c 1st Div. at commissioning May 12, 1942, and was on board on its 2nd and 3rd anniversaries. He resides at PO Box 362, Wauna, WA 98395.

HAFFENRAFFER, CARL W., (Honorary Officer) (Largest Donation) part of "Bring Back Big Mamie" Campaign; (Fleet Admiral) "Massachusetts Navy" and "BB-59 Award" 1968.

HAGAN, EDWARD JOHN, 224-78-69, enlisted April 2, 1942, New York, NY. He is a plankowner and served aboard BB-59 as AS at commissioning May 12, 1942, and was on board on its 2nd anniversary. Memory List 1990.

HAGGARD, ARTHUR A., M Div., resides at 412 St. Jude Circle, Florence, KY.

HAINS, GEORGE KENNETH, 372-43-56, enlisted Jan. 19, 1942, Denver, CO. He is a plankowner and served aboard BB-59 as AS L Div. at commissioning May 12, 1942, and was on board on its 2nd and 3rd anniversary.

In his spare time he had a CB station and made contact with all 50 states on CB. He was a 4th Degree in Knights of Columbus. Was Santa at Christmas parties with a real white beard! He resided at 7457 So. Pierce Court, Littleton, CO. Memory List 1997.

HALL, GEORGE HENRY, 170-24-01, enlisted Jan. 9, 1942, Chicago, IL. He is a plankowner and served aboard BB-59 as MM2/c at commissioning May 12, 1942, and was on board on its 2nd anniversary.

HALL, GEORGE M., COMDR, served aboard BB-59; June 1965 part of "Homecoming Crew" as captain. He resides at 18 Gordon Rd., Needham, MA (1965).

HALL, JOHN C., resides at 3909A Arizona Ave., Los Alamos, NM (1956).

HALL, JOHN CHESTER, 224-70-10, enlisted Jan. 30, 1942, New York, NY. He is a plankowner and served aboard BB-59 as AS E Div. at commissioning May 12, 1942, and was on board on its 2nd anniversary. He resides at Box 3 Guilford, NY 13780.

HALL, JOSEPH EARLY, 296-10-34, enlisted Jan. 30, 1942, Nashville, TN. He is a plankowner and served aboard BB-59 as AS at commissioning May 12, 1942.

HALLETT, WILLIAM D., JR., enlisted USMC, May 8, 1942, Norfolk Navy Yard. He is a plankowner and served aboard BB-59 as PFC 7th Div. at commissioning May 12, 1942.

HALLOCK, WILLIAM JOSEPH, 647-02-86, enlisted Feb. 21, 1942, New York, NY. He is a plankowner and served aboard BB-59 as AS at commissioning May 12, 1942, and was on board on its 2nd and 3rd anniversary.

HALVERSON, GAYLORD HAROLD, 520-33-65, enlisted Feb. 3, 1942, Des Moines, IA. He is a plankowner and served aboard BB-59 as S2/c at commissioning May 12, 1942. Memory List 1977.

HAM, WALLACE EDMUND, 606-56-33, enlisted April 3, 1942, Portland, ME. He is a plankowner and served aboard BB-59 as AS at commissioning May 12, 1942, and was on board on its 2nd and 3rd anniversaries.

HAMANN, ROBERT G., A Div., 5552 No. 26th St., Milwaukee, WI.

HAMBLIN, GOVER MASON, 355-98-76, enlisted Jan. 3, 1942, Dallas, TX. He is a plankowner and served aboard BB-59 as MM1/c at commissioning May 12, 1942.

HAMBLY, RICHARD, JR., (n) 382-24-90, enlisted Aug. 22, 1940, Los Angeles, CA. He is a plankowner and served aboard BB-59 as S1/c at commissioning May 12, 1942, and was on board on its 2nd and 3rd anniversaries.

HAMERSLY, HOWARD LOUIS, 650-32-52, enlisted Feb. 24, 1942, Philadelphia, PA. He is a plankowner and served aboard BB-59 as AS 1st Div. at commissioning May 12, 1942, and was on board on its 2nd and 3rd anniversaries. He resides at Rt. 2 Box 359A, Gladys, VA 24554.

HAMILTON, ALONZO, 552-07-24, enlisted March 30, 1942, Columbia, SC. He is a plankowner and served aboard BB-59 as MATT3/c at commissioning May 12, 1942.

HAMILTON, WILLIAM A., July 1945 MACH.

HAMM, LOUIS GENE, resides at 1207 Virginia St., Waterloo, IA (1966).

HAMM, MANN, LT CMDR, Bat. Div. 8, graduated US Naval Academy Class of 1931 and served aboard BB-59 August 1943; Oct. 1, 1943, Communications Off. Left BB-59 April 21, 1945, at sea off Okinawa.

HAMMOND, PETER, Memory List 1986.

HAMMOND, STANLEY RYDER, served aboard BB-59 as a plankowner LT(jg) P Div.; made lieutenant P Div. Oct. 1, 1943; and left BB-59 on May 12, 1945.

HAMMOND, WILLIAM EDWARD, 650-22-77, enlisted Feb. 24, 1942, Philadelphia, PA. He is a plankowner and served aboard BB-59 as AS at commissioning May 12, 1942, and was on board on its 2nd anniversary.

HAMPTON, JOE ALFRED, 310-84-69, enlisted April 3, 1942, Boston, MA. He is a plankowner and served aboard BB-59 as CRM at commissioning May 12, 1942.

HANDEN, R.D., COMDR MC, served aboard BB-59 as senior medical officer at commissioning April 6, 1944, and left BB-59 Nov. 2, 1944.

HANDLEN, WILLIAM T., born Aug. 20, 1926, San Francisco, CA. With five years of college, he enlisted March 22, 1944, Seattle, WA. Training at Farragut, ID.

Served aboard BB-59 in May 1944 Bremerton, WA, and made S2/c 4th Div. May 1944; SM3/c CS Div. September 1944; and left BB-59 in May 1946. Was also assigned to USN AmphibForce Little Creek, VA; LSM 417; and LSM 399.

After the war he worked for William T. Handlen

HANKINS, MARVIN JAMES, 294-68-41, enlisted April 21, 1939, San Diego, CA. He is a plankowner and served aboard BB-59 as CBmkr at commissioning May 12, 1942.

HANLEY, DANIEL FRANCIS, 610-47-14, enlisted Jan. 26, 1942, Chicago, IL. He is a plankowner and served aboard BB-59 as CSp at commissioning May 12, 1942.

HANNAH, BERNARD ARDEN, 258-20-55, born Aug. 9, 1918, Wallace, WV. He enlisted June 28, 1938, Baltimore, MD, and trained at Norfolk Naval Base. Was assigned to USS *West Virginia*, 1938 and USS *Balch* DD-359. He is a plankowner and served aboard BB-59 as GM2/c 2nd Div. at commissioning May 12, 1942, and was on board on its 2nd and 3rd anniversaries #2 Turret CAPT. Left BB-59 in July 1945.

After the war he worked for Monongahela Power Company in the customer service department. In his spare time he is involved in VFW #573 Clarksburg, WV, and keeping in touch with members of BB-59 Turret #2.

He married Mary Lee in 1950 and has one son, Michael. He resides at 520 Harrison St., Bridgeport, WV.

HANNAN, DENNIS EDWARD, 385-78-09, born Jan. 30, 1921, Chicago, IL. A high school graduate with two years of college, he enlisted March 5, 1941, San Francisco, CA. He was assigned to USS *Maryland*, Pearl Harbor.

He is a plankowner and served aboard BB-59 as GM2/c 2nd Div. at commissioning May 12, 1942, also Turret Captain 1/c also X Div. In 1943 stationed at Instructor Gunner's Mate School, Washington, DC; USS *New Jersey* and USS *Des Moines*. He retired as CWO2 (gunner) in 1958.

After the war he was stationed at Naval Torpedo Station, Keyport, WA. In his spare time he spent 26 years as volunteer fireman and fire commissioner for Jefferson County fire district, Port Ludlow, WA. He has three children. He died Feb. 21, 1993. (Mrs.) resides 231 Puget Loop, Port Ludlow, WA 98365.

HANNAN, THOMAS JOSEPH, 223-65-44, enlisted Feb. 8, 1940, New York, NY. He is a plankowner and served aboard BB-59 as F2/c at commissioning May 12, 1942.

HANSON, DEWAYNE B., 982-02-91, born April 20, 1926, St. Paul, MN. Graduated from high school and attended Dale Carnegie Watchmaking and Jewelry Schooling. He enlisted April 1944 Portland, OR, and trained at Camp Farragut, ID.

He served aboard BB-59 in June 1944 as AS (Snipe Eng. Room Throttle); August 1944 S1/c (Signalman CS Div.). Left BB-59 in May 1946 Portsmouth, VA.

After the war he became owner of two Guild Jewelry Stores with 47 years in jewelry work. He retired at 58 (health problems) but is very healthy now (1993). In his spare time he enjoys garden work (nine acres), golf and "RV ing."

He married Bernice Nov. 7, 1948, in Portland, OR, and has two sons and four grandchildren. He resides at 22300 S. Penman Rd., Oregon City, OR 97045.

HANSON, HERBERT, JR., 202-40-44, born June 6, 1924, Portsmouth, NH. He attended the R.W. Traip Academy, Kittery, ME, in June 1942. He enlisted Aug. 3, 1942, Boston, MA, and attended Electrical School, Newport, RI.

Company (consulting company in fluid power) teaching maintenance.

He married Ruth Geldart in 1956 in Seattle and has five sons and eight grandchildren. He resides at 303 1st St., Apt. 29, Raymond, WA.

He served aboard BB-59 in December 1942 as F3/c E Div., 1943 EM3/c. Left BB-59 in March 1944 New Hebrides. Other assignments: Mine warfare school in Virginia; USS *Sereen* AM-369 August 1944-May 1945; I.C. School, Virginia May 1945-July 1945; Portland, ME, 1945-47; USS *Mindoro* CVE-120 and discharged July 31, 1948, Norfolk, VA.

Married Wanita M. May 4, 1944, in York, ME, and has two children. He resides at 37707 March Lane, Zephyrhills, FL.

HANSON, OSCAR H., FC Div., resides at Box 105, Maynard, MN 56260.

HARDISTY, CHARLES EDSEL, 272-27-15, enlisted Jan. 18, 1940, Birmingham, AL. He is a plankowner and served aboard BB-59 as EM3/c E Div. at commissioning May 12, 1942.

HARGRAVES, WINFIELD SCOTT, JR., 650-30-98, enlisted Feb. 20, 1942, Philadelphia, PA. He is a plankowner and served aboard BB-59 as AS FC Div. at commissioning May 12, 1942, and as FC3/c was on board on its 2nd and 3rd anniversaries. Left BB-59 in June 1945.

After the war he was an accountant for Mobil Oil. He was active in the American Legion in his spare time and resided at 561 S. Broadway, Gloucester, NJ (1966). Memory List 1991.

HARKINS, DANIEL LEE, JR., 223-47-79, enlisted Aug. 17, 1938, New York, NY. He is a plankowner and served aboard BB-59 as S1/c at commissioning May 12, 1942.

HARKINS, R.H., resides at 132 Randolph St., Salem, WV (1966).

HARKNESS, LLEWELLYN, JR., ENS, served aboard BB-59 in FC Div. in May 1943. A member of Anniversary Committee, May 12, 1944.

HARLAN, HARMON ROSS, 328-64-25, enlisted Jan. 9, 1940, Minneapolis, MN. He is a plankowner and served aboard BB-59 as S1/c at commissioning May 12, 1942.

HARLAND, RICHARD SQUIRE, 650-32-27, enlisted Feb. 24, 1942, Philadelphia, PA. He is a plankowner and served aboard BB-59 as AS 1st Div. at commissioning May 12, 1942, and was on board on its 2nd and 3rd anniversaries. He resides at 411 E. Carlisle Rd., Lakeland, FL.

HARLOW, PHILIP H., resides in ElDara, IL (1966).

HARM, ALVIN, (n) resides in Sioux City, IA (1966).

HARMAN, JOHN EATON, 372-04-75, enlisted Jan. 10, 1942, San Francisco, CA. He is a plankowner and served aboard BB-59 as MM2/c at commissioning May 12, 1942.

HARNESS, ROBERT BLANCHARD, served aboard BB-59 as LT(jg) 2nd Div. in August 1942, and as lieutenant 2nd Div. Oct. 1, 1943.

HARNISH, MAX J., 555820, born Dec. 19, 1925, Grand Rapids, MI. Attended Grand Rapids Catholic Central High School, US Naval Academy Prep. School, Grand Rapids Air Service and American Graduate University. He enlisted in the USMC Dec. 17, 1943.

He served aboard BB-59 in 7th Div. PFC later as sergeant on June 16, 1944 and left Feb. 19, 1945. Was also assigned USMC Reserves and recalled to active duty in 1950 during Korean Conflict. Was instructor (DI) in San Diego, CA, and returned to inactive status Jan. 23, 1954.

After the was he was contract manager for Lear Siegler, Inc. and Smiths Industries. He is retired. He spent his spare time boxing, 1940-48 amateur, Golden Gloves/AAU; professional 1947, coach; 1948-62 referee for 31 years (several thousand bouts from 1962-1993. Was inducted in the Michigan Golden Gloves Hall of Fame in 1994.

HARRI, GEORGE W., resides at 2005 Clements, Detroit, MI (1966).

HARRIGAN, E.D., LT(jg) served CR Div. March 1943. He resides in Washington, DC, LCDR (1965).

HARRINGTON, H.L., resides at PO Box 554, Coos Bay, OR.

HARRINGTON, JAMES LEO, 606-05-05, enlisted Dec. 15, 1941, Boston, MA. He is a plankowner and served aboard BB-59 as EM3/c at commissioning May 12, 1942.

HARRIS, ELDRIDGE GRADY, JR., 359-85-52, enlisted Feb. 19, 1941, Houston, TX. He is a plankowner and served aboard BB-59 at commissioning May 12, 1942.

HARRIS, GORDON WOODSON, 355-43-04, enlisted Jan. 13, 1940, Norfolk, VA. He is a plankowner and served aboard BB-59 as Bmster at commissioning May 12, 1942.

HARRIS, JAMES JAY, 342-04-27, enlisted March 18, 1942, New York, NY. He is a plankowner and served aboard BB-59 at commissioning May 12, 1942.

HARRIS, LON, (n) resides at 720 Lafayet, Tacoma 44, WA (1959).

HARRIS WILFRED L., served in R and 4th Div. Memory List 1986. (Mrs.) resides at 7418 N. Regal St., Spokane, WA.

HARRIS, WILLIAM RANDOLPH, 265-59-79, enlisted June 6, 1938, Los Angeles, CA. He is a plankowner and served aboard BB-59 as SC1/c at commissioning May 12, 1942.

HART, EARL ALEXANDER, 328-79-94, enlisted Nov. 27, 1940, Minneapolis, MN. He is a plankowner and served aboard BB-59 as RM3/c at commissioning May 12, 1942.

HART, EUGENE CHARLES, 202-24-29, enlisted March 31, 1942, Boston, MA. He is a plankowner and served aboard BB-59 as AS at commissioning May 12, 1942.

HART, JAMES JOSEPH, 606-48-90, enlisted March 11, 1942, Boston, MA. He is a plankowner and served aboard BB-59 as AS at commissioning May 12, 1942.

HART, ROBERT PARKER, served aboard BB-59 as ENS R Div. on Sept. 5, 1943; in CS Div. JO LT(jg) Dec. 9, 1944; and left BB-59 Dec. 2, 1945. He resides at 75-233 Nani Kailua Dr., Kailua-Kona, HI.

HART, WILLIAM A., resides at 821 N.E. Union Ave., Portland, OR (1966).

HART, YULEE WESLEY, 171-17-45, enlisted Dec. 11, 1941, Birmingham, AL. He is a plankowner and served aboard BB-59 as EM1/c at commissioning May 12, 1942.

HARTLEY, JOHN, (n) 171-36-11, enlisted March 7, 1942, Jacksonville, FL. He is a plankowner and served aboard BB-59 as Mus1/c at commissioning May 12, 1942.

HARTRANFT, CHARLES THOMAS, 650-30-93, enlisted Feb. 20, 1942, Philadelphia, PA. He is a plankowner and served aboard BB-59 as AS at commissioning May 12, 1942.

HARVEY, JAMES B., served aboard BB-59 as S1/c Supply Div. operating ship's and small stores in December 1945. Left BB-59 in 1946.

After the war he worked for TWA in technical services at Main Overhaul Base in Kansas City. Served in USNR Patrol Squadron 881 and recalled to active duty 1961-62. He is active in NER Assoc. and was national vice president.

He has three children and resides at 5016 NE 56th Terr., Kansas City, MO 64119 (1966).

HARVEY, JESSIE RAY, served in 4th Div. and resides in Dunbar, WV (1966).

HASKELL, H. LELAND, CDR (Honorary Officer) 1st president of USS *Massachusetts* and part of Memorial Committee 1963-65. Received BB-59 Award in 1966.

HASSBERGER, JOHN BAXTER, LT COMDR, served aboard BB-59 in H Div. in December 1942 as assistant medical officer October 1943. Resided at 483 W. Brown, Birmingham, MI. Memory List 1990.

HATMAKER, LUTHER L., resides at 6823 Britton Ave., Cincinnati, OH (1966).

HATTER, HARRY V., born July 9, 1922, Stamford, CT. He enlisted in 1942 in Stamford, CT. He served aboard BB-59 in R Div. on Aug. 1, 1942, and left Sept. 6, 1945, R Div.

After the war he owned and operated Waterside Cottages, Provincetown, MA, for 20 years. In his spare time he helped to refurbish BB-59 in Fall River and was a member of BOPE.

Married Erma (died 1985) and they had two children and six grandchildren. He died on May 17, 1993. Memory List 1993. Judy Andrade (daughter) resides at 16 Jared Hall Rd., Sterling, CT 06377.

HAUGAN, ROBERT DAVID, 321-53-63, enlisted Dec. 10, 1940, Des Moines, IA. He is a plankowner and served aboard BB-59 as S1/c at commissioning May 12, 1942.

HAUSER, D.F., F2/c on March 8, 1943, from A Div. to ComSerForSoPac.

HAUSER, KENNETH ALFRED, 608-14-06, enlisted March 19, 1942, Buffalo, NY. He is a plankowner and served aboard BB-59 as AS at commissioning May 12, 1942.

HAUSMAN, WALTER H., 7th Div., resides at 517 Grandview Ave., Bellevue, KY.

HAUSMAN, WILLIAM FREDERICK, 608-14-06, enlisted Feb. 25, 1942, Philadelphia, PA. He is a plankowner and served aboard BB-59 as AS at commissioning May 12, 1942, and was on board on its 2nd and 3rd anniversaries.

HAVILAND, ARTHUR PIERCE, 646-33-97, enlisted Jan. 7, 1942, New York, NY. He is a plankowner and served aboard BB-59 as SK3/c at commissioning May 12, 1942. Memory List 1977. He had three children and two grandchildren (Oct. 30, 1991) A.P. Jr. (son) resides at 16 Orangeburg Rd., Old Tappan, NJ 07675.

HAWN, KENNETH F., resides at Oak and Central Ave., Blackwood Terrace, NJ (1966).

HAYES, JACK TRUMAN, 268-19-19, born Sept. 21, 1917, enlisted Feb. 3, 1942, San Diego, CA. He is a plankowner and served aboard BB-59 as GM1/c 6th Div. at commissioning May 12, 1942, and was on board on its 2nd and 3rd anniversaries. Left BB59 Dec. 19, 1944, CGM Trans. to (NTSch GM and Electric Hydr.) Washington, DC.

After the war he worked as a salesman for J.P. Manning Company in Boston, MA. In his spare time he is active in the VFW #6800 and a committee worker for USS *Massachusetts* Memorial Committee. Received BB-59 Award in 1987. He resides at 87 Marion St., Somerville, MA.

HAYS, CECIL ROY, 380-69-41, enlisted April 13, 1939, Hampton Roads, VA. He is a plankowner and served aboard BB-59 as CWT at commissioning May 12, 1942, and was on board on its 2nd anniversary. Was B Div. May 19, 1944, transferred to Water Tender Classification Center, San Francisco.

HAYSLETT, ALLEN RICHARD, 321-05-55, enlisted Jan. 6, 1942, Richmond, VA. He is a plankowner and served aboard BB-59 as MM2/c at commissioning May 12, 1942.

HEADINGS, HOWARD, (n) I Div. resides at Rt. 1 Box 67, Guntown, MS.

HEALION, WILLIAM ELMER, 299-88-75, enlisted March 12, 1942, San Francisco, CA. He is a plankowner and served aboard BB-59 as S1/c at commissioning May 12, 1942, and was on board on its 2nd anniversary. On March 11, 1943, V Div. to N Div.

HEARN, GALEN EDWARD, 652-24-32, enlisted March 3, 1942, Pittsburgh, PA. He is a plankowner and served aboard BB-59 as AS A Div. at commissioning May 12, 1942, and was on board on its 2nd and 3rd anniversaries. He resides at Route 1 Box 24, Williamsburg, PA.

HEARNE, JAMES B., B Div. resided at 1 Walnut Place, Angleton, TX. Memory List 1986.

HEATH, HAROLD E., SR., 5th Div., Forest St., RR #1, Box 436, Lee, MA.

HEATH, RICHARD PUTNAM, 622-25-37, enlisted Dec. 26, 1941, Detroit, MI. He is a plankowner and served aboard BB-59 as S2/c at commissioning May 12, 1942, and was on board on its 2nd and 3rd anniversaries.

HEATH, WALTER JOHN, 238-58-15, enlisted Dec. 12, 1931, Albany, NY. He is a plankowner and served aboard BB-59 as Msmth2/c at commissioning May 12, 1942.

HEATON, HARRY DEWITT, 342-64-03, enlisted Jan. 23, 1942, Kansas City, MO. He is a plankowner and served aboard BB-59 as AS at commissioning May 12, 1942.

HEATON, ROBERT, 387-02-37, born March 22, 1927, Block Island, RI. Graduated from high school and enlisted March 22, 1944, Seattle, WA. Trained at NTS Farragut, ID. Served aboard BB-59 in B Div. S2/c to F1/c on May 23, 1944, and left on March 7, 1946, San Francisco, CA.

Other assignments: USS *Omeida* March 8, 1946, (APA-221); Jan. 30, 1947, USS *Miami* (CL-89); June 30, 1947, USS *Shangri La* (CV-38); and discharged Feb. 13, 1948, San Francisco, CA.

After the war he worked for the city of Seattle, WA, in the water department October 1948. Retired as electrical foreman March 15, 1985. In his spare time he enjoys bowling, golf and travel. Married Joyce on Feb. 25, 1949, and has two children. He resides at 10618 35th SW, Seattle, WA 98146.

HEINZ, ROBERT HENRY, 372-26-24, enlisted Jan. 27, 1941, Denver, CO. He is a plankowner and served aboard BB-59 as S1/c at commissioning May 12, 1942, and was on board on its 2nd anniversary.

HEITCZMAN, JAMES, (n) 650-33-13, enlisted Feb. 25, 1942, Philadelphia, PA. He is a plankowner and served aboard BB-59 as AS at commissioning May 12, 1942.

HEITZMAN, ROBERT JAMES, 224-78-71, enlisted April 2, 1942, New York, NY. He is a plankowner and served aboard BB-59 as AS 3rd Div. at commissioning May 12, 1942, and as S1/c 1943. After the war he was self-employed as a plumbing and heating contractor and is a commander in the American Legion. He has two children (1966).

HELBERT, HENRY H., 234-19-35, enlisted Jan. 11, 1939, Buffalo, NY. He was a plankowner and served aboard BB-59 as GM3/c at commissioning May 12, 1942. He resided at 13104 Avenida Grande, San Diego, CA 92129. Memory List 1997

HELM, OTHO WILLIAM, 266-21-87, enlisted Oct. 7, 1940, Richmond, VA. Was assigned to USS *Chester* as AS February 1941. He is a plankowner and served aboard BB-59 as S1/c 4th Div. at commissioning May 12, 1942, and as GM2/c 3rd Div., May 12, 1944. Left BB-59 in May 1945. In June 1945 served aboard USS *Seapoacher* (SS-346); San Diego Elec./Hydraulics School; and Groton, CT, Submarine School.

After the war he earned a BS from Virginia Poly. Inst. 1953; a MA from George Washington University 1954; and an MA from Harvard University 1962.

Married Emily Brookshelm in 1950 in Roanoke, VA, and has one daughter and one granddaughter. He resides at 3618 Annadale Rd., Annadale, VA.

HELM, STANLEY LEROY, 602-04-62, enlisted Dec. 16, 1941, Baltimore, MD. He is a plankowner and served aboard BB-59 as AS at commissioning May 12, 1942.

HELMA, ALLEN EDWARD, 316-68-21, enlisted Sept. 18, 1940, Omaha, NE. He is a plankowner and served aboard BB-59 as S1/c at commissioning May 12, 1942.

HELMS, JOSEPH BRYANT, 267-83-71, enlisted Nov. 8, 1939, San Diego, CA. He is a plankowner and served aboard BB-59 as SF1/c at commissioning May 12, 1942.

HENAULT, THEODORE VALMOR, 666-19-93, enlisted March 6, 1942, Springfield, MA. He is a plankowner and served aboard BB-59 as AS at commissioning May 12, 1942, and was on board on its 2nd and 3rd anniversaries.

HENDERSON, BURT F., resides at 36 Cloudrest St., Dillon, MT.

HENDERSON, DEE EDWARD, 337-24-82, enlisted Dec. 19, 1939, St. Louis, MO. He is a plankowner and served aboard BB-59 as F2/c at commissioning May 12, 1942.

HENDERSON, THEODORE EDWARD, 263-56-12, enlisted April 1, 1942, Raleigh, NC. He is a plankowner and served aboard BB-59 as Matt3/c at commissioning May 12, 1942.

HENDERSON, WILLIAM, resides at Colorado City, TX (1966).

HENDRICKS, LAWRENCE EDWARD, 201-05-15, enlisted March 28, 1942, Pearl Harbor, HI. He is a plankowner and served aboard BB-59 as EM1/c at commissioning May 12, 1942.

HENLEY, JAMES A., enlisted USMC, May 8, 1942, Norfolk Navy Yard. He is a plankowner and served aboard BB-59 as a Pvt. 7th Div. at commissioning May 12, 1942.

HENLEY, WILLIAM J., 4th Div., resides at 818 Dunwood, Toledo, OH 43609.

HENNIGAN, JOHN A., JR., served CY X Div.

HENNINGER, ROBERT JAMES, 243-10-64, enlisted Aug. 1, 1935, New London, CT. He is a plankowner and served aboard BB-59 as RM1/c at commissioning May 12, 1942.

HENNISSEY, WILLIAM M., Memory List 1993.

HENRY, RICHARD JAMES, 238-61-11, enlisted June 21, 1939, Albany, NY. He is a plankowner and served aboard BB-59 as FC2/c at commissioning May 12, 1942, F Div. to FC Div. March 10, 1943, and was on board on its 2nd anniversary.

HENSLEY, MERLE VESPER, 620-33-19, enlisted Feb. 2, 1942, Des Moines, IA. He is a plankowner and served aboard BB-59 as AS at commissioning May 12, 1942, and was on board on its 2nd and 3rd anniversaries. Memory List 1977. (Mrs.) resides at PO Box 4, Bourbon, MO.

HENSON, I., resides in Lebanor, OK (1966).

HENSON, LOUIS BRIAN, A Div., born Dec. 18, 1906, Pittsburg, TX, and graduated from Pittsburg High School. He enlisted in 1929. He served aboard BB-59 on Nov. 27, 1944, appointed machinist on Nov. 28, 1944, A Div. JO Dec. 9, 1944; and left BB-59 Aug. 14, 1945 after Solomon Islands and Philippines.

After the war he worked for South Western Bell Telephone Company and was involved in the Masons – Temple Lodge, Worshipful Grand Master, past patron of Eastern Star Chapter #305.

He married Ann Scott in 1929 (died in May 1978) and had one daughter, Delores Ann Whatley (three children and four grandchildren).

He then married Helen Mercer in September 1978. He died March 11, 1992, and part of Memory List 1992. (Mrs.) resides at Rt. 6 Box 1865, Mt. Pleasant, TX.

HENZELOFF, EDWARD ELIA, 647-02-88, enlisted Feb. 21, 1942, New York, NY. He is a plankowner and served aboard BB-59 as AS at commissioning May 12, 1942, and was on board on its 3rd anniversary.

HERBERT, LYLE JUNIOR, 311-19-57, enlisted Nov. 17, 1936, Detroit, MI. He is a plankowner and served aboard BB-59 as BM2/c at commissioning May 12, 1942.

HERNANDEZ, JAMES CARLOS, served aboard BB-59 as ENS CR Div. in March 1943 and Oct. 1, 1943, as LT(jg) CR Div. (censor).

HERNDON, CARLE WILLARD, 265-61-59, enlisted July 27, 1941, San Francisco, CA. He is a plankowner and served aboard BB-59 as GM3/c at commissioning May 12, 1942.

HERRMANN, RICHARD JACK, 355-98-63, enlisted Dec. 27, 1941, Dallas, TX. He is a plankowner and served aboard BB-59 as MM1/c A Div. at commissioning May 12, 1942, and MACH A Div. Dec. 9, 1944. He resides at HC 1 Box 377, Canyon Lake, TX.

HESSER, GEORGE W., B Div., Memory List 1991. (Mrs.) resides at 223 Cedar Ave. Woodlynne, NJ 08107.

HESSON, JAMES EDWARD, 650-32-43, enlisted Feb. 24, 1942, Philadelphia, PA. He is a plankowner and served aboard BB-59 as AS at commissioning May 12, 1942, and was on board on its 2nd and 3rd anniversaries.

He is married to Catherine and has two children (1966 survey). He resides at 801 Burgess St., Philadelphia, PA.

HESTBECK, DOUGLAS MARINUS, 328-72-36, enlisted July 30, 1940, Minneapolis, MN. He is a plankowner and served aboard BB-59 as S1/c at commissioning May 12, 1942.

HEWELL, EDWARD A., CEM E Div., Feb. 5, 1945, Trans. Elec. Mate Classification Center.

HIATT, M. RAY, born Feb. 16, 1922, Spanish Fort, UT. He graduated from Payson, UT, High School, Class of 1940 and attended Utah State University. He was a welder in shipyards at Alameda, CA, and enlisted Sept. 2, 1942, in San Francisco, CA, with train-

ing at Machinist Mate School, Great Lakes, Chicago, IL. Assignments were Rec. Station San Francisco, CA; via Liberty Ship, USS *Paul Revere* to Nouma, New Caledonia (March 15, 1943).

He served aboard BB-59 as MM2/c P Div. on April 1, 1943, and served on BB-59 with Fleets 3, 5 and 7 under Adm. Halsey and Adm. Nimitz. Left BB-59 in 1945 Bremerton, WA, and was assigned to the US Naval Hospital, Bremerton for operation on double hernia. Was discharged Nov. 25, 1945, MM1/c.

After the war he was self-employed in mining, trucking, automobile businesses and commercial building construction. In his spare time he is active in city government, Payson, UT; city council 1978-1994; also active in American Battleship Association; traveled to their Bahamas, Pearl Harbor and Russia meetings and to the ABA memorial service in Japan, August 1995, also traveled to China in 1995.

He married Maurine Gardner on June 9, 1942, and has six children, 26 grandchildren and three great-grandchildren. He resides at 618 South 700 West, Payson, UT 84651.

HICKS, HENRY JACKSON, General Delivery, Princeton, WV (1966).

HICKS, WILLIAM H., 321-85-02, born Feb. 9, 1926, Jackson, NE. He enlisted Feb. 10, 1943, Sioux City, IA, and attended training at Farragut, ID, NTS and Class A Gunner's Mate School.

He served aboard BB-59 as S1/c 1st Div. Turret #1 and loader on 40mm Quad #2 in December 1943. He left BB-59 in October 1946 Norfolk, VA. Was assigned to USS *Rutland* for four months and discharged in 1947.

After the war he worked construction as a plasterer in Milwaukee, WI, for 40 years. His 2nd wife died in 1988 and he married Betty Lou on Dec. 14, 1990, Quimby, IA. He has one daughter and two grandchildren and resides at 3364 DuPont St., Sioux City, IA.

HIDALGO, ZARAGOZA, resides at 4652 Sierra Springs Dr., Pollock Pines, CA 95626.

HIGGINS, JOHN THOMAS, 336-99-91, enlisted Sept. 6, 1937, St. Louis, MO. He is a plankowner and served aboard BB-59 as COX at commissioning May 12, 1942, and in R Div. CBM in 1945.

HIGH, ELVIN COTTREL, 360-47-91, enlisted Sept. 29, 1941, Houston, TX. He is a plankowner and served aboard BB-59 as Matt2/c at commissioning May 12, 1942.

HILBERER, WILLIAM HENRY, 646-70-43, enlisted Feb. 9, 1942, New York, NY. He is a plankowner and served aboard BB-59 as AS at commissioning May 12, 1942, and was on board on its 2nd anniversary.

HILL, CHARLES EDWARD, 295-41-71, enlisted March 4, 1942, Pearl Harbor, HI. He is a plankowner and served aboard BB-59 as Matt2/c at commissioning May 12, 1942.

HILL, F.M., served aboard BB-59 as ENS L Div. in February 1943.

HILL, FRANKLIN MAYNARD, LT(jg) served aboard BB-59 in CR Div. Radio Officer on Jan. 6, 1943, and left BB-59 July 30, 1944, lieutenant.

HILL, GENE ROSS, M Div. resides at 2222 Sacramento St., St. Joseph, MO 64507.

HILL, GEORGE, JR., served aboard BB-59 as ENS in May 1943 and Oct. 1, 1943, Transferred as CommWatchOff/ComBatDiv8.

HILL, JAMES, (n) resides at 1785 Mortewson, Berkley, MI (1955).

HILL, KENNETH RALPH, 274-11-58, enlisted March 16, 1942, Boston, MA. He is a plankowner and served aboard BB-59 as WT1/c at commissioning May 12, 1942.

HILL, ROBERT WILLIAM, 385-81-05, born Dec. 22, 1918, Vancouver, B.C., Canada. Graduated from high school in Port Orchard, OR, and enlisted on June 12, 1939, Seattle, WA. Training was at Optical School Mare Island, 1940; served aboard USS *Arizona* from September 1939 to November 1941; and San Diego, CA, 1941-42. He served aboard BB-59 Quincy, MA, March 1942 as FC2/c FC Div. at commissioning May 12, 1942, as a plankowner.

He left BB-59 on Sept. 30, 1945, as CFC.

Was in the US Naval Reserve, 1946-51; Active Naval Reserve 1958-78; and retired in Bremerton NSY November 1945 and June 1974. He enjoys hunting and traveling in his spare time. He has two sons, two daughters, eight grandchildren and two great-grandchildren. He resides at 3300 Carpenter Rd. SE, C-76, Lacey, WA 98503.

HILLELSON, UPTON MERWIN, served aboard BB-59 as ENS 4th Div. 40mm Sky Off. on May 21, 1944, and 4th Div. JO Dec. 9, 1944. He left BB-59 in 1946 as LT(jg). After the war he became owner of Andrew Worsted Mills, Inc. in Pascoag, RI. He has three children (1966).

HILLPOT, JOSEPH DAVID, served aboard BB-59 as Pharm. H Div. on Dec. 26, 1944, and asst. to SMO ChPharm.

HILLSTROM, ORLY WILLIAM, 262-62-46, enlisted July 23, 1940, Raleigh, NC, and served aboard BB-59 as F1/c at commissioning May 12, 1942. He is a plankowner.

HILLYER, CLIFFORD LAROY, 328-48-86, enlisted May 6, 1941, San Francisco, CA. He is a plankowner and served aboard BB-59 at commissioning May 12, 1942. Memory List 1979. (Mrs.) resides at 109 Wilson Ave., Weymouth, MA 02188.

HINDMAN, WILLIAM GORGE, 347-02-24, enlisted Jan. 14, 1942, Little Rock, AR. He is a plankowner and served aboard BB-59 as S2/c at commissioning May 12, 1942.

HINES, THOMAS HOWARD, 337-03-98, enlisted Jan. 11, 1938, St. Louis, MO. He is a plankowner and served aboard BB-59 as S1/c at commissioning May 12, 1942.

HINRICHS, HERMAN JOSEPH, 328-86-05, born Jan. 23, 1921, St. Paul, MN. He enlisted Feb. 6, 1941, Minneapolis, MN, and trained at Machinist Mate School, Ford Motor Company in 1941. Was assigned to USS *Oklahoma*, which was sunk in Pearl Harbor and then assigned to USS *Helena*. He is a plankowner and served aboard BB-59 as F2/c A Div. Machine Shop MM1/c A Div. at commissioning May 12, 1942, and left BB-59 in May 1945 Mog Mog, Ulithi. Was assigned to USS *Grand Canyon*.

After the war he worked as a tool and die maker, as a foreman for tool & die and a tooling coordinator. In his spare time he is involved in the Pearl Harbor Survivors Assoc. holding various offices including state chairman. Was president of B-Dale Club; part of A.S.T.M.E. Board; and the USS *Oklahoma* Assoc. He holds state honors for veteran's work and county honors for civic activities. He married Lorraine on June 12, 1948, in Minneapolis, MN, and has two children and four grandchildren. He resides at 696 Shryer Ave., St. Paul, MN.

HIRSCH, ARNOLD J. ENS, 4th Div., served aboard BB-59 in 4th Div. JO 40mm SkyOff on Sept. 29, 1944. He left BB-59 on Jan. 2, 1946, and on Memory List 1983. (Mrs.) resides at 4212 SW 10th Ave., Cape Coral, FL 33914.

HIRST, JOHN RAYMOND, 650-33-04, enlisted Feb. 25, 1942, Philadelphia, PA. He is a plankowner and served aboard BB-59 as AS at commissioning May 12, 1942.

HIRST, JOHN WAINWRIGHT, born April 20, 1919, Syracuse, NY. Attended Syracuse University, Graduated from United States Naval Academy Class of 1941, and the Naval War College. He joined the US Navy in Annapolis, MD, 1937 and assigned to USS *Niblack* DD; and USS *Swanson* DD (Eng. and Plotting Room Off.).

He served aboard BB-59 as ENS in March 1942 Quincy and as a plankowner May 12, 1942, LT(jg) F Div. January 1943 LT 6th Div.; and in 1944 Sec. Battery OffAirDef; LCDR CIC Off. He left as LCDR in Bremerton, WA, January 1946. Other USN assignments: 1946 USS *Nevada*; 1946 USS *Oakland* CL Gunnery Off.; 1946-47 Navy Supply School, Bayonne, NJ; Asst. Off. in Charge, Navy Purchasing Off. New York City; 1948-50 USNA Teaching Ordnance and Gunnery; 1950-51 LCDR/ CDR USS *Amphion* AR Supply Off.; 1951-54 CDR

Director of Purchasing, Gen. Stores Sup. Off. Philadelphia; 1954-56 CDR. Purchasing, BuS&A, Washington, DC; 1956-58 Supply and Fiscal Off. NAS Agana, Guam; 1958-59 CDR/CAPT Staff Sup. Off. Chief Naval Air Adv. Training; 1959-62 Capt. of Dir. of Purch. Aviation Sup. Off. Philadelphia; 1962-63 Naval War College, Newport, RI; 1963-67 Supply Off. NAS Pensacola, FL; retired in July 1967.

He has five daughters and eight grandchildren (as of November 1993). He resides at 5909 Strickland Pl., Pensacola, FL. He is an assistant editor of this book.

HOBAN, JOSEPH JAMES, 650-31-00, enlisted Feb. 20, 1942, Philadelphia, PA. He is a plankowner and served aboard BB-59 as AS at commissioning May 12, 1942, and was on board on its 2nd and 3rd anniversaries. Memory List 1990. (Mrs.) resides at Township Line/N. Drexel Ave., Havertown, PA 19083.

HOBAN, JAMES PATRICK, 243-74-19, enlisted Aug. 14, 1940, Philadelphia, PA. He is a plankowner and served aboard BB-59 as RM3/c at commissioning May 12, 1942.

HOBBS, HAROLD LLOYD, Memory List 1986.

HOBBS, RALPH EDGAR, 668-31-17, enlisted Jan. 21, 1942, St. Louis, MO. He is a plankowner and served aboard BB-59 as AS N Div. at commissioning May 12, 1942, and was on board on its 2nd and 3rd anniversaries. He resides at R#3 6 Corners, Sheboygan Falls, WI.

HOCHE, HERMAN EMANUEL, H Div., served aboard BB-59 in Pharmacy on April 28, 1943, and left BB-59 as ENS H Div. J.O. Jan. 26, 1945.

HODNICKI, THEODORE JOHN, 311-55-50, enlisted Nov. 22, 1940, Detroit, MI. He is a plankowner and served aboard BB-59 as S1/c at commissioning May 12, 1942.

HOERMANN, ALBERT, JR., (n) 874-06-00, born Jan. 13, 1926, St. Louis, MO. A high school graduate he enlisted March 21, 1944, St. Louis, MO, with training at NAVTRASTA Farragut, ID. He served aboard BB-59 as F1/c A Div. Air Cond. in May 1944 and left BB-59 in May 1946.

After the war he was a steelworker at Donco Steel Erection Company; member of Bridge and Structural Iron Workers Local #396; and last worked for EME Construction Company. In his spare time he is active in the VFW and Masonic Blue Lodge Pyramid #180 AF&AM.

He married Audrey Ward July 4, 1947, St. Louis, MO, and has three children, nine grandchildren and two great-grandchildren. He died June 20, 1987; Memory List 1989. (Mrs.) resides at 1105 Meadowgrass Drive, Florissant, MO 63033.

HOFFAY, WESTON, (n) 647-02-91, enlisted Feb. 21, 1942, New York, NY. He is a plankowner and served aboard BB-59 as 4th Div. at commissioning May 12, 1942, and left in 1945. After the war he worked as a patrolman in Kingston, NY. He was active in VFW #1386 and the Masonic Lodge. #10 (Kingston, NY). Memory List 1987. (Mrs.) resides at 62 Clearview Circle, Hopewell Jct., NY.

HOFFELT, JOHN FRANCIS, 368-39-49, enlisted Jan. 29, 1942, Minneapolis, MN. He is a plankowner and served aboard BB-59 as EM2/c at commissioning May 12, 1942. Left BB-59 April 17, 1945 CEM to USS *Kaskaskia* FFT RS.

HOGAN, DANIEL JOSEPH, 606-48-96, enlisted March 11, 1942, Boston, MA. He is a plankowner and served aboard BB-59 as AS at commissioning May 12, 1942, and was on board on its 2nd anniversary.

HOHRATH, EMIL WALTER, 650-30-92, born Jan. 14, 1918, Philadelphia, PA. A high school graduate he enlisted Feb. 20, 1942, Philadelphia, PA, and received training at Newport, RI. He is a plankowner and served aboard BB-59 as AS 2nd Div. at commissioning May 12, 1942, and as S1/c N Div. Dec. 12, 1942. He left BB-59 in September 1945.

After the war he was self-employed for 11 years and a stainless steel precision fabricator for 25 years. Retired in 1981. Enjoys working in his vegetable garden and crafts in his spare time. He has four children and eight grandchildren (as of January 1992). He resides at 2061 Bridge Rd., Schwenksville, PA 19473.

HOLBERG, NORMAN RAGNAR, 646-81-32, enlisted Feb. 18, 1942, New York, NY. He is a plankowner and served aboard BB-59 as AS at commissioning May 12, 1942.

HOLDEN, LIVINGSTON LEE, 624-19-27, enlisted in December 1941, Houston, TX. He is a plankowner and served aboard BB-59 S2/c at commissioning May 12, 1942.

HOLLANDSWORTH, EARL MARVIN, 668-30-68, enlisted Jan. 21, 1942, St. Louis, MO. He is a plankowner and served aboard BB-59 as AS 4th Div. at commissioning May 12, 1942, and was on board on its 2nd and 3rd anniversaries. Memory List 1991. (Mrs.) resides at 9397 Hayes Dr., Overland Park, KS 66212.

HOLLINGSWORTH, GEORGE LEO, 650-20-69, enlisted Feb. 20, 1942, Philadelphia, PA. He is a plankowner and served aboard BB-59 as AS at commissioning May 12, 1942.

HOLLEY, IRA DAN, 560-12-68, born April 29, 1925, Huntington, WV. Graduated from East High School, Huntington, WV, and enlisted Aug. 25, 1942, Huntington, WV; training Norfolk, VA. Assigned to NRS Charleston, WV; NTS NOB Norfolk, VA, and aboard BB-59 from 1942-45.

After the war he was service station dealer/owner; auto repair/owner and was semi-retired in 1987, limousine driver. In his spare time he was active in Charles Galey Post VFW #7340.

Married Mary Jane and had two daughters, three sons and seven grandchildren. He died Oct. 16, 1995. (Mrs.) resides at 7409 Martin St., Cincinnati, OH 45231.

HOLLEY, REEDER RUSHING, 295-12-01, enlisted March 10, 1942, Norfolk, VA. He is a plankowner and served aboard BB-59 as Mus1/c at commissioning May 12, 1942.

HOLLMAN, WILLIAM J., resides at 1718 Sylvan Way, Lodi, CA 95242.

HOLTON, RICHARD EARL, 321-55-63, enlisted Jan. 2, 1941, Des Moines, IA. He is a plankowner and served aboard BB-59 as S1/c at commissioning May 12, 1942.

HOLTZ, HOWARD W., resides at 5129 Wright Terr., Skokie, IL.

HOOKER, C.P., ENS 2nd Div., served aboard BB-59 as J.O. Turret H.R. on May 21, 1944, and left BB-59 Nov. 7, 1944.

HOPKINS, CHARLES FERGUSON, 243-81-03, enlisted Nov. 19, 1940, Philadelphia, PA. He is a plankowner and served aboard BB-59 in Quincy, MA, May 5, 1942, and at commissioning May 12, 1942, F1/c M Div. (after engine room). Left BB-59 as MM1/c M Div. 1945-46.

After the war he was maintenance machinist at the Naval Air Eng. Center. He has three boys (1966). Memory List 1979. (Mrs.) resides at Box 578A, Rd. 3 Williamstown, NJ 08094.

HOPKINS, CLARENCE A., CSK S Div., left BB-59 April 17, 1945, transferred to USS *Kaskaskia* FFT RS.

HOPKINS, JOHN, (n) P Div. served aboard BB-59 March 25, 1943; Oct. 1, 1943 LT(jg) Asst. Eng. Educ. Off. Dec. 9, 1944, lieutenant B Div.; left BB-59 Sept. 15, 1945.

HOPP, LAVERNE D., has one son, one daughter and two grandchildren (son in Alaska February 1992). He resides at PO Box 2074, Marysville, CA.

HORB, T.H., May 12, 1945 RM2/c CR Div. captain.

HORBATT, PAUL, resides at 1709 Marlot St., Fairlawn, NJ (1963).

HORN, THOMAS E., 939-31-09, born Dec. 28, 1925, Amarillo, TX. Graduated from high school and joined the Navy March 13, 1944, Amarillo, TX. He served aboard BB-59 as AS, S2/c, F2/c, F1/c and WT3/c and was discharged March 20, 1946. He resides at Box 2753, Ruidoso, NM 88345.

HORNE, CALVIN, resides in Lin Oak, FL (1964).

HORNER, WILBERT DAVID, 258-15-46, enlisted Jan. 10, 1942, Charleston, WV. He is a plankowner and served aboard BB-59 as WT2/c at commissioning May 12, 1942, and was on board on its 2nd and 3rd anniversary.

HORNUNG, ORLANDO RON, 279-65-35, enlisted Jan. 9, 1940, Cincinnati, OH. He is a plankowner and served aboard BB-59 as F1/c at commissioning May 12, 1942.

HORVATH, JOHN, (n) 299-86-14, born Aug. 17, 1916, Austria. Graduated from high school and enlisted Jan. 23, 1942, Chicago, IL and served aboard USS Lexington DD-218 and DD-222. He served aboard BB-59 as MM2/c M Div. at commissioning May 12, 1942. He is a plankowner. He has two children and three grandchildren. He resides at RR1 Box 600, Lake Geneva, WI.

HOUCHEN, GLEN E., served as CY A Div.

HOUFF, WILLIAM C., Memory List 1989.

HOUSTON, JOHN CECIL, 342-63-75, enlisted Jan. 20, 1942, Kansas City, MO. He is a plankowner and served aboard BB-59 as AS at commissioning May 12, 1942.

HOUTS, COYDEN DALE, 316-23-92, enlisted May 8, 1939, San Diego, CA. He is a plankowner and served aboard BB-59 as SF1/c at commissioning May 12, 1942.

HOVIS, CHARLE, Memory List 1996.

HOWARD, DONALD H., born July 2, 1922, Moville, IA. A high school graduate with two years of junior college, he enlisted July 22, 1942, Des Moines, IA, and was assigned to USS *Alabama.* He served aboard BB-59 in A Div.

After the war he worked for the US Post Office retiring in 1972. He was active in the American Legion as a life member and the Elks.

Married Dorothy and had two children. He died Nov. 25, 1989; Memory List 1990. (Mrs.) resides at 27180 Cornell St., Hemet, CA.

HOWARD, GOLDEN R., served aboard BB-59 in October 1943 as S1/c 1st Div. and left BB-59 in November 1945. After the war he joined the US Navy as aviation machinist mate 1/c. He has three children and resides at 1769 Halley St., San Diego, CA (1966).

HOWARD, THOMAS E., 876-62-73, born April 25, 1925, Snyder, TX. Graduated from high and enlisted in 1943 with training at Farragut, ID. Served aboard BB-59 as WT1/c B Div. and was discharged April 7, 1946, San Francisco, CA. He married Eunice April 14, 1947, in Montrose, CO, and resides at 1305 Laguna, Farmington, NM.

HOWARD, THOMAS WILLIAM, 393-19-04, enlisted Sept. 22, 1939, San Diego, CA. He is a plankowner and served aboard BB-59 as RM1/c at commissioning May 12, 1942.

HOWELL, ELBERT JEROME, served aboard BB-59 as LT(jg) I Div. on Aug. 11, 1944; Dec. 9, 1944 J.O. I Div.; and left BB-59 Dec. 15, 1945. Memory List 1981.

HOWELL, ROBERT JACKSON, 328-49-79, enlisted Jan. 6, 1942, New York, NY. He is a plankowner and served aboard BB-59 as WT2/c at commissioning May 12, 1942.

HOY, CHARLES E., enlisted USMC, May 8, 1942, Norfolk, Navy Yard. Served aboard BB-59 as FM 7th Div. at commissioning May 12, 1942.

HRUGGER, JAMES, (n) F/c from Missouri. (Note received from C.L. Klein December 1993) "We both rode same school bus to high school – did not see again until aboard BB-59 Dec. 19, 1942."

HRYZAK, JOSEPH M., served aboard BB-59 on July 13, 1944; Dec. 9, 1944, lieutenant 3rd Div. and left BB-59 May 29, 1945 M Div. Memory List 1977.

HUBBARD, ROBERT, (n) 223-80-65, enlisted Aug. 21, 1940, New York, NY. He is a plankowner and served aboard BB-59 as MATT1/c at commissioning May 12, 1942.

HUBBERT, DONALD B., resides at 7160 Nottingham, West Bloomfield, MI 48322.

HUDEK, HENRY HARRY, 650-32-44, enlisted Feb. 24, 1942, Philadelphia, PA. He is a plankowner and served aboard BB-59 as AS at commissioning May 12, 1942, and was on board on its 2nd and 3rd anniversaries.

HUDDLESTON, LOUIS HADLEY, 346-68-70, enlisted Dec. 10, 1937, Little Rock, AR. He is a plankowner and served aboard BB-59 as COX at commissioning May 12, 1942.

HUDSON, HERMAN D., enlisted USMC, May 8, 1942, Norfolk Navy Yard. He is a plankowner and served aboard BB-59 in 7th Div. as PLT SGT at commissioning May 12, 1942.

HUDSON, JOSEPH JAMES, 239-15-89, enlisted March 2, 1937, Norfolk, VA. He is a plankowner and served aboard BB-59 as SM1/c at commissioning May 12, 1942.

HUFFMAN, W.L., USMC Major 7th Div. Memory List 1986.

HUFFMIRE, CALVIN JOSEPH, 646-17-84, enlisted Dec. 17, 1941, New York, NY He is a plankowner and served aboard BB-59 as SF2/c at commissioning May 12, 1942, and was on board on its 2nd anniversary. He resides at 93-23 209th St., Queens Village, NY (1955).

HUGALL, H.R., 113 Linden St., Freemont, MI 49412.

HUGGON, ROBERT VINCENT, 606-57-44, enlisted April 27, 1942, Boston, MA. He is a plankowner and served aboard BB-59 as GM3/c R Div. at commissioning May 12, 1942. He resides at 30 Holly Hill Circle, South Weymouth, MA 02190.

HUGHES, CARLEY M., JR., 7231 Hargrove Rd., East, Cottondale, AL.

HUGHES, LAWRENCE HENRY, 666-19-75, enlisted March 5, 1942, Springfield, MA. He is a plankowner and served aboard BB-59 as AS at commissioning May 12, 1942.

HUGHEY, GEORGE HARING, 389676, born May 2, 1922, Honolulu, HI. He holds a BS from USNA Class of 1944 and an MS from Princeton University 1954. Joined the Navy in June 1941, Annapolis, MD. Attended EM School TI 1946; Flight Training 1948; Fleet Air Gunnery Unit 1957.

He served aboard BB-59 as ENS FC Div. on Oct. 11, 1944, and left BB-59 in March 1946 as LT(jg). Was assigned to USS *Stickell* DD-888 1946-47; Flight Training 1947-48; VA 25 1948-50; USPGS 1950-54; VC-4 1954-57; and BuAer 1957-60.

After the war he worked for General Electric as systems engineer, satellites and missiles; Fairchild engineering manager; American Satellite as engineering manager; Contel as engineering director. In his spare time was vice-president Potomac C of C.

Married Ann C. Oct. 27, 1945, in Washington, DC, and has one daughter and two grandchildren. He resides at 11208 Spur Wheel Lane, Potomac, MD.

HUMES, JAMES E., USMC GySgt. 7th Div.

HUMMEL, RALPH M., Memory List 1996.

HUMMEL, RONALD E., resides at Box 753 2505 Nevada St., Hutchinson, KS.

HUMPHREYS, JAMES W., resides at 508 W 4th Ave., Derry, PA.

HUNT, HARRY MONROE, 346-77-33, enlisted Jan. 9, 1940, Little Rock, AR. He is a plankowner and served aboard BB-59 as S1/c 5th Div. at commissioning May 12, 1942, and was on board on its 2nd anniversary. He resides at 14333 Seaforth Ave., Norwalk, CA.

HUNT, ROBERT SHERWOOD, born July 14, 1917, Postville, IA. Obtained an AB from Oberlin College, 1939; AM Harvard 1940; LLB from Yale 1947; and SJD from University of Wisconsin 1952. Joined the Navy in 1940 USNR. He served aboard BB-59 FC Div. as an ENS on commissioning May 12, 1942 and was a plankowner. Other duty with L Div. from Oct. 1, 1943, to May 12, 1944. Other assignments were to USS *Flint* LTCdr.

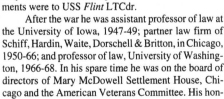

After the war he was assistant professor of law at the University of Iowa, 1947-49; partner law firm of Schiff, Hardin, Waite, Dorschell & Britton, in Chicago, 1950-66; and professor of law, University of Washington, 1966-68. In his spare time he was on the board of directors of Mary McDowell Settlement House, Chicago and the American Veterans Committee. His honors include the Everest Prize in Wisconsin Economic History for his book, *Law and Locomotives*, 1958.

He married Claudette Marie Leers in April 1984, Seattle, WA. He has four stepchildren, two step-grandsons and one step-granddaughter. He died Nov. 2,

1990; Memory List 1991. (Mrs.) resides at 1415 38th Ave., Seattle, WA.

HUNTER, A.O., JR., resides at 3514 Wyandate St., Kansas City, MO (1962).

HUNTER, CLIFFORD EUGENE, Capt. 3590145B2, born Sept. 23, 1922, Taylorville, IL. He holds a BS from USNA Class of 1944; MA from George Washington University 1964; and an MS from George Washington University 1965. He served aboard BB-59 as ENS 5th Div. on Sept. 29, 1944, Saipan and left BB-59 Dec. 20, 1945, Bremerton, WA. Other assignments were DE-152, DDR-842; DESDIV-232; and DESRON-2.

After the war he taught social studies and became assistant principal at NCHS, Norfolk, VA, 1976-88. In his spare time he was chairman of building committee for Donation Episcopal Church, Virginia Beach, VA; and the Convenor in Order of St. Luke.

He married Margaret T. Sept. 11, 1948, in Annapolis, MD, and has three children and one grandchild. He resides at 4191 Wakefield CT., Virginia Beach, VA 23455.

HUNTOON, ALFRED T., 224-08-10, born in New York, NY. Graduated from Madison High School, Brooklyn, NY, and enlisted Jan. 28, 1941, New York. Training and assignments include: Newport, RI; AM School Pensacola, FL, May 1941 to August 1941; NAS Kodiak, AL, October 1941 to December 1943; and NAS Seattle January 1944 to June 1944.

He served aboard BB-59 as AM1/c V Div. in July 1944 and left BB-59 September 1945 Bremerton, WA. Assigned to SOSU Alameda, CA, October 1945 to April 1946; USS *Boxer* CV-21 May 1946 to December 1946; USS *Curtiss* AV-4 October 1950 to December 1951.

After the war he worked for the Civil Service NAS Alameda, CA, from January 1947-July 1977. He married Janice March 1946 in Oakland, CA, and had three children. He resided at PO Box 2122, Arnold, CA 95223. Memory List 1996.

HURST, JOHN, (n) LT Memory List 1993.

HUSSEMAN, ARNOLD JAMES, 385-80-71, enlisted April 11, 1939, Seattle, WA. He is a plankowner and served aboard BB-59 as QM1/c N Div. at commissioning May 12, 1942.

HUSSEY, STEPHEN MONROE, 372-00-27, enlisted Jan. 8, 1937, Denver, CO. He is a plankowner and served aboard BB-59 as MM1/c at commissioning May 12, 1942.

HUSTON, EDWARD B., served in I Div. Memory List 1989. (Mrs.) resides at 3887 East 54th St., Cleveland, OH 44105.

HUTCHINGS, MELVILLE D., Memory List 1983.

HUTCHINSON, MARK FRANCIS, 650-32-48, born Dec. 19, 1919, Philadelphia, PA. Graduated from high school and enlisted Feb. 24, 1942, Philadelphia, PA. Trained at Newport, RI. He is a plankowner and served aboard BB-59 as AS S Div. at commissioning May 12, 1942, became Baker1/c. He left BB-59 in September 1945 Bremerton, WA.

After the war he worked for a small local bakery for 15 months then was employed at A & P Tea Company Bakery in Philadelphia for 36 years (1977).

He married Anna Elsa Nov. 23, 1942, in Philadelphia and has four children, and as of November 1991

five grandchildren. He resides at 4723 Oakmont St., Philadelphia, PA.

HUTCHINSON, R.G., S2/c, served aboard BB-59 on March 10, 1943, transferred CR Div. to FR Div.

HUTCHINSON, WARREN, 329-55-57, born March 3, 1927, Duluth, MI. Graduated from high school and enlisted March 15, 1944, Duluth, MI. He served aboard BB-59 May 1944 as AS 4th Div. and left BB-59 March 1946. Also assigned to *Skagit, Pickaway, Yorktown, Lowe;* shore duty in San Diego, CA; Washington, DC, retired from the Navy Sept. 20, 1963.

After the war he worked for the Potomac Electric Power for 26 years, two months, in Washington, DC. Retired March 30, 1990.

Married Martha, Delray, VA, and has one daughter and one grandson. He resides at 6943 Willow Tree Lane, Huber Heights, OH 45424.

HUTZLER, JAMES ARTHUR, 646-17-85, born June 18, 1919, Jersey City, NJ. Graduated from high school and enlisted Dec. 17, 1941, New York, NY. Before the war worked as a general contractor in California and a masonry and shipfitter.

He is a plankowner and served aboard BB-59 as Msmth2/c at commissioning May 12, 1942, and left BB-59 in Boston as the result of a fractured neck. He spent 18 months in the hospital.

After the war he worked as a general contractor and married Ora F. Sept. 16, 1950, in Portland, OR. He has one son and one daughter. He resides at 820 Blue Falls Place, Reno, NV.

HYLAN, PAUL FRECERIO, 606-48-18, enlisted March 9, 1942, Boston, MA. He was a plankowner and served aboard BB-59 as AS 2nd Div. at commissioning May 12, 1942, and was on board on its 2nd and 3rd anniversaries COX. He left BB-59 in November 1945.

After the war he worked for General Dynamics as an electrician and has five children (1966). He resides at 521 Willard St., Quincy, MA.

IANNACO, ALFRED J., Memory List 1977.

IANNARINO, GUS A., served aboard BB-59 in the 3rd and R Div. He resides at 4965 Shadycrest Rd., Columbus, OH 43229.

ILLINGSWORTH, CHARLES, (n) served aboard BB-59 in L Div. He resides at 3 Primrose Lane #3-S, Fords, NJ 08863.

INGRASSIA, STEPHEN JOSEPH, 606-18-09, enlisted Jan. 9, 1942, Boston, MA. He is a plankowner and served aboard BB-59 as GM2/c at commissioning May 12, 1942.

INSELMAN, DONALD, (n) 372-14-39, enlisted April 10, 1940, Denver, CO. He is a plankowner and served aboard BB-59 as S1/c at commissioning May 12, 1942.

IPPOLITO, PETER, (n) 238-85-08, enlisted March 30, 1942, Albany, NY. He is a plankowner and served aboard BB-59 as AS S Div. at commissioning May 12, 1942, and was on board on its 2nd and 3rd anniversaries. Was assigned as Bk1/c S Div. and left BB-59 in June 1947. Other Naval assignments in Naval Reserve, Albany, NY.

After the war he was self-employed as contractor, Tile Marble & Slate Company. He was active in VFW Boyd Hilton Post 7062, Altamont, NY. Memory List 1991. (Mrs.) resides at 50 Prescott St. #315, Albany, NY 12205-4442.

IRELAND, F.M.

IRELAND, JAMES MORRISON, ENS, born July 4, 1914, Sherman, TX. Holds a BA from Southern Methodist University. He enlisted Sept. 14, 1940, USS *Prairie State* and commissioned ensign June 6, 1941.

He is a plankowner and served aboard BB-59 as ensign X Div. at commissioning May 12, 1942, and was on board on its 2nd anniversary. Was assigned ensign F Div. LT(jg) 3rd Div. and left BB-59 April 18, 1945. Was also assigned March to May 1950 Staff Armed Forces College; August 1950 to August 1954 Staff CincPacFleet. Aug. 5, 1954 to June 27, 1956 Opr. officer USS *Manchester*; Sept. 18, 1956, to Sept. 14, 1948, Commanding Officer USS *Charles S. Sperry*; May 12, 1956 to Dec. 31, 1959 Office of CNO; August 11, 1960 to Feb. 11, 1964 Naval Attaché Rio de Janeiro, Brazil; April 11, 1964, to April 15, 1965, Commanding Officer USS *Talladega* APA-208; June 1, 1965, to May 18, 1968, Senior Member SAB Board of Inspection and Survey; June 3, 1968, to Feb. 10, 1970, Chief Labor Section US Forces, Japan; June 1, 1970, to Dec. 1, 1970, assistant chief of staff for Administration 11th Naval District San Diego, CA; and March 1, 1971 retired as captain.

Married Eulah March 23, 1946. Ireland died in January 1977. (Mrs.) resides at 3011 Orleans East, San Diego, CA 92110. Memory List 1997.

IRVIN, PAUL JOSEPH, 600-10-09, enlisted Dec. 26, 1941, Boston, MA. He is a plankowner and served aboard BB-59 as Y3/c at commissioning May 12, 1942. Memory List 1986.

ISANHART, IRWIN E., served aboard BB-59 in 1st Div. Resides at 36401 5 Acre Lane, Zephyrhills, FL 33541.

ISBELL, H. ROY, 753-07-12, born April 25, 1926, Hanna City, IL. Enlisted May 5, 1943, and attended Great Lakes Naval Training Station, USS *Wharton*. Served aboard BB-59 September 1943 Efate, New Hebrides and assigned GM3/c 6th Div. Left BB-59 Jan. 20, 1946, Seattle, WA.

After the war worked in the machine shop for the Brass Foundry Company, Peoria, IL, for 41 years and was mayor of Hanna City, IL, for 11 years. Was Logan Township supervisor for 14 years. In his spare time he is active in the Salvation Army.

He married Mildred Sept. 26, 1946, Hanna City, IL, and has one son, two daughters, seven grandchildren and three great-grandchildren. He resides at RR #1 Box 189, Hanna City, IL 61536.

ISOM, KELSON JAMES, 606-49-94, enlisted March 9, 1942, Boston, MA. He is a plankowner and served aboard BB-59 as AS at commissioning May 12, 1942.

ISYK, DANIEL L., served aboard BB-59 in 1st Div. He resides at 147 Murray St., Meriden, CT 06450.

ISZARD, HOWARD ESTELL, 382-20-13, enlisted May 15, 1940, Los Angeles, CA.

JACKSON, CHARLES, JR., (n) 316-89-82, enlisted March 1, 1942, Omaha, NE. He is a plankowner and served aboard BB-59 as Matt3/c at commissioning May 12, 1942.

JACKSON, DENNIS MARSHALL, 644-02-46, enlisted Aug. 7, 1941, New Orleans, LA. He is a plankowner and served aboard BB-59 as EM3/c E Div. at commissioning May 12, 1942.

JACKSON, GEORGE STEPHEN, 234-26-24, enlisted Aug. 13, 1940, Buffalo, NY. He is a plankowner and served aboard BB-59 as S1/c at commissioning May 12, 1942, and was on board on its 2nd anniversary.

JACKSON, MAURICE, (n) LT, served aboard BB-59 as LT A Div. at commissioning May 12, 1942, as a plankowner and left in December 1942. After the war he was treasurer and controller at Worth's Dept. Store and was active in Jewish War Vets in his spare time. He had one son and one daughter and latest address was 154 Arden Road, Waterbury, CT 06716. Memory List 1977.

JACKSON, ROBERT HAROLD, 243-26-24, enlisted Dec. 16, 1941, Philadelphia, PA. He is a plankowner and served aboard BB-59 as EM2/c E Div. at commissioning May 12, 1942.

JACKSON, ROBERT J., served aboard BB-59 in R and L Div. Latest address was 1734 Ayersville Ave., Defiance, OH 43512. Memory List 1992.

JACOBS, JOHN HOWARD, enlisted March 20, 1942, Columbia, SC. He is a plankowner and served aboard BB-59 as Matt3/c at commissioning May 12, 1942.

JACOBSON, STAN, (n) Memory List 1977. (Mrs.) resides at RFD 1, Cottage Grove, WI 53527.

JACOBUS, PETER GEORGE, 650-30-71, born May 10, 1918, Philadelphia, PA. Graduated from high school and enlisted Feb. 20, 1942, Philadelphia, PA. Received training at Newport Naval Training Station, Newport, RI.

He was a plankowner and served aboard BB-59 as AS 2nd Div. at commissioning May 12, 1942, and was on board on its 2nd anniversary. Left BB-59 in July 1943 as S1/c. Other assignments as plankowner on (minesweeper) USS *Competent* (AM-316).

After the war he was a supervisor for Mack Wholesale Corp. and married Catherine, Jan. 25, 1943, Boston, MA. He had one son and one daughter. Latest address was 36 Pebble Lane, Levittown, PA 19054. Memory List 1994.

JACOBY, EARL F., CGM 4th Div., temporary duty aboard BB-59. Was transferred to AATC, Navy 36 for duty Aug. 8, 1944.

JACQUES, MARJORIE (n) (MISS), Honorary Secretary for USS *Massachusetts* Assoc. and received BB-59 Award in 1968. She resides at 22 Judith Lane Apt. 5, Waltham, MA 02154.

JADACH, WALTER THOMAS, 650-30-73, enlisted Feb. 20, 1942, Philadelphia, PA. He is a plankowner and served aboard BB-59 as AS at commissioning May 12, 1942, and was on board on its 2nd and 3rd anniversaries.

JAKWAY, ELWOOD BAINES, 650-32-10, enlisted Feb. 24, 1942, Philadelphia, PA. He is a plankowner and served aboard BB-59 as AS at commissioning May 12, 1942, and was on board on its 2nd and 3rd anniversaries.

JAMES EDWIN LEWIS, 274-50-32, enlisted Aug. 30, 1940, New Orleans, LA. He is a plankowner and served aboard BB-59 as S1/c at commissioning May 12, 1942, and was on board on its 2nd anniversary.

JAMES, HOMER E., served aboard BB-59 in 5th Div. Memory List 1993. (Mrs.) resides at 111 Alcala Ave., Lehigh Acres, FL 33936.

JAMISON, FRANK W., born Nov. 30, 1908, Bellfontaine, OH. A high school graduate, he enlisted Jan. 31, 1944, Des Moines, IA, and attended Radar School, San Diego, CA, and Officer Training, University of Iowa. Served aboard BB-59 as Rdm3/c in February 1944 and left BB-59 November 1945, San Diego, CA.

After the war he was an agent for Standard Oil Company for 30 years, and West Ridge Nursing Home. In his spare time he teaches Sunday School, sings in the church choir, and teaches oil painting.

He married Mable Aug. 12, 1931, Bellefontaine, OH, and has one son, one daughter, 11 grandchildren and five great-grandchildren. He resides at 1314 North Grant, Knoxville, IA 50138.

JANKOWSKI, CHESTER FRANCIS, 337-33-55, born Oct. 29, 1921, East St. Louis, IL, and graduated from East St. Louis High School. He enlisted Feb. 6, 1941, St. Louis, MO. From April 30, 1941, to Aug. 29, 1941, Navy Service School, Fort Motor Company, Dearborn, MI, USS *Oklahoma,* and USS *Helena.*

He is a plankowner and served aboard BB-59 as F2/c B Div. at commissioning May 12, 1942, and was on board on its 2nd anniversary. Left BB-59 July 23, 1943, Noumea, New Caledonia. Was also assigned to USS *Epping Forest* (LSD-4), USS *Carib* (ATF-82).

After the war from March 26, 1947 to April 1, 1977 was maintenance supervisor for Monsanto Company; April 19, 1978, night supervisor for Eythl Corp.; and retired April 13, 1984. Active in Red Cross Blood Bank, YMCA, golf and traveling.

Married Clara June on June 19, 1948, East St. Louis, IL, and has one son, one daughter and one grandchild. He resides at 12 Roclare Drive, Belleville, IL 62220-4710.

JANNECK, EARL F., served aboard BB-59 as QM3/c N Div. in March 1944. Was assigned as helmsman, general quarters, underway station, quartermaster of watch. Left BB-59 in July 1946.

After the war he was vice-president of Delta Savings and Loan. Was active in Disabled War Veterans and had two sons and one daughter. Memory List 1987.

JANUSIS, ALPHONSE JOSEPH, 207-27-46, enlisted July 9, 1940, New Haven, CT. He is a plankowner and served aboard BB-59 as F2/c at commissioning May 12, 1942.

JANUSIS, ALBERT, Memory List 1985.

JARES, JOE, (n) assigned in charge of catapults. He resides in Erie, PA.

JARRETT, HOWARD R., enlisted USMC, May 8, 1942, Navy Yard, Norfolk, VA. He is a plankowner and served aboard BB-59 as Pvt. 7th Div. at commissioning May 12, 1942.

JARRETT, ROBY J., 658-50-65, born Aug. 13, 1923, Gilliam, WV. Attended Electrical Engineering, Virginia Polytechnic Institute and enlisted April 1942, Roanoke, VA. Attended Newport Naval Training Station, Newport, RI, and Fire Control School, Newport, RI. He served aboard BB-59 as FC2/c FC Div. in June 1942. Left BB-59 December 1945, Bremerton, WA.

After the war he was vice-president of Jarrett Electric Company, Inc. In his spare time he is active in Lakeland No. 190 Masonic Lodge, past master of Roanoke Scottish Rite Kazim Shrine Temple; Royal Arch; Commandery K.T.; past master Masonic Lodge; Orator in Shrine Ceremonial Cast; 33rd Degree Mason. He married Barbara June 7, 1974, Roanoke, VA, and has two stepsons and 6 step-grandchildren. He resides at 910 5th St. SW, Roanoke, VA 24016.

JARVIS, RAYMOND ALVIS, 360-23-56, enlisted Oct. 5, 1940, Houston, TX. He was a plankowner and served aboard BB-59 as S1/c at commissioning May 12, 1942. He resided at Harbor Point Rd., Rte. 3, Mabank, TX 75147. Memory List 1996.

JASA, JERRY, (n) 321-30-00, enlisted Feb. 17, 1939, Washington, DC. He is a plankowner and served aboard BB-59 as SC2/c at commissioning May 12, 1942.

JEANNETTE, ANTHONY AUGUSTUS, 650-32-21, enlisted Feb. 24, 1942, Philadelphia, PA. He is a plankowner and served aboard BB-59 as AS at commissioning May 12, 1942. He resides at 107 North 5th St., Millville, NJ 08332.

JEFFERS, WARREN EDWIN, 311-38-36, enlisted Dec. 11, 1939, Detroit, MI. He is a plankowner and served aboard BB-59 as S1/c at commissioning May 12, 1942, and was on board on its 2nd and 3rd anniversaries. He resides at 315 Jones St.,, Lansing, MI 48909.

JENCUNAS, FRANK JOSEPH, LT(jg) is a plankowner and served in CS Div. at commissioning May 12, 1942, and assigned as signal officer Signal Bridge. Left BB-59 in December 1943.

After the war he worked as a postal inspector for the US Post Office and is active in US Naval Reserve, Navy League and the International Assoc. of Chiefs of Police.

He married Doro and had one son and two daughters. Memory List 1977. (Mrs.) resides at 65 Charles St., Natick, MA 01760.

JENKINS, DWIGHT EDMUND, ENS, served aboard BB-59 with ComBatDiv8 in May 1943. Was assigned as Comm. Watch Officer.

JENKS, NORMAN E., served aboard BB-59 in FC Div. He resides at 42 Emerson Rd., Agawam, MA 01001.

JENSEN, HAROLD E., served aboard BB59 in B Div. Memory List 1978. (Mrs.) resides at 201 Lincoln Ave., Geneva, IL 60134.

JENSEN, NORMAN LOUIS, LT(jg) served aboard BB-59 as Com. in CS Div. on April 29, 1943. Was assigned as signal officer and watch officer. Left BB-59 Jan. 5, 1946, as LT CDR.

JENSEN, STANLEY KEITH, 372-15-34, enlisted June 12, 1940, Denver, CO. He is a plankowner and served aboard BB-59 as FC3/c at commissioning May 12, 1942.

JETER, JAMES EDWARD, LT(jg) served aboard BB-59 in CS Div. on Aug. 23, 1944, and left BB-59 Dec. 2, 1945.

JEZIORO, JOSEPH THOMAS, 610-23-75, enlisted Jan. 2, 1942, Chicago, IL. He is a plankowner and served aboard BB-59 as F2/c at commissioning May 12, 1942. He resides at 7310 West Olive Ave., Chicago, IL 60631.

JIMENEZ, FRANK, (n) 849-12-89, born Oct. 10, 1918, San Antonio, TX. He enlisted Feb. 29, 1944, Oklahoma City, OK, and attended Farragut Naval Training Station, Farragut, ID. Served aboard BB-59 as AS S Div. in May 1944 and assigned to S2/c

and S1/c S Div. Left BB-59 Dec. 11, 1945, Bremerton, WA.

After the war from Sept. 18, 1935, to October 1975 he worked miscellaneous jobs in the bakery industry; 1971-81 owned vending machine business; and 1980-90 landscape business.

He married Marguerite June 17, 1939, Oklahoma City, OK, and has three sons, one daughter, 13 grandchildren and five great-grandchildren. He resides at Rt. 2 Box CW 103A, Tuttle, OK 73089

JODAITIS, FRANCIS CADAMIL, 212-27-17, enlisted Jan. 16, 1942, Boston, MA. He is a plankowner and served aboard BB-59 as MM1/c at commissioning May 12, 1942, and was on board on its 2nd anniversary. He resides at 16 Harvard St., Charlestown, MA 02129. Memory List 1988.

JODOIN, JOSEPH, (n) resides at 51 Walnut St., Lowell, MA 01853 (1966).

JOHANSSON, WALTER HENNING, 201-76-75, born June 22, 1919, Somerville, MA. Graduated from high school and Medford Vocational School. Enlisted Aug. 30, 1940, Boston, MA, and attended Newport Naval Training Station, Newport RI; and on USS *St. Louis.*

He served aboard BB-59 as AS X Div. at commissioning May 12, 1942, and was on board on its 2nd and 3rd anniversaries. He is a plankowner and was assigned to print shop, master-at-arms and BM2/c. Left BB-59 December 1945 Bremerton, WA. Was also assigned to Bremerton Naval Hospital, Bremerton, WA, and discharged Jan. 26, 1946.

After the war worked for Oxford Print, 1946; Daniels Printing Company, Boston, MA, 1947; printer for Boston Herald Traveler Company, Boston, MA, 1949 for 34 years. He married Johnson June 24, 1944, Malden, MA, and had two daughters and two grandchildren. Memory List 1986. (Mrs.) resides at 72A Renwick Rd., Wakefield, MA 01880.

JOHNSON, ALDRED HOLM, 650-33-03, born Nov. 1, 1921, Chester, PA. Earned a BS in business administration and enlisted Feb. 25, 1942, Philadelphia, PA. Attended Newport Naval Training Station, Newport, RI.

He is a plankowner and served aboard BB-59 as AS 1st Div. at commissioning May 12, 1942, and was on board on its 2nd anniversary. Was assigned October 1942 to E Div. EM2/c and left BB-59 in March 1945 Ulithi. Was also assigned to IC School, Camp Perry, Washington, DC; and discharge November 1, 1945, as EM2/c.

Worked for Goodyear Tire Company, Rochester, NY; manager for White Plains Tire & Retreader, White Plains, NY; accountant for White Plains Hospital, White Plains, NY; and retired in 1987.

Married Gladys Sept. 10, 1949, Groveville, NJ, and has two sons and five grandchildren. He resides at 11 Whitehead St., Cranston, RI 02920.

JOHNSON, BUSTER HORACE, 372-05-37, enlisted April 9, 1938, Denver, CO. He served aboard BB-59 as EM1/c E Div. at commissioning May 12, 1942, and is a plankowner.

JOHNSON, CHARLES PAUL, 154-58-93, enlisted July 4, 1939, San Francisco, CA. He is a plankowner and served aboard BB-59 as EM2/c E Div. at commissioning May 12, 1942.

JOHNSON, CLYDE HAROLD, 371-80-35, enlisted Sept. 19, 1939, Denver, CO. He is a plankowner and served aboard BB-59 as S1/c at commissioning May 12, 1942.

JOHNSON, CLYDE T., 656-83-95, born Nov. 12, 1923, Birmingham, AL, and educated in Durham City schools. He enlisted Sept. 2, 1923, Raleigh, NC, and

attended Norfolk Operating Base, Norfolk, VA. He served aboard BB-59 in October 1942 Casco Bay, ME, and assigned as S1/c 4th Div. Left BB-59 December 1945 Bremerton, WA.

After the war he worked for Liggett Myers Company for 39 years retiring March 1, 1985. He enjoys golf, travel and fishing in his spare time. Married Doris March 29, 1948, Durham, NC, and has two daughters. He resides at 1505 Carolina Ave., Durham, NC 27705.

JOHNSON, DOIR, C., CDR, graduated from US Naval Academy, Class of 1926. Served aboard BB-59 as communication officer in March 1943. Memory List 1982.

JOHNSON, DONALD A., Memory List 1996.

JOHNSON, ERNEST HERMAN, 620-33-27, enlisted Feb. 2, 1942, Des Moines, IA. He served aboard BB-59 as S1/c at commissioning May 12, 1942, and was on board on its 2nd anniversary as a plankowner.

JOHNSON, HAROLD MARSHFIELD, 329-14-12, born Aug. 13, 1923, Marchfield, WI. A high school graduate he enlisted June 16, 1942, Chippawa Falls, WI. Attended Naval Training Station, Great Lakes, IL, and Naval Training Station, San Diego, CA.

He served aboard BB-59 in Casco Bay, ME, on Dec. 28, 1942, and assigned bugler buglemaster 3/c in X Div. Left BB-59 October 1946 Naval Operating Base, Norfolk, VA.

After the war he worked as an electrician, cable splicer, operation foreman and is now retired.

Married Consulo in 1958, Reno, NV, and has two sons and one daughter. He resides at 1830 E. Yosemite Ave., Space 151, Manteca, CA 95336.

JOHNSON, JOHN JEROME, 238-44-02, enlisted Aug. 13, 1937, Washington, DC. He is a plankowner and served aboard BB-59 as EM1/c E Div. at commissioning May 12, 1942.

JOHNSON, JOHN THOMAS, 606-19-33, enlisted Jan. 12, 1942, Boston, MA. He is a plankowner and served aboard BB-59 as EM3/c E Div. at commissioning May 12, 1942.

JOHNSON, KARL LEVI, JR., 337-08-68, enlisted Aug. 16, 1938, St. Louis, MO. He is a plankowner and served aboard BB-59 as SC2/c at commissioning May 12, 1942.

JOHNSON, KENNETH L., 6th Div. resides 23360 DeJong Rd., Sheridan, OR 97378.

JOHNSON, LEONARD ALEXANDER, 606-47-72, enlisted March 6, 1942, Boston, MO. He was a plankowner and served aboard BB-59 as SK3/c at commissioning May 12, 1942. Memory List 1977.

JOHNSON, VENNER G., resided at 3512 E. 38th St., Des Moines, IA 50317. Memory List 1996.

JOHNSON, VERNON HARLAND, 610-12-47, enlisted Dec. 12, 1941, Chicago, IL. He is a plankowner and served aboard BB-59 as SF3/c at commissioning May 12, 1942.

JOHNSON, WILLIAM EDWARD, 410-53-34, enlisted April 17, 1939, Duluth, MN. He is a plankowner and served aboard BB-59 as S1/c at commissioning May 12, 1942, and was on board on its 2nd anniversary. He resides at 1119 North 6th Ave., E. Duluth, MN 55801.

JONES, ADRIAN, (n) was stationed aboard USS *Sederstorm* (DE-31). He served aboard BB-59 as S1/c on Sept. 22, 1945.

JONES, FLOYD R., served aboard BB-59 as BKR3/c S Div. in December 1943 and assigned as baker. Left BB-59 in December 1945. After the war he worked as a clerk for Union Pacific Railroad. Memory List 1983. His latest address was 115 N. Buchanan, Topeka, KS 66606.

JONES, FREDERICK WENDELL, 368-58-21, enlisted Jan. 13, 1941, Salt Lake City, UT. He is a plankowner and served aboard BB-59 as S1/c at commissioning May 12, 1942.

JONES, HARRY LOYAL, 652-25-54, born March 31, 1915, Houston, PA. He enlisted March 7, 1942, Pittsburgh, PA, and attended Newport Naval Training Station, Newport, RI.

He served aboard BB-59 as AS S Div. at commissioning May 12, 1942, as a plankowner. Left BB-59 October 1943 Noumea, New Caledonia. Was assigned from Nov. 29, 1943, to Sept. 23, 1945, to USS *Hornet* (CV-12) as SK1/c.

After the war he worked as a plant controller for Consolidated Packaging Corp., Wheeling, WV; office manager for A.J. Wahl Assoc., Brocton, NY; Plant #2 Hazol Atles Glass Company, Washington, PA; and plant manager for Chertiers Concrete Block, Houston, PA.

He married Jean Nov. 15, 1941, Pittsburgh, PA, and has one son, one daughter, two grandchildren and one great-grandchild. He resides at 108 Pine Ave., #304, St. Clairsville, OH 43950.

JONES, JAMES ANDREW, JR., 268-29-24, enlisted Jan. 27, 1942, Macon, GA. He is a plankowner and served aboard BB-59 as MM2/c at commissioning May 12, 1942.

JONES, JOHN WILLIAM, JR., 321-55-61, enlisted Jan. 21, 1941, Des Moines, IA. He is a plankowner and served aboard BB-59 as S1/c L Div. at commissioning May 12, 1942, and was on board on its 2nd and 3rd anniversaries. He resides at Box 415, Crocker, MO 65452.

JONES, LINSTER VERNON, 262-31-40, enlisted Sept. 27, 1938, Raleigh, NC. He is a plankowner and served aboard BB-59 as OS3/c at commissioning May 12, 1942.

JONES, RAYMOND BRUCE, 342-16-52, enlisted Dec. 13, 1939, Kansas City, MO. He is a plankowner and served aboard BB-59 as COX at commissioning May 12, 1942, and was on board on its 2nd anniversary.

JONES, R.C., resides in Burlington, VT (1966).

JONES, WALDON COTESWORTH, 262-26-85, enlisted Jan. 6, 1942, Columbia, SC. He is a plankowner and served aboard BB-59 as MM2/c at commissioning May 12, 1942.

JONES, WILLIAM OSWALD, JR., 261-72-85, enlisted Nov. 15, 1940, Newport, RI. He is a plankowner and served aboard BB-59 as Bkr1/c at commissioning May 12, 1942.

JORDAN, THEODORE WILLIAM, 610-43-31, enlisted Jan. 21, 1942, Chicago, IL. He is a plankowner and served aboard BB-59 as AS at commissioning May 12, 1942, and was on board on its 2nd and 3rd anniversaries.

JORDAN, WILLIAM HENRY, 650-32-31, enlisted Feb. 24, 1942, Philadelphia, PA. He is a plankowner and served aboard BB-59 as AS CR Div. at commissioning May 12, 1942, and was on board on its 2nd and 3rd anniversaries. Was assigned to S2/c FR Div. March 10, 1943.

JOSEPH, JOSEPH PATRICK, 283-49-05, enlisted Jan. 17, 1941, Cleveland, OH. He is a plankowner and served aboard BB-59 as EM3/c at commissioning May 12, 1942.

JOURDAN, THOMAS A., resides at 493 Prospect Place, Brooklyn, NY 11202 (1966).

JULESKUSKY, JOHN ANDREW, 647-01-47, enlisted Feb. 20, 1942, New York, NY. He is a plankowner and served aboard BB-59 as AS 2nd Div. at commissioning May 12, 1942, and was on board on its 2nd and 3rd anniversaries. He resides at 119 Amsterdam Ave., Passaic NJ 07055.

JULIAN, DAVID WILLIAM, JR., 380-98-33, enlisted Sept. 15, 1936, Los Angeles, CA. He is a plankowner and served aboard BB-59 as Bug1/c at commissioning May 12, 1942.

JURGENS, JAMES, Memory List 1997.

JUSTICE, DELBERT, (n) 385-88-56, enlisted July 15, 1940, Seattle, WA. He is a plankowner and served aboard BB-59 as S1/c at commissioning May 12, 1942. After the war he worked for D. Justice & Company, Jamacia Plains, MA. He has one daughter and resides at 50 Wenham St., Jamacia Plains, MA.

KACHILLA, ANDREW, (n) 283-22-17, enlisted Dec. 29, 1917, Cleveland, OH. He is a plankowner and served aboard BB-59 as SM3/c at commissioning May 12, 1942.

KACHITES, WILLIAM BAZIL, 646-79-97, enlisted Feb. 17, 1942, New York, NY. He is a plankowner and served aboard BB-59 as AS at commissioning May 12, 1942, and on board for BB-59 2nd and 3rd anniversaries. Memory List 1977.

KACHUR, JOSEPH T. "SHORTY," 652-25-99, enlisted March 10, 1942, Pittsburgh, PA. He is a plankowner and served aboard BB-59 as AS at commissioning May 12, 1942, and on board for for BB-59 2nd and 3rd anniversaries. Memory List 1984.

KAFKA, JERRY, USMC, served aboard BB-59 7th Div. He resides at 1230 E. Como Blvd., St. Paul, MN.

KAHL, CHARLES ARNOLD, JR., 647-02-95, enlisted Feb. 21, 1942, New York, NY. He is a plankowner and served aboard BB-59 as AS 3rd Div. at commissioning May 12, 1942. He resides at 162 Winnacunnt Rd., Hampton, NH.

KALMANOWITZ, IRVING, (N) enlisted USMC, May 8, 1942, Norfolk Navy Yard. Served aboard BB-59 as Pfc. 7th Div. at commissioning May 12, 1942, as a plankowner.

KALVIN, WILLIAM TERROL, 274-46-30, enlisted June 19, 1940, New Orleans, LA. He is a plankowner and served aboard BB-59 as S1/c at commissioning May 12, 1942, and on board for BB-59 2nd anniversary.

KAMEN, STANLEY WALTER, 122636, born April 30, 1916, New York, NY. Earned a BS from William and Mary and MA from Columbia University. Joined Navy Feb. 5, 1942, Washington, DC, with post graduate studies at US Naval Academy. Was assigned to coding board, Navy Dept., Washington, DC.

He served aboard BB-59 as LT(jg) asst. radio and coding officer CR Div. February 1943, and left BB-59 April 1944 Eniwetok. Was also assigned to Communications Dept. Head LT (CVE-102); Staff Communicator for (COMCAR-DIV25).

After the war he was recreation director for the city of Mansfield, OH, and taught and coached in Mansfield school districts. He is active as ASA softball commissioner in five Ohio counties.

He married Mary Elizabeth, Jan. 6, 1945, San Francisco, CA, and has three sons and four grandchildren. He resides at 38 Parkwood Blvd., Mansfield, OH 44906 (summers in Beulah, MI).

KAMPSCHROEDER, ROLLAND R., Memory List 1983.

KANE, JAMES MICHAEL, aboard LT(jg) CR Div.; Oct. 1, 1943, LT, served aboard BB-59 as radio officer at commissioning May 12, 1942; department head May 12, 1944, communications CR Div. He was a plankowner. Memory List LCDR 1991.

KANE, JOHN JOSEPH WILLIAM, served aboard BB-59 as LT(jg) FC Div. May 20, 1944, and left BB-59 Dec. 13, 1945.

KAPOLKA, FRANK JOSEPH, 666-19-80, born in Whitinsville, MA. Enlisted March 5, 1942, Springfield, MA. He is a plankowner and served aboard BB-59 as AS 3rd Div. at commissioning May 12, 1942; S1/c Oct. 14, 1943; and COX Aug. 9, 1945. Left BB-59 and the Navy in September 1945 in Boston.

After the war he worked for the Whitin Machine Works in stores room. Married Rita Vallee, Sept. 9, 1963, Linwood, MA, and has two daughters. He died Feb. 10, 1993; Memory List 1993. Daughter, Linda Page, resides at 128 Hecla St., Uxbridge, MA 01569.

KARBOWSKI, HENRY, (N) served aboard BB-59 in F Div. July 1942 and left BB-59 as S1/c September 1943. After the war he was self-employed, Feed & Grain Supply Company and active in the American Legion Post 175. He has two daughters and resides at Mill St., East Haven, CT (1966).

KARLSEN, E.V., F3/c A Div., transferred to ComSerForSoPac, March 8, 1943.

KARY, METRO, (n) 647-02-96, enlisted Feb. 21, 1942, New York, NY. He is a plankowner and served aboard BB-59 as AS at commissioning May 12, 1942, and on board for BB-59 2nd and 3rd anniversaries. He has three children and six grandchildren all living in Brooklyn or Staten Island, New York (1992). Memory List 1992. Latest address was 291 Travis Ave., Staten Island, NY 10314.

KASOUF, JOSEPH G., resides at 41 Hayel St., Methuen, MA (1955).

KASOUF, JOSEPH Z., enlisted USMC, May 8, 1942, Norfolk Navy Yard. Served aboard BB-59 as Pvt. 7th Div. at commissioning May 12, 1942, and is a plankowner. Resided at Box 131, Exeter, NH (1966) and Clearwater, FL (1992).

KASUBA, EDWIN A., enlisted USMC, May 8, 1942, Norfolk Navy Yard. Served aboard BB-59 as Pvt. 7th Div. at commissioning May 12, 1942, and is a plankowner.

KAVANAUGH, JOHN MICHAEL, 600-03-02, enlisted Dec. 17, 1941, Albany, NY. He is a plankowner and served aboard BB-59 as SF3/c at commissioning May 12, 1942.

KAVCHAK, STEPHEN MICHAEL, 652-25-46, enlisted March 7, 1942, Pittsburgh, PA. He is a plankowner and served aboard BB-59 as AS at commissioning May 12, 1942.

KAYSER, JOHN ROBERT, 700-07-36, enlisted Dec. 13, 1941, Great Lakes, IL. He is a plankowner and served aboard BB-59 as CM3/c at commissioning May 12, 1942.

KEE, WILLIAM, (N) 650-32-39, born July 2, 1920, Philadelphia, PA, and graduated from high school. He enlisted Feb. 24, 1942, Philadelphia, PA, and attended training at Newport, RI. He is a plankowner and served aboard BB-59 as AS 5th Div. at commissioning May 12, 1942, as S2/c-S1/c in 1942 and to GM3/c May 1, 1943. Left BB-59 in July 1944 Bremerton, WA.

Other assignments were Advanced Gunnery & Hydro School; plankowner on USS *St. Paul* (CA-37); and USS *New Amsterdam* (CL-101). After the war he worked for the Philadelphia Fire Dept. for 29 years. He enjoys traveling in his spare time. Married Veronica Sept. 19, 1942, in Philadelphia, PA, and has five children. He resides at 5926 Shisler St., Philadelphia, PA.

KEFAUVER, ALDEN CASPER, 603-03-24, enlisted Oct. 14, 1941, Washington, DC. He is a plankowner and served aboard BB-59 as EM3/c commissioning May 12, 1942, and on board for BB-59 2nd anniversary. After the war he worked for the Washington, DC, Fire Dept. and resided at 1418 Stateside Dr., Silver Spring, MD (1966). Memory List; 1986.

KEGG, ALDEN FRANK, 652-27-11, enlisted March 17, 1942, Pittsburgh, PA. He is a plankowner and served aboard BB-59 as S2/c at commissioning May 12, 1942.

KEGG, JOHN ANDREW, 652-26-55, enlisted March 13, 1942, Pittsburgh, PA. He is a plankowner and served aboard BB-59 as AS at commissioning May 12, 1942.

KEHR, JOHN HAROLD, 337-49-45, enlisted Jan. 3, 1941, St. Louis, MO, and trained at Great Lakes, IL. Served aboard USS *Tennessee* BB-43. He is a plankowner and served aboard BB-59 as S1/c 3rd Div. at commissioning May 12, 1942, and left BB-59 as BM1/c 3rd Div. November 1945.

Other assignments to USS *Monrouia* from September 1946 to October 1946; NAS Norfolk November 1947 to March 1947; USMC Cherry Point, NC, March 1947 to August 1949; USS *Olympus* from October 1949 to January 1954; USS *Rockwell* January 1954 to February 1955; USS *San Macus* from February 1955 to March 1956; Marine Corps School March 1956 to March 1958; Service Craft NNSY March 1958 to May 1961; LT(jg) June 1961; USS *Intrepid* June 1961 to December 1963; ComSerRon Four December 1963 to January 1967; NavSta Norfolk, VA, January 1967 to February 1969; USS *Capricorn* February 1969 to February 1970; InacShipFac, Norfolk, VA, February 1970 to March 1971; and retired March 1971 as lieutenant.

He married Mary Alice in Boston, 1944, and has two daughters, two grandchildren and one great-grandchild. He resides at 5612 Bingham Dr., Portsmouth, VA.

KEKLAK, PAUL, (n) 238-41-30, enlisted Jan. 28, 1942, Buffalo, NY. He is a plankowner and served aboard BB-59 as Mus2/c at commissioning May 12, 1942.

KELLEY, FRANK, Memory List 1996.

KELLEY, GEORGE WILLIAM, 385-89-01, enlisted July 22, 1940, Seattle, WA. He is a plankowner and served aboard BB-59 as F1/c at commissioning May 12, 1942.

KELLEY, HARRY F., served aboard BB-59 in 5th Div., resides at PO Box 795 Glendale, OR 97442. He died May 26, 1997. Memory List 1997.

KELLEY, J., (N) ENS, served aboard BB-59 in FC Div. J.O. April 8, 1945, and left BB-59 Oct. 15, 1945.

KELLEY, JACK CLAYTON, 321-47-75, enlisted Sept. 25, 1940, Des Moines, IA. He is a plankowner and served aboard BB-59 as F1/c at commissioning May 12, 1942, and on board for BB-59 2nd and 3rd anniversaries.

KELLEY, JOHN JOSEPH, 606-42-75, born Dec. 8, 1907, South Boston, MA. Graduated from South Boston High School and attended Wentworth Institute. Joined the Navy Feb. 28, 1942, Boston, MA, and attended Boot Camp, Newport, RI. He was a plankowner and served aboard BB-59 as F3/c at commissioning May 12, 1942, and left Navy and BB-59 Sept. 26, 1945.

After the war he worked for the Gillette Corp. as general manager of shaving cream department and as an electrician at MBTA, Boston, MA. He enjoyed gardening, bowling and was a member of So. Boston Yacht Club.

He married Helen Oct. 25, 1952, So. Boston, MA, and had two daughters and two grandchildren. He died Oct. 29, 1995. He resided at 62 Great Hill Drive, No. Weymouth, MA. Memory List 1996.

KELLEY, ROBERT EUGENE, 342-10-87, enlisted March 7, 1939, Kansas City, MO. He is a plankowner and served aboard BB-59 as FC3/c at commissioning May 12, 1942. He resides in Medford, MA/Fairfield, CT (1966-67).

KELLEY, WILLIAM MADDOX, 272-77-44, enlisted Nov. 14, 1941, Birmingham, AL. He is a plankowner and served aboard BB-59 as EM3/c at commissioning May 12, 1942.

KELLY, CLYDE, (n) 268-30-74, enlisted April 22, 1942, Boston, MA. He is a plankowner and served aboard BB-59 as QM3/c at commissioning May 12, 1942.

KELLY, HAROLD EVERTT, 393-53-13, enlisted March 24, 1941, Portland, OR. He is a plankowner and served aboard BB-59 as S1/c 4th Div. at commissioning May 12, 1942, and on board for BB-59 2nd and 3rd anniversaries. He married Nancy and has six children and seven grandchildren as of January 1991. He resides at 396 Lucas Creek Rd., Chehalis, WA.

KELLY, HARRY FRANK, 342-23-84, enlisted July 2, 1940, Kansas City, MO. He is a plankowner and served aboard BB-59 as GM3/c at commissioning May 12, 1942.

KELLY, KENNETH JOSEPH, ENS, served aboard BB-59 in FC Div. in April 1945.

KELLY, WILLIAM FRANCIS, 650-32-65, enlisted Feb. 24, 1942, Philadelphia, PA. He is a

plankowner and served aboard BB-59 as AS at commissioning May 12, 1942. He resides at 1702 Riverside Dr., Trenton, NJ.

KEMMER, HARVEY L., served aboard BB-59 in I Div., resides at RR 1 Box 5, Alice, ND 58003.

KENNEDY, ARNOLD, (n) 622-50-82, enlisted Feb. 9, 1942, Detroit, MI. He is a plankowner and served aboard BB-59 as AS at commissioning May 12, 1942. On March 8, 1943 assigned to F3/c P Div. to ComSerForSoPac.

KENNEMORE, GEORGE, (N) Memory List 1977.

KENNEY, JAMES A., CRM CR Div. Memory List 1987.

KENNEY, MARTIN JOSEPH, 650-32-70, enlisted Feb. 24, 1942, Philadelphia, PA. He is a plankowner and served aboard BB-59 as AS 3rd Div. at commissioning May 12, 1942, and on board for BB-59 2nd anniversary. He resides at 203 Catherine St., Philadelphia, PA (1966).

KENNY, JAMES ALOYSIUS, 403-75-89, enlisted Oct. 23, 1940, Brooklyn, NY. He is a plankowner and served aboard BB-59 as RM3/c at commissioning May 12, 1942, and on board for BB-59 2nd and 3rd anniversaries.

KENNY, ROBERT EUGENE, 620-19-87, enlisted Dec. 31, 1941, Des Moines, IA. He is a plankowner and served aboard BB-59 as F1/c at commissioning May 12, 1942.

KEOUGH, WILLIAM J., resides at TA Flower Shop, 6527, Frankford Ave., Philadelphia, PA 19149.

KERN, WILLIAM MCKINLEY, 102-32-72, enlisted Jan. 8, 1942, Albany, NY. He is a plankowner and served aboard BB-59 as WT2/c at commissioning May 12, 1942, and on board for BB-59 2nd anniversary.

KERR, SAMUEL A., 650-86-58, born Nov. 23, 1921 Palmyra, PA. Graduated from high school and enlisted July 1942, Harrisburg, PA. Training at NTS, Newport RI; Aviation Radio & Radar School at JAX, FL; Aerial Gunnery School, Yellow Water, FL; Dive Bomber Training, Cecil Field, FL. Was assigned to CASU #7 ARM3/c; USS *Washington* ARM3/c.

He served aboard BB-59 as ARM2/c V Div. and left BB-59 in 1945 Bremerton, WA. After the war he was in the US Air Force for 20 years and at Penn State University for 17 years. In his spare time he is active in the church, volunteer fire department and Little League baseball.

He married Beverly E. Aug. 14, 1948, in Campelltown, PA, and has two sons and one daughter (November 1993). He resides at RD 3 Box 489, Palmyra, PA 17078.

KESNER, CHARLES H., 4th Div. resides at 103 Hillside Drive, Mt. Holly Springs, PA 17065.

KEYES, THOMAS FRANKLIN, 274-29-57, enlisted Jan. 12, 1942, New Orleans, LA. He is a plankowner and served aboard BB-59 as Ptr3/c at commissioning May 12, 1942.

KEYS, STUART DONALD, LT, served aboard BB-59 in E Div. April 22, 1945.

KIDDER, ARLAND NEWTON, 212-49-46, enlisted May 4, 1938, Springfield, MA. He is a plankowner and served aboard BB-59 as EM2/c at commissioning May 12, 1942.

KIERNAN, JOSEPH WILLIAM, USMCR, served aboard BB-59 as 1st LT 7th Div. June 1945.

KILDUFF, GERARD L., enlisted USMC, May 8, 1942, Norfolk Navy Yard. He is a plankowner and served aboard BB-59 as Pvt. 7th Div. at commissioning May 12, 1942.

KILDUFF, JERRY, (N) Memory List 1990.

KILE, RICHARD LABAGH, 334304, born Aug. 17, 1918, Devine Corners, NY. Graduated from high school and attended training at Newport, RI, 1936. Assigned to USS *Avocet,* Pearl Harbor; Radio Material School, 1942 Bellvue, DC; trained with Seabees at Port Huen, CA, sailed to Solomon Islands to set up mobile radar.

He served aboard BB-59 as ENS CR Div. in December 1944 and left BB-59 in 1946 Norfolk, VA. Was assigned to USS *Juneau* as LT(jg), 1946; Officers Elect. School (Graduated 3rd in his class) lieutenant, 1948; Naval Special Weapons Unit #1233, SandiaBase, Albuquerque, NM; ComSerRon 3, Sasebo, Japan; Electronics Lab. Off. PostGradSch Monterey, CA; LCDR 1956 USS *Norton Sound;* and retired USN April 1, 1958.

After the war he worked for Raytheon, Waltham, MA, 1958; IBM San Jose, CA, 1961; in 1970 formed an import and export company which he operated until his death.

He enjoyed being amateur radio (licensed operator for 50 years) and camping.

Married Jeanne (Eva) June 22, 1944, San Francisco, and had four children and seven grandchildren. He died July 24, 1991; Memory List 1992.

KILMER, EUGENE LEROY, 600-20-96, enlisted March 13, 1942, Albany, NY. He is a plankowner and served aboard BB-59 as AS at commissioning May 12, 1942, and on board for BB-59 2nd and 3rd anniversaries.

KIMBALL, BURNHAM, "WHITEY," 375-73-01, enlisted March 7, 1941, Pearl Harbor, HI. He is a plankowner and served aboard BB-59 as S1/c at commissioning May 12, 1942, and on board for BB-59 2nd and 3rd anniversaries.

He resided at 2020 Main St., Santa Clara, CA. Memory List 1982.

KIMMERLY, GEORGE D., FC Div., resides at 1 LaCrescenta Circle, Madison, WI 53716 (1994).

KING, ALBERT EDWARD, 381-25-19, enlisted March 12, 1942, Pearl Harbor, HI. He is a plankowner and served aboard BB-59 as S1/c at commissioning May 12, 1942.

KING, ARTHUR LEE, 262-91-06, enlisted March 2, 1936, Raleigh, NC. He is a plankowner and served aboard BB-59 as Matt1/c commissioning May 12, 1942.

KING, CHRISTOPHER C., L Div., Memory List 1989. (Mrs.) resides at 10348 Park St., Bellflower, CA.

KING, DANIEL, (N) 201-02-59, enlisted June 3, 1940, Pearl Harbor, HI. He is a plankowner and served in 1st Div. at commissioning May 12, 1942. Received a letter from Leo Kolb with a bit of history about Danny King. Said his hometown was near Boston and had 18 years service before 1940. Was turret captain USS *Oklahoma* Dec. 7, 1941. He had also survived a turret explosion aboard the USS *Mississippi* in 1927. Was also the lightweight boxing champ of the battleship fleet around 1927-28. On BB-59 was chief turret captain (Turret #1).

KING, EARL, (N) Memory List 1978.

KING, HERBERT LLOYD, served aboard BB-59 as ENS P Div. June 23, 1943, and as LT(jg) A Div. Left BB-59 on Nov. 1, 1945.

KING, HOWARD RAY, 608-09-24, enlisted Feb. 5, 1942, Buffalo, NY. He is a plankowner and served aboard BB-59 as AS 4th Div. at commissioning May 12, 1942, and on board for BB-59 2nd and 3rd anniversaries. Was assigned COX 4th Div.

KING, JAMES JOSEPH, 650-32-64, enlisted Feb. 24, 1942, Philadelphia, PA. He is a plankowner and served aboard BB-59 as AS at commissioning May 12, 1942, and on board for BB-59 2nd and 3rd anniversaries.

KING, JOSEPH EARL, 295-71-15, enlisted July 17, 1940, Nashville, TN. He is a plankowner and served aboard BB-59 as S1/c at commissioning May 12, 1942.

KING, JOE H., REV., 2nd Div. resides at 3345 Statesville Blvd. #27, Salisbury, NC 28144.

KING, LESLIE L., (no data) resides at 1310 Lake St., South Detroit Lakes, MI.

KINGERY, FORREST GLENN, 668-31-29, enlisted Jan. 21, 1942, St. Louis, MO. He is a plankowner and served aboard BB-59 as AS at commissioning May 12, 1942.

KINGSTON, ELVIS PHILIP, 310-87-93, enlisted April 2, 1942, Boston, MA. He is a plankowner and served aboard BB-59 as EM2/c at commissioning May 12, 1942.

KINLEY, JOHN NORMAN, 359-58-92, enlisted Jan. 2, 1940, Houston, TX. He is a plankowner and served aboard BB-59 as BM2/c at commissioning May 12, 1942. Memory List 1988.

KINNER, ROBERT T., 828-47-18, born July 16, 1925, Ashland, KY. After attending Marshall University, Huntington, WV, for two and half years he enlisted July 1943 with training at Great Lakes, IL. Was assigned to New Caledonia in 1943.

He served aboard BB-59 as S1/c F Div. November 1943, starboard catapult, 1943-46. He left BB-59 in 1946 San Francisco, CA. After the war he worked for Dekalb Police Dept., Dekalb, IL, as sergeant; GTE computer programmer, Genoa and Northlake, IL (retired).

He married Marna R. in 1965 in Dekalb, IL, and has one son. He resides at 1630 Maness Ct., Sycamore, IL.

KINNEY, JAMES FRANKLYN, 614-24-27, enlisted Feb. 6, 1942, Cleveland, OH. He is a plankowner and served aboard BB-59 as AS at commissioning May 12, 1942.

KINOSIAN, KAYAJAN, (N) Memory List 1992.

KINSELA, ARTHUR JOHN, 608-08-35, enlisted Feb. 2, 1942, Buffalo, NY. He is a plankowner and served aboard BB-59 as AS R Div. at commissioning May 12, 1942, and on board for BB-59 2nd anniversary. He died Nov. 23, 1993; Memory List 1994. (Mrs.) Nina, 745 Lawnsdale Rd., Medford, OR 97501.

KINSELLA, JAMES FRANCIS, 238-56-56, enlisted Jan. 6, 1937, Albany, NY. He is a plankowner and served aboard BB-59 as QM3/c at commissioning May 12, 1942.

KINSEY, JOHN DANIEL, 263-56-07, enlisted April 1, 1942, Raleigh, NC. He is a plankowner and served aboard BB-59 as Matt3/c at commissioning May 12, 1942.

KIRK, EMERY C., 4th Div., Memory List 1988. (Mrs.) resides at Box 231, Bloomingrose, WV.

KIRK, LEWIS PAUL, L Div., served aboard BB-59 in CS Div. in November 1943 and left BB-59 in March 1946 as signalman. After the war he worked as a salesman for Allied Security Insurance Company. He was active in the VFW Post 7726, Independence, VA. He has one daughter, Lisa, and resides at PO Box 113, Elk Creek, VA 24326 (1966).

KIRKHART, ROBERT EDWIN, 321-13-81, enlisted Jan. 10, 1942, Washington, DC. He is a plankowner and served aboard BB-59 as EM2/c at commissioning May 12, 1942.

KIRVES, ELMER EDWARD CARL, 291-33-12, enlisted July 20, 1935, Tsingtae, China. He is a plankowner and served aboard BB-59 as GM1/c at commissioning May 12, 1942.

KISSINGER, GEORGE, (N) Memory List 1983. (Mrs.) resides at 50 Tinder Rd., Levittown, PA 19056 (1994).

KITCHINGS, ALTON D., Esq., resides at 553 Suncrest Blvd., Savannah, GA 31410.

KITE, WALTER MATTHIS, 272-76-86, enlisted Oct. 31, 1941, Birmingham, AL. He is a plankowner and served aboard BB-59 as Matt2/c at commissioning May 12, 1942.

KITTAY, MORTON VICTOR, I Div. JO, served aboard BB-59 as LT(jg) January 1944.

KLAMUT, MICHAEL JOSEPH, 652-18-44, enlisted Feb. 5, 1942, Pittsburgh, PA. He is a plankowner and served aboard BB-59 as AS at commissioning May 12, 1942.

KLEIN, ALFRED, (N) resides at 16913 Martha Rd., Cleveland, OH.

KLEIN, CHARLES L., 669-97-01, born July 19, 1922, Auxvasse, MO. A high school graduate, he enlisted June 30, 1941, St. Louis, MO. Attended Merchant Marine Training, Hoffman Island, NY; United Fruit Co. Bananas between Central America and New Orleans. In 1942 he was on that famous convoy run to Murmansk, Russia.

He served aboard BB-59 and was assigned to personnel office X Div. working with H. Bowman, D Lewicki, P Bates, E.C. Little and Paul Miller, Dec. 18, 1943. Left BB-59 in August 1944 and sent to USNH Base 8; USNH Nave10; USNH Seattle; and USNH Great Lakes, IL; and dismissed Feb. 18, 1945. After the war he rejoined the Merchant Marines, April 1945 to April 1949; to St. Louis, MO, to the wholesale meat industry. Retired in April 1987.

He married Catherine Feb. 23, 1952, and has two children. He resides at 1507 Wind River Dr., Arnold, MO.

KLEIN, DANIEL, (N) 5th Div., resides at 7729 Encino Ave., Northridge, CA.

KLEPACH, GREGORY H., 642-14-52, enlisted Feb. 28, 1942, New Haven, CT. He is a plankowner and served aboard BB-59 as AS at commissioning May 12, 1942, and on board for BB-59 2nd and 3rd anniversaries. Memory List 1992. (Mrs.) resides at 66 Sunnybrook Bend, Waterbury, CT (mail returned November 1993).

KLEPRIS, MICHAEL, JR., (n) 646-63-72, enlisted Feb. 3, 1942, New York, NY. He is a plankowner and served aboard BB-59 as AS at commissioning May 12, 1942, and on board for BB-59 2nd anniversary.

KLINE, CHARLES, (N) (Letter of July 13, 1994, from Paul Miller) C. Kline medical discharge from Navy and joined Merchant Marines.

KLOEPPEL, LAWRENCE SYLVESTER, 410-86-33, born June 29, 1922, Dixon, MO. Graduated from high school and enlisted July 27, 1940, St. Louis, MO, with training at San Diego, CA. Stationed on USS *Utah* and USS *Minneapolis*. He is a plankowner and served aboard BB-59 as S1/c 3rd Div. at commissioning May 12, 1942, and left BB-59 in Bremerton, WA.

After the war he worked on a dairy farm, dairy plant and General Motors. In his spare time is active in church bingo, picnic, serves senior citizens hunting and fishing.

He married Mary Feb. 15, 1947, in Vienna, MO, and has five children, 12 grandchildren and one great-grandchildren (as of January 1994). He resides at 1112 Sunhaven Dr., Bldg. 3, Unit C, St. Louis, MO 63129.

KLOSS, HENRY, (N) 359-80-91, enlisted Jan. 6, 1938, Houston, TX. He is a plankowner and served aboard BB-59 as FC1/c at commissioning May 12, 1942, served as ENS, May 12, 1944. He left BB-59 on May 2, 1945.

KLUBAK, FRANK C., M Div., resided at 126 N. Dean St., PO Box 387, Royalton, IL 62983. Memory List 1997.

KMIEC, EDWARD MATTHEW, 300-39-43, enlisted March 7, 1941, Chicago, IL. A Pearl Harbor survivor, he is a plankowner and served aboard BB-59 as COX 1st Div. at commissioning May 12, 1942. He married Camille (died June 1992) and has one daughter and one grandson. In his spare time he enjoys dancing with new partner. He resides at 4674 Scarlett Ct., Jacksonville, FL 32210.

KNAPPER, HENRY, (N) 952-61-47, born Feb. 3, 1926, Kalamazoo, MI. Graduated from high school and enlisted May 10, 1944, Kalamazoo, MI, with training at Great Lakes, IL. He served aboard BB-59 as F1/c M Div. July 1944 and left BB-59 May 21, 1946, Norfolk, VA.

After the war he worked for the Eaton Corp. as a production machinist for 38 years. In his spare time Henry, with the help of wife, Josephine, spent eight years helping daughter Carolyn restore her 1889 home in Almena, Van Buren County. (Great story in *Kalamazoo Gazette*, Jan. 16, 1994.) Great job!

He married Josephine in Kalamazoo on Aug. 26, 1949, and has four children and eight grandchildren as of Jan. 31, 1994. He resides at 2963 S. 11th St., Kalamazoo, MI.

KNIGHT, ARTHUR M., CAPT, vice-president of Mystic Steamship Company, (Mystic & Boston Tow Boat Company both parts of Eastern Gas & Fuel Company) Had the responsibility for towing *Big Mamie* to Fall River. Capt. Knight was a strong supporter for saving BB-59. Was Honorary Officer and awarded BB-59 Award in 1967.

KNIPLING, ALBERT J., 5th Div., has three sons and two grandchildren. He resides at 106 Church St., New Rochelle, NY 10805.

KNISELEY, JOHN W., born in Tishomingo, OK, and earned an AB from the University of Oklahoma with one year graduate school. He joined the Navy on May 15, 1943, Tucson, AZ, and attended Indoc. Tucson and Naval Communication, Harvard University. He served aboard BB-59 as LT CR Div. February 1944. He left BB-59 in March 1945.

Was also assigned to Staff ComBatDiv 5 and ComBatRon 3. After the war he worked in motion picture theaters and is active in Camp Fire Girls, American Cancer Society and Telephone Help Line.

He married Helen A., Jan. 24, 1969, in Wilburton, OK, and has two daughters and three grandchildren. He resides at 807 Schulze Dr., Norman, OK 73071.

KNOTEK, ALOIS ALBER, 638-10-35, enlisted Dec. 30, 1941, Minneapolis, MN. He is a plankowner and served aboard BB-59 as F2/c at commissioning May 12, 1942.

KNOWLES, FRED M., part of Homecoming Crew 1965. Resides at So. Braintree, MA (1966).

KNOWLES, ROBERT HEALD, 606-61-59, born Nov. 30, 1919, Quincy, MA. Graduated from high school and attended Embalming School. Enlisted April 13, 1942, Boston, MA. He is a plankowner and served aboard BB-59 as SF3/c R Div. at commissioning May 12, 1942, and on board for BB-59 2nd anniversary. Left BB-59 and transferred at sea off the Philippines; to Fleet School (welding) San Diego, CA; to USS *Kent Isle*; and discharged Dec. 20, 1945, Boston.

After the war he became an embalmer, So. Portland, ME; sold caskets in Maine, New Hampshire and Vermont for 10 years; moved to California in 1962; and retired from Naval shipyard, Long Beach, CA, in 1980. In his spare time he attended first BB-59 reunion at Parker House; active in Lions Club; raised seeing eye dogs for the blind; hosted high school students from Australia.

He married Dorothy Johnson in 1951 in So. Portland, ME, and has one son and one daughter and four grandchildren. He resides at 34112 Harrow Hill Rd., Lake Elsinore, CA 92532.

KNOX, HERBERT MACK, 295-27-18, enlisted May 13, 1941, Pearl Harbor, HI. He is a plankowner and served aboard BB-59 as CFC at commissioning May 12, 1942.

KNOX, JOHN WESLEY, JR., 608-10-84, enlisted Feb. 16, 1942, Buffalo, NY. He is a plankowner and served aboard BB-59 as AS at commissioning May 12, 1942, and on board for BB-59 2nd and 3rd anniversaries.

KOBLICK, DON, (N) USMC 857896, born July 19, 1925, San Francisco, CA. Earned a BA at San Jose State University and joined the USMC in August 1943. Trained at sea school in San Diego, CA, and was assigned to the USS *Charleston* (gunboat) and the USS *Colorado*.

He served aboard BB-59 in July 1944 as Pfc. 7th Div. and left BB-59 in February 1946. Was assigned to Bremerton, WA; Pearl Harbor, HI; and Mare Island, NY.

After the war he worked in sales and service, diesel engines, generator sets and marine engines; also owned and operated a commercial fishing boat (still doing it in January 1994). He is active in Sea Scouts in his spare time and resides at 155 Brookwood Rd., Woodside, CA.

KOCHN, BILL, (N) resides at 2737 So. 27th St., Milwaukee, WI (1966).

KOEPPEN, JOHN, JR., 729-92-85, born Sept. 12, 1923, LaPorte, IN. Graduated from high school and joined the Navy in May 1944, Chicago, IL. Training at Great Lakes, IL, and stationed at Shoemaker, CA, July 1944; Hawaii August 1944; South Pacific Islands-Japan coast.

He served aboard BB-59 as S2/c 2nd Div. October 1944 and S1/c at the end of the war. Left BB-59 May 1, 1946, Norfolk, VA. Was also assigned to US Maritime Service, November 1942 to May 1944.

After the war he worked as sales manufacturing representative in the glass industry and owner of glass business (architectural and insulated). In his spare time he is on the Zoning Board of Appeals, 1961-62; elected trustee of Village of Wheeling, IL, 1965-75 (10 years); and president of Wheeling Diamond Jubilee 1969. He was appointed Illinois Governor's advisory commission, 1969; "Man of the Year" President's Award, May 20, 1969, Wheeling, IL (Leadership and Community Service); Historical Society, August 1967 to May 1972. He married Shirley Oct. 6, 1945, in Chicago, IL, and had one son and one daughter and three grandchildren (Jan. 12, 1994). (Mrs.) resides at

1625 Sheridan Rd., Wilmette, IL 60091. He died May 7, 1989; Memory List 1990.

KOESTER, WILLIAM HERBERT, 647-02-99, enlisted Feb. 21, 1942, New York, NY. He is a plankowner and served aboard BB-59 as AS at commissioning May 12, 1942.

KOLB, LEON CHARLES, 355-98-48, born May 22, 1918, Spencer, OK. Earned USC Extension Public Administration and joined the Navy June 12, 1936, Dallas, TX. Received basic training at San Diego, CA; GM School Washington, DC; Advanced Gunner's Mate School, Norfolk, VA. Was assigned to USS *Texas* 1936-37; USS *Balch* 363, Pearl Harbor; USS *Oklahoma* (survivor) (also on USS *St. Paul*).

He is a plankowner and served aboard BB-59 as GM2/c 3rd Div. at commissioning May 12, 1942, and left BB-59 May 25, 1945 (transfer at sea). Was assigned to Gunner's School, Washington, DC, and retired as warrant gunner.

After the war he worked for the US Post Office, 1946-47; Los Angeles Fire Dept. for 26 years; licensed California State Electric Contractor 1967-94. In his spare time he is active in Pearl Harbor Survivors Assoc., Elks, American Legion and USS *Oklahoma* Historical Assoc.

He has one son, two grandchildren (February 1992) and resides at 5705 Camellia Ave., North Hollywood, CA 91601.

KOLB, ROBERT J., USMC 7th Div. Memory List 1996. (Mrs.) resides at 121 Payne Beach Rd., Hilton, NY.

KOLBERG, IRVIN, (N) Memory List 1977.

KOLODNICKI, BASIL ANDREW, 647-01-51, enlisted Feb. 20, 1942, New York, NY. He is a plankowner and served aboard BB-59 as AS at commissioning May 12, 1942, and on board for BB-59 2nd and 3rd anniversaries.

KOMACK, MICHAEL, (n) 652-17-36, enlisted Feb. 1, 1942, Pittsburgh, PA. He is a plankowner and served aboard BB-59 as AS R Div. at commissioning May 12, 1942. He resides at 3003 Harding Ave., Aliquippa, PA.

KONCEWICZ, LEO JOHN, 650-31-36, enlisted Feb. 21, 1942, Philadelphia, PA. He is a plankowner and served aboard BB-59 as AS at commissioning May 12, 1942, and on board for BB-59 2nd anniversary. He resides at 426 W. Atlantic St., Shenandoah, PA (1966).

KONOPKA, JAN EDWARD, 212-38-05, enlisted Dec. 3, 1938, San Pedro, CA. He is a plankowner and served aboard BB-59 as COX at commissioning May 12, 1942.

KONTUL, GEORGE, (n) 650-22-32, born Dec. 8, 1923, Phoenixville, PA. Graduated from high school with some college. He enlisted Feb. 23, 1942, Philadelphia, PA. He is a plankowner and served aboard BB-59 as AS CR Div. at commissioning May 12, 1942; March 10, 1943, S2/c CR Div. to FR Div.; and May 12, 1944, Radarman 3/c I Div. He left BB-59 Nov. 11, 1945, Seattle, WA.

After the war he was in the US Air Force from August 1946 to January 1963 and retired Jan. 1, 1963, as master sergeant (20 years of military service).

He married Ruth Dewaele (the third marriage for both). Both lost their previous spouses. He resides at 532 S. Crescent Dr., Apt. 101, Hollywood, FL 33021.

KOPASZ, WILLIAM P., enlisted USMC May 8, 1942, Norfolk Navy Yard. He is a plankowner and served aboard BB-59 as Pvt. 7th Div. at commissioning May 12, 1942.

KOPPENHAVER, GLENN D., 249-60-10, born Oct. 22, 1925, Orwin, PA. Graduated from Porter Township High School in 1943 and enlisted Aug. 23, 1943, Pottsville, PA. Trained at NTS Great Lakes, IL, and assigned to Shoemaker'sville, CA, 1943 and New Caledonia, 1943. He served aboard BB-59 as S1/c FC Div. December 1943 and as GM3/c catapult until September 1946 Portsmouth, VA, for mothballing. Was transferred to USS *Bennington*, aircraft carrier, and discharged Nov. 16, 1946.

After the war he worked as an auto mechanic on trucks, tanks, combined support maintenance shop (support for the Pennsylvania National Guard). Retired in March 1984. He is active in the Pennsylvania National Guard. Received Army Achievement Medal.

Married Jacqueline July 24, 1948 (died in 1993 after 45 years of marriage) and has two sons and three grandchildren (as of December 1993). He resided in 16 Snyder Ave., Orwin, PA 17980.

KOSIEK, EDWARD JACOB, 650-32-66, enlisted March 24, 1942, Philadelphia, PA. He is a plankowner and served aboard BB-59 as AS at commissioning May 12, 1942.

KOSLOWSKI, JOHN G., SR., resides at 3121 Georgetown Rd., Baltimore, MD.

KOSMYNA, MICHAEL, (n) 647-03-00, enlisted Feb. 21, 1942, New York, NY. He is a plankowner and served aboard BB-59 as AS at commissioning May 12, 1942.

KOSTOPOULOS, JOHN ADAM, 382-14-39, enlisted Long Beach, CA, as S1/c.

KOUSTUBARDIS, NICHOLAS, (N) 647-03-01, enlisted Feb. 21, 1942, New York, NY. He is a plankowner and served aboard BB-59 as AS at commissioning May 12, 1942.

KOVACH, PAUL, (n) 642-14-23, enlisted Feb. 25, 1942, New Haven, CT. He is a plankowner and served aboard BB-59 as AS at commissioning May 12, 1942.

KOWALCZYK, CHESTER STEVENS, 606-78-74, enlisted May 25, 1942, Boston, MA. He served aboard BB-59 as EM3/c at commissioning May 31, 1942.

KOWALCZYK, STANLEY, (n) 212-51-75, enlisted July 19, 1939, Springfield, MA, and stationed at NTS Newport, RI. He served aboard BB-59 as GM3/c 4th Div. at commissioning May 12, 1942, and left BB-59 after North Africa. Was also assigned to the USS *Claxton*, the USS *General John Pope* and R/S NYD Washington, DC; Naval Mine Warfare, Yorktown, VA; AS, NYD Philadelphia, PA.

After the war he worked for S.D. Warren Paper Mill, Westbrook, ME. In his spare time he is involved in church work and Masonic. He died Feb. 14, 1991; Memory List 1992. (Mrs.) resides at 41 Maple St., Westbrook, ME.

KOWITZ, VERN M., R Div. resided at 5050 West Byron St., Chicago, IL 60641. Memory List 1996.

KOWOLASKI, JOSEPH DAVID, 299-93-48, enlisted Jan. 17, 1939, Chicago, IL He is a plankowner and served aboard BB-59 as FC3/c FC Div. at commissioning May 12, 1942. He resides at 109 So. Bend Rd., Glen Burnie, MD.

KOZIEL, VICTOR ADAM, 647-01-52, enlisted Feb. 20, 1942, New York, NY. He is a plankowner and served aboard BB-59 as AS at commissioning May 12, 1942, and on board for BB-59 2nd anniversary.

KOZLOWSKI, FELIX WILLIAM, 224-78-74, enlisted April 2, 1942, New York, NY. He is a plankowner and served aboard BB-59 as AS at commissioning May 12, 1942.

KRAFT, CHARLES H., SR., 1st Div., resides at 48 Salem St. #601, Portland, ME.

KRAJASKI, STANLEY JOHN, 224-77-74, enlisted March 31, 1942, New York, NY.

KRAMER, FRANK GEORGE, 202-17-63, enlisted Feb. 23, 1942, Boston, MA. He is a plankowner and served aboard BB-59 as AS at commissioning May 12, 1942, and on board for BB-59 2nd and 3rd anniversaries. He resides at 1675 9th St., NW, Cedar Rapids, IA 52450.

KRAMER, SYLVESTER A., 6th Div., has six children and 10 grandchildren (as of January 1992). Resides 252 The Boulevard Pittsburgh, PA 15210.

KRAMER, WILLIAM, (N) A Div., resides at Parkersburg, WV 26101.

KRAUS, DR. HERBERT H., resides at 8320 Spring Valley Drive, Cincinnati, OH 45236.

KRECEK, JAMES ARTHUR, E Div., served aboard BB-59 as LT(jg) Sept. 29, 1944, and resides at 39 Garry Hampton Rd., West Yarmouth, MA 02673.

KREMP, PHILIP, JR., (n) 647-01-53, enlisted Feb. 20, 1942, New York, NY. He is a plankowner and served aboard BB-59 as AS at commissioning May 12, 1942, and on board for BB-59 2nd and 3rd anniversaries.

KRESS, R.W., CRT, Feb. 10, 1943, CR Div. to FR Div.

KRESSEN, HAROLD, (N) Memory List 1977.

KRETZSCHMAR, DONALD, (N) resides at RR 1 Box 109, Willow Lake, SD 57268 (name submitted by D.A. Krough August 1992).

KROESE, DONALD, (N) 860-28-60, born Jan. 16, 1926, Sanborn, IA. Joined Navy at Camp Dodge, IA, March 21, 1944, and received training at Farragut, ID. Served aboard BB-59 as S1/c 4th Div. May 1944 and SK3/c S Div. Left BB-59 May 20, 1946, Norfolk, VA.

After the war he worked for the Assoc. Milk Producers for 41 years and spent his spare time in E911, church boards and in upper Des Moines Food for Life. He married Eunice June 24, 1926, and has three children. He resides at 505 Sunrise Ave., Sanborn, IA 51248.

KROGH, DEWAYNE A., served aboard BB-59 as F11/c A Div. May 1944 and left in May 1946 (water king-evaporators). After the war he was self-employed as a farmer. He is active in the American Legion as commander, adjutant, finance officer, and Americanism chairman. Wife, Corinne, was executive secretary for the American Legion Auxiliary. He has one son, one daughter and two grandchildren. They reside in Bruce, SD 57220.

KROWIALIS, LEONARD E., Memory List 1996.

KRUPIKA, WALTER, (N) served aboard BB-59 as MM2/c M Div. February 1943 and left BB-59 in August 1945. After the war he worked for Polaroid Corp. as a modelmaker. He had one son as of 1966. Memory List 1987. (Mrs.) resides at 1124 W. Boylston St., Worcester, MA 01606.

KROLLMAN, KARL F., enlisted USMC, May 8, 1942, Norfolk Navy Yard. He is a plankowner and served aboard BB-59 as 1st Sgt. 7th Div. at commissioning May 12, 1942. He resides at Armed Services YMCA, Newport, RI, as of 1956.

KRYIAK, VINCENT E., 6th Div., resides at 4406 Linden Lane, Rolling Meadows, IL 60008.

KUDASIK, CASIMIR WALTER, 642-14-45, enlisted Feb. 27, 1942, New Haven, CT. He served aboard BB-59 in April 1942 Quincy, MA, and as plankowner in 4th Div. at commissioning May 12, 1942. Also in 40mm guns on the ships 2nd anniversary and left BB-59 in Bremerton, WA. Memory List 1977. Latest residence was 581 No. Main St., Seymour, CT (1966).

KUJLSKI, STANLEY, (N) resides at 262 Franklin St., Brooklyn NY (1966).

KUNERT, VERNON, (N) 306-44-21, born Aug. 8, 1925, Milwaukee, WI. Graduated from high school plus a course in business. He enlisted Aug. 10, 1943, Milwaukee, WI, with training at USNTC, Great Lakes, IL. He served aboard BB-59 in F Div. December 1943 South Pacific and left BB-59 Sept. 12, 1946, Norfolk, VA.

After the war he worked for Allis Chalmers Mfg. from 1947-56 (advertising production); Meltzer Adv. Agency (production manager), Los Angeles 1956-57; McDonnell-Douglas Aircraft (printing and publication) Space Systems Center, Santa Monica, CA and Huntington Beach, CA 1957-88. Retired April 29, 1988. He enjoys woodworking and bowling in his spare time.

He married Jane Oct. 11, 1947, West Allis, WI, and has five children and 11 grandchildren. He resides at 8154 Great House Way, Antelope, CA 95843.

KURKE, VINCENT JOSEPH, 244-06-28, enlisted Feb. 26, 1942, Philadelphia, PA. He is a plankowner and served aboard BB-59 as AS at commissioning May 12, 1942, and on board for BB-59 2nd anniversary.

KURR, NORMAN J., born June 14, 1914, St. Cloud, MN. A high school graduate with two years of college, he enlisted in St. Cloud, MN. Received training at Coeur D'Alene, ID. He served aboard BB-59 as EM3/c E Div. and left BB-59 Dec. 7, 1945, Bremerton, WA. After the war he worked in the ice business as manufacturing shop foreman. He married Helen in St. Cloud, MN, and has five boys. He resided at 6724-46th Ave., St. Cloud, MN. Memory List 1997.

KURTYKA, GEORGE ALBERT, 642-12-55, enlisted Feb. 10, 1942, New Haven, CT. He is a plankowner and served aboard BB-59 as AS at commissioning May 12, 1942, and on board for BB-59 2nd and 3rd anniversaries. Memory List 1977. At Otis Air Force Base, S/Sgt. (1959).

KURTZ, CLAUDE JENNINGS, 383593, born Berwick, PA, he holds a BS and MS in chemical engineering from Lehigh University. Joined USN in Annapolis, MD, May 1944 and attended Midshipman's School. He served aboard BB-59 as ENS B Div. Nov. 24, 1944, and as ENS A Div. 1946. Left BB-59 March 15, 1946, San Francisco, CA. After the war he worked in

the chemical and explosives industries. He married Betty in 1944, Bethlehem, PA, and resided at 1931 Grove Way, Castro Valley, CA 94546 (1994). Memory List 1996.

KURTZ, JOSEPH FRANCIS, 647-01-55, enlisted Feb. 20, 1942, New York, NY. He is a plankowner and served aboard BB-59 as AS at commissioning May 12, 1942. He resides at 3250 Perry Ave., 3M, Bronx, NY.

KWIATRK, MECIALAUS STANLEY, 224-78-75, enlisted April 2, 1942, New York, NY. He is a plankowner and served aboard BB-59 as AS at commissioning May 12, 1942, and on board for BB-59 2nd anniversary.

LABAR, WILLIAM EDWIN, 650-24-24, enlisted Feb. 3, 1942, Philadelphia, PA. He is a plankowner and served aboard BB-59 as AS at commissioning May 12, 1942.

LABOON, JOE T., enlisted USMC May 8, 1942, Norfolk Navy Yard. He was a plankowner and served aboard BB-59 as Corp 7th Div. at commissioning May 12, 1942. Memory List 1989. (Mrs.) resides at 1037 N. Jamestown Rd. #A, Decatur, GA 30030.

LACEY, WILBUR J., born Oct. 3, 1921, Richford, NY. Graduated from Newark Valley High School, enlisted July 1942 Owego, NY, and trained at Rhode Island. He served aboard BB-59 in 3rd Div. and S Div. S1/c also baker July 1942. Left BB-59 in November 1945.

After the war he worked for NCR Adding Machine Div. (assembly work) for 37 years from November 1946 to November 1983. In 1985 began a two year battle with cancer. He won and is doing well. In his spare time he enjoys gardening, some cooking and baking.

He married Jean Goodrich May 14, 1949, in Richford, NY, and has four children and two grandchildren (as of Jan. 10, 1994). He resides at 404 Comfort Rd. #4, Ithaca, NY 14850.

LACKEY, ROBERT JOSEPH, 342-64-10, born Dec. 4, 1922, enlisted Jan. 24, 1942, Frankfort, KS, and trained at Great Lakes, IL. He served aboard BB-59 as AS 1st Div. plankowner at commissioning May 12, 1942, and left BB-59 Aug. 14, 1945, off the coast of Japan.

Was also assigned to Hydraulic School, San Diego, CA; Naval Base, Newport, RI; aboard USS *Robert L. Wilson* DD-847 in Boston; June 1946 went to Europe transferred November 1946 and discharged Jan. 20, 1947.

After the war he worked as a machinist for Kenworth Trucks, Kansas City, MO. Retired in 1986. In his spare time he is a volunteer driver for cancer patients to Kansas City and St. Joseph, MO.

He married Rita Oct. 10, 1945, in Atchison, KS, and has five children, 10 grandchildren and one great-granddaughter. He resides at 1316 So. 10th St., Atchison, KS.

LACY, JOHN CLEMENT, born in Brookline, MA, attended Choate; earned an AB from Harvard University; and JD from Boston College Law School. Joined the US Navy at the Harvard Naval ROTC September 1937 and trained summer cruises aboard USS *Wyoming* and USS *St. Augustine* 1941. He was a plankowner and served aboard BB-59 in February 1942 at Quincy. Was ENS L Div. at commissioning May 12, 1942, LT(jg) 6th Div. Oct. 1, 1943, and lieutenant 6th Div. 1944. Left BB-59 in July 1944 Bremerton, WA.

Also assigned July 1944 to USS *Bon Homme Richard*, Tokyo Bay 1945. After the war involuntary recall to active duty, office of naval intelligence, Pentagon 1951; assistant Naval attaché Saigon, Vietnam, 1953; staff CINCPAC/CINCPACFLT 1951; Chief Counter Intelligence ONI 1958; staff, Joint Chiefs of Staff 1960; staff, US Naval Forces Japan 1962; Defense Intelligence Agency 1966; CO Naval Investigative Service Office 3rd Naval District; retired captain USNR 1970. Received Navy Commendation Medal and BB-59 Award 1976.

He married Yvonne Archen in October 1955, Eze, France, and has one son, one daughter and one granddaughter. He resides at Place du Verger, 06640 St. Jeannet, France.

LA DUKE, CLYDE A., 635-21-22, born Aug. 22, 1926, Louisville, KY. Graduated from high school and enlisted Aug. 23, 1943, Louisville, KY. Trained at Great Lakes, IL (eight weeks); San Francisco, CA (two weeks); via troop ship to New Caledonia. He served aboard BB-59 as S1/c L Div. on Dec. 5, 1943, and left BB-59 Dec. 5, 1945, Bremerton, WA. Was assigned to Navy Reserve in Louisville, KY, 1945-55.

After the war he went to work in a packing house January 1946 (14 years) from labor to supervisor. Took sales job selling liquor and wines for 31 years. He enjoys bowling and played ball in his younger years.

He had one son, one daughter and six grandchildren. He resided at 9904 Grassland Dr. Apt. #13, Louisville, KY 40299. Memory List 1996.

LA FONTAINE, OSCAR R., born July 15, 1924, Frankfort, KY. Attended Good Shepherd School, enlisted in August 1943 and trained at Great Lakes, IL. He served aboard BB-59 in 5th Div. at commissioning December 1943 and left BB-59 in April 1946 Seattle, WA. He married Theressa Aug. 3, 1946, Frankfort, KY, and has one daughter, two sons and four grandchildren. He resides at 908 Crosshill Dr., Frankfort, KY.

LA FORCADE, G.H., AMM3/c V Div. to Commandant Fleet Air, Noumea, New Caledonia on March 8, 1943.

LA FRANCE, ROLAND A. Born Fall River, MA, May 27, 1920. Attended Prevost H.S., became a meat cutter for A&P store. Enlisted in Air Force 1942 and became chef for officers mess at Gulfport and Biloxi Airfields, and Okinawa. Purchased White's Spa in 1945, became a caterer and later developed White's Restaurant in Westport. Was cook aboard BB59 on her Homecoming trip. In 1944 married Rita Fallon and they had one son and four grandchildren. He died in 1995.

LA GAMBA, VINCENT ANTHONY, 243-60-26, enlisted Jan. 25, 1938, Philadelphia, PA. He is a plankowner and served aboard BB-59 as EM3/c at commissioning May 12, 1942.

LA GROSSA, ANTHONY DONATE, 404-76-49, enlisted March 24, 1942, New York, NY. He is a plankowner and served aboard BB-59 as BM2/c at commissioning May 12, 1942.

LAKE, EUGENE ROBERT, 341-99-65, born June 23, 1918, Bucklin, MO. Graduated from high school, enlisted Nov. 17, 1936, Kansas City, MO, and trained at Radio Material School, Hertzel Jr. College, Chicago; College of the Ozarks, Clarksville, AR; and Navy Pier, Chicago. Was stationed aboard the USS *Utah* BB-1 April 1937 to August 1938, RM3/c; USS *Pinola* an AT August 1938 to February 1942 RM1/c.

He served aboard BB-59 February 1942, in Quincy; plankowner RM1/c CR Div. at commissioning May 12, 1942; and CRM Sept. 11, 1942. Left BB-59 in April 1944 Majuro Atoll South Pacific. Was also assigned to Industrial Command Repo. Base San Diego, CA, July 9, 1945; USS *Avery Island* Sept. 11, 1945; USS *Piedmont Ad* Japan, Nov. 12, 1945; USS *Avery*

Island -AG Bikini Test Gr. March 5, 1946; Fleet Training Command PHTH, May 1946 to December 1947; NATTU Olathe, KS, January 1948 to July 1951; USS *Monterey* CVL NAS Pensacola, FL, July 1951 to September 1953; and CICOFF School, Glenview, IL, September 1953 to June 1957.

After the war he retired from Contel, Jan. 1, 1984, (now GTE) Toll Test Board. In his spare time he is active in the Boy Scouts, local church, church buildings and grounds and Sunday School teacher.

He married Mozelle Harrison, Dec. 2, 1944, Chicago, IL, and has two daughters and seven grandchildren. He resides at 900 So. Ithaca Ave., Russellville, AR.

LALLY, JOHN JOSEPH, JR., 647-03-02, enlisted Feb. 21, 1942, New York, NY. He is a plankowner and served aboard BB-59 as AS at commissioning May 12, 1942.

LALLY, TOM, (N) served aboard BB-59 June 30, 1945, and left BB-59 in September 1945 in California. He has two sons both were in pro ranks of boxing. Brett still boxing and wears a "BB-59" patch on his trunks. He resides at 1769 Newburgh Rd., Westland, MI 48185.

LAMBERT, LLOYD HOWARD, 337-72-20, enlisted Oct. 31, 1941, St. Louis, MO. He is a plankowner and served aboard BB-59 as F3/c at commissioning May 12, 1942. He resided in Everett, MA (1955) and Wilmington, MA (1963).

LAMBERT, MELVIN THEODORE, 328-74-37, enlisted Sept. 10, 1940, Minneapolis, MN. He served aboard BB-59 as F1/c and plankowner at commissioning May 12, 1942.

LAMBERT, RUSSELL, (N) served aboard BB-59 in January 1942, at Quincy, MA, and in A Div. as a plankowner at commissioning May 12, 1942, air conditioning and refrigeration, CMM. Left BB-59 in September 1945 (over the side in cargo net to a barge and a tug pushed them to a dock), Strait of Juan de Fuca (Seattle, WA).

After the war he worked for Kraft Foods as plant engineer for 30 years. Awarded life membership in the American Society of Heating and Refrigeration Engineers (ASHRAE).

He married Dolores and has two daughters. He resides at 3646 Floramar Terr., New Port Richey, FL 34652.

LA MONICA, JOSEPH G., M Div., has one son, two daughters and seven grandchildren. He resides at 304 Villinger Ave., Cinnaminson, NJ 08077.

LANCASTER, J.E., S2/c, March 10, 1943, transferred CR Div. to FR Div.

LANDIS, QUENTIN J., served aboard BB-59 in November 1943 2nd Div. and left February 1946. After the war he worked for the Tasty Baking Company of Philadelphia. He resides at 120 Penwood Rd., York, PA 17402.

LANDRUM, FRANK GRAY, JR., 356-46-44, enlisted Dec. 28, 1940, Dallas, TX. He is a plankowner and served aboard BB-59 as S1/c at commissioning May 12, 1942.

LANDRY, LOUIS GERARD, 202-29-01, enlisted April 2, 1942, Boston, MA. He is a plankowner and served aboard BB-59 as AS at commissioning May 12, 1942.

LANE, CHARLES ARTHUR, JR., served aboard BB-59 as lieutenant I Div. RCM officer on May 19, 1944, and left BB-59 as LT CMDR Dec. 1, 1945.

LANG, EDWARD ADOLPH, 606-34-81, enlisted Feb. 14, 1942, Boston, MA. Served aboard BB-59 as a plankowner and AS 3rd Div. at commissioning May 12, 1942. After the war he worked in the Mill Room, Dorchester High School. He resides at 64 Bigelow Ave., Watertown, MA.

LANE, JAMES LAVERNE, 250-73-14, enlisted April 2, 1942, Pittsburgh, PA. He served aboard BB-59 as plankowner as AS 2nd Div. at commissioning May 12, 1942. He resides at 211 Ohio St., Monroeville, PA.

LANG, JOHN HENRY, 327-85-04, enlisted Oct. 6, 1941, Cincinnati, OH. He is a plankowner and served aboard BB-59 as CQM N Div. at commissioning May 12, 1942.

LANGLEY, JULIUS LEE, 336-62-30, enlisted Nov. 23, 1938, San Pedro, CA. He is a plankowner and served aboard BB-59 as BM1/c at commissioning May 12, 1942.

LANNI, PAUL VINCENT, 650-22-14, enlisted Feb. 20, 1942, Philadelphia, PA. He is a plankowner and served aboard BB-59 as AS at commissioning May 12, 1942. He resides at 8 Fairview Ave., Malden, MA.

LAPLANTE, ARTHUR R., enlisted USMC, May 8, 1942, Norfolk Navy Yard. He is a plankowner and served aboard BB-59 as PVT 7th Div. at commissioning May 12, 1942.

LA PORT, EDWARD, (N) enlisted USMC, May 8, 1942, Norfolk Navy Yard. He is a plankowner and served aboard BB-59 as PVT 7th Div. at commissioning May 12, 1942.

LAPREL, HENRY, (N) Memory List 1981.

LARGE, HOBERT F., E Div., resided at 628 W. Elm St., Carmi, IL. Memory List 1997.

LARITY, WILLIAM R., served aboard BB-59 in 3rd Div. July 1942 and Turret 3 – loader. Left BB-59 in December 1945. After the war he worked for the post office department as a truck mechanic. He had one son and two grandchildren. He died Feb. 1, 1989; Memory List 1989. (Mrs.) resides at 58 Cottage Ave. #1, Winthrop, MA 02152.

LA ROCCA, ANTHONY FRANCIS, 647-03-03, enlisted Feb. 21, 1942, New York, NY. He is a plankowner and served aboard BB-59 as AS CS Div. at commissioning May 12, 1942, and left BB-59 Nov. 13, 1945, as SM3/c. After the war he worked for the US Post Office, Linden, NJ, as a mailman. He is active in the VFW, American Legion and Hawthorne Caballeros Drum Corps. He has three children and resides at 78A Wavecrest Ave., Winfield Park, NJ 07037 (1994).

LARSEN, W.L., FC Div., resides at 131 Mockingbird Lane, Marathon, FL 33050.

LARSON, RALPH DUANE, 371-65-19, enlisted Feb. 6, 1942, Bremerton, WA. He is a plankowner and served aboard BB-59 as CMM at commissioning May 12, 1942.

LA RUSSO, MARTIN, (N) resides at 1653 Bailgate Ave., Bronx, NY (1966).

LASARD, GEORGE, (N) resides at 29 Hale Ave., Manchester, NH.

LATRAVERSE, NORMAND JOSEPH, 202-26-39, enlisted Feb. 27, 1942, Boston, MA. He is a plankowner and served aboard BB-59 as AS at commissioning May 12, 1942.

LAVELL, JOHN, (N) 224-78-30, enlisted April 1, 1942, New York, NY. He served aboard BB-59 as AS 1st Div. plankowner at commissioning May 12, 1942, and on board for BB-59 2nd and 3rd anniversaries as Turret 1 GM2/c. After the war he worked for the Erie Railroad as a brakeman. He is active in the VFW #1477, Sparrow Hill. He has two sons and resides at 181 Ogden Ave., Jersey City, NJ (1966).

LAWRENCE, ROBERT LEONARD, 382-40-08, enlisted Feb. 19, 1941, Los Angeles, CA. He is a plankowner and served aboard BB-59 as F2/c at commissioning May 12, 1942.

LAWSON, HERMAN DANIEL, 310-99-90, enlisted Feb. 18, 1942, San Pedro, CA. He is a plankowner and served aboard BB-59 as EM2/c at commissioning May 12, 1942.

LAWSON, THOMAS SEAY, LT I Div., Supreme Court of Alabama and joined the Navy in 1943. Trained at Hollywood Beach, FL; Washington, DC, Bureau of Personnel and JAB. Served aboard BB-59 in communications CIC. After the war in early fall of 1945 assigned as JAB and State Supreme Court from 1972 to retirement. He resides at 1-104, 3567 Carter Hill Rd., Montgomery, AL 36111.

LAWTON, ALFRED ABBOTT, ENS S Div., served aboard BB-59 Nov. 24, 1944, and left BB-59 Jan. 25, 1946 (ship's service).

LAX, MORRIS HENRY, ENS 6th Div., served aboard BB-59 Sec. Batt. Off. Sept. 29, 1944, and left BB-59 July 20, 1945.

LAZERATION, JOSEPH, (N) resides in Indiana, PA (1966).

LEAHY, GEORGE A., RADM, Memory List 1982.

LEAMAN, THOMAS H., married Edith and had one daughter and two grandchildren (as of November 1992). He died May 7, 1963; Memory List 1988. (Mrs.) resides at 4585 Stauffer Ave. S.E. Apt., 201, Kentwood, MI 49508.

LEARNARD, ROBERT GUY, 606-37-35, born June 3, 1924, Boston, MA, enlisted March 4, 1942, Boston, MA. Trained at Newport, RI, and Fire Control School, Great Lakes, IL, S2/c to Rec.Sta. Casco Bay ME.

He served aboard BB-59 on Sept. 12, 1942, as S1/c June 1, 1943; and FC3/c June 1, 1944. He left BB-59 in 1945. Was assigned to USS *Garrard* (APA-84) via USS *De Haven* and USS *Bennington* Aug. 21, 1945, FC3/c; Nov. 18, 1945, Rec.Sta. Seattle, WA; Nov. 27, 1945, PSC Boston, MA; and discharged Nov. 29, 1945.

After the war he was a sergeant for the Arlington, MA, Police Dept. He was an active fund-raiser for BBBM Campaign and received the BB-59 Award in 1984.

He married Muriel Jan. 28, 1951, in Medford, MA, and had two sons and one daughter. Memory List 1990. (Mrs. and son) reside at Box 427 Lakewood Rd., S. Casco, ME 04077.

LEBENBERG, BERNARD, (N) 714-69-83, born Nov. 7, 1926, Brooklyn, NY. Earned a BA from Brooklyn College and MA from Columbia University. Joined the Navy Oct. 11, 1944, Brooklyn, NY, and trained at Sampson, NY, QM School.

He served aboard BB-59 as S1/c (QM) N Div. in May 1945 and left BB-59 in May 1946 Bremerton, WA, to USS *Alabama* to Los Angeles for discharge. Bernie's nickname was "Whale Killer." While in the South Pacific, steering BB-59, he hit a whale.

After the war he worked as a postal worker, wallpaper salesman, office clerk and high school English teacher, 1951-91. Was teacher of famous athletes: Tommie Davis, Lennie Wilkens and Connie Hawkins, Brooklyn Boys High School. Hawkins and Wilkens made Basketball Hall of Fame.

He married Marie April 2, 1961, and has two daughters. He resides at 298 Maple St., West Hempstead, NY.

LEBRODA, STANLEY ADAM, 606-30-70, enlisted Feb. 4, 1942, Boston, MA. He is a plankowner and served aboard BB-59 as S2/c at commissioning May 12, 1942.

LEBRUN, RAYMOND LOISE, 606-47-41, enlisted March 7, 1942, Boston, MA. He served aboard BB-59 as a plankowner at commissioning May 12, 1942. Memory List 1993.

LEDFORD, G.B., enlisted USMC, May 8, 1942, Norfolk Navy Yard. He served aboard BB-59 as PVT 7th Div. and plankowner at commissioning May 12, 1942.

LEE, BENJAMIN F., H Div. doctor, served aboard BB-59 as Jr. Med. LT on Oct. 30, 1944, and left BB-59 as Asst. Med. LT COMDR Dec. 3, 1945. After the war he went into private practice (general surgery) 1966 and had one daughter. Memory List 1977.

LEE, GERALD J., Memory List 1985.

LEEWE, MILTON WILLIAM, X Div. LT, served aboard BB-59 as aide to executive officer July 5, 1944.

LEGASEY, LEROY A., resides at 15 Ames St., Medford, MA (1966).

LEGAULT, GEORGE, (n) 238-58-42, enlisted Sept. 29, 1937, Albany, NY. He is a plankowner and served aboard BB-59 as F1/c at commissioning May 12, 1942.

LEGER, LLOYD JOSEPH, 360-31-83, enlisted Jan. 17, 1941, Houston, TX. He served aboard BB-59 as S1/c 3rd Div. at commissioning May 12, 1942. Memory List 1986. (Mrs.) resides at 3304 Pocahontas St., Baton Rouge, LA 70805.

LEGERE, ALBERT E., enlisted USMC, May 8, 1942, Norfolk Navy Yard. He is a plankowner and served aboard BB-59 as PVT 7th Div. at commissioning May 12, 1942.

LE GRANDE, NUNZIO, (n) 250-44-33, enlisted Jan. 8, 1942, Pittsburgh, PA. He is a plankowner and served aboard BB-59 as SF2/c R Div. at commissioning May 12, 1942. Transferred to CSF May 12, 1945, USS *Chipola* FFT RS, WC for duty by ComWes-SeaFron. Memory List 1996.

LEIGHTON, RUSSELL EUGENE, 299-64-92, enlisted Aug. 22, 1940, San Diego, CA. He is a plankowner and served aboard BB-59 as CEM at commissioning May 12, 1942.

LEINENBACH, MYRON, (n) 291-27-79, enlisted April 9, 1938, Norfolk, VA. He is a plankowner and served board BB-59 as CMM at commissioning May 12, 1942.

LELNEIER, ARTHUR R., resides at 113 Cutler St., Waterbury, CT (1964).

LENERT, WALTER, (N) M Div., resides at 5150 So. Lorel, Chicago, IL.

LENGES, STEPHEN WILLIAM, 291-53-70, enlisted Feb. 3, 1938, Indianapolis, IN. He is a plankowner and served aboard BB-59 as COX at commissioning May 12, 1942.

LENIHAN, JOHN W., 715-11-56, born Sept. 21, 1927, Hoboken, NJ. Enlisted Dec. 21, 1944, New York, NY, and trained at Sampson, NY (10 weeks); NTC Gulfport, MS; and USS *Indiana* BB-58. He served aboard BB-59 as S1/c CR and R Div. in February 1946 and left BB-59 in April 1946; NTC Gulfport, MX, seven months ship's company.

After the war he worked as a printer for Composter Union for 26 years and as a letter carrier for NALC for 20 years. In his spare time he has been a service officer for VFW Post #809 Little Ferry, NJ, since 1985 with other assignments. Was All-State Post Commander from 1969-70.

He married Arlene Feb. 27, 1971, in Little Ferry, NJ, and has two daughters and four grandchildren. He resides at 120 Main St., Box 488, Little Ferry, NJ 07643.

LENTZ, CLIFFORD LEO, 381-28-56, enlisted Sept. 8, 1939, San Diego, CA. He is a plankowner and served aboard BB-59 as GM3/c at commissioning May 12, 1942.

LESLIE, FRANK HALLETT, 647-21-42, enlisted March 23, 1942, New York, NY. He is a plankowner and served aboard BB-59 as AS at commissioning May 12, 1942.

LE TOURNEAU, FRANCIS GERARD, 202-26-33, enlisted Feb. 27, 1942, Boston, MA. He served aboard BB-59 as AS 4th Div. and plankowner at commissioning May 12, 1942.

He was president of the USS *Massachusetts* Assoc. in 1962 and on the board of directors from 1961-66. He resides at 2 Eastmor Lane, Hampton, NH.

LETTEREST, DICK, (N) resides at 614 Ann Eliza St., Pekin, IL (1966).

LETTEST, RICHARD J., resides at 25241 Nueva Vista Dr., Laguna Niguel, CA 92677.

LETTIE, GEORGE, JR., (N) 652-17-20, enlisted Jan. 31, 1942, Pittsburgh, PA. He is a plankowner and served aboard BB-59 as AS at commissioning May 12, 1942.

LEVESQUE, FRANCIS L., resides at 8031 Highpoint Blvd., Brooksville, FL 34613.

LEWICKI, JOSEPH JAMES, 207-38-07, enlisted Feb. 27, 1942, New Haven, CT. He is a plankowner and served aboard BB-59 as AS at commissioning May 12, 1942. Latest address is 5624 Murdock Ave., Sarasota, FL.

LEWIS, DEAN LOYD, 610-23-74, enlisted Jan. 2, 1942, Chicago, IL. He is a plankowner and serve aboard BB-59 as F2/c at commissioning May 12, 1942.

LEWIS, FLOYD MARTIN, 212-78-07, born Feb. 22, 1925, Barre, VT. Graduated from high school, enlisted April 2, 1942, Springfield, MA, and trained at NTS Newport, RI. He served aboard BB-59 as AS 1st Div. and plankowner at commissioning May 12, 1942. He left BB-59 as S1/c in March 1946.

After the war he was in the Teamsters Local 315 and married Martha April 17, 1947, in Barre, VT. He has one son, one daughter and four grandchildren. He resides at 2535 Kenny Dr., San Pablo, CA.

LEWIS, GERALD WILSON, 337-38-90, enlisted Sept. 24, 1940, St. Louis, MO. He is a plankowner and served aboard BB-59 as S1/c at commissioning May 12, 1942.

LEWIS, HAROLD D., 957-50-68, born May 6, 1925, Greensburg, KS. Graduated from high school, enlisted June 28, 1944, Kansas City, MO, and trained at Farragut, ID. He served aboard BB-59 as F1/c M Div. Sept. 28, 1944, and left BB-59 May 20, 1946, Norfolk, VA.

After the war he was a farmer and rancher. In his spare time he was commander of American Legion Post 138, Stratton, CO, for two years.

Married Esther Aug. 15, 1947, and had one son and one daughter. He lost son, Robert, to cancer in 1976. He resides at 25931 County Rd. #29, Stratton, CO 80836.

LEWIS, JOHN ALLO, 381-36-19, enlisted Aug. 16, 1940, San Diego, Ca. He is a plankowner and served aboard BB-59 as S1/c at commissioning May 12, 1942.

LEWIS, PAUL JOHN, 282-89-65, enlisted Nov. 18, 1936, Mare Island, CA. He is a plankowner and served aboard BB-59 as COX at commissioning May 12, 1942.

LEWIS, ROBERT JOHN, 300-00-39, enlisted Nov. 21, 1939, Chicago, IL. He is a plankowner and served aboard BB-59 as S1/c at commissioning May 12, 1942.

LEWTON, THEODORE GRAHAM, JR., served aboard BB-59 as LT C Div. communications officer July 31, 1944. He left BB-59 on Oct. 7, 1945. After the war he worked as a consultant for agricultural chemicals. He resides at 6615 Reeds Drive, Mission, KS.

LICHTE, JOHN, (N) Chicago, IL, March 7, 1922, mail was returned.

LICKLITER, JOSEPH B., resides at PO Box 1763, Silver City, NM 88062.

LIFORD, BOYD, (N) resides at Beards Fort, WV (1966).

LIGHT, ROBERT BURTON, Memory List 1992.

LIINATAINEN, PETER E., enlisted USMC, May 8, 1942, Norfolk Navy Yard. He is a plankowner and served aboard BB-59 as PVT 7th Div. at commissioning May 12, 1942.

LINCOLN, CHARLES E., Memory List 1979.

LINDELL, OLAVI, (N) Memory List 1992.

LINDEN, FRANCIS BERNARD 647-03-04, enlisted Feb. 21, 1942, New York, NY. He is a plankowner and served aboard BB-59 as AS at commissioning May 12, 1942. Memory List 1977.

LINDSEY, WILLIAM CLYDE, 616-13-25, enlisted Dec. 28, 1941, Dallas, TX. He is a plankowner and served aboard BB-59 as EM3/c at commissioning May 12, 1942.

LINDSEY, WILLIAM M., Served three years. Memory List 1977.

LINN, COLIN CHURCHILL, enlisted Jan. 30, 1942, New York, NY. He was a plankowner and served aboard BB-59 as AS at commissioning May 12, 1942, and on board for BB-59 2nd and 3rd anniversaries as forward store and space parts storeroom S Div. SK1/c.

After the war he worked for T.C. Moffat & Company in the executive department, Nutley, NJ. Memory List 1977.

LIOTTI, LOUIS, (N) 614-65-77, born Sept. 26, 1921, Canton, OH. Graduated from East Canton High School, enlisted July 1942, Great Lakes, IL, and electrical training for eight weeks at Teachers College, Morehead, KY. He served aboard BB-59 in January 1943 as EM3/c E Div., EM2/c and EM1/c Heavy Power. He left BB-59 in December 1945 Bremerton, WA.

After the war he worked as a maintenance foreman for Timken Roller Brg. and retired December 1982. Married Virginia July 23, 1949, and resides at 7680 Fawn Dr., No. Canton, OH.

LIPHAM, EVERETT, (n) 650-07-24, enlisted Dec. 3, 1941, Philadelphia, PA. He is a plankowner and served aboard BB-59 as MM2/c at commissioning May 12, 1942, and on board for BB-59 2nd and 3rd anniversaries.

LIPPOLD, WALTER WILLIAM, served aboard BB-59 as LT CDR H Div. June 10, 1944, and as senior dental officer COMDR. Left BB-59 in September 1945 and retired as captain.

After the war he had a part-time, private practice in dentistry. Memory List 1984.

LIPSCHUTZ, WILLIAM MAX, 239-30-71, enlisted Feb. 12, 1942, Albany, NY. He was a plankowner and served aboard BB-59 as Mus2/c at commissioning May 12, 1942. Memory List 1977.

LISEMBY, JOHN WOODS, 269-00-55, enlisted Oct. 27, 1941, Macon, GA. He is a plankowner and served aboard BB-59 as EM3/c at commissioning May 12, 1942.

LISHING, CARL, (n) 283-11-75, enlisted Dec. 15, 1941, Cleveland, OH. He was a plankowner and served aboard BB-59 as WT2/c B Div. at commissioning May 12, 1942. Memory List 1989.

LISHING, FRANK, (n) 283-10-15, born Cleveland, OH, Feb. 7, 1915. Graduated from high school and enlisted Dec. 15, 1941, Cleveland, OH. Trained as boilermaker also four years in the Navy 1934-38 USS *Texas,* USS *Peary,* USS *Indianapolis* and USS *Louisville.*

He served aboard BB-59 as WT2/c E Div. and plankowner at commissioning May 12, 1942. Left BB-59 in May 1944 in the Pacific to Philadelphia assigned to the USS *Chicago* and made chief petty officer; and in April 1945 back to the Pacific.

After the war he worked for Eaton Manufacturing Company (external grinding) Cleveland, OH. In his spare time he played golf five days a week.

Married Honora April 13, 1942, in Quincy, MA, and had two daughters and three grandchildren. He died Aug. 8, 1988; Memory List 1992. (Mrs.) resides at 24280 Devoe Ave., Euclid, OH.

LITTERST, RICHARD J., 852-65-90, born April 3, 1925, Pekin, IL. Graduated from high school and enlisted June 1943, Great Lakes, IL. Served aboard BB-59 as S2/c 4th Div. in October 1943 and left BB-59 March 1946, Long Beach, CA, as GM3/c to duty on LST-1141 for 16 months.

After the war he worked as a brick layer in Steel Mill for 30 years then masonry contractor for 15 years until he retired. In his spare time he is active in Elks Lodge, Mission Viejo, CA, and is an artist (oil painting).

He married Vivian Sept. 22, 1945, in Delavan, IL, and has two sons, seven grandchildren and six great-grandchildren (December 1993). He resides at 25241 Nueva Vista Dr., Laguna Niguel, CA 92677.

LITTLE, CHARLES ROBERT, served aboard BB-59 as LT(jg) H Div. junior medical officer Feb. 5, 1943. Left BB-59 Oct. 31, 1944, lieutenant. He resides at 241 Cape Arrow, Corpus Christi, TX.

LITTLE, ERNEST C., 250-77-13, born May 13, 1923, Raleigh, NC. Graduated from high school and attended Carnegie Tech. He enlisted May 29, 1942, Pittsburgh, PA, and trained at NTS Newport, RI.

He served aboard BB-59 as Y3/c X Div. July 1942 and left BB-59 in 1945 in the South Pacific via USS *Lexington* to US for shore duty 1st Naval Dist., Boston for one year; staff, ROTC Unit at Harvard University and finished last Navy year on light cruiser. Enlisted in Naval Reserve, and recalled to duty for 16 months (1951) with fleet training, Norfolk, VA.

After the war he was production manager for a large advertising agency with headquarters in Pittsburgh, PA. Transferred to Fort Lauderdale, FL, to retirement at age 62.

Married Ruth Feb. 4, 1956, Pittsburgh, PA, and has three children and four grandchildren (as of January 1994). He resides at 1732 NE 37th St., Fort Lauderdale, FL 33334.

LITTLE, RILEY MCMILLAN, served aboard BB-59 as ENS B Div. May 21, 1944, and in B Div. JO and JW LT(jg).

LLOYD, RALPH LLEWELLYN, 620-33-39, enlisted Feb. 3, 1942, Des Moines, IA. He was a plankowner and served aboard BB-59 as AS at commissioning May 12, 1942. Memory List 1984.

LOCKE, FREDERICK, (N) born Feb. 5, 1922, Upland, PA. Graduated from high school and attended Temple Technical. He joined the Navy July 1, 1942, NRS Philadelphia, PA, and trained at NTS Newport, RI. He served aboard BB-59 as S2/c R and 1st Div. Aug. 16, 1942; USNH, Bremerton, WA, Nov. 29, 1945, as SF1/c; aboard BB-59 SF1/c Dec. 11, 1945.

Additional Naval duties: March 21, 1946, USNH San Francisco, CA; June 20, 1946, Rec. Sta. San Francisco; Aug. 30, 1946, USS *Sierra;* Jan. 2, 1947, Rec. Sta. San Francisco; Jan. 8, 1947 USNH Bethesda, MD; and Feb. 11, 1948, discharged. After the war he worked as a machinist for Westinghouse Electric.

He married Margaret June 12, 1948, Chester, PA, and has two sons, two daughters and five grandchildren. He died July 21, 1995. (Mrs.) Locke resides at 2312 Graywood Rd., Wilmington, DE.

LOCKHART, ROBERT, (N) 4th Div., resides at 4306 Valley View, Luray, VA.

LOCKWOOD, GEORGE ASHTON, 342-11-16, enlisted April 7, 1939, Kansas City, MO. He was a plankowner and served aboard BB-59 as S1/c at commissioning May 12, 1942. Memory List 1984.

LOCKWOOD, WILLIS A., served aboard BB-59 as CQM N Div. Transferred March 12, 1945, to USS *Admiral R.E. Coontz* FFT RS, WC, US for discharge from Naval service.

LODDIGS, HERMAN WILLIAM, 223-47-45, enlisted Aug. 3, 1938, Brooklyn, NY. He is a plankowner and served aboard BB-59 as EM1/c at commissioning May 12, 1942.

LOEBER, EDWARD CONRAD, 646-64-84, enlisted Feb. 4, 1942, New York, NY. He is a plankowner and served aboard BB-59 as AS at commissioning May 12, 1942.

LOGAN, CHARLES EDWARD, 652-20-61, enlisted Feb. 13, 1942, Pittsburgh, PA. He was a plankowner and served aboard BB-59 as AS at commissioning May 12, 1942. Memory List 1984.

LOGAN, HUGH JAMES, 244-07-07, born Dec. 24, 1920, Darby, PA. Graduated from Darby High School and enlisted Feb. 27, 1942, Philadelphia, PA. He is a plankowner and served aboard BB-59 as AS 4th Div. at commissioning May 12, 1942, and again on board for BB-59 2nd and 3rd anniversaries. He left BB-59 as GM1/c in August 1945. After the war he worked for Westinghouse Steam Div. as a blader for 23 years. He married Elinor June 3, 1944, Philadelphia and has five children and 14 grandchildren. He resides at 15 Avenue "A," Tabernacle, NJ.

LOMASNEY, JAMES G., 862-89-34, born Jan. 19, 1925, Detroit, MI. Graduated from high school and UM extension courses. He enlisted Aug. 9, 1943, Detroit, MI, and trained at Great Lakes, IL, to Advance Naval Base (3) Noumea. He served aboard BB-59 as SF3/c R Div. in November 1943 and left BB-59 in December 1945 Bremerton, WA.

Was assigned to USS *Lyons* APA-71. After the war he worked for Grose Point Sheet Metal Company as a sheet metal worker; APP Local #58 IBEW 1951; worked for W.D. Gale Electric for 20 years as journeyman foreman; and electrical inspector for the city of Fraser, 1964 to present (1993). He spends his spare time attending electrical meetings and giving electrical exams for journeymen and master licenses.

He married Marjorie June 5, 1951, in Detroit, MI, and has four children and three grandchildren (August 1993). He resides at 16170 Kingston St., Fraser, MI.

LONG, CARLETON G., CAPT, Memory List 1982.

LONG, DALE E., 5th Div., resides at 24 Homewood Rd., Wilmington, DE.

LONG, EDWARD BEDFORD, 346-84-31, enlisted Aug. 30, 1940, Little Rock, AR. He is a plankowner and served aboard BB-59 as S1/c at commissioning May 12, 1942.

LONG, HARRY EDWARD, JR., 647-01-59, enlisted Feb. 20, 1942, New York, NY. He was a plankowner and served aboard BB-59 as AS at commissioning May 12, 1942. Memory List 1997.

LONG, JAMES ANDREW, 606-45-99, enlisted March 4, 1942, Boston, MA. He is a plankowner and served aboard BB-59 as AS at commissioning May 12, 1942.

LONG, JOHN, (N) 299-83-45, born in Gary, IN, and raised in Joliet, IL. Earned a BS in occupational education from the University of Southern Illinois. He enlisted Oct. 20, 1936, Chicago, IL, and trained at Great Lakes, IL.

He was assigned to the USS *San Francisco* April 1937 to August 1939; USS *Mustin* September 1939 to June 1941; and USS *Hamman* November 1941 to February 1942. He served aboard BB-59 as SC3/c S Div. as plankowner at commissioning May 12, 1942, July 1, 1942, as SC2/c and April 1, 1943, as SC1/c.

He left BB-59 Jan. 21, 1944, at Funa Futi Atoll; plankowner aboard USS *Wren* DD-568; assigned to Div. 2 Squad 57, Task Force 94; Adak, AK, and tail end of Okinawa Campaign on radar picket duty in Tokyo Bay; duty in American Samoa; USS *Dixie,* shore duty in Alameda; USS *Breakinridge,* Adak, AK;

Great Lakes NTS, taught swimming; and retired Sept. 20, 1957. Made chief in January 1945.

After the war he worked at the Mare Island Shipyard as an equipment specialist (ships) in the allowance section and retired in 1980. Spends time in community service with his wife. Married Norma March 2, 1944, Chicago, and has four children and two grandchildren. He resides at 106 Lasson Circle, Vacaville, CA.

LOPERFIDO, FRANK, (n) 224-78-32, enlisted April 1, 1942, New York, NY. He is a plankowner and served aboard BB-59 as AS 2nd Div. at commissioning May 12, 1942. He resides at 312 Cedar Ave., Allenhurst, NJ.

LOTT, RAYMOND S., resides at Route 1, Omega, GA (1966).

LOUGHLIN, THOMAS JOSEPH, 646-63-80, enlisted Feb. 3, 1942, New York, NY. Served aboard BB-59 as a plankowner AS I Div. at commissioning May 12, 1942; March 10, 1943, RDM3/c CR Div. to FR Div. Memory List 1995. (Mrs.) resides at Box 51, Bloomingburg, NY 12721.

LOUNSBURY, CHARLES FAWCETT, JR., 212-62-39, enlisted Nov. 25, 1940, Springfield, MA. He is a plankowner and served aboard BB-59 as PhM3/c at commissioning May 12, 1942.

LOVE, LAWRENCE, (N) c/o L.D. Love Rt. 6, Box 107A, Bristol, VA.

LOVE, OCIE BROWN, 287-16-77, enlisted May 6, 1936, Louisville, KY. He is a plankowner and served aboard BB-59 as Matt1/c at commissioning May 12, 1942.

LOVELL, PALMER, (N) resides at Bigstone Gap, VA (1966).

LOVERCAMP, FREDERICK, (N) resides at 1904 Liberty Park Blvd., Sedalia, MO 65301.

LOWE, CHARLES EDWIN, 328-36-25, enlisted July 2, 1940, San Diego, CA. He is a plankowner and served aboard BB-59 as Sm1/c at commissioning May 12, 1942.

LOWE, MARCUS L., CAPT, Memory List 1982.

LOWRY, JAMES DOUGLAS, 200-79-70, enlisted Dec. 3, 1941, Philadelphia, PA. He is a plankowner and served aboard BB-59 as MM2/c at commissioning May 12, 1942.

LOWRY, LEONARD ROBERT, 628-17-51, enlisted Jan. 7, 1942, Kansas City, MO. He is a plankowner and served aboard BB-59 as S2/c at commissioning May 12, 1942.

LUCIANI, LOUIS JOHN, 311-48-53, enlisted Aug. 20, 1940, Detroit, MI. He is a plankowner and served aboard BB-59 as S1/c at commissioning May 12, 1942.

LUCKEY, RUSSEL JOSEPH, 337-02-20, born May 2, 1918, Springfield, IL. Enlisted Nov. 15, 1937, St. Louis, MO, and attended boot camp Norfolk, VA, November 1937 to February 1938. Was assigned to USS *Texas* BB-41, USS *Enterprise* CV-6 (plankowner) and USS *Yorktown* October 1938 to November 1941.

He re-enlisted Jan. 6, 1942, St. Louis, MO. He served aboard BB-59 Jan. 15,

1942, Quincy, MA, and was plankowner at commissioning May 12, 1942, as MM2/c A Div. and MM1/c – CMM. Left BB-59 Nov. 1, 1945, Bremerton, WA. He was also assigned to the USS *Curtis,* May 1946 to March 1950; USNTC Great Lakes March 1950 to March 1953; USS *Kula Gulf* AV-107, March 1953 to October 1955; USS *Coral Sea* CV-43 October 1955 to October 1956; USS *Leyte* CV-32 October 1956 to May 1957; recruiting duty, Kenosha, WI, three months; promoted to warrant officer USNTC Great Lakes to September 1959; to USS *Passumpsic* AD-107, September 1959 to July 1962; Reserve fleet, Bremerton, WA, 1962-64; USS *Staten Island* AGB-5 September 1964 to February 1966; USS *Currituck* AV-7 February 1966 to March 1968; retired May 1, 1968, with 30 years of service; and promoted to lieutenant May 1962 and LCDR 1968.

After the war he was chief engineer of Washington State Ferries for 12 years and retired in 1980. In his spare time he was active in the Boy Scouts, 1962-64; and a hobby farmer raising beef, sheep, fish and hay.

He married Helen 1947, Las Vegas and has four children, eight grandchildren and one great-grandchild. He resides at 2630 Garfield Ave., Port Orchard, WA 98366.

LUDWICK, JOHNIE ALVIN, 256-15-36, enlisted Sept. 6, 1939, Dallas, TX. He is a plankowner and served aboard BB-59 as SK2/c at commissioning May 12, 1942.

LUDWICK, MAX EUGENE, 359-96-15, born May 6, 1920, Mt. Carroll, IL. Graduated from high school and attended the University of Missouri, School of Journalism. Joined the Navy Sept. 10, 1937, Houston, TX, and trained at NTS San Diego, CA. Was assigned to USS *Colorado* BB-45 and Fargo Barracks, Boston.

Served aboard BB-59 in March 1942 Quincy, MA, and at commissioning May 12, 1942, F1/c S Div. plankowner. Left BB-59 in June 1944 to USS *Kwajalein* CVE-98 Bkr1/c S Div.; NRS Watertown, NY 1945; Com P10 Great Lakes 1948; 1950-52 CINCPAL Fleet, Ch Joint Chiefs of Staff; in charge of USN recruits, sub-station Watertown, NY; Com 9 Pub. Info. Office, Great Lakes, Journalism School; assigned to CINCPACFLT Headquarters 1950, to ADM A.W. Radford as press representative; retired from Navy June 1957 from Chr. JCS as chief journalist.

After the war he was administrative assistant to vice-president Pacific Gas & Electric Company, San Francisco for four years; September 1961 Pub.Info.Off. USN Propellant Plant, Indian Head, MD; in 1971 worked for Navy Legislative affairs in Pentagon (legislative writer). He retired in March 1976 with 34 years of government service.

In his spare time he is active in Elks Lodge. He worked through chairs and became Exalted Ruler of Waldorf Lodge #2421, Waldorf, MD. Was awarded Elk "Citizen of the Year" in 1993 (approved by Grand Lodge in Chicago). He has one son and resides at 924 Sloane Ave., Waldorf, MD.

LUDWICK, RALPH WALDO, 109734, born 1916 in Lincoln, NE. He holds a DDS joined the Navy in 1941, Great Lakes and Annapolis. He served aboard BB-59 as a plankowner LT H Div. at commissioning May 12, 1942, and as dental officer. Left BB-59 Jan. 3, 1944, CAPT to New York Navy Yard; Dental School, Bethesda, MD. After the war he retired as dentist Jan. 1, 1978. He married Hope in 1944, Lincoln, NE, and has three children and one grandchild. He resides at 2921 Stratford Ave., Lincoln, NE.

LUHR, ALLEN WILLIAM, 642-14-37, enlisted Feb. 27, 1942, New Haven, CT. He is a plankowner and served board BB-59 as AS at commissioning May 12, 1942. He is director of engineering services, Paramount General Hospital and resides at 16453 So. Colorado Ave., Paramount, CA.

LUKAS, MICHAEL STANLEY, 610-43-33, enlisted Jan. 21, 1942, Chicago, IL. He is a plankowner and served aboard BB-59 as AS at commissioning May 12, 1942, and as F3/c A Div. to ComSerForSoPac March 8, 1943.

LUKE, OWEN BURNELL, 283-22-46, enlisted March 12, 1942, San Francisco, CA. He is a plankowner and served aboard BB-59 as S1/c at commissioning May 12, 1942.

LUKEN, ROBERT WALKER, enlisted July 25, 1940, St. Louis, MO. He is a plankowner and served aboard BB-59 as F2/c at commissioning May 12, 1942.

LUMBERG, LAWRENCE, (N) 224-78-33, enlisted April 1, 1942, New York, NY. He is a plankowner and served aboard BB-59 as AS 6th and 4th Div. at commissioning May 12, 1942, and left BB-59 January 1945. After the war he was employed by the United States Line Ship Company. He died May 20, 1992; Memory List 1993. Latest address: Savannah, GA (Information supplied by Dennis Rauch of Savannah.)

LUNGHI, ALBERT DOMINIC, 666-15-38, enlisted Feb. 5, 1942, Springfield, MA. He was a plankowner and served aboard as AS R and 3rd Div. at commissioning May 12, 1942, and on board for BB-59 2nd and 3rd anniversaries MAA. After the war he worked for Hurley & David Refrigeration & Air Conditioning. He resided at 86 Peekskill Ave., Springfield, MO 01129. Memory List 1996.

LUTENEGGER, WALTER JOSEPH, 321-30-22, born May 26, 1920, Burlington, IA. He enlisted March 8, 1939, Des Moines, IA, and assigned to Gunnery School and the USS *Oklahoma* BB-37 (left Dec. 7, 1941). He served aboard BB-59 as S1/c 5th Div. at commissioning May 12, 1942, as a plankowner. He resides at 2704 So. Central, Burlington, IA 52601.

LYDECKER, ALBERT A., enlisted USMC May 8, 1942, Norfolk Navy Yard. He is a plankowner and served aboard BB-59 as PVT 7th Div. at commissioning May 12, 1942.

LYDECKER, BERT, (N) attended 1955 reunion. He resided at 50 Waverly Ave., Newton, MA (1955). Memory List 1977.

LYDECKER, WILLIAM W., enlisted USMC, May 8, 1942, Norfolk Navy Yard. He is a plankowner and served aboard BB-59 as PVT 7th Div. at commissioning May 12, 1942. Was captain's orderly 20 mm guns PVT1/c. After the war he worked for Fairchild-Hill Republic Div. as a security guard. He spent his spare time as chaplain in the American Legion and had two step-children (Leon USN). Memory List 1977.

LYNCH, MICHAEL KENNETH, 600-13-82, enlisted Feb. 4, 1942, Albany, NY. He is a plankowner and served aboard BB-59 as AS at commissioning May 12, 1942.

LYNCH, WILLARD SANFORD, 382-17-17, enlisted Feb. 15, 1940, Los Angeles, CA. He is a plankowner and served aboard BB-59 as S1/c at commissioning May 12, 1942.

LYONS, PAUL ALBERT, served aboard BB-59 Dec. 18, 1942, in B Div. WT2/c (in charge of #1 machinery space). He left BB-59 in July 1946. Last address was Keegan, ME. He had six children and spent his spare time in Fleet Reserve Assoc., Holy Name Society and the Boy Scouts. Memory List 1977.

LYONS, WILLIAM FREDERIC, 606-69-64, enlisted May 1, 1942, Boston, MA. He is a plankowner and served aboard BB-59 as SF3/c R Div. at commissioning May 12, 1942, and on board for BB-59 2nd and 3rd anniversaries CSF.

MACAFEE, DONALD W., served aboard BB-59 as PhotoM3/c V Div. in 1944. Was assigned as ship's photographer and left BB-59 in 1945. After the war he worked as chief photographer for the *Alexandria Gazette* newspaper, Alexandria, VA.

In his spare time he was honorary member of the Lions Club; in the Rotary, Optimists, Kiwanis Clubs, National Press Photographer's Assoc., American Philatelic Society, Alexandria Mt. Vernon Stamp Club, Northern Virginia Camera Club and founder of International Assoc. of Pipe Smokers. He has two daughters and resided at 7133 Layton Drive, Springfield, VA 22150. Memory List 1985.

MACAVOY, RICHARD R., USMC, May 8, 1942, Norfolk Navy Yard, VA. He is a plankowner and served aboard BB-59 as PVT 7th Div. commissioning May 12, 1942. His latest address is (Son) resides at 2130 Fairton Rd., Millville, NJ 08332. Memory List 1996.

MACCULLOCH, DONALD, 650-32-05, enlisted Feb. 21, 1942, Philadelphia, PA. He is a plankowner and served aboard BB-59 as AS at commissioning May 12, 1942, and on board for BB-59 2nd and 3rd anniversaries as a plankowner.

MACDONALD, CHARLES, JR., 202-29-17, born July 18, 1924, Wakefield, MA. He graduated from high school and attended various real estate and banking studies. Enlisted April 8, 1942, Boston, MA, and trained at Great Lakes Training Station, IL, and Henry Ford Machinist's Mate School, Detroit, MI.

He served aboard BB-59 as MM2/c M Div. commissioning Nov. 24, 1942, and assigned to Control Engine Room #3. He left BB-59 Aug. 18, 1944. After the war he worked for the post office for nine years; sales for six years; banking for 30 years; second assessor (selectman) four years; first assessor (selectman/mayor) one year, Monhegan Island, ME; banking vice-president; construction mortgage lending Essex Bank, Peabody, MA.

In his spare time he is president of USS Mass. Assoc., 1983-present. Received the BB-59 Award, 1988. He married Jewel Sept. 21, 1945, Wakefield, MA, and has two sons, one daughter and four grandchildren. He resides at PO Box 383, Monhegan Island, ME 04852-0383.

MACDONALD, HOWARD RONALD, 606-50-62, enlisted March 12, 1942, Boston, MA. He was a plankowner and served aboard BB-59 as SK3/c at commissioning May 12, 1942. He resided at 9 Glenrose Road, Dorchester, MA 02124. Memory List 1977.

MACDONALD, JAMES RICHARD, 606-74-27, enlisted May 1942. He is a plankowner and served aboard BB-59 as MM2/c at commissioning May 12, 1942. After the war he worked for the Chemical Process Corp. in Stamford, CT. He resided at 654 Columbia Road, Dorchester, MA 02124. Memory List 1977.

MACDONALD, JOHN F., served aboard BB-59 as CEM E Div. at commissioning May 12, 1942, as a plankowner. Was assigned to electric and left BB-59 October 1943. After the war he worked as a highway supervisor in Boston, MA. He was a delegate to Na-

tional Convention of American Legion. He resided at 1273 Hyde Park Ave., Boston, MA 02136. Memory List 1992.

MACEL, WILLIAM PETER, 652-25-51, born June 16, 1924, Pittsburgh, PA. Graduated from high school and enlisted March 7, 1942, Pittsburgh, PA. He is a plankowner and served aboard BB-59 as AS 5th Div. at commissioning May 12, 1942. He left BB-59 November 1944, Seattle, WA.

After the war he worked at Tracy's Machine Shop; Machine Shop Research, University of Pittsburgh; Special Products Westinghouse Company; Printing Devices Pannier Stamp Company; Clerk District Attorney of Pittsburgh, PA. In his spare time he was a little league coach.

He married Margaret in September 1947, Pittsburgh, PA. He has two sons, one daughter and three grandchildren. He resided at 909 California Ave. #208, Avalon, PA 15202-2744. Memory List 1993.

MACFADYEN, HARRY, 647-01-63, enlisted Feb. 20, 1942, New York, NY. He is a plankowner and served aboard BB-59 as AS at commissioning May 12, 1942.

MACHARA, VINCENT JOHN, 652-26-16, enlisted March 11, 1942, Pittsburgh, PA. He is a plankowner and served aboard BB-59 as AS at commissioning May 12, 1942, and on board for BB-59 2nd and 3rd anniversaries.

MACHEN, ARTHUR WEBSTER, JR., ENS, 185178, born Dec. 16, 1920, Baltimore, MD. Attended Princeton University, 1942 and Harvard Law School, 1948. He enlisted Dec. 16, 1942, Baltimore, MD, and attended the V-7 Program Columbia University and officer training Notre Dame University.

He served aboard BB-59 as ENS 4th Div. Dec. 18, 1942, Casco Bay, ME. He was assigned LT(jg) N Div. and LT(jg) DRX. Left BB-59 May 2, 1945. Was promoted to LT; Dec. 9, 1945, to Jan. 15, 1946 on USS *Fargo* and released from active duty Jan. 15, 1946.

After the war he worked as a lawyer from 1948-51; 1951-57; 1957-92; 1992-senior; and retired in 1995. In his spare time he was in Phi Beta Kappa, numerous activities for Episcopal Church, chancellor for Episcopal Diocese of Maryland, Maryland Bar Assoc. Committee for ABA, Who's Who in America.

He married Rose Purves Jan. 24, 1948, Cambridge, MA. He has three sons (one deceased) and four grandchildren. He resides at 1400 Malvern Ave., Ruxton, MD 21204.

MACUIN, ALGARD FRANK, 650-34-21, enlisted Feb. 3, 1942, Philadelphia, PA. He is a plankowner and served aboard BB-59 as AS 3rd Div. at commissioning May 12, 1942. He was assigned as ship's taylor 1/c and left BB-59 in 1945. After the war he was truck driver for Ma's Old Fashion Corp. He was involved in the Catholic War Veterans and the American Legion. He has one son and two daughters. He resides at 76 South Main St., Ashley, PA 18706.

MACK, CLARENCE JAMES, 283-22-54, enlisted Jan. 19, 1938, Cleveland, OH. He is a plankowner and served aboard BB-59 as COX at commissioning May 12, 1942.

MACKEY, WILLIAM DELANEY, 647-01-64, enlisted Feb. 20, 1942, New York, NY. He is a plankowner and served aboard BB-59 as AS at commissioning May 12, 1942, and on board for BB-59 2nd anniversary as a plankowner.

MACLEAR, THOMAS JOSEPH, 224-70-78, enlisted Feb. 24, 1942, New York, NY. He is a plankowner and served aboard BB-59 as AS at commissioning May 12, 1942, and on board for BB-59 2nd and 3rd anniversaries.

MACNEIL, JOHN WILFRED, 212-34-18, enlisted March 29, 1942, Los Angeles, CA. He is a plankowner and served aboard BB-59 as CEM at commissioning May 12, 1942.

MACSISAK, STEPHEN, USMC, May 8, 1942, Norfolk Navy Yard. He is a plankowner and served aboard BB-59 as corporal 7th Div. commissioning May 12, 1942.

MADAU, MAURICE, (n) 234-12-43, born July 27, 1915, Hornell, NY. Graduated from high school and enlisted Dec. 29, 1936, Buffalo, NY. Was stationed aboard USS *Richmond*. He served aboard BB-59 Jan. 28, 1942, Quincy Shipyard as MM2/c A Div. commissioning May 12, 1942, as a plankowner.

Was assigned evaporators MM1/c and left BB-59 in 1943. Other Naval assignments: Feb. 2, 1944, aboard USS *Houston* (CL-81) for commissioning, Portsmouth, VA, left July 1944; assigned to USS *Audubon* (APA-149) to Nov. 29, 1944; Dec. 27, 1944 to Small Craft Training Center, San Pedro, CA, to USS YR-74 April 3, 1945, to Sept. 3, 1945.

After the war he was in the ice cream business, 1946-49 California; worked for Emery Ind. Inc. California 1950-77; and retired in 1977. In his spare time he was involved in the Special Olympics coaching bowling and basketball; received 1991 Oregon Special Olympics Outstanding Family Award; was a five year volunteer in Shakespeare Festival; volunteer for the Northwest Museum of National History.

He married Charlotte Dec. 1, 1944, St. Josephis Church, Quincy, MA, and has one son, two daughters and seven grandchildren. He resides at 63 Mallard Street, Ashland, OR 97520-7316.

MADDEN, HARRY, Memory List 1977.

MADDEN, HENRY, (n) 646-57-84, enlisted Jan. 28, 1942, New York, NY. He is a plankowner and served aboard BB-59 as AS at commissioning May 12, 1942.

MADDEN, JOHN PETER, 212-47-86, enlisted Aug. 11, 1937, Springfield, MA. He is a plankowner and served aboard BB-59 as F1/c at commissioning May 12, 1942.

MADDOX, JAMES AUBURN, 295-43-90, born March 27, 1920, Harvest, AL. Graduated from high school and had two years of college. Enlisted Oct. 18, 1938, Nashville, TN, and trained at Naval Training Station, Norfolk, VA; Hospital Corps School, Norfolk, VA; Naval Medical School, Washington, DC; US Naval Hospital, Washington, DC.

He is a plankowner and served aboard BB-59 as PHM1/c H Div. at commissioning May 12, 1942, and assigned to hospital spaces. He left BB-59 April 23, 1943, South Pacific. Was also assigned to USS *Relief* (AH-1). Became CPHM, July 1, 1943, Advanced Base Personnel Depot, San Bruno, CA; Nov. 1, 1944, District Staff Headquarters, 12th Naval District; March 5, 1946, Naval Station, Alameda, CA; Aug. 1, 1946, USS ARD-17; Feb. 22, 1947, Onopnola, New Orleans, LA; Oct. 25, 1946, US Naval Hospital, Oakland, CA; Nov. 14, 1950, USS *Vammer* (DE-644); Feb. 15, 1952, Staff ComCR US Des Pacific; March 31, 1953, US Naval Hospital, Oakland, CA; June 30, 1955, transferred to fleet reserve; and May 7, 1958, inactive.

After the war he worked as a pharmaceutical sales manager hospital territory, Wyeth Labs; training and selling Tennessee Walking horses to follow bird dogs quail hunting. In his spare time he enjoys fishing and quail hunting with pointers and setters.

He married Ruby Jan. 4, 1974, Reno, NV, and has two sons, one daughter and three grandchildren. He resides at 781 Ardmore Highway, Taft, TN 38488.

MAGNER, WILLIAM MICHAEL, 376-27-77, enlisted March 6, 1941, San Francisco, CA. He is a plankowner and served aboard BB-59 as F2/c at commissioning May 12, 1942, and on board for BB-59 2nd and 3rd anniversaries.

MAHAUM, FRANCIS ROBERT, 243-92-11, enlisted May 14, 1941, Philadelphia, PA. He is a plankowner and served aboard BB-59 as HA1/c at commissioning May 12, 1942.

MAHER, VERNON EDWARD, 620-33-55, enlisted Feb. 3, 1942, Des Moines, IA. He trained at Great Lakes Naval Training Station, IL. He served aboard BB-59 as AS S Div. at commissioning May 12, 1942, as plankowner and on board for BB-59 2nd and 3rd anniversaries. Was assigned to SC2/c ship cook and left BB-59 September 1945 to Minneapolis, MN.

After the war he worked as a farmer retiring in 1968 and moving to Iowa City. He married Rosella Oct. 13, 1945, Cedar Rapids, IA, and has one son, two daughters and five grandchildren. (Mrs.) resides at 1124 Spruce St., Iowa City, IA 52240-5723. He died Nov. 17, 1980; Memory List 1981.

MAHON, JOSEPH THOMAS, 650-29-58, enlisted Feb. 18, 1942, Philadelphia, PA. He is a plankowner and served aboard BB-59 as AS at commissioning May 12, 1942, and on board for BB-59 2nd and 3rd anniversaries.

MAHONEY, JOHN EDWARD, ENS, born March 25, 1921, Gloversville, NY. Educated at Yale University in 1943 with a 1948 Yale University Certificate of Transportation. He enlisted January 1943, New Haven, CT, and trained at Officer Training Center, Columbia University.

He served aboard BB-59 as Efate ENS 5th Div. commissioning Sept. 26, 1943. Was assigned to 5th Div. 5" Control 3, LT(jg) and left BB-59 May 2, 1945, Ulithi on USS *Intrepid*. Was also assigned to Training School, Washington, DC; training Newport, RI; 1946 Boston, MA, USS *Oregon City*.

After the war he worked as assistant trainmaster, Supt. of Transportation, 1947-63; assistant to president, Research and Development; assistant to chairman, Delaware, Lackawanna & Western Railroad; 1963 Tri-State Regional (New York, New Jersey and Connecticut) Planning Commission; 1978 consultant New Jersey Transit; 1980-88 New Jersey Transit; and 1988 retired.

Married Patricia July 17, 1947, Forest Hills, NY, and has three sons, three daughters and three grandchildren. He resides at PO Box 1004, 16 Heritage Drive, South Orleans, MA, 02662.

MAIER, PHILLIP LIBERATUS, 310-75-99, enlisted Jan. 8, 1938, San Pedro, CA. He is a plankowner and served aboard BB-59 as MM1/c commissioning May 12, 1942. He resides at 6 East Logan Terrace, Danville, IL 61832.

MAINS, H. EARL, 945-00-61, born Oct. 2, 1917, Danville, IL. Graduated from high school and attended Millikin University. He enlisted May 2, 1944, and trained at Great Lakes Naval Training Station, IL. He served aboard BB-59 as S1/c N Div. August 1944 left BB-59 Dec. 18, 1945, Bremerton, WA.

After the war he worked as manager for Leath Furniture Company and is active at the St. James

Methodist Church and the Kiwanis Club. He has two sons, four grandchildren and one great grandchild.

MAJKA, JOSEF, (n) 283-22-37, enlisted Jan. 28, 1942, Boston, MA. He is a plankowner and served aboard BB-59 as WT2/c B Div. at commissioning May 12, 1942, and on board for BB-59 2nd and 3rd anniversaries. He was assigned CWT.

MAJOR, MALCOLM C., ACMM, left BB-59 Jan. 26, 1945, to R/S Navy 128 FFT to ComAirPac for assignment.

MALCOLM, DON Q., resides at 2465 Sherwood Drive, Ventura, CA 93001.

MALLON, CHARLES EDWARD, 646-62-65, enlisted Feb. 2, 1942, New York, NY. He is a plankowner and served aboard BB-59 as AS at commissioning May 12, 1942. He was assigned to radio striker, Y3/c communications and left BB-59 March 1945.

After the war he worked as a dispatcher for Humble Oil Company, Linden, NJ. He has one daughter and resides at 438 W 6th Avenue, Roselle, NJ 07203.

MALLORY, GEORGE BARRON, ENS, born April 25, 1919, New York, NY. Earned a BA from Yale University 1941 and LLB 1947. He is a plankowner and served aboard BB-59 as ENS FC Div. at commissioning May 12, 1942, and on board for BB-59 2nd anniversary.

He was assigned March 1943 LT(jg) F Div. watch officer; October 1943 LT optical officer Gun Dept. and left BB-59 July 15, 1944. After the war 1960-68 was president; 1968-70 chairman of board P.R. Mallory & Company, Inc. Indianapolis, IN; 1970-80 law firm counselor, Jacobs, Persinger & Parker. He is active in Alcoholics Anonymous; board of directors Mystic Seaport Museum, Mystic, CT; and the Episcopal Church.

Married his first wife, Eleanor, in 1941, Greenwich, CT; divorced in 1970; married second wife, Margaret, in 1971 in Texas; and divorced in 1981. He has two sons, two daughters and five grandchildren. (Son) George Mallory Jr. resides at 446 N. Warson Road, St. Louis, MO 63124. He died April 6, 1986; Memory List 1986.

MALONEY, BERNARD JOHN, 647-01-66, enlisted Feb. 20, 1942, New York, NY. He is a plankowner and served aboard BB-59 as AS at commissioning May 12, 1942. He was assigned to F1/c A Div., mechanical operation and auxiliary maintenance, and left BB-59 November 1944. After the war he was an operating engineer for General Services Administration. He is active in the American Legion Post 172, Jersey City, NJ. He resides at 219 Clendenny Ave., Jersey City, NJ 07304.

MANNIX, WILLIAM R., Memory List 1977.

MANSFIELD, JOHN JOSEPH, 606-32-02, enlisted Feb. 9, 1942, Boston, MA. He is a plankowner and served aboard BB-59 as S2/c at commissioning May 12, 1942, and on board for BB-59 2nd and 3rd anniversaries. (Mrs.) resides at 127 Mill St., Foxboro, MA 02035. Memory List 1992.

MANZIE, THORLOW WINSFIELD, 222-87-56, enlisted Oct. 7, 1940, Whitestone, NY. He is a plankowner and served aboard BB-59 as EM2/c E Div. at commissioning May 12, 1942.

MAPLES, JOHN BERNARD, 616-13-34, enlisted Dec. 29, 1941, Dallas, TX. He is a plankowner and served aboard BB-59 as EM2/c E Div. at commissioning May 12, 1942. Memory List 1977.

MARANVILLE, MARSHALL, (n) 606-29-20, enlisted Jan. 30, 1942, Boston, MA. He is a plankowner and served aboard BB-59 as AS at commissioning May 12, 1942.

MARCANTONIO, FRANK PETER, 652-26-34, enlisted March 11, 1942, Pittsburgh, PA. He is a plankowner and served aboard BB-59 as AS at commissioning May 12, 1942, and on board for BB-59 2nd and 3rd anniversaries. He resided at 529 Freeport Road, New Kensington, PA 15068.

MARCARELLI, DIONISIO, (n) 642-14-01, enlisted Feb. 24, 1942, New Haven, CT. He is a plankowner and served aboard BB-59 as AS 3rd Div. at commissioning May 12, 1942, and on board for BB-59 2nd and 3rd anniversaries. He resided at 39 N. Whittlesey St., Wallingford, CT 06492. He died May 6, 1995; Memory List 1995.

MARCHANT, WALTER EDMUND, 652-22-27, enlisted Feb. 19, 1942, Pittsburgh, PA. He is a plankowner and served aboard BB-59 as AS at commissioning May 12, 1942. He resides at Curtis St., Follansbee, WV 26037.

MARCU, NATHAN C., USMC, Norfolk Naval Yard, Norfolk, VA. He is a plankowner and served aboard BB-59 as PVT 7th Div. commissioning May 12, 1942.

MARCUS, FRANCIS A., served aboard BB-59 as CEM E Div.

MARCY, CARL JOSEPH, 606-49-34, enlisted March 12, 1942, Boston, MA. He is a plankowner and served aboard BB-59 as AS 1st Div. at commissioning May 12, 1942. Was assigned as seaman, EM2/c E Div. and left BB-59 in July 1945.

After the war he was a signal maintainer for the Boston & Maine Railroad. He is local chairman of Veterans of Foreign Wars and active in Brotherhood of Railroad Signalmen of America.

He married Alice and has one son, three daughters and 11 grandchildren. He resides at 532 Woburn St., Wilmington, MA 01887.

MARION, FRANK, JR., 646-62-67, born March 7, 1922, Windber, PA. Graduated from high school and enlisted Feb. 2, 1942, New York, NY. Trained at Newport Naval Training Station, Newport, RI. He is a plankowner and served aboard BB-59 as AS L Div. at

commissioning May 12, 1942. Was assigned as 20mm gunner, air defense lookout, R Div. and left BB-59 November 1945, Bremerton, WA. After the war he worked in bridge and road construction. He married Dorothia, Newark, NJ, and has one son. He resides at HC Rt. 1, Box 19, Margaretville, NY 12455.

MARKHAM, JOHN E., served aboard BB-59 as QM2/c N Div. February 1943 and left BB-59 November 1945. After the war he was an office manager in product engineering department for Behr-Manning Div. of Norton Company. In his spare time he was past director of Behr-Manning Employee Credit Union, Service Committee Men's Council C.C.H.S., Boy Scout Troop # 5 and church fraternal societies. He had three sons and two daughters and resided at 598 3rd Ave., Troy, NY 12182. Memory List 1986.

MARKWARD, FRANK FRANCIS, 650-20-60, enlisted Jan. 27, 1942, Philadelphia, PA. He is a plankowner and served aboard BB-59 as AS at commissioning May 12, 1942. He resides at RD3 Box 120, Coatesville, PA 19320.

MARLEY, ALBERT JOSEPH, 202-28-77, enlisted March 31, 1942, Boston, MA. He is a plankowner and served aboard BB-59 as AS at commissioning May 12, 1942, and on board for BB-59 2nd and 3rd anniversaries. He resided at 47 Main St., Somerville, MA 02143. Memory List 1981.

MARSDEN, HERBERT L., resides at 5890 49th Ave., North, St. Petersburg, FL 33733.

MARSDEN, WILLIAM FRANCIS, 201-64-33, enlisted Sept. 7, 1938, Boston, MA. He is a plankowner and served aboard BB-59 as S1/c at commissioning May 12, 1942.

MARSHALL, JOHN ROBERT, 337-06-72, enlisted May 10, 1938, St. Louis, MO. He is a plankowner and served aboard BB-59 as COX at commissioning May 12, 1942.

MARSHALL, LLOYD M., served aboard BB-59 as CTC 1st Div.

MARSHALL, RICHARD OLIVER, 606-32-13, enlisted Feb. 15, 1942, Boston, MA. He is a plankowner and served aboard BB-59 as AS at commissioning May 12, 1942, and on board for BB-59 2nd and 3rd anniversaries as plankowner.

MARSLAND, JOHN, JR., (n) 606-41-58, enlisted Feb. 26, 1942, Boston, MA. He is a plankowner and served aboard BB-59 as AS at commissioning May 12, 1942. (Mrs.) resides at 560 Mendon Rd., #129, South Attleboro, MA 02703. Memory List 1984.

MARSON, EARL W., resides at 1667 Glenmount Ave., Akron, OH 44309.

MARTENS, WILLIAM FRANK, JR., 223-52-76, enlisted June 7, 1939, New York, NY. He is a plankowner and served aboard BB-59 as GM3/c at commissioning May 12, 1942.

MARTIN, DAVID PAUL, 606-34-84, enlisted Feb. 14, 1942, Boston, MA. He is a plankowner and served aboard BB-59 as AS at commissioning May 12, 1942. He was assigned F3/c A Div. and left BB-59

March 8, 1943, to ComServForSoPac. Memory List 1977.

MARTIN, FREDERICK LESLIE, 228-01-94, enlisted May 11, 1939, New York, NY. He is a plankowner and served aboard BB-59 as Mus1/c at commissioning May 12, 1942.

MARTIN, FREDERICK MICHAEL, 658-20-19, enlisted Jan. 28, 1942, Norfolk, VA. He is a plankowner and served aboard BB-59 as SK3/c at commissioning May 12, 1942.

MARTIN, GORDON WILLIAM, LT(jg) 107102, born Nov. 21, 1918, Seattle, WA. Received a BA from Western Washington University and BS from University of Washington. Enlisted in 1936 Seattle, WA, and trained at Naval Reserve Officer Training Center, University of Washington; Sept. 1, 1941, commissioned ensign; Sept. 1, 1941 to June 1, 1942, Naval Training Station, Newport, RI; June 9, 1942, Boston, MA.

He served aboard BB-59 as LT(jg) R Div. July 1942 and assigned duty JO, Battle Station Repair 1-A. He left BB-59 July 31, 1943, Noumea, New Caledonia. Was also assigned from Aug. 1, 1943, to March 14, 1944, commander South Pacific Fleet; July 22, 1944, to Aug. 3, 1944, PCO training LSM's; Aug. 3, 1944, to Nov. 30, 1945, CO USS LSM-233; Feb. 15, 1946 to June 24, 1946, staff LST Squadron 2; June 28, 1946, to May 29, 1947, General Line School, Newport, RI; June 1, 1947, to June 26, 1948, commander LSM Div. 21; Aug. 10, 1948, to July 31, 1950, CO USS *Purvis.*

Marine Corps Schools, Aug. 16, 1950, to Dec. 22, 1950; Jan. 1, 1951, to July 2, 1953, CO USS *Bowers;* July 8, 1953, Fleet Sonar School, Key West, FL; Aug. 27, 1953, to Nov. 6, 1953, commander in chief Atlantic Fleet, Norfolk, VA; November 1953 to June 1954 Naval Hospital, Portsmouth, VA; June 1954 to July 1954 Fifth Naval District; July 26, 1954, to Oct. 31, 1956, Office of Naval Research, Washington, DC; Dec. 7, 1956, to Oct. 25, 1958, Military Sea Transportation Service, Anchorage, AK; Nov. 15, 1958, to July 20, 1960, staff commander Western Sea Frontier, San Francisco, CA; Aug. 10, 1960, to Sept. 1, 1961, commander Columbia River Group Pacific Reserve Fleet, Astoria, OR.

Retired from active duty as LT CMDR Sept. 1, 1951, after 21 years, eight months and 16 days of service. He received Command-At-Sea and qualified for Command of Destroyers awards. Retired after 15 years as head of mathematics department at Tyee High School, Seattle, WA, and sold real estate for three years. He enjoys trail rides, hunting and fishing and traveling in motor-home.

He married Dorothy and has one son, one daughter and one grandchild. He resides at 19232 33rd Ave. So., Seattle, WA 98188.

MARTIN, HARRY RALPH, 244-06-34, born Sept. 12, 1923, Middle Township, NJ. He enlisted Feb. 25, 1942, Philadelphia, PA, and trained at Naval Training Station, Newport, RI. He is a plankowner and served aboard BB-59 as AS 1st Div. at commissioning May 12, 1942.

He was assigned July 1943 S1/c 1st Div. and Nov. 21, 1945, COX 1st Div. He left BB-59 in Norfolk, VA, and assigned to USS LSM-547. Discharged Dec. 23, 1946, Brooklyn, NY.

After the war he earned his pilot's license and was employed crop dusting for Young's Flying Service, Wildwood, NJ; worked in a service station; body and fender repair shop; owned a custard; sold his business and retired. He is active in the American Legion, Disabled Americans Veterans, 4-H Clubs, and is president of Volunteer Fire Company.

He has two daughters and five grandchildren. He resides at 675 Dias Creek Rd., Cape May Courthouse, NJ 08210.

MARTIN, HENRY DENNIS, JR., LT, 098277, born Sept. 5, 1916, North Bergen, NJ. Attended St. Francis College, Loretto, PA, and enlisted August 1940, New York, NY. Attended Midshipman School USS *Prairie State*, NY 1941; August 1940 to Oct. 21, 1942, USS *Hornet* (CV-8); January 1942 to June 1943 USS *Lexington* (CV-12); June to September 1943 Naval Flight Training; and August 1943 to May 1944 USS *Franklin*.

He served aboard BB-59 as LT 4th Div. at commissioning May 20, 1944, and assigned machine gun officer, Quadrant Control. He left BB-59 as LCDO Dec. 13, 1945, Bremerton, WA.

After the war he was a distributor for Chevron Oil Company and a franchisee for Sheraton Hotel. He is active in the Naval Reserve; Trenton, NJ, County Club; and founding member of Adios Golf Club, Coconut Creek, FL.

He married Victoria May 21, 1955, Burlington, NJ, and has two sons and one daughter. He resides at 2455 S. Ocean Blvd., Highland Beach, FL 33487.

MARTIN, J.H., LT(jg) served aboard BB-59 July 1942 as LT(jg) CR Div. and was assigned March 1943 duty officer, Battle Station Radio III.

MARTIN, ROBERT F., 258-44-23, born Feb. 22, 1925, Everett, MA. He attended Bentley School of Accounting and holds a degree in hypnotherapy and psychic science from Providence College. He enlisted April 1942 in Baltimore, MD, and trained aboard USS *Alabama*. He served aboard BB-59 as AS FC Div. June 1942 and left BB-59 March 2, 1946, S1/c Bainbridge, MD. He was also assigned oil tanker.

After the war he worked as a salesman and an accountant. In his spare time he was a practicing hypnotherapist.

He married Jean in 1955 at St. Catherine's Church, Norwood, MA, and had three sons and nine grandchildren. (Mrs.) resides at 19 William Shyne Circle, Apt. 14, Norwood, MA 02062. He died Nov. 17, 1992; Memory List 1992.

MARTINEZ, ANGEL, (n) 342-63-80, enlisted Jan. 20, 1942, Kansas City, MO. He is a plankowner and served aboard BB-59 as AS at commissioning May 12, 1942, and on board for BB-59 2nd and 3rd anniversaries.

MARTO, WILLIAM, 652-26-30, enlisted March 11, 1942, Pittsburgh, PA. He is a plankowner and served aboard BB-59 commissioning May 12, 1942.

MASON, CLIFTON EARLE, served aboard BB-59 as MoMM2/c A Div. and was assigned MoMM1/c. After the war he worked as a lubrication engineer and is active in Veterans of Foreign Wars #799. He resides at PO Box 202, Hooksett, NH 03100.

MASSECCI, JOHN L., USMC, May 8, 1942, Norfolk Navy Yard. He is a plankowner and served aboard BB-59 as PVT 7th Div. at commissioning May 12, 1942.

MASSENZIO, JOHN J., USMC, May 8, 1942, Norfolk Naval Yard. He is a plankowner and served aboard BB-59 as PVT 7th Div. at commissioning May 12, 1942. He resides at 3 Ring Liquor Store, Plainfield St., Providence, RI 02940.

MASSEY, JAMES KARL, 267-89-62, enlisted Oct. 7, 1941, Pearl Harbor, HI. He is a plankowner and served aboard BB-59 as GM1/c at commission-

ing May 12, 1942, and on board for BB-59 2nd anniversary.

MASTERSON, RAYMOND D., served aboard BB-59 as EM2/c E Div. commissioning November 1942 and was assigned to #3 and 4 switchboard. He left BB-59 in December 1945. After the war he was a metalsmith for the US Navy. He has one son, one daughter and three grandchildren. He resides at 63 Pembroke Lane, Coventry, RI 02816.

MATHESON, CARTER, resides at Vilas, NC 28692.

MATHIAS, PETER JOHN, 652-19-88, enlisted Feb. 11, 1942, Pittsburgh, PA. He is a plankowner and served aboard BB-59 as AS at commissioning May 12, 1942, and on board for BB-59 2nd and 3rd anniversaries. He resides at 1334 Pierce Ave., Sharpsville, PA 16150.

MATHIESON, LOUIS RAYMOND, 328-69-44, born Dec. 19, 1920, Minneapolis, MN. Graduated from high school and enlisted May 22, 1940, Minneapolis, MN. Trained at Naval Training Station, Great Lakes, IL; served aboard USS *Oklahoma* (BB-37), USS *Hull* (DD-350) and USS *Whitney* (AD-4). He served aboard BB-59 as F1/c A Div. at commissioning May 12, 1942, and is a plankowner. Assigned After Emergency Diesel Generator Room, Foreward Emergency Generator Room, (2) Forward Pump Rooms, Air System and MM2/c. He left BB-59 Dec. 23, 1943, Efate, New Hebrides.

Other Naval assignments include: Naval Training Diesel School, Cleveland, OH; instructor Naval Training Center, Great Lakes, IL; discharged May 19, 1946, as MoMM1/c. He was honored for his account on the attack Dec. 7, 1941, on USS *Oklahoma*. Trip to Oklahoma, OK with Admiral Arleigh Burke, chief of Naval Operations in Secretary of the Navy's plane. Made honorary colonel by J.E. Wilson, governor of Oklahoma.

After the war he worked for Standard Oil Company for 22 and a half years as a truck driver; captain and relief chief engineer on tanker *SS Cape Anne Socony* for 16 years; master electrician; and electrical contractor, Mathieson Electric Inc. He spends his spare time with Coastal Transport taking cancer patients for treatment, electrical work for town of Owl's Head, Habitat for Humanity, the Rockland Congregational Church.

He married Vera Feb. 6, 1944, Rockland, ME, and has two sons, three daughters, nine grandchildren and four great-grandchildren. He resides at HC 32, Box 325, Rockland, ME 04841.

MATIGZECK, JOHN FRANCIS, 647-01-67, enlisted Feb. 20, 1942, New York, NY. He is a plankowner and served aboard BB-59 as AS at commissioning May 12, 1942, and on board for BB-59 2nd anniversary. Memory List 1980.

MATTEI, SILVIO, (n) 207-29-80, born Jan. 30, 1922, New Haven, CT. He enlisted Oct. 22, 1940, New Haven, CT, and served aboard USS *Colorado*. He is a plankowner and served aboard BB-59 as S1/c 5th Div. at commissioning May 12, 1942, and on board for BB-59 2nd anniversary. He was assigned GM1/c.

After the war he worked for 11 years at the *New Haven Register* newspaper, New Haven, CT. He was active in the Knights of Columbus, Father Club, Sacred Heart Academy, and Blessed Sacrament Church.

He married Amelia July 12, 1945, New Haven, CT, and has two sons, three daughters and eight grandchildren. Mary Mattei (daughter) resides at 49 Beechwood Ave., Hamden, CT 06514. He died October 21, 1991; Memory List 1992.

MATTHEWS, GLENN BURR, served aboard BB-59 as CGM FC Div. April 6, 1944, and assigned JO, assistant SB Plot Office Ordnance. He left BB-59 Oct. 11, 1945.

MATTHEWS, JOSEPH PATRICK, 606-48-72, enlisted March 10, 1942, Boston, MA. He was a plankowner and served aboard BB-59 as AS 3rd Div. at commissioning May 12, 1942. He was assigned #3 Turret, Gun Elevation Layer, Gun CAPT 40mm Mount, GM3/c and left BB-59 May 10, 1944. After the war he worked as a pressman for Fashion Press. He was a commander and chaplain for the American Legion in his spare time. He resided at 884 Olympic Ave., Banning, CA 92220. He died Feb. 19, 1994; Memory List 1994.

MATYKA, CHESTER TEOPHILO, 606-16-26, enlisted Jan. 5, 1942, Boston, MA. He is a plankowner and served aboard BB-59 as CM3/c at commissioning May 12, 1942.

MAURIER, LIONEL EUGENE, 606-33-95, enlisted Feb. 12, 1942, Boston, MA. He is a plankowner and served aboard BB-59 as AS at commissioning May 12, 1942, and on board for BB-59 2nd and 3rd anniversaries. He resides at 154 Grove St., Haverhill, MA 01830.

MAURER, RUDOLPH JOHN, 299-25-71, enlisted Jan. 3, 1942, Chicago, IL. He is a plankowner and served aboard BB-59 as MM2/c M Div. at commissioning May 12, 1942, and was assigned to M Div. CMM.

MAVROGEORGE, AVION ALEXANDER, 606-33-56, born Nov. 29, 1921, Manchester, NH. Graduated from high school and enlisted Feb. 9, 1942, Boston, MA. Trained at Naval Training Station, Newport, RI. He served aboard BB-59 April 1942 Quincy Shipyard and as AS 4th Div. at commissioning May 12, 1942 as a plankowner. Was assigned as gunner 40mm, yeoman striker, S1/c CR Div. and left BB-59 November 1945. He was discharged Dec. 2, 1945, Boston, MA.

After the war he worked for 11 years in Mills Dry Cleaners; 11 years owner and manager One Hour Martiniging; and 25 years owner and manager A&A Cleaners; He is retired. In his spare time he was chief of staff Manchester Veterans Council; Honorable Mention from Veterans Council; received BB-59 Award, 1989; and Field Day (crew chief), Fall River, MA. He resides at 39 Fairmount Ave., Manchester, NH 03104-5612.

MAYES, JAMES L., served aboard BB-59 in FC Div. He resides at 205 South 4th, Shelbina, MO 64368.

MAYHEW, SAMUEL AUGUSTUS, JR., 602-04-47, enlisted Dec. 16, 1941, Baltimore, MD. He is a plankowner and served aboard BB-59 as SF1/c at commissioning May 12, 1942.

MAYNE, RALPH ELMER, 666-15-72, enlisted Feb. 9, 1942, Springfield, MA. He is a plankowner and served aboard BB-59 as AS at commissioning May 12, 1942.

MAYNOR, SAM FORREST, 262-30-00, enlisted Dec. 19, 1941, Pearl Harbor, HI. He is a plankowner and served aboard BB-59 as S1/c N Div. at commissioning May 12, 1942. He resides at Rock Hill, SC 27730.

MAYOTTE, HENRY ALAN, JR., 606-49-27, enlisted March 12, 1942, Boston, MA. He is a plankowner and served aboard BB-59 as AS 2nd Div. at commissioning May 12, 1942, and on board for BB-59 2nd and 3rd anniversaries. He resides at 3305 Leonard Rd., Grants Pass, OR 97526.

MAZZANTI, FIORE, resides at PO Box 388, Lake Village, AR 71653.

MCALEER, CHARLES LEO, 650-32-14, enlisted Feb. 24, 1942, Philadelphia, PA, and trained at Naval Training Station, Newport, RI.

He is a plankowner and served aboard BB-59 as AS X Div. commissioning May 12, 1942, and on his 2nd anniversary. He was assigned SK3/c S Div. and left BB-59 January 1945 after Philippines Operations. He was assigned to Wildwood Naval Air Station, Wildwood, NJ, SK2/c and discharged September 1945.

In his spare time he is a finance officer for Philadelphia American Legion Council, and treasurer for Philadelphia American Legion Convention Corp.

He married Marie 1951, Philadelphia, PA, and has one daughter. He resides at 6519 Walnut Park Drive, Philadelphia, PA 19120-1031.

MCALEER, FRANCIS RAYMOND, 256-33-90, enlisted Dec. 12, 1939, Washington, DC. He is a plankowner and served aboard BB-59 as S1/c 5th Div. commissioning May 12, 1942. He resides at 8110 Riggs Road, Adelphi, MD 20783.

MCALLISTER, RICHARD GEORGE, 646-01-64, enlisted June 10, 1941, New York, NY. He is a plankowner and served aboard BB-59 as PHM1/c H Div. commissioning May 12, 1942. He left BB-59 in June 1944. After the war he was an agent for Prudential Insurance Company. He married Ruth (deceased) and has six sons, seven daughters, 19 grandchildren and six great-grandchildren. He resides at 9 Potomac St., West Roxbury, MA 02132.

MCAVENE, STEPHEN EDWARD, 337-48-03, enlisted Dec. 12, 1940, St. Louis, MO. He is a plankowner and served aboard BB-59 as S1/c at commissioning May 12, 1942.

MCAVOY, RICHARD, Memory List 1996.

MCBLAIN, WILLIAM LEO, LT, served aboard BB-59 as LT N Div. Aug. 7, 1943, and assigned chaplain. He left BB-59 July 10, 1944. Memory List 1977.

MCBRIDE, JAMES DEWEY, 640-04-14, born in McMinnville, TN. Graduated from high school and enlisted Sept. 26, 1941, Nashville, TN. He trained at Navy Radio School.

He was a plankowner and served aboard BB-59 as S2/c May 12, 1942. He was assigned to radio, copied news broadcasts, RM1/c and left BB-59 September 1945 Bremerton, WA. After the war he worked for three and a half years for Power Matic Machine Company and 31 years a machine (fixer) Rockford Textile Company.

He enjoyed fishing in his spare time. He married Kassie in 1957 and had one son, one stepson and one stepdaughter. (Mrs.) resides at 581 East Rivercliff Road, McMinnville, TN 37710. Memory List 1996.

MCBRIDE, JULIAN PERRITT, 261-55-33, enlisted Jan. 12, 1942, Washington, DC. He is a plankowner and served aboard BB-59 as WT1/c at commissioning May 12, 1942. He was assigned CWT and left BB-59 July 12, 1944. Was also assigned to Water Tender Center, San Francisco, CA.

MCCABE, CHARLES H., born Jan. 31, 1912, Ansonia, CT. Graduated from high school and enlisted Aug. 12, 1942, Newburgh, NY. Trained at Naval Training Station, Newport, RI, and Radio School, Bedford Springs, PA.

He served aboard BB-59 as RM3/c CR Div. at commissioning Jan. 31, 1943, and assigned Radio Watch RM2/c CR Div. He left BB-59 Sept. 13, 1945, Bremerton, WA. After the war he worked 1945-54 Typewriter Service State Store; 1954-63, owned service and sales business; 1963-87, serviced office machines; and 1987 retired. Is active in Civil Defense and Rotary Club.

He married Marjorie Sept. 13, 1932, Ithaca, NY, and has one son. He resides at 519 Lombardy Blvd., Brightwater, NY 11718.

MCCABE, JOHN JEROME, 647-01-60, enlisted Feb. 20, 1942, New York, NY. He is a plankowner and served aboard BB-59 as AS at commissioning May 12, 1942.

MCCABE, ROBERT JEROME, 652-25-78, enlisted March 9, 1942, Pittsburgh, PA. He is a plankowner and served aboard BB-59 as AS at commissioning May 12, 1942, and on board for BB-59 2nd anniversary.

MCCAMMAN, PERCY KELLY, 375-51-32, enlisted April 21, 1942, Boston, MA. He is a plankowner and served aboard BB-59 as CEM E Div. at commissioning May 12, 1942. He was assigned electric line jr. officer and left BB-59 Jan. 26, 1945.

MCCANN, GERALD FRANCIS, 224-77-61, enlisted March 30, 1942, New York, NY. He is a plankowner and served aboard BB-59 as AS at commissioning May 12, 1942, and on board for BB-59 2nd and 3rd anniversaries.

MCCARTHY, EDWARD, Memory List 1990.

MCCARTHY, WILLIAM E., served aboard BB-59 as YEO3/c F Div. on August 1942. He was assigned 16" battery gunnery yeoman and left BB-59 October 1945. After the war he worked as an investigator for 1st National City Bank; detective for the New York Police Dept. for 20 years and is retired. He is active in the American Legion. He has one son and one daughter. He resides at 2123 E 38th St., Brooklyn, NY 11202.

MCCARTY, CLEYLOR L., DR., his wife resides at 1304 Kitchen St., Jonesboro, AR 72401.

MCCHESSNEY, WILLIAM T., ENS, served aboard BB-59 as ENS CS Div. at commissioning December 1942 and assigned assistant signal officer, coding, battle station FC Tower, LT. He resides at 302 High St., Dayton, VA 22821.

MCCLAIN, BARTON WILLIAM JR., Memory List 1996.

MCCLISTER, JOSEPH WILLIAM, 244-06-35, enlisted Feb. 25, 1942, Philadelphia, PA. He is a plankowner and served aboard BB-59 as AS at commissioning May 12, 1942.

MCCOLEY, BERNARD C., resides at 320 E 73rd St., New York, NY 10001.

MCCOLLOUGH, P.R., 294-42-79, resides at 515 Malaga St., Wenatchee, WA 98801.

MCCOY, LOWELL LANNING, ENS 187390, born July 16, 1919, Mount Vernon, OH. He received a BA in business from Ohio University in 1942. He enlisted September 1942 Mansfield, OH, and trained at V-7 Program, Notre Dame University; Officer Training, Northwestern University; January 1943 Coastal Patrol, Morrow Bay, CA; Exec. officer USS YP-369; communication relay ship, *SS Paul Revere* to Noumea, New Caledonia.

He served aboard BB-59 as ENS JO 4th Div. May 23, 1943, Noumea, New Caledonia. Was assigned LT(jg) JO 3rd Div. in October 1943 and LT command 1st Div., Turret 1 officer June 1944. He left BB-59 Sept. 15, 1945, Seattle, WA. After the war he worked as a US Treasury agent 1945-74 and retired in 1974. He spends his spare time in sports, reading, travel and music.

He married Fran May 24, 1944, North Canton, OH, and has one son and three daughters. He resides at 75 Long Ben Lane, Nokomis, FL 34275.

MCCRADY, JOE E., served aboard BB-59 in B Div. and resides at 108 Fairview Box 882, Smyrna, TN 37167.

MCCREA, JOSEPH JAMES, 207-38-33, enlisted April 1, 1942, New Haven, CT. He is a plankowner and served aboard BB-59 as AS at commissioning May 12, 1942.

MCCUE, JOHN KENNETH, LT COMDR, Naval Academy 1928, served aboard BB-59 in September 1942 and assigned LT COMDR engineering officer March 1943 and damage control welfare aud. commander Oct. 1, 1943.

MCCULLOGH, E.L., served aboard BB-59 in 4th Div. He resides at 2300 West Broadway, Moses Lake, WA 9883.

MCCULLOUGH, PAUL RANDALL, 245-42-79, enlisted July 12, 1942, Nashville, TN. He is a plankowner and served aboard BB-59 as EM3/c E Div. at commissioning May 12, 1942. He resides at 139 Fairview Drive, Maryville, TN 37801.

MCCUTCHEON, GILBERT L., resides at 268 Q Avenida Sevilla, Laguna Hills, CA 92653.

MCDANIEL, WILBUR LESLIE, ENS, served aboard BB-59 in 5th Div. May 31, 1944, and assigned LT(jg) 5th Control Spot July 1945.

MCDONALD, THOMAS J., (Mrs.) resides at 240 Lake St., Newburgh, NY 12550. Memory List 1979.

MCDONNELL, JAMES L., USMC, May 8, 1942, Norfolk Navy Yard. He is a plankowner and served aboard BB-59 as corporal 7th Div. at commissioning May 12, 1942.

MCDOWELL, JOHN CHARLES, 375-13-86, enlisted Jan. 3, 1942, San Francisco, Ca. He is a plankowner and served aboard BB-59 as CCM R Div. at commissioning May 12, 1942, and left BB-59 July 13, 1944, Bremerton, WA.

MCDOWELL, ROBERT HAMILTON, 250-73-12, enlisted April 2, 1942, Pittsburgh, PA. He is a plankowner and served aboard BB-59 as AS at commissioning May 12, 1942. Memory List 1990.

MCFARLAND, EUGENE CLARK, 668-30-90, enlisted Jan. 21, 1942, St. Louis, MO. He is a plankowner and served aboard BB-59 as AS at commissioning May 12, 1942.

MCFAYDEN, HARRY, served aboard BB-59 as SM3/c CS Div. at commissioning May 12, 1942. A plankowner. Was assigned to L Div. and left BB-59 November 1945. After the war he worked as a plumber foreman for L.A. Dobson, Inc. (Mrs.) resides at 86 West 33rd St., #403, Bayonne, NJ 07002. Memory List 1989.

MCGARRAUGH, MAURY MAVERICK, ENS, served aboard BB-59 as ENS P Div. at commissioning May 12, 1942, and is a plankowner. He was assigned to W and JO LT(jg) A Div. March 13; and W & JO, Battle Station Mach #2, LT Oct. 1, 1943. He left BB-59 on Nov. 1, 1945.

MCGARRY, JOHN R., served aboard BB-59 in 4th Div. He resides at 1656 Country Club Rd., Youngstown, OH 44514.

MCGEE, CLARENCE E., USMC, May 8, 1942, Norfolk Navy Yard. He is a plankowner and served aboard BB-59 as corporal 7th Div. commissioning May 12, 1942.

MCGEE, FRANCIS WILEY, 616-12-75, enlisted Dec. 31, 1941, Dallas, TX. He is a plankowner and served aboard BB-59 as EM3/c E Div. at commissioning May 12, 1942, and on board for BB-59 2nd and 3rd anniversaries.

MCGOLDRICK, LOUIS H., served aboard BB-59 as WT3/c B Div. November 1944 and was assigned Water Tender #1 Fireroom. He left BB-59 in June 1946.

After the war he worked as secretary-manager for the Memphis Chapter National Electrical Contractors Assoc., Inc. He is active in the American Legion in his spare time. He resides at 3782 Norriswood Ave., Memphis, TN 38111.

MCGOWAN, WILLIAM EUGENE, 650-26-74, born May 4, 1913, Wilmington, DE. Attended St. Patrick's Parochial School and enlisted Feb. 10, 1942,

Philadelphia, PA. Trained at Newport Naval Training Station, Newport, RI.

He is a plankowner and served aboard BB-59 as AS 1st Div. at commissioning May 12, 1942. Was assigned COX 1st Div. and left November 1945 Bremerton, WA. He was discharged Nov. 10, 1945, Bainbridge, MD.

After the war he worked as keyman inventory, receiving and shipping departments for Electric Hose & Rubber Company. He enjoys gardening and sports in his spare time.

He married Mary July 30, 1946, and resides at 4668 Malden Drive, Wilmington, DE 19803.

MCGRAW, ROBERT L., resides at 6345 Jackson Ave., St. Louis, MO 63134.

MCGUIRE, EDMUND JAMES, 646-52-33, enlisted Jan. 22, 1942, New York, NY. He is a plankowner and served aboard BB-59 as AS at commissioning May 12, 1942, and on board for BB-59 2nd and 3rd anniversaries.

MCGUIRE, JOHN, resides in Denton, TN 41053.

MCGUIRE, JULIUS PAUL, 287-52-04, enlisted Jan. 23, 1941, Louisville, KY. He is a plankowner and served aboard BB-59 as S1/c commissioning May 12, 1942.

MCGURN, EDWARD MARTIN, 204-37-60, enlisted Jan. 29, 1936, Washington, DC. He is a plankowner and served aboard BB-59 as CRM CR Div. at commissioning May 12, 1942. He was assigned assistant to radio officer, radio reports and left BB-59 Nov. 30, 1944.

MCHALE, JOHN JOSEPH, LT(jg) 225464, born Oct. 3, 1917, Philadelphia, PA. Earned a BA from LaSalle College, 1941 and enlisted August 1942 Philadelphia, PA. Trained at Army Air Corp., Maxwell Field, Montgomery, AL, January to August 1942; Basic Training, Dorr Field, Arcadia, FL; Primary Flight School, Shaw Field, Sumpter, SC; Basic Flight School, Army Air Corps Base, Nashville, TN.

Discharged August 1942 and sworn into Navy in Philadelphia, PA. On Dec. 7, 1942, Midshipman School, Columbia University, New York; Lookout School, Columbus, OH; Navy Signal School University of Illinois, Champaign, IL; Advance Recognition and Refresher Class Recognition, Columbus, OH; LT(jg) General and Recognition Instructor Sampson Navy Base, NY; Recognition Instructor Signal School, Champaign, IL.

He served aboard BB-59 Sept. 29, 1944, Saipan as LT I Div. and assigned lookout officer, recognition officer and gunnery department. He left BB-59 Jan. 25, 1946.

After the war he was a livestock and corn bean farmer, Ivesdale, IL; custom hay baler and salesman; licensed title, licensed remitter and notary public; and multi-township assessor. He has been a 4-H leader, softball manager, Farm Bureau member, Democratic precinct committee man and Champaign County chairman.

He married Catherine Oct. 3, 1945, St. Boniface, Seymour, IL, and has four sons, 10 daughters and 25 grandchildren. He resides at 202 4th St., Box 144, Ivesdale, IL 61851.

MCHOUL, SAMUEL, (n) 202-18-40, enlisted Feb. 23, 1942, Boston, MA. He was a plankowner and served aboard BB-59 as AS at commissioning May 12, 1942. Memory List 1987.

MCHUGH, WILLIAM ROBERT, 202-22-38, enlisted Feb. 23, 1942, Boston, MA. He is a plankowner and served aboard BB-59 as AS at commissioning May 12, 1942.

MCILVAINE, EDWARD JOSEPH, 650-32-04, enlisted Feb. 24, 1942, Philadelphia, PA. He is a plankowner and served aboard BB-59 as AS at commissioning May 12, 1942.

MCKAIG, WILLIAM V., LT COM, attended US Naval Academy, 1931 and served aboard BB-59 as senior assistant engineer, captain March 1943. Memory List 1981.

MCKAY, ROBERT DONALD, 666-19-91, born Nov. 20, 1921, Ware, MA. Graduated from high school and enlisted March 6, 1942, Springfield, MA. He served aboard BB-59 as AS 3rd Div. at commissioning May 12, 1942, and left December 1943 South Pacific. Was also assigned to USS *Tulazi* COX Dec. 23, 1943; Naval Air Station, Jacksonville, FL, BM2/c October 1944; and was discharged Oct. 1, 1945.

After the war he worked as a truck driver for a grain store for five years; 25 years for the Massachusetts Department of Public Works as a highway repair foreman. He retired Nov. 20, 1979. In his spare time he worked for volunteer fire department, Wales, MA, and volunteer police department, Wales, MA.

He married Alice October 1944 (deceased Aug. 3, 1985). He married Buella March 13, 1989. He has two sons, two daughters and 12 grandchildren. He resides at PO Box 927, Hermando, FL 34442.

MCKEE, ARTHUR LAWRENCE, 274-66-35, enlisted March 26, 1941, New Orleans, LA. He is a plankowner and served aboard BB-59 as S1/c at commissioning May 12, 1942.

MCKEE, CALVIN CRAWFORD, 652-27-48, enlisted March 19, 1942, Pittsburgh, PA. He is a plankowner and served aboard BB-59 as AS at commissioning May 12, 1942.

MCKEE, LEO, (n) 311-42-42, born Dec. 28, 1914, North Baltimore, OH. Graduated from high school and enlisted March 13, 1940, Detroit, MA. Trained at Naval Training Station, Great Lakes, IL; USS *New Mexico*; and Flight Service School Navy Base, San Diego, CA.

He was a plankowner and served aboard BB-59 as S1/c F Div. at commissioning May 12, 1942, and assigned GM1. He was discharged April 10, 1946.

He married Mildred July 2, 1942, Findlay, OH, and had one son and one grandchild. Last address was 334 Edith Ave., Findlay, Oh 45840. He died Feb. 9, 1989, Memory List 1993.

MCKEE, RICARD JOSEPH, 647-01-62, enlisted Feb. 20, 1942, New York, NY. He is a plankowner and served aboard BB-59 as AS at commissioning May 12, 1942, and on board for BB-59 2nd anniversary.

MCKEEVER, DANIEL JOSEPH, JR., 650-32-13, enlisted Feb. 24, 1942, Philadelphia, PA. He is a plankowner and served aboard BB-59 as AS 2nd Div. at commissioning May 12, 1942, and on board for BB-59 3rd anniversary. He resides at 412 Kent Road, Bala Cynwyd, PA 19004.

MCKENNEY, REGINALD T., served aboard BB-59 in L and A Div. He resides at PO Box 27, Dexter, ME 04930.

MCKENZIE, JOHN CHASE, LT, served aboard BB-59 as LT X Div. commissioning July 28, 1943, and assigned aide to executive officer, personnel ship store treasurer. He left BB-59 May 19, 1944.

MCLAIN, BARTON WILLIAM, JR., 606-34-61, enlisted Feb. 9, 1942, Boston, MA. He is a plankowner and served aboard BB-59 as AS 3rd Div. at commissioning May 12, 1942, and on board for BB-59 2nd anniversary.

He resided at 38 Brown St., Whitefield, NH 03598. Memory List 1996,

MCLAIN, IRWIN A., served aboard BB-59 as Mach July 1945.

MCLAINE, V.A., resided at Charlestown, SC (1965).

MCLAUGHLIN, JOHN F., resided at RFD #5, Brewer, ME 04412 (1955).

MCLAUGHLIN, THOMAS FRANCIS, 650-32-06, enlisted Feb. 24, 1942, Philadelphia, PA.

He is a plankowner and served aboard BB-59 as AS at commissioning May 12, 1942, and on board for BB-59 2nd and 3rd anniversaries.

MCLEAN, HEBER H., CAPT, commanding officer from Jan. 22, 1946, to Aug. 5, 1946.

MCLEOD, KENNETH JAMES, 300-41-59, born in 1923, Minneapolis, MN. Graduated from high school and enlisted March 26, 1941, Chicago, IL. Trained at Naval Training Station, Great Lakes, IL, and USS *Idaho* (YTB-539).

He served aboard BB-59 April 1942 Quincy, MA, Shipyard and as S1/c 2nd Div. at commissioning May 12, 1942, and on board for BB-59 2nd and 3rd anniversaries as a plankowner. Was assigned BM1/c 6th Div. and master at arms 2nd Div.

After the war he worked for 28 years for Trane Company, Mac's Sealing, DePere, WI. He is a life member of Disabled American Veterans, Veterans of Foreign Wars, American Legion, Scoutmaster Troop #86, Decora Lodge #177 AF&AM, and Chapter 206 OES.

He has three sons and seven grandchildren. He resides at 310 So. Main St., Ehrick, WI 54627.

MCLIN, STANLEY WAYNE, 291-58-68, enlisted June 13, 1939, Indianapolis, IN. He is a plankowner and served aboard BB-59 as F2/c at commissioning May 12, 1942.

MCMANUS, JOHN, Memory List 1988.

MCNALLY, JAMES ANTHONY, COMDR, attended US Naval Academy 1925. Served aboard BB-59 as COMDR January 1944 and assigned executive officer May 12, 1944. Was also assigned as rear admiral. (Mrs.) resides at 18 Elizabeth Road, Upper Montclair, NJ 07043. Memory List 1979 RADM.

MCNALLY, WILLIAM JOHN, 133-70-78, enlisted Sept. 16, 1935, San Diego, CA. He is a plankowner and served aboard BB-59 as CWT at commissioning May 12, 1942.

MCNAMARA, BERTRAM MATHIAS, ENS, served aboard BB-59 ENS I Div. and assigned assistant R.C.M. officer.

MCNAUL, ROBERT J., born Aug. 29, 1925, Butte, MT. Graduated from high school and attended Technical Trade School, San Diego, CA. He enlisted Seattle, WA, Aug. 20, 1943, and trained V12A Aviation Cadet, Farrigut, ID; Livermore Naval Air Station and V12A Helena College, MT.

He served aboard BB-59 as S2/c and assigned Ship Fitters S1/c, Radar Counter Measures and Radar Operator RDM3/c. He left BB-59 in San Francisco, Ca. After the war he was owner and operator of Bob's Auto Repair & Towing Service; worked at Spar Electronics, Inc., Electronics Engineer Ryam; owner and operator of Modular Power, Inc., San Diego, CA.

In his spare time he is director of the Mobile Home Owners Assoc., San Diego, CA; responsible for new state and county legislation; earned his pilot license; designer and manufacturer of 100 products (electronic); and enjoys sailing.

He has one son and seven grandchildren and resides at 4938 Old Cliff's Road, San Diego, CA 92120.

MCNEIL, C.R., resides at 172 Morgan St., Fall River, MA 02722.

MCNUTT, VELMER RAY, 346-82-20, enlisted July 10, 1940, Little Rock, AR. He is a plankowner and served aboard BB-59 as F2/c at commissioning May 12, 1942.

MCPEAK, GREGORY, W., 898-69-32, joined the Navy May 11, 1944, Syracuse, NY, and trained at USNTS Sampson, NY. He served aboard BB-59 as S1/c radar operator. He resides at 4791 State Rd. 19 South, Belmont, NY.

MCQUADE, PETER JOHN, 628-05-11, enlisted Oct. 24, 1941, Kansas City, MO. He is a plankowner and served aboard BB-59 as F2/c B Div. at commissioning May 12, 1942, and on board for BB-59 2nd anniversary. He resides at 414 East 6, Ellinwood, KS 67526.

MEADE, JAMES DONALD, Memory List 1993.

MEDAGLIO, MICHAEL JOHN, 224-78-79, born in New York, NY. He graduated from high school and enlisted April 2, 1942, New York, NY. Trained at Newport Naval Training Station, Newport, RI. He is a plankowner and served aboard BB-59 as AS 1st Div. at commissioning May 12, 1942, and on board for BB-59 2nd and 3rd anniversaries. He was assigned COX 1st Div. and left BB-59 April 4, 1946, San Francisco, CA.

After the war he worked as an oil burner serviceman for V.S. Smyth Fuel Service & Sure Fire Fuel Company for 40 years. He retired March 31, 1987. He enjoys traveling in his spare time.

He has two sons, one daughter and three grandchildren. He resides at 134 Ridgewood Road, Washington Twp., NJ 07675-5123.

MEDLIN, EDWARD LEE, 266-15-28, enlisted Aug. 7, 1940, Norfolk, VA. He is a plankowner and served aboard BB-59 as S1/c at commissioning May 12, 1942.

MEDVETZ, EDWARD JOHN, 646-63-83, enlisted Feb. 3, 1942, New York, NY. He is a plankowner

and served aboard BB-59 as AS at commissioning May 12, 1942, and on board for BB-59 2nd and 3rd anniversaries.

MEEHAN, FRANCIS WILLIAM, 642-14-20, enlisted Feb. 25, 1942, New Haven, CT. He was a plankowner and served aboard BB-59 as AS at commissioning May 12, 1942, and on board for BB-59 2nd and 3rd anniversaries. Memory List 1977.

MEEHAN, JOHN EDWARD, 321-22-13, enlisted Dec. 14, 1937, Des Moines, IA. He is a plankowner and served aboard BB-59 as F1/c at commissioning May 12, 1942.

MEEKS, WILLIAM HENRY, JR., 287-37-42, enlisted Feb. 28, 1940, Louisville, KY. He is a plankowner and served aboard BB-59 as S1/c commissioning May 12, 1942.

MEGAHAN, EARL JOHN, 258-29-87, enlisted Aug. 20, 1940, Baltimore, MD. He is a plankowner and served aboard BB-59 as S1/c at commissioning May 12, 1942, and on board for BB-59 2nd and 3rd anniversaries. He was assigned CMB R Div.

MEIER, MAX O., resides at 8550 Chevy Chase Dr., La Mesa, CA 92041.

MEKUS, RALPH PAUL, 234-39-10, enlisted March 30, 1942, Buffalo, NY. He is a plankowner and served aboard BB-59 as AS at commissioning May 12, 1942.

MELLI, RALPH D., Memory List 1977.

MELNIK, DANIEL, USMC, May 8, 1942, Norfolk Navy Yard. He is a plankowner and served aboard BB-59 as PFC 7th Div. at commissioning May 12, 1942.

MENARY, GERARD LIONEL, 300-77-91, enlisted Jan. 29, 1942, Chicago, IL. He is a plankowner and served aboard BB-59 as AS at commissioning May 12, 1942, and on board for BB-59 2nd and 3rd anniversaries. He resides in Nahma, MI.

MENARY, ROBERT, Memory List 1991.

MENGLE, OLIVER KNIGHT, 650-32-11, enlisted Feb. 24, 1942, Philadelphia, PA. He was a plankowner and served aboard BB-59 as AS at commissioning May 12, 1942. Memory List 1987.

MERCHANT, HARRY A., served aboard BB-59 in 6th Div. He resides at PO Box 1064, Alton, NH 0380.

MERREY, ROBERT JAMES, 606-65-23, enlisted April 21, 1942, Boston, MA. He is a plankowner and served aboard BB-59 as MM2/c A Div. and assigned auxiliary machines. He left BB-59 in December 1942. After the war he was owner of R.M. Burner Services, Inc. He was active in Veterans of Foreign Wars in his spare time. He had two son and four daughters and resided at 104 Hollis St., Brockton, MA 02402. Memory List 1993.

MERRILL, AUTHUR, resides at Box 264, Flaxton, ND 58737.

MERRITT, JOHN STEPHEN, 646-63-83, enlisted Feb. 3, 1942, New York, NY. He is a plankowner and served aboard BB-59 as AS at commissioning May 12, 1942.

MERRY, ROBERT J., Memory List 1980.

MESIARRO, JOHN, resides at 27 Forrester St., Newburyport, MA 01950.

METZ, GEORGE, resides at 1102 Terry Ave., Billings, MT 59107.

METZEL, WILLIAM EDWARD, JR., born Feb. 23, 1921, Annapolis, MD. Graduated from high school and attended trade school painting and paper-hanging, New York, NY. He enlisted Feb. 22, 1941, New York, NY, and trained at Great Lakes Naval Training Station, IL.

He is a plankowner and served aboard BB-59 as AS 4th Div. at commissioning May 12, 1942. He was assigned as S2/c, S1/c, COX and BM2/c and left BB-59 in San Francisco, CA. He was discharged Oct. 30, 1945, Lido Beach, LI, NY.

After the war he was in painting and decorating with his father and in 1952 owned his own paper-hanging business. In his spare time he was a PAL boxing coach and painted Camp Rainbow for retarded children.

He married Helen July 16, 1949, Bergenfield, NJ. (Mrs.) resides at 117 Harcount Ave., Bergenfield, NJ 07621. He died Oct. 19, 1990; Memory List 1993.

METZENHUBER, ANTON STEVEN, 143-35-00, enlisted Dec. 12, 1941, Minneapolis, MN. He is a plankowner and served aboard BB-59 as MM2/c at commissioning May 12, 1942, and on board for BB-59 2nd anniversary.

MEUSE, FRANCIS VICTOR, 212-78-08, enlisted April 2, 1942, Springfield, MA. He is a plankowner and served aboard BB-59 as AS at commissioning May 12, 1942, and on board for BB-59 2nd and 3rd anniversaries.

MEYERS, DONALD WILLIAM, 610-12-48, enlisted Dec. 12, 1941, Chicago, IL. He is a plankowner and served aboard BB-59 as SF3/c at commissioning May 12, 1942.

MEYERS, ROY, born March 17, 1926, Baraboo, WI. He enlisted Nov. 11, 1943, Milwaukee, WI, and trained at Farragut Naval Training Station, ID and Signal Training School, Chicago University, Chicago, IL. He served aboard BB-59 as SM3/c CS Div. June 1944. He left BB-59 April 6, 1946, Shoemaker, CA.

After the war he was a painting contractor. He married Betty Dec. 17, 1949, Baraboo, WI, and resides at 1309 East Road 1350S, Kokomo, IN 46901.

MEYERS, THOMAS, M Div. Engine Room #3. He resides in Milwaukee, WI.

MICHALAKES, THOMAS JOHN, 614-23-24, enlisted Feb. 2, 1942, Cleveland, OH. He is a plankowner and served aboard BB-59 as AS S Div. at commissioning May 12, 1942, and on board for BB-59 2nd and 3rd anniversaries. He resides at 5803 Bradley Ave., Parma, OH 44129.

MICHALENKA, M., JR., is a plankowner and served aboard BB-59 as S2/c CR Div. at commissioning May 12, 1942, and on board for BB-59 2nd and 3rd anniversaries. He was transferred to FR Div. I March 10, 1943.

MIGNOGNA, PASQUALE, USMC Norfolk Navy Yard, Norfolk, VA. He is a plankowner and served aboard BB-59 as PVT 7th Div. at commissioning May 12, 1942.

MIGNONE, ANTHONY, served aboard BB-59 Sept. 29, 1944, Ch.Sh.Clk. Was assigned as ship's secretary and coding officer. He left BB-59 Nov. 26, 1945.

MIHALENKO, MICHAEL, JR., 652-26-17, enlisted March 11, 1942, Pittsburgh, PA. He is a plankowner and served aboard BB-59 as AS at commissioning May 12, 1942, and on board for BB-59 2nd and 3rd anniversaries.

MIKUSZEWSKI, FRANK PAUL, 666-18-00, enlisted Feb. 18, 1942, Springfield, MA. He is a plankowner and served aboard BB-59 as AS at commissioning May 12, 1942, and on board for BB-59 2nd anniversary. He resides at 38 School St., South Hadley Falls, MA 01075.

MILAM, WILLIAM PATRICK, 272-37-33, enlisted Aug. 6, 1940, Birmingham, AL. He is a plankowner and served aboard BB-59 as S1/c at commissioning May 12, 1942, and on board for BB-59 2nd anniversary. He resides at Route #1, Riderwood, AL.

MILICH, BOEZEDER, (n) 650-32-12, enlisted Feb. 24, 1942, Philadelphia, PA. He is a plankowner and served aboard BB-59 as AS at commissioning May 12, 1942, and on board for BB-59 2nd anniversary.

MILLER, BERNARD OWEN, served aboard BB-59 as CHMach A Div. March 24, 1943, and left Aug. 21, 1945.

MILLER, CHARLES DAVID, 375-62-20, enlisted March 18, 1939, Guantanamo, Cuba. He is a plankowner and served aboard BB-59 as EM1/c E Div. at commissioning May 12, 1942.

MILLER, CHARLES EDWARD, 316-88-04, enlisted Jan. 11, 1942, Omaha, NE. He is a plankowner and served aboard BB-59 as S2/c CR Div. at commissioning May 12, 1942, and on board for BB-59 2nd and 3rd anniversaries as a plankowner. He was assigned to FR Div. March 10, 1943.

MILLER, EDWIN C., ENS, served aboard BB-59 in FR Div. March 24, 1943, and assigned to LT(jg) I Div. Intr. officer. He left BB-59 Sept. 27, 1944.

MILLER, HAROLD ERVIEN, 244-06-37, enlisted Jan. 31, 1942, Philadelphia, PA. He is a plankowner and served aboard BB-59 as AS at commissioning May 12, 1942.

MILLER, JOHN EDWARD, 244-06-53, enlisted Feb. 26, 1942, Philadelphia, PA. He is a plankowner

and served aboard BB-59 as AS at commissioning May 12, 1942, and on board for BB-59 2nd anniversary.

MILLER, NERVAN LEROY, 258-38-24, enlisted Nov. 3, 1941, Baltimore, MD. He served aboard BB-59 as EM3/c E Div. at commissioning May 12, 1942, and on board for BB-59 2nd anniversary as plankowner.

MILLER, ROY DAVID, USMC, May 8, 1942, Norfolk Navy Yard, VA. He is a plankowner and served aboard BB-59 as 2nd LT 7th Div. at commissioning May 12, 1942. He was assigned to Defense Aft. and left BB-59 June 12, 1944, as CAPT.

MILLER, ROYAL F., USMC, 469121, born June 28, 1925, Huntington Park, CA. Graduated from high school, Huntington Park, CA, and enlisted Oct. 8, 1942, Los Angeles, CA. Trained in 30 Cal-Air-Cooled Machine Gun from September 8 to April 25, 1943, 1st Marine Amphibious Corps, Noumea, New Caledonia and assigned to Staff ComBattDiv. 8 aboard USS *Indiana* April 28 to Sept. 27, 1944.

He served aboard BB-59 as PFC 7th Div. Sept. 8, 1943, and assigned 20mm guns. He left BB-59 in September 1945 Bremerton, WA. After the war he worked in the trucking industry and is active in the Veterans of Foreign Wars, MOC.

He married Delma, Las Vegas, NV, and has three sons, one daughter and five grandchildren. He resides at PO Box 748, 2665 Truckee St., Silver Springs, NV 89429.

MILLER, TESTER CHARLES, 600-13-76, enlisted Feb. 4, 1942, Albany, NY. He is a plankowner and served aboard BB-59 as AS at commissioning May 12, 1942.

MILLER, THOMAS PAUL, born Feb. 21, 1920, Van Wert, OH. Graduated from high school in Van Wert, OH, and enlisted Nov. 24, 1941, Detroit, MI. Passed test at enlistment for Y2/c, Great Lakes Naval Training Station, IL.

He is a plankowner and served aboard BB-59 as Y2/c X Div. at commissioning May 12, 1942, and on board for BB-59 2nd anniversary. Was assigned to captain's office, navigator's yeoman and exec's office. He left BB-59 Nov. 30, 1944. He was assigned to Treasure Island, San Francisco, CA; commander Western Frontier Intelligence Unit, San Francisco, CA; and discharged Sept. 19, 1945, Great Lakes, IL.

Did apprenticeship as assistant make-up man, head make-up man; compositor for *Daily Newspaper,* Van West, OH; compliance supervisor and dispatcher for a trucking company; and dispatcher for Van Wert County Sheriff Office. In his spare time he was scorer for city league softball games; is active in veterans organizations; creative writing; and river and reservoir fishing.

He married Elizabeth May 25, 1947, Hicksville, OH, and has one son and three grandchildren. He resides at 611 State Street, Van Wert, OH 45891-2248.

MILLER, WALTER, JR., (n) 355-63-05, enlisted Jan. 11, 1938, San Diego, CA. He is a plankowner and served aboard BB-59 as WT1/c 3rd Div. at commissioning May 12, 1942.

MILLER, WALTER ELROY, 224-78-80, enlisted April 2, 1942, New York, NY. He is a plankowner and served aboard BB-59 as AS at commissioning May 12, 1942, and on board for BB-59 2nd anniversary. He resides at 283 Larson Road RR4, North Brunswick, NJ 08902.

MILLER, WILLIAM B., DR., ENS, 423731, born July 27, 1923, Bethlehem, PA. Earned a BS in English, MA in math and Ph.D. in math from Lehigh University. He enlisted December 1942 Philadelphia, PA, and trained V-12 MIT, Midshipman School, Columbia University, Communication School Harvard University and Amphibious Forces, Coronado, CA.

He served aboard BB-59 as ENS CS Div. in November 1945 and left BB-59 July 19, 1946, Norfolk, VA. Was assigned to Philadelphia Navy Yard.

After the war he worked as an engineer for Western Electric; engineer for Laros Textile; 1953 mathematics teacher Moravian College; and professor of mathematics Worcester Poly Institute. He is active in his church, the Food Cupboard, choir, has written several mathematics books, was in Who's Who for Scientists & Engineers and is part of Pi Mu Epsilon Fraternity.

He married Geraldine 1948, Pennsylvania and has three sons, one daughter and nine grandchildren. He resides at 624 Grove St., Worcester, MA 01605.

MILLHOUSE, ROBERT, born Aug. 10, 1918, Wolf Point, MT. Graduated from high school and enlisted Nov. 2, 1936, St. Louis, MO. Trained at Great Lakes Naval Training Station and the USS *Lexington* (CV-2). He is a plankowner and served aboard BB-59 as COX 3rd Div. at commissioning May 12, 1942.

Was assigned Pointer Turret # 3 and left BB-59 July 1944 New Hebrides. Was also assigned to USS *Clelloisel* (DE-750), Nov. 1, 1944, CWO; 1946-60 served on various amphibious ships and Naval stations; and retired Jan. 1, 1961, as WEO with 25 years of service. After retirement from the Navy he managed a hotel, restaurant and club. He is active in the Oregon Food Bank and the United Way.

He married Vera September 1981 in Reno, NV, and has one son and one daughter. He resides at 9508 NE Wygant Ave., Portland, OR 97220-4228.

MILLIGAN, FREDERICK MANSFIELD, ENS, served aboard BB-59 from May 1945 to July 1945.

MILLS, R.G., LT, served aboard BB-59 in E Div. June 10, 1944, and left April 11, 1945.

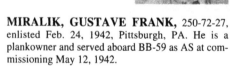

MIRALIK, GUSTAVE FRANK, 250-72-27, enlisted Feb. 24, 1942, Pittsburgh, PA. He is a plankowner and served aboard BB-59 as AS at commissioning May 12, 1942.

MITALE, MICHAEL ALFRED, 600-21-88, enlisted March 17, 1942, Albany, NY. He is a plankowner and served aboard BB-59 as AS at commissioning May 12, 1942.

MITCHELL, ALEXANDER, 652-26-04, enlisted March 10, 1942, Pittsburgh, PA, He was a plankowner and served aboard BB-59 as AS at commissioning May 12, 1942. Memory List 1977.

MITCHELL, ALLEN, resided at 59 Evans Road, Marblehead, MA 01945. Memory List 1978.

MITCHELL, ELDREN ALLEN, JR., 201-65-50, enlisted Feb. 7, 1939, Boston, MA. He is a plankowner and served aboard BB-59 as SM2/c CS Div. at commissioning May 12, 1942. He was assigned CSM and left BB-59 Nov. 30, 1944 to CBD-8. He resides at 2 Harding Lane, Marblehead, MA 01945.

MITCHELL, GILBERT HESSER, LT COMDR, graduated US Naval Academy Class 1932. He was a plankowner and served aboard BB-59 as COMDR at commissioning May 12, 1942. Was assigned Air Defense officer, Battery Problem, D.C. Recreation, March 1943 Main Battery assistant and gunnery officer. He left BB-59 Dec. 9, 1944. Memory List 1979.

MITTELBRUNN, ANDREW, (n) 223-47-47, enlisted Aug. 3, 1938, Brooklyn, NY. He is a plankowner and served aboard BB-59 as S1/c at commissioning May 12, 1942, and on board for BB-59 2nd anniversary.

MOCHEN, DANIEL THOMAS, 606-71-95, born Nov. 7, 1920, Quincy, MA. Graduated from high school 1940 Quincy, MA, and enlisted May 8, 1942, Boston, MA. Had no Naval Training School but was accepted into Navy in Apprentice Program at Fore River Shipyard, MA.

He is a plankowner and served aboard BB-59 as F2/c A Div. at commissioning May 12, 1942, and left BB-59 October 1943 South Pacific. Was assigned to the USS *Hornet* (CV-12) till the end of WWII; attended various service schools, ET Conv. Great Lakes, IL; GCA (Tech) Maint. School; GCA (Engineman) Maint. School, Instructor Training School, Counselor and Guidance School; April 1949, re-enlisted in Navy USS *Salem*, (CA-139) until October 1958.

After the war he worked at Fore River Shipyard until re-enlistment in Navy in 1949. In April 1968 USN Dept. NA VELEC SYSCOM for Navy Air performing consulting and technical assistance duties at various GCA units around the world. In his spare time he enjoys woodworking.

He married Alice (deceased) August 1946 Chatham, MA. He resides at 52 Oval Road RR-1, Chatham, MA 02633.

MOEHRING, EDWIN WHITAM, 647-01-73, enlisted Feb. 20, 1942, New York, NY. He is a plankowner and served aboard BB-59 as AS at commissioning May 12, 1942, and on board for BB-59 2nd anniversary.

MOFFA, PATRICK EDWARD, 606-48-65, enlisted March 10, 1942, Boston, MA. He is a plankowner and served aboard BB-59 as AS at commissioning May 12, 1942, and on board for BB-59 2nd and 3rd anniversaries.

MOLDEREG, PITO, resides at 81 Blucher St., Manchester, NH 03108.

MOLDEREZ, PETER, (n) 606-49-37, enlisted March 12, 1942, Boston, MA. He is a plankowner and served aboard BB-59 as AS at commissioning May 12, 1942.

MOLLISON, PRESCOTT JAMES, 400-77-91, enlisted Aug. 9, 1940, Boston, MA. He is a plankowner and served aboard BB-59 as Y2/c at commissioning

May 12, 1942, and assigned to executive office, captain's office. He left BB-59 December 1942. After the war he was a credit man. He is active in the American Legion and Veterans of Foreign Wars. He had one son and resided at 41 Fisher St., Norwood, MA 02062. Memory List 1984.

MOMEYER, FREDERICK GRANT, 608-13-05, served aboard BB-59 as AS at commissioning May 12, 1942. He is a plankowner.

MONINGER, WILLIAM F., resides at Blackstone Hotel, Omaha, NE 68103.

MONIZ, ANTONE, JR., 606-33-94, enlisted Feb. 12, 1942, Boston, MA. He is a plankowner and served aboard BB-59 as AS at commissioning May 12, 1942.

MONROE, JOHN A., ENS, served aboard BB-59 in July 1945.

MONTAGUE, ROBERT E., 821-27-88, born July 19, 1923, Danville, PA. He earned a BS in business from Bloomsburg University, PA, with graduate studies at Bucknell University, PA. He enlisted March 5, 1943, Wilkes-Barre, PA, and trained at Sampson Navy Training Station, NY; Machinist Mate School, Great Lakes, IL; and USS *Conway* (DD-507).

He served aboard BB-59 as F2/c A Div. September 1943 Espirito Santo and assigned MM3/c M Div. August 1944. He left BB-59 Nov. 13, 1945, Puget Sound Navy Yard for discharge. After the war he worked as a cost accountant, chief accountant, secretary/treasurer for Kennedy Van Saun Corp. for 38 years. He retired June 1, 1986.

He was active as a volunteer for Mended Hearts Support Group, Geisinger Medical Center, Danville, PA; a member of Hospital Artists, made cakes and candy; active Red Cross worker, Elks, Cancer Society, United Way and had many volunteer hours explaining heart surgery to patients. Received Mr. Elk Award in 1991.

He married Jane May 8, 1943, Danville, PA, and had one daughter and four grandchildren. He died Aug. 29, 1995. (Mrs.) resides as 112A N. George St., Millersville, PA.

MONTGOMERY, HOWARD HOWLETT, JR., LT, Graduated from United States Naval Academy, class of 1941, served aboard BB-59 as LT 1st Div. at commissioning May 12, 1942, and on 2nd assignment. Was assigned treasury mess officer, March 1943 F Div. Battle Station Spot coordinator Turret I officer. He left BB-59 June 14, 1944.

Other Naval assignments: USS *Washington*, gunnery officer USS *Portsmouth;* captain USS *Borie;* master's degree in electronics MIT; staff of services Atlantic Fleet; Bureau of Ordnance; Military Assistance Advisory Group, Paris, Naval Proving Ground Dahlgren; and retired after 20 years of service.

After retirement from the Navy, he was a contractor for Tri-Service Electromagnetic Compatibility Analysis Center (ECAC). His primary job was computer programming for maintenance data base to support the military radio frequency interference studies. He enjoyed sailing in his spare time.

Married first wife Nancy; divorced and married second wife Ishbel. (Mrs.) resides at 1204 Dreams Landing Way, Annapolis, MD 21401. Memory List 1993.

MONTGOMERY, JAMES FRED, 291-57-29, enlisted Jan. 17, 1939, Indianapolis, IN. He is a plankowner and served aboard BB-59 as S1/c at commissioning May 12, 1942, and on board for BB-59 2nd and 3rd anniversaries.

MOODY, JOSEPH N., LT, born April 18, 1904, New York, NY. He attended Sacred Heart Catholic School, Mt. Vernon, NY; St. Joseph Seminary (Dunwoody), Yonkers, NY; was history professor Cathedral College; and assistant pastor and chaplain College of New Rochell, NY. He enlisted 1941. He is a plankowner and served aboard BB-59 as LT N Div. at commissioning May 12, 1942, and assigned chaplain. He left BB-59 December 1943 to USS *Yorktown* and discharged in 1946.

After the war he taught at Cathedral College, New York City. Had a weekly radio show on all subjects in New York City. Was pastor of parishes in Congers and Valley Cottage, NY, and pastor at Sacred Heart Highland Falls, NY, teaching at Catholic University, Washington, DC. Continued studies at Georgetown University, Washington, DC, Georgia Southern University, St. Mathew's Church, Statesboro, GA, Rt. Rev. Msr.

In his spare time he loved eating good fish dinners, walking, working out. He was founding member and twice president of National French History Society, and received highest award Georgetown University along with many other awards. He resided at 111-B Gromatie Drive, Statesboro, GA 30458. He died March 2, 1994; Memory List 1994.

MOODY, RAYMOND, (Mrs.) resides at 204 Crestview Lane, Nekoosa, WI 54457. Memory List 1989.

MOONEYHAM, JAMES DONIE, JR., 342-63-88, enlisted Jan. 21, 1942, Kansas City, MO. He is a plankowner and served aboard BB-59 as AS at commissioning May 12, 1942.

MOORE, A.J., Memory List 1977.

MOORE, BENJAMIN LANCASTER, 272-10-94, enlisted Aug. 29, 1939, Washington, DC. He is a plankowner and served aboard BB-59 as COX at commissioning May 12, 1942, and on board for BB-59 2nd anniversary.

MOORE, CECIL RAY, 360-34-79, enlisted March 4, 1941, Houston, TX. He is a plankowner and served aboard BB-59 as S1/c at commissioning May 12, 1942.

MOORE, E.C., ENS, served aboard BB-59 as ENS R Div. Jan. 23, 1943. Was assigned bomb disposal officer, Cobbler Shop, Battle Station – General Repair, LT(jg). He left BB-59 June 15, 1944.

MOORE, IRA TRUMAN, 143-57-03, enlisted Dec. 27, 1941, Chicago, IL. He is a plankowner and served aboard BB-59 as WT2/c at commissioning May 12, 1942, and on board for BB-59 2nd anniversary.

MOORE, "J" DOUGLAS, 360-54-68, born Sept. 2, 1925, Houston, TX. He enlisted Dec. 23, 1941, Houston, TX and trained at Great Lakes Naval Training Station, IL. He is a plankowner and served aboard BB-59 as S2/c 3rd Div. at commissioning May 12, 1942. Was assigned S1/c N Div. and left BB-59 Nov. 28, 1945, Seattle, WA as QM1/c.

After the war he was a Merchant Marine, part of Master, Mates & Pilots' Union and worked for Lykes Bros. Steam Ship Company. He retired in 1992.

He married Raedel June 1949 (deceased) and Barbara Feb. 16, 1962, Houston, TX. He has three sons

and two grandchildren and resides at 11711 N. Nottingham Circle, Houston, TX 77071.

MOORE, JACK D., served aboard BB-59 in M Div. and resides at PO Box 41, Shasta, CA 96087.

MOORE, JAMES T., resides at 41 Lenning St., Lanett, AL 36863.

MOORE, JEFFERSON M., born Aug. 30, 1925, High Springs, FL. He enlisted 1942 Raleigh, NC, and trained at Norfolk Naval Training Station, VA. He served aboard BB-59 as S3/c M Div. July 1942 and assigned machinist mate Boiler Room. He left BB-59 Guantanamo, Cuba. He had 22 years, seven months in Navy aboard several ships and shore duties and was discharged July 19, 1965.

After Naval service he attended school for boiler inspection and was licensed for state and national boiler inspections. He worked for the post office, Doubleday Book Company, Hanover, PA; four years inspector for Commercial Union Insurance Company, Cleveland, OH; inspector in Williams, PA; six years with Burman Boiler Company, Lancaster, PA, as inspector; and retired in 1983 due to disability. He enjoys bowling and is a volunteer at Muncy Valley Hospital, PA.

He married Shirley July 7, 1963, Hagerstown, MD. He resides at 208 Sprout Road, Muncy, PA 17756.

MOORE, JOHN PARRY, 650-31-02, enlisted Feb. 20, 1942, Philadelphia, Pa. He is a plankowner and served aboard BB-59 as AS X Div. at commissioning May 12, 1942. He resides at RR2 Box 2198, Shohola, PA 18458.

MOORE, OTIS, (n) 646-35-53, enlisted Dec. 6, 1939, Houston, TX. He is a plankowner and served aboard BB-59 as F2/c at commissioning May 12, 1942.

MOORE, PAUL CHARLES, 291-45-98, enlisted Dec. 31, 1941, Indianapolis, IN. He was a plankowner and served aboard BB-59 as MM1/c at commissioning May 12, 1942. Memory List 1981.

MOORE, ROBERT HERBERT, 646-35-53, born Aug. 6, 1921, Bronx, NY. Graduated from high school and enlisted Jan. 8, 1942, New York, NY. Stationed Jan. 18, 1942, Newport Naval Training Station, RI, and held as witness in a general court martial until May 9, 1942.

He is a plankowner and served aboard BB-59 as AS 6th Div. at commissioning May 12, 1942. He was assigned S1/c June 1, 1943, and left BB-59 Sept. 7, 1943. Other Naval assignments: USS *North Carolina* Nov. 8, 1943, Rec.Sta. Bremerton, WA; Nov. 18, 1943,COX; Dec. 18, 1943, Rec. Sta. Astoria, OR; Dec. 21, 1943, USS *Tulagi* (CVE-72); June 20, 1944, Naval Air Training Center, Corpus Christi, TX, BM2/c; discharged Nov. 7, 1945, BM2/c Lido Beach, NY.

From 1946 to 1952 worked for the US Government Staten Island Army Base, NY; 1952 to 1980 licensed mate Staten Island Ferry, NY; and retired in 1980. In his spare time he enjoys golf, traveling and Atlantic City casinos.

He married Gertrude in 1949, St. Ritas Church, Staten Island, NY, and has two sons, three daughters and 11 grandchildren. He resides at 24 Kramer Place, Staten Island, NY 10302.

MOOSE, ROBERT F., 269-57-42, born Nov. 15, 1920, Charlotte, NC. A high school graduate with two year of college, he enlisted Sept. 19, 1939, Richmond, VA. Trained at Norfolk Naval Training Station, VA. Was stationed on USS *Oklahoma* from December 1939 to May 1940 and USS *Drayton* (DD-366) from May 1940 to March 1942.

He served aboard BB-59 as S1/c 5th Div. commissioning June 1942 and assigned COX 1943,

BM2/c Deck petty officer 5th Div. 1944. He left BB-59 September 1945 Bremerton, WA, and discharged as BM2/c Nov. 12, 1945.

From 1945-46 gas station attendant; 1946-50 truck driver; 1950-52 two years college; 1952-59 accountant for General Electric Company; 1959-62 property administration Raytheon Company; 1962-85 property administration RCA; and retired April 30, 1985. He is active in the American Legion and Veterans of Foreign Wars.

He married Claire Nov. 25, 1945, Cambridge, MA, and has three sons, one daughter and six grandchildren. He resided as PO Box 941, Burlington, MA 01803. Memory List 1997.

MORAN, EDWARD P., 706-09-87, born July 21, 1921, New York, NY. Graduated from high school and enlisted July 27, 1942, New York, NY. Trained at Newport Naval Training Station, RI, and Signal School, Chicago University, IL. He served aboard BB-59 as SM3/c CS Div. January 1943 and assigned Signal Bridge. He left BB-59 December 1945 Bremerton, WA, and discharged Lido Beach, NY. After the war he worked for the US Postal Service, New York, NY, and retired. He married Irene Nov. 1, 1958, Linden, NJ. He resides at 20 Acme Place, Colonia, NJ 07067.

MORGAN, HARRY GORDON, 385-81-37, enlisted July 10, 1939, Seattle, WA. He is a plankowner and served aboard BB-59 as CM3/c at commissioning May 12, 1942.

MORGAN, RICHARD R., Memory List 1990.

MORIARTY, FRANK MAURICE, 606-37-11, was a graduate of Everett, MA, schools. He was a talented left-handed pitcher and played semi-pro baseball. He enlisted Feb. 17, 1942, Boston, MA. He is a plankowner and served aboard BB-59 as AS CR Div. at commissioning May 12, 1942, and on his board for BB-59 anniversary. He was assigned S2/c FR Div. After the war he worked for the Boston Gas Company for 46 years. He married Stella (Olsen) who died at the age of 39. He had two daughter and one son. He died Sept. 9, 1996. Memory List 1997.

MORIN, JOSEPH SARTO, 204-22-24, enlisted Dec. 16, 1941, Albany, NY. He is a plankowner and served aboard BB-59 as MoMM2/c A Div. at commissioning May 12, 1942. He was assigned to MoMM1/c A Div. and left BB-59 in September 1945. After the war he worked as a mechanic for the New York State Highway Dept. He had two sons and one daughter and resided at Riverside Trailer Court, 163 Hudson River Road, Waterford, NY 12188. Memory List 1977.

MORLEY, FRANCIS WAYLAND, ENS, born June 6, 1920, Toledo, OH. Attended University of Michigan and enlisted Nov. 7, 1942, Chicago, IL. He attended V-7 Midshipman School. He served aboard BB-59 as ENS FR Div. April 1943 and left BB-59 December 1943 Egate, New Hebrides.

Received an Honorable Discharge for chronic seasickness. After the war he was chairman of EPACO (Employer Plan Administrators and Consultants Company) Chicago, IL. He is active in the Sons of the American Revolution and the Sons of the Revolution.

He married Jean March 6, 1943, Ann Arbor, MI, and has two sons, one daughter and seven grandchildren. He resides at 835 Surrey Lane, Glenview, IL 60025.

MORRIS, MARVIN L., served aboard BB-59 in R Div. He resides at 6708 Lakewood, Box 140106, Dallas, TX 75214.

MORRIS, THOMAS MATHIAS, 647-01-74, enlisted Feb. 20, 1942, New York, NY. He is a plankowner and served aboard BB-59 as AS at commissioning May 12, 1942.

MORRIS, WILLIAM DUFFY, 359-67-92, served aboard BB-59 as FC1/c at commissioning May 12, 1942, and is a plankowner.

MORRISON, ROBERT LEONARD, 642-14-05, enlisted Feb. 24, 1942, New Haven, CT. He is a plankowner and served aboard BB-59 as AS F Div. at commissioning May 12, 1942, and on board for BB-59 2nd and 3rd anniversaries. He resides at PO Box 123, Danielson, CT 06239.

MORRISON, ROGER WILLIAM, 224-78-81, enlisted April 2, 1942, New York, NY. He is a plankowner and served aboard BB-59 as AS 3rd Div. at commissioning May 12, 1942, and on board for BB-59 2nd and 3rd anniversaries. He resides at 508 Lynn Ave., East Northport, NY 11731.

MORRISSETTE, JOSEPH MELVIN, 341-85-84, enlisted Jan. 8, 1942, Trinidad, British West Indies. He is a plankowner and served aboard BB-59 as SF1/c R Div. at commissioning May 12, 1942, and on board for BB-59 2nd anniversary. Was assigned CSF, and appointed ensign Nov. 24, 1944.

MORSE, WILLIAM F., resides at RR1 Box 101, Ratcliff, OK 73081.

MORSS, STRAFFORD, was a 1965-90 member of the Memorial Committee (Engineering & Preservation Expert) and received BB-59 Award, 1975.

MOSER, CHARLES A., LT(jg) served aboard BB-59 as LT(jg) L Div. and CR Div. June 4, 1943. Was assigned ship's secretary, Communication Dept. and legal assistance officer. He left BB-59 Sept. 19, 1945, and assigned captain of US Naval Reserve. After the war he was an attorney and on the board of directors of the Building & Loan Assoc. He was active in the Rotary Club and Masons in his spare time.  (Mrs.) resides at 715 East Noble Ave., Guthrie, OK 73044. Memory List 1983.

MOSS, CORNELIUS, (n) 365-93-85, enlisted Oct. 18, 1939, Norfolk, VA. He is a plankowner and served aboard BB-59 as Matt1/c at commissioning May 12, 1942.

MOSS, H.G., served aboard BB-59 as FC1/c FC Div. and assigned May 12, 1945, to FC Div. captain.

MOSTELLER, LEO, (n) 144-01-94, is a plankowner and served aboard BB-59 as CSK at commissioning May 12, 1942.

MOTO, KIOKI, JR., served aboard BB-59 in L Div. Latest address: c/o Iwamoto 626 Coral St., Honolulu, HI 96813.

MOTTRAM, F.R., 1966, name submitted by A. Vigeant.

MOUDY, DALE, born May 25, 1923, Omaha, NE. A high school graduate with some college, he enlisted in May 1940, Omaha, NE. Trained at Radio School, Norfolk, VA; C & V Div. USS *Quincy*; and Quincy, MA, April 1942.

He served aboard BB-59 as ARM1/c V Div. at commissioning May 12, 1942, and appointed warrant officer. He left BB-59 July 30, 1942, to Pearl Harbor,

HI. He is a plankowner. Was assigned radio material officer, Naval Air Station, Kingsville, TX.

After the war he was vice-president and director of engineering Storz Broadcasting Company; general manager of radio stations WING, WSAT, KNBB,WKIS, WRMF; chief engineer Y106 Radio Orlando, FL; and retired. In his spare time he is secretary and director of Sandlake Townhouses Assoc.

He married Eleanora March 16, 1946, Omaha, NE, and has three sons, two daughters and seven grandchildren. He resides at 7925 Bayside View Drive, Orlando, FL 32819.

MOULTON, JAMES ALVIN, 355-95-32, enlisted March 4, 1940, Seattle, WA. He is a plankowner and served aboard BB-59 as BM2/c X Div. at commissioning May 12, 1942. Was assigned BM1/c 4th Div. DC MAA and left BB-59 December 1943. After the war he was a maintenance engineer for Children's Cancer Research Foundation. Memory List 1985.

MOYE, WILLIAM HENRY, 291-21-30, enlisted Jan. 6, 1940, San Pedro, CA. He is a plankowner and served aboard BB-59 as TC1/c at commissioning May 12, 1942.

MOYER, WILLIAM WARREN, 266-66-14, enlisted Dec. 18, 1941, Richmond, VA. He is a plankowner and served aboard BB-59 as S2/c at commissioning May 12, 1942.

MROCZEK, STANLEY WALTER, 234-22-72, enlisted Dec. 27, 1939, Buffalo, NY. He is a plankowner and served aboard BB-59 as EM3/c E Div. at commissioning May 12, 1942.

MUIR, ROBERT ALEXANDER, 355-81-27, enlisted Dec. 28, 1941, San Francisco, CA. He served aboard BB-59 as CEM E Div. Aug. 29, 1943, and assigned Fire Control and Interior Communications. He left BB-59 Aug. 11, 1944.

MULHERN, JAMES ROBERT, 201-49-01, enlisted Dec. 6, 1941, San Francisco, CA. He was a plankowner and served aboard BB-59 as WT2/c at commissioning May 12, 1942. Memory List 1977.

MULKERN, JOSEPH LAWRENCE, 606-42-50, enlisted March 2, 1942, Boston, MA. He was a plankowner and served aboard BB-59 as Y3/c at commissioning May 12, 1942. Memory List 1991.

MULLER, CHARLES FREDRICK, 224-78-37, enlisted April 1, 1942, New York, NY. He is a plankowner and served aboard BB-59 as AS A Div. at commissioning May 12, 1942. He was assigned to F3/c A Div. and left BB-59 March 8, 1943, ComSerForSoPac.

MULLER, LAWRENCE R., 224-75-77, born March 20, 1925, Clifton, NJ. Was educated at St. Nicholas School, Passaic, NJ, and St. Mary's High School, Rutherford, NJ. He enlisted at New York, NY, and trained at Class A Gunner's Mate School, Great Lakes, IL.

He served aboard BB-59 as GM3/c 1st Div. September 1942 Portland, ME. He was assigned to Turret #1 Crew and left BB-59 July 8, 1944, Pearl Harbor, HI. Assigned to Class B Gunners Mate School, Treasure Island, San Francisco, CA, September 1944; US Naval Ammunition Depot, Port Chicago, CA, December 1944.

Discharged March 19, 1946; rejoined the Navy May 1948; Fleet Reserve inactive retired November 1963. He was recalled to active duty from May 1966 to June 1971 and retired senior chief petty officer. After Naval service he was boiler repairman crew chief for Oleum Plant Pacific Gas & Electric Company. He has been active in the Knights of Columbus for 40 years; Fleet Reserve Assoc., 40 years; and 15 years in German-American Club.

He married Joyce May 15, 1945, Martinez, CA, and has four sons and three daughters. He resides at 928 Lawhon Drive, Switzerland, FL 32259.

MULLIGAN, JERRY, (n) 360-08-58, born Jan. 13, 1921, Houston, TX. Holds a AA from Junior College and enlisted Nov. 15, 1939, Houston, TX. Trained at Naval Training Station, USS *Tennessee* (BB-43). He served aboard BB-59 as F1/c P Div. at commissioning May 12, 1942, and is a plankowner.

He left BB-59 in Boston, MA, and assigned shore duty, Lion I, AROU I and AROU II. After the war he worked for South California Edison Company and was a power house operator for a local electric company.

He has one daughter and three grandchildren. He resides at 2347 Stanbridge Ave., Long Beach, CA 90815-1932.

MUNSEY, CLARENCE JENNINGS, 658-08-34, enlisted Nov. 17, 1941, Richmond, VA. He is a plankowner and served aboard BB-59 as RM3/c on commissioning May 12, 1942.

MURPHY, CHARLES R., is a plankowner and served aboard BB-59 in R Div. at commissioning May 12 1942, and on board for BB-59 2nd and 3rd anniversaries. He resided at 234 Knox St., Rumford, ME 04276. Memory List 1997.

MURPHY, FRANCIS JAMES, 646-64-97, enlisted Feb. 4, 1942, New York, NY. He is a plankowner and served aboard BB-59 as AS at commissioning May 12, 1942. Was assigned RT1/c CR Div. and left BB-59 Nov. 20, 1945.

After the war he was manager for administrative services for Frigidaire Sales Corp. and is active in the GM Club. He has three sons and one daughter and resides at 78 Joseph Road, Framingham, MA 01706.

MURPHY, JAMES CHARLES, 666-15-81, born June 28, 1913, Danvers, MA. A high school graduate with one year of business school, he enlisted Feb. 9, 1942, Springfield, MA. Trained at Newport Naval Training Station, RI.

He is a plankowner and served aboard BB-59 as AS FC Div. at commissioning May 12, 1942. He left BB-59 November 1944 in the Pacific. Attended Naval Training School, Washington, DC; Anacostia Fire Control School; USS *Macon;* and discharged October 1945.

After the war he was district plant regional credit manager for Swift & Company. He retired 1977 with 47 years service and worked for Son's Wholesale Greenhouse, Kenner, LA. He is a 25 year Scoutmaster.

He married Eveline June 27, 1944, Navy Chapel, Bremerton, WA. He has one son and one daughter and resides at 513 Rosewood Drive, Metairie, LA 70001.

MURPHY, JAMES JOSEPH, 242-78-58, enlisted Aug. 26, 1938, San Diego, Ca. He is a plankowner and served aboard BB-59 as S1/c at commissioning May 12, 1942.

MURPHY, MALCOLM JOE, 360-57-14, enlisted Jan. 30, 1942, Houston, TX. He is a plankowner and served aboard BB-59 as AS at commissioning May 12, 1942, and on board for BB-59 2nd and 3rd anniversaries.

MURPHY, RICHARD THOMAS, 642-14-02, enlisted Feb. 24, 1942, New Haven, CT. He is a plankowner and served aboard BB-59 as AS 6th Div. at commissioning May 12, 1942. Was assigned S1/c gunner and left BB-59 November 1945. After the war he worked as an industrial engineer for United Aircraft Corp. and is active in the Elks Club as selectman New Britain, CT. He has one son and one daughter and resides at 87 New Hampshire Drive, New Britain, CT 06052.

MURPHY, ROBERT, (n) 266-14-39, enlisted July 18, 1940, Richmond, VA. He is a plankowner and served aboard BB-59 as F1/c at commissioning May 12, 1942

MURPHY, ROBERT JEROME, 600-00-91, born June 20, 1920, Clifton Springs, NY. With education background in Naval science and electrical engineering, he enlisted Jan. 6, 1942, Albany, NY. Trained at Newport Naval Training Station, RI.

He is a plankowner and served aboard BB-59 as EM3/c E Div. at commissioning May 12, 1942. Was assigned EM2/c and made EM2/c second time at Panama City, Panama for helping to get #1 Turret operative, EM1/c. Left BB-59 October 1943 Kwajalein. Attended V-12 Program, Union College, ROTC Program, Georgia Tech; commissioned ensign October 1944 USS *Supply* (IX-147); AVS1 until November 1945; and stayed in Naval Reserve until retirement.

After Naval service, he was chief electrician for Westuseo, Mechanicsville, NY; sales engineer Louis Allis Company, Atlanta, GA; Supt. O-I Jacksonville, FL; chief engineer O-I Valdosta, GA; chief engineer O-I Orange, TX; mill manager O-I Lufkin, TX; engineer and power supt. Big Island, VA. He is active in the "Meals on Wheels" program, AARP, (TCE) Tax Counseling for the Elderly and 1967-68 Who's Who South West.

He married Doris Oct. 23, 1944, and has three sons, four daughters and 15 grandchildren (one deceased). He resides at 1808 Heather, Nacogdoches, TX 75961.

MURRAY, FRANCIS LEVERETT, 201-53-98, enlisted March 4, 1942, Boston, MA. He is a plankowner and served aboard BB-59 as S1/c at commissioning May 12, 1942.

MURRAY, HARRY RICHARD, 201-69-47, enlisted Dec. 4, 1939, Boston, MA He is a plankowner and served aboard BB-59 as S1/c at commissioning May 12, 1942.

MURRAY, MATTHEW T., JR., served aboard BB-59 in N Div. He resides at 38 Greenhill Drive, Fishkill, NY 12524.

MURRAY ROBERT J., served aboard BB-59 in 6th Div. He resided at 701 Sherwood Road, Norfolk, NE 68701. Memory List 1994.

MUSSER, DONALD HESTER, 244-07-05, enlisted Feb. 26, 1942, Philadelphia, PA. He is a plankowner and served aboard BB-59 as AS at commissioning May 12, 1942.

MYERS, CLARENCE JACKSON, 382-06-84, enlisted July 15, 1938, Los Angeles, CA. He is a plankowner and served aboard BB-59 as COX at commissioning May 12, 1942, and on board for BB-59 2nd anniversary.

MYERS, MAC L., resides at RR #6, Kokomo, IN 46901.

MYERS, ROBERT JOHNSON, 403-70-00, enlisted Sept. 4, 1940, New York, NY. He is a

plankowner and served aboard BB-59 as RM2/c at commissioning May 12, 1942.

NAANOS, VINCENTE, (n) 497-71-10, enlisted Jan. 11, 1941, San Pedro, CA. He is a plankowner and served aboard BB-59 as OS1/c S Div. commissioning May 12, 1942, and on board for BB-59 2nd and 3rd anniversaries as CSt.

NAAS, W.B., LT, served aboard BB-59 in CS Div. March 5, 1944, and left May 8, 1945.

NACE, LUTHER, resided at Confluence, PA 15424. Memory List 1997.

NAPARSTEK, HAROLD, served in V Div. and resides at 8 Belmart Rd., Hicksville, NY.

NAPIER, ALEXANDER, JR., (n) 606-36-98, enlisted Feb. 17, 1942, Boston, MA. He was a plankowner and served aboard BB-59 as S2/c at commissioning May 12, 1942, and on board for BB-59 2nd and 3rd anniversaries. Memory List 1996.

NAPIER, HORACE "D," 376-06-37, enlisted June 6, 1940, San Francisco, CA. He is a plankowner and served aboard BB-59 as QM3/c at commissioning May 12, 1942.

NAPIER, JAMES SYLVESTER, 382-34-31, enlisted Dec. 28, 1940, Los Angeles, CA. He is a plankowner and served aboard BB-59 as S1/c at commissioning May 12, 1942; as RDM3/c CR to FR Div. March 10, 1943; and on board for BB-59 2nd anniversary.

NAPLES, MARIO PHILIP, 650-26-61, enlisted Feb. 11, 1942, Philadelphia, PA. He is a plankowner and served aboard BB-59 as AS at commissioning May 12, 1942.

NARJAS, JOHN, (n) 224-71-12, born June 18, 1912, Mahwar, NJ. Worked as a forklift operator for American Brake Shoe and a steward aboard *Grace Line* (passenger). He enlisted Feb. 25, 1942, New York, NY, and trained at Newport, RI.

He is a plankowner and served aboard BB-59 as AS L Div. at commissioning May 12, 1942, and on board for BB-59 2nd and 3rd anniversaries. He left BB-59 as (cook) S Div., Bremerton, WA, after a six year hitch and left the service in 1948.

After the war he worked on the Hudson River in mothball fleet ship's maintenance for two years; Lederle Lab-Pearl River, NY, for 24 years; and counter clerk and cook in a cafeteria. In his spare time he sails in a 18 foot boat, traveled up and down the Hudson River and Long Island Sound. Played sax in a marching and concert band and volunteer band in nursing homes.

He married Evelyn Oct. 31, 1949, Elkton, MD, and resides at 173 Democracy Ln., Washingtonville, NY 10992.

NASH, W.O., elected E Div. Served aboard BB-59 Oct. 30, 1944, and left Dec. 31, 1944.

NAUMAN, MYLES HULL, 256-39, enlisted Dec, 12, 1941, Washington, DC. He is a plankowner and served aboard BB-59 as QM3/c at commissioning May 12, 1942.

NAVA, FRANK, (n) 647-0177, enlisted Feb. 20, 1942, New York, NY. He is a plankowner and served aboard BB-59 as AS at commissioning May 12, 1942.

NEARING, HEWITT, (n) 337-83-15, enlisted March 21, 1942, St. Louis, MO. He is a plankowner and served aboard BB-59 as Matt3/c at commissioning May 12, 1942, and on board for BB-59 3rd anniversary.

NEARY, JOHN JOSEPH, 642-14-17, born May 12, 1924. He enlisted Feb. 25, 1942, New Haven, CT, and trained at Newport, RI. He is a plankowner and served aboard BB-59 as AS 3rd Div. at commissioning May 12, 1942, and on on board for BB-59 2nd and 3rd anniversaries as Gun Capt. as COX. He left BB-59 in August 1945 South Pacific.

After the war he worked for Rilling-Dermetics Company as traffic manager. He is a Long Hill Volunteer Fire Co. #1 as president, board of directors and commissioner.

He married Mildred Jan. 18, 1947, in Trumbill, CT, and has six children and 12 grandchildren. He resides at 940 Groveland Rd., Venice, FL.

NEARY, PETER FRANCIS, 606-39-43, enlisted Feb. 20, 1942, Boston, MA. He was a plankowner and served aboard BB-59 as SK S Div. at commissioning May 12, 1942, and on board for BB-59 2nd and 3rd anniversaries. Memory List 1990. (Mrs.) resides at 46 Fairfield St., Needham, MA 02192.

NEBESNI, JOHN, (n) 647-01-78, enlisted Feb. 20, 1942, New York, NY. He is a plankowner and served aboard BB-59 as AS at commissioning May 12, 1942.

NEBLICK, EDWARD J., 372-21-70, born Dec. 19, 1921, Pueblo, CO. Graduated from Pueblo, CO, High School 1939 and attended the University of Colorado, Boulder, CO, 1951. He enlisted Nov. 27, 1940, Denver, CO, and assigned to USS *Pensacola*.

He is a plankowner and served aboard BB-59 as F2/c at commissioning May 12, 1942, and on board for BB-59 2nd and 3rd anniversaries as MM2/c. He left BB-59 in July 1945 Leyte Gulf as MM2/c. Was assigned to USS *Macon* and the USS *Randolf* and was discharged Dec. 26, 1946.

After the war he was an accountant for Colorado State Hospital from September 1951 to March 1982. He retired in March 1982. He enjoys fishing, hiking and golf in his spare time. He resides at 321 W. Adams Ave., Pueblo, CO.

NEDELL, RICHARD, USMC, 372585, born Sept. 16, 1921, Brooklyn, NY. Earning a BA from CCNY and an MS from Platz State, NY, he enlisted Feb. 18, 1942, New York, NY. He trained at Parris Island, SC and Sea School, Portsmouth, VA, May 8, 1942.

He is a plankowner and served aboard BB-59 as PVT 7th Div. at commissioning May 12, 1942, and on board for BB-59 2nd and 3rd anniversaries as orderly/

assigned 20 and 40 mm guns (PFC). He left BB-59 October 1945 Bremerton, WA.

After the war he worked for Chase Bank, NYC (foreign department) for eight years; elementary teacher, Plainview, NY, schools for 29 years; and retired July 1984. He enjoys traveling the US by motor home in his spare time.

He married Joan June 8, 1942, Brooklyn, NY, and has four children and seven grandchildren (as of July 1994). He resides at 130 Lee Ave., Hicksville, NY.

NEILSON, S., CHElect. E Div., served aboard BB-59 Jan. 27, 1945, and left BB-59 May 15, 1945.

NELSON, CARL LLOYD, served aboard BB-59 as S1/c (signalman) in July 1944. He left BB-59 in CS Div. in December 1945. After the war he worked as a lineman for Iowa/Illinois Gas & Electric Company. He has two children and resides at 4721 18th Ave. Court, Moline, IL.

NELSON, EARL M., 891-21-43, born July 25, 1920, Seattle, WA. Graduated from high school and Puget Sound Naval Shipyard Apprenticeship (pipefitter). He enlisted June 20, 1944, Seattle, WA, and trained at E School, Great Lakes, IL, for eight weeks; NTS, Farragut, ID; and NAS Whidbey Island, WA. He served aboard BB-59 as F1/c A Div. at commissioning Sept. 20, 1945, and left BB-59 Jan. 27, 1946, Bremerton, WA.

After the war he worked for 34 years at the Puget Sound Shipyard and retired with ship scheduler rate (pipe-fitter); commercial fishing for salmon and shrimp for six years in Alaska summers; 1973-83 worked for QED checking fire fighting equipment several times on all of the big carriers.

He married Louise Sept. 14, 1944, in Seattle, WA, and has two sons. He resides at 313 Olympic Ave., Bremerton, WA.

NELSON, HARLAND E., born Sept. 23, 1920, Minneapolis, MN. On Jan. 17, 1939, CCC (cook); October 1940 to December 1941 Moline Iron Works, Moline, IL, core room laborer; and enlisted Dec. 30, 1941, Rock Island, IL. Trained at Cooks and Bakers School, Great Lakes, IL, for 16 weeks. He served aboard BB-59 as AS, S2/c and SC3/c in 1942 and 1945 as SC1/c. He left BB-59 Oct. 19, 1945. He married Bertha June 15, 1946, in Moline, IL, and had three children and eight grandchildren. He died July 11, 1989; Memory List 1990. (Mrs.) resides at 2067 Coral Lane, Eagan, MN.

NELSON, JOHN JAMES, LT(jg) BatDiv8, served aboard BB-59 from June 1943 to Oct. 1, 1943, CommWatchOff.

NELSON, S.O., ENS 5th Div., served aboard BB-59 July 1942 JW and JD.

NETTS, GEORGE W., LT CDR July 1945 in S Div. and CDR. He resides at 1609 Briteway Court, Bowling Green, KY 42103.

NEUMAN, ROBERT EUGENE, 328-80-68, born in Washburn, WI. A high school graduate, he enlisted Dec. 6, 1940, Minneapolis, MN, and trained at Great Lakes, IL. He was assigned to USS *Nevada*, Pearl Harbor. He was a plankowner and served aboard BB-59 as S1/c N Div. at commissioning May 12, 1942, and QM3/c 1942. Left BB-59 November 1942 to Aleutian

Islands aboard minesweeper. After the war he worked as a salesman for G&H Poultry. He married Rita and had two sons and one granddaughter. He died Aug. 6, 1969; Memory List 1981. (Mrs.) Bos resides 891 64 Victoria Rd., W. Chatham, MA 02669.

NEVILLE, FRANCIS EUGENE, 250-55-15, enlisted April 23, 1940, Pittsburgh, PA, and served aboard BB-59 as FC3/c at commissioning May 12, 1942. He is a plankowner.

NEW, CECIL ATHELSTANE, JR., 2nd Div., served aboard BB-59 as LT(jg) March 25, 1943, and left BB-59 Sept. 15, 1945, as LT.

NEWELL, FRANCIS JOSEPH, 606-69-10, enlisted April 30, 1942, Boston, MA. He is a plankowner and served aboard BB-59 as S1/c X Div. at commissioning May 12, 1942. He resides at 2046 Grundy Place, Merrick, NY.

NEWMAN, HULON THROVILLE, 644-06-18, enlisted Oct. 31, 1941, New Orleans, LA. He is a plankowner and served aboard BB-59 as EM3/c E Div. at commissioning May 12, 1942. On March 8, 1943, was F2/c E Div. to ComSerForSoPac.

NEWMAN, PHILIP, 223-43-71, enlisted Jan. 19, 1938, Brooklyn, NY. He is a plankowner and served aboard BB-59 as COX at commissioning May 12, 1942.

NEWMAN, ROBERT GEORGE, LT CR Div., served aboard BB-59 March 6, 1945, and left Oct. 9, 1945.

NEWMAN, WALTER MONROE, 646-69-14, enlisted Feb. 7, 1942, New York, NY. He is a plankowner and served aboard BB-59 as AS at commissioning May 12, 1942.

NEWPORT, THEODORE CHARLES, 606-47-62, enlisted March 7, 1942, Boston, MA. He is a plankowner and served aboard BB-59 as AS commissioning May 12, 1942.

NICHOLSON, JOHN R., 761-58-98, born Nov. 28, 1925, Gloucester, MA. Graduated from Gloucester High School and enlisted Jan. 6, 1943, Boston, MA. He trained at Sampson, NY, and Naval Training (radio), University of Wisconsin, and assigned to USS *Alabama* from Aug. 9, 1943 to Sept. 22, 1943.

He served aboard BB-59 as FC3/c FC Div. at commissioning Sept. 22, 1943, in FC Plotting Rms. and maintenance of 40mm quads and directors. He left BB-59 Jan. 25, 1946. After the war he was employed as a fishcutter for five years and mason/bricklayer for Faulk Bros. Inc. He is active in USS *Massachusetts* Assoc. as officer and board of directors; and American Legion. Received BB-59 Award 1983.

He married Virginia Jan. 12, 1947, in Gloucester and has three daughters and four grandchildren. He resides at 93 Centennial Ave., Gloucester, MA.

NICHOLSON, THOMAS GILBERT, 646-69-15, enlisted Feb. 7, 1942, New York, NY. He is a plankowner and served aboard BB-59 as AS at commissioning May 12, 1942, and on board for BB-59 2nd anniversary.

NICKETAKIS, PETER JOHN, 202-27-26, enlisted March 9, 1942, Boston, MA. He was a plankowner and served aboard BB-59 as AS at commissioning May 12, 1942, and on board for BB-59 2nd and 3rd anniversaries. Memory List 1977.

NICOLO, WILLIAM ALEXANDER, 650-32-72, enlisted Feb. 24, 1942, Philadelphia, PA. He is a plankowner and served aboard BB-59 as AS at commissioning May 12, 1942, and on board for BB-59 2nd and 3rd anniversaries. On March 10, 1943, served as S2/c CR to FR Div.

NICOSON, WILLIAM FRED, CHCarp, served aboard BB-59 as DamgContMaint May 22, 1944.

NIEDOSIK, LEONARD S., USMC, May 8, 1942, Norfolk Navy Yard. He is a plankowner and served aboard BB-59 as PVT 7th Div. at commissioning May 12, 1942. Memory List 1977.

NIERADKA, JOHN, (n) 600-22-30, enlisted March 20, 1942, Albany, NY. He is a plankowner and served aboard BB-59 as AS at commissioning May 12, 1942.

NITKIN, MORRIS, (n) 647-01-80, enlisted Feb. 20, 1942, New York, NY. He is a plankowner and served aboard BB-59 as AS A Div. at commissioning May 12, 1942, and as F3/c A Div. to ComSerForSoPac March 8, 1943.

NIX, HASKELL KARL, 346-76-27, enlisted Dec. 5, 1939, Little Rock, AR. He is a plankowner and served aboard BB-59 as F2/c at commissioning May 12, 1942, and on board for BB-59 2nd anniversary. He resides at 242 Barbara Dr., Clute, TX.

NJIRICH, FRANK ARTHUR, 375-87-39, enlisted Dec. 11, 1941, Pearl Harbor, HI. He is a plankowner and served aboard BB-59 as COX at commissioning May 12, 1942.

NOAH, GEORGE JAMES, 376-04-26, enlisted April 4, 1940, San Francisco, CA. He is a plankowner and served aboard BB-59 as S1/c at commissioning May 12, 1942.

NOLAN, EMMITT LOUIS, 620-03-20, enlisted Aug. 14, 1941, Des Moines, IA. He is a plankowner and served aboard BB-59 as S1/c commissioning May 12, 1942.

NORMAN, LESLIE PURNELL, 265-68-83, enlisted Feb. 26, 1942, Richmond, VA. He is a plankowner and served aboard BB-59 as WT2/c B Div. at commissioning May 12, 1942. He resides at PO Box 11, Dagsboro, DE 19939.

NORTH, ARTHUR HERBERT, ENS, served aboard BB-59 June 1943 and CommWatchOff ComBatDiv 8 Oct. 1, 1943.

NORTON, FRANK L., JR., 606-30-74, born in Alexandria, VA. Graduated from high school and enlisted July 4, 1942, Washington, DC. Trained at NTC Newport, RI, and Electric School.

He served aboard BB-59 as EM3/c E Div. Dec. 12, 1942, and left Nov. 20, 1945, Seattle, WA. At the only burial at sea, he was one of the electricians to serve as a pall-bearer and honor guard. (Remember #1 Turret that was flooded during gale off North Carolina coast on our way to South Pacific and all new wiring before Panama Canal.)

After the war he worked for C & P Telephone Company (now Bell Atlantic) for 37 years; and was cable splicer and installer of PBX – special service. He retired in 1978. In his spare time he is a handy man serving many seniors (Telephone Pioneers).

He married June Aug. 2, 1947, in Alexandria, VA, and has two sons and three grandchildren. He resides at 2417 Cavendish Dr., Alexandria, VA 22308.

NORTON, HERBERT L., CMus X Div. May 12, 1945, Band Master.

NORWOOD, EMMETT GORDON, 341-96-72, born Sept. 24, 1915, Owensville, MO. Graduated from high school and enlisted April 13, 1936, Kansas City, MO. He was assigned USS *Beaver* 1936-37; USS *Keosanqua* 1939; USS *Dent* (DD-116) 1939-42. He served aboard BB-59 Quincy, MA, Feb. 14, 1942; as Mm1/c M Div. (plankowner) May 12, 1942; and MMC #3 Engine Room M Div. May 1, 1943, (plankowner). He left BB-59 July 27, 1943, Noumea, N. Caledonia.

Was assigned to USS *Catskill* LSVI at Portland, OR, commissioning June 30, 1944 to May 16, 1945; plus USS *Toledo* (CA-133); USS *Planter* (engineering officer); USS *Neshoba* APA-216; USS *Taussig* (DD-746); recruiting duty 1948-51 St. Louis, MO; Korean War aboard USS *Memifeea* (APA-202) 1951-55; shore duty, 1955-57; USS *Roanoke* 1957-58 and retired Jan. 31, 1959, CWO3.

After retiring from the Navy he worked for General Electric and spent 22 years in a boiler house doing what he loved to do "make steam" and drink coffee. He retired in 1981.

He married Betty March 7, 1942, in San Diego, CA, and has one son and two grandchildren. He resides at 926 E. McGee, Springfield, MO 65807.

NOTT, HOWARD CLAUDIOS, JR., 647-00-11, enlisted Feb. 19, 1942, New York, NY. He is a plankowner and served aboard BB-59 as AS at commissioning May 12, 1942, and on board for BB-59 2nd and 3rd anniversaries.

NOVAK, GEORGE JERRY, 300-76-16, enlisted Jan. 21, 1942, Chicago, IL. He is a plankowner and served aboard BB-59 as AS at commissioning May 12, 1942.

NOVAK, HARRY STEPHEN, 224-74-01, enlisted March 11, 1942, New York, NY. He was a plankowner and served aboard BB-59 as AS at commissioning May 12, 1942, and on board for BB-59 2nd and 3rd anniversaries. He resided at 57 Dalton St., Long Beach, NY. Memory List 1997.

NOWAK, JOHN, JR., 600-14-66, enlisted Feb. 5, 1942, Albany, NY. He is a plankowner and served aboard BB-59 as AS at commissioning May 12, 1942, and on board for BB-59 2nd and 3rd anniversaries.

NUNES, JOHN, H Div., resides at 24 Sherrick Ave., Holbrook, MA.

NUNNALLY, JAMES RAY, ENS 4th Div. served aboard BB-59 April 26, 1945.

NUZZO, ANDREW D., USMC, May 8, 1942, Norfolk Navy Yard. He is a plankowner and served aboard BB-59 as PVT 7th Div. at commissioning May 12, 1942. He resided at 972 Grace Terrace, Teaneck, NJ. Memory List 1997.

NYE, HAROLD FRANCIS, 606-35-08, enlisted Feb. 16, 1942, Boston, MA. He is a plankowner and served aboard BB-59 as AS at commissioning May 12, 1942, and on board for BB-59 2nd and 3rd anniversaries in S Div. He is an active committee chairman for BBBM Campaign and on the board of directors (1977 to present) of BB-59 Assoc. Was a cook on Homecoming Crew (1965).

After the war he worked as a florist. In his spare time he is involved in Masonic Work, Master of Lodge; member of committee for 50th Anniversary of BB-59 Commissioning. Received BB-59 Award in 1969.

He married Margare and has one son, one daughter and two grandchildren. He resides at Box 301, 248 Converse Rd., Marion, MA 02738.

OATES, THOMAS FRANCIS, 646-44-22, enlisted Jan. 19, 1942, New York, NY. He is a plankowner and served aboard BB-59 as AS at commissioning May 12, 1942.

O'BEIRNE, EMMET, RADM, Memory List 1991.

O'BRIEN, EDWARD JAMES, 606-33-73, born Aug. 29, 1916. Graduated from Salem High School and enlisted Feb. 11, 1942, Boston, MA. Trained at Newport, RI. He is a plankowner and served aboard BB-59 as AS FR Div. at commissioning May 12, 1942, and was on board for its 2nd and 3rd anniversaries. Left BB-59 as RDM1/c September 1945, Japan.

After the war he was a firefighter for the city of Salem from 1949 to 1981. He was president from 1977-79, board of directors for USS *Massachusetts* Assoc., Inc. Received BB-59 Award in 1982. He married Margaret and has two children. He resides at 91 Ord St., Salem, MA 01970.

OBRYAN, RALPH L., 528776, born Oct. 29, 1917, Elkland, PA. He graduated from Elkland High School; Massey Tech. Institute, Jacksonville, FL; plus correspondence courses in industrial electronics. He enlisted April 29, 1944, Wellsboro, PA, and trained at Bainbridge, MD. Basic Training for three days, Shoemaker, CA, and 27 days on a troop ship.

He served aboard BB-59 as S2/c 6th Div. August 1944; and S1/c August 1945. He left BB-59 Dec. 18, 1945, Bremerton, WA.

After the war he earned his journeyman's card in electronics and was an electrician for Ingersoll Rand Company, Inc., Painted Post, NY, for 16 years until retirement. He was an active Boy Scout leader; active for 46 years in Grange as an officer, most of the time (7th Degree Club); Rand Retirement Club; and local seniors, "Nifty 50 Club." He married Ardis Albee Aug. 10, 1938, in Elkland, FL, and has two children, six grandchildren and four great-grandchildren. He resides at RD #1 Box 4, Lawrenceville, PA.

OBSZARNY, JOHN, (n) 646-69-19, enlisted Feb. 7, 1942, New York, NY. He is a plankowner and served aboard BB-59 as AS at commissioning May 12, 1942.

OCHE, H.E., LTCDR, c/o McCulloch D-14, Harvard Business School (1966).

O'CONNOR, JOHN H., 189750, born May 28, 1919, Milwaukee, WI. Attended Marquette University and received a BA in business and Law LLB. Joined the Navy Sept. 15, 1942, Columbia University and trained at Columbia Midshipman School, Ohio State Aircraft Recog. and USNT Newport, RI.

He served aboard BB-59 as LT(jg) N Div. July 8, 1944; division officer and assistant navigator. He left BB-59 Dec. 5, 1945, to Naval Reserve for four years retiring as LCDR.

After the war he was an attorney for State Farm Mutual Insurance Company. In his spare time he is active in the St. Vincent De Paul Society (conference president), teacher of Wisconsin Literacy Service and Benedict Center Citizens Advisory. Was honored as "Parishioner of the Year" St. John Cathedral. He married Mary F. June 26, 1943, in Newport, RI, and has four children and nine grandchildren. He resides at 1328 N. Jefferson St., #310, Milwaukee, WI 53202.

ODENING, ROBERT ERNEST, joined the Navy, Annapolis Class of 1936. He served aboard BB-59 as LTCDR on May 20, 1944, as gunnery officer and dept. head commander. CAPT Odening resides at 1133 Daniels Dr., Los Angeles, CA 90035.

ODOM, DOUGLAS H., 606-74-67, born in 1914 Quincy, MA. Graduated from high school and attended Wilbraham Academy. Trained as a Cadet engineer, Eastern Steamship Lines and joined USN May 5, 1942.

He is a plankowner and served aboard BB-59 as F1/c M Div. on commissioning May 12, 1942, and #1 Engine Room and #3 Engine Room as M2/c and MM1/c. Left BB-59 at Puget Sound, WA, Sept. 25, 1945.

After the war he owned and operated Monhegan General Store, Monhegan Island, ME. He is also a lobster fisherman. He resides at PO Box #67, Monhegan Island, ME 04852.

O'DONEIL, FREDDIE LEE, 342-64-17, enlisted Jan. 26, 1942, Kansas City, MO. He is a plankowner and served aboard BB-59 as AS at commissioning May 12, 1942, and was on board for its 2nd and 3rd anniversaries. He resides at Anderson Home, Lexington, KY (1966).

O'DONNELL, THOMAS, 606-37-08, enlisted Feb. 17, 1942, Boston, MA. He is a plankowner and served aboard BB-59 as AS 5th Div. at commissioning May 12, 1942, and was on board for its 2nd and 3rd anniversaries. He resides at 24 Lake Ave., Woburn, MA 01801.

OEDEL, HOWARD TREDENNICK, born July 9, 1921, Boston, MA. Earned an AB from Harvard University 1943; a MAT from Harvard 1947; and Ph.D. from Boston University 1960. Joined the Navy September 1943, Naval ROTC at Harvard University. Served aboard BB-59 as ENS R Div. September 1943 and left BB-59 as LT(jg) Bremerton, WA, December 1945.

After the war he taught prep school 1946-57; Lesley College, Cambridge, MA, 1957-61; Southern Connecticut State University 1961-81 as professor of history. In his spare time he is an antique dealer; involved in historic restoration and preservation; travel; gardening and photography. He married Carolyn Townsend May 28, 1943, Wellesley, MA, and has one son, one daughter, and four grandchildren (August 1993). He resides at Uriah Pike Place, E. Hebron, NH.

OGNIBENE, JOSEPH ANDREW, 646-69-22, born in Morristown, NJ. Graduated from high school and enlisted Feb. 7, 1942, New York, NY, with training at Coddington Point, Newport, RI. He is a plankowner and served aboard BB-59 as S2/c 5th Div. at commissioning May 12, 1942; was on board for its 2nd anniversary as F2/c A Div. and for its 3rd anniversary as MM3/c A Div. He left BB-59 at Pearl Harbor, HI. He was assigned to USS *Maggoffin* (APA-199).

After the war he war he was STA. ENG for the city of New York. In his spare time he is involved in the K of C (4th Degree) and American Legion; Senior Citizens; and enjoys traveling, bowling, golf, hunting and archery. He married Sadie Rosaria April 23, 1950, and has three children and three grandchildren. He resides at 96-20 159th Ave., Howard Beach, NY 11414.

O'KEEFE, THOMAS RICHARD, 223-49-20, enlisted Jan. 3, 1942, San Francisco, CA. He is a plankowner and served aboard BB-59 as MM2/c at commissioning May 12, 1942.

OLBERG, STIRLING MEACHAM, 413-47-00, born in Petaluma, Sonoma County, CA. Graduated from high school and attended US Naval Radio School, Stanford, CA. He enlisted Aug. 2, 1940, Santa Rosa, CA, and assigned to USS *Maryland*, Pearl Harbor, HI. Also trained at Radio Engineering and USN Radio School, San Francisco.

He is a plankowner and served aboard BB-59 as RM3/c CR Div. at commissioning May 12, 1942, and was on board for its 2nd and 3rd anniversaries. He left BB-59 Oct. 6, 1946, Oakland, CA. He was assigned to US Naval Intelligence School, PHN Yard; PHTH US Embassy, Christ Church, New Zealand; (CRRM) to Stanford, CA, for BSEE and Physics Master.

After the war he was an engineer at radio astronomy lab at Harvard College Observatory; GTE Lab engineer, Fiber Optics Lab; lab tech for Ewen Knight Corp.; and engineer in charge of Needham Radio Telescope facility. Part of Homecoming Crew, 1965 (operated Ham radio broadcasting from ship for five days.) In his spare time he operates an amateur radio station W2SNN Satellite AO17; member of Pearl Harbor Survivors and Amateur Radio Net. Holds MA Pearl Harbor License Plate PJ16HIHI. He married Florence April 27, 1947, and has two daughters. He resides at 19 Loretta Ave., Waltham, MA.

OLCOTT, FRANK EDMOND, JR., 600-21-97, enlisted March 18, 1942, Albany, NY. He is a plankowner and served aboard BB-59 as AS at commissioning May 12, 1942, and was on board for its 2nd and 3rd anniversaries. Memory List 1977.

OLEJACK, JOSEPH E., USMC, May 8, 1942, Norfolk Navy Yard. He was a plankowner and served aboard BB-59 as PVT 7th Div. at commissioning May 12, 1942. Memory List 1977.

OLFSON, J.N., name appears on 3rd anniversary of commissioning as a plankowner.

OLINGER, ROBERT HAMILTON, 652-19-36, born Aug. 12, 1921, Pittsburgh, PA. Graduated from high and attended one year of vocational at Carnegie Tech. Enlisted Feb. 9, 1942, Pittsburgh, PA, and trained at Newport, RI.

He is a plankowner and served aboard BB-59 as AS 6th Div. at commissioning May 12, 1942, and was

on board for its 2nd and 3rd anniversaries; became gun captain Mount #4 BM2/c. Left BB-59 on Sept. 27, 1945.

After the war he was a stage technician for KDKA TV for 34 years and J.P. Harris Theatre for seven years. In his spare time is involved with Meals on Wheels, American Legion, Lodge 743 F&AM and deacon in Presby Church. Received Meritorious Service Award aboard BB-59.

He married Juanita E. May 6, 1949, in Pittsburgh, and has three children and four grandchildren. He resides at 598 Century Drive, Winter Haven, FL.

OLINS, BENNET SEYMOUR, 642-13-73, enlisted Feb. 21, 1942, New Haven, CT. He was a plankowner and served aboard BB-59 as AS at commissioning May 12, 1942. Memory List 1978.

OLIVA, FRANK ANTHONY, 201-46-36, enlisted Sept. 28, 1938, Mare Island, CA. He is a plankowner and served aboard BB-59 as CEM at commissioning May 12, 1942.

OLIVER, JAMES BROWN, JR., 258-12-99, enlisted June 10, 1936, Baltimore, MD. He is a plankowner and served aboard BB-59 as S1/c at commissioning May 12, 1942.

OLIVERIA, JOSEPH, JR., part of Homecoming Crew; 1965 Field Day crew member and received BB-59 Award, 1969.

OLNEY, HENRY WESTPHAL, 646-72-19, enlisted Feb. 10, 1942, New York, NY. He is a plankowner and served aboard BB-59 as AS at commissioning May 12, 1942.

OLSEN, KENNETH ARTHUR, 224-73-73, enlisted March 10, 1942, New York, NY. He is a plankowner and served aboard BB-59 as AS 5th Div. at commissioning May 12, 1942. He resides at 213 West County Line Rd., Calimesa, CA 92320.

OLSON, ARCHIE LEONARD, served aboard BB-59 as ChRadElec Jan. 27, 1945. Memory List 1989.

OLSON, REX EUGENE, 393-55-20, enlisted May 26, 1941, Washington, DC. He is a plankowner and served aboard BB-59 as Mus3/c X Div. at commissioning May 12, 1942.

O'MALLEY, WILLIAM FRANCIS, 242-88-99, enlisted Nov. 17, 1937, New York, NY. He is a plankowner and served aboard BB-59 as CFC at commissioning May 12, 1942, and was on board for its 2nd anniversary.

O'NEILL, HENRY JOSEPH, 602-04-05, enlisted Dec. 15, 1941, Baltimore, MD. He is a plankowner and served aboard BB-59 as SF2/c at commissioning May 12, 1942. He resides at Box 204 RFD #2, Middleboro, MA. Memory List 1996.

O'NEILL, HOWARD RAYMOND, 224-74-28, enlisted March 12, 1942, New York, NY. He is a

plankowner and served aboard BB-59 as AS at commissioning May 12, 1942.

O'NEILL, JOHN ALOYSUIS, 652-13-70, enlisted Jan. 20, 1942, Pittsburgh, PA. He is a plankowner and served aboard BB-59 as AS at commissioning May 12, 1942, and was on board for its 2nd and 3rd anniversaries, plankowner.

O'NEILL, JOHN HENRY, JR., 606-34-50, born in Cambridge, MA. Graduated from high school Lowell, MA, and business course at Lowell. Enlisted Feb. 9, 1942, Boston, MA, and boot camp, Gunnery and Communications Training.

He was a plankowner and served aboard BB-59 as AS 4th Div. at commissioning May 12, 1942, and was on board for its 2nd and 3rd anniversaries, RN2/c CR Div. Left BB-59 in September 1945. Assigned to USNTC San Diego, CA; USNTC Bainbridge, MD; USS *T.J. Gary;* USS *Rhodes;* USS *Kitty Hawk;* COMSTA London, England; NTC Newport, RI; Yokuska, Japan; USNRTC Santa Monica, CA; and retired as master chief radioman in San Diego, CA, September 1969.

After the war he had various US Navy assignments (Navy Intelligence); three years Washington, DC; three in Tehran, Iran; and two years in Istanbul, Turkey. He spends his spare time at VFW Thrift Shop and one day a week at Camp Verde.

He married Tamara, State Line, NV, and had four children and two grandchildren. He resided at HC-62-3858 Aspen Way, Camp Verde, AZ 86322. Memory List 1996.

O'NEIL, PETER F., LT, resided at Pray's Dept. Store, 132 Tremont St., Boston and Shirley St., Winthrop, MA. Memory List 1977.

O'NEILL, RAYMOND FRANCIS, 646-62-82, enlisted Feb. 2, 1942, New York, NY. He is a plankowner and served aboard BB-59 as AS at commissioning May 12, 1942.

ONGARO, FRANK NONDO, 385-49-57, enlisted Dec. 13, 1941, San Francisco, CA. He is a plankowner and served aboard BB-59 as CCM at commissioning May 12, 1942.

OPALENIK, MIKE, 283-14-89, enlisted Aug. 30, 1941, Portland, ME. He is a plankowner and served aboard BB-59 as SM1/c at commissioning May 12, 1942, and was on board for its 2nd and 3rd anniversaries. He left BB-59 July 13, 1944, to R/S, PSNY Bremerton, WA.

ORCHULEK, STANISLAS ALBERT, 212-32-55, enlisted June 22, 1939, Springfield, MA. He is a plankowner and served aboard BB-59 as COX at commissioning May 12, 1942.

ORD, HARVEY L., has two daughters and three grandchildren (as of March 30, 1992). He resides at 207 Wildwood Rd., Council Bluffs, IA 51503.

ORLANDO, JOSEPH, (n) 214-55-74, enlisted Dec. 15, 1941, Albany, NY. He was a plankowner and served aboard BB-59 as EM1/c E Div. at commissioning May 12, 1942. After the war he worked for the Boston Naval Shipyard (1955). He resided at 12 Otis St., Somerville, MA (1955). His son resides at 21 Applewood Drive, Saco, ME 04072. Memory List 1996.

ORURELAR, BENJAMIN, resides at 630 Price St., Santa Barbara, CA (1966).

OSBORN, JOHN AMBROSE, 250-72-70, enlisted March 11, 1942, Pittsburgh, PA. He is a plankowner and served aboard BB-59 as AS 2nd Div. and his 2nd and 3rd anniversaries, plankowner. He left BB-59 November 1945 S1/c.

After the war he was an ironworker and has two children. He resides at 131 Campbell St., Kittanning, PA.

OSBORNE, CROCKETT, resides at 5014 Meadowlark Lane, Roswell, NM.

OSBORNE, JAMES BRADFORD, 279-69-66, enlisted July 10, 1940, Cincinnati, OH. He is a plankowner and served aboard BB-59 as Bkr3/c at commissioning May 12, 1942.

OSBORNE, THOMAS KEEFE, 606-34-65, enlisted Feb. 9, 1942, Boston, MA. He is a plankowner and served aboard BB-59 as SK3/c S Div. at commissioning May 12, 1942, disbursing storekeeper – in charge of disbursing office. He left BB-59 Dec. 29, 1945.

After the war he was office manager for Cutler Motor Sales, Inc. and was VFW commander in his spare time. Memory List 1986. Last resided at 15 Clapp St., Malden, MA.

O'SULLIVAN, THOMAS, USMC, born Aug. 19, 1917, and attended South Boston High School. Trained CCC's 1933; and USMC Parris Island, April 1940. Served aboard BB-59 as PVT 7th Div. 1942, and assigned to Attu, Kiska, AK; joined 6th Marine Div. forming in Linda Vista, CA, and went to Okinawa, Easter Sunday 1945. Received the Bronze Star and Purple Heart 1945.

He married Katherine (died 1973) and then Geraldine 1979, Boston. He has four children and resides at 60 Joan Drive, Quincy, MA.

OSWALT, HARRY P., Memory List 1977.

OUTCALT, CHARLES THOMAS, 371-89-54, born May 6, 1915, Denver, CO. Graduated from Moreno, CO, High School and enlisted June 12, 1934, Sterling, CO. Trained at San Diego, CA, NTS and assigned USS *Kanawha* (tanker) to Panama Canal Zone; USS *Louisville*, 1934-38; 1940 San Diego destroyer base, working on four pipers going to England; 1940-42 USS *Pennsylvania*, (S1/c to BM2/c) Pearl Harbor attack.

He is a plankowner and served aboard BB-59 January 1942, Quincy, MA, and as BM2/c 1st Div. at commissioning May 12, 1942, BM1/c to CMB to ENS. He left BB-59 in June 1944 Bremerton, WA. Was also assigned NavPhibTraining, Norfolk; training XO LSM class ships; commissioned LSM-105 as XO; South Pacific-high octane gas to Guadalcanal to Eniwetok; transported USMC and 51st CB's to various islands. After WWII to ConusGreenCoveSprings to decommission LSM-105. At his own request reverted to CBM. In 1946-48 in charge air sea rescue at US NavAirFac, John Rogers Air Station, Honolulu, HI, December 1948-51; chief master at arms NavPhibBase, Coronado, CA; 1951-52 USS *Washburn*; 1952-55 USS *Los Angeles* (CA-135); June 1951 to April 1953 Korean Theater of Operations; Fleet Reserve F6; and retired CBM July 18, 1955.

After his Navy career, 1956-79 worked for GMRD, STL, TRW (security) and retired December 1979. He married Charlotte June 8, 1944, Denver, CO, and has two children, five grandchildren and one great-grandson (as of August 1994). He died Dec. 8, 1992; Memory List 1993. (Mrs.) resides at 4207 W. 173rd St., Torrance, CA.

OVERBEY, JOHN KIRKWOOD, USMC, served aboard BB-59 2nd LT 7th Div. on Oct. 30, 1944, and left BB-59 1st LT (no date).

OWCZARSKI, FRANK JOHN, 610-18-58, enlisted Dec. 22, 1941, Chicago, IL. He is a plankowner and served aboard BB-59 as F1/c at commissioning May 12, 1942.

OWEN, IRLAM BLACKLEDGE, 660-18-11, enlisted Jan. 29, 1942, Salt Lake City, UT. He is a plankowner and served aboard BB-59 as AS CR Div. at commissioning May 12, 1942, and S2/c CR to FR Div. March 10, 1943, and on board for its 2nd anniversary.

OWENS, FRANK TOLBER, served aboard BB-59 as ENS CR Div. on May 21, 1944, and left BB-59 as LT(jg) Oct. 16, 1945.

PABLISKI, JOSEPH, Memory List 1983.

PACZKOWSKI, JOSEPH JAMES, 646-70-82, enlisted Feb. 9, 1942, New York, NY. He is a plankowner and served aboard BB-59 as AS at commissioning May 12, 1942, and was on board for its 2nd and 3rd anniversaries.

PADDOCK, JAMES ROBERT, 355-65-82, enlisted Oct. 31, 1940, Mare Island, CA. He is a plankowner and served aboard BB-59 as CPhM at commissioning May 12, 1942.

PAGETT, ROBERT L., Memory List 1989. (Mrs.) resides at 111 Highland Dr., Duncan, SC.

PAGE, WILLARD GARDNER, 606-49-41, enlisted March 12, 1942, Boston, MA. He is a plankowner and served aboard BB-59 as AS at commissioning May 12, 1942, and was on board for its 2nd and 3rd anniversaries.

PALMA, JOHN TONY, 646-69-29, born in Newark, NJ. He enlisted Feb. 7, 1942, New York, NY, and trained at NTS Newport, RI, and R/Sta. Fargo, Boston.

He was a plankowner and served aboard BB-59 as S1/c 6th Div. at commissioning May 12, 1942, and was on board for its 2nd and 3rd anniversaries. He left BB-59 Sept. 15, 1945, Seattle, WA.

After the war he worked as a longshoreman (foreman). He married Florence May 30, 1944, Newark, NJ, and had two sons and two grandsons. He resided at 10 Seely Terr., Bloomfield, NJ 07003. Memory List 1996.

PALMER, EDWARD WALLACE, 606-36-77, born Sept. 24, 1917, Winchester, MA. Graduated from Stoneham, MA, High School, 1935 and Boston University College of Commerce, 1947. Worked at the New England Telephone Company and enlisted Feb. 13, 1942, Boston, MA. Was assigned Y3/c Boston Recruiting Station (fingerprinting).

He served aboard BB-

59 April 1942, Quincy, MA, and was plankowner at commissioning May 12, 1942. Served in chaplain's, yeoman, librarian, editor of ship's newspaper and was also D.J. He left BB-59 April 1943 Nouema; transferred via HMS *Engadene* to US to US Navy School of Photography, Pensacola, FL, September 1943 graduated PhoM2/c, and appointed an instructor of photography to September 1945.

After the war he returned to New England Telephone Company in charge of audio-visual department. Worked later for AT&T Company in public relations in New York City as exhibits and display supervisor. In 1949 he returned to Boston and pioneered the use of video for training. In his spare time he organized professional audio-visual and television associations; Audio-Visual Mgmt. Assoc., International Television Assoc. (first chairman, board of directors); also active in local town committees, school committees, historical commission and others.

Was past president of BB-59 Assoc. and formed USS *Massachusetts* Memorial Inc. and became first chairman, board of directors. Homecoming Crew, 1965 and signed for the ship in Norfolk, VA, for the Memorial Committee. Received BB-59 Award, 1967; Silver Anvil Award from the Public Relations Society of America, 1966; and name appears in many Who's Who publications, including *Who's Who in the World*. He married Grace Storti March 16, 1944, US Naval Chapel, Pensacola, FL. He has five children and four grandchildren and resides at 45 Pratt St., Reading, MA 01867.

PALMER, HAROLD BROWN, 238-69-92, enlisted Oct. 22, 1940, Albany, NY. He is a plankowner and served aboard BB-59 as S1/c at commissioning May 12, 1942.

PALMER, JOHN LEWIS, 382-88-44, enlisted March 24, 1942, Los Angeles, CA. He is a plankowner and served aboard BB-59 as Matt3/c at commissioning May 12, 1942.

PALMITER, HOWARD ELLIOT, 393-33-03, born June 27, 1914, Kennewick, WA. Graduated Palouse, WA, High School, Class of 1932 and enlisted Dec. 13, 1939, Portland, WA. Trained before USN-CCC 1934-39, Arctic and Maryland. He was a plankowner and served aboard BB-59 as SC3/c S Div. at commissioning May 12, 1942, and as SC2/c to SC1/c to chief commissary steward. Left BB-59 in November 1945.

After the war he worked at Madigan General Hospital, Ft. Lewis, WA, (Dept. of Army) as a cook. He was active in the American Legion; VFW; Disabled American Vets; American Fed of Government Employees Navy League; Fleet Reserve; and Asbury Methodist Church. Was honored as Federal Employee of the Year at Madigan, 1970.

He married Lillian (died) and had one son, three grandchildren and three great-grandchildren. He died July 7, 1989; Memory List 1990. John D. (son) resides at 29 Maybury Rd., Gray, ME 04039. (Howard was adopted at age 3 months.)

PAPA, PAUL PIETRO, 274-52-38, enlisted Oct. 8, 1940, New Orleans, LA. He is a plankowner and served aboard BB-59 as GM3/c at commissioning May 12, 1942.

PAPINEAU, CLAUDE WELDON, 600-15-71, enlisted Feb. 11, 1942, Albany, NY. He is a plankowner and served aboard BB-59 as AS at commissioning May 12, 1942, and was on board for its 2nd anniversary.

PARCHI, JOHN P., resides at 13 Coolidge St., Everett, MA.

PARDEE, HOWARD OWEN, 608-13-04, enlisted March 9, 1942, Buffalo, NY. He is a plankowner and served aboard BB-59 as AS at commissioning May 12, 1942, and was on board for its 2nd and 3rd anniversaries.

PARKE, FRANKLIN EDWARD, FC Div., served aboard BB-59 as ENS March 1943 and in 1st Div. May 1943. He left BB-59 Nov. 7, 1944, LT(jg).

PARKHURST, JOHN SULLIVAN, 337-28-54, enlisted March 26, 1940, St. Louis, MO. He is a plankowner and served aboard BB-59 as S1/c at commissioning May 12, 1942, and was on board for its 2nd anniversary.

PARKS, JIMMIE, (n) 337-11-41, enlisted Jan. 12, 1939, St. Louis, MO. He is a plankowner and served aboard BB-59 as Matt2/c at commissioning May 12, 1942.

PARKS, MARVIN DAVID, 261-71-06, enlisted Sept. 6, 1935, Norfolk, VA. He is a plankowner and served aboard BB-59 as MM1/c at commissioning May 12, 1942.

PAROLA, FREDERICK ERNEST, 647-01-81, enlisted Feb. 20, 1942, New York, NY. He served aboard BB59 Feb. 20, 1942, Quincy, MA, and as COX 5th Div. at commissioning May 12, 1942. He was a plankowner and on board for its 2nd and 3rd anniversaries. Left BB-59 Sept. 23, 1945.

After the war he was assessor for Nassau County, Assessment Dept. He was active in the VFW; American Legion and Wantagh Republican Club.

He had one son, Fred Jr. Memory List 1977. He resided at 2 Beverly Rd., Bellmore, NY (1966).

PARROTT, ALTON RAY, 656-11-63, enlisted Nov. 4, 1941, Raleigh, NC.

He is a plankowner and served aboard BB-59 as F3/c E Div. at commissioning May 12, 1942, and was on board for its 2nd and 3rd anniversaries. Memory List 1990. (Mrs.) resides PO Box 53, Branchville, SC.

PARTCH, WILLARD SOOFIELD, 380-87-13, enlisted Oct. 1, 1938, San Diego, CA. He is a plankowner and served aboard BB-59 as SC1/c at commissioning May 12, 1942.

PARTIN, EMMETT B., born July 19, 1923, Durham, NC. Graduated from Chapel Hill High School, 1942, and enlisted Oct. 21, 1942, Raleigh, NC. Trained at Great Lakes, IL.

He served aboard BB-59 as S1/c 6th Div. on Dec. 10, 1942, and left November 1945, Seattle, WA. Was discharged from Separation Center in Nashville, TN, Dec. 22, 1945.

After the war he worked for Western Electric Manufacturing July 15, 1946, retiring July 15, 1981 (35 years). Later he was a US Postal worker (RCA) a rural carrier sub.

He married Irene Jan. 4, 1947, in Hillsboro, NC, and has three children. He resides at 1466 Morningside Drive, Burlington, NC 27215.

PASEUR, JOHN LARK, LT M Div., served aboard BB-59 March 8, 1945, as LT and left Nov. 29, 1945, as LT CDR.

PATTESON, WALTER RANDOLPH, 375-91-66, enlisted Oct. 13, 1938, San Francisco, CA. He was a plankowner and served aboard BB-59 as COX at commissioning May 12, 1942. He died in 1978; Memory List 1979. (Mrs.) resides at PO Box 64, Tracy, CA.

PATTON, CRAIG LYCOS, 652-20-52, enlisted Feb. 12, 1942, Pittsburgh, PA. He is a plankowner and served aboard BB-59 as AS CR Div. at commissioning May 12, 1942; March 10, 1943, as S2/c CR to FR Div.; and May 12, 1944, aboard for the 2nd anniversary of BB59's commissioning.

PATTON, THOMAS FURRY, 652-18-03, enlisted Feb. 3, 1942, Pittsburgh, PA. He is a plankowner and served aboard BB-59 as AS at commissioning May 12, 1942, and was on board for its 2nd and 3rd anniversaries. Old address was Westville, PA.

PATZ, WILLIAM, (n) 224-73-30, enlisted March 9, 1942, New York, NY. He is a plankowner and served aboard BB-59 as AS at commissioning May 12, 1942.

PAULEY, FRANK, 726-77-73, born Nov. 19, 1925, Chicago, IL. Graduated from high school and trained at Great Lakes, IL. Served aboard BB-59 as S1/c L Div. (forward lookout) and left BB-59 Long Beach, CA. After the war he was in Ironworker's Local Union #1 as secretary/treasurer, Forest Park, IL. Is active in children's charities as a board member. He married Jean November 1971 and has one son, three grandsons and one great-grandson. He resides at 5161 So. LaPorte, 2W, Chicago, IL.

PAULINE, JOSEPH V., S Div., resides at 140 W. Court Manor Place, Decatur, IL 62522.

PAULK, BROOKS, Memory List 1982.

PAULSEN, GEORGE WILLIAM, 328-63-93, enlisted Jan. 3, 1940, Minneapolis, MN. He is a plankowner and served aboard BB-59 as S1/c at commissioning May 12, 1942,

PAUSTIAN, EARL EDGAR, 371-96-37, enlisted Dec. 16, 1941, Pearl Harbor, HI. He is a plankowner and served aboard BB-59 as RM2/c at commissioning May 12, 1942.

PAVIK, MICHAEL, (n) 646-69-31, enlisted Feb. 7, 1942, New York, NY. He is a plankowner and served aboard BB-59 as AS at commissioning May 12, 1942. He resides at 25 W. 26th St., Bayonne, NJ.

PEACH, CLYDE, 607-05-21, born Oct. 2, 1923, Chelsea, MA. Graduated from Saugus, MA, High School and attended Northeastern University for two years. Enlisted March 1942 and trained at Newport, RI, Electrical School. He served aboard BB-59 as EM3/c E Div. December 1942, and EM2/c 1943. He left BB-59 December 1945 Seattle, WA.

After the war he was an apprentice orthotist for BusLenfeldt Company; certified orthotist for Michael Reese Hospital; orthotic engineer for PapeBiareDir.; president/owner of Indiana Brace Company; and retired in 1989. Enjoys fishing, golf and Rotary Club. He married Helen March 1992 in Indianapolis, IN. He has

three children, seven grandchildren and resides at 7018 Castle Manor Drive, Indianapolis, IN 46214.

PEARSALL, ARTHUR WILLIAM, 228-12-03, enlisted Dec. 31, 1941, New York, NY. He is a plankowner and served aboard BB-59 as Pmkr2/c at commissioning May 12, 1942.

PEARSON, JAMES R., 943-18-02, born Nov. 30, 1920, Watseka, IL. Graduated from high school and trained at Fire Control School, San Diego, CA. Served aboard BB-59 as S1/c FC Div. in August 1944 and left December 1945, Bremerton, WA.

After the war he worked in purchasing and production control, 1946-87; director of purchases for Bohn Heat Transf. Company, Danville, IL, 1966-73; director of purchasing and materials for the Tridan Tool & Machine, Inc. in Danville, IL, 1973-87; and retired in 1987 to consulting work. He married Alberta Aug. 10, 1941, in Danville, IL, and has one son.

PEASE, THOMAS CLIFFORD, 239-30-20, enlisted Dec. 12, 1941, Albany, NY. He is a plankowner and served aboard BB-59 as SF3/c at commissioning May 12, 1942.

PECOR, STEPHEN FRANCIS, JR., 642-11-72, born Jan. 9, 1919, Bridgeport, CT. Graduated from high school and attended Singer Co. Enlisted Feb. 4, 1942, New Haven, CT. He was a plankowner and served aboard BB-59 as AS at commissioning May 12, 1942, and was on board for its 2nd and 3rd anniversaries.

After the war he worked for the Singer Sewing Machine Company as a tool maker and later in the engineering department. In his spare time he enjoys art and did it as a hobby.

He married Lola Jan. 26, 1946, in Bridgeport, CT, and has two children and three grandchildren. He died April 3, 1968; Memory List 1977. (Mrs.) resides at 41 Corntassle Rd., Naugatuck, CT 06770 (October 1994).

PEDERSON, ERNEST WALTER, 328-92-34, enlisted June 10, 1941, Minneapolis, MN. He is a plankowner and served aboard BB-59 as F3/c at commissioning May 12, 1942.

PEKERA, DANIEL, JR., (n) 207-38-13, born Feb. 8, 1925, Shelton, CT. Graduated from Shelton High School and enlisted Feb. 27, 1942, New Haven, CT. Trained at Newport, RI 132.

He is a plankowner and served aboard BB-59 as AS 5th Div. at commissioning May 12, 1942, and as S1/c – COX. Left BB-59 at Nouema, New Caledonia. Additional service included Sub Base, New London, CT; Sub School – failed physical in pressure tank but remained in ship's company; then to Chelsea Naval Hospital to receive medical discharge.

After the war he worked for the police department Shelton, CT; director public works 1957-59; foreman public works 1960-68; and retired April 1968. In his spare time he was chairman of War Memorial Committee for 25 years and 1st commander VFW Post 1236, Shelton, CT. Was honor graduate of New Haven Police Academy (3.9 average). He married Christine Sept. 21, 1946, and has two children. He resides at 72 New St., Shelton, CT 06484.

PELLARIN, VICTOR LOUIS, 223-24-87, born May 1, 1918, New York, NY. A high school graduate with some college experience, he enlisted Oct. 1, 1935. Trained at NTC Newport, RI; School of Hospital Administration, Bethesda, MD; and Armed Forces Staff College, Newport. He was assigned to Naval Hospital, Brooklyn, NY; Naval Hospital, Washington, DC; USS *Pennsylvania* (BB-38); RecSta. San Francisco; Destroyer Base, San Diego, CA; and USS *Ortolen*.

He served aboard BB-59 Feb. 10, 1942, Quincy, MA, for ship "fitting out"; Quincy to Boston and as Phm1/c H Div. at commissioning May 12, 1942, as a plankowner. He was appointed CPhM Nov. 1, 1942, on way to Casablanca. He left BB-59 on Nov. 26, 1942. Was assigned to USS *Relief*; USS *Curtis*; NTC Great Lakes; Naval Hospital Quantico, VA; Air Trans., Evacuation Squadron One; NATS VR 6 Bureau of Medicine and Surgery and retired CDR #283663.

After the war he worked for Montgomery Public Schools, Rockville, MD. He enjoys golf in his spare time. He married Elizabeth Aug. 30, 1939, in Long Beach, CA, and has four sons and eight grandchildren. He resides at 193 Monterey Isle, So., Longwood, FL 32779.

PELLICONE, MYER JOSEPH, "MIKE," 642-14-21, born Sept. 26, 1916, Westport, CT. Graduated from Staples High School and enlisted Feb. 25, 1942, New Haven, CT. Trained at Newport, RI. He is a plankowner and served aboard BB-59 as AS 1st Div. at commissioning May 12, 1942, and was on board for its 2nd and 3rd anniversaries. Left BB-59 October 1945 as GM3/c Turret #1.

After the war he worked as an electrical contractor and in electrical installations. He is active in the VFW; as a volunteer firemen, Westport, CT; golf; and softball.

He married Eleanor Sept. 11, 1952, in Westport, and has two step-children, six grandchildren and three great-grandchildren. He resides at 40 Salem Rd., Weston, CT.

PELPIER, GEORGE, resides at 1883 Birch Lake Ave., White Bear Lake, MN 55110.

PENDER, SAMUEL T., USMC, May 8, 1942, Norfolk Naval Yard. He is a plankowner and served aboard BB-59 as SGT 7th Div. at commissioning May 12, 1942.

PENDERGAST, GEORGE W., Memory List 1985.

PENIRIAN, ROBERT L., served aboard BB-59 as S2/c 4th Div. November 1943 Deck 20mm and 40mm. Left BB-59 in March 1946. After the war he was a route salesman (1966) for Challenge Dairy. He has three children and resides at 2982 Bush St., San Francisco, CA (1966).

PENKERT, RAYMOND WALKER, 321-75-36, enlisted Feb. 24, 1942, Des Moines, IA. He is a plankowner and served aboard BB-59 as AS at commissioning May 12, 1942.

PEPPER, JOSEPH W., USMC 7th Div., Memory List 1991. (Mrs.) resides at Box 397, Clayton, NM 88415.

PEREZ-GUERRA, ALFRED ANTHONY, 4th Div., served aboard BB-59 April 6, 1944, Class of 1943 and July 1945 LT USN.

PERISHO, DONALD MAX, 300-42-43, enlisted April 4, 1941, Washington, DC. He is a plankowner and served aboard BB-59 as Mus2/c X Div. at commissioning May 12, 1942.

PERKINS, CHARLES WARREN, 200-84-14, enlisted Oct. 28, 1935, Boston, MA. He is a plankowner and served aboard BB-59 as CWT at commissioning May 12, 1942.

PERKINS, LESLIE, (n) 606-36-63, enlisted March 16, 1942, Boston, MA. He is a plankowner and served aboard BB-59 as AS at commissioning May 12, 1942, and was on board for its 2nd and 3rd anniversaries. He resides at 30 Doughty Rd., No. Yarmouth, ME 04097.

PERKINS, PAUL, USMC, May 8, 1942, Norfolk Navy Yard. He is a plankowner and served aboard BB-59 as SGT 7th Div. at commissioning May 12, 1942.

PERKOSKI, STANLEY MICHAEL, 606-47-29, enlisted March 12, 1942, Boston, MA. He is a plankowner and served aboard BB-59 as AS at commissioning May 12, 1942. He resides at 136 Metcalf Rd., No. Attleboro, MA (1955).

PERRAS, WILBERT EDWARD, 212-60-68, enlisted Oct. 21, 1940, Springfield, MA. He is a plankowner and served aboard BB-59 as S1/c E Div. at commissioning May 12, 1942, and was on board for its 3rd anniversary as BM1/c (MAA).

After the war he worked for the Mother of Pearl Cross Company in manufacturing. He is active in the American Legion #343 and the DAV #116 in his spare time. He resides at Fowler St., Northbridge, MA (1966).

PERRY, CHARLES MATTHEW, 646-69-33, enlisted Feb. 7, 1942, New York, NY. He was a plankowner and served aboard BB-59 as AS at commissioning May 12, 1942, and was on board for its 2nd and 3rd anniversaries. Memory List 1977.

PERRY, EDWARD ALBERT, 400-87-63, enlisted Oct. 19, 1940, Boston, MA. He is a plankowner and served aboard BB-59 as S1/c at commissioning May 12, 1942.

PERRY, JOHN HOPPER, 647-01-82, enlisted Feb. 20, 1942, New York, NY. He was a plankowner and served aboard BB-59 as AS at commissioning May 12, 1942, and was on board for its 2nd anniversary. Memory List 1993. (Mrs.) resides at Box 888, N. Eastham, MA 02651.

PETERS, EDWARD IRVING, ENS M Div., served aboard BB-59 May 21, 1944, and July 1945 as LT(jg).

PETERS, HOWARD J., USMC, May 8, 1942, Norfolk Navy Yard. He is a plankowner and served aboard BB-59 as PFC 7th Div. at commissioning May 12, 1942.

PETERS, WILLIAM LAVERNE, 316-88-81, enlisted Jan. 26, 1942, Omaha, NE. He is a plankowner and served aboard BB-59 as AS at commissioning May 12, 1942, and was on board for its 2nd anniversary.

PETERSON, WALTER D., a father of three children (as of March 1992), resides at 32 Virginia Hills, Council Bluffs, IA 51503.

PETRACCI, PELLIGRINO, 647-02-21, enlisted Feb. 20, 1942, New York, NY. He is a plankowner and served aboard BB-59 as AS at commissioning May 12, 1942, and was on board for its 2nd anniversary.

PETRILLO, THOMAS JOHN, 606-46-38, enlisted March 10, 1942, Boston, MA. He is a plankowner and served aboard BB-59 as AS 5th

Div. at commissioning May 12, 1942, and as shell loader mount 5 S1/c. Left BB-59 September 1943.

After the war he worked for AF Electronic Systems Div., Bedford, MA, as a carpenter. He has four children (as of 1966).

In his spare time he is involved in the American Legion # 122; VFW Post #1617, Derry, NH; and Military Order of the Purple Heart post #334, Lowell, MA. He resides at 11 Florence Rd., Methuen, MA 01844.

PETROCCI, RALEIGH R., USMC, May 8, 1942, Norfolk Navy Yard. He is a plankowner and served aboard BB-59 as PVT 7th Div. at commissioning May 12, 1942, and was on board for its 2nd and 3rd anniversaries.

PETROCCIA, WILLIAM J., served aboard BB-59 in A Div. June 1942 and ice machines two and a half years MM2/c.

After the war he worked for Wtby Store & Fixtures Company in refrigeration and AC serviceman.

He married Marie and has one daughter (as of 1966). He resides at 43 Ball Farm Rd., Oakville, CT 06779.

PETTI, ANTHONY VICTOR, 608-05-04, enlisted Jan. 6, 1942, Buffalo, NY. He is a plankowner and served aboard BB-59 as EM2/c E Div. at commissioning May 12, 1942. He resides at 56 Hawthorne Ave., Buffalo, NY 14223.

PETTITT, CLAUDE S., "BOB," 392957, USMC, born Jan. 22, 1924, Siront Royal, VA. He graduated from Kenmore High School. Enlisted USMC July 8, 1942, Buffalo, NY, and trained at PT Sea School, Norfolk, VA, and Gunnery School in several places in Virginia. He served aboard BB-59 in 7th Div. AA FC man 594 Quads 8 and 9. Left BB-59 Oct. 12, 1945, Bremerton, WA.

After the war he worked for the New York Telephone Company, 1945-79 as an installer/repair, switching SVC, carrier, and microwave SVC. He was active in VFW Post #4287, Orlando, FL, as post trustee and honor guard.

He married Dolores in New York and has four children, seven step-children, 24 grandchildren and one great-granddaughter (as of January 1995). He resides at 6820 Pompeii Rd., Orlando, FL 32822 (1995).

PETTY, GEORGE E., USMC, May 8, 1942, Norfolk Navy Yard. He is a plankowner and served aboard BB-59 as SGT 7th Div. at commissioning May 12, 1942.

PEVEAR, RICHARD CLAYTON, 606-12-37, enlisted Dec. 23, 1941, Boston, MA.

He served aboard BB-59 in Quincy, MA, as Y3/c at commissioning May 12, 1942, as a plankowner and was on board for its 2nd and 3rd anniversaries.

PHILIPS, LOUIS CHARLES, ENS S Div., served aboard BB-59 May 1943 and 2nd anniversary May 12, 1944, as boxing judge.

PHILIPS, L.C., LT(jg) CR Div. served aboard BB-59 as Div. JO CBO on March 5, 1944.

PHILLIPS, CHARLES KLINGELHOFER, S Div., served aboard BB-59 as LT CDR supply officer on May 3, 1943, and left Sept. 24, 1945, as COMDR.

PHILLIPS, FRANCIS W., born in Hughsonville, NY, joined the Navy in 1942, Poughkeepsie, NY. Was assigned to USS *Sentinel* minesweeper. He served aboard BB-59 1943, Casco Bay, ME, as qualified gunners mate 4th Div. Left BB-59 December 1945, Bremerton, WA. After the war he became a master plumber for 40 years and spent his spare time farming and gardening. He married Maxine 1946 in Wappingers Falls, NY, and has four children, five grandchildren and one great-granddaughter. He resides at RR #2 Box 160, Springfield, IL 62707 (1994).

PHILLIPS, JAMES AUBREY, 337-53-92, enlisted Feb. 11, 1941, St. Louis, MO. He is a plankowner and served aboard BB-59 as S1/c at commissioning May 12, 1942, and was on board for its 2nd anniversary.

PHILLIPS, WILLIAM RAY, 342-04-12, enlisted Jan. 14, 1942, Bremerton, WA. He is a plankowner and served aboard BB-59 as SC2/c at commissioning May 12, 1942.

PICKETT, CONDY EVERETT, 294-85-74, enlisted Dec. 16, 1941, Nashville, TN. He is a plankowner and served aboard BB-59 as S1/c at commissioning May 12, 1942.

PIERCE, BURTON F., 203-28-22, born July 27, 1916, Seekonk, MA. He graduated from E. Providence High School and enlisted Oct. 10, 1942, Boston, MA, SF3/c and trained at USNTS Great Lakes, IL. He served aboard BB-59 Jan. 11, 1943, Boston, MA, as SF2/c and SF1/c. He left BB-59 Oct. 11, 1945, Bremerton, WA, and left the Navy Oct. 25, 1945, Boston, MA.

After the war he worked as a burner/welder for the Draper Corp.; and Beebe River, NH, Plant as machinist, millwright and production supervisor. He retired in 1976. In his spare time he drives patients to cancer treatment centers.

He married Jane Higgins July 2, 1941, Riverside, RI, and has three children and three grandchildren. (Burt adds that his son Steve served in USN 1971-91 and retired as intelligence officer on the USS *Carl Vinson*, at a much better rating than his dad!) He resides at Box 33, Rt. 49, Campton, NH 03223.

PIETRAS, BEN H., served aboard BB-59 in H Div. on June 7, 1944, and left Feb. 21, 1946, as PhM3/c. After the war he worked for the plastics division of Swedish Crucible Steel Company (leader) and is active in the VFW 4162. He resides at 11467 Klinger St., Hamtramck, MT 48212 (1966).

PIGNOTTI, NUNZIO FRANK, 648-10-00, enlisted Jan. 8, 1942, Omaha, NE. He was a plankowner and served aboard BB-59 as S2/c at commissioning May 12, 1942, and was on board for its 2nd and 3rd anniversaries. Memory List 1985. He resided at 3312 Corley St., Omaha, NE.

PILATO, GEORGE, born Jan. 30, 1919, Lowell, MA. Educated at St. Peter's School and Lowell High School and was a roofer from 1935-42. He enlisted Aug. 20, 1943, and trained at Newport, RI; Iowa State College, Ames, IA (EE School); to USS *Indiana* and USS *South Dakota*.

He served aboard BB-59 as EM3/c E Div. in 1944 and left BB-59 November 1945 Bremerton, WA.

After the war he worked as a roofer foreman for the city of Lowell, 1948-88 and retired in 1988 with 40 years of service. He is active in Veteran Affairs.

He married Rose M., in 1941, Lowell, MA, and has six children, 12 grandchildren and one great-grandson (as of September 1994). He resides at 56 Lyons St., Lowell, MA 01852.

PILGRIM, OLLASTER CONNORS, 648-15-11, enlisted Dec. 9, 1941, Richmond, VA. He is a plankowner and served aboard BB-59 as SF1/c at commissioning May 12, 1942, and was on board for its 2nd anniversary.

PIMER, RICHARD K., F Div., resides at Box 15 RD 2, Pennsburg, PA 18073.

PINI, SANTE ALBERT, 652-26-84, enlisted March 16, 1942, Pittsburgh, PA. He is a plankowner and served aboard BB-59 as AS at commissioning May 12, 1942.

PIPTO, MICHAEL THOMAS, 650-16-92, enlisted Jan. 16, 1942, Philadelphia, PA. He is a plankowner and served aboard BB-59 as AS at commissioning May 12, 1942.

PISCITELLI, LOUIS, (n) 224-73-76, enlisted March 10, 1942, New York, NY. He is a plankowner and served aboard BB-59 as AS at commissioning May 12, 1942, and was on board for its 2nd and 3rd anniversaries.

PITERA, FRANK T., B Div., resides at 9 Georgian Dr., Clark, NJ 07066.

PITMAN, ROY MELVIN, 656-10-90, enlisted Oct. 10, 1941, Raleigh, NC. He is a plankowner and served aboard BB-59 as EM3/c at commissioning May 12, 1942, and was on board for its 2nd and 3rd anniversaries.

PITTS, ARTHUR FRANCIS, 606-29-63, enlisted Jan. 31, 1942, Boston, MA. He is a plankowner and served aboard BB-59 as AS 5th Div. at commissioning May 12, 1942, and was on board for its 2nd and 3rd anniversaries. He resides at 1510 W. Ariana St., Lot 386, Lankland, FL 33803.

PLATE, CHARLES ALOYSIUS, 153-38-62, enlisted Dec. 27, 1941, Detroit, MI. He is a plankowner and served aboard BB-59 as EM2/c at commissioning May 12, 1942.

PLAYER, HEBER, Naval Academy 1933, served aboard BB-59 as LT 1st Div. March 1943. Memory List 1977-81 (LT Reginald H.) and 1982 (CDR Heber).

PLEMMONS, CHARLES, "FIREMAN," A Div., Oil King Gang, came from Buena Vista, PA. At the time of death he lived in Orlando, FL. His wife's name was Marie and he had two children. Memory List 1996. (Information supplied by Bob Emerick, Ephrata, PA, on Oct. 29, 1994.)

PODBIELSKI, JOSEPH JOHN, 646-60-43, enlisted Jan. 30, 1942, New York, NY. He is a plankowner and served aboard BB-59 as AS at commissioning May 12, 1942, and was on board for its 2nd and 3rd anniversaries.

PODSAID, JOHN S., USMC, May 8, 1942, Norfolk Navy Yard. He is a plankowner and served aboard BB-59 as PVT 7th Div. at commissioning May 12, 1942.

POGOR, EDWARD J., (was Pogorzelski before 1954), born Oct. 9, 1890, Philadelphia, PA. Graduated from high school and enlisted February 1942 Philadelphia, PA. Trained at Newport, RI.

He served aboard BB-59 in April 1942, firewatch on board in Quincy Shipyard. He served as COX 6th Div. at commissioning May 12, 1942, as a plankowner and left September 1945 Puget Sound, WA.

After the war he was a US Merchant Marine and an organizer of the National Maritime Union. He was business agent from 1960-65; research director 1967-70; and safety director 1970-77. Worked for handicapped blind veterans in N.E. and Pennsylvania area. He has one son, one daughter and four grandchildren and resides at PO Box 1017 PCP, Tobyhanna, PA.

POIOR, G.J., a plankowner, served aboard BB-59 at commissioning May 12, 1942.

POIRIER, GERARD JAMES, 642-12-50, enlisted Feb. 10, 1942, New Haven, CT. He is a plankowner and served aboard BB-59 as F2/c at commissioning May 12, 1942, and was on board for its 2nd anniversary.

POLICHUK, WOODROW, A Div., resides at 698 Easton Ave., San Bruno, CA.

POLITANO, CHARLES, (n) 223-78-94, enlisted Aug. 8, 1940, New York, NY. He is a plankowner and served aboard BB-59 as F2/c at commissioning May 12, 1942, and was on board for its 2nd anniversary.

POLLACK, JEROME P., "JERRY," CQM N Div., resides at 8316 TurpenHocken Ave., Elkins Park, PA 19117.

POLLARD, WILLIAM JAMES, 207-23-86, enlisted Sept. 9, 1939, New Haven, CT. He is a plankowner and served aboard BB-59 as F1/c at commissioning May 12, 1942.

POLONSKY, GRAHAM M., served aboard BB-59 as ET2/c CR Div. January 1943 and left September 1945. After the war he was a machinist at Boston Naval Shipyard. He married Barbara and has three children (1966). He resides at 35 Hampshire Ave., Sharon, MA..

POLTORAK, HENRY T., L and 4th Div., resided at 48 Esther St., Worcester, MA. Memory List 1996.

POLYAK, STEPHEN JOHN, 646-70-85, born June 28, 1921, Passaic, NJ. Trained at Newport, RI, to Fargo barracks, Boston. He is a plankowner and served aboard BB-59 as AS 1st Div. at commissioning May 12, 1942, and as S1/c, GM3/c and GM2/c. Left BB-59 1943 Noumea, New Caledonia. Was assigned to USS *Epping Forrest* (LSD-4) September 1943 to July 1945; USNH Corvalis, OR, from July 27, 1945, to Aug. 1, 1945; USNH St. Albans, L.I., NY, Aug. 1, 1945, to Jan. 7, 1946; USNSH Asbury Park, NJ, July 1, 1946, as GM2/c.

After the war he worked as a draftsman for Meycalex Corp. for five years; foreman and quality control for Sundial and Panel Corp., Caldwell, NJ, for 33 years. Enjoys bowling and is president of Passic County Bowling Assoc.

He married Anne, Sept. 11, 1943, in Passic, NJ, and has three daughters, seven granddaughters and one great-granddaughter (as of September 1994). He resides at 185 Lester Rd., Toms River, NJ.

POMEROY, GEORGE FRANKLIN, 622-25-45, enlisted Dec. 26, 1941, Detroit, MI. He is a plankowner and served aboard BB-59 as S2/c at commissioning May 12, 1942.

POND, WILLIAM EVERETT, ENS, served aboard BB-59 as OinC TDD Unit 63 on June 29, 1945, and left Aug. 7, 1945.

POOLE, THOMAS JUDSON, JR., 262-27-19, enlisted Feb. 23, 1938, Raleigh, NC. He is a plankowner and served aboard BB-59 as WT1/c at commissioning May 12, 1942.

POOLE, VERNNON H., resides at Rt. 3, Box 5541/2, Petersburg, VA (1966).

POOR, BURTON ROBERT, 646-62-87, born Dec. 14, 1922, Hillsdale, NJ. A high school graduate with some college, he enlisted Feb. 2, 1942, New York, NY. Training at Newport, RI, Boot Camp and Gunnery School.

He is a plankowner and served aboard BB-59 as AS 3rd Div. at commissioning May 12, 1942, and was on board for its 2nd and 3rd anniversaries as S1/c – X Div. laundry, P Div. 1st mach. space. Left BB-59 Nov. 30, 1945, Bremerton, WA.

After the war he worked as plant manager for Wright Metalcoater, Inc. (plating company) for 23 years; plant engineer for B. Blumenthal Company Inc. 17 years. Worked part-time at information center on I-80 in New Jersey near Delaware Water Gap. In his spare time he was Scoutmaster for 10 years, VFW and American Legion. Is a member of Sons of American Revolution (related to Brig. Gen. Poor).

Married Irmgard Aug. 7, 1977, in Paramus, NJ, and has two daughters and four grandchildren. He resides at RD#2 Box 374A, Kunkletown, PA 18058 (1994).

POPIELARSKI, ADOLPH JOSEPH, 650-73-98, enlisted Jan. 13, 1942, Philadelphia, PA. He is a plankowner and served aboard BB-59 as AS at commissioning May 12, 1942.

POPLOFSKY, ISADORE JOSEPH, 223-73-40, enlisted June 11, 1940, New York, NY. He is a plankowner and served aboard BB-59 as S1/c at commissioning May 12, 1942, and was on board for its 2nd and 3rd anniversaries.

POPOLO, JOSEPH, (n) 212-33-45, enlisted Nov. 20, 1939, Springfield, MA. He is a plankowner and served aboard BB-59 as F1/c at commissioning May 12, 1942.

POPPAS, EDWARD, (n) 291-50-73, enlisted Jan. 22, 1942, Indianapolis, IN. He is a plankowner and served aboard BB-59 as MM1/c at commissioning May 12, 1942.

POPTIEDWELL, G.D., served aboard BB-59 as GM1/c 6th Div. at commissioning May 12, 1942. He is a plankowner. He has four children and resides at Brown St., Westbrook, ME (1966).

PORCO, BRUNO, resides at 220-39th St., Pittsburgh, PA (1966).

PORTER, HARRY CLINTON, 642-00-97, born May 4, 1920, New Haven, CT. He finished high school with credits earned while in the Navy and worked for Vought Sikorsky, CT. Joined the Navy Sept. 9, 1941, New Haven, CT, and assigned NTS, Newport, RI and NTS (Electrical School) St. Louis, MO.

He is a plankowner and served aboard BB-59 as F3/c at commissioning May 12, 1942. Was also as-signed RS San Francisco, CA; RS Brooklyn, NY; NAS Banana River, FL; RS So. Annex, NOB, Norfolk, VA; and USNPSC, Lido Beach, LI, NY, Sept. 1, 1945.

After the war he worked for So. N.E. Telephone Company as installer, radio operator license and repaired mobile phones, and Telephone Headquarters, New Haven as foreman of installers. He retired after 37 years.

He married Evelyn, Oct. 16, 1948, St. Johns Church, Bridgeport, CT, and has three daughters, one son and 11 grandchildren. He resides at 185 Walnut Tree Hill Rd., Shelton, CT.

POST, MARK E., born Feb. 7, 1915, Shelby, OH. Attended high school and correspondence school, Scranton, PA. He enlisted March 4, 1942, Cleveland, OH, and trained at Great Lakes and Fire Control School. He served aboard BB-59 Oct. 12, 1942, Boston, MA, in FC Div. S2/c; Aug. 1, 1945, as FC1/c. Left BB-59 Oct. 10, 1945, Bremerton, WA.

After the war he was in Air Force Shelby, OH, as heavy equipment mechanic and operator for 12 years; heavy equipment inspector; sales writer for used aircraft in Tucson, AZ, for 21 years. Both retired in 1980. He enjoys traveling, church work and active Elks Lodge member for 18 years (Lodge 385).

He married Lucy July 28, 1946, in Tavares, FL (died March 8, 1989), and has two sons, one daughter, eight grandchildren and 10 great-grandchildren. He resides at 114 N. Avenida Carolina, Tucson, AZ 85711-3012.

POSTON, CLIFFORD, (n) 375-69-82, enlisted April 7, 1941, Manila, P.I. He is a plankowner and served aboard BB-59 as EM1/c at commissioning May 21, 1942.

POTRIKUS, LEO, Memory List 1985.

POTTHOFF, ROBERT H., Memory List 1983.

POULOS, ALEXANDER, 4th and FC Div., served aboard BB-59 as GM3/c in October 1944 and left BB-59 May 1946. After the war he worked for the Boston Gas Company - appliance repair. Part of the USS *Massachusetts* Assoc. Board of Directors from 1977 to present and Homecoming Crew, 1965. Received BB-59 Award, 1985. He married Patricia and has three children. He resides at 213 Churchill's Lane, Milton, MA.

POUME, NORMAN JAMES, 668-06-73, enlisted Oct. 22, 1941, St. Louis, MO. He is a plankowner and served aboard BB-59 as S2/c at commissioning May 12, 1942.

POWE, EUGENE E., CR Div., resides at 2709 N. Wilson St., Royal Oak, MI.

POWELL, LEONARD FRANK, 341-62-99, enlisted Jan. 5, 1942, New York, NY. He is a plankowner and served aboard BB-59 as EM2/c at commissioning May 12, 1942.

POWELL, THOMAS MCCLELLAN, 342-26-41, enlisted Aug. 20, 1940, Kansas City, MO. He is a plankowner and served aboard BB-59 as F2/c at commissioning May 12, 1942, and was on board for its 2nd anniversary.

POWELSON, HAROLD MERLE, served aboard BB-59 as ENS F Div. on July 30, 1943, and LT(jg) Main Batt. FC Div. Oct. 1, 1943. Left BB-59 Nov. 30, 1944, as LT 5th Div.

POWER, DURWARD VAUGHN, 223-77-56, enlisted July 25, 1940, New York, NY. He is a plankowner and served aboard BB-59 as FC3/c at commissioning May 12, 1942.

POYORZELSKI, EDWARD JOSEPH, 650-27-97, enlisted March 13, 1942, Philadelphia, PA. He is a plankowner and served aboard BB-59 as AS at commissioning May 12, 1942.

PRADO, FRANCIS JOSEPH, 606-46-08, born March 5, 1922, Taunton, MA. Enlisted March 6, 1942, Boston, MA, and trained at NTS Newport, RI. He is a plankowner and served aboard BB-59 as AS at commissioning May 12, 1942; S2/c, July 1942; and S1/c Feb. 1, 1944. Was on board for its 2nd and 3rd anniversaries 2nd Div. and left BB-59 Nov. 10, 1945, Seattle, WA. Was assigned from Jan. 17, 1947, to Jan. 16, 1952, USNR; Aug. 1, 1957, joined R.I. ARNG as SGT, Oct. 18, 1958; Mass. ARNG SGT E-5 Hq.Btry 104 Arty. Bde. (AD), Taunton, MA, Oct. 27, 1958, to Feb. 1, 1961, BtryB2dBN101Arty; and discharged Nov. 14, 1964.

After the war he worked for Vernery Mills, East Taunton January 1946; New Haven Railroad, brakeman, March 1946; Bristol County Hospital, grounds keeper February 1948; daytime work with Swank Inc. (polisher); night work at Bishop Feenhan High School as bus driver for 10 years. He is chairman of Retarded Children Inc.; Attleboro, Norton, Wrentham, Mansfield, MA, chaplain US Marines Corps for four years; helps brother-in-law at funeral home (Silva Funeral Home).

He married first wife Patricia Wynn, Sept. 1, 1951; and second wife Elsie Costa March 21, 1984, in Taunton. He has five children and resides at 143 Tremont St., Taunton, MA (1994).

PRECOPIO, JOHN, (n) 647-01-85, enlisted Feb. 20, 1942, New York, NY. He is a plankowner and served aboard BB-59 as AS 3rd Div. at commissioning May 12, 1942. After the war worked for the West Long Beach, NJ, Board of Education for 27 years and retired in 1987. He has five children and resides at 214 Maple Ave., Neptune, NJ (1994).

PRICE, CONRAD ELLSWORTH, 342-63-83, enlisted Jan. 21, 1942, Kansas City, MO. He is a plankowner and served aboard BB-59 as AS at commissioning May 12, 1942.

PRICE, JOHN ALBERT, 650-27-99, born Oct. 27, 1922, Philadelphia, PA. Educated at Penn Treaty School and Northeast High, Philadelphia and enlisted Feb. 13, 1942, Philadelphia, PA. Trained at Newport, RI.

Served aboard BB-59 March 9, 1942, Quincy Shipyard at commissioning May 12, 1942, 5th Div. as S2/c, S1/c and MAM3/c (t) (mailman). Left BB-59 Nov. 24, 1945, Bremerton, WA.

After the war he worked as truck driver. He married Joan G. March 14, 1946, in Chicago, IL, and has two daughters and two grandchildren.

PRICE, LOUIS WILLIAM, 368-52-65, enlisted Oct. 18, 1940, Salt Lake City, UT. He is a plankowner and served aboard BB-59 as S1/c at commissioning May 12, 1942.

PRICE, ROBERT HAYWOOD, 262-35-02, born Aug. 7, 1919, Walstonburg, NC. A high school graduate who was active in baseball and football, he enlisted May 22, 1939, Raleigh, NC, and went to Signalman and Radioman School. He is a plankowner and served aboard BB-59 as SM3/c CS Div. at commis-

sioning May 12, 1942. Left BB-59 Oct. 1, 1945, CSM Camp Shelton, VA, discharge Sept. 1, 1966.

After the war worked head retention team; correspondence courses for US Naval Reserve training, Wilmington, NC. Worked for the US Post Office for eight years as a letter carrier; security officer in Wilmington and Kinston, NC; was also salesman for Dunn & Bradstreet; and an active church worker. In his spare time was AARP volunteer tax team.

His 2nd marriage to Isabelle October 1973. He has two daughters, 12 grandchildren and one great-grandchild. In 1993 and 1995 spent time in hospital with heart and cancer problems. He resides at 402 English Sq. Drive, Kinston, NC 28501.

PRINCE, GEORGE A., ENS A Div., served aboard BB-59 as JW and JD Eng. Inst. February 1943 and BS-Fwd Diesel. He resides at 3032 So. Glencoe St., Denver, CO 80222.

PRINCEHORN, HEDGE, Memory List 1992.

PRINCETON, ROBERT TYLER, 606-48-85, born Dec. 20, 1912, Danielson, CT. Graduated from high school 1933 and enlisted March 11, 1942, Boston, MA. Trained at Newport, RI.

He served aboard BB-59 April 1942 Quincy Shipyard as AS A Div. at commissioning May 12, 1942, and 2nd anniversary. Was "Oil King." Left BB-59 in September 1945 as WT1/.

After the war he worked for Connecticut Light and Power as store supervisor retiring in 1974. He has one daughter and two grandsons and resides 34 High St., Danielson, CT 06239.

PRITCHARD, DONALD, (n) 652-21-51, enlisted Feb. 16, 1942, Pittsburgh, PA. He is a plankowner and served aboard BB-59 as AS at commissioning May 12, 1942, and was on board for its 2nd and 3rd anniversary.

PROFETA, LOUIS JULIAN, 224-74-05, enlisted March 11, 1942, New York, NY. He is a plankowner and served aboard BB-59 as AS 1st Div. at commissioning May 12, 1942. He resides at 218 Chestertown Ave., Staten Island, NY 10306.

PROVENCHER, JOSEPH C., Memory List 1977.

PROVOST, ALFRED GEORGE, 212-77-72, enlisted Feb. 25, 1942, Springfield, MA. He is a plankowner and served aboard BB-59 as AS at commissioning May 12, 1942.

PROVOYNIK, MILTON, resides at 473 Mechanic St., Perth Amboy, NJ (1966).

PROZONIC, JOHN, Memory List 1993. (Family) resides at 1560 Washington Ave., Northampton, PA 18067.

PRUETT, JESSE LEROY, 411-35-69, enlisted Nov. 4, 1940, Kansas City, MO. He is a plankowner and served aboard BB-59 as SK1/c S Div. at commissioning May 12, 1942, and was on board for its 2nd anniversary CSK S Div. (senior enlisted plankowner) and also for its 3rd anniversary.

PUFFE, ESTHEL R., FC Div., resides at 2107 St., Benedict Dr., Bismark, ND 58501.

PUGLISI, FRANK, (n) 600-21-52, enlisted March 15, 1942, Albany, NY He is a plankowner and served aboard BB-59 as AS 3rd Div. at commissioning May 12, 1942, and left BB-59 Sept. 23, 1945. After the war he worked for the New York State Thruway Authority

toll collector. He has three children and resides at 16 Highland Rd., Amsterdam, NY 12010.

PUISYS, WILLIAM VINCENT, 214-83-75, enlisted Nov. 6, 1941, Pearl Harbor, HI. He is a plankowner and served aboard BB-59 as BM1/c at commissioning May 12, 1942.

PULLIAM, ROBERT SMITH, 342-64-14, enlisted Jan. 26, 1942, Kansas City, MO. He is a plankowner and served aboard BB-59 as AS at commissioning May 12, 1942.

PURCELL, EDWARD JOSEPH, 606-00-25, born March 8, 1918, Providence, RI. Graduated from high school and enlisted Sept. 9, 1941, Boston, MA, and trained at NTS Hospital Corps School, Brooklyn, NY. Was assigned to Newport Naval Hospital.

He is a plankowner and served aboard BB-59 as HA1/c H Div. at commissioning May 12, 1942, later assigned to Quonset NAS-HMC; Chelsea Naval Hospital Detail officer. Left BB-59 at South Pacific and came back on the *Lexington*. Was called back for the Korean War, 1950-52; and assigned to Newport Train Sta. Dispensary as chief master of arms.

After the war he worked for Providence Gas Company for 41 years retiring in 1980. He married Kathleen June 21, 1944, and has one son and one granddaughter. He resides at 1183 Narrangansett Pkwy., Warwick, RI 02888 (1994).

PURCELL, KENNETH W., 393-83-68, born June 1, 1927, Creswell, OR. A high school graduate with one year of college, he enlisted Aug. 12, 1944, Portland, OR. Trained at NTS Farragut, ID, and assigned to USS *Idaho* (BB-42) December 1944 to May 1946. He served aboard BB-59 May 20, 1946, as member of the decommissioning crew and left BB-59 March 21, 1947, Portsmouth, VA.

After the war he was a plasterer foremen for 40 years; also journeyman moulder making train wheels in Portsmouth, VA, and in Atlanta, GA. He is a volunteer driver for DAV transportation system for over four years; and a member of American Legion Color Guard.

He married Thelma Jean October 1948 in Portsmouth, VA, and has two daughters and five grandchildren. He resides at 754 Vinyard Ave. N.E., Salem, OR 97301.

PUTAANSUU, ONNI PELLERVE, 606-48-19, enlisted March 9, 1942, Boston, MA. He is a plankowner and served aboard BB-59 as AS at commissioning May 12, 1942, and was on board for its 2nd and 3rd anniversaries.

PUTANNSO, ORNI, Memory List 1980.

PUTNOKI, LOUIS STEPHEN, 224-73-79, enlisted March 10, 1942, New York, NY. He is a plankowner and served aboard BB-59 as AS at commissioning May 12, 1942.

PYSHKO, EDWARD, Memory List 1986.

QUANGUANO, CHARLES, Memory List 1989.

QUASNE, WILBUR CHARLES, 376-22-47, enlisted Jan. 23, 1941, San Francisco, CA. He is a plankowner and served aboard BB-59 as F2/c at commissioning May 12, 1942, and was on board for its 2nd and 3rd anniversaries.

QUESENBERRY, GEORGE HAMPTON, 552-95-01, born May 29, 1920, Floyd, VA. Graduated from Floyd High School and attended Lowell Tech. for two years. He enlisted July 10, 1942, Charleston, WV, and trained at Newport Naval Training Station, RI.

He served aboard BB-59 as AS L Div. in August 1942. Was assigned S2/c and S1/c Lookout and left BB-59 Nov. 1, 1945, Bremerton, WA. Was discharged Nov.

1, 1945, and re-enlisted in Navy March 21, 1951, USS *Cone* (DD-866), USS *Borie* and USS *Lewis Hancock*. In 1959 spent six months in Naval hospital and six months limited duty at Charlestown Naval Yard. Was discharged 1959 with disability.

After Naval service was an operator for Reichold Chemicals for 27 years. Retired June 1, 1985. Loves to travel and do yard work in his spare time.

He married Isabel May 31, 1944, Andover, MA, and had one son (deceased), two daughters and three grandchildren. He resides at 140 Autumn Ct., St. Cloud, FL 34771.

QUIGLEY, JOSEPH PETER, 243-75-90, enlisted Sept. 11, 1940, Philadelphia, PA. He is a plankowner and served aboard BB-59 as S1/c at commissioning May 12, 1942. He resides at 34 Maryland Ave. W., Long Beach, NJ 07740.

QUINLAN, DONALD, Memory List 1993.

QUINLAN, JOHN PATRICK, 646-69-68, enlisted Feb. 7, 1942, New York, NY. He is a plankowner and served aboard BB-59 as AS at commissioning May 12, 1942.

QUINN, PHILLIP B., (Mrs.) resides at 151 Mizar Place, Lompoc, CA 93436. Memory List 1981.

QUOTIDOMINE, FRANCIS, is a plankowner and served aboard BB-59 as ChGun FC Div. at commissioning May 12, 1942. He was assigned magazine officer and left BB-59 May 20, 1944.

RABBITT, JAMES EDWARD, 410-65-71, enlisted Jan. 22, 1940, Toledo, OH. He is a plankowner and served aboard BB-59 as S1/c at commissioning May 12, 1942.

RACHELS, ROBERT EDWARD, 606-42-26. enlisted Feb. 28, 1942, Boston, MA. He is a plankowner and served aboard BB-59 as AS R Div. at commissioning May 12, 1942.

RACHT, RICHARD A., 297-86-31, born July 5, 1927, Oak Park, IL. Graduated from high school and enlisted November 1944. Trained at Great Lakes Naval Training Station, IL. Served aboard BB-59 as S1/c S Div. in February 1945 and left BB-59 April 3, 1946, discharged Shoemaker, CA. After the war he was employed by the school. He married Velma Mae, in Niles, MI. He resided at 511 South 3rd St., Niles, MI 49120.

RADCLIFF, MCLEAN MURRAY, 262-22-35, enlisted Jan. 10, 1942, Pearl Harbor, HI. He is a plankowner and served aboard BB-59 as SC2/c at commissioning May 12, 1942.

RADER, RAY EDWARD, 265-85-61, enlisted Feb. 3, 1941, Washington, DC. He is a plankowner and served aboard BB-59 as COX R Div. at commissioning May 12, 1942, and was on board for its 2nd and 3rd anniversaries. He was assigned to CBM and left BB-59 May 12, 1945. Was also assigned to the USS *Chipola* FFT receiving ship for duty by ComWesSeaFron.

RAFFERTY, LAWRENCE JAMES, JR., 610-06-33, enlisted Sept. 30, 1941, Chicago, IL. He is a plankowner and served aboard BB-59 as F3/c at commissioning May 12, 1942, and was on board for its 2nd and 3rd anniversaries.

RAFTERY, CLAIR BYRON, 668-08-59, enlisted Nov. 24, 1941, St. Louis, MO. He is a plankowner and served aboard BB-59 as PTR3/c at commissioning May 12, 1942, and was on board for its 2nd anniversary.

RAGAN, EDWARD, (n) 182-49-28, enlisted July 31, 1938, Lakehurst, NJ. He is a plankowner and served aboard BB-59 as CCStd at commissioning May 12, 1942.

RAGAZZINI, ARTHUR JOSEPH, 606-46-43, enlisted March 6, 1942, Boston, MA. He is a plankowner and served aboard BB-59 as AS at commissioning May 12, 1942.

RAGSDALE, JACOB, (n) 263-55-94, enlisted March 27, 1942, Raleigh, NC. He is a plankowner and served aboard BB-59 as Matt3/c at commissioning May 12, 1942, and was on board for its 2nd and 3rd anniversaries.

RAINEY, JAMES WILLIS, JR., LT(jg) served aboard BB-59 in 1st Div. on March 9, 1944, and assigned JO 1st Div. Turret I. Left BB-59 July 1945. He resides at 1708 Post Oak, Irving, TX 75060.

RAJEWSKI, JOHN F., is a plankowner and served aboard BB-59 at commissioning May 12, 1942, and was on board for its 2nd anniversary. He resides at 38 14th St., Norwich, CT.

RAJNAK, JOHN, (n) 650-26-54, enlisted Feb. 12, 1942, Philadelphia, PA. He is a plankowner and served aboard BB-59 as AS at commissioning May 12, 1942, and was on board for its 2nd and 3rd anniversaries.

RAKER, F.S., CS Div., served aboard BB-59 as ENS on May 11, 1944, and left May 8, 1945, as LT(jg).

RAKOC, GENO J., M Div.; Memory List 1987. (Mrs.) resides at 2 Felt St., Salem, MA 01970.

RAND, RUBIN CHARLES, 650-23-65, enlisted Feb. 4, 1942, Philadelphia, PA. He is a plankowner and served aboard BB-59 as AS at commissioning May 12, 1942, and was on board for its 2nd anniversary.

RANDALL, GEORGE EMORY, 606-56-10, born June 22, 1921, Kingston, MA. A high school graduate he attended launching of BB-59, Quincy, MA, Sept. 23, 1941. He joined the Navy March 28, 1942, Boston, MA, and trained at GRI School (fire control) Great Lakes, IL and USNTS Great Lakes, IL, April 14, 1942.

He served aboard BB-59 August 1942, Norfolk, VA, as FC3/c and left BB-59 Oct. 19, 1945, Seattle, WA. He was discharged Oct. 24, 1945, Boston, MA.

After the war he worked for the New England Telephone Company from Dec. 3, 1945, to Nov. 30, 1982. He was a member of the Telephone Pioneers of America, Selectman, Plymouth, MA, and cemetery commissioner at Plymouth, MA. He married Betsey Jan. 21,

1943, Kingston, MA, and had three daughters. Memory List 1997.

RANDALL, WILLIAM JOHN, 600-14-64, enlisted Feb. 5, 1942, Albany, NY. He is a plankowner and served aboard BB-59 as AS at commissioning May 12, 1942, and was on board for its 3rd anniversary.

RANDOLPH, W.J., is a plankowner and served aboard BB-59 at commissioning May 12, 1942, and was on board for its 2nd anniversary.

RAPPS, CARL D., 305-32-92, born June 26, 1916, Milwaukee, WI. A high school graduate with extension courses at UWM, he enlisted June 26, 1942, Milwaukee, WI. Trained at Great Lakes Naval Training Station, IL, and Training School, Ford Plant, Dearborn, MI.

He served aboard BB-59 in A Div. on Dec. 25, 1942, and assigned Machine Shop MM2/c, MM1/c Watches Boiler and Engine Rooms, volunteer basis. He left BB-59 Nov. 18, 1945, Bremerton, WA, and discharged Nov. 29, 1945, Great Lakes, IL.

After the war he was a journeyman machinist for Allis Chalmers, West Allis, WI; and from 1946-1980 was a clerk and supervisor for US Postal Service, record for non-use of sick leave, one hour in 34 years of service.

In his spare time he is a volunteer for Senior Center, service officer for NARFF, tax counseling for the elderly and works parties at church. He married Verna (deceased) Sept. 26, 1947, Milwaukee, WI, and has one son, one daughter and three grandchildren. He resides 3918 W. Silver Spring Drive, Milwaukee, WI 53209.

RASMUSSEN, JAMES, (n) 620-17-38, enlisted Dec. 28, 1941, Des Moines, IA. He was a plankowner and served aboard BB-59 as S2/c at commissioning May 12, 1942, and was on board for its 2nd and 3rd anniversaries. He resided at RR 1 Box 442, Lot 51, Lake Village, IN 46349. Memory List 1993.

RATCLIFFE, LANDON MCELROY, served aboard BB-59 as ChCarp R Div. on Aug. 23, 1943, and assigned Hull Maintenance. He left BB-59 on Jan. 29, 1945.

RAU, FREDERICK ELLIS, ENS, served aboard BB-59 as ENS 5th Div. on Oct. 26, 1943, and assigned JO 5" Control 3 Spot, LT(jg). Left BB-59 Oct. 31, 1944, as LT(jg).

RAWLING, CARROLL ERNEST, 300-09-19, enlisted June 5, 1940, Chicago, IL. He is a plankowner and served aboard BB-59 as S1/c at commissioning May 12, 1942.

RAY, ELMER A., H Div., March 5, 1945, CPh.M. transferred to USS *Lexington* FFT RS, WC US for reassignment by ComWesSeaFron.

RAY, LYNN R., A Div., born Dec. 27, 1909, Shell Rock, IA. He married Martha June 16, 1934, Cedar Falls, IA. (Mrs.) resides 1109 West 12th, Cedar Falls, IA 50613. He died May 12, 1976; Memory List 1978.

RAYMOND, HENRY P., served aboard BB-59 as S1/c 4th Div. in August 1942 and assigned Deck Work. Left BB-59 November 1945. After the war he was an assembler and cabinetmaker for Harvey Probber Company. In his spare time he is involved with VFW Private Joseph Francis Post 486, Fall River, MA; Blanket Bum Military Order of the Cootie; treasurer Square Deal Social Club. He married Joan and has one son, one daughter and three grandchildren. He resides at 466 Dickinson St., Fall River, MA 02721.

RAYMOND, STILLMAN CURT, 668-31-84, enlisted Jan. 22, 1942, St. Louis, MO. He is a plankowner and served aboard BB-59 as AS at commissioning May 12, 1942, and was on board for its 2nd and 3rd anniversaries.

READ, HILL PATERSON, JR., 355-91-45, enlisted April 30, 1941, Houston, TX. He is a plankowner and served aboard BB-59 as BM2/c R Div. at commissioning May 12, 1942. Was assigned CBM and left BB-59 May 19, 1944, Bremerton, WA.

REARDON, JOSEPH WILLIAM, born July 7, 1921, Brookline, MA. Attended Brookline High School and enlisted 1942. Served aboard BB-59 1942 and left September 1945 Seattle, WA. After the war he worked as a brakeman for Boston & Albany Railroad; worked for Red Cab; United Farmer; Hemingway Motors; and Comm. New Boston Globe. He married Eleanor Sept. 30, 1945, and has two sons, two daughters, six grandchildren and one great-grandchild. He died Sept. 29, 1989; Memory List 1993. (Mrs.) resides at 89 Franklin St., Allston, MA 02134.

REDDING, RICHARD E., DR., 611-51-11, born Sept. 11, 1920, Gary, IN. Graduated from high school and earned a BS from Northwestern University, 1945 and DSS in 1949. He enlisted June 1942 Chicago, IL, and trained at Great Lakes Naval Training Station, IL; Hospital Corps School, Great Lakes, IL; and Naval Medical Center, Bethesda, MD.

He served aboard BB-59 as HA2/c H Div. in November 1942 Boston, MA. He was assigned HA1/c 1942 and PHM3/c 1943. He left BB-59 September 1943 Noumea, New Caledonia. Was also assigned V-12 Training, Northwestern University; 1945 Dental School, Northwestern University; Reserve Commission LT(jg); recalled to active duty on Sub Tender USS *Orion*, Norfolk, VA; relieved as lieutenant 1952; and resigned Reserve 1958.

After the war he worked as a teacher for Northwestern University until 1950. Went into private practice from 1953-1987. In his spare time he is involved in Meals on Wheels, Kiwanis and Rotary Clubs visiting shut-ins; church work; and chairman of committees ships. He married Dorothy in 1950, Gary, IN, and has one son, three daughters and one grandchild. He resides at 753 Rosslare Place, Crown Point, IN 46307-2982.

REDIN, GUSTAF ADOLPH, LT, served aboard BB-59 July 1945.

REDMAN, JOHN ROLAND, Vice Admiral, US Naval Academy Class of 1919. He served aboard BB-59 as captain April 1945 and assigned commanding officer from May 2, 1945, to Jan. 22, 1946. He left BB-59 November 1945 and retired as vice admiral.

In his spare time he was active in the California

Golf Club, St. Francis Yacht Club, San Francisco, CA; and a member of San Francisco, CA, Naval League. Memory List 1977.

REDMOND, HENRY ASHTON, served aboard BB-59 as LT(jg) E Div. in May 1945.

REDMOND, J.A., LT(jg) served aboard BB-59 in E Div. JO, on April 30, 1945.

REED, FRANK O'HARE, 723-63-91, served aboard BB-59 6th Div. He has two sons, one daughter and eight grandchildren. He resides at 91 N. Main St., Mt. Gilead, OH 43338.

REED, H.P., served aboard BB-59 as a plankowner at commissioning May 12, 1942, and was on board for its 2nd anniversary.

REED, JACK, resides at 4120 Lohring Road, Linden, MI 48451.

REED, JOHN WESLEY, 646-37-01, enlisted Jan. 10, 1942, New York, NY. He is a plankowner and served aboard BB-59 as PTR3/c at commissioning May 12, 1942, and was on board for its 2nd anniversary.

REGIEC, JOSEPH ANDREW, 646-72-24, enlisted Feb. 10, 1942, New York, NY. He was a plankowner and serve aboard BB-59 as AS at commissioning May 12, 1942, and was on board for its 2nd and 3rd anniversaries. Memory List 1977-88 (1989 listed as John).

REICHEL, ALVIN SYLVESTER, 224-70-86, born July 21, 1922, Brooklyn, NY. He enlisted Feb. 24, 1942, New York, NY, and trained at Newport Naval Training Station, RI.

He is a plankowner and served aboard BB-59 as AS 4th Div. at commissioning May 12, 1942. Was assigned GM3/c Gunner on 20 and 40mm, Sky Pointer and left BB-59 June 1946. Was also assigned USS *Bennington* and discharged November 1947; re-enlisted 1954 at Naval Air Station, Willow Grove, PA; 1962 Naval Air Station, Twin Cities, MN; 1966 shipped over and transferred to MCB ONE as a Builder-1; two nine month tours in Vietnam; and retired from Navy Feb. 6, 1969.

After the war he was a builder in Narragansett, RI. He married Dorothy 1949 in Pennsylvania. He has one son, two daughters and two grandchildren. He resides at 7804 Coral Lane, Ellentown, FL 34222.

REID, JOHN WARREN, 439-95-61, born Feb. 26, 1921, Greenfield, MA. Earned a BA in English languages and enlisted May 30, 1942. Trained at Midshipman School and Navy School of Oriental Languages.

After the war he was production manager for Starcraft Jensen Marine. He married Evva Lou May 5, 1945, South Bend, IN. He had three sons, two daughters and seven grandchildren. He resided at 2983 Ceylon Drive, Costa Mesa, CA 92626. He died May 29, 1994.

REIKER, RAYMOND NOLAN, 244-06-61, born Aug. 7, 1924, York, PA. He enlisted Feb. 26, 1942, Philadelphia, PA, and trained at Newport Naval Training Station, RI, CO 141.

He is a plankowner and served aboard BB-59 as AS M Div. at commissioning May 12, 1942. He was assigned #4 Engine Room MM2/c and left BB-59

November 1945 Bremerton, WA. Was assigned to the USS *Wallace L. Lind* (DD-703), the USS *Little Rock* (CL-92); discharged Aug. 23, 1947; Naval Reserve till 1949 E-7 master sergeant Pennsylvania National Guard; discharged December 1949; enlisted July 15, 1963, enlisted in the Coast Guard Reserve as CMM; and retired Aug. 7, 1984, as LCDR.

After the war he worked as a utility operator for Doubleday Book Company for five years; utility operator for Caterpillar Tractor Company, York, PA, for 40 years; councilman Dover Boro, PA, for 40 years; police commissioner for Northern York County Region, PA. In his spare time was commander and life member of VFW Post 7374; founder of Tri-Town Boys Club; American Legion; Reserve Officer Assoc., Retired Officer Assoc., and the Knights of Columbus. He married Olga and has one son, one daughter and two grandchildren. He resides at 207 Gross Ave., Dover, PA 17315.

REILLY, JOSEPH WILLIAM, 650-26-43, born Jan. 17, 1919, Philadelphia, PA. He enlisted Feb. 11, 1942, Philadelphia, PA, and trained at Newport Naval Training Station, RI.

He was a plankowner and served aboard BB-59 as AS 6th Div. at commissioning May 12, 1942. Was assigned Radio Communication Mount #5, S1/c CR Div., Y2/c and left December 1944 Ulithia. Other Naval assignments were: USS *Intrepid* December 1945 District Staff HQ 12th Naval District, San Francisco, CA; and discharged Oct. 14, 1944, Shoemaker, CA.

After the war he worked for the Somerville, MA, Fire Department for 24 years. He died in the line of duty June 10, 1974, named Somerville Fire Dept., Central Fire Station "Reilly-Brickley" (in his memory). He was involved in the USS *Massachusetts* Committee and member of 1965 "Homecoming Crew." He married Lucy and had one son. (Mrs.) resides at 1029 Massachusetts Ave., Lexington, MA 02173. Memory List 1992.

REIS, THEODORE L., resides at 7149 4th Section Rd., Brockport, NY 14420.

RENFRO, JOHN R., 082331 LT(jg), born Aug. 26, 1915, Memphis, TN. Enlisted US Naval Academy June 1935 and graduated US Naval Academy Class of 1939. Aboard USS *California* (BB-44), sunk at Pearl Harbor Dec. 7, 1941.

He served aboard BB-59 as LT(jg) in August 1942 and assigned radio officer. Left BB-59 October 1942. Was also assigned from 1942-43 XO USS *Stanley* (DD-478); 1943-44 XO USS *Samiel N. Moore* (DD-747); 1944-45 CO USS *Frazier* (DD-607); CO USS *Donner* (LSD-20); CO USS *Calvert* (APA-32); 1962-69 CO Naval WPNS Station, Charleston, SC; various shore jobs; mission to Brazil; NATO Paris; Bell Labs; and retired June 30, 1969, as captain.

After the war he was in Head Engineering Dept. Technical College, Orangeburg, SC 1970-78. In his spare time he enjoys golf, bridge, oil painting, Pearl Harbor Survivors, Kiwanis, and awarded Bronze Star. He married Nida and resides at 134 Chateau Drive, Columbia, SC 29204.

RENNER, WILLIAM BEACH, ENS, served aboard BB-59 as ENS X Div. in December 1942 and assigned JD X Div., Battle Station Sky 6. He resides at 21 Rope Ferry Road, Hanover, NH 03755.

REPOLI, PAT, resides at 16 Mount Prospect Place, Newark, NJ 07104.

REPPEL, CLARENCE, served aboard BB-59 in S Div. and resides at 103 Ashton St., Gretna, LA 70053.

RESCIGNO, PETER JOHN, 646-31-97, born Sept. 30, 1917, New York, NY. Graduated from high school and enlisted Jan. 4, 1942, New York, NY.

He was a plankowner and served aboard as

SK3/c S Div. at commissioning May 12, 1942. Was assigned Supply Office, GSK Records, SK1/c. He left BB-59 November 1945.

After the war he worked as a cashier/paymaster for Harper & Row Publishers, Inc. and was active in the Knights of Columbus.

He married his first wife (deceased May 22, 1965) and Muriel in 1976. He died Sept. 4, 1993; Memory List 1996. (Mrs.) resides at 6 Elm Road, Fawn Lakes, Manahawkin, NJ 08050.

RESTUCCIA, BARTOLO, (n) 238-47-95, enlisted Jan. 3, 1942, Hvalfjordur, Iceland. He is a plankowner and served aboard BB-59 as MM1/c at commissioning May 12, 1942, and was on board for its 2nd anniversary.

REVAK, ANTHONY, (n) 652-18-80, enlisted Feb. 6, 1942, Pittsburgh, PA.

REYBINE, ROBERT FREDRICK, ENS, served aboard BB-59 as ENS N Div. on Sept. 14, 1942. He was assigned Asst. Nav., Battle Station Conn. Oct. 1, 1943, LT(jg) FC Div.; sail officer for Ships Reg. SCM July 1943 LT(jg). Left BB-59 April 26, 1945. (Mrs.) c/0 Hedman 16 Quail Ave., Berkeley, CA 94708. Memory List 1980.

REYNOLDS, CLARENCE CHAPPELL, 400-87-84, enlisted Oct. 21, 1940, Boston, MA. He is a plankowner and served aboard BB-59 as RM3/c at commissioning May 12, 1942, and was on board for its 2nd anniversary.

REYNOLDS, DON, resides at 848 E. Mechanic St., Bethlehem, PA 18016.

REYNOLDS, GERALD E., (Mrs.) resides at 2610 So. 14th St., Tacoma, WA 98405. Memory List 1993.

REYNOLDS, WILLIAM HENRY, JR., 274-45-31, enlisted May 14, 1940, New Orleans, LA. He is a plankowner and served aboard BB-59 as S1/c at commissioning May 12, 1942.

RHEIN, R.L., resides at 2621 Old Welsh Rd., Willow Grove, PA 19090.

RHOADES, KENNETH WOODFIN, JR., 316-66-14, enlisted July 9, 1940, Omaha, NE. He was a plankowner and served aboard BB-59 as F1/c M Div. at commissioning May 12, 1942, and was on board for its 2nd and 3rd anniversaries. Memory List 1977.

RICCI, THOMAS AUGUSTINE, 244-08-61, enlisted March 11, 1942, Philadelphia, PA. He is a plankowner and served aboard BB-59 as AS 5th Div. at commissioning May 12, 194. He was assigned COX 5th Div. and left BB-59 October 1946.

After the war he was assistant produce manager for Atlantic & Pacific Tea Company. He has one son and one daughter. He resides at 667 6th Ave., Williamsport, PA 17702.

RICCIARDELLI, LOUIS, 642-25-03, born in 1924 New Haven, CT. Attended Hillhouse High School and enlisted June 24, 1942, New Haven, CT. Trained at Newport Naval Training Station, RI. He served aboard BB-59 as S1/c 6th Div. on Aug. 5, 1942 and left Dec. 10, 1945, Lido Beach, NY.

After the war he worked for the Gulf Oil Corp., New Haven, CT, and married Anne 1947, New Haven, CT. He has one son, three daughters and six grandchildren, and resides at 16 Garry Drive, East Haven, CT 06513.

RICE, HAROLD GRAHAM, 614-16-41, enlisted Jan. 13, 1942, Cleveland, OH. He is a plankowner and served aboard BB-59 as S2/c at commissioning May 12, 1942, and was on board for its 2nd and 3rd anniversaries.

RICE, ROBERT JOHN, 224-71-64, born June 22, 1922, Chatham, NY. Enlisted Feb. 27, 1942, New York, NY, and trained at Newport Naval Training Station, RI.

He served aboard BB-59 as AS 4th Div. at commissioning May 12, 1942. He was assigned S1/c 6th Div. and left BB-59 November 1946 Portsmouth, VA, decommissioning.

After the war he worked for the Jersey City, NJ, Fire Dept. March 1, 1956, and retired March 1, 1984, as battalion chief.

In his spare time he enjoys fishing, hunting, reading and golf. He married Alma in East Paterson, NJ, and has two daughters and four grandchildren. He resides at 6 Laverne Drive, Rutland, VT 05701-2506.

RICH, STEPHEN JOHN, 606-47-09, born Nov. 19, 1911, Natick, MA. Graduated from Natick High School, 1930 and enlisted March 6, 1942, Boston, MA. He trained at Newport Naval Training Station, RI.

He is a plankowner and served aboard BB-59 as AS at commissioning May 12, 1942. He was assigned Y2/c CR Div. and left BB-59 Sept. 26, 1945.

After the war he was a serviceman for Worcester Gas Company. In his spare time he is involved in the VFW and Village Club, Needham, MA.

He married Evelyn Dec. 2, 1942, and has two sons, one daughter and three grandchildren. He resides at Box 920, 336 Barlows Landing Road, Pocasset, MA 02559-0920.

RICHARD, RAYMOND R., USMC 270037, born Dec. 5, 1919, Opelousas, LA. A high school graduate with two years of college, he enlisted Feb. 3, 1938, New Orleans, LA. Trained at Parris Island, SC, Marine Corps Training; 4th Marines Shanghai, China; Charleston, SC, Marine Barracks; Sea School, Portsmouth, VA; and May 8, 1942, Norfolk Navy Yard, VA.

He is a plankowner and served aboard BB-59 as SGT 7th Div. at commissioning May 12, 1942, and assigned sergeant of the guard. He left BB-59 at Noumea, New Caledonia. Was assigned 3rd Raider BN operations WWII Guadalcanal; Bouganville; The Marshalls; Guam; Tarawa; duty Parris Island, SC; Camp Lejeune, NC; fired on four Marine Corps Rifle and Pistol Teams; Korean War assigned Baker CO 1st BN, 7th Marine Reg. made landing at Inchon, Korea and capture of Seoul; made North Korean invasion; Yalu River and Chosin Reservoir; back to Hungnam for evacuation to Pusan; returned to States for duty at Norfolk, VA, and Camp Lejeune; two hours of duty in Vietnam War; and retired after 30 years of service as MGY SGT.

After Naval duty he was safety director and purchasing agent for telephone company, Moncks Corner, SC.

He married Irene, Charleston, SC, and has two sons, three grandchildren and one great-grandchild. He resides at 1418 Dennis Blvd., Moncks Corner, SC 29461.

RICHARDS, LOUIS JAMES, LT(jg) served aboard BB-59 as LT(jg) 2nd Div. on May 21, 1944, and assigned JO 2nd Div., Turret III HR. He left BB-59 Jan. 25, 1946.

RICHARDS, ROGER K., 610-53-00, born June 13, 1924, Racine, WI. Graduated from high school, Mineral Point, WI, and took courses at Wisconsin University, Parkside, WI. He enlisted Jan. 30, 1942, Chicago, IL, and trained at Great Lakes Naval Training Station, IL, and 40mm Gun Mount School, York, PA. He served aboard BB-59 as FC3/c FC Div. and discharged Nov. 28, 1945.

After the war he was supervising engineer (outside plant) May 1946 to April 1986 Wisconsin Telephone Company and retired April 1986. In his spare time he was student officer Rotary Foreign Exchange; president from 1982-83 Rotary Club, Kenosha, WI; Rotary Paul Harris Fellow; driver for Red Cross; church council member; nine years Sunday School teacher; rock polishing; Elks Club; and golf.

He married Marjorie June 7, 1947, Kenosha, WI, and had two sons and two grandchildren. (Mrs.) Marjorie Anthonsen resides at 1316 33rd Court, Kenosha, WI 53144. He died May 29, 1987; Memory List 1990.

RICHARDSON, EUGENE, served aboard BB-59 in 3rd Div. He resides at 111 Pine Hills Drive, Hattiesburg, MS 39401.

RICHARDSON, VARNELL, (n) 267-10-50, enlisted July 11, 1940, San Diego, CA. He is a plankowner and served aboard BB-59 as S2/c at commissioning May 12, 1942, and was on board for its 2nd anniversary.

RICKABAUGH, JOHN MASON, LT(jg) Naval Academy Class of 1942. Was a plankowner and served aboard BB-59 in FR Div. at commissioning May 12, 1942, and assigned W(P) and JD Battle Station C.O.C. March 1943; October 1943 W and Jr. Radar Officer, SCM Swimming Officer and made lieutenant October 1943. Was promoted to captain. Memory List 1980.

RIDING, J.P., served aboard BB-59 as EM3/c E Div. at commissioning May 12, 1942.

RIFF, A.L., is a plankowner and served aboard BB-59 at commissioning May 12, 1942, and was on board for its 2nd anniversary.

RIFFER, MARLIN W., served aboard BB-59 in A Div. He resided at 510 Utopia Road, Apollo, PA 15613. Memory List 1997.

RIGGLE, H.V., is a plankowner and served aboard BB-59 at commissioning May 12, 1942, and was on board for its 2nd anniversary.

RIGGS, W.N., "REX," is a plankowner and served aboard BB-59 as member of CE Group at commissioning May 12, 1942, and was on board for its 2nd anniversary.

RIGLEY, JOHN S., 202-01-43, is a plankowner and served aboard BB-59 as CGM 4th Div. at commissioning May 12, 1942, and was on board for its 2nd and 3rd anniversaries. He resides in Bayside, Long Island, NY.

RILEY, J.G., served aboard BB-59 as S2/c CR Div. to FR Div. on March 10, 1943.

RILEY, JAMES MIDDLETON, LT, served aboard BB-59 in H Div. on Sept. 20, 1944, and assigned junior dental officer. After the war he worked as a dentist and resides at 1392 Pilgrim, Birmingham, MI 48009.

RILEY, WILLIAM OLIVER, LT(jg) Naval Academy Class of 1942. He served aboard BB-59 as LT(jg) F Div. on Dec. 20, 1942, assigned lieutenant October 1943 and lieutenant commander Plotting Room. He left BB-59 September 1946.

After the war he was vice-president for Anaconda Wire & Cable Company. He married Ruth and had two sons. He resided at 26 Hillcrest Road, New Canaan, CT 06840. Memory List 1986.

RIMER, JOHN PATTON, ENS April 1943. He served aboard BB-59 as ENS FC Div. on July 26, 1943, and assigned JO FC Div., SB Plotting officer, LT(jg). He left BB-59 June 20, 1945. He resides at 960 West 19th St., Upland, CA 91786.

RINEBARGER, CARL HENRY, 371-63-15, enlisted April 17, 1940, Denver, CO. He is a plankowner and served aboard BB-59 as CBgmstr X Div. at commissioning May 12, 1942, and left BB-59 April 17, 1945. Was assigned USS *Kaskaskia* FFT receiving station and Naval School of Music, Washington, DC.

RINNER, ROBERT T., resides at 800 East Murray St., Macomb, IL 61455.

RIORDAN, FRANCIS M., M Div., resides at 156 Wilson St., Norwood, MA 02062.

RIPP, ALBERT, "L.," 610-23-71, enlisted Jan. 2, 1942, Chicago, IL. He is a plankowner and served aboard BB-59 as F1/c at commissioning May 12, 1942.

RITCHIE, PETER, JR., (n) 606-43-07, born Feb. 24, 1922, Paisley, Scotland. Graduated from high school and enlisted March 2, 1942, Boston, MA. He was a plankowner and served aboard BB-59 as AS 6th Div. at commissioning May 12, 1942. Was assigned to A Div. and has medical discharge 1945, Quonset Point, RI.

After the war he worked for Bay State Bank and Arlington Trust as HUO from 1969-73. Spent his spare time hunting, fishing, antique cars, stamp collecting; active in veteran organizations; and State Dept. commander DAV of New Hampshire. He married Ruth Dec. 15, 1944, Methuen, MA, had one son, two daughters and three grandchildren. He died Dec. 12, 1973. (Mrs.) resides at 214 Lawrence Road, Salem, NH 03079-3907.

RITTER, FREDERICK H., served aboard BB-59 as CEM E Div.

RIVENBARK, JACK, is a plankowner and served aboard BB-59 as CGM 4th Div. at commissioning May 12, 1942. He left BB-59 in X Div. April 17, 1945. Was also assigned to the USS *Kaskaskia* FFT Receiving Station and GM School Washington, DC. He resides at 207 Yorkshire Drive, Birmingham, AL 35202.

RIXFORD, DAVID L., is a plankowner and served aboard BB-59 as SC2/c S Div. at commissioning May 12, 1942,. He left BB-59 in 1945. After the war he worked as a butcher for Big Y Supermarket and was active in the American Legion. He married Rita and had three daughters. Memory List 1986. He resides at 67 Canterburg Road, Springfield, MA 01108.

RIZZELLI, WILLIAM DONALD, 606-27-97, born Aug. 20, 1921, Marlboro, MA. Graduated from high school and enlisted Jan. 28, 1942, Boston, MA, and assigned musician.

He is a plankowner and served aboard BB-59 as AS at commissioning May 12, 1942, and left BB-59 November 1942. Was also assigned to Submarine School, New London, CT; USS *Gunniad*; USS *Hammerhead*; received two Presidential Citations; and was discharged Portsmouth, NH, as MoMM2/c.

After the war he worked for General Motors for 36 years and retired. Enjoys traveling and gardening in his spare time. He married Rita Sept. 21, 1946, Marlboro, MA, and has two sons, two daughters and four grandchildren. He resides at 77 Francis St., Marlboro, MA 01752.

RIZZO, CHARLES L., was a plankowner and served aboard BB-59 as MM2/c A Div. at commissioning May 12, 1942,. Was assigned Fresh Water Maker and in charge of Sea and Port Fueling. Left BB-59 June 1944.

After the war he was fireman for the Needham, MA, Fire Dept. and was active in the VFW, Elks and the Knights of Columbus. He married Madeline and had one son and two daughters. Memory List 1982. He resided at 30 Norfolk St., Needham, MA 01292.

RIZZOTTI, LAWRENCE, born March 23, 1920, Salem, MA. Educated in the Salem schools and enlisted February 1942 Boston, MA. Trained at Newport Naval Training Station, RI.

He is a plankowner and served aboard BB-59 as S1/c 5th Div. at commissioning May 12, 1942, and was on board for its 2nd and 3rd anniversaries. Left BB-59 November 1945.

After the war he was a barber in Marblehead, MA, for 44 years. He is active in AMVETS and VFW. He married Marion in 1962 and resides at 48 Margaret Road, South Hamilton, MA 01982.

ROACH, EDWARD MAURICE, 328-67-57, enlisted April 2, 1940, Minneapolis, MN. He is a plankowner and served aboard BB-59 as S1/c at commissioning May 12, 1942.

ROACH, GALE WARD, 316-88-53, born Oct. 27, 1924, Nebraska City, NE. He enlisted Jan. 20,

1942, Omaha, NE, and trained at Great Lakes Naval Training Station, IL.

He is a plankowner and served aboard BB-59 as AS 4th Div. at commissioning May 12, 1942. Was assigned yeoman striker and anti-aircraft striker. He left BB-59 November 1945 Bremerton, WA. He was discharged November 1945 St. Louis, MO.

After the war 1946-52 worked in the bulldozer business Nebraska City, NE; 1952-84, trucking business La Verne, CA; 1984-94, semi-retired cattle ranch, Meta, MO. In his spare time he enjoys bowling, fishing, hunting and aircraft flying. He married Patsy Nov. 9, 1945, Senaca, KS, and has two sons, one daughter, two grandchildren and two great-grandchildren. He resides at Box 13, Meta, MO 65058.

ROACH, M.E., CAPT USMC, served aboard BB-59 as CAPT 7th Div. on June 8, 1944, and assigned to Defense Aft. He left BB-59 Oct. 31, 1944.

ROBARGE, RONALD DEWAYNE, 510-04-37, enlisted Jan. 30, 1942, Seattle, WA. He is a plankowner and served aboard BB-59 as RM3/c at commissioning May 12, 1942, and was on board for its 2nd anniversary.

ROBBINS, KENNETH H., served aboard BB-59 4th Div. and resided at PO Box 131, Letohatchee, AL 36047. Memory List 1993.

ROBERTS, CHARLES RICHARD, 311-25-20, enlisted Feb. 18, 1938, Detroit, MI. He is a plankowner and served aboard BB-59 as F1/c at commissioning May 12, 1942.

ROBERTS, MARK WALLARD, 355-54-35, enlisted Feb. 22, 1938, Bremerton, WA. He is a plankowner and served aboard BB-59 as WT1/c at commissioning May 12, 1942, and was on board for its 2nd and 3rd anniversaries as CWT B Div.

ROBERTS, OTIS RAYMOND, 346-43-96, enlisted Jan. 7, 1942, San Francisco, CA. He is a plankowner and served aboard BB-59 as MM1/c at commissioning May 12, 1942.

ROBERTS, PAUL LEON, ENS, served aboard BB-59 as ENS V Div. on May 27, 1945, and assigned aviator.

ROBERTS, WALTER ARTHUR, JR., 382-44-94, enlisted April 29, 1941, Los Angeles, CA. He is a plankowner and served aboard BB-59 as S1/c at commissioning May 12, 1942.

ROBERTSON, HAROLD THOMAS, 648-16-47, enlisted Feb. 2, 1942, Omaha, NE. He is a

plankowner and served aboard BB-59 as AS at commissioning May 12, 1942, and was on board for its 2nd anniversary.

ROBICHAUD, EDWARD HAROLD, 606-36-59, enlisted Feb. 19, 1942, Boston, MA. He is a plankowner and served aboard BB-59 as AS at commissioning May 12, 1942, and was on board for its 2nd anniversary.

ROBILLARD, ALBERT J., served aboard BB-59 in L Div. He resides at 2191 Park Drive, Slidell, LA 70458.

ROBINSON, BENJAMIN, USMC May 8, 1942, Norfolk Navy Yard. He is a plankowner and served aboard BB-59 as PFC 7th Div. at commissioning May 12, 1942.

ROBINSON, EARLE W., JR., served aboard BB-59 in A Div. He resides at 110 West Bacon St., Plainville, MA 02762.

ROBINSON, G.A., LT, served aboard BB-59 as LT V Div. on Feb. 4, 1944, and assigned senior aviator. Left BB-59 May 2, 1945.

ROBINSON, OTIS D., Memory 1977.

ROBISON, WILLIAM LEROY, LT, served aboard BB-59 as LT I Div. on July 2, 1944, and left Dec. 20, 1945.

ROCCA, SALVATORE THOMAS, 606-46-70, enlisted March 6, 1942, Boston, MA. He is a plankowner and served aboard BB-59 as AS at commissioning May 12, 1942, and was on board for its 2nd and 3rd anniversaries.

ROCH, EDWIN, resides at 32 Bridge St., South Hadley Falls, MA.

ROCK, EDWIN LEONARD, 666-16-99, enlisted Feb. 18, 1942, Springfield, MA. He is a plankowner and served aboard BB-59 as AS at commissioning May 12, 1942.

ROD, ERNEST DAVID, 666-15-70, enlisted Feb. 9, 1942, Springfield, MA. He is a plankowner and served aboard BB-59 as AS at commissioning May 12, 1942.

RODEEN, CHARLES WILLIAM, 212-56-83, enlisted July 9, 1940, Springfield, MA. He is a plankowner and served aboard BB-59 as S1/c 5th and 7th Div. May 12, 1942. He resides at 523 Thornton Ave. SW, Huntsville, AL 35801.

RODEMICK, FRANCIS E., 4th Div., resides at 8330 Cedar Rd., Elkins Park, PA.

RODINGUEY, ROBERT P., resides at 1017 Buttonwood St., Philadelphia, PA.

RODRIGUEZ, LOUIS MARIANO, 224-77-69, enlisted March 30, 1942, New York, NY. He is a plankowner and served aboard BB-59 as AS at commissioning May 12, 1942, and was on board for its 2nd and 3rd anniversaries.

RODRIGUEZ, JAMES A., Memory List 1979.

RODRIGUEZ, ROBERT RICHARD, 244-07-03, enlisted Feb. 26, 1942, Philadelphia, PA. He is a plankowner and served aboard BB-59 as AS at commissioning May 12, 1942, and was on board for its 2nd and 3rd anniversaries.

ROEMER, CHARLES WILLIAM, 286-86-95, enlisted Oct. 18, 1940, New York, NY. He is a plankowner and served aboard BB-59 as CMM at commissioning May 12, 1942.

ROESCH, CHARLES JOSEPH, 646-69-40, enlisted Feb. 7, 1942, New York, NY. He is a plankowner and served aboard BB-59 as AS at commissioning May 12, 1942, and was on board for its 2nd anniversary.

ROESLER, ROBERT WAYNE, 610-56-94, enlisted Feb. 4, 1942, Chicago, IL. He is a plankowner and served aboard BB-59 as AS at commissioning May 12, 1942, and was on board for its 2nd and 3rd anniversaries.

ROGOE, MILES EDWARD, 274-39-05, enlisted Sept. 13, 1939, New Orleans, LA. He is a plankowner and served aboard BB-59 as S1/c at commissioning May 12, 1942.

ROGERS, ANTHONY PAUL, 212-77-88, enlisted March 10, 1942, Springfield, MA. He is a plankowner and served aboard BB-59 as AS at commissioning May 12, 1942, and was on board for its 2nd and 3rd anniversaries. He resides at 157 Federal St., St. Albans, VT 05478.

ROGERS, HARRY MELVILLE, 447868, born April 24, 1922, Pittsburgh, PA. He holds a BS from USNA and an MS from George Washington University. He joined the Navy June 1942 and was assigned USNA 1942-45.

He served aboard BB-59 in 5th Div. ENS in August 1945 and left BB-59 October 1945 in R Div. Additional Naval assignments were Amphips ASMR; flight training PC, AP DER(XO), AGR(CO); USMC Senior School; Comphiblant Staff USS *Laffrey* (DD-724) CO; guided missile cruiser XO OPNAV and retired as captain.

After the war he owned a waterfront farm in So. Maryland and raised sheep and beef cattle. He also has a tree farm. He was church treasurer for 15 years and a life member of DD-724 Assoc. He married Edith, Dec. 25, 1950, Milford, MA, and has three daughters and one son. He resides at 39209 Maycroft Road, Avenue, MD 20609-2205.

ROGERS, HUBERT, (n) 279-97-25, enlisted March 31, 1942, Cincinnati, OH. He is a plankowner and served aboard BB-59 as Matt3/c at commissioning May 12, 1942.

ROGERS, JAMES, resides at 647 East 16th St., New York, NY 10001 (1966).

ROGERS, JOHN L., served aboard BB-59 as S1/c 6th Div. in August 1942 and assigned Gun Pointer and Radar Operator Mark 37. Left BB-59 December 1945.

After the war he worked at Carpenter Navy Exchange, Quonset, RI. He is active in the American Legion. He married Dorothy and has two daughters and two grandchildren. He resides at 13 Beaton St., Coventry, RI 02816.

ROGERS, ROY W., JR., served aboard BB-59 as S2/c on Sept. 22, 1945, and assigned to USS *Sederstorm* (DE-31).

ROGERS, WOODROW DOUGLAS, 346-67-42, enlisted Jan. 13, 1942, Little Rock, AR. He is a plankowner and served aboard BB-59 as CM2/c at commissioning May 12, 1942.

ROGINSKI, EDWARD STANLEY, 224-73-84, enlisted March 10, 1942, New York, NY. He was a plankowner and served aboard BB-59 as AS C Div. at commissioning May 12, 1942, and was on board for its 2nd and 3rd anniversaries. Memory List 1990. (Mrs.) resides at 1070 Garry Terrace, Secaucus, NJ 07094.

ROLLISON, VERN LESLIE, 623-99-51, born Sept. 25, 1925, Detroit, MI. Enlisted Oct. 15, 1942, Pontiac, MI, and trained at Great Lakes Naval Training Station, IL.

He served aboard BB-59 as AS 4th Div. in November 1942 and assigned S2/c and S1/c. Left BB-59 October 1945, Bremerton, WA, and discharged on Oct. 19, 1945.

He worked for GMC Pontiac Motors after the war and spent his spare time roller skating, boating, Cub Scout leader, soccer coach, baseball coach and projects at St. Hugo's School. He married Elizabeth July 6, 1946, Pontiac, MI, and had one son, three daughters and one grandchild. He died Aug. 18, 1981, Memory List 1983. (Mrs.) resides at 3584 San Mateo Road, Waterford, MI 48329.

ROLOFF, RAYMOND JOSEPH, LT(jg) served aboard BB-59 as LT(jg) R Div. on June 17, 1945.

ROMANO, COSMO, (n) 646-60-49, born in 1915, New York, NY. Graduated from high school and enlisted Jan. 30, 1942, New York, NY. Trained at Newport Naval Training Station, RI.

He was a plankowner and served aboard BB-59 as AS 3rd Div. at commissioning May 12, 1942. Was assigned to S1/c 4th Div. and left BB-59 September 1945 Seattle, WA.

After the war he worked in the supply department for New Jersey Bell Telephone Company for 32 years. Participated in the Civic Watch Neighbor. He married Paula and had two daughters. He died Aug. 31, 1987; Memory List 1988. (Mrs.) resides at 714 Irvington Ave., Maplewood, NJ 07040.

ROMANO, LEONARD, (n) 224-69-87, enlisted Jan. 29, 1942, New York, NY. He is a plankowner and served aboard BB-59 as AS 6th Div. at commissioning May 12, 1942, and transferred to CR Div. March 3, 1943.

ROMANO, PAUL ANTHONY, 224-73-35, enlisted March 9, 1942, New York, NY. He was a plankowner and served aboard BB-59 as AS at commissioning May 12, 1942, and was on board for its 2nd and 3rd anniversaries. He died July 6, 1983. (Mrs.) resides at 1440 East 3rd St., Brooklyn, NY 11215.

ROSA, EVERETT, (n) 606-35-23, enlisted Feb. 10, 1942, Boston, MA. He was a plankowner and served aboard BB-59 as AS 4th Div. at commissioning May 12, 1942. Was assigned to BM3/c maintenance of ship and left BB-59 October 1945. After the war he worked as a grinder for Brown Sharpe. He had one son

and resided at 878 Rock St., Fall River, MA 02720. Memory List 1993.

ROSE, GEORGE J., served aboard BB-59 in 5th Div. and resides at 205 North 2nd St., National Park, NJ 08063.

ROSEK, KENNETH G., 312-08-55, born Oct. 11, 1925, Grand Rapids, MI. Attended East Grand Rapids High School and enlisted Oct. 14, 1942, Detroit, MI. Trained at Great Lakes Naval Training Station, IL.

He served aboard BB-59 as S1/c 4th Div. on Sept. 5, 1942, and assigned 40 MM anti-aircraft gunner. Was injured July 22, 1943, Operation Munda, New Georgia. Was transferred after injury to hospital ship, USS *Solace* then to the USS *Dashing Wave*. Was in Naval Hospital, San Diego, CA, for one and a half years. He was discharged Dec. 22, 1944.

After the war he worked for Lear Products, Grand Rapids, MI. He married Donna Jan. 19, 1974, Muskegon, MI, and had two sons, one daughter and six grandchildren. He died April 5, 1991; Memory List 1996. (Mrs.) resides at 5158 Angermeyer Rd., Ravenna, MI 49451-9445.

ROSEMOND, JOSEPH F., 657-10-93, born July 8, 1923, Hillsborough, NC. A high school graduate with one year of college, he enlisted Oct. 19, 1942, Raleigh, NC. Trained at Great Lakes Naval Training Station, IL.

He served aboard BB-59 as S1/c FC Div. in November 1942. Was assigned Main Battery Plotting Room, 1st Class Pointers, Main Battery and Spot One. Left BB-59 December 1945, Bremerton WA.

After the war he was a timber dealer and worked for the US Postal Service. He enjoys golf, service clubs and church in his spare time. He has four sons, one daughter and seven grandchildren. He resides at 126 East Queen St., Hillsborough, NC 27278.

ROSEN, JAMES STANLEY, 647-01-87, born Feb. 25, 1918, West Hoboken, NJ. Graduated from Emerson High School and attended New York University. He enlisted Feb. 20, 1942, New York, NY, and trained at Newport Naval Training Station, RI. He was a plankowner and served aboard BB-59 as AS FC Div. at commissioning May 12, 1942. Was assigned to FC Plot FC2/c and left BB-59 September 1945. Was also assigned to USS *Relief* and the USS *Solace*.

After the war he worked on a program to control decompression of air workers during construction of the third tube of Lincoln Tunnel; was a New York insurance broker; vice-president of Johnson & Higgins and vice-president of Frelinghuysen Corp. In his spare time he was a guest lecturer at Harvard School of Public Health on applications of safety and medical principles in industry; was member of New York University Club, Board of Governors of Haworth NJ Men's Club; Board of Trustee Haworth, NJ, Swim Club. He married Florence April 27, 1947, St. Michael's Monastery, Union City, NJ. He had two sons and one daughter. He died May 3, 1979; Memory List 1979. (Mrs.) resides 12 Lake Shore Dr. S., Randolph, NJ 07801.

ROSEN, MORTON, born Sept. 23, 1920, graduated from high school and enlisted in 1942 Philadelphia, PA. Trained at Newport Naval Training Station, RI. He is a plankowner and served aboard BB-59 as AS 3rd Div. at commissioning May 12, 1942, and assigned Bos'n Mate. He left BB-59 in 1945, Seattle, WA. After the war he worked as a meat cutter. He married Mollie March 23, 1941, Philadelphia, PA, and has one son, two daughters, eight grandchildren and four great-grandchildren. He resides at K-1 Cooper Valley Village, Edgewater Park, NJ 08010.

ROSEN, DR. OSCAR, born June 21, 1922, Roxbury, MA, the child of Russian-Jewish immigrants. Graduated from Revere, MA, High School, 1939 and attended 7 months Wentworth Institute. He enlisted Dec. 23, 1940, Boston, MA, and trained at Boot Camp, Newport,

RI; Great Lakes, carpentry; and Ford River Rouge, Dearborn, MI. He was assigned to USS *Astoria* (CA-34) June 1941 as carpenter's mate striker and left Pearl Harbor Dec. 5, 1941.

He served aboard BB-59 Portland, ME, 1942 in R Div. then to 3rd Div. He left BB-59 1943 Panama and was sent to Naval Academy Prep. School, Norfolk; Norfolk Navy Yard, carpentry shop; CarpMate3/c; US Naval Testing Range, Montauk Point, LI; amphibious training, Fort Pierce, FL; to USS *Queens* (APA-103); to Iwo Jima then Maui; to Oak Knoll Naval Hospital and Corona Naval Hospital, CA; December 1945 to USS *Kerstin* (AF-34), CM2/c; to Tarawa 7 other islands, then to Pearl Harbor June 1946; transferred to ARD-29; towed to Bikini, Marshall Islands for series of nuclear bomb tests. Was discharged Nov. 23, 1946.

After the war with the GI Bill enrolled Colby College September 1947 and obtained BA in history and government; attended Grad school, University of WI for an MA and in August 1956 Ph.D. in modern European history and East Asian studies; 15 years of college teaching in Pennsylvania and part-time at Salem State College. He married Eileen Aldenburg, 1943 (died 1987) and has one daughter, 2 adopted Korean orphan girls, five grandchildren and two great-grandchildren. Was National commander and newsletter editor for the National Assoc. of Atomic Veterans. He resides at 6A Russell Drive, Salem, MA 01970.

ROSENSTEEL, ROBERT B., served aboard USS *Sederstorm* (DE-31) and BB-59 as S2/c on Sept. 22, 1945.

ROSKOSKI, CHARLES J., resides at 73 Briarwood Drive, Meriden, CT 06450.

ROSS, EUGENE, (n) 626-20-82, enlisted Jan. 28, 1942, Indianapolis, IN. He is a plankowner and served aboard BB-59 as AS at commissioning May 12, 1942, and was on board for its 2nd and 3rd anniversaries.

ROSS, JOHN FRANCIS, 224-69-46, enlisted Jan. 28, 1942, New York, NY. He is a plankowner and served aboard BB-59 as AS at commissioning May 12, 1942, and was on board for its 2nd anniversary.

ROSS, LEONARD, (n) 274-77-69, enlisted Jan. 3, 1942, New Orleans, LA. He was a plankowner and served aboard BB-59 as S2/c at commissioning May 12, 1942, and was on board for its 2nd anniversary. (Mrs.) resides at 40026 Dillingham Lane, Caledonia, MS 39740. Memory List 1993.

ROSS, THOMAS WILLIAM, 202-26-25, enlisted Feb. 26, 1942, Boston, MA. He is a plankowner and served aboard BB-59 as AS at commissioning May 12, 1942, and was on board for its 2nd and 3rd anniversaries.

ROUMPH, FRANCIS LEROY, 316-88-96, enlisted Jan. 29, 1942, Omaha, NE. He is a plankowner and served aboard BB-59 as AS L Div. at commissioning May 12, 1942, and was on board for its 2nd anniversary. He resides at 22355 Lariat Lane, Red Bluff, CA 96080.

ROWLAND, NORMAN ROBERT, 642-12-58, enlisted Feb. 10, 1942, New Haven, CT. He is a plankowner and served aboard BB-59 as AS at commissioning May 12, 1942, and was on board for its 2nd and 3rd anniversaries. He resides at 132 Hunting St., Bridgeport, CT 06601.

ROZENSKY, BERNARD, 252-71-18, born in Pittsburgh, PA. Graduated from high school and enlisted June 17, 1945, Pittsburgh, PA. He served aboard BB-59 as S1/c S Div. in 1945 and assigned Ship's Taylor. He left BB-59 July 1946 Norfolk, VA.

After the war he worked as a store manager of Schwartz S.S. Market, 1946-67; American General

Life Insurance 1967-81; and Principal Financial Group 1981. He is active in JWV Post #49; junior warden/past master Oakland #535 F.A.M.; and past president of Kiwanis. He married Corinne and has one son, one daughter and one grandchild.

RUANE, MARTIN JAMES, 224-70-41, enlisted Jan. 31, 1942, New York, NY. He is a plankowner and served aboard BB-59 as AS at commissioning May 12, 1942, and was on board for its 2nd anniversary.

RUCKER, ROBERT WALSTINE, 311-98-11, enlisted March 25, 1942, Detroit, MI. He is a plankowner and served aboard BB-59 as Matt3/c at commissioning May 12, 1942.

RUDDOCK, THEDORE DAVIS, CAPT, US Naval Academy Class of 1914. Served aboard BB-59 Sept. 23, 1943, and left April 8, 1944, VADM. Memory List 1990.

RUDERMAN, STANLEY GEORGE, 646-61-74, enlisted Jan. 31, 1942, New York, NY. He is a plankowner and served aboard BB-59 as AS A Div. at commissioning May 12, 1942, and assigned F3/c. Left BB-59 March 8, 1943, to ComSerForSoPac. He resides at 104 Patten Drive, Lynchburg, VA 24502.

RUDOKAS, WALTER GEORGE, USMC, May 8, 1942, Norfolk Navy Yard, VA. He was a plankowner and served aboard BB-59 as PVT 7th Div. at commissioning May 12, 1942, and assigned line sergeant. Left BB-59 in November 1945.

After the war he worked in security for Proctor & Gamble Company. He resided at 277 Myrtle St., West Hanover, MA 02339. Memory List 1996.

RUDOLPH, F.L., S1/c N Div., March 3, 1943, transferred to the 4th Div.

RUDOLPH, RAYMOND, resides at 2043 West Ontario St., Philadelphia, PA 19104.

RUDZIK, FRANK FRED (SAILS), 646-59-13, born Dec. 26, 1913, New York, NY. Graduated from Newark, NJ, High School and enlisted Jan. 29, 1942, New York, NY. Trained at Newport Naval Training Station, RI.

He is a plankowner and served aboard BB-59 as AS R Div. at commissioning May 12, 1942. Was assigned Sailmaker 1/c R Div. and left BB-59 November 1945 Bremerton, WA.

After the war he owned an excavation company and a manufacturing company for construction of concrete products. He married Helen (deceased) Nov. 30, 1946, New Jersey, and has one son, six daughters and 13 grandchildren. He resides at 2315 57th St. S., Gulfport, FL 33707.

RUGGERI, ANDREW, (n) 647-12-04, enlisted March 4, 1942, New York, NY. He is a plankowner and served aboard BB-59 as AS at commissioning May 12, 1942.

RUGGERI, PETER JOHN, 646-69-44, born in West Hoboken, NJ. He enlisted Feb. 7, 1942, New York, NY, and trained at Newport Naval Training Station, RI. He is a plankowner and served aboard BB-59 as AS 6th Div. at commissioning May 12, 1942, and left BB-59 at Kwajalein Athol. Was also assigned to Gunners Mate Electric Hyd. School, San Diego, CA, and Adak, AK.

He worked in the general shipping department, Yardley of London, 1936-41; after the war as compounder for Yardley of London; 1968-82, assistant plant manager/plant manager of H. Kotinstamia Company; and retired at age 62. Was a Bethol volunteer ambulance driver, and a member of the Kauneonga Volunteer Fire Dept. He married Lela July 1947 in Bethel, NY, and has one son, one daughter and three

grandchildren. He resides at 511 Laymon Road, Swan Lake, NY 12783.

RUKUS, ANTHONY JOSEPH, 642-07-96, born March 4, 1920, Takottville, CT. He enlisted Jan. 10, 1942, New Haven, CT, and trained at Newport Naval Training Station, RI.

He is a plankowner and served aboard BB-59 as EM3/c E Div. at commissioning May 12, 1942. Was assigned EM1/c E Div. in 1945 and left BB-59 in 1945 Saipan. Was discharged Norfolk, VA, Nov. 2, 1945.

After the war he was an electrician and motor repairs; electrician/master mechanic for GAF Corp., Franklin, MA; and retired Dec. 31, 1985. He enjoys traveling in his spare time. He has one daughter, two grandchildren, and resides at 3300 Sand Key Drive, Palm Harbor, FL 34684.

RULLMANN, ALVIN H., JR., 313-24-16, born To. 4, 1925, Aurora, IN. Graduated from high school and enlisted Aug. 19, 1943, Detroit, MI, and trained at Great Lakes to Signal School to MP duty to troop ship to Kwajalein. He served aboard BB-59 in January 1946, San Francisco and discharged April 6, 1946.

After the war he was a carpenter for 25 years and retired in January 1988. He also taught carpentry at vocational school and built a home 1952-53. In his spare time he enjoys hot air ballooning, licensed in 1988. His wife is "crew chief." His daughter and her husband also enjoys ballooning. He married Marilyn Jan. 15, 1949, Bridgetown, Cincinnati, OH. His wife is a registered nurse, Christ Hospital, Cincinnati. He has one daughter, Kim Martin and resides at 5076 Zion Road, Cleves, OH 45002-9602.

RUMLEY, THOMAS JOSEPH, 606-34-91, enlisted Feb. 13, 1942, Boston, MA. He is a plankowner and served aboard BB-59 as AS 4th Div. at commissioning May 12, 1942, and was on board for its 2nd and 3rd anniversaries. He resides at 33 Woodrow Ave., Medford, MA 02155.

RUMMENS, WILLIAM STEEN, LT CDR, served aboard BB-59 on Oct. 29, 1943, and assigned senior assistant 1st LT Hull Dept. and left BB-59 Sept. 19, 1945. Memory List 1981.

RUNKLE, HARRY LEWELLYN, 385-48-71, enlisted Feb. 16, 1942, Bermuda. He is a plankowner and served aboard BB-59 as CMM at commissioning May 12, 1942.

RUPELL, EARL WESLEY, 224-93-68, born April 15, 1925, Trenton, NJ. He enlisted July 10, 1942, New York, NY, and trained AT Newport Naval Training Station, RI. He served aboard BB-59 as AS CS Div. on Sept. 1, 1942, and assigned S2/c, S1/c, SC3/c and SC2/c. He left BB-59 April 1946 Shoemaker, CA.

From 1965-66 was commander VFW 2525; member of Hibenian Club; Ozark Hunting Club; Hunting Club Fin, Fur & Feather; and enjoys fishing in Buxton, NC, spring and fall. He married Catherine Feb. 28, 1959, Pennington, NJ, and has three sons, two daughters and six grandchildren. He resides at 9 Lamont Ave., Apt. 913, Trenton, NJ 08619.

RUSSELL, FREDERICK WILLIAM, USMC, served aboard BB-59 in the 7th Div. He resides at 40 Warren St., Lawrence, MA 01842.

RUSSELL, LEO STANISLAUS, 207-28-52, enlisted Sept. 10, 1940, New Haven, CT. He is a plankowner and served aboard BB-59 as F1/c at commissioning May 12, 1942.

RUSSELL, RENOUF, LT(jg), born Oct. 10, 1914, Keene, NH. Attended Deerfield Academy and graduated Harvard Class of 1935.
He was a plankowner and served aboard BB-59 as LT(jg) 4th Div. at commissioning May 12, 1942, and assigned JD 4th Div., catapult officer, Battle Station Sky 8 and October 1943 lieutenant. Left BB-59 on April 11, 1945.
After the war he worked for the Gillette Company and a partner investment banking F.S. Moseley. He enjoys hunting, fishing and golf. He married Lily 1934, Beverly Farms, MA, and had two sons, two daughters and eight grandchildren. He resided at 1 Gilson Road, Jaffrey, NH 03452-1626. He died Oct. 14, 1994; Memory List 1995.

RUSSI, EUGENE, (n) 646-69-45, enlisted Feb. 7, 1942, New York, NY. He is a plankowner and served aboard BB-59 as AS at commissioning May 12, 1942, and was on board for its 2nd anniversary.

RUTHER, WILLIAM JOSEPH, 214-55-51, enlisted April 17, 1942, New York, NY. He is a plankowner and served aboard BB-59 as Mus1/c at commissioning May 12, 1942.

RYAN, ARTHUR E., served aboard BB-59 in R Div. (Mrs.) resides at 112 Cowing St., West Roxbury, MA 02132. Memory List 1979.

RYAN, CARL JOSEPH, 201-54-67, enlisted Dec. 18, 1941, Pearl Harbor, HI. He is a plankowner and served aboard BB-59 as Y1/c F Div. at commissioning May 12, 1942. Was assigned chief yeoman Gunnery Department, chief warrant officer Coding Board and ship's secretary Feb. 28, 1945. Retired from the USN.
After the war he worked for the Safety & Security Administration Sylvania Electronic Systems. He is a member of the American Society of Ind. Security; instructor/first aid American Red Cross; life member National Rifleman's Assoc. and chairman of Boys Scouts of America. He has two sons and five daughters and resides at 50 G St., South Boston, MA 02127.

RYAN, DILLON, (Mrs.) resides at 58 Church St., Malden, MA 02148-4432. Ryan died Oct. 12, 1992; Memory List 1993.

RYAN, EUGENE FRANCIS, 201-56-35, enlisted Jan. 27, 1942, Boston, MA. He was a plankowner and served aboard BB-59 as SF3/c at commissioning May 12, 1942. Memory List 1977.

RYAN, JAMES WALTON, 295-71-09, enlisted July 17, 1940, Nashville, TN. He was a plankowner and served aboard BB-59 as FC3/c F Div. at commissioning May 12, 1942, and was on board for its 2nd and 3rd anniversaries. Was assigned March 10, 1943, to FR Div. Memory List 1977.

RYAN, JOHN FRANCIS, 606-35-47, enlisted Feb. 24, 1942, Boston, MA. He was a plankowner and served aboard BB-59 as AS 6th Div. at commissioning May 12, 1942. Was assigned to EM2/c E Div. and left BB-59 Oct. 25, 1945.
After the war he worked in communication pole line construction and repair Western Union Telegraph

Company. He is active in the VFW in his spare time. He resided at 273 Clarendon St., Boston, MA 02116. Memory List 1996.

RYAN, WILLIAM JOSEPH, 600-16-19, enlisted Feb. 12, 1942, Albany, NY. He is a plankowner and served aboard BB-59 as AS FC Div. at commissioning May 12, 1942. He resides at 10596 Shasta Drive, Chardon, OH 44024.

RYBCZYNSKI, WILLIAM DOMINICK, 650-28-05, enlisted Feb. 13, 1942, Philadelphia, PA. He is a plankowner and served aboard BB-59 as AS 6th Div. at commissioning May 12, 1942. He resides at 1930 E. Lippincott St., Philadelphia, PA 19134.

RYDER, CHARLES T., served aboard BB-59 in R Div. and resides at 832 NE 120th St., Seattle, WA 98125.

RYDER, JOHN FRANKLIN, JR., 606-35-42, born July 21, 1916, Boston, MA. Graduated from high school and enlisted Feb. 14, 1942, Boston, MA. Trained at Newport Naval Training Station, RI. He is a plankowner and served aboard BB-59 as AS M Div. at commissioning May 12, 1942. Was assigned F3/c, F2/c, F1/c, MM3/c and MM2/c, and left BB-59 Oct. 24, 1945.
After the war he was a truck driver for Armour & Company. He married Mary (deceased) April 17, 1949, Boston, MA, and has two sons. He resides at 1707 Shoreline Drive #113, Alameda, CA 94501.

RYDER, THOMAS G., served aboard BB-59 as S1/c.

RYERSON, WALTER B., served aboard BB-59 as MM2/c M Div. and assigned to A Div. He has one son, one daughter and six grandchildren. He resides at 5480 S.E. Paramount Drive, Stuart, FL 34997.

SABOURIN, ERNEST JOSEPH, 666-15-20, enlisted Feb. 3, 1942, Springfield, MA. He is a plankowner and served aboard BB-59 as AS at commissioning May 12, 1942, and on board for its 2nd and 3rd anniversaries.

SACHAT, SAMUEL, 700-05-01, born August 1920 in Romania. He enlisted May 1942, New York, NY, and trained at Naval Training Station, Newport, RI, and December 1942 Signalman School, Chicago University, Chicago, IL. He served aboard BB-59 as SM2/c CS Div. at commissioning January 1943 and assigned Admiral's Staff SM2/c. He left BB-59 December 1945 Bremerton, WA. After the war he was a salesman for Hart Schaffner Mark for more than 20 years. He delivers meals to elderly; was past quartermaster of JWV Post and enjoys golf in his spare time. He has two daughters and resides at 2717 W. Jarvis St., Chicago, IL 60645.

SACHTLEBEN, WARREN W., 648-16-52, enlisted Feb. 2, 1942, Omaha, NE. He is a plankowner and served aboard BB-59 as AS 4th Div. at commissioning May 12, 1942, and on board for its 2nd and 3rd anniversaries. He resides at 5750 M St., Lincoln, NE 68510.

SAINT MARY, EUGENE J., resided at 1150 Bracey Ave., Greenville, MI 48838. He died; Memory List 1977.

SAKEMILLER, CLAUDE HENRY, JR., 650-23-81, enlisted Feb. 5, 1942, Philadelphia, PA. He is a plankowner and served aboard BB-59 as AS at commissioning May 12, 1942.

SALE, WILLIAM FRANCIS, 375-82-15, enlisted Feb. 9, 1942, San Francisco, CA. He is a plankowner and served aboard BB-59 as S1/c CR Div.

at commissioning May 12, 1942, and assigned March 10, 1943, RDM3/c FR Div.

SALEM, EDWARD J., served aboard BB-59 in A Div. He resides at 12 Cute St., Pawtucket, RI 02860.

SALERNI, EUGENE, (n) 388-42-02, born Jan. 29, 1920, in Italy. Graduated from Bryant High School, New York, NY, and enlisted Sept. 13, 1938, Salt Lake City, UT. Trained at Naval Training Station, San Diego, CA, and on USS *Louisville*. He is a plankowner and served aboard BB-59 as S1/c 1st Div. at commissioning May 12, 1942.
He was assigned COX Oct. 1, 1942; BM2/c Feb. 1, 1943, and "Rammerman" Left Gun Turret #1. He left BB-59 Nov. 31, 1944, South Pacific. Was also assigned Master at Arms Wescousound Trans. School January 1945 and discharged Sept. 19, 1945.
After the war he was a bus operator for the New York Transit Authority, New York, NY, and received "Commendation" Transit Employee of the Month for 28 years service. He enjoys tennis and golf in his spare time.
He married Rosina in 1951 New York, NY, and has two sons and two grandchildren. He resides at 2192 Sweedish Drive #20, Clearwater, FL 34623.

SALMON, MARCOS, (n) 114-89-56, enlisted Nov. 26, 1949, Bremerton, WA.
He is a plankowner and served aboard BB-59 as OC1/c S Div. at commissioning May 12, 1942, and on board for its 2nd and 3rd anniversaries. He was assigned CCK.

SALTON, P.J., served aboard BB-59 as S1/c CR Div. and assigned to CS Div. March 3, 1943.

SALVA, WALTER GEORGE, 212-78-10, born Feb. 22, 1925, Southbridge, MA. Graduated from high school, enlisted April 2, 1942, Springfield, MA, and trained at Naval Training Station, Newport, RI. He is a plankowner and served aboard BB-59 as AS 2nd Div. at commissioning May 12, 1942. Was assigned 4th Div., GM2/c volunteer, landing force Japan Mainland Yokosuka Naval Base. He left BB-59 San Pedro, CA, 1946. After the war he worked for Massachusetts Electric Company for 40 years and active in Veterans of Foreign Wars in his spare time. He married Alice 1947 Webster, MA, and has three daughters. He resides at 22 Locust Ave., Southbridge, MA 01550.

SALVATORIELLO, VINCENT, resides at 105 N. 15th St., Bloomfield, NJ 07003.

SANDE, OLAV LEONARD, 224-69-09, enlisted Jan. 27, 1942, New York, NY. He is a plankowner and served aboard BB-59 as AS B Div. at commissioning May 12, 1942. Was assigned Engine and Fireroom Repairs, MM1/c M Div. and left BB-59 Aug. 17, 1948. He was awarded the Bronze Star. After the war he worked as a general foreman for Schatz Federal Bearings Company, Inc. He has one son, two daughters and resides at 7300 20th St., #126, Vero Beach, FL 32966.

SANDIN, CARL JAMES, 207-24-04, enlisted Oct. 5, 1939, New Haven, CT. He was a plankowner and served aboard BB-59 as F1/c B Div. at commissioning May 12, 1942. (Mrs.) resides at 495A North Spring St., Naugatuck, CT 06770. He died; Memory List 1989.

SANDOR, STEPHEN BERNARD, 250-72-36, enlisted Feb. 24, 1942, Pittsburgh, PA. He is a plankowner and served aboard BB-59 as AS at commissioning May 12, 1942.

SANDOVAL, RUBEN JUAN, 618-16-40, born 1919 Chimayo, NM. Graduated from high school and enlisted Jan. 21, 1942, Denver, CO. Trained at Great Lakes Naval Training Station, Great Lakes, IL, and Gunnery School, Chicago, IL. He is a plankowner and served aboard BB-59 as AS 2nd Div. at commissioning May 12, 1942.

Was assigned S1/c and left Nov. 8, 1945, Shoemaker, CA, discharged. Re-enlisted in the Navy, and discharged October 1953 with seven years, eight months and 18 days service.

After the war he worked for CCC Camps, telephone construction. In his spare time he is a volunteer for Lincoln County Medical Center Auxiliary and Food Bank Ruidoso, NM.

He married Adelina 1948 Santa Cruz, NM, and has one son, two daughters and four grandchildren. He resides at PO Box 1284, Ruidoso Downs, NM 88346.

SANTA BARBARA, SALVADORE, (n) 238-38-03, enlisted Jan. 7, 1942, Albany, NY. He was a plankowner and served aboard BB-59 as MM2/c at commissioning May 12, 1942. He died; Memory List 1990.

SANTINI, CLEVELAND JOSEPH, 642-12-74, enlisted Feb. 11, 1942, Bridgeport, CT. He is a plankowner and served aboard BB-59 as AS R Div. at commissioning May 12, 1942, and on board for its 2nd anniversary. He resides at 27 Elliot Road, Trumbull, CT 06611.

SANTORA, JOSEPH MICHAEL, 647-01-93, enlisted Feb. 20, 1942, New York, NY. He is a plankowner and served aboard BB-59 as AS A Div. at commissioning May 12, 1942, and left BB-59 March 8, 1943, ComSerForSoPac F3/c.

SARDELIS, CHRISTO PETER, 212-61-70, enlisted Nov. 5, 1940, Springfield, MA. He is a plankowner and served aboard BB-59 as S1/c at commissioning May 12, 1942.

SARIK, ALBERT JOSEPH, 650-23-12, enlisted Feb. 5, 1942, Philadelphia, PA. He is a plankowner and served aboard BB-59 as AS at commissioning May 12, 1942, and on board for its 2nd and 3rd anniversaries.

SARRO, JOSEPH ALBERT, 224-46-66, enlisted Dec. 12, 1941, New York, NY. He is a plankowner and served aboard BB-59 at commissioning May 12, 1942, New York, NY, and on board for its 2nd anniversary.

SATORY, NORMAN T., born Nov. 28, 1911, Warsaw, IL. Graduated from high school 1930 and enlisted July 19, 1943. Trained at Farragut Naval Training Station, ID, and USS *Indiana.* He served aboard BB-59 in E Div. and left Nov. 19, 1945.

After the war he worked at Bushing Grocery for one and half years and Iowa Public Service for 30 years. He retired Dec. 1, 1976. In his spare time he was active in the St. John Lutheran Church, the American Legion, Lions Club and a fire chief Clarksville Fire Dept. for 12 years.

He married Sara May 1, 1938, St. John Parsonage, Clarksville, IA, and had one daughter and two grandchildren. Mrs. M.J. Aissen (daughter) resides at Box 444, Clarksville, IA 50619. He died Feb. 25, 1993; Memory List 1995.

SAUNDERS, ROBERT NEAL, ENS, served aboard BB-59 as ENS 5th Div. April 26, 1945, and assigned JO 5th Div. He left BB-59 July 1945.

SAUNDERS, W.J., served aboard BB-59 as F3/c E Div. and left BB-59 March 8, 1943, to ComSerForSoPac.

SAVIDGE, PAUL SHEPPARD, JR., COMDR, Naval Academy Class of 1934. Served aboard BB-59 July 7, 1944, and assigned navigator. He left BB-59 July 1945. He resided at 19233 Dunbridge Way, Gaithersburg, MD 20879. He died; Memory List 1993.

SAWYER, JAMES FREDERICK, 200-27-27, enlisted Jan. 6, 1942, Boston, MA. He is a plankowner and served aboard BB-59 as Mus1/c at commissioning May 12, 1942.

SBIRAL, ALVIN E., resides at 20 Brook, Keene, NH 03848.

SCACCIAFERRO, JOSEPH, JR., (n) 207-38-11, enlisted Feb. 27, 1942, New Haven, CT. He is a plankowner and served aboard BB-59 as AS at commissioning May 12, 1942, and on board for its 2nd and 3rd anniversaries.

SCANLON, LEO F., 650-23-68, enlisted Feb. 3, 1942, Philadelphia, PA. He was a plankowner and served aboard BB-59 as AS at commissioning May 12, 1942, and left BB-59 in 1944. After the war he worked for Erie Lackawanna Railroad and resided at PO Box 73, Moscow, PA 18444. He died; Memory List 1977.

SCARBOROUGH, CHARLES DAVIDSON, 295-43-42, enlisted Sept. 6, 1938, Jackson, TN. He is a plankowner and served aboard BB-59 as S1/c at commissioning May 12, 1942.

SCHEFFLER, ARLT LEONARD, 382-26-65, enlisted Sept. 26, 1940, Los Angeles, CA. He is a plankowner and served aboard BB-59 as F2/c at commissioning May 12, 1942.

SCHEIDECKER, GEORGE FREDERICK, 223-58-79, enlisted Aug. 6, 1940, New York, NY. He was a plankowner and served aboard BB-59 as F1/c at commissioning May 12, 1942. (Mrs.) resides at 1339 Pine Drive, Bay Shore, NY 11706. He died; Memory List 1991.

SCHELL, JOSEPH N., served aboard BB-59 as CPC Oct. 3, 1943, and assigned General Stores. He left BB-59 Jan. 11, 1946.

SCHEVON, HARRY HENRY, 646-61-75, enlisted Jan. 31, 1942, New York, NY. He is a plankowner and served aboard BB-59 as AS at commissioning May 12, 1942.

SCHINDLER, GEORGE JOSEPH, 202-27-39, enlisted March 10, 1942, Boston, MA. He is a plankowner and served aboard BB-59 as AS at commissioning May 12, 1942, and on board for its 2nd and 3rd anniversaries. He resides at 107 Saunders St., Medford, MA 02155.

SCHLAURAFF, HENRY AUGUSTUS, 646-69-49, enlisted Feb. 7, 1942, New York, NY. He is a

plankowner and served aboard BB-59 as AS at commissioning May 12, 1942.

SCHLOSSER, CHARLES LEO, 328-48-66, born Nov. 3, 1916, Durand, WI. Graduated from high school 1934 and enlisted Sept. 14, 1937, Cheppewa Falls, WI. Trained at Great Lakes Naval Training Center, IL, and stationed aboard USS *Brazos* January 1938 to September 1941.

He is a plankowner and served aboard BB-59 as MM1/c A Div. at commissioning May 12, 1942, and left BB-59 March 15, 1943. Was assigned to USS SC-1322 June 10, 1943, and the USS *Instill* AM-252 Feb. 5, 1944, to Feb. 12, 1946.

After the war he worked as a mechanic for International Harvester for a year and a half, Durand, WI; Dairyland Power Company, Alma, WI, for 31 and a half years and eight summers maintenance at Denali National Park, Alaska. Was a volunteer fireman for Buffalo City, WI, Fire Department for 30 years and 40 years American Legion.

He married Marie April 25, 1944, Savannah, GA, and has two sons, two daughters and three grandchildren. He resides at 388 W. 24th St., Buffalo City, WI 54622-9548.

SCHLOSSER, FLORIAN SYLVESTER, 328-48-17, enlisted Feb. 9, 1942, Minneapolis, MN. He is a plankowner and served aboard BB-59 as MM1/c M Div. at commissioning May 12, 1942, and on board for its 2nd and 3rd anniversaries. Was assigned CMM.

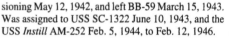

SCHLOSSER, KEITH FRANK, born March 9, 1923, Robbinsdale, MN. A high school graduate with some college, he enlisted Jan. 14, 1943, Minneapolis, MN. Trained at Farragut Naval Training Station, ID, Electrical School and Ship's Company, Farragut, ID; and USS *Indiana.* He served aboard BB-59 as EM2/c E Div. and left BB-59 Jan. 20, 1946, Bremerton, WA.

After the war he was manager of major appliance department, L.S. Donaldson (Allied Stores) for 27 years and real estate sales for 20 years. In his spare time he has been active in the American Legion for 48 years, enjoys traveling, golf, hunting and fishing.

He married Fran Aug. 19, 1950, Minneapolis, MN, and has one son, two daughters and seven grandchildren. He resides at 5724 Drew Ave. N., Brooklyn Center, MN 55429.

SCHMEDDING, JOSEPH, USMC, served aboard BB-59 as major 7th Div. June 1943 and assigned CO Marine Div. Oct. 1, 1943; Combat Intelligence, legal officer, BatDiv 8.

SCHMIDER, ARCHIE, resides at 124 Siebold Place, Apt. 456, Peoria, IL 61601.

SCHMIEDESHOFF, FRED W., DR., served aboard BB-59 in 2nd Div. (Mrs.) resides at Prison Camp Road, Rockingham, NC 28379. He died; Memory List 1987.

SCHMITT, FLOYD LEO, 287-42-56, born Oct. 25, 1919. He enlisted July 30, 1940, Louisville, KY, and trained at Great Lakes Naval Training Station, IL, and USS *Colorado* (BB-45). He is a plankowner and served aboard BB-59 as S1/c 1st Div. at commissioning May 12, 1942. Left BB-59 August 1946 for discharge.

Re-enlisted in the Navy October 1946 and served on various ships mostly minesweepers and harbor crafts,

San Diego; Recruit Training Great Lakes, IL; May 1960 retired to Fleet Reserve Branch 53, Great Lakes, IL. After Naval service he worked for Abbott Labs, North Chicago, IL, December 1960 to December 1981. He enjoys outboard motor repairs and fishing in his spare time.

He married Anna August 1946, High Point, NC, and resides at 40028 Hamilton Rd., Hamilton, MS 39746-9658.

SCHMITTER, WARREN ANTHONY, 646-72-29, enlisted Feb. 10, 1942, New York, NY. He is a plankowner and served aboard BB-59 as AS at commissioning May 12, 1942, and on board for its 2nd and 3rd anniversaries.

SCHOENEBERG, J.F., died; Memory List 1992.

SCHOLL, HAROLD ALEXANDER, 305-25-46, enlisted Jan. 8, 1942, Chicago, IL. He is a plankowner and served aboard BB-59 as WT2/c at commissioning May 12, 1942, and on board for its 2nd anniversary.

SCHONFELD, BERNARD, served aboard BB-59 in 7th Div. He resides at 1141 Holly Ave., Imperial Beach, CA 92032.

SCHOSSLER, CHARLES ARTHUR, served aboard BB-59 in E Div. Jan. 27, 1945, and assigned E Div. junior officer.

SCHRAMM, FLOYD B., served aboard BB-59 as SF3/c R Div. October 1943 and left BB-59 February 1946. After the war he worked as a pipe-fitter for Central Foundry General Motors Corp. He is past commander of American Legion and member VFW. He has two daughters and resides at Rt. 2 Box 151, Oakwood, IL 61858.

SCHREIER, ARTHUR RAYMOND, 207-27-27, born April 16, 1922, Waterbury, CT. A high school graduate with specialized evening training, he enlisted June 25, 1940, New Haven, CT. Trained at Newport Naval Training Station, RI, and the USS *Henley* (DD-391).

He is a plankowner and served aboard BB-59 as F2/c M Div. at commissioning May 12, 1942. Was assigned MM2/c P Div. and left BB-59 1944, Seattle, WA. Was also assigned to USS *Navarro* (APA-215).

After the war he was an electronic technician/salesman for NCR Corp. and salesman in building supply. He is president/secretary Lions Club; treasurer Boy Scouts; treasurer Pearl Harbor Survivors Connecticut Chapter; and state chairman and director 8th District.

He married Ann May 3, 1947, Waterbury, CT, and has one son, three daughters and six grandchildren. He resides at 113 Cutler St., Watertown, CT 06795.

SCHRIEFER, HAROLD JOSEPH, 646-59-20, enlisted Jan. 29, 1942, New York, NY. He is a plankowner and served aboard BB-59 as AS at commissioning May 12, 1942, and on board for its 2nd and 3rd anniversaries. He resides at 18 Bond St. Apt. 209, Lynn, MA 01902.

SCHROIRIER, A.R., served aboard BB-59 commissioning May 12, 1942, and on board for its 2nd anniversary as a plankowner.

SCHROTH, WILLIAM GEORGE, 650-26-08, enlisted Feb. 11, 1942, Philadelphia, PA. He is a plankowner and served aboard BB-59 as AS at commissioning May 12, 1942.

SCHULMAN, BENJAMIN DAVID, LT, born in Decatur, AL. Attended Vanderbilt University (engineering) and enlisted in 1940 Nashville, TN. Served aboard the USS *Tuscaloosa.* He is a plankowner and

served aboard BB-59 as LT 3rd Div. at commissioning May 12, 1942.

Was assigned March 1943 W(P) and JD Battle Station Turret 3 and Oct. 1, 1943, W and D Assist Gunnery Education S.C.M. He left BB-59 in 1944. Was gunnery officer aboard USS *Missouri* and chief gunnery officer aboard USS *Springfield.* After the war from 1946-55 worked for J.A. Cigar Company; 1965-77 president of Liberty Bank; and 1980-93, owner Schulman Studios, Hollywood, CA. A member of the American Legion, Crosscup Vishon, Boston, MA; Honorary Citizen, Nashville, TN; and Honorary Citizen, Los Angeles, CA.

He has two sons, two daughters, and resides at 7529 Gibraltar St., Carlsbad, CA 92009.

SCHULTHEIS, GEORGE ROBERT, (see, WILKINSON, GEORGE ROBERT)

SCHULTZ, CHARLES, (n) 224-64-64, enlisted Jan. 16, 1942, New York, NY. He is a plankowner and served aboard BB-59 as AS at commissioning May 12, 1942, and on board for its 2nd and 3rd anniversaries.

SCHWARTZ, NORMAN, ENS 422024, born Dec. 30, 1924, Bronx, NY. Earned a BA Union College; an MA from Columbia University; and Ed.D New York University. He enlisted July 1, 1943, Schenectady, NY, and trained at V-12 Union College, Midshipman School Northwestern, Miami Training and Edgewood Arsenal Chemical Warfare.

He served aboard BB-59 as ENS R Div. on July 20, 1945, and assigned JO R Div. He left BB-59 January 1946. Was then assigned Naval Supply Depot, Mechanicsburg, PA.

After the war he taught high school English and social studies; a New York State basketball coach; guidance counselor; high school principal at Wyandanch, Kingston and Long Beach, NY; superintendent of schools Syosset, Ellenville, Warwick and Middletown, NY. He is a member of Rotary Club, Syosset, NY; past president of various education associations; earned awards from PTA and other educational groups; and Long Island Administrator of the Year from music teachers.

He married Jean 1951 New York, NY, and has two sons, one daughter and four grandchildren. He resides at 5 Lakes Shore Drive South, Rock Hill, NY 12775.

SCHWARTZ, WILLIAM VINCENT, 638-11-20, enlisted Jan. 2, 1942, Minneapolis, MN. He is a plankowner and served aboard BB-59 as F1/c at commissioning May 12, 1942, and on board for its 2nd and 3rd anniversaries.

SCHWEIGER, JOHN A., resides at 4428 Scotia Road, Baltimore, MD 21227.

SCIOTTI, VINCENT, USMC, served aboard BB-59 in 7th Div. He resides at 21 Elmhurst Ave., Providence, RI 02908.

SCIUTO, ANTONIO JOSEPH, AS, 606-38-42, enlisted Feb. 19, 1942, Boston, MA. He is a plankowner and served aboard BB-59 as AS at commissioning May 12, 1942, and on board for its 2nd anniversary.

SCOTT, EARL GARLAND, 382-00-49, enlisted March 8, 1941, Philadelphia, PA. He is a plankowner and served aboard BB-59 as BM1/c at commissioning May 12, 1942.

SCOTT, HERBERT A., DR., died; Memory List 1979.

SCOTT, LELAND ALVIN, 328-81-94, enlisted Dec. 20, 1940, Minneapolis, MN. He is a plankowner and served aboard BB-59 as S1/c at commissioning May 12, 1942, and on board for its 2nd anniversary.

SCOTT, WALTER ERNEST, 202-27-22, enlisted March 9, 1942, Boston, MA. He is a plankowner and served aboard BB-59 as AS at commissioning May 12, 1942.

SCRAFFORD, CHARLES WILLIAM, 600-13-49, enlisted Feb. 3, 1942, Albany, NY. He is a plankowner and served aboard BB-59 as AS at commissioning May 12, 1942, and on board for its 2nd and 3rd anniversaries.

SCRANTON, DELBERT ELMER, 336-92-59, enlisted Feb. 20, 1941, St. Louis, MO. He is a plankowner and served aboard BB-59 as COX at commissioning May 12, 1942.

SCULL, LEONARD M., 651-77-41, born Nov. 16, 1919, Atlantic City, NJ. Graduated from high school and enlisted September 1942 Philadelphia, PA. He served aboard BB-59 as SF2/c R Div. January 1943 and assigned Damage Control. He left BB-59 May 1944. Also assigned Naval Air Station, Pomona, NJ; Radar Training School, Brigantine, NJ; and discharged October 1945 Philadelphia Navy Yard.

After the war he was a plumber with John H. Moore & Son. In his spare time he was active in Pleasantville, NJ, VFW 2389 and American Legion 430.

He married Ruth June 14, 1941, Atlantic City, NJ, and has two daughters. He resides at 1148 Lodestar Drive, Holiday, FL 3469.

SCURICH, FRANK, (n) 283-69-99, born June 19, 1921, Campbell, OH, and graduated high school, Campbell, OH. He enlisted Jan. 29, 1942, Cleveland, OH, and trained at Great Lakes Naval Training Station, IL, and Naval Hospital, Chelsea, MA.

He was a plankowner and served aboard BB-59 as AS 1st Div. at commissioning May 12, 1942. Left BB-59 July 26, 1945. Was also assigned USS *Kearsarge* (CV-33) and discharged Dec. 10, 1946, as RADM.

After the war he was set-up man for Hynes Industries Roll Formed Products Company, Youngstown, OH, for 32 years.

He married Bernita Aug. 9, 1958, Ellsworth, OH, and had one son, one daughter and three grandchildren. He resided at 318 S. Board St., Canfield, OH 44406. Memory List 1997.

SEABERT, CLAYTON, (n) 359-81-93, enlisted Dec. 30, 1939, Norfolk, VA. He is a plankowner and served aboard BB-59 as COX at commissionig May 12, 1942.

SEABOLT, DANIEL ROY, 265-99-46, enlisted Oct. 13, 1939, Richmond, VA. He was a plankowner and served aboard BB-59 as F2/c at commissionig May 12, 1942. He died; Memory List 1992.

SEALEY, JOHN HERMAN, 268-11-51, enlisted March 15, 1940, San Diego, CA. He is a plankowner and served aboard BB-59 as SF1/c at commissionig May 12, 1942.

SEARBY, ARTHUR F., 809-88-99, born Aug. 23, 1924, Queens Village, NY. Graduated from Jamaica, NY, High School and attended City College of New York. He enlisted Feb. 19, 1943, New York, NY, and trained at Samson Naval Training Station, NY, and Quartermaster Service School, Newport, RI.

He served aboard BB-59 as quartermaster striker N Div. October 1943 and assigned July 1944 QM3/c N Div. Left BB-59 Jan. 25, 1946, Bremerton, WA. From July 1947 to June 1951 in Inactive Naval Reserve.

After the war he worked air cargo sales at JFK

International Airport, NY, and salesman in a retail paint store three days a week. Enjoys golf and walking in his spare time. He married Estelle Nov. 21, 1948, Queensville, NY, and has one son, one daughter and two grandchildren. He resides at 10733 Firestone Court NW, North Fort Myers, FL 33903.

SECHRIST, ARCHIE, served aboard BB-59 in 6th Div. He resides at 1500 South Main, Sapulpa, OK 74066.

SEELEY, H.A., "SLATS," 328-83-71, born May 5, 1923, Pasadena, CA. Graduated from high school and enlisted January 1941 in Minneapolis, MN. Trained at Great Lakes Naval Training, IL; aboard USS *Vessel* and USS *Franklin Bell*. He served aboard BB-59 as EM3/c E Div. and left August 1945. He resides at 9325 E. Nichols St., Bell Flower, CA 90706.

SEELEY, JAMES WILLIAM, 321-25-16, enlisted May 18, 1938, Des Moines, IA. He is a plankowner and served aboard BB-59 as BM2/c at commissionig May 12, 1942.

SEGAL, WILLIAM, (n) 606-05-20, enlisted Dec. 12, 1941, Boston, MA. He is a plankowner and served aboard BB-59 as SF3/c at commissionig May 12, 1942.

SEGER, GLENN ALLEN, 320-66-22, enlisted March 17, 1942, Des Moines, IA. He is a plankowner and served aboard BB-59 as Mus1/c at commissionig May 12, 1942.

SEIFERT, RALPH ERWIN, 243-22-04, enlisted Nov. 26, 1936, Philadelphia, PA. He is a plankowner and served aboard BB-59 as CSM at commissionig May 12, 1942.

SEIP, FRANCIS CHARLES, 243-73-81, enlisted Aug. 7, 1940, Philadelphia, PA. He is a plankowner and served aboard BB-59 as S1/c at commissionig May 12, 1942.

SELMSER, CECIL ROLLIN, JR., 244-06-62, born Aug. 5, 1920, York, PA. Graduated from York, NY, High School, 1938 and enlisted Feb. 26, 1942, Philadelphia, PA. Trained at Newport Naval Training Station, RI.

He was a plankowner and served aboard BB-59 as AS PB Div. at commissioning May 12, 1942. Was assigned July 15, 1943, WT3/c; Sept. 15, 1943, WT2/c and Nov. 1, 1944, WT1/c. He left BB-59 Nov. 13, 1944. Was assigned to the USS *Topeka* and Feb. 15, 1945, Boiler and Turbine Naval Training School, Philadelphia, PA.

Worked for the Department of Defense for 29 years. Married his first wife, Margaret Dec. 26, 1946, and his 2nd wife, Ruth (deceased) July 28, 1957, Maryland. He has four daughters, six grandchildren and one great-grandchild. Cathy Selmser (daughter) resides at 3013 Nutmeg, Garland, TX 75040. Selmser died Dec. 6, 1974; Memory List 1977.

SEMINO, FRANK FELIX, 622-14-30, enlisted Nov. 21, 1941, Detroit, MI. He is a plankowner and served aboard BB-59 as Msmth2/c at commissionig May 12, 1942, and on his 2nd and 3rd anniversaries.

SERAFIN, BERNARD JOHN, 311-13-77, enlisted Jan. 2, 1942, Detroit, MI. He is a plankowner and served aboard BB-59 as Phm2/c at commissionig May 12, 1942.

SEVERSON, EUGENE, L., resides at 12520 50th Ave. N., Minneapolis, MN.

SEYMOUR, IRWIN LEWIS, 401-92-97, enlisted Jan. 5, 1942, Albany, NY. He is a plankowner and served aboard BB-59 as Bkr2/c at commissioning May 12, 1942, and on board for its 2nd and 3rd anniversaries.

SEYMOUR, L.C., died; Memory List 1980.

SGOLINSKI, JOSEPH, died; Memory List 1992.

SHACKELFORD, ROY FARMER, 382-36-60, enlisted Jan. 20, 1941, Los Angeles, CA. He is a plankowner and served aboard BB-59 as S1/c at at commissionig May 12, 1942, and on board for its 2nd and 3rd anniversaries.

SHAFFER, JOHN JOSEPH, JR., 650-26-06, enlisted Feb. 11, 1942, Philadelphia, PA. He is a plankowner and served aboard BB-59 as AS at commissionig May 12, 1942.

SHAFROTH, JOHN F., RADM, served aboard BB-59 in Combat Div. 8 from April 1943 to December 1944 and commander battleship Div. 8 Dec. 24, 1944, to Jan. 28, 1946. He died; Memory List 1977.

SHANNON, G.H., served aboard BB-59 as S1/c CR Div. and assigned to FR Div. March 10, 1943.

SHANNON, JOHN ANDREW, 600-12-03, enlisted Jan. 26, 1942, Albany, NY. He is a plankowner and served aboard BB-59 as AS at commissionig May 12, 1942.

SHANNON, ROBERT CLAIR, 372-27-00, enlisted Feb. 6, 1941, Denver, CO. He is a plankowner and served aboard BB-59 as S1/c at commissionig May 12, 1942, and on board for its 2nd and 3rd anniversaries.

SHARP, CHARLES FREDERICK, 244-05-84, born in Philadelphia, PA. He attended Pitman High School and enlisted Jan. 28, 1942, Philadelphia, PA. Stationed at South Boston Annex March 1942.

He is a plankowner and served aboard BB-59 as AS L Div. at commissionig May 12, 1942. Was assigned to Lookout, SM3/c; CS Div.; SM2/c Flag 3 CB Div. 8. He left BB-59 July 25, 1945. Was also assigned to the USS *Dalphin* APA, USS *Allagash* fleet oiler; discharged February 1947; US Naval Reserve; October 1951 Korean Action USS *Calvert* (APA-32); 1965 US Coast Guard Reserve quartermaster instructor Quartermaster Training Center; 1972 Search/Rescue ODO Cape May Air Station, Cape May, NJ; and February 1984 retired with 27 1/2 years service.

After Naval service was a printer for *Woodbury Times*; shop chairman Local ITU; president Local ITU; night foreman *Gloucester County Times* and retired in 1985 with 34 years service. In his spare time is in the US Coast Guard Office/Berthing Module Training Center, Cape May, NJ, and dedicated "Sharp Hall" in 1984.

He married Dorothy and has one son, two daughters and four grandchildren. He resides at 257 Elm Ave., Mantua, NJ 08051.

SHAW, CALVIN RUSSEL, 372-16-64, enlisted Aug. 5, 1940, Denver, CO. He is a plankowner and served aboard BB-59 as F2/c at commissionig May 12, 1942.

SHAW, ROBERT, (n) 652-03-40, enlisted Dec. 14, 1941, Pittsburgh, PA. He was a plankowner and served aboard BB-59 as EM2/c E Div. at commissionig May 12, 1942. Died Nov. 7, 1944.

SHAWCROSS, RAYMOND J., served aboard BB-59 in V Div. He resided at 25 Whittingham Terrace, Millburn, NJ 07041.

SHEA, GERALD JERAMIAH, 244-06-85, enlisted Feb. 3, 1942, Philadelphia, PA. He is a plankowner and served aboard BB-59 as AS at commissioning May 12, 1942, and on board for its 2nd and 3rd anniversaries.

SHEA, JOSEPH FRANCIS, 244-06-86, enlisted Feb. 3, 1942, Philadelphia, PA. He is a plankowner and served aboard BB-59 as AS at commissionig May 12, 1942. He resides at 721 River Road, Scranton, PA 18501.

SHEATS, RAYMOND R., 952-42-18, born March 2, 1925, Mt. Clemens, MI. Enlisted April 28, 1944, and trained at Great Lakes Naval Training Station, IL, and aboard USS DD-214. He served aboard BB-59 as S2/c 1946 and discharged May 20, 1946.

After the war he was a warehouse manager for Malbin's Furniture retiring with 31 years service and worked for Petitpren, Inc., Mt. Clemens, MI, for three years.

He married Virginia Feb. 1, 1947, Mt. Clemens, MI, and had two sons and two grandchildren. (Mrs.) resided at 45 Englewood St., Mt. Clemens, MI 48043. He died July 31, 1992; Memory List 1992.

SHEDERICK, WILLIAM EDWARD, 600-02-69, enlisted Dec. 16, 1941, Albany, NY. He is a plankowner and served aboard BB-59 as SF3/c at commissioning May 12, 1942.

SHEEHAN, WILLIAM JOSEPH, JR., 212-44-38, enlisted Feb. 9, 1942, Boston, MA. He is a plankowner and served aboard BB-59 as EM3/c E Div. at commissioning May 12, 1942, and left BB-59 Feb. 3, 1943. After the war he worked for Clark College, Vancouver, WA, and resides at 2311 NE 58th St., Vancouver, WA 98663.

SHEFFIELD, CLARENCE LEE, 406-86-65, enlisted July 26, 1940, Lakeland, FL. He is a plankowner and served aboard BB-59 as F3/c at commissioning May 12, 1942.

SHEKER, GENE WENCESLAUS, graduated from high school 1934 and enlisted the same year. Attended Naval Academy Class of 1940 and served aboard USS *California* and USS *Washington*.

He served aboard BB-59 in 1942. He served aboard the USS *Boise*; USS *Richmond*; resigned active duty and entered Naval Reserve 1947; and retired in 1964 as a commander.

After his Naval service he was electrical engineer for Honeywell, Westinghouse and Lockheed retiring 1975. In his spare time he earned his real estate license, enjoys fishing, golf and gambling. He has four daughters and three grandchildren.

SHELDON, H.R., resides at Star Rt. 2, Box 308, Crescent City, FL 32112.

SHEPARD, WINNER K., served aboard BB-59 in CR Div. (Mrs.) resides at 3411 Parkway Blvd., Meridian, MS 39305. He died; Memory List 1990.

SHEPOSH, JOHN RUDOLPH, 250-49-67, enlisted Feb. 6, 1939, Pittsburgh, PA. He is a plankowner and served aboard BB-59 as COX at commissioning May 12, 1942, and on board for its 2nd and 3rd anniversaries.

SHEPPARD, ARTHUR FRED, 551-65-59, served aboard BB-59 in CR Div. He resides at 190 Pine Ave., Pacific Grove, CA 93950.

SHERIDAN, FRANCIS LEONARD, 224-69-88, enlisted Jan. 29, 1942, New York, NY. He is a plankowner and served aboard BB-59 as AS at commissioning May 12, 1942.

SHERIDAN, PETER V., 853-60-75, born Oct. 31, 1915, Carbondale, PA. Graduated from high school and enlisted July 23, 1943, Great Lakes, IL. Trained at Great Lakes Naval Training Station, IL, and Electrical School, Iowa State College and aboard USS *Indiana*.

He served aboard BB-59 as EM3/c E Div. at commissioning April 1944 and assigned to Lighting, Section Battery and Maintenance. He left BB-59 November 1945.

After the war he worked as an electrician for Otis Elevator Company retiring March 1978. He was active in the VFW and on call for senior citizens with electrical problems.

He married Anne Oct. 5, 1940, and had two sons and seven grandchildren. (Mrs.) resides at 930 Taylor Drive 308, Gurnee, IL 60031. He died Sept. 7, 1991; Memory List 1993.

SHERLEY, LEWIS CARROL, 356-25-16, enlisted March 8, 1941, Fort Worth, TX. He is a plankowner and served aboard BB-59 as S1/c at commissionig May 12, 1942.

SHIAVO, ANTHONY, served aboard BB-59 in 2nd Div. He resides at 333 46th St., Pittsburgh, PA 15201.

SHIELDS, MATTHEW JOSEPH, 646-70-72, enlisted Feb. 9, 1942, New York, NY. He was a plankowner and served aboard BB-59 as AS at commissionig May 12, 1942. He died; Memory List 1980.

SHIELS, JOHN EDWARD, 606-54-98, enlisted March 27, 1942 as YN3/c. Reported to Fitting out duty at Fore River Shipyard, Quincy, MA. Aboard for Commissioning and assigned to the Engineer's Office (Log Room) until transferred to Flag Office (COMBATDIV 8). While with Flag was promoted to YN1/c and YNC.

Transferred to shore duty Nov. 1944 and served at West Coast Sound School, San Diego, CA until discharged Aug. 28, 1945. Returned to active duty Oct. 1946 serving various naval air stations. In Dec. 1964 retired as a Master Chief Petty Officer. Served as Secretary, USS Massachusetts Associates until 1958.

He has two sons, one daughter and four grandchildren. He resides at 2345 Vegas Ave., Castro Valley, CA 94546.

SHIFLET, ROBERT L., served aboard the USS *Sederstorm* (DE-31). He served aboard BB-59 as GM3/c Sept. 26, 1945.

SHIMENSKY, WALTER, served aboard BB-59 in 1st and X Div. He resided at 1592 Ridgewood Court, Twinsburg, OH 44087. He died; Memory List 1993.

SHINAVER, JEROME MARTIN, 311-85-63, enlisted Dec. 10, 1941, Detroit, MI. He is a plankowner and served aboard BB-59 as MM2/c at commissioning May 12, 1942, and on board for its 2nd and 3rd anniversaries as CMoMM.

SHIPLEY, JACK DALE, 368-59-12, enlisted Jan. 21, 1941, Salt Lake City, UT. He is a plankowner and served aboard BB-59 as S1/c at commissioning May 12, 1942.

SHOEMAKER, WILLIAM, 342-24-54, born July 15, 1922, Kansas City, KS. He enlisted July 19, 1940, Kansas City, MO, and stationed Dec. 7, 1941, Pearl Harbor aboard USS *Helena*. He was a plankowner and served aboard BB-59 as S1/c. At commissioning May 12, 1942. Was assigned May 1943 as GM2/c; December 1944 GM1/c, #9 Mount captain. He was discharged July 19, 1946, Lido Beach, NY.

After the war he worked as a master electrician for General Electric Company. In his spare time he was a Boy Scout troop leader.

He married June 9, 1945, Fitchburg, MA, and then divorced. He had two sons, one daughter and six grandchildren. Diane Mahoney (daughter) resides at 840 Ashby W. Road, Fitchburg, MA 01420. Shoemaker died April 6, 1993; Memory List 1993.

SHONECK, JOHN JOSEPH, 207-18-02, enlisted Jan. 19, 1942, New Haven, CT. He is a plankowner and served aboard BB-59 as FC3/c at commissioning May 12, 1942.

SHONERD, HENRY GILBERT, JR., LT, Naval Academy Class of 1935. He was a plankowner and served aboard BB-59 as LT 3rd Div. at commissioning May 12, 1942. Was assigned March 1943 LT 3rd Div. officer; October 1943 LT COMDR Turret officer Spot One; E Div. officer, assistant engineering officer; COMDR. He left BB-59 June 30, 1944, and retired as CDR. After the war he was a rocket test engineer for Aerojet General Corp. He had two sons, one daughter, and resided at 8257 Rensselaer Way, Sacramento, CA 95826. He died; Memory List 1984.

SHOWALTER, MARVIN GORMAN, served aboard BB-59 as CEM E Div. Dec. 28, 1942, and assigned JO admiral of personnel. He left BB-59 Feb. 5, 1945.

SHUTTER, TREMAN ALBERT, 244-06-52, enlisted Feb. 26, 1942, Philadelphia, PA. He is a plankowner and served aboard BB-59 as AS at commissioning May 12, 1942.

SIBOLE, JAMES LESLIE WILLIAM, 258-08-57, enlisted Aug. 14, 1939, Baltimore, MD. He is a plankowner and served aboard BB-59 as COX at commissioning May 12, 1942.

SICARD, DONAT MARSEL, 212-77-85, enlisted March 9, 1942, Springfield, MA. He is a plankowner and served aboard BB-59 as AS at commissioning May 12, 1942.

SIDERS, CARL EUGENE, 279-96-08, enlisted Jan. 29, 1942, Cincinnati, OH. He is a plankowner and served aboard BB-59 as AS 2nd Div. at commissioning May 12, 1942, and on board for its 2nd anniversary. He resides at 1962 Fulton Ave., Monterey Park, CA 91754.

SIKES, THEODORE ALLEN, 372-16-75, enlisted Aug. 6, 1940, Denver, CO. He is a plankowner and served aboard BB-59 as FC3/c at commissioning May 12, 1942.

SILVERIA, BERNARD JOSEPH, 202-27-55, born April 10, 1926, Lowell, MA. He enlisted March 10, 1942, Boston, MA, and trained at Newport Naval

Training Station, RI. Served aboard BB-59 as AS 5th Div. at commissioning May 12, 1942.

He is a plankowner and assigned as Mount Captain 5" 38 Cal. #3; GM2/c Starboard #3, #5, #7 5." He left BB-59 Nov. 20, 1945, Bremerton, WA. Was also assigned Nov. 30, 1945, to Dec. 4, 1946, chief master at arms Dutch Harbor Navy Base, Unalaska, AK, and discharged Dec. 9, 1946.

After the war from 1947 to 1956 worked for DeSoto Auto Dealership, Lowell, MA; 1956-57 Desoto Div., Chrysler Corp.; New England field engineer; 1957-66 Studebaker Auto Corp., New England district manager; 1966-88 Fiat Motors of North America, Inc., importation of Italian automobiles for North American continent; and retired as vice-president. In his spare time he is corporate member USS *Massachusetts* Memorial Committee; 1970-90 a leader of BB-59 "Field Days;" organizer, booster USS *Massachusetts* newsletter; a member of the Lions and the Elks.

He married Claire and has three sons, four daughters and 13 grandchildren. He resides at 86 Dayton Road, Lake Worth, FL 33467.

SIMMONS, ELMER MELL, JR., 337-12-57, enlisted Feb. 20, 1939, St. Louis, MO. He is a plankowner and served aboard BB-59 as AS at commissioning May 12, 1942, and on board for its 2nd anniversary.

SIMON, JOHN "B," ENS, 440465, born Sept. 10, 1924, Newark, NJ. Holds a BA in business administration from Duke University. He enlisted September 1942 Durham, NC, and trained as Naval ROTC Duke University. He served aboard BB-59 as LT(jg) 1st Div. April 26, 1945, and assigned JO 6th Div. division officer. He left BB-59 June 12, 1946, Portsmouth, VA. Was assigned recruiting officer, Newark, NJ, 1947.

After the war, from 1949-78 founder of Sunglo Glass Company and 1979 real estate investor. Is president of Los Angeles Chapter Leukemia Society of America; chairman of the board, Israel Cancer Research Fund; board of directors Anthony Industries, Inc.; and member World Presidents Organization.

He married Liona (Boyd) Feb. 2, 1992, Beverly Hills, CA, and has three sons and one grandchild. He resides at 510 Doheny Road, Beverly Hills, CA 90210.

SIMPSON, ALEXANDER GEORGE, 650-26-22, born July 9, 1920, Philadelphia, PA. A high school graduate with two years college, he enlisted Feb. 11, 1942, Philadelphia, PA. Trained at Newport Naval Training Station, RI. He is a plankowner and served aboard BB-59 as AS 6th Div. at commissioning May 12, 1942. Left BB-59 August 1945 Seattle, WA. After the war he was an electrician for a heating, ventilating and air conditioning factory. He married Rita Sept. 28, 1945, and has three daughters and six grandchildren. He resides at 6 Plumbridge Way, Levittown, PA 19056-3543.

SIMPSON, EARL EMMIT, 393-50-26, enlisted Jan. 30, 1941, Portland, OR. He is a plankowner and served aboard BB-59 as F2/c P Div. at commissioning May 12, 1942, and left March 8, 1943, ComSecForSoPac.

SIMPSON, GEORGE H., (Mrs.) resides at 33 Irvine Road, Old Greenwich, CT 06870. He died; Memory List 1989.

SIMPSON, WAYNE DEAN, 393-50-25, enlisted Jan. 30, 1941, Lewiston, ID. He is a plankowner and served aboard BB-59 as F2/c P Div. at commissioning May 12, 1942, and left BB-59 ComSerForSoPac.

SIMS, CLIFFORD RANDOLPH, 268-29-37, enlisted Jan. 10, 1942, Washington, DC. He is a plankowner and served aboard BB-59 as MM1/c M Div. at commissioning May 12, 1942. Was assigned to #2 Engine Room, CMM in charge #1 Engine Room, P Div. He left BB-59 January 1946. After the war he worked as a carpenter for the US Air Force, Hanscom Field. He has two sons, one daughter, and resides at 68 Arcadia Ave., Reading, MA 01867.

SINGLEY, GROVER CLEVELAND, 644-06-12, enlisted Oct. 30, 1941, New Orleans, LA. He is a plankowner and served aboard BB-59 as EM3/c E Div. at commissioning May 12, 1942, and on board for its 2nd anniversary.

SINOPOLI, VINCENT FRANCIS, 202-26-08, enlisted Feb. 27, 1942, Boston, MA. He was a plankowner and served aboard BB-59 as AS at commissioning May 12, 1942, and on board for its 2nd and 3rd anniversaries. He resided at 76 Smith Place, Cohasset, MA 02025. He died; Memory List 1981.

SIPPEL, RICHARD W., resides at 7451 Springhaven Ave., Indiantown, FL 34956.

SIROTAK, WILLIAM KENNETH, 646-32-90, enlisted Jan. 5, 1942, New York, NY. He is a plankowner and served aboard BB-59 as Y3/c at commissioning May 12, 1942.

SISUL, ANDREW, JR., 300-81-33, born Sept. 27, 1924, Gary, IN. Attended Froebel High School and enlisted March 20, 1942, Gary, IN. Trained at Great Lakes Naval Training Station, IL. Served aboard BB-59 as S1/c and assigned assistant train layer #3 Turret, 20 mm Aft. He left BB-59 December 1943.

Other Naval assignments: Dec. 9, 1943, plankowner USS *Fanshaw* (CVE-70) as GM1/c. After the war he worked for Kaiser Steel Company, Fontana, CA, 1945; Royal Typewriter, Portland, OR, 1948; self-employed from 1952-1993 office machines; 1978-90 restaurant; and from 1965 to date on the golf course.

He married Catherine Jan. 19, 1945, San Diego, CA, and has four sons and one grandchild. He resides at 2965 N. Holly, Canby, OR 97013.

SKAGGS, RALPH, served aboard BB-59 as S1/c. He resides at Kankakee, IL 60901.

SKARA, MARNOLD, died; Memory List 1994.

SKELTON, DELBERT MARION, 668-39-10, enlisted Feb. 6, 1942, St. Louis, MO. He is a plankowner and served aboard BB-59 as AS at commissionig May 12, 1942.

SKELTON, JOHN JACOBS, 368-32-07, enlisted May 28, 1941, Salt Lake City, UT. He is a plankowner and served aboard BB-59 as COX at commissionig May 12, 1942.

SKERBA, EUGENE JOSEPH, 250-72-19, enlisted Feb. 24, 1942, Pittsburgh, PA. He is a plankowner and served aboard BB-59 as AS at commissionig May 12, 1942.

SKIBA, CHARLES, (n) 224-72-97, enlisted March 6, 1942, New York, NY. He is a plankowner and served aboard BB-59 as AS at commissioning May 12, 1942, and on board for its 2nd and 3rd anniversaries. He resides at 1200 SW 12th St., Fort Lauderdale, FL 33315.

SKILLINGSTAD, RAMON E., served aboard BB-59 in 2nd Div. He resides at 9960 Haug Ave., NE Monticello, MN 55362.

SKIPWITH, THOMAS AMOS, 266-67-53, enlisted March 26, 1942, Richmond, VA. He is a plankowner and served aboard BB-59 as Matt3/c at commissioning May 12, 1942.

SKLUZACEK, ROBERT RUDOLPH, 328-74-51, enlisted Sept. 10, 1940, Minneapolis, MN. He is a plankowner and served aboard BB-59 as S1/c at commissioning May 12, 1942, and on board for its 2nd anniversary. He resides at PO Box 281, Lonsdale, MN 55046.

SKRLAC, JOHN JAKE, 299-89-55, enlisted Feb. 24, 1938, Chicago, IL. He is a plankowner and served aboard BB-59 as S1/c at commissioning May 12, 1942.

SKVOLKA, ANDREW MARTIN, 652-07-44, enlisted Dec. 31, 1941, Pittsburgh, PA. He is a plankowner and served aboard BB-59 as SK3/c S Div. at commissioning May 12, 1942. He resides at RR #1 Box 210, Carlton, PA 16311.

SLAFF, ALLAN PAUL, LT(jg) 390013, born Feb. 2, 1923, Mount Vernon, NY. Graduated Naval Academy Class of 1944; Naval Post Graduate School, Naval War College; and Advanced Management Program, Harvard Business School. He entered the US Naval Academy July 1, 1944.

He served aboard BB-59 as ENS 3rd Div. Oct. 30, 1944. Was assigned JO 3rd Div.; LT(jg) commanding officer Turret III; May 12, 1945 editor of *Baystater*. He left BB-59 February 1946 San Francisco, CA. Was assigned to USS *Houston* (CL-81); 1947 Staff Comm. Crv. Div. 12; 1947-49 OP Naval; 1949-50 P.C. School Com. Nav. FE; 1950-51 USS *Holder* DD-819; 1952-54 P.G. School; 1953-54 USS *Hazelwood* (DD-519); 1956-58 USS *Laiter* (DE-1022); 1956-58 Aide Comm. Dailant; 1959 War College; 1961 personal aide CNO Admiral Arleigh Burke; 1961-63 USS *Davis* (DD-937); 1963-64 USS *Luce* (DLGM); 1964-67 office of Secretary of Navy; 1967 Harvard Business School; 1967-68 senior advisor Vietnam; 1968-70 USS *Albany* (CG-10). From 1970-79 administrative dean and faculty member of Harvard Business School; 1979-86 president and chief editor of *Luzerne County News Co.*; 1982 to present chairman of Labsphere, Inc.

He enjoys golf in his spare time. He has one son and one daughter. He resides in the summer at PO Box 1836, New London, NH 03257 and 3101 Green Dolphin Lane, Naples, FL 33940.

SLAUGHTER, E.W., served aboard BB-59 as S1/c V Div. and left BB-59 March 8, 1943, Noumea to Commandant Fleet Air.

SLEVIN, WILLIAM JAMES, 646-66-61, enlisted Feb. 5, 1942, New York, NY. He was a plankowner and served aboard BB-59 as AS S Div. at commissioning May 12, 1942. He was assigned SSML2/c laundry and left BB-59 September 1945. After the war he was a trim repairman for Ford Motor Company. He had two sons and one daughter. (Mrs.) resides at 218 Broad Ave., Leonia, NJ 07605. He died; Memory List 1989.

SLICK, ROBERT W., served aboard BB-59 as Mus2/c X Div. and band member January 1943. He left BB-59 January 1945. After the war he was a driving instructor for Fitzgerald's Driving School. He resides at 19 Shelbourne Lane, Stony Brook, NY 11790.

SLOAN, JOSEPH, USMC, born in Vivian, SD, and enlisted October 1943 USMC. Was stationed in San Diego, CA, and Sea School, San Diego, CA. He served aboard BB-59 as PFC 7th Div. 1944 and left December 1945 Seattle, WA. After the war he was a merchant and enjoys golf in his spare time. He married Doris Feb. 3, 1946, Seattle, WA, and resides at 135 Fairway Blvd., Kalispell, MT 59901.

SLOVER, WALTER PETER, 223-07-19, enlisted March 17, 1942, San Diego, CA. He is a plankowner and served aboard BB-59 as GM2/c at commissioning May 12, 1942.

SLUSARZ, CHESTER FRANK, 224-73-38, enlisted March 9, 1942, New York, NY. He is a plankowner and served aboard BB-59 as AS at commissioning May 12, 1942.

SLUSKI, JOHN PETER, 299-83-81, enlisted Jan. 6, 1942, Chicago, IL. He was a plankowner and served aboard BB-59 as Bmkr1/c E Div. at commissioning May 12, 1942. He resided at 871 N. 14th St. #B, Laramie, WY 82070. He died Jan. 11, 1994; Memory List 1994.

SMALASZ, ADAM JOSEPH, 224-71-31, enlisted Feb. 26, 1942, New York, NY. He is a plankowner and served aboard BB-59 as AS at commissioning May 12, 1942, and on board for its 2nd and 3rd anniversaries.

SMALL, EUGENE EDGAR, 202-26-10, enlisted Feb. 27, 1942, Boston, MA. He was a plankowner and served aboard BB-59 as AS at commissioning May 12, 1942, and on board for its 2nd anniversary. He resided at 30 Wentworth St., Biddeford, ME 04005. He died; Memory List 1977.

SMALLECK, ALEXANDER, JR., enlisted Jan. 29, 1942, Cleveland, OH. He is a plankowner and served aboard BB-59 as AS at commissioning May 12, 1942.

SMART, ERNEST GLENN, 261-64-25, enlisted Feb. 18, 1936, Raleigh, NC. He is a plankowner and served aboard BB-59 as Mus1/c X Div. and band member at commissioning May 12, 1942.

SMALLWOOD, DONALD R., resides at 116 Center St., Charlestown, WV 25414.

SMALLWOOD, JOHN, served aboard USS *Sederstorm* (DE-31). He served aboard BB-59 as S2/c Sept. 22, 1945.

SMILEY, ROGER, resides at Fritzlyn Farms, Pipersville, PA 18747 (1963).

SMITH, ANGIE FRANK, LT(jg) served aboard BB-59 as LT(jg) L Div. June 4, 1943, and assigned instrument recognition, LT and assistant navigator Oct. 1, 1943. He left BB-59 Sept. 19, 1945. He resided at 3420 Piping Rock Lane, Houston, TX 77027. He died July 4, 1994; Memory List 1994.

SMITH, ARTHUR E., born Jan. 8, 1922, Carthage, TX. Graduated from high school Marshall, TX, and enlisted July 18, 1942, Dallas, TX. Trained at Naval Training Station, San Diego, CA; Machinist Mate School; Landing Craft School and USS *Barnett*. He served aboard BB-59 April 9, 1943, and left Oct. 28, 1945, Bremerton, WA.

After the war he worked as a car man apprentice for Texas and Pacific Railroad. In his spare time he is involved with Meals on Wheels, hospice, church activities and voted "Man of the Year" Christian Men's Fellowship.

He married Loyda Aug. 1, 1946, Marshall, TX, and has one son and two grandchildren. He resides at 505 Deanne Drive, Longview, TX 75603.

SMITH, AUSTIN TURNER, 606-33-36, enlisted Feb. 9, 1942, Boston, MA. He is a plankowner and served aboard BB-59 as AS at commissioning May 12, 1942.

SMITH, BEN HILL, JR., 268-06-80, enlisted March 10, 1942, Mare Island, CA. He is a plankowner and served aboard BB-59 as COX at commissioning May 12, 1942.

SMITH, CHARLES B., ENS, served aboard BB-59 as ENS FC Div. Oct. 26, 1943, and assigned JO FC Div. J.O.R.K. officer. He left BB-59 Aug. 12, 1944.

SMITH, CHARLES H., 244-08-97, born in Utica, NY. He enlisted March 4, 1942, Philadelphia, PA, and trained at Newport Naval Training Station, RI; USS *Indiana*, SM2/c staff Admiral Davis Com.Bat. Div. 8.

He served aboard BB-59 in CS Div. and left November 1944 Eniwetok. He taught Signal School Seattle, WA; USS *Brevard* (AK-164); and discharged Jan. 26, 1946, Bainbridge, MD. After the war he was an apprentice mechanic Chevey Garage for two years; heavy equipment operator for construction company 42 years; and does gun smithing at home. He enjoys boating, shooting and hunting in his spare time.

He married Ethel in 1946 Perkasie, PA. He has one son, three daughters and six grandchildren, and resides at 837 Spring Hill Road, Secane, PA 19018.

SMITH, CLARENCE, (n) 646-65-24, enlisted Feb. 4, 1942, New York, NY. He is a plankowner and served aboard BB-59 as AS at commissioning May 12, 1942.

SMITH, DAVID FRANCIS, 287-23-12, enlisted Jan. 19, 1938, Louisville, KY. He is a plankowner and served aboard BB-59 as COX at commissioning May 12, 1942.

SMITH, ELDEN LEWIS, 268-57-96, enlisted Nov. 9, 1940, Macon, GA. He is a plankowner and served aboard BB-59 as S1/c at commissioning May 12, 1942.

SMITH, EUGENE WILLIAM, JR., 606-33-05, enlisted Feb. 14, 1942, Boston, MA. He was a plankowner and served aboard BB-59 as AS at commissioning May 12, 1942, and on board for its 2nd and 3rd anniversaries. He died; Memory List 1985.

SMITH, HAROLD DEWEY, 359-99-85, enlisted July 12, 1938, Houston, TX. He is a plankowner and served aboard BB-59 as S1/c at commissioning May 12, 1942.

SMITH, JOHN E., resided at PO Box 201, Norridgewock, ME 04957. He died; Memory List 1993.

SMITH, JOHN PERSHING, 300-06-48, enlisted April 3, 1940, Chicago, IL. He is a plankowner and served aboard BB-59 as S1/c at commissioning May 12, 1942.

SMITH, JOYE WAYNE, 654-03-83, enlisted Oct. 2, 1941, Portland, OR. He is a plankowner and served aboard BB-59 as S2/c A Div. at commissioning May

12, 1942. Was assigned to MM1/c refrigeration A Div. and left BB-59 Nov. 1, 1945, Bremerton, WA. He was discharged Nov. 1, 1945.

After the war he worked as a meat cutter; and in 1970 senior weight and measures inspector for Sacramento County, CA. He retired Nov. 1, 1980. He is senior advisor for Sacramento Fire Dept. Reserve and enjoys traveling in his recreational vehicle.

He married Margaret Nov. 18, 1945, Oregon and has one daughter and one grandchild. He resides at 1257 Rodeo Way, Sacramento, CA 95819.

SMITH, KIRBY, JR., 346-63-22, enlisted Jan. 5, 1942, Little Rock, AR. He is a plankowner and served aboard BB-59 as SK2/c at commissioning May 12, 1942.

SMITH, LAWRENCE EDWIN, 201-59-99, enlisted Feb. 13, 1942, Boston, MA. He is a plankowner and served aboard BB-59 as GM3/c at commissioning May 12, 1942, and on board for its 2nd anniversary.

SMITH, LITTLETON K., Major USMC, 142-10-7851, born April 19, 1917, New Brunswick, NJ. Attended Rutgers University 1941 and enlisted Sept. 2, 1941, Marine Barracks, Philadelphia Navy Yard, PA. In May 1941 2nd LT Army Infantry Reserve; 2nd LT USMC January 1942 OCS Basic School, Parris Island, SC; and Marine Barracks Portsmouth Navy Yard, NH.

He is a plankowner and served aboard BB-59 as 2nd LT 7th Div. at commissioning May 12, 1942, and assigned 1st LT and CAPT. Left BB-59 in spring 1943 Noumea, New Caledonia. Other assignments include: BN Ex. officer Transit Camp Noumea; October 1944 returned to US; 1945 Command Staff School Quantico, VA; 1945 Manila/Philippines and Joint Planning Staff Japan Invasion; 1947 6th Base Supply Service Depot, Pearl Harbor; 1947-49 assistant director 3rd Marine Corps Reserve District New York, NY; 1952-53 Korea; Feb. 7, 1953, 2nd Marine Div.; 1953 Quantico, VA; 1956-61 Marine Corps Base, 29 Palms, CA; and retired.

After his Naval service he taught history and government at University of California, and Riverside High School. He retired after 13 years.

He married Dorothy Oct. 21, 1944, Rochester, NY, and has one son, two daughters and seven grandchildren. He resides at 186 Martin Luther King Blvd., Riverside, CA 92507-5402.

SMITH, MARION EDWARD, 311-55-67, born Nov. 19, 1923, Flint, MI. Graduated from high school and enlisted Nov. 25, 1940, Detroit, MI. Trained at Great Lakes Naval Training Station, IL; aboard USS *Oklahoma* (BB-37) and USS *Chester.*

He is a plankowner and served aboard BB-59 as S1/c 1st Div. at commissioning May 12, 1942. Was assigned GM3/c Turret #1, Gun Captain Center Gun. He left Jan. 18, 1944, Philippines. On Feb. 19, 1944, Advanced Gunners Mates School and Electrical Hydraulic Course, San Diego, CA; USS *W.L. Lind* (DD-703); USS *Indiana*; Naval Repair Base, San Diego, CA; USS *Ingram* (APD-43); and Jan. 19, 1947, discharged with four years Naval Inactive Reserve. After the war he was a construction supt. sprinkler work and retired Sept. 5, 1986, with 40 years service.

He is active in the VFW, American Legion, DAV and Pearl Harbor Survivors Assoc. He has two sons, two daughters, 10 grandchildren and three great-grandchildren. He resides at 8921 NE Afton Road, Kansas City, MO 64155-2506.

SMITH, R.M., served aboard BB-59 as EM1/c E Div. May 12, 1945.

SMITH, RALPH TINER, 642-13-87, enlisted Feb. 23, 1942, New Haven, CT. He is a plankowner and served aboard BB-59 as AS at commissioning May 12, 1942.

SMITH, ROBERT ROLAND, 600-14-52, enlisted Feb. 5, 1942, Albany, NY. He is a plankowner and served aboard BB-59 as AS at commissioning May 12, 1942, and on board for its 2nd and 3rd anniversaries.

SMITH, R.Z., resided at 800 So. Salisbury St., Lexington, NC 27292. He died; Memory List 1977.

SMITH, THOMAS EARL, 243-18-32, enlisted May 11, 1940, Cincinnati, OH. He is a plankowner and served aboard BB-59 as CMM at commissioning May 12, 1942.

SMITH, WILLIAM CHARLES, 652-13-88, enlisted Jan. 20, 1942, Pittsburgh, PA. He is a plankowner and served aboard BB-59 as AS at commissioning May 12, 1942, and on board for its 2nd and 3rd anniversaries.

SMITH, WILLIAM DORSEY, 646-61-83, enlisted Jan. 31, 1942, New York, NY. He was a plankowner and served aboard BB-59 as AS CR Div. at commissioning May 12, 1942, and on board for its 2nd and 3rd anniversaries. Was assigned March 4, 1943, RDM3/c to FR Div. He resided at 181 Foreside Road, Falmouth, ME 04105. Memory List 1996.

SMITH, WILLIAM HARRISON, 359-99-32, enlisted May 17, 1938, San Diego, CA. He is a plankowner and served aboard BB-59 as GM2/c at commissioning May 12, 1942.

SMITHSON, GEORGE W., served aboard BB-59 in 2nd Div. He resides at 48 Mayetta Landing Road, Mayetta, NJ 08092.

SMOLINSKY, FERDINAND, JR., 600-13-68, enlisted Feb. 3, 1942, Albany, NY. He is a plankowner and served aboard BB-59 as AS at commissioning May 12, 1942, and on board for its 2nd and 3rd anniversaries. He resides at RD #1, Binghamton, NY 13902.

SMONKO, GEORGE, 652-17-21, enlisted Jan. 31, 1942, Pittsburgh, PA. He is a plankowner and served aboard BB-59 as AS at commissioning May 12, 1942, and on board for its 2nd and 3rd anniversaries.

SNODA, JOSEPH JOHN, 385-39-06, enlisted Jan. 5, 1942, Chicago, IL. He is a plankowner and served aboard BB-59 as Mldr1/c at commissionig May 12, 1942.

SNOWER, MAURQUIS, resides in Zearing, IA.

SOBOLOSKI, STEVEN, (n) 646-59-24, enlisted Jan. 29, 1942, New York, NY. He is a plankowner and served aboard BB-59 as AS at commissionig May 12, 1942.

SOIOTTI, VINCENT T., USMC, May 8, 1942, Norfolk Navy Yard, Norfolk, VA. He is a plankowner and served aboard BB-59 as PVT 7th Div. at commissionig May 12, 1942.

SOKOLOWSKI, CHESTER J., served aboard BB-59 in 4th Div. He resides at 40105 Capitol Drive, Sterling Heights, MI 48313.

SOLARI, MARIO LOUIS, 642-11-92, enlisted Feb. 5, 1942, New Haven, CT. He is a plankowner and served aboard BB-59 as AS at commissioning May 12, 1942, and on board for its 2nd anniversary.

SOMMERS, RUDOLPH TURRILL, JR., 606-31-24, born Sept. 18, 1921, Milford, MA. He enlisted Feb. 18, 1942, Newport, RI, and trained at Newport Naval Training Station, RI.

He was a plankowner and served aboard BB-59 as AS 4th Div. at commissioning May 12, 1942. He was assigned S2/c and S1/c and left BB-59 Nov. 14, 1945.

He was married and divorced; married 2nd wife,

Florence in 1967. He had two sons, one daughter and one grandchild. (Mrs.) resides at 16288 N5200W Garland, UT 84312. He died July 16, 1993; Memory List 1993.

SOPER, GEORGE LEONARD, 385-76-97, enlisted Feb. 16, 1938, Seattle, WA. He was a plankowner and served aboard BB-59 as SC2/c at commissioning May 12, 1942. He died; Memory List 1988.

SOSSI, JOHN A., served aboard BB-59 in E Div. He resides at 5044 Lanno St., Detroit, MI 48236.

SOTTILE, JOHN, (n) 224-68-74, enlisted Jan. 26, 1942, New York, NY. He is a plankowner and served aboard BB-59 as AS at commissioning May 12, 1942, and on board for its 2nd and 3rd anniversaries.

SOURS, PAUL EDWARD, ENS, served aboard BB-59 as ENS S Div. October 1942.

SOUTH, R.D., 224-71-16, enlisted Feb. 25, 1942, New York, NY. He is a plankowner and served aboard BB-59 as AS at commissioning May 12, 1942, and on board for its 2nd and 3rd anniversaries.

SOUTHWICK, GEORGE ARNOLD, 646-58-13, born Sept. 13, 1924, Massapequa, NY. Graduated from high school and enlisted Jan. 28, 1942, New York, NY. Trained at Newport Naval Training Station, RI.

He is a plankowner and served aboard BB-59 as AS I Div. at commissioning May 12, 1942. Was assigned to Radar School, Virginia Beach, VA; March 10, 1943, S2/c CR Div. and RDM2/c FR Div. He left BB-59 November 1945 Seattle, WA.

After the war he managed and co-owned truck stop and restaurant for 20 years. In his spare time he plays golf and is member of VFW and the American Legion.

He married Noni Aug. 20, 1947, Freeport, NY, and has one son, one daughter and one grandchild. He resides at 2036 N. Lambert Drive, Normal, IL 61761-5263.

SPARROW, JOSEPH PAUL, 310-55-17, enlisted April 25, 1941, New York, NY. He is a plankowner and served aboard BB-59 as CSF at commissioning May 12, 1942.

SPATARO, GENNARINO J., USMC, 378529, born April 12, 1916, New York, NY. He enlisted March 4, 1942, Boston, MA, and trained at USMC School, Norfolk, VA; Parris Island, SC; Sea School, Norfolk, VA; and May 8, 1942, Norfolk Navy Yard, VA. He is a plankowner and served aboard BB-59 as PVT 7th Div. at commissioning May 12, 1942, and assigned 20 and 40 mm Gun Crew. He left BB-59 April 18, 1944.

Was also assigned USS *Relief*; Naval Hospital, Hawaii and Oakland, CA; St. Albens Hospital, Brooklyn Navy Yard; Feb. 21, 1945, medical survey for disability.

After the war he part of investigation of Barbers Comm. of Massachusetts and from Dec. 1, 1948, to Dec. 30, 1978, self-employed as a barber. He is past commander of VFW Post 2188; Elks #1274; DAV #36, and past commander Marine Corps League, Quincy, MA.

He married Mae May 23, 1942, Boston, MA, and has one son, one daughter and four grandchildren. He resides at 9 Reland St., Middleboro, MA 02346-2218.

SPEAGLE, DEWEY L., USMC, May 8, 1942, Norfolk Navy Yard, VA. He is a plankowner and served aboard BB-59 as corporal 7th Div. at commissioning May 12, 1942.

SPENCER, WILLIAM CLAYTON, LT, served aboard BB-59 as LT CR Div. April 22, 1945, and assigned radio officer.

SPERNACK, ANTHONY, died; Memory List 1988.

SPEWOCK, SAMUEL, resides at 320 Chestnut Ridge Road, Latrobe, PA 15650.

SPIES, ROYAL LEO, 258-01-33, enlisted Feb. 15, 1937, Baltimore, MD. He is a plankowner and served aboard BB-59 as Mus1/c at commissioning May 12, 1942.

SPINKS, A.T., served aboard BB-59 as BM2/c M.A.A., and assigned Feb. 25, 1943, to 5th Div.

SPRIG, FRANK LUDWIG, 646-65-27, born Feb. 16, 1924, West New York, NY. He enlisted Feb. 4, 1942, New York, NY, and trained at Newport Naval Training Station, RI.

He is a plankowner and served aboard BB-59 as AS 3rd Div. at commissioning May 12, 1942. He was assigned S2/c, F2/c and F1/c, and left BB-59 November 1945 Bremerton, WA.

He married Olga in 1948 Union City, NJ, and has two sons, one daughter and two grandchildren. He resides at 316 10th St., Carlstadt, NJ 07072.

SPRINGER, PAUL LEWIS, 321-46-23, enlisted Aug. 20, 1940, Des Moines, IA. He is a plankowner and served aboard BB-59 as S1/c at commissioning May 12, 1942, and on board for its 2nd anniversary.

SPURLOCK, EDWARD MARSHALL, 274-23-88, born Sept. 24, 1915, Big Bend, LA. Graduated from high school and enlisted Jan. 6, 1942, New Orleans, LA. Served aboard USS *Texas* 1936-38 and USS *Seagull* 1938-39.

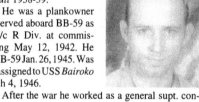

He was a plankowner and served aboard BB-59 as CM2/c R Div. at commissioning May 12, 1942. He left BB-59 Jan. 26, 1945. Was also assigned to USS *Bairoko* March 4, 1946.

After the war he worked as a general supt. construction company and 1978-90 owned a construction company. Was chairman of Television Ministry for Church Building Committee for church. He married Helen Nov. 22, 1952, Baton Rouge, LA, and had one son, two daughters and five grandchildren. (Mrs.) resides at 3826 Greenway Drive, Baton Rouge, LA 70814. Memory List 1997.

SPYTKOWSKI, STANLEY, served aboard BB-59 as S1/c 4th Div. Feb. 5, 1943, and left BB-59 Nov. 4, 1945.

After the war he worked as a plant special laborer for Westchester County Sewage Plant. He resides at 56 Park Ave., Terrace, Yonkers, NY 10703.

SGOUNSKI, JOSEPH, died; Memory List 1992.

STAFFORD, LEO ELI, 224-71-33, born May 20, 1923, Little Egg Harbor, NJ. He enlisted Feb. 2, 1942, New Brunswick, NJ. He is a plankowner and served aboard BB-59 as AS 4th Div. commissioning May 12, 1942, and on his 2nd and 3rd anniversaries.

Was assigned to L and FC Div. and left BB-59

February 1945. Rates held were S2/c, S1/c, CS3/c, CS2/c, CS1/c. He was also assigned March 2, 1945, to Aug. 2, 1945, Naval Barracks, Lake Union, Seattle, WA; Aug. 4, 1945, to March 1, 1947, Naval Receiving Station, Seattle, WA; March 10, 1947, to Dec. 10, 1947, USS *Takelma* (ATF-113); inactive duty Dec. 21, 1947, to July 25, 1950.

Back to active duty July 25, 1950, Naval Air Station, Sand Point, Seattle WA; July 30, 1950, to Nov. 12, 1954, Naval Air Station, Alameda, CA; Nov. 12, 1954, to Nov. 2, 1959, Korean and Japan Service; Dec. 7, 1959, to March 7, 1960, USS *Orca* (AVP-49); April 23, 1960, to Sept. 5, 1961, USS *Shield* (DD-596); Oct. 7, 1961, to Dec. 1, 1961, USS *Robison* (DDG-12); transferred to Fleet Reserve and retired Feb. 3, 1965.

He married Frances (second wife) and has one son, one daughter and three grandchildren. He resides at 32 Deanna Drive Apt. 72, South Somerville, NJ 08876.

STALLO, EUGENE V., USMC May 8, 1942, Norfolk Navy Yard, VA. He is a plankowner and served aboard BB-59 as PVT 7th Div. at commissioning May 12, 1942.

STANARD, WILLIAM B., ENS, served aboard BB-59 as ENS B Div. Oct. 26, 1943, and assigned JO and JW B Div. LT(jg). He left BB-59 Oct. 2, 1944.

STANFORD, A.G., LCDR, died; Memory List 1982.

STANISLAWSKI, ANTHONY STANLEY, 646-59-26, born Oct. 11, 1915, Bayonne, NJ. Graduated from Bayonne High School Class of 1934, and enlisted Jan. 29, 1942, New York, NY. Trained at Newport Naval Training Station, RI.

He is a plankowner and served aboard BB-59 as AS 5th Div. at commissioning May 12, 1942. He left BB-59 Oct. 25, 1945, Bremerton, WA. Was discharged Lido Beach, Long Island, NY. On Nov. 8, 1946, worked as unloader and stockman for General Motors Assembly Div., Linden, NJ. He retired on Oct. 1, 1972, with 32 years of service.

In his spare time he enjoys sports, softball, bowling, horse racing and gardening. He resides at 24 Pointview Terrace, Bayonne, NJ 07002.

STANKUS, ALFRED, resides at 3524 Frederick, Detroit, MI 48226.

STANTON, SAMUEL, (n) 272-31-23, enlisted May 7, 1940, Birmingham, AL. He is a plankowner and served aboard BB-59 as Matt1/c at commissioning May 12, 1942, and on board for its 2nd anniversary.

STARK, H.B., LT, Naval Academy Class of 1936. He served aboard BB-59 March 1943 and assigned Asst. Air Defense.

STASTNY, CHARLES EUGENE, ENS, Naval Academy 1943, served aboard BB-59 as ENS A Div. July 1942 and assigned March 1943 W(P) and JD 1st Div.; Battle Station Comp. Turret #1; Oct. 1, 1943, JW and JD Boxing Officer, LT(jg). Was assigned to captain. He died; Memory List 1990.

STEFFEN, LOUIS ERNEST, 638-11-26, enlisted Jan. 2, 1942, Minneapolis, MN. He is a plankowner and served aboard BB-59 as EM3/c E Div. at commissioning May 12, 1942.

STEIB, CONRAD J., resides at 1108 11th Ave. So., Fort Dodge, IA 50501 (1966).

STEIGER, ELMER ELLSWORTH, 646-64-18, enlisted Feb. 3, 1942, New York, NY. He is a plankowner and served aboard BB-59 as AS at commissioning May 12, 1942, and on board for its 2nd anniversary.

STEIN, FRANCIS CAMILLUS, 652-18-40, enlisted Feb. 4, 1942, Pittsburgh, PA. He is a plankowner and served aboard BB-59 as AS at commissioning May 12, 1942, and on board for its 2nd and 3rd anniversaries.

STEINHELFER, RICHARD LEE, 279-58-82, enlisted Jan. 11, 1939, Cincinnati, OH. He is a plankowner and served aboard BB-59 as S1/c at commissioning May 12, 1942.

STEINKRAUS, JACK DONALD, 610-44-04, enlisted Jan. 21, 1942, Chicago, IL. He was a plankowner and served aboard BB-59 as AS at commissioning May 12, 1942, and on board for its 2nd and 3rd anniversaries. Was assigned to S1/c 1st Div.

After the war he was a machinist for Britt Mfg. Corp. He was active in the American Legion and Elks. He married Hazel. (Mrs.) Hazel Weymouth resides at 966 E. Wisconsin St., Delavan, WI 53115. Memory List 1977.

STEINMANN, MARTIN, ENS, born March 3, 1915, Minneapolis, MN. He holds a BA, MA and Ph.D. in English from the University of Minnesota. He served aboard BB-59 as ENS FR Div. July 25, 1943, and assigned I Div. JO; Asst. FC C.I.C. officer and LT(jg). He left BB-59 May 4, 1945.

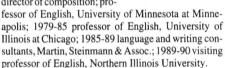

After the war from 1946-79 was director of freshman English; director of Minnesota Center for Advanced Studies in Language; director of composition; professor of English, University of Minnesota at Minneapolis; 1979-85 professor of English, University of Illinois at Chicago; 1985-89 language and writing consultants, Martin, Steinmann & Assoc.; 1989-90 visiting professor of English, Northern Illinois University.

Membership: American Society for Aesthetics, Assoc. for Professional Writing Consultants, British Society of Aesthetics, Linguistics Society of America, Powys Society of America and of Great Britain and Rhetoric Society of America.

He married Jane in 1958 Wakefield, MI, and has one son, two daughters and three grandchildren. He resides at 525 Grove St. #3D, Evanston, IL 60201.

STELZENMULLER, G.V., JR., LT(jg) served aboard BB-59 as LT(jg) I Div. May 12, 1944, and assigned I Div. JO; C.I.C. Air Plot Officer. He left BB-59 Nov. 21, 1944.

STEPHENS, HARRY RICHARD, 337-0-77, enlisted July 11, 1938, St. Louis, MO. He is a plankowner and served aboard BB-59 as F1/c at commissioning May 12, 1942, and on board for its 2nd anniversary.

STEPHENS, VERNE EDWARD, 342-24-29, born March 6, 1921, Kansas City, KS. Graduated from Wyandotte High School Class of 1940 and enlisted July 10, 1940, Kansas City, MO. Trained at Great Lakes Naval Training Station, IL, and stationed aboard USS *Honolulu* (CL-48) from September 1940 to March 1942.

He is a plankowner and served aboard BB-59 as S1/c F Div. at commissioning May 12, 1942. Assigned rates FC3/c, FC2/c, FC1/c; July 1942 to September 1942 Fire Control School, Norfolk, VA. He left BB-59 December 1945 Bremerton, WA. Other Naval assignments: December 1945 to February 1946 Bremerton Naval Hospital, WA; February 1946 to March 1946 Lake Union Barracks; March 1946 to April 1946 USS *Dixie* (AD-14); April 1946 to May 1946 TAD CEN Camp Elliot San Diego, CA; May 1946 to July 1946 Rec. Sta. San Diego, CA, and discharged July 9, 1946.

From July 1946 to February 1949 laborer and hood carrier Kansas Staten University, Kansas City, KS; June 28, 1950, April 14, 1951, insurance rep. Winter, VA; Hospital Topeka, KS; April 7, 1952, electrical apprenticeship; Feb. 10, 1953, journey wireman. From September 1961 to July 1964 apprenticeship instructor humanities, Topeka Civic Theatre; active in church, secretary/treasurer I.B.E.W. 226 Retirees; Cub and Boy Scouts; Kansas Hunter Safety instructor; was awarded Carmie Wolfe and Volunteer of the Year Topeka Civic Theatre; plaque from USS *Topeka*; plaque Troop 26 Boy Scouts; and plaque from Cub Pack 5.

He married Wanda in 1958 Topeka, KS, and has two sons and four grandchildren. He resides at 1019 SW Munson Ave., Topeka, KS 66604-1131.

STEPIEN, JOSEPH PETER, 666-15-63, enlisted Feb. 7, 1942, Springfield, MA. He was a plankowner and served aboard BB-59 as AS S Div. at commissioning May 12, 1942. Was assigned S1/c Store Keeper. He left BB-59 1945. After the war he worked as an inspector for Thompson Wire and had three children. He resides at 47 Old Worcester Road, Oxford, MA 01540. He died; Memory List 1980.

STERLING, CHARLES ANDREW, 342-14-56, born in 1921 Milan, MO. A high school graduate with some college, he enlisted Oct. 10, 1939, Kansas City, MO. Was stationed aboard USS *Argonne* and British ship, *Aquatania*.

He is a plankowner and served aboard BB-59 as BM2/c 5th Div. at commissioning May 12, 1942. He left BB-59 November 1944. Was also assigned US Navy Pilot Training. Attended school and married Ruth.

He has two daughters and four grandchildren. He resides at 170 Deer Meadow Lane, Chatham, MA 02633.

STEVENS, FRANK H., served aboard BB-59 in M Div. He resides at 1347 Ana Maria Circle, Port Orange, FL 32119.

STEVENS, OSCAR J., 862-53-36, born April 14, 1925, Flushing, MI. Graduated from Flushing, MI, High School Class of 1943 and enlisted July 14, 1943, Detroit, MI. In July 1943 Great Lakes Naval Training Station, IL, and USS *Indiana*. He served aboard BB-59 as F1/c E Div. at commissioning April 21, 1944, and assigned EM3/c, EM2/c Heavy Power E-3. Left BB-59 April 1946 Shelton, VA, ship mothballed.

After the war he worked as an installer central office equipment, Western Electric Company for four and a half years; General Telephone Company of Michigan for 35 and a half years and retired as division manager. He is a life member of VFW Post #5666 Flushing, MI; member of (6) Kiwanis Clubs; member of (6) Chambers of Commerce; past president Kiwanis; past distinguished lieutenant governor Michigan District.

He married Doris Aug. 19, 1950, Angola, MI, and resides at 3122 Cherry Tree Lane, Elkhart, IN 46514.

STEVENSON, ARTHUR RAYMOND, 321-18-25, enlisted July 13, 1937, Des Moines, IA. He is a plankowner and served aboard BB-59 as SK2/c at commissioning May 12, 1942.

STEWART, HAMPTON ARTHUR, 238-55-99, enlisted Oct. 5, 1936, Albany, NY. He is a plankowner and served aboard BB-59 as RM1/c at commissioning May 12, 1942.

STEWART, HAROLD VAN ALLEN, JR., ENS, served aboard BB-59 as ENS FC Div. May 21, 1944, and assigned FC Div. JO RK officer. He left BB-59 May 12, 1945.

STEWART, HERBERT V., served as 7th Div. GY SGT.

STEWART, JACK JEFF, 346-75-72, enlisted Nov. 15, 1939, Little Rock, AR. He is a plankowner and served aboard BB-59 as F1/c at commissioning May 12, 1942.

STEWART, JESSIE LEROY, 360-06-23, enlisted Sept. 20, 1939, Houston, TX. He is a plankowner and served aboard BB-59 as Matt1/c at commissioning May 12, 1942.

STICKNEY, HAROLD JUDSON, 636-15-37, enlisted Dec. 17, 1941, Macon, GA. He is a plankowner and served aboard BB-59 as RM3/c at commissioning May 12, 1942, and on board for its 2nd anniversary.

STOCK, LOREN A., resides at Box 125, Dumont, IA 50625 (1966).

STOKES, THOMAS MURRAY, CAPT, Naval Academy Class of 1922 and made captain June 1942. He served aboard BB-59 ComBatDiv 8 June 1943 and assigned chief of staff and aide to operations.

STOLLEY, GEORGE J., resides at 421 Livalda St., Aurora, CO 80011.

STOMSKI, WILLIAM ZIGMONT, 238-22-44, enlisted Nov. 27, 1936, Des Moines, IA. He is a plankowner and served aboard BB-59 as CBM at commissioning May 12, 1942.

STONE, HAROLD, served aboard BB-59 in 1st and E Div. He resides at 2980 Plaimore Ave., Palm Springs, CA 92262.

STONE, JAMES ALOYAIUS, 243-59-24, born in Millville, NJ. Enlisted Sept. 21, 1937, Philadelphia, PA, and trained at Newport Naval Training Station, RI, and Squadron 3 USS *Saratoga*. He is a plankowner and served aboard BB-59 as PTR2/c R Div. at commissioning May 12, 1942. Was assigned PTR1/c R Div. in 1943 and left in Bremerton, WA.

Was also assigned Philadelphia Navy Yard Shore Patrol and Atlantic City Shore Patrol. After the war he worked as painting contractor for Hyman & Son for five years; Oim Company to 1965; Pacemaker Boats & C.P. Leek for 15 years; Ocean and Fiberglass Yachts for four years; and retired at age 68. He is a member of the VFW,

American Legion, Exchange Club, Goodfellows and the Knights of Columbus.

He married Mary, Egg Harbor, NJ, and resides at 310 St. Louis Ave., Egg Harbor City, NJ 08215.

STONE, JOHN THOMAS, 336-80-70, enlisted Jan. 14, 1942, St. Louis, MO. He is a plankowner and served aboard BB-59 as FC2/c at commissioning May 12, 1942.

STRAHAN, FLOYD WILLS, 375-74-75, enlisted Feb. 14, 1940, Boston, MA. He is a plankowner and served aboard BB-59 as MM1/c at commissioning May 12, 1942.

STRAUSBAUGH, HOWARD K., served aboard BB-59 in S Div. He has one son, two grandchildren and one great-grandchild. He resides at 263 Long St., Chillicothe, OH 45601.

STRETCH, DAVID A., CDR, died; Memory List 1982.

STRICKLIN, WILLIAM PERSHING, 624-18-54, born May 20, 1918, Birmingham, AL. Attended Sam Houston High School and several trade school. He enlisted Dec. 24, 1941, Houston, TX, and trained at Great Lakes Naval Training Station, IL. He is a plankowner and served aboard BB-59 as EM3/c E Div. at commissioning May 12, 1942. Was assigned EM2/c damage control electrician and EM1/c turret electrician. He left BB-59 October 1945.

He returned to the Navy during the Korean War aboard USS *Tombigbee* (AOG-11). After the war he worked as a cable splicer assistant for Houston Lighting & Power Company, Texas and electrician for Shell Oil Company, Deer Park, TX, for 46 years. Spends his spare time doing church work and walking.

He married Bernice Sept. 17, 1955, Houston, TX, and has two sons, one daughter and five grandchildren. He resides at 1607 Zapp Lane, Pasadena, TX 77502.

STRIVING, SILAS, assignments included tenor sax – band.

STROM, ARNOLD, served aboard BB-59 as S1/c 4th Div. November 1942 and assigned L Div. He left BB-59 May 1946. After the war he was a mechanic for Alameda-Contra Costa Transit District. He married Dorothy and has one son. He resides at 24785 Willimet Way, Haywood, CA 94544.

STROM ARTHUR EDWARD, 618-19-51, enlisted Jan. 31, 1942, Denver, CO. He is a plankowner and served aboard BB-59 as AS at commissioning May 12, 1942.

STROM, FRANK ANDERS, LT(jg) served aboard BB-59 as LT(jg) 4th Div. July 25, 1943, and assigned LT Fire Control Div. officer, machine gun instructor and catapult officer. He left BB-59 May 10, 1945. After the was president of Oil Stone Bank, Providence, RI. He was involved with several civic organizations and had one son and one daughter. He died; Memory List 1977.

STUBBS, JAMES E., 383-20-34, born Aug. 1, 1926, Mankato, MN. A high school graduate with a corrections course at American University, Washington, DC, he enlisted Aug. 12, 1943, San Diego, CA. Stationed at San Diego, CA, Naval Training Station; EMA School University of Minnesota; EMR School Great Lakes, IL, and USS *Indiana*.

He served aboard BB-59 as F2/c E Div. at commissioning April 1944 and assigned Electric Shop,

EM3/c Boats and Batteries and EM2/c I.C. Group. He left BB-59 Portsmouth, VA, September 1946. Other Naval assignments: Naval Station Treasure Island, San Francisco, CA Naval Air Station, Jacksonville, FL; USS *Perkins* (DDR-877); USS *Boyd* (DD-594); USS *Shangri La* (CV-38); USS *Seminole* (AKA-104); USS *Oak Hill* (LSD-7); USS *Bellatrix* (AF-62); USS *Pictor* (AF-54); retired July 1, 1973, as CWO 4 after 30 years of service. In his spare time he enjoyed hunting, fishing, model railroads and ships.

He married Phyllis Sept. 16, 1955, Buffalo, NY, and had one son. He resided at 4553 Zambito Ave., Jacksonville, FL 32210. He died Nov. 14, 1996. Memory List 1997.

STUCKEY, ALFRED, Memory List 1986.

STUMP, JAMES B., 659-26-58, born in Copperhill, VA, enlisted October 1942. Trained at Great Lakes Naval Training Station, IL. Served aboard BB-59 as AS 3rd Div. December 1942 and left BB-59 at Marshall Islands. Was also assigned to the USS *North Carolina* and discharged December 1945. After the war he worked as a baker at Sunbeam Company. He enjoys bowling and golf. Married Beatrice August 1946, and has one son and one daughter. He resides at 2308 Highland Farm Rd. NW #5, Roanoke, VA 24017.

STURWOLD, FRANK J., 862-47-63, born Jan. 9, 1925, Lincoln Park, MI. He enlisted June 30, 1943, Detroit, MI, and trained at Great Lakes Naval Training Station, IL; Electrical School Purdue University, San Francisco to Pearl Harbor on USS *Lexington*, Pearl Harbor to Admiralty Islands on USS *Indiana*. Served aboard BB-59 as EM3/c E Div. April 28, 1944, and assigned to I.C. Room, switchboard operator (E1), movie operator and church setting up (E-8). He left BB-59 Norfolk, VA, April 27, 1946.

After the war he worked as an electrician Allied Signal Company 1946-68 for 21 and a half years; 1968-87 electrician General Motors Company for 19 and a half years and retired January 1987. He is an avid sports fan, loves travel and gardening.

He married Mary Bernice May 26, 1951, St. Henry's, Lincoln Park, MI. He has two sons, three daughters, eight grandchildren and one great-grandchild. He resides at 15570 O'Conner St., Allen Park, MI 48101.

STYLES, WALTER H., served aboard BB-59 as CTC 3rd Div.

SUBA, THEODORE GOLDEN, 207-21-39, enlisted Dec. 28, 1937, New Haven, CT. He is a plankowner and served aboard BB-59 as COX at commissioning May 12, 1942.

SUGARMAN, BERNARD LOUIS, 666-15-77, enlisted Feb. 9, 1942, Springfield, MA. He is a plankowner and served aboard BB-59 as AS at commissioning May 12, 1942, and on his 2nd anniversary.

SUGGS, THOMAS IRWIN, 261-92-59, enlisted May 20, 1936, Raleigh, NC. He is a plankowner and served aboard BB-59 as GM1/c at commissioning May 12, 1942.

SULLIVAN, ALBERT FRANK, 385-78-08, enlisted July 14, 1938, Seattle, WA. He is a plankowner and served aboard BB-59 as S1/c commissioning May 12, 1942.

SULLIVAN, JOHN R., born Dec. 10, 1913, Bronx, NY. He enlisted July 28, 1942, New York, NY, and trained at Newport Naval Training Station, RI. He served aboard BB-59 as GM2/c January 1943 and assigned Turret #1. He left BB-59 September 1945. After the war he worked as a butcher for Gresleah Bros. and a social director for AARP. He married Sept. 29, 1945, New York, NY, and had one son, two daughters and seven grandchildren. (Mrs.) resides at 1490 East Ave., Bronx, NY 10462-7531. He died Nov. 19, 1988; Memory List 1990.

SUMMERVILLE, EDWARD CLARK, 652-15-03, born in 1918 Evans City, PA. Enlisted Jan. 23, 1942, Pittsburgh, PA, and trained at Newport Naval Training Station, RI. He is a plankowner and served aboard BB-59 as AS CR Div. at commissioning May 12, 1942. He left BB-59 1945 Manila Bay, Philippines, and assigned to Philadelphia Navy Yard. After the war he worked as desk clerk for Penn Lincoln Motel, Pennsylvania. He married Bertha 1945, Butler, PA, and has one daughter and two grandchildren. He resides at 4009 Liberty St., Erie, PA 16509-1623. Memory List 1997.

SUPPLEE, JOSEPH T., 650-81-15, born March 9, 1920, Philadelphia, PA. He graduated from Pierce College and enlisted July 1942 Philadelphia. He trained at Newport Naval Training Station, RI. He served aboard BB-59 as QM2/c N Div. at commissioning January 1943 and assigned to P Div. He left BB-59 February 1944 and assigned to USS *General S.D. Sturgis*, QM1/c. He was discharged December 1945.

After the war he was assistant treasurer for Elliot Lewis Corp.; credit manager for Bayard Sales Corp. and semi-retired. He has been a volunteer fireman for 41 years. He has one daughter and resides at 23 W Laurel Road, PO Box 129, Stratford, NJ 08084-1718.

SUTCLIFFE, JOHN, (n) 244-06-19, enlisted Jan. 30, 1942, Philadelphia, PA. He is a plankowner and served aboard BB-59 as AS at commissioning May 12, 1942, and on board for its 2nd and 3rd anniversaries.

SUTTER, ANTHONY, (n) 336-12-72, enlisted Dec. 23, 1941, San Francisco, CA. He is a plankowner and served aboard BB-59 as CWT at commissioning May 12, 1942.

SWANSON, MELVILLE E., USMC, born Dec. 16, 1920, Columbus, OH. A high school graduate with less than a year at Ohio State University, he enlisted Feb. 23, 1942, Cincinnati, OH. Trained at Marine Corps Training Parris Island and May 8, 1942, Norfolk Navy Yard.

He is a plankowner and served aboard BB-59 as PVT 7th Div. at commissioning May 12, 1942, and on board for its 2nd anniversary. He was assigned 20 mm guns and 40 mm guns after training in Seattle, WA, Sgt. Admiral Davis Flag Group, Platoon SGT 7th Div. He left BB-59 Nov. 10, 1943, with Admiral Davis to USS *Indiana*; Feb. 5, 1944, returned to BB-59; Sept. 28, 1945, left BB-59 Bremerton, WA, and was discharged Oct. 3, 1945. Occupied Yokosuka Navy Base, Japan.

After the war he worked in car sales, repair, estimates cases, West Insurance adjuster; manager DD Minehart; hourly employee, foreman, general foreman, production supt. for General Motors Corp. He is active in the VFW.

He married Shirley and has two sons, one daughter and five grandchildren. He resides at 5671 Rings Road, Dublin, OH 43017-1229.

SWEENEY, GEORGE ARTHUR, 606-61-65, enlisted April 11, 1942, Boston, MA. He is a plankowner and served aboard BB-59 as S2/c S Div. at commissioning May 12, 1942. He resides at 321 Neponset Ave., Dorchester, MA 02122.

SWEET, FLOYD, (n) 328-11-16, enlisted Feb. 5, 1942, Dutch Harbor, AK. He is a plankowner and served aboard BB-59 as CEM E Div. at commissioning May 12, 1942.

SWENSON, OWEN HOWARD, ENS 256120, born May 15, 1921, Kindred, Cass County, SD. Earned a BA in electrical engineering University of Minnesota. He enlisted in the Naval Reserve RM3/c 1938 Minneapolis, MN, and trained 1939-43 Naval ROTC University of Minnesota, MN, and June 1943 V3 commissioned ensign.

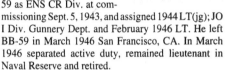

He served aboard BB-59 as ENS CR Div. at commissioning Sept. 5, 1943, and assigned 1944 LT(jg); JO I Div. Gunnery Dept. and February 1946 LT. He left BB-59 in March 1946 San Francisco, CA. In March 1946 separated active duty, remained lieutenant in Naval Reserve and retired.

After Naval service in August 1947 field engineer with assignments in Pacific Northwest, Alaska and Europe; industrial and marine power propulsion, automation systems for General Electric Company, Schenectady, NY, Syracuse, NY, and Seattle, WA, and retired May 1981. In his spare time he is an amateur radio operator (W7ZGF), enjoys photography, big band music, history, languages and computers.

He married Bernice (deceased) April 1946 San Francisco, CA, and has three sons, one daughter and two grandchildren. He resides at 3127 SW 169th St., Seattle, WA 98166.

SWING, HOWARD BUCHANAN, 261-75-03, enlisted July 2, 1940, Philadelphia, PA. He is a plankowner and served aboard BB-59 as COX at commissioning May 12, 1942.

SWINSON, FLOYD ORVAL, 337-27-87, enlisted March 5, 1940, St. Louis, MO. He is a plankowner and served aboard BB-59 as S1/c at commissioning May 12, 1942.

SWITZER, GEORGE L., MD Memory List 1989.

SWOPE, WILLIAM MOUNTS, 404-65-98, enlisted Jan. 2, 1942, Raleigh, NC. He is a plankowner and served aboard BB-59 as MM1/c at commissioning May 12, 1942, and on board for its 2nd anniversary.

TABLERT, FRANK X., USMC served aboard BB-59 as master sergeant and left Aug. 14, 1944, transferred to Administration FMF, Pacific.

TALBOT, GEORGE ARTHUR, 202-23-78, enlisted Feb. 23, 1942, Boston, MA. He is a plankowner and served aboard BB-59 as AS at commissioning May 12, 1942, and on board for its 2nd and 3rd anniversaries.

TALLMAN, ALLEN DAVID, 565-43-79, born Aug. 18, 1925, Anaheim, CA. He enlisted Aug. 11, 1943, San Diego, CA, via US *Nechas* to Effate. He served aboard BB-59 as S1/c 5th Div. Dec. 12, 1943, also Y3/c CR Div. He re-enlisted July 21, 1948, Long Beach, CA; November 1949 US Naval School of Photography, graduated June 9, 1950.

Assigned to Naval Station Long Beach, CA, to ADM Hendren; December 1951 to USS *Kearsarge* (CVA-33) April 16, 1952, PhotgM1/c; June 1952 Naval Photo Intelligence School; to Korean War in charge of photo lab on carrier; assigned as personal photographer to ADM J.J. "Jocko" Clark; while assigned to staff, served aboard USS *New Jersey*, USS *Missouri*, USS *Wisconsin* and USS *Rochester*; stayed with 7th Fleet Commd. ADM A.M. Pride; November 1954 to Naval

Photographic Center, Washington, DC; discharged April 1955.

After the war he worked as an accountant and computer programmer and is now retired. He enjoys researching family history in his spare time.

He married May Davies June 26, 1961, and has two step-children and 10 grandchildren. He resides at 551 No. 1100 East, Bountiful, UT 84010.

TAMEZ, ROY CRESPIN, 375-78-58, enlisted Dec. 5, 1941, San Diego, CA. He is a plankowner and served aboard BB-59 as SF3/c R Div. at commissioning May 12, 1942, and left BB-59 May 19, 1944, as CSF to R/S Bremerton, WA.

TARANGO, LOUIS DOUGLAS, 376-16-15, enlisted Nov. 14, 1940, San Francisco, CA. He was a plankowner and served aboard BB-59 as S1/c at commissioning May 12, 1942, and on board for its 2nd anniversary. Memory List 1978.

TARLTON, DENNIS CLARENCE, 262-60-20, enlisted June 26, 1940, Raleigh, NC. He is a plankowner and served aboard BB-59 as SC3/c at commissioning May 12, 1942.

TATE, JAMES EDWARD, 262-58-36, enlisted June 13, 1940, Raleigh, NC. He is a plankowner and served aboard BB-59 as F2/c at commissioning May 12, 1942, and on board for its 2nd anniversary.

TAUSS, ALFRED EUGENE, 223-99-12, born Jan. 5, 1923, Chicago, IL. Graduated from high school and attended electric and trade schools. He enlisted Dec. 12, 1940, New York, NY. He served aboard BB-59 April 16, 1942, Quincy, MA, and is a plankowner commissioning May 12, 1942, as S1/c E Div. Served as EM3/c E Div. Dec. 2, 1942, and left BB-59 Feb. 5, 1943, Boston, MA, to Norfolk, VA.

Commissioned April 15, 1943, to USS *Yorktown*; June 30, 1943, to Carrier Aircraft Service Unit #22 Quonset Point, RI; Sept. 1, 1943, C.R. to A. EM2/c; May 1, 1944, T & R to Carrier Service Unit #26; July 1, 1944, C & R to A.E. M1/c; Oct. 10, 1944, T & R to USNH Newport, RI; Nov. 30, 1944, honorably discharged Vets Hospital, Beacon, NY.

After the war he worked as a lab. elec. technician Bendix Corp., Teterboro, NJ (27 years) and retired in 1986. Prior to retirement worked as shipyard electrician New York Naval Shipyard for eight years; aircraft electrician B.O.A.C. for two years; and trade electrician for contractors for three years. He is involved in various church activities in his spare time.

He married Josephine July 30, 1943, Appaunaugh, RI, and has three children and five grandchildren. He resides at 124 Coles Ave., Hackensack, NJ 07601.

TAYLOR, J.R., F3/c P Div., left BB-59 March 8, 1943, to ComSerForSoPac.

TAYLOR, JOSEPH M., 606-15-72, born June 12, 1919, Fall River, MA. Has a degree in pharmacy and enlisted Jan. 23, 1942, Boston, MA. Trained at Naval Hospital, Newport, RI; USN Mobile Hospitals #6, #4, #5 and #2 (part of 1st Marine Div.); Phm1/c USS *Hermitage;* Naval Torpedo Station, Newport, RI; and USS *Zenobia* (Iceland). He served aboard BB-59 as ship rider Norfolk to Fall River 1965.

After the war he owned Taylor's Pharmacy 1950-68 (sold out after heart attack); 1969-82 managed building for the handicapped under Fall River Housing Authority. In his spare time he was active with Wheelchair Sports 1970-82 and an AARP volunteer for IRS Aid.

He married Pauline May 16, 1981, Westport, RI, and has five children and five grandchildren. He resides at 185 Linden St., Fall River, MA 02720.

TAYLOR, LOUIS, (n) 300-80-19, enlisted March 31, 1942, Chicago, IL. He is a plankowner and served aboard BB-59 as Matt3/c at commissioning May 12, 1942.

TAYLOR, RALPH ARTHUR, 610-41-22, enlisted Jan. 19, 1942, Chicago, IL. He is a plankowner and served aboard BB-59 as AS at commissioning May 12, 1942, and on board for its 2nd and 3rd anniversaries. He resided at 63 East 69th St. Chicago (1966).

TAYLOR, RICHARD BAXTER, 261-67-84, enlisted Sept. 26, 1939, Norfolk, VA. He is a plankowner and served aboard BB-59 as Mus1/c at commissioning May 12, 1942.

TAYLOR, WALTER CARROLL, ENS, served aboard BB-59 in N Div. JW and JD May 2, 1943; October 1943 Roster CS Div. as LT(jg) and left BB-59 Oct. 12, 1945, as signal officer. He resides at 2110 Observatory Rd., Martinsville, IN 46151.

TEGELER, ELMER F., USMC, 7th Div., resides at 913 8th Ave., Dyersville, IA.

TELTHORST, ERWIN H., P Div., resides at 6622 Kingsway Dr., Afton, MO.

TENACE, JAMES, S Div., resides at 534 New Castle St., Butler, PA.

TERESCO, JOSEPH, (n) 224-70-91, enlisted Feb. 24, 1942, New York, NY. He is a plankowner and served aboard BB-59 as AS at commissioning May 12, 1942, and on board for BB-59 2nd and 3rd anniversaries. On March 10, 1943, was RDM3/c CR Div. to FR Div.

TERMINE, PAUL JOSEPH, JR., 223-79-34, enlisted Aug. 9, 1940, New York, NY. He is a plankowner and served aboard BB-59 as S1/c at commissioning May 12, 1942.

TERMYNA, ANDREW WALTER, JR., 646-58-16, enlisted Jan. 28, 1942, New York, NY. He was a plankowner and served aboard BB-59 as AS L Div. at commissioning May 12, 1942. Served Lookout and Paint Locker R Div. and left BB-59 August 1945. After the war he worked as a pressman for Raybestos Manhattan, Inc., Passaic, NJ. Memory List 1986. He resided at 37 Lisbon St., Clifton, NJ.

TERRELL, "J" PETE, JR., 321-73-06, enlisted Dec. 19, 1941, Des Moines, IA. He is a plankowner and served aboard BB-59 as S2/c at commissioning May 12, 1942.

TERRANO, WALTER RICHARD, 224-71-19, enlisted Feb. 25, 1941, New York, NY. He is a plankowner and served aboard BB-59 as AS at commissioning May 12, 1942.

TERRY, JAMES FRANKLIN, 274-38-90, enlisted Sept. 13, 1939, New Orleans, LA. He is a plankowner and served aboard BB-59 as F2/c at commissioning May 12, 1942.

TETEN, CARL, resided at Talmage, NE (1966).

TEW, JAMES L., USMC 358857, born March 8, 1918, Mobile, AL. He enlisted USMC Feb. 8, 1942, Mobile, AL, and trained at Parris Island, SC. Was assigned May 8, 1942, Norfolk Sea School. He served aboard BB-59 as PVT 7th Div. at commissioning May 12, 1942; 1943 corporal; 1944 SGT 7th. He left BB-59 in 1944 after Battle of Philippines. Was assigned Naval Hospital, Corvallis, OR, 1945; Marine Corps Base, San Francisco, CA; and discharged Sept. 28, 1945. He married Lucille Aug. 3, 1945, Corvallis Chapel, Corvallis, OR. They were married 50 years in 1995). He resides at 6316 Southridge Rd. N., Mobile, AL 36693-3423.

THACKER, ROBERT D., 657-12-15, born Oct. 18, 1925, Greensboro, NC. Attended Lexington schools and enlisted Oct. 20, 1942, Raleigh, NC. Trained at Great Lakes, IL, and Gunnery School, Prices Neck, RI, and was assigned Fargo Barracks, Boston, MA.

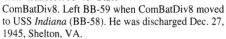

He served aboard BB-59 Jan. 1, 1943, as S2/c 4th Div. transferred to L Div. and then to CS Div. SM3/c. Was then transferred to Staff ComBatDiv8. Left BB-59 when ComBatDiv8 moved to USS *Indiana* (BB-58). He was discharged Dec. 27, 1945, Shelton, VA.

After the war he attended barber school, Durham, NC (under GI Bill of Rights). Barbered for 20 years and sang with singing group quartet for four years; worked in radio for six years and retired. He was VFW Post commander in his spare time.

He married Frances 1947 in South Carolina, and has one daughter and one grandson. He resides at 964 Floyd Church Rd., Lexington, NC 27292.

THATCHER, RICHARD M., 1st Div., resides at 9773 N. Keno Rd., Saint Helen, MI.

THEOBALD, RUDOLF HERBERT, 305-15-81, enlisted Jan. 24, 1942, San Diego, CA. He is a plankowner and served aboard BB-59 as CM1/c at commissioning May 12, 1942.

THODE, HENRY FREDRICK, JR., 646-59-30, enlisted Jan. 29, 1942, New York, NY. He is a plankowner and served aboard BB-59 as AS at commissioning May 12, 1942.

THOMALLO, ROBERT FRANCIS, 328-45-22, enlisted Dec. 12, 1941, Minneapolis, MN. He is a plankowner and served aboard BB-59 as MM2/c A Div. at commissioning May 12, 1942, and in A Div. JO & JW Mach. He left BB-59 May 19, 1944.

THOMAS, ALVIN, ENS 2nd Div. served aboard BB-59 as JO Turret #2 HR Oct. 26, 1943. He left BB-59 Aug. 28, 1944.

THOMAS, EDGAR A., E Div., resides at 2215 47th St., Los Alamos, NM.

THOMAS, FRANK LINCOLN, JR., served aboard BB-59 as ENS 3rd Div. July 1942. Graduated United States Naval Academy Class of 1943 and was JW and JD BS h.r. Turret #3. He was LT(jg) Oct. 1, 1943, in 3rd Div. W(P) and JD.

THOMAS, LLOYD HOWDEN, COMDR, Naval Academy Class of 1924, served aboard BB-59 as supply officer from February 1943 to October 1943. Memory List 1996.

THOMAS, WILLIAM SPENCER, 96434, born Dec. 18, 1920, Los Angeles, CA. Received a BS from University of California, Berkeley, CA, 1947. Joined the Navy 1940 in V-7 Program serving aboard USS *New York* as midshipman, August 1940. Trained at various gunnery and fire control schools and served on USS *Tennessee*.

He served aboard BB-59 several months before commissioning Quincy and made lieutenant 5th Div. as a plankowner. He left BB-59 November 1943, Fiji Islands. Was gunnery officer, Jeep carriers. After the war he worked various management jobs and then Pan Am Airways. He is involved in various environmental organizations; (1994) was a member of board of Mohonk Preserve (a nature preserve, New Paltz, NY).

He married his wife September 1945 Santa Barbara, CA, (she died October 1985), and has one son, one daughter and five grandchildren. He resides at 3010 Hermosa Rd., Santa Barbara, CA 93105.

THOMPSON, ERWIN JESSE, 382-52-77, enlisted Aug. 11, 1941, Los Angeles, CA. He is a plankowner and served aboard BB-59 as S1/c at commissioning May 12, 1942.

THOMPSON, EDW M., Executive Officer, Naval Academy 1921, served aboard BB-59 as COMDR March 1943. He was a plankowner. In 1964 was RADM living in Mt. Vernon, VA. He purchased five "Big Mamie" bumper stickers. Memory List 1985.

THOMPSON, ERNEST WEBSTER, 272-09-45, enlisted Feb. 17, 1942, Birmingham, AL. He is a plankowner and served aboard BB-59 as EM2/c at commissioning May 12, 1942.

THOMPSON, J., ENS, served aboard BB-59 in 6th Div. J.D. July 1942.

THOMPSON, LELAND RAY, 336-67-40, enlisted June 9, 1941, Los Angeles, CA. He is a plankowner and served aboard BB-59 as CTC at commissioning May 12, 1942.

THOMPSON, LEWIS F., JR., resided at RFD #1, Box 390, Mt. Vernon Hills, Alexandria, VA (1966).

THOMPSON, ROBERT WILLIAM, served aboard BB-59 as LT 6th Div. May 3, 1945, and left I Div. J.O. on Jan. 15, 1946.

THORNTON, LAWRENCE JOSEPH, 201-68-70, enlisted Nov. 6, 1939, Boston, MA. He is a plankowner and served aboard BB-59 as S1/c 6th and X Div. COX M.A.A. at commissioning May 12, 1942. He left BB-59 Dec. 18, 1943. After the war he worked for the Boston Fire Dept. He is a member of Pearl Harbor Attack Vets, the American Legion and VFW. He resides at 50 Pleasant St., Brookline, MA.

THORSON, JOHN DUDLEY, ENS B Div., served aboard BB-59 in B Div. J.O. March 6, 1945. He resides at 433 E. Pierce St., Council Bluffs, IA.

TIEDWELL, GEORGE DEWEY, 104-23-50, enlisted Jan. 17, 1942, Little Rock, AR. He is a plankowner and served aboard BB-59 as GM3/c at commissioning May 12, 1942. Memory List; 1981.

TIERNAN, FRANK, resided at 95 1177th St., Ozone Park, LI, NY (1955).

TIERNEY, EDWARD WARREN, 646-57-05, enlisted Jan. 27, 1942, New York, NY. He is a plankowner and served aboard BB-59 as AS at commissioning May 12, 1942, and on board for BB-59 2nd and 3rd anniversaries.

TIERNEY, RAYMOND JOSEPH, 606-75-00, enlisted April 19, 1942, Boston. He is a plankowner and served aboard BB-59 as CM2/c at commissioning May 12, 1942.

TIMLIN, JOSEPH PATRICK, 610-43-45, enlisted Jan. 21, 1942, Chicago, IL. He is a plankowner and served aboard BB-59 as AS at commissioning May 12, 1942, and on board for BB-59 2nd and 3rd anniversaries.

TIMMONS, CARROLL EDWARD, resided at Rt. 1, Box 411-B, Springhill, LA 71075 (1995).

TISKO, LEO JOHN, 214-24-57, enlisted Jan. 20, 1941, San Francisco, CA. He is a plankowner and served aboard BB-59 as CEM E Div. at commissioning May 12, 1942.

TODARO, DOMINIC, resided at 5th St., Newell, PA 15466 (1995).

TOLLE, GENE L., 957-69-74, born Dec. 4, 1925, Dawson, IA. Graduated from Dawson High School, Dawson, IA, and enlisted Aug. 18, 1944, Kansas, MO. Trained in Idaho and assigned to DD-527. He served aboard BB-59 in A Div. later aboard USS *Alabama*.

After the war he was a salesman and is a member of the Kiwanis Club. He married Eugenia July 5, 1957, and resided at 224 4th Ave. E., Cresco, IA 52136. Memory List 1997.

TOLLESTRUP, ALVIN V., LT(jg) resides at 29 W 254 Renouf, Warrenville, IL 60555.

TOMALLO, R.E., MACH, served aboard BB-59 May 12, 1944.

TONE, RALPH WILLIAM, 646-58-18, enlisted Jan. 28, 1942, New York, NY. He was a plankowner and served aboard BB-59 as AS at commissioning May 12, 1942. Memory List 1983.

TOPNICK, CHARLES, (n) 224-68-04, enlisted Jan. 31, 1942, New York, NY. He is a plankowner and served aboard BB-59 as AS at commissioning May 12, 1942. He resides at 50 Island Rd., Mahwah, NJ 07430.

TOPORCER, JOHN MICHAEL, 650-24-19, enlisted Feb. 3, 1942, Philadelphia, PA. He is a plankowner and served aboard BB-59 as AS at commissioning May 12, 1942.

TOUSSAINT, WILFRED RAYMOND, 202-24-05, enlisted Feb. 23, 1942, Boston, MA. He was a plankowner and served aboard BB-59 as AS at commissioning May 12, 1942. Memory List 1993.

TOWNE, DONALD LEE, ENS 5th Div., served aboard BB-59 May 6, 1943, and left Oct. 15, 1945, as LT(jg).

TOWNSEND, JAMES EDWARD, ENS 6th Div., served aboard BB-59 May 25, 1943, and left 1945 LT(jg).

TOWNSEND, J.B., resided in Madison, FL.

TOWNSEND, ROBERT ARNOLD, ENS FC Div., served aboard BB-59 in 6th Div. J.O. Aug. 10, 1943. He left BB-59 as LT(jg) Nov. 2, 1944. Memory List 1978.

TRACY, ALLEN CARL, 238-26-30, enlisted Jan. 8, 1942, Albany, NY. He was a plankowner and served aboard BB-59 as EM2/c at commissioning May 12, 1942. Memory List 1992.

TRAINOR, MARTIN FRANCIS, 202-25-66, enlisted Jan. 31, 1942, Boston, MA. He is a plankowner and served aboard BB-59 as AS at commissioning May 12, 1942.

TRBOJAVIC, NICHOLAS, USMC, May 8, 1942, Norfolk Sea School. He is a plankowner and served aboard BB-59 as PVT 7th Div. at commissioning May 12, 1942 as SGT. He left BB-59 in May 1944.

After the war he was a tavern proprietor. He is married with three kids and a member of the Marine League and American Legion. He resided at 103 Roland Place, Bel Air, MD 21014 (1995).

TRENCHERY, HAROLD ATKINS, 372-05-10, enlisted March 11, 1938, Denver, CO. He is a plankowner and served aboard BB-59 as QM3/c N Div. at commissioning May 12, 1942. He resides at 1125 So. Adams Ave., Fullerton, CA 92632.

TRIEST, CYRUS KELCHNER, 104-67-77, U.S.F.R., is a plankowner and served aboard BB-59 as CWT at commissioning May 12, 1942.

TRUAIR, WILLIAM DATIS, 321-31-51, enlisted May 3, 1939, Des Moines, IA. He is a plankowner and served aboard BB-59 as S1/c at commissioning May 12, 1942.

TUCKER, CLARE ADDISON, ENS R Div., served aboard BB-59 May 31, 1944, and as LT(jg) 1st Div. J.O. in July 1945.

TUCKER, DONALD ALEXANDER, 660-09-59, enlisted Dec. 27, 1941, Salt Lake City, UT. He served aboard BB-59 January 1942 in Quincy, MA, and as MM2/c P Div. at commissioning May 12, 1942. He was throttleman Main Control Engine Room and left BB-59 June 1943 as MM1/c. After the war he worked for the Idaho Power Company, Southern Div. Services as dispatcher. He is married with four children and resided in Twin Falls, ID.

TUCKER, EUGENE, resided in Randelman, NC (1966).

TUCKER, LEO CLINTON, 201-69-65, enlisted Dec. 4, 1939, Boston, MA. He is a plankowner and served aboard BB-59 as COX at commissioning May 12, 1942.

TURNER, FRANKLIN KENNETH, 646-59-33, enlisted Jan. 29, 1942, New York, NY. He is a plankowner and served aboard BB-59 as AS 6th Div. at commissioning May 12, 1942, and on board for BB-59 2nd and 3rd anniversaries. He resides at Barger St., Putnam Valley, NY 10579.

TUROCK, FRANCIS J., resided at 319 No. 2nd St. #22, Olean, NY (1995).

TUTTLE, ROBERT FRANK, born 1920 Springfield, OH. Attended Wittenberg University (business) and joined the Navy 1942, New York, NY. Trained at Columbia University and American University (bomb disposal) and assigned to USS *Harris* (attack transport). He served aboard BB-59 as LT(jg) R Div. in July 1944 and left Bremerton in 1945.

After the war he was president of The Tuttle Brothers Company. He was a member of the Jaycees and board member of OAWA (Ohio Automotive Wholesale Assoc.).

He married Ruth and has three sons and seven grandchildren. He died April 6, 1990; Memory List 1991. (Mrs.) resides at 2199 Pebble Beach Dr., Spring Hill, FL 34606.

TWIRAGA, ANTHONY, 606-35-52, enlisted Feb. 11, 1942, Boston, MA. He is a plankowner and served aboard BB-59 as AS at commissioning May 12, 1942, and on board for BB-59 2nd and 3rd anniversaries.

TYCZKOWSKI, JOHN EDWARD, 104-87-61, enlisted Nov. 6, 1941, Mare Island, CA. He is a plankowner and served aboard BB-59 as CFC at commissioning May 12, 1942.

TYLER, EDWARD W., JR., A Div., resides at 15 Ledgewood Rd., Shelton, CT 06484.

TYLER, FREDERICK CHARLES, 223-89-87, enlisted Oct. 15, 1940, New York, NY. He is a plankowner and served aboard BB-59 as S1/c at commissioning May 12, 1942, and on board for BB-59 2nd anniversary.

TYLER, SAM J., 765-17-70, born Nov. 14, 1925, Spokane, WA. Attended U. Gonzaga, Spokane, WA and enlisted Sept. 27, 1943, Spokane, WA. Trained at Farragut, ID, and assigned USNABPD, San Bruno, CA, N-29 Unit 98, Navy 167; USNB 717. He served aboard BB-59 as Y2/c X Div. Personnel Office Jan. 24, 1946, and left BB-59 Norfolk, VA, May 1946.

After the war he was a farmer, self-employed as Benewah County commissioner; Idaho Wheat Commissioner and Idaho Governor Ag Task Force. He is a part of Democratic Party; several farm groups; and chairman of Western Wheat Assoc. 1978-79.

He married Donna, Spokane, WA, and has two daughters and seven grandchildren. He resides at Route 1 Box 64, Plummer, ID 83851.

UMFLEET, EDWARD, (n) 668-31-56, enlisted Jan. 22, 1942, St. Louis, MO. He is a plankowner and served aboard BB-59 as AS at commissioning May 12, 1942.

UMINSKI, FRANK S., served aboard BB-59 as S1/c 4th Div. November 1942 and assigned lookout air defense. He left BB-59 November 1945. After the war he worked for the US Postal Service as a carrier for 10 years. He is active in the Post 124, Men's Club and St. Mary's Church. He married Eileen and has four daughters. He resides at 35 Southgate Ave., Westfield, MA 01085.

UNDERWOOD, GEORGE, resides at 102 New York St. #B, Lowell, MA 01854.

UPCHURCH, DONALD WILLIAM, 311-70-01, enlisted April 4, 1941, Detroit, MI. He is a plankowner and served aboard BB-59 as COX at commissioning May 12, 1942. He was assigned N Div. captain.

URQUHART, JOHN R., enlisted Oct. 19, 1940, and served aboard USS *Indiana* and USS *Chester*. He served aboard BB-59 as CY0 and engaged in communication intelligence (cryptology), warrant officer and finally lieutenant commander. He retired Dec. 1, 1940. He married Willie J. in 1946 and has two sons and four grandchildren.

UTLEY, WALLACE ALFRED, born July 26, 1916, Oak Park, IL. Enlisted June 1936 in the Naval Academy and graduated in 1940 with a BS and MS in engineering. From July 1940 to November 1941 served aboard USS *West Virginia* (BB-48) and from November 1941 to April 1942 Radar School and NRL.

He is a plankowner and served aboard BB-59 as LT CR Div. at commissioning May 12, 1942, and on board for BB-59 2nd anniversary. He was assigned radar officer, battle station radar plot; October 1943 FR Div. W.(P) and D-F.D.O.; and May 1944 R Div. He left BB-59 Sept. 10, 1944, Efate, New Hebrides. Was also assigned USNA Post Grad. School, 1944-47; ComServPac Staff, 1947-50; BUSHIPS, 1950-53; assist repair supt. and industrial manager, Philadelphia Naval Yard, 1953-56; industrial manager 15th Naval District, 1956-58; director, Navy Applied Science Lab, 1959-60; and retired as commander 1960. After Naval service was assistant to chief engineer Marine Div. Sperry Gyro Company, 1961-62; engineering professor Temple University, 1962-64; electronics and physics professor Bucks County, PA, College 1965-66; physics professor

Camden County College, NJ, 1967-85; and retired in 1985.

He enjoys sailing, tennis, bridge and travel. He married Helyn April 15, 1942, Maple Shade, NJ, and has two sons, two daughters, six grandchildren and one great-grandchild. He resides at 1205 Fleet Landing Blvd., Atlantic Beach, FL 32233.

UZAS, FRANK, 312-44-98, born May 4, 1907, Kaunas, Lithuania. He enlisted Nov. 14, 1942, Detroit, MI, and attended Great Lakes Naval Training Station, IL. He served aboard BB-59 as CM3/c R Div. December 1942 and assigned CM2/c. He was discharged Sept. 28, 1945, USN Separation Center, Minneapolis, MN.

After the war he worked as a spindler carver for Mueller Furniture Company, Grand Rapids, MI, 1946-57; and for John Widdecomb Furniture Company 1957-72. He retired 1972. He was a life member of American Legion Post #258, active in Golden Gloves American Legion, sports skating, running, softball, health spa and traveling.

He married Sophie (deceased) in 1930 South Bend, IN, and had one daughter and one grandchild. Jachie Rothfuss (daughter) resides at 636 Hinchman Road, Berrien Springs, MI 49103. He died March 30, 1993; Memory List 1993.

VAITSES, PAUL STEPHEN, JR., ENS, born Aug. 31, 1919, Melrose, MA.

He graduated Melrose High School and attended Tabor Academy and Dartmouth College. He enlisted January 1942, Boston, MA, V-7 USNR Program. Attended V-7 Columbia University, NY, and Mid-shipman's School from August 1942 to November 1942. He served aboard BB-59 as ENS R Div. December 1942. Was assigned Hull Department as LT(jg) A Div. and Engineering Department. He left BB-59 June 1944 Seattle, WA.

Was also assigned July 1944 to October 1944 Amphibious Training, Norfolk, VA; executive officer, commanding officer USS LSMR-193; Okinawa Campaign; and was awarded Bronze Star Medal May 11, 1945. He was vice-president of USS *Massachusetts* Assoc. 1991-92; active fund raiser and committee member. He was chairman of board 1965-70 of Memorial Committee and executive director of BB-59, at Battleship Cove, Fall River, MA 1970-90. After his Naval service worked in an investment business, Hutchins, Miscter & Parkinson Boston, MA, 1946-70; was mayor of Melrose, MA, 1964-67; town assessor of Swansea, MA, 1982-present; and was chairman/full-time assessor from 1991-93.

He is a member of American Legion, VFW, Sons of American Revolution, Family Service Assoc., trustee Massachusetts Maritime Academy, Mayflower Descendants Society, 1994-current trustee Fall River 5c Savings Bank, MA.

He has one son and one grandchild and resides at 15 Bay Point Rd., Swansea, MA 02777.

VANDENBERG, JOHN, JR., (n) 622-40-21, enlisted Jan. 20, 1942, Detroit, MA. He is a plankowner and served aboard BB-59 as AS at commissioning May 12, 1942, and on board for BB-59 2nd anniversary.

VAN DYKE, JOSEPH CONRAD, 316-87-91, enlisted Jan. 9, 1942, Omaha, NE. He is plankowner and served aboard BB-59 as S2/c 4th Div. at commissioning May 12, 1942, and was assigned deck hand. He left BB-59 November 1942. After the war he was self-employed and has one son. He is active in the D.A.V. and resides at PO Box 851, Columbus, NE 68601.

VAN DYKE, RICHARD LEE, ENS, served aboard BB-59 as ENS 1st Div. April 5, 1943, and assigned 1st Div. J.O. and LT(jg) Turret H.R. He left BB-59 May 5, 1944.

VAN HORN, ROBERT LAVERNE, 328-81-96, enlisted Dec. 20, 1940, Minneapolis, MN. He is a plankowner and served aboard BB-59 as S1/c at commissioning May 12, 1942.

VAN HUISON, G.H., resides at 11985 Marsh Road, Shelbyville, MT 49344.

VAN LIEW, VERNON BRUCE, 372-44-18, born Jan. 24, 1925, Des Moines, IA. He enlisted Jan. 30, 1942, Denver CO. He is a plankowner and served aboard BB-59 as AS CS Div. at commissioning May 12, 1942. He left BB-59 1944 to new construction. Was also assigned USS *Shields* (DD-596) till the end of WWII. He was on various ships and stations until retirement in 1965. His highest rate was CQM-CSM.

After the war he was an aircraft painter at North Island Naval Air Station, CA, for five years; raised cattle Maryville, CA, 1971-1992; and retired in 1992. He enjoys hunting, fishing, travel and just smelling the roses along the way.

He married LaVonda 1949, San Francisco, CA, and has two sons and six grandchildren. He resides at 5189 Loop Rd., Maryville, CA 95901.

VAN ORNUM, GLEN Z., 413-27-29, enlisted Dec. 21, 1941, San Francisco, CA. He is a plankowner and served aboard BB-59 as WT2/c FC Div. at commissioning May 12, 1942, and on board for BB-59 2nd anniversary. He resides at PO Box 2052, Oroville, CA 95965.

VARIS, FRANK, JR., (n) 608-34-17, born July 25, 1920. He enlisted Jan. 27, 1942, St. Louis, MO, and trained at Great Lakes Naval Training Station, IL. He is a plankowner and served aboard BB-59 as AS S Div. at commissioning May 12, 1942. Was assigned Baker 1/c and left BB-59 Sept. 20, 1945. After the war he worked as a coal miner and is retired. He enjoys fishing and auto repairs. He married Mary (deceased) 1938, Benton, KY, and has one son and two grandchildren. He resides at 411 N. Cherry St., West Frankfort, IL 62896-1517.

VARNUM, GEORGE E., served aboard BB-59 in E Div. He resides at 3 Freeman St., Arlington, MI 02174.

VAUGHAN, GREY GOLSON, JR., 272-04-81, enlisted Feb. 19, 1938, Birmingham, AL. He is a plankowner and served aboard BB-59 as Mus1/c at commissioning May 12, 1942.

VEACH, SHERMAN LEE, 382-34-65, enlisted Dec. 31, 1940, Los Angeles, CA. He served aboard BB-59 as F2/c at commissioning May 12, 1942.

VELDMAN, ROBERT MARTIN, 622-42-95, born Dec. 25, 1923, Detroit, MI. Graduated from Our Lady of Lake Huron High School, Harbor Beach, MI, and enlisted Jan. 26, 1942, Detroit, MI. He trained at Newport Naval Training Station, RI. He was a plankowner and served aboard BB-59 as AS at commissioning May 12, 1942. He left BB-59 Oct. 8, 1945, Bremerton, WA.

After the war he worked for the Port Orchard Police Dept., WA; Huron Milling Company, Harbor Beach, MI; sailing Cleveland Cliff's Iron Company,

Cleveland, OH; owned Sunoco Gas Station, Harbor Beach, MI; sailing Kensman Transit Company; joined Lake Pilots Assoc., Port Huron, MI, 1964; attended Marine School, Buffalo, NY, for captain's license, also received US pilot's license.

He is a member of American Legion Post #197 and enjoys woodworking and golf. He married Myrtle Nov. 29, 1942, Harbor Beach, MI, and had two sons, four daughters (two deceased) and seven grandchildren. (Mrs.) Myrtle M. Veldman resides at 266 Tucker St., Harbor Beach, MI 48441-1159. He died Dec. 6, 1978; Memory List 1979.

VELMER, GEORGE, (n) 652-17-25, enlisted Jan. 31, 1942, Pittsburgh, PA. He is a plankowner and served aboard BB-59 as AS at commissioning May 12, 1942, and on board for BB-59 2nd and 3rd anniversaries.

VENDOLOSKIE, WALTER STANLEY, 650-21-61, enlisted Jan. 31, 1942, Philadelphia, PA. He is a plankowner and served aboard BB-59 as AS at commissioning May 12, 1942.

VERDERESE, ANGELO, served aboard BB-59 in A Div. He resides at 17 Wilson Ave., Amsterdam, NY 12010.

VESEY, EDWARD JOSEPH, 224-70-92, enlisted Feb. 24, 1942, New York, NY. He is a plankowner and served aboard BB-59 as AS at commissioning May 12, 1942, and on board for BB-59 2nd and 3rd anniversaries. He resides at 39 Kenneth Place, Clark, NJ 07066.

VESTAL, S.W., resides at Matoaka, WV 24736.

VICARIO, AMODEO, (n) 606-32-92, enlisted Feb. 10, 1942, Boston, MA. He is a plankowner and served aboard BB-59 as AS at commissioning May 12, 1942, and on board for BB-59 2nd anniversary. He resides at 141 Grove St., Providence, RI 02940.

VICTOR, LOUIS, served aboard BB-59 in 1st Div. He resides at 1970 Killarney Drive, Winter Park, FL 32789.

VIELLIEUX, THOMAS EDWARD, 638-11-15, enlisted Jan. 2, 1942, Minneapolis, MN. He is a plankowner and served aboard BB-59 as S1/c at commissioning May 12, 1942.

VIGEANT, ARMAND ALPHONSE, 202-26-42, born Sept. 20, 1922, Fall River, MA. He enlisted Feb. 27, 1942, Boston, MA, and trained at Newport Naval Training Station, RI. He is a plankowner and served aboard BB-59 as AS 6th Div. at commissioning May 12, 1942.

He was assigned May 1942 to December 1942 as AS, S2/c, S1/c 6th Div.; December 1942 to September 1946 SK3/c, SK2/c, SK1/c S Div. He left BB-59 Sept. 12, 1946, Portsmouth, VA. He was also assigned to USS *Rutland*, USS *Xanthus* (AR-19), USS *Oregon City* and discharged Dec. 23, 1947, Korean War USMCB. He was a corporate member of USS *Massachusetts* Memorial Committee, 1990-93 and "Field Day" Crew member 1980-90, volunteer 1990-present. He received BB-59 Award 1995.

After the war he worked as a meat cutter at A & P Tea Company. He enjoys sailing, gardening and travel. He has one son, two daughters and two grandchildren. He resides at 140 Carolina Ave., Somerset, MA 02725.

VISCONTI, NICKOLAS LOUIS, 606-34-83, enlisted Feb. 14, 1942, Boston, MA. He is a plankowner and served aboard BB-59 as AS at commissioning May 12, 1942, and on board for BB-59 2nd and 3rd anniversaries.

VISE, CHARLES MCKINLEY, 381-32-11, enlisted Feb. 9, 1940, San Diego, CA. He is a plankowner and served aboard BB-59 as EM2/c E Div. at commissioning May 12, 1942.

VITELLO, JAMES JOSEPH, 202-25-10, enlisted Jan. 28, 1942, Boston, MA. He was a plankowner and served aboard BB-59 as AS M Div. at commissioning May 12, 1942, and on board for BB-59 2nd and 3rd anniversaries. He resided at 102 Cass St., West Roxbury, MA 02132. Memory List 1993.

VITTI, SAMUEL JOHN, 646-60-63, enlisted Jan. 30, 1942, New York, NY. He is a plankowner and served aboard BB-59 as AS commissioning May 12, 1942.

VLK, T.J., served aboard BB-59 as F3/c P Div. and left BB-59 March 8, 1943, ComSerForSoPac.

VLK, W.L., served aboard BB-59 as F3/c P Div. and left BB-59 March 8, 1943, ComSerForSoPac.

VOGEL, SAMUEL FREDERICK, 368-73-20, enlisted Jan. 20, 1942, Salt Lake City, UT. He is a plankowner and served aboard BB-59 as AS at commissioning May 12, 1942, and on board for BB-59 2nd and 3rd anniversaries. He resides at Havre, MT 59501.

VOLCK, HARRY EDWARD, JR., 646-64-25, enlisted Feb. 3, 1942, New York, NY. He is a plankowner and served aboard BB-59 as AS commissioning May 12, 1942.

VOLK, GEORGE MATHEW, 224-70-66, enlisted Feb. 23, 1942, New York, NY. He is a plankowner and served aboard BB-59 as AS at commissioning May 12, 1942, and on board for BB-59 2nd and 3rd anniversaries.

VOLLMER, PAUL WARREN, 646-65-36, born April 29, 1921, Staten Island, NY. He enlisted Feb. 4, 1942, New York, NY, and trained at Newport Naval Training Station, RI. He is a plankowner and served aboard BB-59 as S2/c 3rd Div. at commissioning May 12, 1942.

He was assigned November 1942 Mess Cook Chief's Quarters; December 1942 S1/c Boiler Room #2 B Div., WT3/c, WT2/c and B Div. Capt. He left BB-59 November 1945 Bremerton, WA, and discharged November 1945, Lido Beach, NY, as WT2/c.

After the war he worked for the New York City Transit; 1957-80 loading and unloading cargo Seaboard World Air Line, Idlewild Airport, NY; 1980-83 Flying Tiger Air Line; May 1983 retired from Cargo Air Lines after 26 years of service. He enjoys gardening and horse shoe pitching.

He married Edith, Staten Island, NY, and has two sons, two daughters and seven grandchildren. He resides at 906 Alcala St., Augustine, FL 32086-7167.

VOLLENWEIDEN, LEO ANDREW, 274-54-96, enlisted Nov. 15, 1940, New Orleans, LA. He is a plankowner and served aboard BB-59 as S1/c at commissioning May 12, 1942.

VON DER HULLS, KURT ENGLEBART, 223-52-44, enlisted June 1, 1939, New York, NY. He is a plankowner and served aboard BB-59 as S1/c at commissioning May 12, 1942.

VON DREELE, WILLIAM H., CAPT, Memory List 1989. (Mrs.) resides at 4000 Mass. Ave. #518, Washington, DC 20016.

VON RUDEN, FRANCIS DONALD, 382-26-64, born Jan. 30, 1921, Faribault, MN. He enlisted Sept. 26, 1940, Los Angeles, CA, and trained at San Diego Naval Training Station, CA, and USS *Salt Lake City*. He is a plankowner and served aboard BB-59 as EM3/c E Div. at commissioning May 12, 1942. He left BB-59 February 1943 Boston, MA.

Other Naval assignments: March 1943 to August 1944 USS *Yorktown* (CV-10) EM2/c; August 1944 to May 1945 USS *Merryweather* EM1/c; September 1945 to November 1945 USS LSM-472; November 1945 to June 1946 Philippines; June 1946 to September 1946 Sea Going Tug Philippines.

After the war he was a dealer and bartender October 1946-1963; part-time insurance agency 1954-63; full-time insurance agency 1963 to now. He enjoys dancing, flying, fishing, hunting, motor home, former civic clubs BPOE and Lions Club.

He married Julie Dec. 1, 1946, and has one son, one daughter and eight grandchildren. He resides at 441 Smithridge Park, Reno, NV 89502.

VUILLEMOT, ROBERT F., 666-22-84, born July 19, 1924, Pittsfield, MA. Graduated from high school and enlisted April 16, 1942, Pittsfield, MA, and trained at Great Lakes Naval Training Station, IL; Fleet Service School Norfolk, VA; and USS *Alabama*.

He served aboard BB-59 as EM3/c E Div. April 1943 and left August 1945. Was also assigned to USS *Randall* (APA-224). After the war he worked as a sprayer for P.N. Zoll Company for 25 years and a route service rep. for Met Path Inc. for 20 years.

He married Elizabeth Jan. 24, 1948, New York, NY. He has two sons, four daughters and 14 grandchildren. He resides at Regency at Sussex 92, Sussex, NJ 07461.

WADDELL, CHARLES ELSON, 272-33-60, enlisted June 19, 1940, Birmingham, AL. He is a plankowner and served aboard BB-59 commissioning May 12, 1942.

WADE, JAMES THOMAS, served aboard BB-59 as S1/c 5th Div. September 1943 and assigned leading seaman and COX CAPT Gig. He left BB-59 December 1945. Retired from the Navy as BM1/c Aug. 16, 1961. After the war he worked as a guard for South Carolina State Ports Authority. He has two sons. He resides at 2103 St. James Drive, Charleston, SC 29412.

WAGNER, ADRIAN DEWITT, 279-44-58, enlisted Dec. 9, 1939, San Diego, CA. He is a plankowner and served aboard BB-59 as FC1/c at commissioning May 12, 1942.

WALDEN, HARTFORD DRAKE, 382-05-73, enlisted May 17, 1938, Los Angeles, CA. He is a plankowner and served aboard BB-59 as PhM2/c at commissioning May 12, 1942.

WALDEN, JAMES W., 603-12-97, born April 28, 1921, Douglas, GA. He earned a MBS in accounting and enlisted Feb. 23, 1942, Washington, DC. He trained at Naval Training Station, Norfolk, VA, and Naval Radio Training School, Auburn, AL. He served aboard BB-59 as S1/c CR Div. September 1942 and assigned RM3/c and RM2/c. He left BB-59 Nov. 20, 1945, Bremerton, WA.

After the war he worked as a public auditor for T.J. Lipton, Inc., accounting and headquarters distribution for 30 years. In his spare time he does tax preparation, is church treasurer, enjoys travel, beach, golf, Ham radio and computer.

He married Virginia Oct. 23, 1948, Washington, DC, and has four sons, one daughter and eight grandchildren. Memory List 1995. (Mrs.) resides at 9079 Ocean Pines, Berlin, MD 21811-7362.

WALDROP, DURWOOD OSCAR, 274-47-52, enlisted July 9, 1940, New Orleans, LA. He is a plankowner and served aboard BB-59 as FC3/c at commissioning May 12, 1942.

WALKER, EDWARD, USMC 371983, born June 9, 1924, Lackawanna, NY. Attended Onondaga Community College, Syracuse University. He enlisted March 4, 1942, Buffalo, NY, and trained at Marine Corps Training Parris Island, SC; Sea School, Portsmouth, VA, and May 8, 1942, Norfolk Navy Yard.

He is a plankowner and served aboard BB-59 as PVT 7th Div. at commissioning May 12, 1942, and assigned anti-aircraft crewman, corporal and executive officer's orderly. He left BB-59 Jan. 20, 1943, Noumea, New Caledonia. Was also assigned 4th Defense Battalion; Dec. 4, 1944, 2nd Guard CO, Brown Field, Quantico, VA; Feb. 12, 1946, (name changed) Circuit Court, Prince William County, VA (name formerly Wicenciuk, Frank E.).

After the war he worked as a bricklayer, furnace repairs, bridge and iron worker Bethlehem Steel Company, Iron Workers Local #6, Buffalo, NY; Iron Workers Local #60, Syracuse, NY; draftsman, O'Brien & Gare Engineers, Syracuse, NY; instructor Ironworkers Local #60, Syracuse, NY; investigator New York State Department of Labor and State Insurance Fund.

He has one son, four daughters and eight grandchildren. He resides at 503 Rowland St., Syracuse, NY 13204.

WALKER, FRANCIS JOHN, 224-71-21, enlisted Feb. 25, 1942, New York, NY. He is a plankowner and served aboard BB-59 as AS at commissioning May 12, 1942.

WALKER, GEORGE VINCENT, 606-35-75, born Sept. 11, 1919, East Boston, MA. Graduated from East Boston High School and enlisted Feb. 14, 1942, Boston, MA. Attended Naval Training Station, Newport, RI. He is a plankowner and served aboard BB-59 as AS B Div. at commissioning May 12, 1942, and assigned F2/c. He left BB-59 April 1944 at sea. Was also assigned USS *Tate* (AKA-70) from August 1944 to December 1945.

After the war he was a plaster and helper for the fire department on land. He ended service as fire lieutenant on fire boat with 35 years service. He does volunteer work on church and rectory repairs.

He married Mildred April 28, 1951, Arlington, MA, and has two sons, three daughters and eight grandchildren. He resides at 178 Falcon St., East Boston, MA 02128-2509.

WALKER, HARRY JUNIOR, 337-80-28, enlisted Jan. 21, 1942, St. Louis, MO. He is a plankowner and served aboard BB-59 as AS at commissioning May 12, 1942, and on his 2nd anniversary.

WALKER, RAYMOND LESLIE, 606-43-23, born Jan. 15, 1915, Lawrence, MA. Graduated from Lawrence, MA, High School and enlisted March 2, 1942, Boston, MA. He trained at Naval Training Station, Newport, RI.

He was a plankowner and served aboard BB-59 as AS 6th Div. at commissioning May 12, 1942, and assigned 5" guns. He left BB-59 and transferred to a CVE. He was discharged Sept. 18, 1945, Bainbridge, MD, as GM2/c. After the war he worked for American Woolen Company, Lawrence, MA, and retired in 1977 from Gillette Company, Andover, MA. He enjoyed fishing and boating.

He married Sybil and has one daughter and two grandchildren. (Wife) resides at 1249 Jamaica Road, Marco Island, FL 33937.

WALKER, ROY DANIEL, served aboard BB-59 as CEM E Div. June 14, 1945, and assigned Maintenance I.C.-F.C. and material.

WALKER, WARREN, JR., LT born in Philadelphia, PA. A high school graduate with six years college, Naval Academy Class 1940, he enlisted in the Naval Academy 1936. He served aboard USS *California*, Pearl Harbor survivor, July 1940-42. He is a plankowner and served aboard BB-59 as LT N Div. at commissioning May 12, 1942. Assigned assistant navigator, 2nd Div., Battle Station Turret #2, Main

Battery Asst., Spot I and left BB-59 March 1946.

Other Naval assignments were executive officer USS *Chevalier*; June 1947 contracted polio and hospitalized Naval Hospital, Aiera, HI; September 1947 transferred to Naval Hospital, Philadelphia, PA; and retired May 1948 as LT CR. He received two Commendation Ribbons.

After the war he returned to Philadelphia, PA, for six years was a sales engineer for Minneapolis-Honeywell Company; eight years general warehouse manager Colorado Fuel & Iron Company; and 26 years real estate broker and appraiser Emlen & Company.

He married Louise Bremerton, WA, and has one son and one grandchild. He resided at 41 Shawnee Road, Ardmore, PA 19003. He died July 21, 1994, at VA Medical Center, Philadelphia, PA. Memory List 1994.

WALLACE, DONALD F., served aboard BB-59 in R Div. and resides at 2716 Texas St. NE, Albuquerque, NM 87101.

WALLACE, HOWARD "J.," 650-29-80, enlisted Feb. 18, 1942, Philadelphia, PA. He is a plankowner and served aboard BB-59 as AS at commissioning May 12, 1942.

WALLACE, JOHN JOSEPH, 606-33-58, enlisted Feb. 10, 1942, Boston, MA. He is a plankowner and served aboard BB-59 as AS at commissioning May 12, 1942.

WALLACE, STONEWALL JACKSON, served aboard BB-59 as Mach. M Div. at commissioning June 24, 1944, and assigned J.O. and J.W. M Div.

WALLS, DWAYNE CHAPMAN, 337-34-46, enlisted July 25, 1940, St. Louis, MO. He is a plankowner and served aboard BB-59 as S1/c at commissioning May 12, 1942.

WALLS, ROBERT, resides at Box 767, Republic, PA 15475.

WALSH, FRANCIS, resides at RR 2, Box 160, Springfield, IL.

WALSH, JOSEPH ARTHUR, 646-59-37, enlisted Jan. 29, 1942, New York, NY. He is a plankowner and served aboard BB-59 as AS at commissioning May 12, 1942, and on board for BB-59 2nd and 3rd anniversaries.

WALSH, WILLIAM SEBASTION, 652-21-82, enlisted Feb. 17, 1942, Pittsburgh, PA. He is a plankowner and served aboard BB-59 as AS at commissioning May 12, 1942, and on board for BB-59 2nd and 3rd anniversaries.

WALTHER, WILLIAM JACOB, JR., ENS, 330841, born March 28, 1923, New York, NY. He holds a college degree in electrical engineering and enlisted 1942, New York, NY. Attended Union College V-12, Midshipman School, Range Finder and Radar Operator's School. He served aboard BB-59 as ENS A Div. May 21, 1944, and assigned A Div. J.O. and J.W., LT(jg). He left BB-59 May 15, 1946, Norfolk, VA.

After the war he was test man for Engineer Telephone Company and an income tax preparer for H & R Block. He enjoys making furniture, wood crafts and barber shop singing.

He has one son, five daughters and six grandchildren. He resides at 65 Pascack Road, Pearl River, NY 10965.

WALTHER, WILLIAM MAX, JR., 646-61-90, enlisted Jan. 31, 1942, New York, NY. He is a plankowner and served aboard BB-59 as AS at commissioning May 12, 1942, and on board for BB-59 2nd and 3rd anniversaries.

WALTON, ANDREW J., served aboard BB-59 in M Div. and resides at 600 West 26th St., Richmond, VA 23225.

WALTON, PAUL A., 207-78-57, born Aug. 20, 1928, Rossville, PA. He is a Tech School grad with one year of college. He enlisted Aug. 20, 1928, New Haven, CT, and trained Naval Training Station Camp Perry, VA.

He served aboard BB-59 as S1/c 6th Div. Feb. 6, 1946, and assigned 5" Twin Gun-Port Side. He left BB-59 Aug. 16, 1946. He was also assigned to Atlantic Reserve Fleet; Norfolk Group; USS *Barnwell*; USS *Gage*; USS *North Carolina*; USS *Huntington* (CL-107); New York Group, USS *Cascade*; and Naval Receiving Station, Philadelphia, PA.

After the war he worked as tool and die foreman for Die Sinking Company, New Haven, CT. He married June Feb. 23, 1957, Ansonia, CT, and has one son, one daughter and three grandchildren. He resides at 38 Shepard Lane, Orange, CT 06477.

WALZ, HELMUTH JOHN, 632-39-18, enlisted Jan. 27, 1942, Los Angeles, CA. He is a plankowner and served aboard BB-59 as Mus1/c at commissioning May 12, 1942.

WARD, EDWARD J., USS *Massachusetts* Assoc., Memorial Committee, Honorary Crew Member, and received BB-59 Award 1977.

WARD, JOHN JOSEPH, 646-63-13, enlisted Feb. 2, 1942, New York, NY. He is a plankowner and served aboard BB-59 as AS at commissioning May 12, 1942.

WARD, ROBERT ELDON, 311-37-13, enlisted Nov. 15, 1939, Detroit, MI. He is a plankowner and served aboard BB-59 as S1/c at commissioning May 12, 1942.

WAREHIME, JOHN THOMAS, 646-78-18, enlisted Feb. 14, 1942, New York, NY. He is a plankowner and served aboard BB-59 as AS 5th Div. commissioning May 12, 1942. He was assigned 5" Gun Mount #7 and left BB-59 November 1945.

After the war he worked for John H. Terry, Inc., building construction and was in the Coast Guard Auxiliary in his spare time. He had one son, one daughter and five grandchildren. (Mrs.) resides at 934 Capstan Drive, Forked River, NJ 08731. Memory List 1990.

WARENCZAK, JULIUS, (n) 646-63-14, enlisted Feb. 2, 1942, New York, NY. He is a plankowner and served aboard BB-59 as AS at commissioning May 12, 1942, and on board for BB-59 2nd anniversary.

WARREN, A.A., Memory List 1996.

WATERMAN, JAMES ANDREW, 606-33-09, born Jan. 10, 1925, Belfast, ME. He enlisted Feb. 11, 1942, Boston, MA, and trained at Newport Naval Training Station, RI. He is a plankowner and served aboard BB-59 as AS 4th Div. at commissioning May 12, 1942. He was assigned L Div. and left BB-59 November 1945 Bremerton, WA.

After the war he worked for Maplewood Poultry for 31 years; Crowe Rope, Inc., two and a half years; Penobscot Frozen Foods for 12 years all in Belfast, ME.

He married Evelyn Jan. 10, 1971, Waterville, ME. He has three sons, five grandchildren and four great-grandchildren. He resides at RR#2 Box 648, Fire Rd. #7 Knox, Brooks, ME 04921-9615.

WATPPE, W.G., resides at RR 1, Fall Creek, WI 54742.

WARWICK, WILLIAM WALTER, CAPT, resided at 131 Charles St., Annapolis, MD 21404. RADM Memory List 1992.

WARREN, ALBURN ANDREWS, 359-78-98, enlisted Nov. 28, 1941, New York, NY. He served aboard BB-59 as CGM 4th Div. Oct. 1, 1943. He was assigned ENS LT(jg) J.O. 4th Div. 40 mm Sky officer. He left BB-59 Oct. 15, 1945. Memory List 1992.

WARNER, FREDERICK GERALD, 162-96-28, enlisted April 16, 1936, Philadelphia, PA. He is a plankowner and served aboard BB-59 as CTC on May 12, 1942.

WARREN, A.A., ENS, is a plankowner and served aboard BB-59 as ENS at commissioning May 12, 1942, and on board for BB-59 2nd and 3rd anniversaries. Memory List 1996.

WASCHE, CHARLES ELWIN, 244-05-03, enlisted Jan. 27, 1942, Philadelphia, PA. He is a plankowner and served aboard BB-59 as AS at commissioning May 12, 1942.

WASHINGTON, PHILIP OLIVER, 632-14-32, enlisted Nov. 19, 1941, Los Angeles, CA. He was a plankowner and served aboard BB-59 as S2/c 5th Div. (Mrs.) resides at 3643 Padua Ave., Claremont, CA 91711. Memory List 1989.

WASHINGTON, SAMUEL, (n) 300-79-62, enlisted March 17, 1942, Chicago, IL. He is a plankowner and served aboard BB-59 as Matt3/c at commissioning May 12, 1942.

WASILUK, JOSEPH, resides at 128 Woodbine Ave., St. Paul, MN 55165.

WASKICK, JOSEPH, resides at 2 Rechard St., Wilkes Barre, PA 18703.

WATSON, KENNETH LAWRENCE, 606-34-69, born Dec. 7, 1917, Boston, MA. Graduated from Boston English High School and earned a BS in criminology from Northeastern University. He enlisted Feb. 13, 1942, Boston, MA, and trained at Newport Naval Training Station, RI.

He is a plankowner and served aboard BB-59 as AS FC Div. at commissioning May 12, 1942. He was assigned S2/c, GM3/c, GM2/c and GM1/c. He left BB-59 May 1945 by Breeches Buoy to Tanker off Okinawa. Was also assigned GM1/c, Naval Gun Factory, Anacostia, MD, and discharged Bainbridge, MD.

After the war he worked in law enforcement and retired Dec. 31, 1991, as chief of police Boston College after 25 years. He enjoys gardening in his spare time.

He married Eleanor June 24, 1944, Boston, MA, and has one son, two daughters and four grandchildren. He resides at 237 Maple St., West Roxbury, MA 02132.

WATSON, PETER PAUL, r 646-80-77, born July 27, 1924, Queens Village, NY. Graduated from Berkeley High School, CA, and attended San Diego Community College, CA. He enlisted Feb. 17, 1942, New York, NY, and trained at Newport Naval Training Station, RI. He is a plankowner and served aboard BB-59 as AS 2nd Div. at commissioning May 12, 1942. He was assigned Oct. 1, 1942, S1/c, RDM3/c CR Div. and March 10, 1943, RDM2/c FR Div. He left BB-59 July 27, 1944, Pearl Harbor. Other assignments: July 1944 RDM2/c Instructor Radar Operators School, Pearl Harbor, HI; November 1944 RDM1/c Instructor Fleet Service Schools, Norfolk, VA; May 1945 RDM1/c Radar Operators School, Point Loma, San Diego, CA; and April 20, 1966, retired Navy as master chief radarman with 24 years of service.

After Naval service he was a material program manager for the Navy Dept. and retired Jan. 3, 1987, with 20 years of service. He is involved with Meals on Wheels program, Coast Guard Auxiliary and National Assoc. of Retired Federal Employees.

He married Catherine Ruth March 2, 1946, Springfield Gardens, NY. He has one daughter and two grandchildren. He resides at 1015 Monterey Court, Chula Vista, CA 91911-2419.

WATSON, RAYMOND ELMER, 610-60-05, enlisted Feb. 9, 1942, Chicago, IL. He is a plankowner and served aboard BB-59 as AS at commissioning May 12, 1942.

WATSON, WILLIAM EDGAR, JR., 262-95-59, enlisted Sept. 23, 1941, Raleigh, NC. He is a plankowner and served aboard BB-59 as F3/c at commissioning May 12, 1942, and on board for BB-59 2nd and 3rd anniversaries.

WATTEL, HAROLD LOUIS, ENS, born Sept. 30, 1921, New York, NY. He holds a BA from Queens College; an MA from Columbia University and a Ph.D. from New School for Social Research. He served aboard BB-59 as ENS 6th Div. May 7, 1943, and assigned LT J.O. CR Div. edited Bay *Stater* and daily newspaper. He left BB-59 Jan. 25, 1946.

After the war he worked as an economist for the Dept. of Agriculture, 1946; an economic consultant for National Economic Research Assoc., 1952; economic consultant to Governor Harriman of New York, 1955-56; instructor to Professor Faculty Member Hofstra University, 1947-86; dean, School of Business Hofstra University, 1961-73; present professor emeritus of economics, Hofstra University, 1986; current Who's Who in America, *American Men of Science*; 1951 Fellowship Hazen Foundation; 1960 Fellowship Ford Foundation; 1986 Distinguished Service Award Hofstra University; many publications written.

He has membership National Assoc. of Forensic Economists, membership American Economics Assoc., board member and former president Cornell Cooperative Extension of Nassau County, board member and treasurer Consumer Farmer Foundation, public representative on Public Island Peer Review Organization, corporate member and former vice-president American Lung Assoc. of New York State.

He married Sara Sept. 1, 1946, and has two daughters and two grandchildren. He resides at 181 Shepherd Lane, Roslyn Heights, NY 11577.

WATTERS, WILLIAM ANDREW, 328-66-69, enlisted March 12, 1940, Minneapolis, MN. He is a plankowner and served aboard BB-59 as F2/c at commissioning May 12, 1942.

WATZ, BASIL D., resides at 3360 Davison Road, Lapeer, MI 48446.

WAWRYSZYN, RAYMOND FRANCIS, 666-15-27, enlisted Feb. 4, 1942, Springfield, MA. He is a plankowner and served aboard BB-59 as AS CR Div. at commissioning May 12, 1942, and on his 2nd and 3rd anniversaries. Assigned to RDM3/c FR Div. commissioning March 10, 1943.

WEATHERBURN, HARRY, (n) 606-15-43, enlisted Feb. 5, 1942, Springfield, MA. He is a plankowner and served aboard BB-59 as AS at commissioning May 12, 1942, and on his 2nd and 3rd anniversaries.

WEATHERWAX, HAZLETT PAUL, LT COMDR Naval Academy Class of 1931. He is a plankowner and served aboard BB-59 as LT COMDR 2nd Div. at commissioning May 12, 1942, and on board for BB-59 2nd anniversary. Assigned machine gun officer, gunnery officer, S.C.M., athletic officer, air defense officer and left BB-59 in 1944. Was also assigned 1965 RADM, OPNAV (OP-07B) Navy Dept., Washington, DC and retired. Memory List 1977.

WEAVER, FRANCIS, (n) 342-29-33, enlisted Sept. 24, 1940, Kansas City, MO. He is a plankowner and served aboard BB-59 as F1/c commissioning May 12, 1942, and on his 2nd anniversary.

WEAVER, HARRY FERNANDAS, GUN, served aboard BB-59 as GUN FC Div. Aug. 18, 1944, and assigned J.O. FC Div., Asst. Rep. VI officer. He left BB-59 Dec. 20, 1945.

WEBSTER, ROBERT L., born July 17, 1922, Grant County, KY. Attended Machine Shop, Mechanical Drawing, Steam Engineering Training. He enlisted Nov. 22, 1942, Cincinnati, OH. He served aboard BB-59 as MM3/c M Div. July 1943 and left BB-59 Feb. 1, 1946, Seattle, WA.

After the war he worked for KD Lamp Company, Cincinnati, OH, for a total of 33 years, the city of Florence, KY, for seven years Public Works Director Baptist Convalescence Center; three years maintenance engineer ; 21 years city council and retired as public works director. He is involved in the Park & Recreation Commission, Water & Sewer Commission, Planning & Zoning Commission, Industrial Park Commission, youth director Florence Baptist Church and was honored as a Kentucky Colonel.

He married Georgia, Covington, KY, and has one son, one daughter and seven grandchildren. He resides at 29921 Briarthorn Loop, Wesley Chapel, FL 33543.

WEDDINGTON, HOWARD C., resides at Rt. 3 Box 308, Mooresville, NC 28115.

WEHNER, JOHN A., served aboard BB-59 in 6th Div. and resides at 10204 20th SW, Seattle, WA 98146. Memory List 1996.

WEINBERG, JOSEPH, resides at 1436 5th Ave., Pittsburgh, PA 15201.

WEINGARTNER, WILLIAM EDWARD, JR., 650-08-14, enlisted Dec. 16, 1941, Philadelphia, PA. He is a plankowner and served aboard BB-59 as SF3/c at commissioning May 12, 1942.

WEIS, ANTHONY L., Memory List 1989.

WEISS, STANLEY WILLIAM, 646-60-64, enlisted Jan. 30, 1942, New York, NY. He is a plankowner and served aboard BB-59 as AS F Div. at commissioning May 12, 1942. He was assigned FC3/c 5" Battery Fire Control and left BB-59 September 1944. After the war he worked as V.P. salesman for Supreme Notion Inc. He has two daughters and resides at 123 Valentine Lane, Yonkers, NY 10701.

WELCH, JOHN WILLIAM, 202-15-18, enlisted March 24, 1942, Boston, MA. He was a plankowner and served aboard BB-59 as AS 2nd Div. at commissioning May 12, 1942. (Mrs.) resides at 5 Huron Drive, Framingham, MA 01701. He died May 1994; Memory List 1994.

WELCOME, CLIFFORD, resided at 7042 Whiflaker, Detroit, MI 48226. Memory List 1977.

WELDON, NATHANIEL WARREN, JR., LT(jg), served aboard BB-59 as LT(jg) 4th Div. March 24, 1943, and assigned 1st J.O. R Div. SCM Catapult officer. He left BB-59 July 13, 1944.

WELLE, TELLEF, (n) 224-71-74, enlisted Feb. 27, 1942, New York, NY. He is a plankowner and served aboard BB-59 as AS at commissioning May 12, 1942.

WELLS, IRA WALTER, 360-37-90, enlisted May 9, 1941, Houston, TX. He is a plankowner and served aboard BB-59 as S1/c at commissioning May 12, 1942.

WEMER, NORMAN G., resides at 610 South Milner, Ottumwa, IA 52501.

WERNER, GEORGE LLOYD, 283-42-23, enlisted Oct. 16, 1940, Cleveland, OH. He is a plankowner and served aboard BB-59 as PhM3/c at commissioning May 12, 1942.

WERNER, SHERWOOD HARRY, LT(jg), Naval Academy Class of 1942, served aboard BB-59 as LT(jg) 5th Div. March 1943. He was assigned W.(P) and J.D. baseball coach, Battle Station Sec. Spot 1.

WERY, KENNETH FRANCIS, 393-30-14, born March 6, 1916, Moscow, ID. A graduate of Palouse High School, Palouse, WA, he enlisted Aug. 14, 1939, Portland, OR. Trained at San Diego Naval Training Station, CA, USS *Oklahoma* and USS *Chester*. He was a plankowner and served aboard BB-59 as S1/c 1st Div. at commissioning May 12, 1942.

He was assigned GM3/c, GM2/c and TC1/c and left BB-59 October 1944. Was assigned to Fleet Service School, Norfolk, VA, USS *Providence* and discharged Sept. 9, 1945, Lido Beach, NY, as turret captain 1st Class.

After the war he worked as a logger, 1945-57; letter carrier US Post Office, 1957-81; and doorman and user Opera House, Seattle, WA, 1965-90. He had two daughters, one grandchild and resided at 1724

North 137th, Seattle, WA 98133-7735. He died Nov. 7, 1995, Seattle, WA.

WESNER, LAWRENCE JOSEPH, LT, born Jan. 19, 1915, Johnstown, PA. Attended St. Vincent College and Temple University Dental School, Philadelphia, PA. He enlisted 1942 Philadelphia, PA. He served aboard BB-59 as LT Dec. 26, 1944, and assigned assistant dental officer. He left BB-59 Nov. 15, 1945. He was assigned to USS *Susan B. Anthony.* After the war he  worked as a dentist GP DMD for 42 years. He married Irene Feb. 26, 1949, and had one son (deceased) and four daughters. (Mrs.) resides at 204 Pallister St., Johnstown, PA 15905-2557. He died May 31, 1993; Memory List 1994.

WESNESKI, RAYMOND, served aboard BB-59 in S Div. (Mrs.) resides at 811 Walnut St., Elmira, NY 14901. Memory List 1990.

WESTBROOM, ALBERT EUGENE, 283-32-02, enlisted Dec. 18, 1941, Pearl Harbor, HI. He is a plankowner and served aboard BB-59 as GM2/c at commissioning May 12, 1942.

WHALEN, FRANK, JR., (n) 380-82-15, enlisted Jan. 3, 1942, San Francisco, CA. He is a plankowner and served aboard BB-59 as MM1/c at commissioning May 12, 1942.

WHALEY, GEORGE RAYMOND, 204-34-83, enlisted Nov. 29, 1941, San Francisco, CA. He is a plankowner and served aboard BB-59 as CSK at commissioning May 12, 1942.

WHEATLEY, CLARENCE C., served aboard BB-59 in B Div. and assigned M Div. Memory List 1993.

WHEELER, CLIFFORD EUGENE, 163-75-53, enlisted Dec. 15, 1941, Des Moines, IA. He is a plankowner and served aboard BB-59 as EM2/c E Div. at commissioning May 12, 1942.

WHELESS, DESEY CLARENCE, 267-98-60, enlisted June 7, 1939, Shanghai, China. He is a plankowner and served aboard BB-59 as FC1/c at commissioning May 12, 1942.

WHITE, JAMES HOUGHTON, 346-29-99, born July 27, 1907, Chicago, IL. Enlisted (first tour) US Navy 1925-29, San Diego, CA, and (second tour) on March 12, 1942, Kansas City, MO. He is a plankowner and served aboard BB-59 as Mus2/c at commissioning May 12, 1942. He was assigned Mus1/c September 1942 and left BB-59 Nov. 29, 1942, Norfolk, VA.

Other Naval assignments: December 1942 to January 1945 Camp Peary, Williamsburg, VA; January 1945 to March 1945 School of Music, Washington, DC; March 1945 to October 1945 Saipan Island, band; and discharged Nashville, TN.

After the war he worked as night supervisor at Boston State Hospital, Boston, MA, 1948-72 and retired Dept. of Mental Hygiene, Boston, MA, June 1972.

He married Rita Jan. 22, 1943, Newport News, VA, and has one two sons, one daughter and six grandchildren. He resides at Box 232 (June to October) South Chatham 02659; PO Box 2452 (October to June) Lake Placid, FL 33862.

WHITE, ROBERT BUSS, 616-12-91, enlisted Jan. 3, 1942, Dallas, TX. He is a plankowner and served aboard BB-59 as EM3/c E Div. at commis-

sioning May 12, 1942, and on board for BB-59 2nd and 3rd anniversary. He was assigned CEM E Div.

WHITE, S.L., served aboard BB-59 as S1/c V Div. and left March 8, 1948, Noumea, New Caledonia. He was assigned Comd. Fleet Air.

WHITE, STANTON MCCONNELL, 300-44-45, enlisted April 29, 1941, Chicago, IL. He is a plankowner and served aboard BB-59 as S2/c at commissioning May 12, 1942, and on board for BB-59 2nd and 3rd anniversaries.

WHITE, WALTER ADELBERT, JR., born March 25, 1910, Dedham, MA. He was educated at Harvard University.

He worked for the US Post Office, Dedham, MA; 1965-68 Urban Renewal Dedham, MA; 1968-72, Urban Renewal Framingham, MA; and 1963-72, Minot Light Inn, Situate, MA. He is a selectman Dedham, MA.

He married Helen (deceased) Nov. 25, 1937, Dedham, MA, and had three sons, one daughter, five grandchildren and one great-grandchild. He died Aug. 30, 1972; Memory List 1977. (Son) resides at 25 Netta Road, Dedham, MA 02026.

WHITEMAN, EARL MYRON, 385-95-79, enlisted Jan. 15, 1941, Seattle, WA. He is a plankowner and served aboard BB-59 as S1/c at commissioning May 12, 1942, and on board for BB-59 2nd and 3rd anniversaries.

WHITFIELD, IRA, (n) 272-81-90, enlisted Jan. 3, 1942, Birmingham, AL. He is a plankowner and served aboard BB-59 as S2/c at commissioning May 12, 1942, and on board for BB-59 2nd and 3rd anniversaries. He resides at 131 Cotton Ave., Pelham, GA 31779.

WHITING, FRANCIS E.M., BB-59's first CAPT-plankowner-aboard May 12, 1942-was assigned VADM. He resided at New York Yacht Club, 37 W 44th St., New York, NY 10001. Memory List 1979.

WHITING, WAYNE WILLIAM, 320-79-04, enlisted Nov. 2, 1939, New York, NY. He is a plankowner and served aboard BB-59 as BM2/c at commissioning May 12, 1942.

WHITT, O.F., served aboard BB-59 as F3/c P Div. and left BB-59 March 8, 1943, ComSerFltSoPac.

WHITTLE, FRANK R., USMC May 8, 1942, Norfolk Navy Yard, VA. He is a plankowner and served aboard BB-59 as PVT 7th Div. at commissioning May 12, 1942.

WICENCIUK, FRANK E., (see WALKER, EDWARD).

WICK, JAMES F., served aboard BB-59 as BM1/c and assigned USS *Rochester* (CA-124). He retired Aug. 1, 1957, from the Navy.

WICKERSHAM, TAYLOR VERN, 360-27-48, enlisted Sept. 18, 1941, Houston, TX. He is a plankowner and served aboard BB-59 as MM2/c at commissioning May 12, 1942.

WIDEMAN, ARNOLD JUSTIN, 346-82-44, enlisted July 17, 1940, Little Rock, AR. He is a

plankowner and served aboard BB-59 as RM3/c at commissioning May 12, 1942.

WIGHTMAN, JOHN WILLIAM, 376-43-02, enlisted Oct. 23, 1941, San Francisco, CA. He is a plankowner and served aboard BB-59 as F3/c at commissioning May 12, 1942, and on board for BB-59 2nd and 3rd anniversaries.

WILBUR, HERBERT ORAN, 238-69-71, enlisted Oct. 22, 1940, Albany, NY. He is a plankowner and served aboard BB-59 as S1/c at commissioning May 12, 1942.

WILDE, ARTHUR JOSEPH, 606-42-59, enlisted Feb. 28, 1942, Boston, MA. He is a plankowner and served aboard BB-59 as S2/c at commissioning May 12, 1942, and on board for BB-59 2nd and 3rd anniversaries. Memory List 1984.

WILDE, DANIEL AUGUSTUS, 204-42-13, enlisted March 28, 1939, Portsmouth, NH. He is a plankowner and served aboard BB-59 as WT1/c B Div. at commissioning May 12, 1942. Was assigned CWT, in charge #1 Fireroom and left BB-59 November 1945.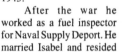

After the war he worked as a fuel inspector for Naval Supply Deport. He married Isabel and resided at 5 Farnum Terrace, Middleton, RI 02840. Memory List 1990.

WILKIN, VERN LOWELL, 342-17-32, enlisted Dec. 27, 1939, Kansas City, MO. He is a plankowner and served aboard BB-59 as EM3/c E Div. at commissioning May 12, 1942.

WILKINSON, GEORGE ROBERT, 646-60-52, (Note: Formerly listed as SCHULTHWIS, GEORGE ROBERT but name changed when adopted by foster mother) born Jan. 14, 1921, Jamaica, NY. He graduated from high school, attended night school and had many special courses. He enlisted Jan. 30, 1942, New York, NY, and trained at Newport Naval Training Station, RI.

He is a plankowner and served aboard BB-59 as S1/c at commissioning May 12, 1942. He was assigned Smoke Watch F2/c and left BB-59 January 1943 Boston, MA. Other Naval assignments: Fire Dept. Submarine Base, New London, CT; June to September 1945 Underwater Demolition School, Norfolk, VA; recalled to active duty during Korean War and served on board USS *Herbert J. Thomas* (DD-833) until 1952.

After the war he worked in soft drink sales and management Coca Cola and 7-Up. He is active in many civic organizations and fraternal groups. He married Mary Alice May 12, 1945, Submarine Base, New London, CT. He has two daughters and four grandchildren. He resides at 361 South River Drive #207, Stuart, FL 34997.

WILKINSON, HAROLD RALPH, 341-99-33, born June 20, 1919, Kansas City, MO. He enlisted Oct. 20, 1936, Kansas City, MO. He was a plankowner and served aboard BB-59 as COX 3rd Div. at commissioning May 12, 1942, and on board for BB-59 2nd anniversary. Was assigned 3rd Div. leading petty officer, BM1/c and left BB-59 Nov. 30, 1944.

After the war he worked in the Supply Dept. Civil Service Submarine Base, New London, CT. He was active in the VFW and Fleet Reserve Assoc. (Mrs.) resides at RFD #5 Holdsworth Rd., Norwich, CT 06360. He died Dec. 16, 1992; Memory List 1992.

WILKY, N.L., ENS, served aboard BB-59 as ENS 6th Div. April 6, 1944, and assigned J.O. 6th Div. Quadrant, LT(jg). He left BB-59 May 1, 1945.

WILLESS, HENRY, 356-28-10, born Nov. 23, 1920, Rockwall, TX. Enlisted May 20, 1940, Dallas, TX, and trained at San Diego Naval Training Station, CA, USS *Arizona* (BB-39) and USS *Idaho*. He is a plankowner and served aboard BB-59 as MM1/c M Div. at commissioning May 12, 1942, and left 1945 in the Pacific. In 1946 put out of commission at San Diego, CA; USS *Albert W. Grant* (DD-649); put in commission USS *Manchester* (CL-83); and duty to USS *Mississippi* (EAR-128). After the war he worked as a trucker until retiring in 1992. He has six sons and two daughters and resides at 301 South Clark St., Rockwall, TX 75087.

WILLETT, JAMES L., served aboard BB-59 in M Div. and resides at 52 Jasper St., Haverhill, MA 01830.

WILLEY, CLIFFORD ALLEN, 666-12-27, enlisted Jan. 16, 1942, Springfield, MA. He was a plankowner and served aboard BB-59 as AS 4th Div. (Mrs.) resides at 42 Holyoke Road, Westfield, MA 01085. Memory List 1993.

WILLEY, GEORGE WILLIAM, 212-20-80, enlisted March 26, 1940, San Diego, CA. He is a plankowner and served aboard BB-59 as S1/c at commissioning May 12, 1942.

WILLIAMS, DON B., resides at 7404 South Park, Tacoma, WA 98401.

WILLIAMS, EARL, (n) 646-68-26, enlisted Feb. 6, 1942, New York, NY. He is a plankowner and served aboard BB-59 as AS P Div. at commissioning May 12, 1942, and on board for BB-59 2nd anniversary. He resides at Rt. 32 Box 2213, Saugerties, NY 12477.

WILLIAMS, HERBERT BYRON, LT, is a plankowner and served aboard BB-59 as LT 3rd Div. at commissioning May 12, 1942. He was assigned assistant D.C. officer; Oct. 1, 1943, R Div.; W. (P) & D Watch officer, chemical warfare officer, Battle Station Repair LT CDR. He left BB-59 Aug. 21, 1945.

WILLIAMS, LAUREL GLEA, 337-25-25, enlisted Dec. 27, 1939, St. Louis, MO. He is a plankowner and served aboard BB-59 as BKR3/c S Div. at commissioning May 12, 1942. He resides at 9 Grove Ave., Wilmington, MA 01887.

WILLIAMS, RAYMOND BERYL, 628-22-65, enlisted Jan. 24, 1942, Kansas City, MO. He is a plankowner and served aboard BB-59 as AS at commissioning May 12, 1942.

WILLIAMS, ROYAL, (n) 372-12-73, enlisted Jan. 3, 1940, Denver, CO. He is a plankowner and served aboard BB-59 as Y3/c at commissioning May 12, 1942.

WILLIAMS, WILLIAM H., born July 30, 1915, Washington, DC. Attended Naval Academy, 1939 and assigned Anti-Aircraft Defense 1940, Pearl Harbor; USS *Oklahoma* from June 1, 1939, to August 1941; to

Naval Supply School, Harvard University. He served aboard BB-59 as LT(jg) disbursing officer March 1942 and left August 1943.

Other assignments included: Efate, Vanuatu Islands; assistant supply officer Tillimook, OR, August 1943 to August 1944; supply officer Marine Air Station, El Centro, CA, August 1944 to August 1945; staff ComServDiv 3 Okinawa August 1945 to December 1945; staff ComServSquad 3, Shanghai, China December 1945 to Dec. 31, 1946; resigned commission March 1947.

After the war he was assistant general manager Stockton Division, American Forest Products Corp., board of directors 1954-72 and retired October 1972. He is on the Stockton Chamber of Commerce; United Way; Friends of Chamber Music; fund-raising for Feather River Inn, Blairsden, CA, and University of the Pacific.

He married Marjorie Webster Sept. 7, 1941, Linden, CA, and has three children and nine grandchildren. (Wife died May 23, 1993) He resides at 800 N. Clements Rd., Linden, CA.

WILLIAMSON, HARRY PAUL, JR., LT, served aboard BB-59 as LT H Div. July 1943 and assigned dental officer October 1943.

WILLIS, CHARLES FRANK, 668-30-69, enlisted Jan. 21, 1942, St. Louis, MO. He is a plankowner and served aboard BB-59 as AS at commissioning May 12, 1942, and on board for BB-59 2nd and 3rd anniversaries.

WILLIS, CLARENCE LAFAYETTE, 262-26-03, enlisted Dec. 21, 1937, Raleigh, NC. He is a plankowner and served aboard BB-59 as S1/c at commissioning May 12, 1942.

WILLIS, FRED, (n) 287-14-26, enlisted Aug. 7, 1941, Pearl Harbor, HI. He is a plankowner and served aboard BB-59 as SC2/c at commissioning May 12, 1942.

WILLIS, MILAN, (n) 262-62-39, enlisted July 18, 1940, Raleigh, NC. He is a plankowner and served aboard BB-59 as S1/c at commissioning May 12, 1942.

WILLNESS, HENRY FRANCIS, 356-28-10, enlisted May 24, 1940, Dallas, TX. He is a plankowner and served aboard BB-59 as F2/c at commissioning May 12, 1942.

WILLS, ROBERT IVAN, 268-49-36, enlisted July 23, 1940, Macon, GA. He is a plankowner and served aboard BB-59 as S1/c at commissioning May 12, 1942, and on board for BB-59 2nd and 3rd anniversaries.

WILSON, CHARLES EDGAR, 295-45-08, enlisted Feb. 21, 1939, Nashville, TN. He is a plankowner and served aboard BB-59 as PhM2/c H Div. at commissioning May 12, 1942. He resided at 423 E. 4th Way, Long Beach, CA 95551.

WILSON, GEORGE EMIEL, 402-99-92, enlisted June 8, 1939, New York, NY. He is a plankowner and served aboard BB-59 as S1/c at commissioning May 12, 1942.

WILSON, JACK, USMC, May 8, 1942, Naval Yard Norfolk, VA. He is a plankowner and served aboard BB-59 as PVT 7th Div. at commissioning May 12, 1942.

WILSON, JOHN RUSSELL, JR., born Aug. 11, 1924, Hagerstown, MD. Graduated from high school Stroudsburg, PA, and enlisted March 4, 1942, Philadelphia, PA. Trained at Newport Naval Training Station, RI. He is a plankowner and served aboard BB-59 as AS 3rd Div. at commissioning May 12, 1942. He

left BB-59 April 1945 Ulithi. Was also assigned USS *Washington*.

After the war he worked for Bell Telephone Company of Pennsylvania for 35 years. He is on United Way Board; Easter Seals; Lions Club; Exchange Club; Delaware Water Gap Dutch Museum, PA; Boro Council; YMCA Board; Monroe County General Authority, Stroudsburg, PA; Good Citizens Award by Boro of Delaware Water Gap, PA; Golden Deeds Award Exchange Club of Monroe County, PA; and several awards from Delaware Water Gap Lions Club.

He has two sons and three grandchildren and resides at PO Box 142, Delaware Water Gap, PA 18327.

WILSON, WILLIAM, Memory List 1992.

WILSON, WINTHROP, (n) 606-42-91, enlisted March 2, 1942, Boston, MA. He is a plankowner and served aboard BB-59 as AS at commissioning May 12, 1942. Was assigned WT1/c and left BB-59 September 1945. Returned to active duty during the Korean War and served aboard USS *Laffey* (DD-724) and USS *Greenwood* (DE-679). After the war he worked as a power plant controlman for High Pressure Main Power Plant and Naval Air Station, Quonset Point, RI. He resided at 16 West St., Jamestown, RI 02835. Memory List 1992.

WINE, RAYMOND L., resided at 452 South Deweter Drive, Freeport, IL 61032.

WINEINGER, RAYMOND, resided at 8526 Midvale Ave. No., Seattle, WA 98103.

WINGET, FRANCIS WAYNE, 668-31-06, enlisted Jan. 21, 1942, St. Louis, MO. He is a plankowner and served aboard BB-59 as AS at commissioning May 12, 1942. Was assigned WT1/c and left BB-59 September 1945. Returned to active duty during Korean War and served aboard the USS *Laffey* (DD-724) and USS *Greenwood* (DE-679).

WINN, ALPHA L., served aboard BB-59 in 1945 as CEM E Div.

WINTER, JAMES FREDERIC, 368-22-55, enlisted Sept. 19, 1939, San Pedro, CA. He is a plankowner and served aboard BB-59 as TC1/c.

WIRTH, JAMES J., served aboard BB-59 in 7th Div. He resides at 49 Nelson St., St. Paul, MN 55119.

WIRTHLIN, MILTON ROBERT, COMDR, served aboard BB-59 as COMDR H Div. December 1942 and was assigned senior medical officer.

WISNIEWSKI, EDWARD FRANK, 224-72-41, enlisted March 3, 1942, New York, NY. He is a plankowner and served aboard BB-59 as AS at commissioning May 12, 1942, and on board for BB-59 2nd and 3rd anniversaries.

WOLF, FRANK JOSEPH, 646-59-41, enlisted Jan. 29, 1942, New York, NY. He is a plankowner and served aboard BB-59 as AS 2nd Div. at commissioning May 12, 1942, and on board for BB-59 2nd and 3rd anniversaries. Was assigned CAPT 2nd Div. BM2/c. He resided at 3884 Beechwood Place, Seaford, NY 11783.

WOLF, I.D., JR., ENS, served aboard BB-59 in R Div. and assigned J.D. Battle Station C.O.C.

WOLF, JOHN ARTHUR, 646-58-29, enlisted Jan. 28, 1942, New York, NY. He is a plankowner and served aboard BB-59 as AS R Div. at commissioning May 12, 1942. He was assigned SF1/c and left BB-59 October 1945. After the war he worked as a plumber and married Peggy. He had one son and resided at 74 North Kinsico Ave., White Plaines, NY 10604. Memory List 1992.

WOLF, W., resided at 98 Harding Ave. A-4, White Plains, NY 10606.

WOLFE, FRANK A., resided at 15094 150th St. NW #4B, Oak Harbor, WA 98277.

WOLLETT, CLARENCE JUNIOR, 614-23-58, enlisted Feb. 4, 1942, Cleveland, OH. He is a plankowner and served aboard BB-59 as AS at commissioning May 12, 1942, and on board for BB-59 2nd and 3rd anniversaries.

WOLNY, WALTER ANTHONY, 652-17-86, enlisted Feb. 3, 1942, Pittsburgh, PA. He is a plankowner and served aboard BB-59 as AS at commissioning May 12, 1942, and on board for BB-59 2nd and 3rd anniversaries.

WOOD, CHARLES E., 666-45-35, born June 18, 1924, Westfield, MA. He graduated from Westfield High School and enlisted Aug. 10, 1942, Springfield, MA. Trained at Newport Naval Training Station, RI, and Wentworth Institute, Boston, MA. He served aboard BB-59 as S1/c 4th Div. December 1942 and assigned gunner's mate striker. He left BB-59 December 1945 Bremerton, WA.

After the war he was president general manager of H.E. Wood & Sons, Inc., Westfield, MA, for 44 years. He retired June 1986 and held two part-time jobs picking up cars for two dealerships and survey for service follow-up for another dealership. In his spare time he builds plank on frame ship models and is active in the American Legion Post 124, Westfield, MA.

He married Dorothy (deceased 1983) May 26, 1946, Cambridge, MA. He has two sons, one daughter and three grandchildren. He resides at 34 Briarwood Place, Westfield, MA 01085.

WOOD, ORVILLE, Memory List 1992.

WOOD, THOMAS BENTON, 224-71-35, born Sept. 29, 1924, Brooklyn, NY. He enlisted Feb. 26, 1942, New York, NY, and was a plankowner. He served aboard BB-59 as AS 4th Div. at commissioning May 12, 1942, and assigned radar operator. He left BB-59 at Tulagi.

After the war he worked as a tile setter. He married Jytte in 1949, Plainfield, NJ, and had two sons, one daughter and two grandchildren. (Mrs.) resides at 161 Brook Ave., North Plainfield, NJ 07060. He died Oct. 25, 1993; Memory List 1994.

WOOD, WILLIAM, resides at 4409 Deering, Forth Worth, TX 76114.

WOODALL, JERE WILLIAM, 224-44-68, born Sept. 2, 1924, Nanpa, ID. He enlisted Nov. 25, 1941, New York, NY. He is a plankowner and served aboard BB-59 as S2/c 5th Div. at commissioning May 12, 1942. Was assigned COX, BM2/c and 5th Div. CAPT and left BB-59 March 1, 1946, Bremerton, WA.

Other Naval assignments: USS *Fazes* (MS-214) and decommissioned to Reserve Fleet, Orange, TX; BM1/c, Salvage School Bayonne, NJ; USS *Mosopeles* (ATF-148); First Class Diving School, Washington, DC; Shore Duty Submarine Base, New London, CT; ASR Sky Lasky, BMC; USS *Fulton* submarine tender, ASR Sky Lask, made master diver, Torpedo Range,

Newport, RI; ARS-24 Shore Patrol Offices and Base Security Offices, Newport, RI; USS *Alstede* (AF-48); Command Harbor Clearance #2 and retired.

He married Jacqueline July 24, 1945, Wayline, IN, and has three sons, one foster son and one daughter. He resides in the summer at 557 Harton Circle, Virginia Beach, VA 23452; winter at 2008 Arches Lane, Mobile, AL 36605.

WOODARD, HENRY LEWIS, served aboard BB-59 as CSP(a) 4th Div. May 19, 1944. He left BB-59 to Com Twelve FUR-ASPERS.

WOODBURN, RONALD, (n) 316-88-99, enlisted Jan. 30, 1942, Omaha, NE. He is a plankowner and served aboard BB-59 as AS at commissioning May 12, 1942.

WOODRUM, DALE EVERETT, 279-67-68, enlisted April 22, 1940, Cincinnati, OH. He is a plankowner and served aboard BB-59 as EM2/c E Div. at commissioning May 12, 1942.

WOOLBRIGHT, REV. T. ALFRED, served aboard BB-59 in I Div. He was Marquis Who's Who in America, Who's Who in Religion in the South/Southwest. He married Lila and resides at 1401 North Main Street, Mount Holly, NC 28120.

WOOLDRIDGE, JOHN, latest address is c/o C.T. Wells, RFD #8 Box 525, Osborn, OH.

WOOLDRIDGE, JOHN WILLIAM, 634-03-86, enlisted Dec. 10, 1941, Louisville, KY. He is a plankowner and served aboard BB-59 as S2/c at commissioning May 12, 1942, and on board for BB-59 2nd anniversary.

WOOLFORD, CHARLES EDWARD, 266-50-79, enlisted Sept. 19, 1941, Norfolk, VA. He is a plankowner and served aboard BB-59 as EM3/c E Div. at commissioning May 12, 1942.

WOOLSEY, FREDERICK ARTHUR, 253-08-04, enlisted Dec. 17, 1941, Albany, NY. He is a plankowner and served aboard BB-59 as EM2/c E Div. at commissioning May 12, 1942, and on board for BB-59 2nd and 3rd anniversaries.

WOOTEN, JOSEPH ALLEN, JR., ENS, Naval Academy Class of 1945. He served aboard BB-59 as ENS CS Div. Oct. 30, 1944, and assigned J.O. CS Div., S.W.O. Communication Dept. He left BB-59 Dec. 13, 1945.

WORTHINGTON, GEORGE W., resided at 205 Brookhaven Drive, Greenwood, SC 29646.

WOS, BOLESLAW WILLIAM, 646-66-82, enlisted Feb. 5, 1942, New York, NY. He is a plankowner and served aboard BB-59 as AS at commissioning May 12, 1942.

WOTHERS, GEORGE WIL, 650-14-47, enlisted Jan. 1, 1942, Philadelphia, PA. He is a plankowner

and served aboard BB-59 as S2/c at commissioning May 12, 1942.

WOZELLA, ANTHONY, USMC, May 8, 1942, Norfolk Navy Yard. He is a plankowner and served aboard BB-59 as PVT 7th Div. at commissioning May 12, 1942.

WREN, BILLY JOE, resided at 2812 Northaven, Denton, TX 76205.

WRIGHT, CHARLES E., resided at 320 West Grant St., Willcox, AZ 85643.

WRIGHT, EDGAR LEE, 346-67-23, enlisted July 3, 1941, Bremerton, WA. He is a plankowner and served aboard BB-59 as COX at commissioning May 12, 1942, and on board for BB-59 2nd anniversary.

WRIGHT, EDWARD, (n) 360-38-26, enlisted Dec. 7, 1940, Houston, TX. He is a plankowner and served aboard BB-59 as F2/c at commissioning May 12, 1942, and on board for BB-59 2nd anniversary.

WRIGHT, HERBERT WELLS, 385-95-32, enlisted Jan. 4, 1941, Seattle, WA. He is a plankowner and served aboard BB-59 as F2/c at commissioning May 12, 1942.

WRIGHT, JAMES J., served aboard BB-59 as a plankowner on commissioning May 12, 1942. He married June 1938 and has two sons. (Mrs.) resides at 2615 N. 4th St., Suite 718, Coeur d'Alene, ID 83814. He died May 5, 1992; Memory List 1992.

WRIGHT, JAMES LECESTER, 262-22-61, enlisted Aug. 18, 1937, Raleigh, NC. He is a plankowner and served aboard BB-59 as FC3/c at commissioning May 12, 1942.

WRIGHT, JOHN S., USMC, 383207, born Dec. 20, 1918, Reading, PA. He enlisted March 18, 1942, Philadelphia, PA, and trained at Marine Corps Training, Parris Island, SC, and Sea School, Norfolk, VA. He served aboard BB-59 as CPL 7th Div. June 1942 and assigned director 40mm guns. He left BB-59 in 1945 Bremerton, WA.

After the war he was a machinist and inspector for Dana Corp., Reading, PA, and retired after 38 years service. In his spare he was mite and midget football coach, track coach, hunting, woodworking, hiking and active in Senior Citizens.

He married first Mabel 1943 Reading, PA, and second Cideannette July 3, 1947, Elkton, MD. He has two sons, one grandchild and three great-grandchildren. He resides at 3725 East Ave., Reiffton, Reading, PA 19606.

WRIGHT, ROBERT L., (Mrs.) resides at 2340 Gen Longstreet Dr., Virginia Beach, VA 23454. Memory List 1990.

WYNN, JOHN BARTTLEY, 267-96-57, enlisted Aug. 20, 1938, San Pedro, CA. He is a plankowner and served aboard BB-59 as SF1/c at commissioning May 12, 1942.

YALCH, MATEY, JR., (n) born April 4, 1917, Pittsburgh, PA. Graduated from high school and became a barber, hairdresser and watchmaker engineer. He enlisted April 3, 1942, Pittsburgh, PA, and trained at Newport Naval Training Station, RI.

He served aboard BB-59 as S1/c 2nd Div. Aug. 25, 1942. He was assigned Port Magazine, CAPT #2 Turret, COX boat for CAPT during air attack first Superstructure Deck Starboard Side, Port Side Leadsman, Barber 2nd Div. before inspection and won first prize twice in ship's handicraft contests. He left BB-59 November 1945 Bremerton, WA, and discharged Nov. 29, 1945, Sampson Naval Base, NY.

After the war he worked as a bartenders for hotels and first class night clubs. He married Sarah in 1946 Pittsburgh, PA, and has one son and one grandchild. He resides at 5903 Babcock Blvd., Pittsburgh, PA 15237.

YARBER, ROY ALBERT, 294-96-26, enlisted Aug. 21, 1941, Pearl Harbor, HI. He is a plankowner and served aboard BB-59 as CMM at commissioning May 12, 1942.

YARBROUGH, GERALD W., 315-39-46, born Nov. 25, 1927, Flint, MI. He earned a BS at Michigan State and enlisted July 13, 1945, Flint, MI. He served aboard USS *Alabama* (BB-60) and USS *Greenwood* (DE-679). He served aboard BB-59 as S1/c 1st Div. March 30, 1946, and assigned captain's orderly. He left BB-59 Sept. 2, 1946, Norfolk, VA. Was also assigned to USS *Bennington* (CV-20), USS *Scott* (DE-214), USS *Otter* (DE-210) and USS *Marlboro* (APB-38).

After the war he worked for the *Hillsdale Daily News*, Adrian Telegram, *Michigan Daily Newspaper* and vice-president and account supervisor for Campell-Ewald Company retiring after 31 years. He was adult leader Junior Carmber-Hillsdale Boy Scouts; 1991-92 president of Clowns Galore Alley 194; 1993 vice-president South East Clown Assoc.; and 1993 southeast director of World Clown Assoc.

He married Conme June 17, 1950, and has four sons, two daughters and eight grandchildren. He resides at 11611 Parkview Lane, Seminole, FL 34642.

YOCHUM, GILBERT R., served aboard BB-59 as COX 5th Div. January 1943 and assigned ComBatDist 8, Battle Station Control #1, 5" Gun Mount #9 and Flag Plotting Room. He left BB-59 July 1945.

After the war he worked as a processor of milk Country Bell Coop Farmers Dairy, Pittsburgh, PA. He was a member of the VFW. He had three sons and two daughters and resided at 63 Lauch Way, Pittsburgh, PA 15201. Memory List 1982.

YORIK, PAUL, 238-49-52, enlisted Jan. 5, 1942, Albany, NY. He is a plankowner and served aboard BB-59 as WT2/c at commissioning May 12, 1942, and on board for BB-59 2nd and 3rd anniversaries.

YOUNG, FRANCIS E., Memory List 1992.

YOUNG, HAROLD THEODORE, 600-15-73, enlisted Feb. 11, 1942, Albany, NY. He is a plankowner and served aboard BB-59 as AS M Div. at commissioning May 12, 1942, and on his 2nd anniversary. He resides at 89 Virginia St., Waterloo, NY 13165.

YOUNG, JAMES H., born May 19, 1922, Grand Haven, MI. Graduated from high school and attended Pontiac Motor Trade School. He enlisted Oct. 14, 1942, Pontiac, MI, and trained at Great Lakes. He served aboard BB-59 as S1/c 3rd Div. and left Oct. 19, 1945.

After the war he was a tradesman for Pontiac Motor and lineman for Michigan Bell. He was a member of Waterford Eagles # 2887.

He married Oct. 8, 1945, and had two sons, one daughter and four grandchildren. He died July 18, 1995, Pontiac, MI, and resided at 101 Ascot St., Waterford, MI 48328. Memory List 1996.

YOUNG, JAMES M., served aboard BB-59 in 3rd Div. (Mrs.) resides at 34 Parkview, 4614 Old Spartanburg Road, Taylors, SC 29687. Memory List 1989.

YOUNG, MERLE NEWCOMER, LT CR, served aboard BB-59 as LT CR April 30, 1945, and assigned chaplain (Prot.) CDR.

YOUNG, M.V. MD, LT(jg) served aboard BB-59 in H Div. October 1943. Memory List 1977.

YOUNG, RICHARD ARTHUR, 279-74-30, enlisted Oct. 21, 1940, Cincinnati, OH. He is a plankowner and served aboard BB-59 as Phm3/c at commissioning May 12, 1942. He resides at 5594 Argyle Way, Riverside, CA 92506.

YOUNGBLOOD, W.C., served aboard BB-59 as RT1/c CR Div. and assigned FR Div. March 10, 1943.

YOUNGBLOOD, WILLIAM OLIVER, 174-24-63, enlisted Jan. 3, 1942, Detroit, MI. He is a plankowner and served aboard BB-59 as RM2/c at commissioning May 12, 1942, and on board for BB-59 2nd anniversary.

YOUNGS, ROBERT DEE, 359-88-96, enlisted Dec. 14, 1941, Pearl Harbor, HI. He is a plankowner and served aboard BB-59 as QM2/c at commissioning May 12, 1942, and on board for BB-59 2nd anniversary.

ZADROGA, STANISLAUS C., born Dec. 1, 1920, Clinton, MA. A high school graduate with a background in electronics, he enlisted Oct. 21, 1940, Springfield, MA. He trained at Newport Naval Training Station, RI; USS *Tennessee*; and Naval Air Station, Pensacola, FL. He is a plankowner and served aboard BB-59 as Y2/c X Div. at commissioning May 12, 1942, and assigned Enlisted Personnel Records. He left BB-59 in Boston, MA.

Other Naval assignments: USS *Nelson* (DD-623); Airship Group 2; Blimp Headquarters Squad 2; Blimp Hedron One; Detachment 2; and Rec. Station South Annex, Norfolk, VA. After the war he worked at Wire Mill, Clinton, ME; plastic fasteners, carpenter work and civil service until retirement. He enjoys walking and watching grandson play football, basketball and baseball.

He married Yvonne May 28, 1944, Coral Gables, FL, and has two sons, one daughter, 11 grandchildren and one great-grandchild. He resides at 74 Shirley Road, Lancaster, MA 01523.

ZAMOJSKI, STANLEY, (n) 600-17-33, enlisted Feb. 19, 1942, New York, NY. He is a plankowner and

served aboard BB-59 as AS at commissioning May 12, 1942, and on his 2nd anniversary.

ZBDROWSKI, SEVERYN ALBERT, JR., 646-61-94, born Aug. 21, 1918, New York, NY. A high school graduate he enlisted Jan. 31, 1942, New York, NY, and trained at Newport Naval Training Station, RI.

He is a plankowner and served aboard BB-59 as AS S Div. at commissioning May 12, 1942, and on board for BB-59 2nd anniversary. He was assigned canteen operator and all provision storerooms SK1/c and left BB-59 December 1944. Was then assigned Frontier Base, San Pedro, CA, for nine months and discharged.

After the war he was a furniture salesman for R.H. Macy Company,, White Plains, NY, for 43 years. He married Edie 1985 Ben Salem, PA, and has four sons and eight grandchildren. He resides at 426 Thrush Court East, New Hope, PA 18938-1526.

ZELLER, JOHN KENNETH, 328-74-65, enlisted Sept. 11, 1940, Minneapolis, MN. He was a plankowner and served aboard BB-59 as F1/c at commissioning May 12, 1942. Memory List 1989.

ZEMBLIDGE, LEROY WILLIAM, 668-31-90, enlisted Jan. 22, 1942, St. Louis, MO. He was a plankowner and served aboard BB-59 as AS 2nd Div. at commissioning May 12, 1942. (Mrs.) resides at 3202 Delor, St. Louis, MO 63111.

ZEMLIN, MICHAEL, (n) 2 50-71-78, enlisted Jan. 24, 1942, Pittsburgh, PA. He is a plankowner and served aboard BB-59 as AS at commissioning May 12, 1942, and on board for BB-59 2nd anniversary.

ZEPPENFELD, STERLING, ENS 420420, born Nov. 24, 1922, Allentown, PA. He holds a BE and ME from Steven's Institute and an M.Ed. from Rutgers University. He enlisted in 1943 New York, NY, and trained at Midshipman School, Naval Academy, MD; and received ensign commission Dec. 20, 1944.

He served aboard BB-59 as ENS E Div. April 1945 and assigned J.O. E Div. A Div. officer. He left BB-59 June 1946, Norfolk, VA, and was discharged. After the war he worked for Ebasco Services, New York, NY; Federal Electric & Telephone Company, Clifton, NJ; Lehman Bros., Newark, NJ; and Essex County Vocational School, Bloomfield, NJ.

He had four sons, one daughter and four grandchildren. (Mrs.) Lincoln Titus resides at 43 Crestview Drive, East Sandwich, MA 02537. He died June 1, 1975; Memory List 1981.

ZINGER, ISADORE, 646-59-44, enlisted Jan. 29, 1942, New York, NY. He is a plankowner and served aboard BB-59 as AS at commissioning May 12, 1942.

ZIRKLE, JOSEPH C., LT(jg) 579-10-2313, born Aug. 25, 1917, Washington, DC. Attended Naval Academy Class of 1941, enlisted Feb. 6, 1941, and served aboard USS *California*. He served aboard BB-59 as LT(jg) 5th Div. March 1943 and assigned 5th Div. (P) and D, Battle Station Sec. Dir. 1. He left BB-59 1944 Noumea, New Caledonia.

Other Naval assignments: USS *Guam*, Naval War College, VA-24/VF-24 and VS-23, OPS and Exec. USS *Ticonderoga*, Staff ComNavAirPac and AirOps, Staff Com7thFlt., CO NAAS Whiting Field, Pensacola; 1961-64 and 1967-71 Pentagon Director Logistics Plans Div. and retired 35 years service. After Naval service became a civil contractor Navy

Dept., 10 years Man Tech International, five years Cerberonice, two years Northern Virginia Community College. He belongs to Blue & Gold officer Naval Academy, bowling and golf.

He married Virginia April 26, 1942, Naval Academy, and has one son and one daughter. He resides at 3509 Redwood Court, Fairfax, VA 22030.

ZISER, GEORGE JOHN, ENS, served aboard BB-59 as ENS 6th Div. October 1943.

ZOOK, DAVID GEORGE, 311-14-58, enlisted Dec. 12, 1941, Pearl Harbor, HI. He is a plankowner and served aboard BB-59 as EM1/c E Div. at commissioning May 12, 1942.

ZUBROVICH, JOSEPH FRANCIS, 646-66-89, enlisted Feb. 5, 1942, New York, NY. He was a plankowner and served aboard BB-59 as AS A Div. at commissioning May 12, 1942. He resided at 93 Diamond St., Brooklyn, NY 11222. Memory List 1987.

Good thing we took the mast off...we cleared by ten feet.

"Bring Back Big Mamie" was a statewide effort. Children, business professionals, and veterans raised money and volunteered their time.

Chapter Nine
Reunions

REUNIONS

Big Mamie welcomes her boys home.

Howard (Bud) Burkhalter, June 1991.

Paul Lanni and John Chudy, 1st Div., Turret 1, after Battle of Casablanca, November 1942, Boston, MA.

Paul Lanni and John Chudy, 54 years later. Reunion, June 1996.

L to R Alex Poulos, Ace Mavrogeorge, Ed Palmer and Bernie Silveria 1991.

M Division, USS Massachusetts, Reunion, June 1995.

L to R Bob Doran, Alfred Johnson, Kieth Schlosser, Norman Davidson, Frank Norton, Bob Vuillmot, kneeling, Bill Stricklin, Reunion June 1995.

L to R Bob Doran, Oscar Stevens, Frank Norton, Alfred Johnson, Reunion June 1995.

Charles MacDonald (President of USS Massachusetts Associates) and wife, and Capt. Cummings, Reunion, June 1996.

Capt. Archambault (Exec Off of USS Massachusetts) and wife, and Cpt. Bowerman, Reunion, June 1996.

Ed Palmer welcomes Fr. Joe Moody to the 20th Reunion, 1966.

L to R Lt (jg) Renouf Russell; Ed Palmer; Capt. F.E.M. Whiting; and LCDR Robert A. Grimes.

USS Massachusetts Associates 20th reunion, 1996, Fall River, MA.

(Above and Below) Big Mamie's boys return for their 20th Reunion aboard Big Mamie in Battleship Cove, 1966.

Big Mamie's boys return for their 20th Reunion aboard Big Mamie in Battleship Cove, 1966.

Ed Palmer, Bill Canfield, Grace Palmer, Reunion, June 1995.

U. S. S. Mass. Associates

22nd Anniversary Reunion

Fall River Mass, May 13, 1967

THE BAY STATER
USS MASSACHUSETTS ASSOCIATES INC

39th

ANNUAL REUNION

THE BAY STATER
USS MASSACHUSETTS ASSOCIATES INC

40th

ANNUAL REUNION

THE BAY STATER
USS MASSACHUSETTS ASSOCIATES INC

41st

ANNUAL REUNION

THE BAY STATER
USS MASSACHUSETTS ASSOCIATES INC

42nd

ANNUAL REUNION

Bill Canfield drew humorous sketches for The Bay Starter while he was on aboard the USS Massachusetts, and continues to entertain us by designing our reunion invitations.

THE BAY STATER
U S S MASSACHUSETTS ASSOCIATES INC

43rd
ANNUAL REUNION

THE BAY STATER
U S S MASSACHUSETTS ASSOCIATES INC

44th
ANNUAL REUNION

THE BAY STATER
U S S MASSACHUSETTS ASSOCIATES INC

45th
ANNUAL REUNION

THE BAY STATER
U S S MASSACHUSETTS ASSOCIATES INC

46th
ANNUAL REUNION

211

THE BAY STATER
U S S   M A S S A C H U S E T T S   A S S O C I A T E S   I N C

47th
ANNUAL REUNION

50th Anniversary of Ship's Commissioning

THE BAY STATER
U S S   M A S S A C H U S E T T S   A S S O C I A T E S   I N C

48th
ANNUAL REUNION

THE BAY STATER
U S S   M A S S A C H U S E T T S   A S S O C I A T E S   I N C

49th
ANNUAL REUNION

THE BAY STATER

U.S.S. MASSACHUSETTS ASSOCIATES INC.

51st

ANNUAL REUNION

Battleship Cove
Fall River, MA

June 17 and 18, 1996

INDEX

Paul Dias had quite a "line" and how he could throw it.

Ed looks North from the bridge and thinks "Can it be true? Are we really bringing "Big Mamie" home?"

Marty Adler

Larry Bennett smiles as he sweeps.

N

Gately, Cassidy, and Beaton, pulling ropes for Big Mamie.

O

P

(L to R) Cassidy and Beaton check "Big Mamie" for repairs.

Jim Burt

Dinner table at the USS Massachusetts Associates Reunion 1996, Fall River, MA.

U.S.S. MASSACHUSETTS WAR MEMORIAL